Scottish Arbitration Handbook

Scottish Arbitration Handbook

A Practitioner's Guide

Second Edition

David R. Parratt QC,
Peter Foreman and Angela Grahame QC

EDINBURGH
University Press

Edinburgh University Press is one of the leading university presses in the UK. We publish academic books and journals in our selected subject areas across the humanities and social sciences, combining cutting-edge scholarship with high editorial and production values to produce academic works of lasting importance. For more information visit our website: edinburghuniversitypress.com

First edition published 2011 by Avizandum Publishing Ltd

Edinburgh University Press Ltd
The Tun – Holyrood Road
12 (2f) Jackson's Entry
Edinburgh EH8 8PJ
www.euppublishing.com

Typeset in 10/12 Palatino by
Servis Filmsetting Ltd, Stockport, Cheshire
and printed and bound in Great Britain

A CIP record for this book is available from the British Library

ISBN 978 1 4744 7893 9 (paperback)
ISBN 978 1 4744 8277 6 (webready PDF)
ISBN 978 1 4744 8278 3 (epub)

Contents

Foreword   xiv

Table of Statutes   xv

Table of Statutory Instruments   xxiii

Table of Cases   xxv

INTRODUCTION   **1**

ARBITRATION (SCOTLAND) ACT 2010   **5**

Introductory provisions

Founding principles   5

   Object of arbitration   6

   Fairness and impartiality (and independence)   7

   Delay and expense   8

   Party autonomy   10

   Clarity of language   12

   Court intervention   12

   Human rights compliance   14

   Article 6 of the European Convention on Human Rights   14

   A linked issue – identity of arbitrators   16

   Arbitration in consumer matters   17

Key terms   18

   Dispute   18

Seat of arbitration   19

   Place of the seat   19

   Comparison with English position   20

   Designation   22

Arbitration agreements

Arbitration agreement   23

   Agreement to arbitrate   23

   Written and oral agreements   24

   Commercial element in addition   28

   An arbitration agreement with no mention of arbitration?   28

   Incorporation of arbitration provisions by reference   29

   'One-stopness'   29

End of the right to arbitrate   31
Separability   32
    The English position   34
Law governing arbitration agreement   34
Scottish Arbitration Rules – Mandatory and Default Rules   35
Mandatory rules   35
Default rules   37
    Scottish seat and the *lex arbitri*   38

Suspension of legal proceedings

Suspension of legal proceedings   39
    Procedural considerations   39
    Court   40
    Underlying considerations   40
    Meaning of sist   41
    Structure of section 10   46
    UK Supreme Court decision on international commercial
        arbitration   53
    Who can apply?   53
    Notice of application   54
    Losing entitlement to a sist   55
    Void, inoperative or incapable of being performed   56
    Multiple applications   56
    No contracting out   57
    Seated in Scotland   57

Enforcing and challenging arbitral awards etc

Arbitral award to be final and binding on parties   57
    Through and under   59
    Final and binding   61
Enforcement of arbitral awards   61
    Procedural issues   62
    Lack of jurisdiction and s 12(3) and (4)   63
    Registration of awards in the Books of Council and Session   64
    Foreign seats   64
    New York Convention requirements   65
Court intervention in arbitrations   65
    Where UNCITRAL applies   66
Persons who take no part in arbitral proceedings – The 'empty chair'
        defence   68
    Interpretation of similar provisions in 1996 Act   69
    Effect of an unsuccessful challenge   72
Anonymity in legal proceedings   73
    Anonymity and the Rules of Court   75

Statutory arbitration

Statutory arbitration   75

Supplementary

Prescription and limitation   77
  Changes to positive prescription provisions   77
  Changes to negative prescription provisions   78
  Limitation period interruption by arbitration proceedings   79
  Amendments to consumer protection provisions   80
Arbitral appointments referee   81
Power of judge to act as arbitrator or umpire   83
Arbitrability of disputes   84

**SCHEDULE 1 TO THE ARBITRATION (SCOTLAND)
ACT 2010 – SCOTTISH ARBITRATION RULES**   **88**

**COMMENCEMENT, CONSTITUTION AND IMMUNITY
OF TRIBUNAL (PART 1)**   **88**
Commencement of arbitration   88
  Giving notice   89
  Equivalent notice procedure in England   91
  'In accordance with the agreement'   92
  'Claiming through and under'   93
Appointment of tribunal   93
Identity of and eligibility to act as an Arbitrator   94
  Legal capacity   95
  Bankruptcy and capacity   96
Number of arbitrators   96
  Agreement   97
  Odd numbers not required   97
  No requirement for a clerk   98
Method of appointment   98
  Who should be appointed?   100
Failure of appointment procedure   100
  Arbitral appointments referee   100
Duty to disclose any conflict of interests   101
  Arbitrators and bias   104
  IBA Guidelines on Conflicts of Interest in International Arbitration   107
Arbitrator's tenure   109
Challenge to appointment of arbitrator   109
  Grounds for objection   110
  Facts not allegations   111
  Time limits   111
Removal of arbitrator by parties   112
Removal or dismissal of arbitrator by court   114
  'Application by any party'   115
Dismissal of tribunal   116
  'Application by a party'   117
  'Dismissal' and removal   117
  Failure to conduct the proceedings   117
  Notification   118
  Representations   118

Court must be satisfied   119
The continuing arbitration   119
Resignation of arbitrator   120
Liability etc of arbitrator when tenure ends   122
  Tenure ends   122
  Repayment   123
  Liability   123
  Finality   123
Reconstitution of tribunal   124
  Objection or appeal not removed   124
Arbitrators nominated in arbitration agreements   125
Immunity of tribunal etc   125
  Limited immunity?   126
Immunity of appointing arbitral institution etc   127
Immunity of experts, witnesses and legal representatives   128
Loss of right to object   129
  English provisions   131
Independence of arbitrator   131
Consideration where arbitrator judged not to be impartial
  and independent   132
Death of arbitrator   133
Death of party   133
Unfair treatment   134
Rules applicable to umpires   134
Formal communications   134
Periods of time   136

JURISDICTION OF TRIBUNAL (PART 2)   **136**
Jurisdiction of the tribunal   136
  Competence/competence generally   137
  Types of challenge   139
  'May rule'?   141
  Power to 'rule' on jurisdiction only   141
  What does the tribunal do if there is no jurisdiction?   142
  Matters submitted to the arbitration   142
  Tribunal properly constituted (rule 19(b))   142
Objections to the tribunal's jurisdiction   143
  Making an objection   143
  'May'   143
  Timing of the objection   144
  Objection to the tribunal   145
  Options open to the tribunal   145
  When can the arbitrator make a determination?   145
  Provisional, part and final awards and the operation of
  the arbitral proceedings   146
  Time limits   147
  Conflicts between tribunal and parties   147
  What does 'setting aside' mean?   147
  Entertaining a late objection   148

Losing the right to object   148
Termination of tribunal or setting aside for no or exceeded
  jurisdiction   149
Delay ruling on objection   149
Appeal against tribunal's ruling on jurisdictional objection   150
  Appeal by petition   150
  Appeal time limited   152
  Lodging a petition   152
Discretion vested in tribunal to continue proceedings pending court's
  decision   153
Obstacles to making an application   155
  No appeal   -   156

GENERAL DUTIES (PART 3)   **156**
Introduction   156
Impartiality, bias and independence   158
  Previous appointments and instructions as counsel   160
  Apparent bias   161
  Waiver of a right to object   162
  Barristers in the same chambers as arbitrators   162
  Solicitors   164
  Test for bias/impartiality   164
  Treating the parties fairly   167
  Consequences of failure to act impartially and fairly   167
  Unnecessary delay and expense   168
  Tension between party autonomy and tribunal's duties   169
  Some English examples   169
  Other examples of independence/impartiality clauses   170
'Unnecessary' delay and expense   172
  Application to arbitration?   172
  Duty to ensure   173
Default rule 26 and the concept of confidentiality in arbitral
  proceedings   174
  The new Scottish approach   174
  The confidential information   **175**
  Continuing obligation of confidentiality?   176
  Exceptions   177
  Preventing unauthorised disclosure by third parties   179
  Remedies for breach   179
  Disapplication or modification of rule 26   179
  English position   179
Tribunal's deliberations   183

ARBITRAL PROCEEDINGS (PART 4)   **183**
Power of the tribunal to determine procedure   183
  The pro-active arbitrator   185
  The common law and the civil law traditions   187
  Documents and electronically stored information (ESI)   189
  Evidence   190

Approach of the appellate courts 191
When and where 192
Recording of evidence 193
Who may appear? 193
Claims and defences and 'pleadings' 194
Disclosure of documents (or recovery or even discovery?) 195
Examination in chief, cross-examination and re-examination 196
Hearings, arguments, documents 197
Written pleadings and submissions 199
Counterclaims 199
New claims at later stages 200
'Scott Schedules' 200
Language 201
The civil and common lawyer compromise 201
The Rules on the Efficient Conduct of Proceedings in International
    Arbitration (the 'Prague Rules') 202
Place of arbitration 209
Overall control of the arbitration 210
Tribunal decision-making 211
Tribunal directions 211
Preliminary issues 212
Power to appoint clerk, agents or employees etc 212
Tribunal secretaries in arbitration 213
Delegation not permitted 215
Party representatives 215
Experts and the tribunal 216
Powers of the tribunal relating to property 218
Oaths or affirmations 219
Failure to submit claim or defence timeously 220
Failure to attend a hearing or provide evidence 221
Failure to comply with tribunal direction or arbitration agreement 221
Failure to comply? 222
Sanctions 222
Order following direction 222
Consolidation of proceedings 223
Contractual provision 223

POWERS OF COURT IN RELATION TO ARBITRAL
PROCEEDINGS (PART 5) **224**
Referral of point of law 224
Referral 224
Any 'point' or 'question' 224
Discretion 225
Relationship with rule 42 226
Application 226
No appeal 227
No delay 227
Continuing arbitration 228
Variation of time limits set by parties 228

Time limits   229
The court and the discretionary nature of the jurisdiction   229
'Substantial injustice'?   230
Extent   231
Continuing arbitration   231
Finality   231
The court's power to order attendance of witnesses and disclosure
   of evidence   232
  Power of the tribunal   232
  Under the jurisdiction of the court   232
  Disclosure of evidence   232
  Application   233
  Scope of the court's order   235
  Finality   235
  Other material evidence   235
  Entitled to refuse   236
The court's other powers in relation to arbitration   236
  Analogous provisions   237
  Default provision   237
  Court   237
  Finality?   237
  Pre-conditions   238
  Relief at the start of the process   238
  Power to make an order under Administration of Justice
   (Scotland) Act 1972   238
  Court powers to appoint a person to safeguard interests of
   person lacking capacity   240
  Court powers to order the sale of any property in dispute in the
   arbitration   240
  Power to make an order securing any amount in dispute   241
  Power to preserve evidence and allow recovery pre-litigation   241
  Power to grant warrant for arrestment or inhibition   242
  Power to grant interdict   242
  Powers of the Court in England and Wales   242
  Power to grant any other interim or permanent order   244
  Tribunal ongoing   245

AWARDS (PART 6)   **245**
Rules applicable to the substance of the dispute   245
  Party choice of law   245
  Tribunal choice   245
  English provisions   248
  Shari'a law as a basis   248
Power to award payment and damages   249
Other remedies available to tribunal   250
  Declarator   250
  Interdict and specific implement   251
  Rectification   252
  Reduction   252

Interest   253
    Interest as a matter of procedure   255
Form of award   255
    Seat and date   255
    Reasons   255
    Award made   256
    Previous provisional or part awards   257
Award treated as made in Scotland   257
Provisional awards   257
Different types of award   257
Part awards   260
Draft awards   260
Power to withhold award on non-payment of fees or expenses   261
Arbitration to end on last award or early settlement   262
    Continued operation of the Rules   263
Correcting an award   263
    Interaction with rule 55   263
    Error or ambiguity   264
    Application or tribunal initiative   264
    Conditions of validity   264
    Reasonable opportunity   265
    Corrections   265
    English examples   266

ARBITRATION EXPENSES (PART 7)   **266**
Arbitration expenses   266
    Arbitrator's fees and expenses   267
    The parties' legal and other expenses   267
Arbitrators' fees and expenses   268
    Several liability   268
    Agreed fees and expenses   269
    Taxation of accounts   269
    Power to order repayment of fees already paid   270
    Increasing costs in arbitration   270
Recovery of arbitration expenses   271
    Recoverable arbitration expenses   272
    Basis of determination   272
    English provisions   273
Liability for recoverable arbitration expenses   274
    Apportionment   274
    Award   274
Ban on pre-dispute agreements about liability for arbitration expenses 276
Security for expenses   277
    Outwith the UK   277
    Can the tribunal itself order security?   279
    Sealed offers and security   279
    Dismissal of the claim   279
Limitation of recoverable arbitration expenses   280
Awards on recoverable arbitration expenses   281

CHALLENGING AWARDS (PART 8)   **281**
Challenging an award: substantive jurisdiction   282
Challenging an award: serious irregularity   284
  Serious irregularity and substantial injustice   285
  Kinds of 'serious irregularity'   287
  Outer House – options   295
  Arbitrators' expenses   295
  Further appeal   296
Challenging an award: legal error   296
Legal error appeals: procedure etc   297
Challenging an award: supplementary   299
Reconsideration by tribunal   302

RECOGNITION AND ENFORCEMENT OF AWARDS
IN SCOTLAND   **303**
Rules of Court   304
Grounds for refusal of recognition and enforcement   305

MISCELLANEOUS (PART 9)   **307**
Immunity of tribunal etc   307
  Limited immunity?   308
Immunity of appointing arbitral institution   309
Immunity of experts, witnesses and legal representatives   310
Loss of right to object   311
  'Participates in an arbitration'   312
  English provisions   312
Independence of arbitrator   313
Consideration where arbitrator judged not to be impartial
  and independent   313
Death of arbitrator   314
Death of party   314
Unfair treatment   315
Rules applicable to umpires   315
Formal communications   316
Periods of time   318
Index of interpretation of terms   318

CONCLUSION   **320**

Appendix 1: Arbitration (Scotland) Act 2010   321
Appendix 2: The Rules of Court   366
Appendix 3: New York Convention States   372
Appendix 4: Recognition and Enforcement of Convention Awards   375
Appendix 5: United Nations Convention on International Settlement
  Agreements Resulting from Mediation (the 'Singapore Convention
  on Mediation')   376

Index   385

Foreword

It has long been recognised, as senior judges have commented, that the health of a legal system depends to no small extent on the aptitude of its procedure. In the field of arbitration, it became increasingly clear some years ago that radical modification was needed in order for our legal system to provide fair, modern and practical governance of the subject-area. The Arbitration (Scotland) Act 2010 was designed to achieve that purpose.

Since those key legislative changes, momentum has continued to gather towards an increased use of arbitration. It is therefore necessary to have up-to-date and useful contributions from academics and practitioners to the legal literature on the subject. One of the great features of the law of arbitration in Scotland is that we are blessed with having several leading textbooks which are of major assistance to lawyers and judges and others involved in the area. The first edition of this book added to that distinguished body of work and it has now been updated and developed further in this second edition.

Building upon the first edition, the authors have continued to put in a great deal of hard work and careful thought to provide a practical, clear and comprehensive account and analysis of the law of arbitration. The book does so by examining the statutory provisions, rules and case law from Scotland and also by analysing these in the context of the often highly relevant developments in the English jurisprudence on the subject. In addition, it takes into account how important issues in the field have been dealt with in many other jurisdictions. The lucidity, breadth and depth of the discussion by the authors are very impressive features and I am confident that this work will continue to play its part in assisting all of those involved in this subject-area in understanding the law and procedure.

The Honourable Lord Clark

Table of Statutes

Administration of Justice (Scotland) Act
1933
s 16 239
Administration of Justice (Scotland) Act
1972
s 1 . . . . 237, 238–40
s 3 . . . . 1, 14, 65, 168, 195, 224, 283, 296
Adults with Incapacity (Scotland) Act
2000 . . . . 114, 240
s 1 (6) 95, 293
Agricultural Holdings Act 1986 77
Agricultural Holdings (Scotland) Act
2003 76
Arbitration Act 1598 (APS iv 233, c 31). 1
Arbitration Act 1894 1
Arbitration Act 1950
s 26 62
Arbitration Act 1979 287
Arbitration Act 1996 . . . 2, 3, 5, 17, 126–7
s 1 6
(a) 6
(b) 6
(c) 6
s 3 . . . . 14, 20, 22
s 5 . . . . 24, 97
(2)(a) 27, 135
(3) 24
s 6 28
(2) 29
s 7 34
s 8 133
s 9 . . . . 49, 50, 70
(1) 49, 52
(4) 51
s 12 300
(3) 81
s 14 92
(4) 91, 91–2
s 15 97
(2) 97

Arbitration Act 1996 (*cont.*)
s 16 99
(3) 91
s 18 . . . . 23, 44
s 24 . . . . 115, 117, 159
(1)(d) 117, 214
s 26 . . . . 133, 314
s 27 208
s 29 . . . . 125, 126, 308
s 30 . . . . 51, 138
s 31 143
(1) 144
(2) 144, 148
(3) 148
(4) 143, 146, 149
(5) 153
s 32 154
(6) 156
s 33 . . . . 9, 117, 167, 170, 183, 186, 187,
196, 220
(1)(a) 170
s 34 . . . . 11, 183, 186, 233
s 38 278
(3) 279
s 39 259
(1) 259
s 40 172
(1) 172
s 41
(3) 221
(3)(b) 220
s 42 . . . . 173, 222
(2)(b)(i) 224
s 43 . . . . 232, 233
s 44 . . . . 43, 237, 243
(5) 244
s 45 226
(1) 224
s 46 248
(2) 248

Arbitration Act 1996 (*cont.*)
s 47 258
s 48 (5) 251
s 52 . . . . 147, 256
s 56 261
    (2) 261, 262
    (4) 262
s 57 263
    (3)(a) 266
s 60 276
s 63 273
s 65 280
s 66 (3) 64
s 67 . . . . 71–2, 181, 248, 286
    (1) 147
    (4) 15
s 68 . . . . . . 72, 161, 167, 170, 181, 182,
                 183, 248, 250, 256, 286
    (2)(a) 117
    (2)(b) 117, 248
    (2)(c) 117
    (2)(d) 266, 290
    (2)(i) 294
    (3) 105
s 69 . . . . 84, 226, 250
s 70 (3) 147
s 72 . . . . 68, 69, 70, 71, 72
s 73 . . . . 131, 312
    (1) 149
s 79 230
s 82
    (1) 224
    (2) 59
ss 89–91 17
s 95 (2) 76
s 103 (2)(b) 45
Arbitration Act 2000 (Alberta)
s 6 31
Arbitration Act 2010 (Ireland)
s 14 38
Arbitration and Conciliation Act 1996
    (India) 11
s 7(4) 27
Arbitration Ordinance (Hong Kong)
    2011 7
Arbitration (Scotland) Act 2010 1,
                                     321–73
s 1 . . . . . . 5–6, 11, 14, 36, 66, 97–8, 114,
                152, 158, 169, 207, 208, 227,
                228, 234, 259, 292–3, 321
    (a) 5, 6, 10, 94, 96, 119, 311
    (b) 10, 93
    (c) 12

Arbitration (Scotland) Act 2010 (*cont.*)
s 2 . . . . 18, 318, 319, 321
    (1) 6
s 3 . . . . 10, 17, 19, 20, 34, 209, 322
    (1) 318
    (1) (a) 11
    (2) 20, 319
s 4 . . . . 23, 29, 34, 79, 318, 323
s 5 . . . . 32, 50, 136, 139, 323
    (3) 32
s 6 . . . . 10, 34, 38, 323
s 7 . . . . 35, 324
s 8 . . . . 3, 35–6, 268, 318, 324
s 9 . . . . 37, 39, 46, 51, 325
    (1) 318
    (4) 46
s 10 . . . . . . 13, 32, 39, 40, 41, 46, 56, 58,
                 139, 326
    (1) 47, 48, 49
    (1)(a) 48, 50
    (1)(b) 50, 53–4
    (1)(c) 47, 54
    (1)(d)(i) 39, 55
    (1)(d)(ii) 47, 55, 57
    (1)(e) 46, 56, 57
    (2) 57
    (3) 57
s 11 . . . . 50, 58, 257, 303, 326
    (1) 57
    (2) 58
    (3) 61
    (4) 58, 61
s 12 . . . . . 61, 62–5, 66, 69, 73, 303, 304,
                 327
    (1) 61, 303
    (2) 62, 63, 305
    (3) 62, 63–4, 69, 305
    (4) 62, 63–4
    (5) 64
    (6) 64
    (7) 64
ss 12–14 13
s 13 . . . . 13, 64, 65, 67, 94, 328
    (2) 293
    (4) 66, 67
s 14 . . . . 60, 68–9, 329
    (1) 68
    (1)(a) 68
    (1)(b) 68
    (2) 69
s 15 . . . . 73, 75, 175, 176, 177, 329
    (1) 74, 176
    (2) 176

Arbitration (Scotland) Act 2010 (*cont.*)
   (3) 176
  s 16 . . . . 76, 330
   (1) 76, 319
   (3) 76
   (4) 76
   (5) 76
   (6) 76
  ss 16–17 . . . . 4, 75–6
  s 17 331
   (a) 77
   (b) 77
  s 18 . . . . 257, 331
   (1) 303, 305
  ss 18–22 . . . . 27, 64, 303
  s 19 332
   (1) 303
   (2) 303
  s 20 . . . . 307, 332
   (1) 305
   (2)(a) 305, 306
   (2)(b) 84, 305
   (2)(c) 305, 306
   (2)(d) 305, 306
   (3)(a) 306
   (3)(b) 306
   (3)(c) 306
   (3)(d) 307
   (4) 307
   (4)(a) 84
   (5) 307
  s 21 . . . . 304, 333
   (2) 27
  s 22 334
  s 23 . . . . 77, 80, 86, 89, 229, 334
   (3) 79
   (4) 79
   (6) 80
  s 24 . . . . . 22, 81, 82, 83, 94, 96, 100, 113,
       127, 160, 289, 290, 293, 295, 310,
                             318, 335
   (2) 81
   (2)(b) 81
   (3) 81
  s 25 . . . . 83, 84, 336
   (3) 83–4
  s 26 336
  s 27 337
  s 28 337
  s 29 338
  s 30 . . . . 84, 338
  s 31 . . . . 67, 338
   (1) 3, 6, 35, 40, 50, 61, 176, 237

Arbitration (Scotland) Act 2010 (*cont.*)
  s 32 339
  s 33 340
  s 34 340
   (1) 86
   (2) 86
   (3) 86
  s 35 341
  s 36 341
  s 37 342
  Sch 1. *See* Scottish Arbitration Rules
   (2010)
  Sch 2 373

Bankruptcy and Diligence etc (Scotland)
  Act 2007 244

Civil Evidence (Scotland) Act
  1988 189
Commercial Arbitration Act 1984
  (New South Wales) 256
Companies Act 1985
  s 459 49
Companies Act 2006 85
  ss 994–996 49
Consumer Protection Act 1987
  s 2 80
Contracts (Third Party) (Scotland)
  Act 2017 60–1
  s 9(1) 60
Court of Session Act 1988
  s 10 244
  s 46 244
  s 47(2) 218, 219, 244
Court Reform (Scotland) Act
  2014
  s 108 272
Crown Proceedings Act 1921
  s 21 251
  s 43 251
Crown Proceedings Act 1947
  s 47 240

Electronic Communications Act
  2000 26
Employment Rights Act 2006
  s 203 86
Equality Act 2010 16
  s 144 86

Family Law Reform Act 1969
  s 1 95
Fraud Act 2006 292

Housing Grants, Construction and
    Regeneration Act 1996 .... 127, 261
  s 108 36–7
Human Rights Act 1998
  s 1 (2) 14
  s 3 14

International Arbitration Act 1974
    (Australia)
  s 28 ....125, 308
International Private and Procedural
    Law (Turkey)
  Art 23 85

Late Payment of Commercial Debts
    (Interest) Act 1998 254
Law of Property (Miscellaneous
    Provisions) Act 1989
  s 2 (3) 26
Law Reform (Miscellaneous
    Provisions) Act 1980 83
Law Reform (Miscellaneous
    Provisions) (Scotland) Act 1990
  s 8 252
  s 9 252
  s 66 6
  Sch 7 ....1, 6
Local Democracy, Economic
    Development and Construction
    Act 2009 127
  Part 8 37

Malaysian Arbitration Act 2005
  s 9
    (4) 24
    (4) (c) 24

Prescription and Limitation (Scotland)
    Act 1973 ....77, 86
  s 1 77
  s 2 77
  s 3 77–8
Prescription and Limitation (Scotland)
    Act 1973 (cont.)
  s 4 77

    (2) 78
    (2)(c) 78
    (3) 78
    (4) 78
    (4)(b)..........................89
  s 6 78
  s 7 78
  s 8A............................78
  s 9 ....77, 78
    (3) 78
  s 17
    (2) 79
  s 18A
    (1) 79
  s 19D..........................77, 79
  s 22A..........................77, 80
    (4) 80
  s 22B
    (2) 80
    (4) 80
  s 22C............................80
    (2) 80
  s 22CA 77, 80
  s 23
    (2) 77
    (3) 77
Prescription (Scotland) Act 2018 .. 77, 78
  s 5
    (4) 112
    (5) 112

Requirements of Writing (Scotland) Act
    1995
  s 1
    (2) 24
    (2)(b)..........................24
  s 12 24

Scotland Act 1998.................77
Senior Courts Act 1981
  s 37 43
Sheriff Courts (Scotland) Act 1971
  s 32 239
Singapore International Arbitration
    Act 25

Scottish Arbitration Rules (2010)

Scottish Arbitration Rules (2010) . . . 3, 7,
35, 88, 343–72
r 1 . . . . 79, 88, 89–90, 343
r 2 . . . . 10, 93, 94, 99, 100, 112, 343
(d) 94
r 3 . . . . 35, 36, 94, 314
r 4 . . . . 35, 94–5, 99, 101, 109, 114, 142,
240, 343
(a) 95, 294
(b) 95, 293
r 5 . . . . 18, 96, 142, 212, 343
r 6 . . . . 94, 98–9, 100, 120, 124,
142, 343
(a) 101
(h) 97
r 7 . . . 35, 81, 94, 99, 100, 101, 110, 120,
124, 127, 310, 344
(2) 81
(5) 82
(6) 101
(8) 82, 100
r 8 . . . . 7, 35, 101–2, 114, 132, 157, 164,
165, 166, 313, 314, 345
(2) 131, 132, 162, 313, 314
(2)(b) 102
r 9 . . . . 109, 113, 114, 116, 120, 125,
208, 345
(a) 137
(c) 208
rs 9–13 103
r 10 . . . . 7, 109, 114, 118, 119, 120,
121, 144, 345
(2) 131
(2)(a) 313
(2)(a)(i) 110
(2)(iii) 142
r 11 . . . . 109, 112, 114, 117, 119,
179, 208, 346
(1) 208
(2) 208
r 12 . . . . 7, 109, 113, 114, 117, 118,
119, 120, 121, 123, 132, 164,
179, 293, 346
(a) 116
(b) 116
(c) 114
(e) 36, 114
rs 12–16 35
r 13 . . . . 109, 113, 116, 117, 118,
119, 120, 121, 123, 132,
165, 313, 346
r 14 . . . . 113, 117, 118, 346
(1)(b)(ii) 113
(3) 119
r 15 . . . . . . 109, 120, 122, 123, 169, 347
(1)(e) 121
(2) 121
r 16 . . . . 122, 124, 169, 208, 347
(1) 132, 313, 314
(1)(c) 122, 123, 125, 126, 127,
308, 309
r 17 . . . . 120, 124, 208, 347
(1) 124
(2) 208
r 18 . . . . 125, 348
r 19 . . . 136, 154, 175, 199, 283, 284, 348
(a) 141
(b) 137, 141, 142
(c) 137, 142
rs 19–23 . . . . 284, 288
r 20 . . . . 137, 143, 154, 252, 282,
283, 284, 312, 348
(1) 143
(2) 143
(2)(a) 144
(2)(b) 144
(3) 142, 263, 283
(4) 143, 147, 283, 284
(4)(b) 145
rs 20–23 282

r 21 . . . . . 13, 66, 147, 156, 283, 284, 349
    (1) 150
    (2) 152
    (3) 152
r 22 . . . . 66, 115, 117, 142, 143, 153,
            154, 155, 156, 283, 284, 349
r 23 . . . . 142, 143, 153, 155, 349
    (2)(b)(i) 153, 155
    (2)(b)(ii) 153, 155
    (2)(b)(iii) 153, 155
    (3) 152
r 24 . . . . 7, 9, 35, 114, 116, 124, 132,
            156, 157, 165, 169, 185, 207,
            208, 212, 216, 227, 228, 234,
            259, 279, 280, 313, 349
    (1)(a) 131, 288, 293, 313
    (1)(c)(i) 119
    (2) 167, 222
r 25 . . . . 7, 10, 31, 35, 124, 150, 172,
                227, 350
r 26 . . . . 37, 73, 113, 174–83, 350
    (1) 175, 177
    (1)(a) 180
    (1)(d) 178
    (1)(e) 180, 183
    (1)(f) 180
    (2) 114, 179
    (3) 175
    (4) 174, 175, 177, 179
r 27 . . . . 183, 350
r 28 . . . . . . 10, 183, 185, 195, 215, 217,
                219, 233, 351
    (1)(b) 190
    (2) 183
    (2)(a) 209
r 29 . . . . 10, 209, 351
r 30 . . . . 211, 351
    (2)(a) 211
    (2)(b) 211
rs 30–40 11
r 31 . . . . 211, 352
r 32 . . . . 98, 212, 352
r 33 . . . . 193, 215, 352
r 34 . . . . 121, 216–17, 218, 352
    (1) 120, 121
    (2) 217
r 35 . . . . 218, 240, 353
r 36 . . . . 38, 219, 353
r 37 . . . . 169, 220, 221, 353
    (1) 263
    (1)(b) 220
rs 37–39 229
r 38 . . . . 169, 221, 353

r 39 . . . . 76, 221, 354
    (1) 221
    (1)(b) 222
    (2) 222
r 40 . . . . 223, 354
r 41 . . . . 115, 117, 224, 226, 227,
                231, 233, 354
r 42 . . . . . . 35, 224, 226, 227, 230, 231,
                247, 355
    (2) 226
r 43 . . . . 228, 229, 231, 300, 355
r 44 . . . . 35, 231, 300, 355
    (1) 229
r 45 . . . . 35, 197, 232, 233, 355
    (2) 232
r 46 . . . . 218, 236, 237, 277, 356
    (1)(a) 240
    (1)(b) 240
    (1)(c) 277
    (2) 244
    (4)(b)(i) 236
r 47 . . . . 245, 246, 248, 249, 356
    (2) 246
    (3) 246
r 48 . . . . 35, 249, 254, 255, 357
r 49 . . . . 251, 357
    (b) 242
r 50 . . . . 35, 253, 255, 357
    (3) 253
    (4) 254
r 51 . . . . 255, 256, 358
    (2)(c) 289, 296, 300, 301
    (2)(d) 259, 260
    (3) 256–7, 265
r 52 . . . . 257, 358
r 53 . . . . 58, 146, 257, 259, 263, 319, 358
r 54 . . . . 36, 147, 259, 260, 319, 358
    (1) 274
    (2) 147, 274
    (3) 260
r 55 . . . . 260, 263–4, 265, 358
    (a) 261
    (b) 261
r 56 . . . . 36, 257, 261, 359
r 57 . . . . 262, 359
    (1) 262, 275
    (2) 263
    (3) 263
    (4) 263
    (5) 263
r 58 . . . . 260, 263–4, 299, 305, 359
    (1) 263
    (2)(b) 291

(4)(a) 265
(4)(b) 265
(5) 264, 265
(6) 265
(6)(a) 265
(6)(b) 265
(7) 265
r 59 . . . . 121, 266, 267, 268, 271,
                              274, 318, 360
(a) 271
(c) 271
rs 59–61 271
r 60 . . . . 36, 121, 261, 267, 268,
                              275, 361
(1)(b)(i) 267
(1)(b)(ii) 217
(3) 269
(3)(a) 270
(3)(b) 270
(5) 270
r 61 . . . 267, 271, 273, 274, 277, 319, 361
(1) 271
(2) 271, 273
(3) 271, 272, 273
(3)(a) 273
(3)(b) 273
r 62 . . . . 252, 274, 276, 281, 362
(1) 275
(2)(a) 271
(3) 269, 274, 275
(3)(b) 275
(4)(a) 275
r 63 . . . . 36, 37, 269, 276, 281, 362
r 64 . . . . 277, 278, 363
(1) 279
(2) 277, 278
r 65 . . . . 280, 281, 363
r 66 . . . . 268, 281, 363
r 67 . . . . . 36, 66, 69, 115, 117, 141, 144,
            146, 147, 149, 153, 154, 281,
            282, 283, 284, 288, 295,
                              296, 363
(1) 116, 151, 227, 282, 283
(2) 282, 283, 284, 295
(3) 282
(4) 282
(5) 282, 284, 285
(6) 282
(7) 282
r 68 . . . . 36, 69, 112, 114, 115, 117,
            132, 195, 240, 265, 281, 283,
            284, 286, 287, 292, 295,
                              296, 313, 364

(1) 288
(2) 284, 285, 287
(2)(a) 288, 294, 295
(2)(a)(ii) 36
(2)(d) 289, 290
(2)(e) 291
(2)(f)(i) 291
(2)(f)(ii) 291
(2)(g) 288, 293, 295
(2)(h) 293, 295
(2)(j) 111, 290
(2)(k) 285, 295
(2)(k)(i) 295
(2)(k)(ii) 295
(4) 132, 285, 295, 314
(4)(b) 102
(5) 285
(6) 285
(7) 285
(8) 285
rs 68–77 114
r 69 . . . . 114, 191, 195, 281, 283,
                    295, 296, 299, 365
(1) 116, 227
(2) 301
(4) 313
r 70 . . . . 36, 299, 301, 365
(1) 299
(2) 297
(2)(a) 298, 300
(2)(b) 298
(2)(c) 298
(3) 297, 300
(3)(a) 297
(3)(b) 297
(3)(c)(i) 297
(3)(c)(ii) 297
(4) 297
(5) 297, 298
(6) 298
(7) 298, 300
(8) 295, 298
(8)(a) 298
(9) 298
(10) 298
(11) 298
(12) 298
r 71 . . . . 36, 296, 299, 301, 302, 366
(1)(c) 299
(2) 69, 282, 291, 299
(3) 299
(4) 282, 299, 300
(5) 300

(6) 300, 302
(7) 300
(8) 184, 256, 300, 301
(8)(b) 300, 302
(9) 301
(10) 301
(10)(b) 301
(11) 301
(12) 301
(12)(a) 301
(12)(b) 301
(13) 302
(14) 302
(15) 302
(16) 302
(17) 302
r 72 . . . . 36, 298, 302, 368
r 73 . . . . 36, 122, 125, 127, 307–8,
                                    310, 368
(2)(b) 122, 127
(3) 128, 310
r 74 . . . . . 36, 82, 100, 127, 128, 309–10,
                                         369
r 75 . . . . 36, 128, 129, 310–11, 369
r 76 . . . . 36, 64, 69, 129–30, 155–6,
                         283, 290, 305, 311, 369
(1) 130
(1)(b) 162
(1)(d) 148–9
(2) 130, 311

(2)(a) 131, 312
(2)(c) 130, 312
(3) 130, 149, 312
r 77 . . . . 7–8, 12, 36, 99, 110, 131,
                   132, 157, 158, 159, 165, 169,
                   293, 313, 314, 318, 370
r 78 . . . . 102, 132, 157, 165, 169,
                                    313, 314, 370
r 79 . . . . 36, 109, 133, 314, 315, 370
(1) 317
r 80 . . . . 133, 314–15, 370
r 81 . . . . 134, 315, 371
r 82 . . . . 36, 102, 134, 315, 371
(2) 134, 315
r 83 . . . . 90, 134, 135, 256, 316, 371
(1) 90, 134, 317
(1)(a) 90
(1)(b) 90
(1)(b)(i) 90
(1)(b)(ii) 90
(1)(b)(iii) 90
(2) 90, 134, 317
(3) 317
(3)(a) 90
(3)(c) 90
(4) 90, 134, 317
(5) 90, 91, 135, 317
(6) 90, 135, 317
(7) 90, 135, 317
r 84 . . . . 136, 318, 372

Table of Statutory Instruments

Act of Sederunt (Rules of the Court of
    Session 1994) (SI 1994/1443) 8
    r 7.5 249
    r 14 151
    r 14.4 150
    r 14.6 54
    r 14.7 . . . . 54, 151
    r 14.8 54
    r 33 278
    r 33.2 (1) 278
    r 35.2.7 236
    r 35.8 (1) 236
    r 42 269
    r 42.4 270
    r 53 252
    r 62 304
    r 62.2 304
    r 62.3 304
    r 62.56 . . . . 305, 374
    r 62.57 . . . . 305, 374
      (2)(d) 304
    r 62.58 . . . . 305, 375
    r 62.59 . . . . 305, 375, 383
    r 62.60 . . . . 305, 375
    r 62.61 305
    r 62.62 305
    r 65.4 41
    r 100 . . . . 151, 228, 304
    r 100.1 376
    r 100.2 . . . . 54, 118, 376
    r 100.3 . . . . 54, 57, 150, 151, 283–4,
                               304, 377
    r 100.4 . . . . 54, 151, 377
    r 100.5 . . . 39, 54, 118, 150, 151, 234, 377
      (1) 54, 62, 63, 115, 117, 123,
                            226, 233, 304
      (2) 123, 304
      (3) 118, 119, 151, 234, 304
      (5) 75, 118, 121, 176, 304
    r 100.6 377

Act of Sederunt (Rules of the Court of
    Session 1994) (SI 1994/1443) (*cont.*)
    r 100.7 . . . . 151, 284, 378
      (1) . . 115, 116, 117, 150, 226, 227, 233
      (2) 226
      (2)(b) 296
      (3) 115, 117, 150, 226
      (3)(f) 284
    r 100.8 378
    r 100.9 . . . . 74, 176, 177, 379
      (2) 75
    r 100.10 . . . . 304, 379
      (1) 63
      (1)(b) 63
      (2) 63
    r 100.591 150
Act of Sederunt (Rules of the Court
    of Session Amendment No 4)
    (Miscellaneous) 2010 (SSI
    2010/205) 374
    r 10(3) 383
Act of Sederunt (Sheriff Court
    Ordinary Cause Rules 1993)
    (SI 1993/1956) 8, 10
    r 9.12 9
Appointment of Judges as Arbiters
    (Fees) Order 1993
    (SI 1993/3125) 83
Arbitral Appointments Referee
    (Scotland) Order 2010
    (SSI 2010/196) 81
Arbitration (Scotland) Act 2010
    (Transitional Provisions) Order
    2016 (SSI 2016/435) 4

Civil Procedure Rules 1998
    (SI 1998/3132) 31, 146, 148, 181
    r 3.1(2)(m) 389
    r 62.8 52
    r 62.10 15

Commercial Agents (Council
  Directive) Regulations 1993
  (SI 1993/3053) 33
Cross-Border Mediation (EU
  Directive) Regulations 2011
  (SI 2011/1133) 385
Cross-Border Mediation (Scotland)
  Regulations 2011
  (SSI/2011/234). 385

Employment Equality (Religion
  or Belief) Regulations 2003
  (SI 2003/1660) 16
Employment Tribunals (Constitution
  and Rules of Procedure)
  Regulations 2004 (SI 2004/1861)
Sch 1 (18) 173

Scotland Act 1998 (Transitory
  and Transitional Provisions)
  (Publication and Interpretation etc
  of Acts of the Scottish Parliament)
  Order (SSI 1999/1379)
  Sch 2 27

Unfair Arbitration Agreements
  (Specified Amount) Order 1996
  (SI 1996/3211) 17
Unfair Terms in Consumer
  Contracts Regulations 1999
  (SI 1999/2083) 17

Table of Cases

A v B [2018] EWHC 1370 (Comm)...52, 73
A v B [2016] EWHC 3003 (Comm)..139
A and others v B and another [2011] EWHC 2345 (Comm)....................160
A v OOO Insurance Company Chubb and others [2019] EWHC 2729 (Comm) .44, 59
Abberley v Abberley [2019] EWHC 1564 (Ch)..................................391
Accentuate Ltd v Asigra Inc [2009] EWHC 2655................................33
AES Ust-Kamenogorsk Hydropower Plant LLP v Ust-Kamenogorsk
    Hydropower Plant JSC [2011] EWCA Civ 647...............................43
AES Ust-Kamenogorsk Hydropower Plant LLP v Ust-Kamenogorsk
    Hydropower Plant JSC [2013] UKSC 35 155
Africa Express Line Ltd v Socofi SA [2009] EWHC 3222 (Comm) 29
Agrimex Ltd v Tradigrain SA [2003] EWHC 1656 215
Airbus SAS v Generali Italia SpA and others [2019] EWCA Civ 805.............52
Aird v Prime Meridian Ltd [2006] EWCA 1866................................207
Al Naimi (t/a Buildmaster Construction Services) v Islamic Press Agency Inc
    [2000] 1 Lloyd's Rep 522...52, 142
Albon (t/a NA Carriage Co) v Naza Motor Trading Sdn Bhd [2007] EWHC 665
    (Ch) 52
Ali Shipping Corp v Shipyard Trogir [1998] 2 All ER 136......................180
Allianz Insurance plc and another v Tonicstar Ltd and others [2018] EWCA
    Civ 434 82
Allianz SpA v West Tankers Inc (Case C-185/07) ECLI:EU:C:2009:69 ....42, 86
Almazeddi v Penner [2018] UKPC 3..8
American Cyanamid Co v Ethicon Ltd [1975] AC 396; [1975] 2 WLR 316 ....175, 252
AmTrust Europe Ltd v Trust Risk Group SpA [2015] EWCA Civ 437 138
Anderson v Gibb 1993 SLT 726 238
Anton Piller KG v Manufacturing Processes Ltd [1976] Ch 55.................244
Aoot Kalmneft JSC v Glencore International AG [2001] 2 All ER (Comm) 577 145
Apollo Engineering Ltd v James Scott Ltd [2009] CSIH 39; 2009 SC 525......268, 274
Apollo Engineering Ltd v James Scott Ltd [2012] CSIH 4 194
Apollo Engineering Ltd v United Kingdom (Admissibility) (2019) 69 EHRR
    SE12..2, 15–16
Aqaba Container Terminal (PVT) Co v Soletanche Bachy France SAS [2019]
    EWHC 471 (Comm) 43
Arab National Bank v El-Abdali [2004] EWHC 2381 (Comm) 70
Arbitration Appeals
    [2019]
    No 1 CSOH 60 13
    No 2 51 263
    No 4 CSOH 46 191

Arbitration Appeals (*cont.*)
  [2018]
    No 2 of 2017 CSOH 12 286
Arbitration Applications
  [2014]
    No 1 CSOH 83 ....4, 286, 287, 288
  [2011]
    No 2 CSOH 186 ....177, 184
    No 3 CSOH 164; 2012 SLT 150 .....2, 66, 75, 151–2, 176, 190, 194, 282, 287, 296, 297
  [2001]
    No 3 SLT 150 4
ArcelorMittal USA LLC v Essar Steel Ltd [2009] EWHC 724 (Comm) 243
Arenson v Casson Beckman Rutley & Co [1977] AC 405.................126, 308–9
Argyll (Duke of) v Duchess of Argyll 1962 SLT 333............................189
Arnwell Pty Ltd v Teilaboot Ltd [2010] VSC 123 13
Arthur J S Hall & Co v Simons [2003] 3 WLR 543........................128, 311
ASM Shipping Ltd v Harris [2007] EWHC 1513 (Comm) 161, 162
ASM Shipping Ltd of India v TTMI Ltd of England [2006] EWCA Civ 1341.......15
ASM Shipping Ltd of India v TTMI Ltd of England [2005] EWHC 2238
    (Comm); [2006] 1 Lloyd's Rep 401 ....104, 108, 160, 293
Assimina Maritime v Pakistan National Shipping Corpn (The Tasman Spirit)
    [2004] EWHC 3005 (Comm)..241
Associated Electric & Gas Insurance Services Ltd v European Reinsurance Co
    of Zurich [2003] UKPC 11 182
Asturcom Telecommunications SL v Rodriguez Nogueira (Case C-40/08)
    [2009] ECR I-9579 17
Atlanska Plovidba v Consignaciones Asturianas SA (The Lapad) [2004] EWHC
    1273 (Admlty) 91
Atlas Power Ltd v National Transmission and Despatcch Co Ltd [2018] EWHC
    1052 (Comm) 22
Austin Rover Group Ltd v HM Inspector of Factories [1990] 1 AC 619 ......130, 311
Australia (Commonwealth of) v Cockatoo Dockyard Pty Ltd [1995] 36 NSWLR
    662 178
Autauric Ltd v Glasgow Stage Crew Ltd [2019] CSOH 111 31
Azumi Ltd v Zuma's Choice Pet Products Ltd [2017] EWHC 45 (IPEC).........163

B v A [2010] EWHC 1626 (Comm)...............................247, 248, 250
BAA Ltd v Competition Commission [2009] CAT 35.........................158
Babanaft International Co SA v Avanti Petroleum Inc (The Oltenia) [1982] 1
    WLR 871 225
Baillie v Pollock (1829) 7 S 619 304
Baker v Quantum Clothing Group [2011] UKSC 17; [2009] EWCA Civ 499...130, 311
Bandwidth Shipping Corp v Intaari [2008] 1 Lloyd's Rep 141 293
Barnmore Demolition and Civil Engineering Ltd v Alandale Logistics (no
    5910P) 11 November 2010, Irish High Ct, no 5910P.....................47
Batt Cables plc v Spencer Business Parks Ltd [2010] CSOH 81..................92
BC v BG [2019] EWFC 7 85
Beauty Star Ltd v Janmohamed [2014] EWCA Civ 451 391
Beck Peppiatt Ltd v Norwest Holst Construction Ltd [2003] EWHC 822 (TCC)....48
Beggs v Motherwell Bridge Fabricators Ltd 1998 SLT 1215 ....130, 312
Belair LLC v Basel LLC [2009] EWHC 725 (Comm)........................243
Ben Cleuch Estates Ltd v Scottish Enterprise [2006] CSOH 35...................92
Ben Cleuch Estates Ltd v Scottish Enterprise [2008] CSIH 1, 2008 SC 252...92, 135, 317

Benaim (UK) Ltd v Davies Middleton Ltd (No 2) [2005] EWHC (TCC) 117
Berebon, King v Shell Petroleum Development Co of Nigeria Ltd [2018] EWHC
    1377 (TCC) 390
Berkeley Burke SOPP Administration LLP v Charlton [2017] EWHC 2396 (Comm). . 32
BGS SGS SOMA JV v NHPC Ltd [2019], Indian Supreme Ct, Civil appeals
    9307/9308/9309 of 2019 11
Bilta (UK) Ltd (in liquidation) v Nazir [2010] EWHC 1086 (Ch) 50
Birkett v James [1978] AC 297 173
Birse Construction v St David [1999] BLR 194. 51–2
BLCT (13096) Ltd v Sainsbury plc [2003] EWCA 884. 15
BN Rendering Ltd v Everwarm Ltd [2018] CSOH 45. 30
BNP Paribas SA v Open Joint Stock Company Russian Machines and another
    [2011] EWHC 308 (Comm). 45
BNP Paribas v Deloitte & Touche LLP [2003] EWHC 2874 (Comm) 235
Bolkiah v Brunei Darussalam [2007] UKPC 62 159
Boulos Gad Tourism & Hotels Ltd v Uniground Shipping Co Ltd (The
    Serenade) 16 November 2001, QBD (Comm) 198
Boyd & Forrest v Glasgow & South Western Railway Co (No 1) 1912 SC
    (HL) 93 292
Braes of Doune Wind Farm (Scotland) Ltd v Alfred McAlpine Business
    Services Ltd [2008] EWHC 426 (TCC); [2008] 2 All ER (Comm) 493. . . . . . . 11, 21,
                                                                                    22–3, 297
Brandeis Brokers Ltd v Black [2001] 2 Lloyd's Rep 359 215
Bridgehouse (Bradford No 2) Ltd v BAE Systems PLC [2020] EWCA Civ 759 50
Bridgeway Construction Ltd v Tolent Construction Ltd [2000] CILL 1662
    (TCC). 36, 269
Briggs v First Choice Holidays [2017] EWHC 2012 (QB). 389
British Sky Broadcasting plc v Virgin Media Communications Ltd (formerly
    NTL Communications Ltd) [2008] EWCA 612 207
Broda Agro Trade (Cyprus) Ltd v Alfred C Toepfer International GmbH [2010]
    EWCA Civ 100. 71
Brown v Rice [2007] EWHC 625 (Ch) 207
Brown v Rysaffe Trustee Company (CI) Ltd [2011] CSOH 26 252
Burmah Oil Co v Bank of England [1979] 1 WLR 473 188
Buyuk Camlica Shipping Trading & Industry Co Inc v Progress Bulk Carriers
    Ltd [2010] EWHC 442 (Comm). 229, 266
DXD v Watch Tower and Bible Tract Society of Pennsylvania [2020] EWHC 656
    (QB). 389

C v D [2007] EWCA Civ 1282. 21
C v D1 [2015] EWHC 2126 (Comm) 138, 140
Cable & Wireless v IBM United Kingdom Ltd [2002] EWHC 2059 (Comm) . .40–1, 47
Canadian Natural Resources Ltd v Flatiron Constructors Canada Ltd 2018
    ABQB 613 31
Caparo Group Ltd v Fagor Arrasate Sociedad Cooperativa [2000] ADRLJ 254;
    [1998] 8 WLUK 75 68
Capital Trust Investment Ltd v Radio Design AB [2002] EWCA Civ 135. 50
Caravel Shipping Services Private Ltd v Premier Sea Foods Exim Private Ltd
    [2018] Indian Supreme Ct, Civil appeals 10800–10801 of 2018. . . . . .27, 29
Cavendish Square Holding BV v Talal El Makdessi; Parking Eye Ltd v Beavis
    [2015] UKSC 67 254
Celtic Bioenergy Ltd v Knowles Ltd [2017] EWHC 472 (TCC); [2018] 1 All ER
    (Comm) 608 292

Cetelem SA v Roust Holdings Ltd [2005] EWCA Civ 618. .243
Chalbury McCouat International Ltd v PG Foils [2010] EWHC 2050 (TCC) 23
Chartered Institute of Arbitrators v B [2019] EWHC 460 (Comm). 182–3
Charterer (Norway) v Shipowner (Russian Federation) 16 August 1999 (2002)
    XXVII Ybk Comm Arb 519-22 (Norway No 1) 26
Checkpoint Ltd v Strathclyde Pension Fund [2003] EWCA Civ 84 . . . . . .186, 256, 286
China Pacific Property Insurance Corpn v Beijing COSCO Logistics Co Ltd
    [2009] Chinese Supreme People's Ct 59
Chung v Silver Dry Co Ltd [2019] EWHC 1479 (Comm). .181
CIB Properties Ltd v Birse Construction Ltd [2004] EWHC 2365 (TCC). 48
City Inn Ltd v Shepherd Construction 2002 SLT 781 254
Club Atlético de Madrid SAD v Sport Lisboa E Benfica - Futebol SAD and
    Fédération Internationale de Football (FIFA), 13 April 2010, Swiss
    Supreme Ct, decision 4A_490/2009 . . . . .62, 292
Clyde & Co LLP v Krista Bates van Winkelhof [2011] EWHC 668 (QB) 86
Cockett Marine Oil DMCC v ING Bank NV and another [2019] EWHC 1533 139
Cofely Ltd v Bingham [2016] EWHC 240 (Comm) 161
Cogentra AG v Sixteen Thirteen Marine SA [2008] EWHC 1615 (Comm) 243
Collins (Contractors) Ltd v Baltic Quay Management (1994) Ltd [2004] EWCA
    Civ 1757 48
Commerzbank AS v Large 1977 SC 375 249
Company 1 v Company 2 [2017] EWHC 2319 (QB) 243
Company X v Company Y 17 July 2000 (unreported) 82
Connell v Grierson (1865) 3 M 1166 41
Continental Transfert Technique Ltd v Federal Government of Nigeria [2010]
    All ER (D) 184 63
Cramaso LLP v Viscount Reidhaven's Trustees 2012 SC 240 252
Crawford Bros v Commissioners of Northern Lighthouse [1925] SC (HL)22,
    1925 SLT 341. 106

Dalian Huarui Heavy Industry Group Co Ltd v Forge Group Construction Pty
    Ltd [2017] Chinese Supreme People's Ct. 85
Dallah Estate and Tourism Holding Co v Ministry of Religious Affairs of the
    Government of Pakistan [2010] UKSC 46 . . . . 43, 53, 56, 64, 69,
                                                                       71, 138, 305
Dallas McMillan (Partners of), Petitioners [2015] CSOH 136 . . . . .105, 307
Daniels v Commissioner of Police of the Metropolis [2005] EWCA Civ 1312 390
David Clark v Argyle Consulting Ltd [2010] CSOH 154 80
David T Morrison & Co Ltd v ICL Plastics and others [2014] UKSC 48 . . . .112, 130–1
David Wilson Homes Ltd v Survey Services Ltd (now in liquidation) [2001]
    EWCA Civ 34. 28
Dawes v Treasure and Son Ltd [2010] EWHC 3218 (TCC) .258
Decision of the 11th Chamber of the Turkish Court of Appeals, 10 December
    2009 E2008/7283, K2009/12746 85
Dedon GmbH v Janus et Cie (1911) US Dist LEXIS 112131 .71
Denel (Proprietary) Ltd v Bharat Electronics Ltd (2010) 6 SCC 394. 103
Department of Economic Policy and Development of the City of Moscow v
    Bankers Trust Co [2004] EWCA Civ 314 . . . . .15, 181
Dera Commercial Estate v Derya Inc [2018] EWHC 1673 221
Derry v Peek (1889) 14 App Cas 337. 292
Derry City Council v Brickkiln Ltd, Professor Stephen Willetts [2012] NIQB 84. . .166
Deutsche Bank AG v Sebastian Holdings Inc [2009] EWHC 3069 (Comm) 45
Diamond v PJW Enterprises Ltd 2004 SC 430 80

Dickson v Grant (1870) 8 March 566 106
Director General of Fair Trading v Proprietary Association of Great Britain
    [2001] 1 WLR 700. 161
Dolling-Baker v Merrett [1990] 1 WLR 1205 180
Dreymoor Fertilizers Overseas Pte Ltd v Eurochem Trading GmbH [2018]
    EWHC 909 19
Drika BVBA v Giles [2018] CSIH 42 . . . . .150, 152
DSN v Blackpool Football Club [2020] EWHC 670 (QB) .389
DTEK Trading SA v Morozov [2017] EWHC 94 (Comm) .235
Dubai Islamic Bank PJSC v Paymentech Merchant Services Inc [2001] 1 Lloyd's
    Rep 65 20

Econet Wireless Ltd v Vee Networks Ltd [2006] EWHC 1568 243
Edmunds' Application for Judicial Review, Re [2019] NIQB 50. 390
EDO Corpn v Ultra Electronics Ltd [2009] EWHC 682 (Ch) 49
Edwards v Bairstow 1956 AC 14 225
Edwards v National Coal Board [1949] 1 KB 704 .130, 144, 311
Elektrim SA v Vivendi Universal SA [2007] EWHC 11 (Comm); [2007] 1
    Lloyd's Rep 693 . . . . .172, 291
Emirates Trading Agency LLC v Prime Mineral Exports Private Ltd [2014]
    EWHC 2104 (Comm) 41
Emirates Trading Agency LLC v Sociedade de Fomento Industrial Private Ltd
    [2015] EWHC 1452 (Comm). 208
Emmott v Michael Wilson & Partners Ltd [2008] EWCA Civ 184 . . . . .13, 178, 181
Emmott v Michael Wilson & Partners Ltd (No 2) [2009] EWHC 1 (Comm). 243
English v Emery Reimbold & Strick Ltd [2002] EWCA 605 15
Enka Insaat Ve Sanayi AS v OOO Insurance Company Chubb [2020] UKSC 38. . . .22
Equatorial Traders Ltd v Louis Dreyfus Trading Ltd [2002] EWHC 2023
    (Comm). 230
Equitas Insurance Ltd v Municipal Mutual Insurance Ltd [2019] EWCA Civ
    718 84
Equity and Law Life Assurance Society v Tritonia Ltd 1943 SC (HL) 88 194
ERDC Construction Ltd v HM Love & Co (No 2) 1996 SC 523. . . . . 105–6, 168,
                                                                                     184, 195, 224
Erdenet Mining Corpn LLC v ICBC Standard Bank plc [2017] EWHC 1090
    (Comm). 301
FRJ Lovelock v Exportles [1968] 1 Lloyd's Rep 163 28
Errington v Wilson 1995 SC 550. 158
Esso Australia Resources Ltd v Plowman (1995) 183 CLR 10 . . . . .74, 178
Esso Exploration & Production UK Ltd v Electricity Supply Board [2004]
    EWHC 723 (Comm) 154
Etihad Airways PJSC v Flother (2019) EWHC 3107 (Comm) 30
European Grain v Johnston [1982] 2 Lloyd's Rep 550 211
Evans v Commissioner of Police of the Metropolis [1993] ICR 151 173
Evison Holdings Ltd v International Co Finvision Holdings [2019] EWHC 3057
    (Comm). 43, 45
Excalibur Ventures LLC v Texas Keystone Inc [2011] EWHC 1624 (Comm) . . .43, 138
Exchange and Commodities Ltd Re [1983] BCLC 186 96
Exeter City AFC Ltd v Football Conference Ltd [2004] 1 WLR 2901 49

Farm Assist Ltd (in liquidation) v Secretary of State for the Environment, Food
    and Rural Affairs (No 2) [2009] EWHC 1102 (TCC). 208
Farstad Supply AS v Enviroco Ltd 2013 SC 302 254–5

Federal Electric (1976) Ltd v McDonald Brothers Construction [2019] ONSC
    496 86
Fence Gate Ltd v NEL Construction Ltd (2001) 82 Con LR 41 (QBD (TCC)) 191
Fernhill Properties (Northern Ireland) Ltd v Mulgrew [2010] NICh 20 254
Field v Network Rail Infrastructure Ltd [2020] EWHC 3440 (Ch) 105, 185
Film Finance Inc v Royal Bank of Scotland [2007] EWHC 195 (Comm) 154
Fiona Trust & Holding Corpn v Privalov [2007] EWCA Civ 20 . . . . . . .18, 50–1, 70, 87
Fiona Trust & Holding Corpn v Privalov (sub nom Premium Nafta Products
    Ltd v Fili Shipping Co Ltd) [2007] UKHL 40 . . . . .13, 15, 18, 19, 30, 34, 140
Fiona Trust & Holding Corpn v Privalov [2010] EWHC 3199 (Comm). 51
Five Oceans Salvage Ltd v Wenzhou Timber Group Co [2011] EWHC 3282
    (Comm). 144
Flaherty v National Greyhound Racing Club Ltd [2005] EWCA Civ 1117 115
Fleetwood Wanderers Ltd (t/a Fleetwood Town Football Club) v AFC Fylde
    Ltd [2018] EWHC 3318 (Comm) 105
Fleming's Trustee v Henderson 1962 SLT 401 162
Flight Training International Inc v International Fire Training Equipment Ltd
    [2004] EWHC 721 (Comm). 28
Fulham Football Club (1987) Ltd v Sir David Richards and another [2010]
    EWHC 3111 (Ch). 49, 85
Fulton v AIB Group (UK) plc [2018] NICh 11 216

G1 Venues for Orders under Schedule 1 to the Arbitration (Scotland) Act 2010
    to set aside a decision of an 'arbiter' dated 10 May 2013 [2013] CSOH 202 . . .282
Gao Haiyan v Keeneye Holdings Ltd [2011] HKEC 514 . . . . .289, 291
Gazprom OAO v Lietuvos Respublika (Case C-536/13) [2015] ECLI:EU:C:2015:
    216 42
Gbangbola v Smith & Sheriff Ltd [1988] 3 All ER 730 167
General Construction Company Ltd v Silver Leaf Developments Ltd 3 March
    2018, Cyprus Supreme Ct, Petition 68/2016 8
General Feeds Inc v Slobodna Plovidba Yugoslavia [1999] 1 Lloyd's Rep 688. 291
Geogas SA v Trammo Gas Ltd (The Baleares) [1993] 1 Lloyd's Rep 215. 191
Gerald Metals SA v Timis [2016] EWHC 2327 (Ch) 243
Glencairn IP Holdings Ltd v Product Specialities Inc (t/a Final Touch) [2019]
    EWHC 1733 (IPEC). 208
Glencore Agriculture BV v Conqueror Holdings Ltd [2017] EWHC 2893
    (Comm). 72
Glidepath BV v Thompson [2005] EWHC 818 (Comm). .180
Gold Coast Ltd v Naval Gijon SA (The Hull 53) [2006] EWHC 1044 (Comm). 230
Goodwood Investments Holdings Inc v Thyssenkrupp Industrial Solution AG
    [2018] EWHC 1056 (Comm). 226
Gordian Runoff Ltd v Westport Insurance Corpn [2010] NSWCA 57. 256
Grahame House Investments Ltd v Secretary of State for the Environment
    [1985] SC 201, 1985 SLT 502. 105
Grindrod Shipping Pte Ltd v Hyundai Merchant Marine Co Ltd [2018] EWHC
    1284 220
Groundshire v VHE Construction [2001] BLR 395 293

Habas Sinai Ve Tibbi Gazlar Isthisal Endustri AS v Sometal Sal [2010] EWHC
    29 (Comm) 29, 140
Hackwood Ltd v Aren Design Services Ltd [2005] EWHC 2322 (TCC). 72
Haden Young Ltd v William McGrindle & Son Ltd 1994 SLT 221 65
Haiti v Duvalier (No 2) [1990] 1 QB 202 243

Haley v Haley [2020] EWCA Civ 1369 85
Halki Shipping Corpn v Sopex Oils Ltd [1997] EWCA Civ 3062 48
Halliburton Company v Chubb Bermuda Insurance Ltd [2020] UKSC 48 . . . . . 8, 101,
                                                   103, 107, 115, 131, 157, 159, 162, 207
Halliday v Duke of Hamilton's Trs (1903) 5 F 800 106
Halsey v Milton Keynes General NHS Trust [2004] EWCA Civ 576 389
Hamlyn & Co v Talisker Distillery (1894) 21 R (HL) 21 . . . . .16, 41
Haryana (Government of) PWD Haryana (B and R) Branch v M/s G F Toll
     Road Pvt Ltd and others [2019] Indian Supreme Ct, Civil appeal 27/2019 . . .103
Hassneh Insurance Co of Israel v Stuart J Mew [1993] 2 Lloyd's Rep 243 . . . .173, 180
Haven Insurance Company Ltd v EUI Ltd (t/a Elephant Insurance) [2018]
     EWCA Civ 2494. 81
Haven Insurance Company Ltd v EUI Ltd (t/a Elephant Insurance) [2018]
     EWHC 143 (Comm) 300
Hayter v Nelson Home Insurance [1990] 2 Lloyd's Rep 265. 48
HC Trading Malta Ltd v Tradeland Commodities SL [2016] EWHC 1279
     (Comm). 154
Heart of Midlothian Football Club plc v Scottish Professional Football League
     Ltd [2020] CSOH 68 . . . . .55, 85
Heifer International Inc v Christiansen [2007] EWHC 3015 (TCC) 17
Helow v Advocate General for Scotland [2008] UKHL 62. . . . . .159, 161
Henry Schein, Inc v Archer & White Sales, Inc 586 US 139 S Ct 524 (2019) 85
Hines v Overstock.com Inc [2010] US App LEXIS 11265 (2nd Cir, June 3, 2010). . . .26
Hiscox v Outhwaite [1992] 1 AC 562. 257
Hiscox Dedicated Corporate Member v Weyerhaeuser [2019] EWHC 2671
     (Comm). 28, 47–8, 140
Hoe International v Anderson 2017 SC 313; [2017] CSIH 9. . . . . .92, 136
Hrvatska Elektroprivreda v Republic of Slovenia (ICSID) Case No
     ARB/05/24. . . . . .104, 164
Hussmann (Europe) Ltd v Al Ameen Development & Trade Co [2002] 2
     Lloyd's Rep 83 . . . . .149, 217

Imperial Chemical Industries Ltd v Merit Merrell Technology Ltd [2018]
     EWHC 1577 (TCC) 390
India (Union of) v Hari Singh [2010] Indian Supreme Ct, Civil Appeal 7970/
     2010 32
India (Union of) v Pradeep Vinod Construction Co SC [2019] Indian Supreme
     Ct, Civil Appeal No 6400/2016 103
Ingmar GB Ltd v Eaton Leonard Technologies Ltd (Case C-381/98) ECLI:EU:C:
     2000:605 EUEC. 33
International Tank & Pipe SAK v Kuwait Aviation Fuelling Co KSC [1975] 1
     Lloyd's Rep 8 23
IS Prime Ltd v TF Global Markets (UK) Ltd [2020] EWHC 3375 (Comm) 44

J (Lebanon) v K (Kuwait) EWHC 899 (Comm) 45
Javor v Francoeur [2003] BCSC 350. 71
Jawaby Property Investment Ltd v The Interiors Group [2016] EWHC 557
     (TCC). 90
Jaya Sudhir a/l Jayaram v Nautical Supreme Sdn Bhd and others [2019]
     Federal Malaysian Ct, Civil appeal 02(i)-83-09/2018(W) 52
Jivraj v Hashwani [2009] EWHC 1364. . . . . .14, 16, 294
Jivraj v Hashwani [2010] EWCA Civ 712 14
Jivraj v Hashwani [2011] UKSC 40 . . . . .14, 16, 111, 294

John G McGregor (Contractors) Ltd v Grampian Regional Council 1991 SLT
    136 253
Jones v DAS Legal Expenses Insurance Co Ltd [2003] EWCA Civ 1071 158
Jones v Kaney [2011] UKSC 13. . . . . .127, 128, 309, 311

K v P [2019] EWHC 589 (Comm). 9
K v S [2019] EWHC 2386 (Comm) 183
Kabab-Ji SAL (Lebanon) v Kout Food Group (Kuwait) [2020] EWCA Civ 6 45
Kalmneft JSC v Glencore International AG [2002] 1 All ER 76 230
Karling v Purdue 2004 SLT 1067 . . . . .128, 310
Kazakhstan v Istil Group Inc [2007] EWCA Civ 471 15
Kazeminy v Siddiqi [2010] EWHC 201 (Comm) 15
Korsnäs Aktiebolag v AB Fortum Värme 9 June 2010, Swedish Supreme Ct
    Case T 156-09 103
Kruppa v Benedetti [2014] EWHC 1887 (Comm) 28
Kyle & Carrick District Council v A R Kerr and Sons 1992 SLT 629 65

Lafarge (Aggregates) Ltd v London Borough of Newham [2005] EWHC 1337
    (Comm). 142
Lahey v Pirelli Tyres Ltd [2007] EWCA Civ 91 389
Laker Airways Inc v FLS Aerospace Ltd [1999] 2 Lloyd's Rep 45 . . . . .115, 163
Laporte v Commissioner of Police of the Metropolis [2015] EWHC 371 (QB) 390
Larsen Oil and Gas Pte Ltd v Petroprod Ltd [2011] SGCA 21. 85
Law Debenture Trust Corp plc v Elektrim Finance BV [2005] EWHC 1412
    (Ch) 68, 70
Lawal v Northern Spirit Ltd [2003] UKHL 35 104
Lesotho Highlands Development Authority v Impregilo SpA [2005] UKHL 43;
    [2006] 1 AC 221 . . . . 247–8, 249–50,
                                                                255, 288, 289, 306–7
LG Caltex Gas Co v China National Petroleum Corpn [2001] EWCA Civ 788. 142
Locabail (UK) Ltd v Bayfield Properties Ltd [1999] EWCA Civ 3004; [2000] QB
    4510 162
Lomax v Lomax [2019] EWCA Civ 1467. 389
Lorand Shipping Ltd v Davof Trading (Africa) BV (Ocean Glory) [2014] EWHC
    3521 (Comm) 290
Louis Dreyfus Commodities Kenya Ltd v Bolster Shipping Company Ltd
    [2010] EWHC 1732 44

M's Application (Leave Stage) [2011] NIQB 4 166
MacDonald Estates plc v NCP Ltd 2010 SC 250 80
McKenzie v McKenzie [1971] P 33. 216
Mace (Russia) Ltd v Retansel Enterprises Ltd [2016] EWHC 1209 (Comm). 45
Magi Capital Partners LLP, Re [2003] EWHC 2790 (Ch) 49–50
Main v City of Glasgow District Licensing Board 1987 SLT 305. 152
Mains v Uniroyal Englebert Tyres Ltd (No 1) 1995 SC 518 . . . . .130, 311–12
Manchester Associated Mills Ltd v Mitchells & Butler Retail Ltd [2013] CSOH
    2; 2013 SCLR 440 297
Mangistaumunaigaz Oil Production Association v United World Trade Inc
    [1995] 1 Lloyd's Rep 617. 28
Mareva Compania Naviera SA v International Bulkcarriers SA [1975] 2 Lloyd's
    Rep 509 243
Margulead Ltd v Exide Technologies [2004] EWHC 1019 (Comm); [2004] 2 All
    ER (Comm) 727 . . . . .199, 286, 288

Marshall v Gotham [1954] AC 360. 144
Maximus Securities Ltd, Re [2016] EWCA Civ 1057. 159
Menini v Banco Popolare Società Cooperativa (Case C-75/16)
    ECLI:EU:C:2017:457 385
Merthyr (South Wales) Ltd v Cwmbargoed Estates Ltd [2019] EWHC 704 (Ch). . .146
Michael Wilson & Partners v John Emmott [2018] EWCA Civ 5 19
Michael Wilson & Partners v Sinclair and others [2017] EWCA Civ 3 58
Micula and others v Romania [2020] UKSC 5 33
Midgulf International Ltd v Groupe Chimique Tunisien [2010] EWCA Civ 66. 53
Millar v Dickson [2001] UKPC D4. . . . . .102, 158, 159
Millchris Developments Ltd v Waters [2020] 4 WLUK 45. 297
Milsom v Ablyazov [2011] EWHC 955 (Ch). 180
Minermet SpA Milan v Luckyfield Shipping Corpn SA [2004] 2 Lloyd's Rep 348 .142
Minister of Finance (Inc) v International Petroleum Investment Co [2019]
    EWCA Civ 2080. 286
Mi-Space (UK) Ltd v Lend Lease Construction (EMEA) Ltd [2013] EWHC 2001
    (TCC). 235
Mobil Cerro Negro Ltd v Petroleos de Venezuela SA [2008] EWHC 532
    (Comm); [2008] 1 CLC 542. 243
Mobile Telecommunications Co KSC v HRH Prince Hussam Bin Saud Bin
    Abdulaziz Al Saud [2019] EWHC 3109 (Comm) 263
Monde Petroleum SA v Westernzagros Ltd [2015] EWHC 67 (Comm) 141
Morris v Harris [1927] AC 252. . . . . .133, 315
Mostaza Claro v Centro Móvil Milenum SL (Case C-168/05) [2006] ECR
    I-1421. 18
Muir Construction Ltd v Hambly Ltd 1990 SLT 830 . . . . .135, 317
Mutu and Pechstein v Switzerland [2018] ECHR, Applications 40575/10 and
    67474/10. 16
Mylcrist Builders Ltd v Buck [2002] EWHC 2172 17

National Boat Shows Ltd v Tameside Marine [2001] WL 1560826. 215
National Navigation Co v Endesa Generacion SA (The Wadi Sudr) [2009]
    EWCA Civ 1397. . . . . .42, 56
Nea Agrex SA v Baltic Shipping Co Ltd (The Agios Lazarus) [1976] QB 933. 91
Neocleous and another v Rees [2019] EWHC 2462 (Ch) 26, 135
New Age Alzarooni 2 Ltd v Range Energy Natural Resources Inc [2014] EWHC
    4358 (Comm) 186
Newfield Construction Ltd v Tomlinson [2004] EWHC 3051   191, 286, 288
No Curfew Ltd v Feiges Properties Ltd [2018] EWHC 744 (Ch). 263
Nobiskrug GmbH v Valla Yachts Ltd [2019] EWHC 1219 (Comm). 297
Noble Denton Middle East v Noble Denton International Ltd [2010] EWHC
    2574 44
Norbrook Laboratories Ltd v Tank [2006] EWHC 1055 (Comm) 105, 115
Nori Holdings Ltd and others v Bank Okritie Financial Corporation PJSC
    [2018] EWHC 1343 (Comm). 42
Norscot Rig Management PVT Ltd v Essar Oilfields Services [2010] EWHC 195
    (Comm). 29
North Lanarkshire Council v Stewart and Shields Ltd [2017] CSOH 76; 2017
    SLT 741 . . . . .74, 177
North Range Shipping Ltd v Seatrans Shipping Corpn (The Western Triumph)
    [2002] EWCA Civ 405 15
Northern Regional Health Authority v Derek Crouch Construction Co Ltd
    [1984] 2 All ER 175 60

Northrop Grumman Mission Systems Europe Ltd v BAE Systems (Al Diriyah
    C41) Ltd [2014] EWHC 3148 (TCC) 390
Norwest Holst v Carfin Developments Ltd [2008] CSOH 138 48
Nova (Jersey) Knit v Kammgarn Spinnerei [1977] 1 WLR 713 19

OAO Northern Shipping Co v Remolcadores de Marin SL (The Remnar) [2007]
    2 Lloyd's Rep 302 170
O'Donnell Developments Ltd v Build Ability Ltd [2009] EWHC 2288 (TCC) 266
O'Donoghue v Enterprise Inns plc [2008] EWHC 2273 (Ch)....................167
Ohpen Operations UK Ltd v Invesco Fund Managers Ltd [2019] EWHC 2246
    (TCC)...41, 390
Oldham v QBE Insurance (Europe) Ltd [2018] 1 All ER (Comm) 1044 293
Omnibridge Consulting Ltd v Clearsprings (Management) Ltd [2004] EWHC
    2276 (Comm) 170
Orascom TMT Investments SRL v Veon Ltd [2018] EWHC 985 (Comm); [2018]
    Bus LR 1787 289
Orkney Islands Council v Charles Brand 2002 SLT 1000......................48
Oxford Shipping Co Ltd v Nippon Yusen Kaisha (The Eastern Saga) (No 2)
    [1984] 3 All ER 835 ....180, 223

P v D [2019] EWHC 1277...196
P v Q [2017] EWHC 194 (Comm)..213–14
Pacol Ltd v Joint Stock Company Rossakhar [1999] 2 All ER (Comm) 169–70
Pakistan v Broadsheet LLC [2019] EWHC 1832 (Comm)......................256
PAO Tatneft v Ukraine [2019] EWHC 3740..................................166
Parker Lloyd Capital Ltd v Edwardian Group Ltd [2017] EWHC 3207 (QB).....390
Party E v Party C BT/109/2016 [2018] 1 WLUK 108 182
Patel v Patel [1999] All ER (Comm) 923 50
Paul Smith Ltd v H&S International Holding Co Inc [1991] 2 Lloyd's Rep
    127 28
PEC Ltd v Asia Golden Rice Ltd [2012] EWHC 846 (Comm) 147
Pedriks v Grimaux [2019] EWHC 2165 (QB) 386, 391
Peel v Coln Park LLP (2010) 154 Sol Jo 38 77
Petroleum Investment Co Ltd v Kantupan Holdings Co Ltd [2002] 1 All ER
    (Comm) 124 243
Petroships Pte Ltd of Singapore v Petec Trading & Investment Corpn of
    Vietnam (The Petro Ranger) [2001] 2 Lloyd's Rep 348 ....186, 289
Politakis v Spencely [2017] ScotSAC Civ 19.................................303
Porter v Magill [2001] UKHL 67, [2002] 2 AC 357.....104, 105, 106, 115, 159, 161, 164
Process & Industrial Developments Ltd v Nigeria [2019] EWHC 2241......10, 11, 21
Premium Nafta Products Ltd v Fili Shipping Co Ltd, see Fiona Trust & Holding
    Corpn v Privalov
Prasad v Monnet Finance Ltd Civil Appeals [2010] Indian Supreme Ct, Civil
    appeals 9224/2010 and 9225/2010 60
Profilati Italia SrL v Painewebber Inc [2001] EWHC 24 (Comm); [2001] 1
    Lloyd's Rep 715..291–2
Profile Projects Ltd v Elmwood (Glasgow) Ltd [2011] CSOH 64; 2011 SLT 975.... 37,
                                                                        269, 276
Progas Energy Ltd v Pakistan [2018] EWHC 209 (Comm) 302
PT Permata Hijau Sawit v Pacific Inter-Link Sdn Bhd [2011] 6 AMR 343.........82

R v Bow Street Magistrates, ex parte Pinochet Ugarte (No 2) [2000] 1 AC 119 158
R v Gough (Robert) [1993] AC 646 163

R (on the application of Toovey) v Law Society [2002] EWHC 391 (Admin)......158
Ranko v Antarctic Maritime SA (1998) LMLN 492............................147
RBRG Trading (UK) v Sinocore International Co Ltd [2018] EWCA 838; [2019] 1
    All ER (Comm) 810...65, 306, 307
Reid v Buckinghamshire Healthcare NHS Trust [2015] EWHC B21.............390
Reliance Industries Ltd v Union of India [2018] EWHC 822 (Comm)...........170
Reynolds v Kingston (City) Police Services Board (2007) 84 OR (3d) 738
    (Ont CA)...129
Richard Wales (t/a Selective Investment Services) v CBRE Managed Services
    Ltd [2020] EWHC 1050 (Comm)..389
Rinehart v Hancock Prospecting Pty Ltd [2019] HCA 13......................19
Ritchie v Maersk 1994 SCLR 1038..152
Rolls-Royce plc v Riddle [2008] IRLR 873.................................173
Rompetrol Group NV v Romania (ICSID Case No ATB/06/3).............104, 164
Roundstone Nurseries Ltd v Stephenson Holdings Ltd [2009] EWHC 1431
    (TCC)...390
Rustal Trading Ltd v Gill & Duffus SA [2000] 1 Lloyd's Rep 14.........115, 130, 312

SAB Miller v East African Breweries Ltd [2010] EWCA Civ 1564..............237
Sabbagh v Khoury [2018] EWHC 1330 (Comm)..............................44
Sabbagh v Khoury [2019] EWCA Civ 1219..................................52
St Andrews Bay Development Ltd v HBG Management Ltd 2003 SLT 740......261
Saloman v A Saloman and Company Ltd [1897] AC 22......................17
Sanderson & Son v Armour & Co Ltd 1922 SC (HL) 117....................40, 41
Schillings International LLP v Scott [2019] EWHC 1335 (Ch)................243
Seabridge Shipping AB v AC Orsleff's Eftf's A/S [1999] 2 Lloyd's Rep 685.......92
Secretary of State for Business, Enterprise and Regulatory Reform v UK
    Bankruptcy Ltd [2010] CSIH 80.......................................194
Secretary of State for the Foreign and Commonwealth Office v Percy Thomas
    Partnership (1998) 65 Con LR 11......................................29
Secretary of State for the Home Department v Raytheon Systems Ltd [2015]
    EWHC 311 (TCC)...290, 295
Serbia (Republic of) v ImageSat International NV [2009] EWHC 2853
    (Comm)..144, 148
Serpentine Trust Ltd v HMRC [2018] UKFIT 535 (TC).......................391
SGL Carbon Fibres Ltd v RBG Ltd [2011] CSOH 62; 2011 SLT 417....148, 186–7, 282
Shagang South-Asia (Hong Kong) Trading Co Ltd v Daewoo Logistics [2015]
    EWHC 194 (Comm), [2015] 1 All ER (Comm) 545.........................11
Shalson v DF Keane Ltd [2003] EWHC 599 (Ch)............................49
Shanks & McEwan (Contractors) Ltd v Mifflin Construction Ltd 1993 SLT 1124...65
Shashoua v Sharma [2009] EWHC 957 (Comm)..............................21
Shell Egypt West Manzala GmbH v Dana Gas Egypt Ltd [2010] EWHC 2097
    (Comm)..281
Shirayama Shukusan Co Ltd v Danovo Ltd [2003] EWHC 3006 (Ch)...........389
Sierra Fishing Co v Farran [2015] EWHC 140 (Comm)...................159, 209
Slovak Republic v Achmea BV (Case C-284/16) EU:C:2018:158................33
Smith v Kvaerner Cementation Foundations Ltd [2006] EWCA Civ 242.....162, 163
Sodzawiczny v Ruhan and others [2018] EWHC 1908 (Comm).................49
Soleimany v Soleimany [1998] EWCA Civ 285; [1998] 3 WLR 811...........62, 248,
                                                                          292, 307
Soletanche Bachy France SAS v Aqaba Container Terminal (Pvt) Co [2019]
    EWHC 362 (Comm)...162
Somerville v Scottish Ministers [2007] UKHL 44...........................150

Sonact Group Ltd v Premuda SpA (The Four Island) [2018] EWHC 3820
    (Comm)...30
Sonatrach v Statoil [2014] EWHC 875 (Comm)..............................186
Sovarex SA v Romero Alvarez SA [2011] EWHC 1661 (Comm)...................68
Squirrel Film Distribution v SPP Opportunities Fund LLP [2010] EWHC 706
    (Ch)..231
SSE Generation Ltd v Hochtief Solutions AG and another [2016] CSOH 177 187
ST Group Co Ltd and others v Sanum Investments Ltd [2019] SGCA 65.........305
Stanton v Callaghan [2000] QB 75.................................128, 311
Star Reefers Pool Inc v JFC Group Co Ltd [2010] EWHC 3003 (Comm)...........44
Stellar Shipping Co LLC v Hudson Shipping Lane [2001] EWHC 2985...........29
Sterling v Rand [2019] EWHC 2560 (Ch)...................................251
Sterling v Rand [2020] EWHC 2899 (Ch)...................................248
Stewart v Stewart 1984 SLT (Sh Ct) 58 123
Stewart Hill v Stewart Milne Group [2011] CSIH 50 254
Strathmore Building Services v Greig (t/a Hestia Fireside Design) 2000 SLT
    815...48
Sumukan Ltd v Commonwealth Secretariat [2007] EWHC 188 (Comm).........165
Straume, (A) UK Ltd v Bradlor Developments Ltd [2000] BCC 333 96
Suncor Energy Products Inc v Howe Baker Engineers Ltd [2010] AJ No 618.......79
Sutcliffe v Thackrah [1974] AC 727.................................126, 308
Symbion Power LLC v Venco Imtiaz Construction Company [2017] EWHC 348
    (TCC)..181
Syska v Vivendi Universal SA [2009] EWCA Civ 677 96

TAG Wealth Management v West [2008] EWHC 1466 (Comm)............196, 220
Taiwan Scot Co v Masters Golf Co [2009] EWCA Civ 685....................254
Tajik Aluminium Plant v Hydro Aluminium AS [2005] EWCA Civ 1218 235
Tamil Nadu Electricity Board v ST-CMS Electric Co Private Ltd [2007] EWHC
    1713 (Comm) 34
Taylor v Lawrence [2002] EWCA Civ 90 ....161, 162, 163
Taylor Woodrow Construction Ltd v Barnes & Elliott Ltd [2006] EWHC 1693
    (TCC)..225
Taylor Woodrow Construction Ltd v RMD Kwikform Ltd [2008] EWHC 825
    (TCC)...92
Terna Bahrain Holdings Co WLL v Al Shamsi [2012] EWHC 3283 (Comm)......300
Thomson v Glasgow Corporation 1961 SLT 237............................189
Tomkins v Cohen 1951 SC 22...152
Tor Corporate v Sinopec Group Star Petroleum Corpn Ltd 2008 SC 303; [2008]
    CSIH 9..65, 150, 153
Townmore (K&J) Construction Ltd v Kildare & Wicklow Education and
    Training Board [2019] IEHC 666 5–8
Trafigura Beheer BV v Yieh Phui (China) Technomaterial Co Ltd [2009] EWHC
    2054 (Comm) 154
Transition Feeds LLP v Itochu Europe plc [2013] EWHC 3629 (Comm).........290
Travelers Insurance Co Ltd v Countryside Surveyors Ltd [2010] EWHC 2455
    (TCC)..235
Trésor Public v Galakis 1966 Revue de l'Arbitrage 99 306

UBC Group Ltd v Atholl Developments (Slackbuie) Ltd [2010] CSOH 21.........50
UBS AG v HSH Nordbank AG [2009] RWCA Civ 585....................30, 140
UMS Holdings Ltd v Great Station Properties SA [2017] EWHC 2473 (Comm);
    [2018] 1 All ER(Comm) 856 ....181, 288

Union Marine Classification Services LLC v Comoros [2015] EWHC 508
    (Comm)..138
United States v Panhandle Eastern Corpn 119 FRD 346 (D Del 1988)............74
Uttam Galva Steels Ltd v Gunvor Singapore Pte Ltd [2018] EWHC 1098
    (Comm)...19

Van der Giessen-de-Noord Shipbuilding Division BV v Intech Marine &
    Offshore BV [2008] EWHC 2904 (Comm); [2009] 1 Lloyd's Rep 273........256,
                                                                      288, 289
Vaughan Engineering Ltd v Hinkin and Frewin 2003 SLT 428 148
Vee Networks Ltd v Econet Wireless International Ltd [2005] 1 Lloyd's Rep
    192...139, 170
Villa Denizcilik Sanayi Ve Ticaret AS v Longen SA (The Villa) [1998] 1 Lloyd's
    Rep 195...91
Virdee v Virdi [2003] EWHC Civ 41 111

W v X Co [2017] EWHC 3430 (Comm)....................................222
W Ltd v M Sdn Bhd [2016] EWHC 422 (Comm).........................108, 166
Walsall Metropolitan Borough Council v Beechdale Community Housing
    Association Ltd [2005] EWHC 2715....................................286
Warborough Investments Ltd v S Robinson & Sons (Holdings) Ltd [2003]
    EWCA Civ 751..187, 288
Watts v Watts [2015] EWCA 1297 163
Webb v Lewis Silkin LLP [2015] EWHC 687 (Ch)......................180, 182
West Tankers Inc v RAS Riunione Adriatica di Sicurta SpA ('The Front Comor)
    [2007] UKHL 4...42
Westacre Investments Inc v Jugoimport-SPDR Holding Co Ltd [2000] QB 288
    (CA)...307
Wicketts v Brine Builders [2001] CILL 1805................................279
Wilson v Dunbar Bank plc 2008 SC 457 255
Wiltshier Construction (Scotland) Ltd v Drumchapel Housing Co-Operative
    Ltd 2003 SLT 443..168
World Trade Corporation Ltd v C Czarnikov Sugar Ltd [2004] EWHC 2332
    (Comm)..256
Wu Chunying v Zhang Guiwen [2010] Chinese Supreme People's Ct............84

Xstrata Coal Queensland Pty Ltd v Benxi Iron and Steel (Group) International
    Economic and Trading Co Ltd [2016] EWHC 2022 (Comm) 263

YCMS Ltd (t/a Young Construction Management Services) v Grabiner [2009]
    EWHC 127 (TCC) 266
Yuanda (UK) Co Ltd v WW Gear Construction Ltd [2010] EWHC 720 (TCC);
    [2011] 1 All ER (Comm) 550...................................36, 37, 269
Yukos International Ltd v Russian Federation, UNCITRAL, PCA Case
    no 2005-04/AA227 213

Zaporozhye Production Aluminium Plan Open Shareholders Society v Ashly
    Ltd [2002] EWHC 1410 (Comm).......................................69
Zermalt Holdings SA v Nu-Life Upholstery Repairs Ltd [1985] 2 EGLR 14.......170

Introduction

The Arbitration (Scotland) Act 2010 marked a completely new start to Scottish arbitration, but it would be wrong to suggest that this method of dispute resolution does not have a long history within Scotland. It is not the purpose of this book to go into distant history, but arbitration was certainly well established in Scotland by medieval times. It is interesting that the formalisation of Scots law on this subject appears to have developed from about the fifteenth century and this coincides with the expansion of Scotland as a trading nation. It is significant that in most countries arbitration on commercial disputes goes hand in hand with the development of trading, particularly in an international context. Traders wish to have their disputes settled by 'men of affairs' and often see arbitration as a quick and relatively cheap method of resolving commercial disputes without getting into detailed legalistic arguments. Unfortunately, in many jurisdictions, problems arose either because arbitration turned into a mirror of court proceedings or because the courts became too ready to intervene in arbitrations, meaning that the parties finished up with two sets of proceedings 'for the price of two'!

While arbitration law has developed in Scotland through case law, there had previously been relatively little legislation on the subject. There is an Act of 1598 (APS iv 233, c 31), which dealt with what was, in effect, arbitration, requiring parties to submit to two or three 'friends' on either side, but the general view appears to be that this Act has fallen into desuetude and it is certainly the case that the 2010 Act assumes that the 1598 Act did not require to be repealed. The Articles of Regulation 1695 make reference to arbitration (Article 25) but there is then no further legislation until the Arbitration (Scotland) Act 1894 which dealt with a small number of technical points such as abolishing the requirement to name an arbiter but not really dealing with substantive issues. The Administration of Justice (Scotland) Act 1972 had one provision (s 3) that dealt with arbitration. Unfortunately, this was to introduce the 'stated case' procedure into Scots law. The motivation behind this appeared to be to bring Scotland into line with what was then the practice in England. However, this was done very shortly before English law decided to abolish the procedure, and it can be suggested that the decline in the use of arbitration to settle commercial disputes since that date owes a great deal to what, with hindsight, appears to have been an unnecessary piece of legislation. The only other major legislative development was through the Law Reform (Miscellaneous Provisions) (Scotland) Act 1990 where s 66 and Sch 7 introduced the UNCITRAL Model Law. As opposed to the position in 1972 where Scotland was attempting to bring itself into line with English practice, this decision moved in the opposite direction. England decided not to introduce the UNCITRAL Model Law but Scotland took the view that it was a useful piece of internationally recognised model legislation that would give Scotland an international profile in arbitration. (See also the comments of Lord Glennie in *Arbitration Application No 3 of 2011* 2012 SLT 150.) England and Wales diverged and went down the route of what was to become the Arbitration Act 1996. It is suggested that, unlike the unfortunate 1972 legislation, this made a lot of sense.

It is not felt valuable to dwell on the historical issues concerning arbitration in Scotland, but it is worth stating why both domestic, and more particularly international, arbitration became less used during the latter part of the twentieth century. As noted above, the introduction of the stated case process in 1972 is considered to have been broadly unhelpful. It allowed a party, dissatisfied with an ongoing arbitration, a very wide ability to take the matter to the courts, often on an interim basis thereby permitting a challenge to an interim decision of the arbiter or to generally delay it. Businesses in particular were often willing to use arbitration on the basis that it would be quick, cheap and private, and the matter would be dealt with by people who had experience in their field of business, if this was what they required. The stated case procedure gave them none of these advantages, and permitted of adjunct or satellite litigation adding to the costs incurred in going into the arbitration in the first place. In time, businesses came to the view that there was little point in resolving their disputes by arbitration in Scotland, and chose to go to the courts for resolution of their dispute. Alternatively, if the parties did want arbitration (for example, for reasons of confidentiality) to resolve the dispute they would not choose Scotland as a seat but go to a jurisdiction (frequently England and Wales) where the courts were very much more reluctant to intervene.

The Scottish approach resulted in enormous delays as matters of law were litigated by the parties up the appellate levels. The recent case of *Apollo Engineering Ltd v United Kingdom (Admissibility)* (2019) 69 EHRR SE12 in the European Court of Justice relates to a Scottish case under the old regime where an action was raised in 1991 which was sisted to arbitration in 1993, and where the final award was not issued until 2007 (and then after the original arbiter had retired and a new one been appointed in 2004). The ongoing litigation arising from the arbitration reached the European Court of Human Rights in 2019, some twenty-eight years after the original proceedings. One of the authors was involved in the 1980s in a judicial arbitration in Scotland which involved stated case procedures going to the House of Lords on one issue, and a second issue proceeding to the Inner House. The dispute was settled by negotiation some eleven years after it had started, with the matter never having got anywhere close to an arbitral evidential hearing. As a result of this, the substantial international company where the author was then working took the decision that a Scottish arbitration clause would not thereafter be inserted into any of its future contracts. This illustration was simply symptomatic of the way in which international companies had come to view Scottish arbitration. The major development of contractual matters with the arrival of North Sea oil and gas from the 1970s onwards illustrates the point. Certainly until recently, it is believed that very few, if any, substantial engineering and construction contracts in the North Sea have used Scottish arbitration as a dispute resolution method, even in the standard form industry suite of contracts. Some examples of arbitration clauses have been seen recently, albeit restricted to use where the contractor is a non-UK company to aid enforcement amid Brexit uncertainties. It may be that this is driven as much by concern at enforceability of court judgments in the European Union after Brexit as by a genuine preference for arbitration. The seat for the arbitration clauses seen has also remained London as has an English law substantive law clause and an English law arbitration clause. The option of using Scottish arbitration seems not to be considered, or quickly discounted. As noted above, the introduction of the UNCITRAL Model Law was seen as a very positive move to try and bring Scotland into the international arbitration community. However, the failure to bring the procedural law of Scotland into line, the failure to incorporate amendments to the Model law and the continuing existence of the stated case procedure made the process unattractive. Since arbitration is by its nature private, it is of course impossible to tell the number of times that the Model Law was used, but it is conjectured that in the twenty years between 1990 and 2010 the average use was probably less than one case a year. (The general figure quoted is around a dozen cases in total.)

Finally, a short paragraph about how the 2010 Act is put together. As is discussed in the commentary to s 8, the structure of the Act follows the design of the Arbitration Act 1996. However, the Scottish Act additionally incorporates a set of Rules within a Schedule to the Act itself – a matter of some debate during the passage of the Arbitration (Scotland) Bill, but having worked well in practice.

There are both mandatory provisions which cannot be excluded, even by the agreement of the parties, and also 'non-mandatory' or, in the language of the Act, 'default' provisions which the parties can agree (in the language of the Act) to 'disapply' or 'modify'.

So the Act gives effect to party autonomy both in principle (s 1) and through the parties' powers to disapply or modify default rules, whilst managing the framework of arbitrations in Scotland under the 'mandatory' provisions.

In practice, it has been seen that references by parties in arbitration agreements to the 'Scottish Rules' are to the rules as encapsulated in Schedule 1 to the Act and s 31(1) provides for that where the phrase 'Scottish Arbitration Rules' is used. The Schedule sets out the Rules in the form of a single code and they (together with the sections of the Act) will govern every arbitration seated in Scotland as a matter of Scots law, and not completely as a matter of contract between the parties. In effect, by agreeing to seat an arbitration in Scotland, the parties have, contractually, incorporated the Rules (with possible disapplication or modification of default rules) into their dispute resolution clause.

This of course is all subject to such of those default provisions as are modified or disapplied by the agreement of the parties. For example, if the parties adopt a different set of rules (eg LCIA Rules) then those rules will apply, but only to the extent that they do not conflict with the mandatory rules. In addition, the default rules will continue to apply to the extent that they are not contradicted or modified by any institutional rules unless they have been specifically excluded. It will, of course, also be open to parties to adopt the Scottish Arbitration Rules for arbitrations seated outside Scotland, subject to this being allowed under local law, but this will be by operation of contract, not the Act itself.

It should be noted that, since the First Edition of this book, the transitional provisions in s 36 have been removed by the Arbitration (Scotland) Act 2010 (Transitional Provisions) Order 2016 (SSI 2016/435). This closes off the right to continue to use pre-2010 arbitration law in an ongoing arbitration, although it was never clear there was any great demand for this choice. However, the Scottish Government have yet to bring into force the provisions on statutory arbitrations in ss 16–17, and this is discussed below.

It will be noted that many of the reported cases cited in this work are from England and Wales. In the First Edition, due to the lack of relevant Scottish authorities, those authorities were helpful to give context to often very similar sections and rules, and while there have been some Scottish cases since then, which are referred to, there have continued to be many more in England. As there are considerable similarities between the 1996 and 2010 Acts, and the judges in Scotland have continued to look at English authorities as persuasive (see in particular the comments of Lord Glennie in *Arbitration Application No 3 of 2011* 2012 SLT 150 and Lord Woolman in *Arbitration Application No 1 of 2013* [2014] CSOH 83) even though they are not, of course, binding, this policy has been continued. Examples from other jurisdictions, including some outside the Common Law world, have been included to illustrate how issues which are common in international arbitration have been dealt with in those jurisdictions.

Arbitration (Scotland) Act 2010

Introductory provisions

Founding principles

Section 1 of the 2010 Act states that

> The founding principles of this Act are –
> (a) that the object of arbitration is to resolve disputes fairly, impartially and without unnecessary delay or expense,
> (b) that parties should be free to agree how to resolve disputes subject only to such safeguards as are necessary in the public interest,
> (c) that the court should not intervene in an arbitration except as provided by this Act.
> Anyone construing this Act must have regard to the founding principles when doing so.

It was stated in the Explanatory Notes to the Arbitration (Scotland) Bill that the purpose of the draftsmen in inserting the founding principles was to provide a basis for informing and steering the interpretation and application of the Act. Although this approach is unusual, in Scottish legislation it is not unknown and, while traditionally one has looked to the courts for interpretation of legislation using the usual canons of construction, this Act requires any court, and indeed anyone (which must include the arbitral tribunal), to have regard to the founding principles in any construction of these provisions. Hence any submission or application to a tribunal or court will have to be examined, or at least viewed, through the lens of the 'object' stated in s 1(a) that the dispute should be resolved 'fairly, impartially and without unnecessary delay or expense'. This gives arbitrators a useful tool when seeking to apply robust, but fair, case management.

The draftsmen of the Act appear to have looked to the rest of the United Kingdom and the Arbitration Act 1996, which is regarded as a successful piece of legislation regulating domestic and international arbitration in a similar jurisdiction. Indeed, the draftsmen explain in the Notes commenting on the Bill stage that 'The principles reflect the principles found in the Arbitration Act 1996.' Note, though, that the English legislation was not adopted wholesale, thereby recognising the different traditions and the need to ensure that the 2010 Act works in a Scottish context. This contrasts with the earlier decision to adopt into Scots law the UNCITRAL Model Law without adjustment (Law Reform (Miscellaneous Provisions) (Scotland) Act 1990 s 66 and Sch 7).

The 2010 Act follows the approach taken in s 1 of the 1996 Act. Section 1(a) of the 1996 Act provides that 'the object of arbitration is to obtain the fair resolution of disputes by an impartial tribunal without unnecessary delay or expense'. Section 1(b) provides that 'the parties should be free to agree how their disputes are resolved, subject only to such safeguards as are necessary in the public interest', and s 1(c) provides that 'in matters governed by this Part the court should not intervene except as provided by this Part'.

Object of arbitration

Turning to the 'object of arbitration' as stated in s 1(a), 'arbitration' itself is defined by virtue of s 2(1) and s 31(1) as including domestic arbitration, arbitration between parties residing or carrying on business anywhere in the UK, and international arbitration. What is undefined are the terms 'domestic arbitration', 'arbitration between parties … in the UK' and 'international arbitration'. The first two would usually be taken to be either arbitrations between Scottish parties seated in Scotland in terms of the Act or arbitrations between parties in the different jurisdictions of the UK (even conceivably two parties neither of whom is Scottish), again with the arbitration seated in Scotland. As to 'international', at a general level the term can be used to differentiate between the other two types, namely those 'domestic' and those transnational disputes which fall into the international category in that at least one party or the subject-matter of the dispute is outside the UK. In international jurisprudence this concept has not always been applied or understood in this way, with some countries defining 'international' by reference to a 'foreign' element in the contract between them even though the parties are nationals of the same country. Other countries have defined it by reference to the nationality or residence or places of business of the parties.

However, this is not simply a jurisprudential academic question, as the Convention on the Recognition and Enforcement of Foreign Arbitral Awards 1958 ('the New York Convention') regulates what are referred to as 'foreign awards' – namely awards made in the territory of a state other than the state in which recognition and enforcement are sought. But: 'It shall also apply to arbitral awards not considered as domestic awards in the State where their recognition and enforcement are sought' (New York Convention 1958 Art I(1)).

This then leads to differences between states as to which awards are domestic in their laws and which are international and so enforceable. To give an example, the courts in Brazil have ruled that an arbitration between Brazilian and foreign parties is 'domestic' because the arbitration took place in Brazil, despite relating to international trade. This would not be the case under the 2010 Act but reflects the fact that Brazilian law is different on this point. By way of contrast, it is interesting to note that the distinction between domestic and international arbitration is fading somewhat, with Hong Kong formally removing the distinction altogether in its Arbitration Ordinance 2011.

The Convention seems to equate states with contracting states or with countries having membership of the United Nations or related organisations which has led in the past to further confusion. As examples, both the UK and the United States signed the Convention, which seems to imply that they, rather than their constituent jurisdictions (such as, in the UK, England and Wales, Northern Ireland and Scotland), are 'states' for this purpose. This has not seemed to be a major issue in practice. It is suggested that an international arbitration for the purposes of this Act will be one which involves parties of different nationalities, or where the subject-matter of the dispute is located in a country 'foreign' to the parties or has as its subject-matter an 'international dispute', ie a dispute with an 'international' flavour.

To look at an example, if a Scottish company and an English company agree to arbitration under the Act, with the 'seat' in Scotland but hearings in Bermuda, this would still seem to be a UK domestic arbitration, and not international. This is on the principle that it is the seat that is determinative and not the venue of the proceedings. This is, of course, only an issue if the winning party wishes to use the Convention to enforce against assets outside the UK.

Fairness and impartiality (and independence)

The overarching obligations of fairness and impartiality are followed throughout the 2010 Act in various rules. Thus Schedule 1 to the Act is infused with references to these concepts: see, eg, mandatory rule 24, the general duty of the tribunal to be impartial and also independent. Rule 24 continues that the tribunal must treat the parties fairly (including giving each party a reasonable opportunity to put its case and to deal with the other party's case), and conduct the arbitration '(i) without unnecessary delay, and (ii) without incurring unnecessary expense'.

The corollary of this is a duty imposed on the parties under mandatory rule 25 to ensure that the arbitration is conducted 'without unnecessary delay' and 'without incurring unnecessary expense'.

Other examples of this overarching obligation can be found in rule 8, where there is a duty of disclosure placed on the tribunal or prospective arbitrators to disclose anything which 'might reasonably be considered relevant when considering whether the individual is impartial and independent'; in default rule 10, which permits a challenge to the appointment of an arbitrator if, *inter alia*, the objection is on the basis that the arbitrator is 'not impartial and independent' or 'has not treated the parties fairly'; and in mandatory rule 12 (removal of arbitrator by court) if the court is 'satisfied' that the arbitrator is not impartial and independent, or that he has not treated the parties fairly. Lastly, mandatory rule 77 does actually make provision for the independence of the arbitrator but defines it in the negative. He or she is not independent if their relationship with any party, their financial or other commercial interests or anything else gives rise to 'justifiable doubts' as to their impartiality. The issue of notice to the parties has recently been considered by the UK Supreme Court in the English case of *Halliburton Company v Chubb Bermuda Insurance Ltd* [2020] UKSC 48 arising from multiple arbitrations following the *Deepwater Horizon* disaster in the Gulf of Mexico where notice of later appointments should have been given, but the arbitrator was not removed on the facts. On this subject, there is also a decision of the Privy Council (on appeal from the Cayman Islands) in *Almazeedi v Penner* [2018] UKPC 3 which explores the complex interconnections that may arise with senior arbitrators with international practices (in this case a former English High Court judge). Neither case really relates to any accusation of impropriety, or suggests that there has necessarily been actual bias – the test is very much about perceptions of possible bias, and the need to ensure everyone is aware of all relevant facts. The antiseptic effect of sunlight tends to apply in such situations.

Independence *per se* is not expressly a requirement in terms of the overriding principles to be applied to the Act, but independence as a quality is required in certain parts and is implicit in the structure of the Act and the rules. This and the subject of conflicts of interest are returned to under rule 8 below.

Discussions in this area tend to focus on relationships (real or perceived) between an arbitrator and the parties or their legal representatives. However, in the Cypriot case of *General Construction Company Ltd v Silver Leaf Developments Ltd* Petition 68/2016, 3 March 2018, the Limassol District Court had to deal with a complaint that the arbitrator was a majority shareholder in a Greek shipping company, and another shareholder was the brother of a main witness in the arbitration. There were also business connections between the Greek company and a Cypriot business of which the witness and his brother were directors. The court upheld the complaint and removed the arbitrator. It should be noted that no notice of this relationship had been given to the parties, which might have cured the problem.

Delay and expense

The principle of minimising delay and expense may throw up some interesting decisions. To what extent is one arbitration different from another? Can comparisons in delay and expense properly be made? One approach may be that tribunals adopt an approach akin to the particular 'expedition requirements' in the Rules of the Court of Session ('RCS') and the sheriff court Ordinary Cause Rules ('OCR') and, in particular, the requirement in commercial cause procedure that the commercial judge shall be 'pro-active' (Practice Note No 1 of 2017, n 6 and also n 11 which states that 'Both parties should consider carefully and discuss whether all or some of the dispute may be amenable to some form of alternative dispute resolution', often seen as language encouraging mediation, but it could equally apply to arbitration) and in the sheriff court that the sheriff 'shall seek to secure the expeditious progress of the cause' (OCR 9.12).

The pro-active approach of the courts in Scotland and England and Wales in their approach to case management may well provide guidance for arbitrators and their management of the arbitral process using these principles enshrined in the Act.

At an international level, the market is increasingly demanding that arbitrations become quicker and less expensive. There have been a number of initiatives and reports, including the ICC Arbitration Commission Report on *Techniques for Controlling Time and Costs in Arbitration* (2nd edn, 2018) (https://iccwbo.org/content/uploads/sites/3/2018/03/icc-arbitration-commission-report-on-techniques-for-controlling-time-and-costs-in-arbitra tion-english-version.pdf) which follows on from the initial report in 2007. There is also an annual *Costs of International Arbitration Survey* undertaken by the Chartered Institute of Arbitrators.

The reason for these and similar initiatives is that many commercial users of arbitration around the world have become exasperated over the years with certain arbitrations turning into a mirror image of the litigation process, particularly with regard to disclosure. Issues also arise with arbitrators not taking a firm grip on procedure by being too forgiving in permitting parties additional time to file pleadings or to take steps in the arbitration for fear of denying them the opportunity to 'make their case', which can later be a ground of resisting enforcement under the New York Convention (what is colloquially referred to as 'due process paranoia'). The whole structure of the Act is intended to encourage the arbitrator to be the master of procedure, within limits such as those in rule 24 mentioned above, to treat the parties fairly, and to do so within the overriding duties imposed – ie to act in accordance with principles of natural justice, and the right to a fair trial enshrined in the European Convention on Human Rights ('ECHR') and the Human Rights Act 1998 derived from the same. This is to be welcomed, and commercial users of arbitration will look to arbitrators working under the Act to take robust, but fair, steps to return the reputation of arbitration to being quick and cost-effective.

The English courts addressed this issue in passing in *K v P* [2019] EWHC 589 (Comm). One of the issues raised was that the award had not been issued until two years after the final submissions by the parties. On the facts, the court held that there had been no breach of duties in s 33 of the 1996 Act (which do not specifically require a prompt disposal) and there had been no 'substantial injustice' as a result. However, while the case was decided on other issues, the judge was critical of the tribunal, saying the delay was 'inordinate and unacceptable' and suggesting that the delay may have led to the arbitrator having 'forgotten what points were raised and required' and possibly having had to rush the eventual production of the award. It would be interesting to see whether a similar set of facts in a Scottish seated arbitration would withstand a challenge on the basis that the arbitrator breached the principles in s 1(a).

However, the burden is not exclusively on the tribunal; it is also important for parties and their lawyers to encourage and support robust case management within the parameters mentioned, and to be mindful of their own duties under rule 25.

Party autonomy

The second principle (s 1(b)) is that the parties should be able (subject to some safeguards) to decide their dispute the way they want to. This is called 'party autonomy' and is a key issue in arbitration. Arbitration is sometimes referred to as a 'creature of consent' – ie that the parties can agree to what is to be arbitrated, how their arbitration will be conducted and what powers they give to the arbitral tribunal. The Act follows this in allowing the parties to pick their procedure. This is not uncommon in international arbitration. The Arbitration Act 1996 uses almost identical wording, and the Model Law, Art 19(1) states that: 'Subject to the provisions of this Law, the parties are free to agree on the procedure to be followed by the arbitral tribunal in conducting the proceedings'. The London Court of International Arbitration (LCIA) Rules, Art 14 (conduct of the proceedings), and the International Chamber of Commerce (ICC) Rules, Art 19 (rules governing the proceedings) provide similar measures.

This principle is also reflected throughout the Act both in the sections and the mandatory and default rules. The word used above was 'infused' and it applies equally here. Thus s 3 allows the parties to agree that the arbitration is seated in Scotland; s 6 provides (in the absence of other provision) that Scots law applies. The parties may provide for the appointment of the tribunal and its form (default rule 2); they may give the tribunal power to determine the procedure to be followed during the arbitration and the admissibility, relevance, materiality and weight of any evidence as well as when and where the arbitral tribunal will meet, and whether, and if so how, claims and defences are to be submitted etc (default rule 28), or they may determine that themselves in their agreement. Even if the seat is Scottish, the parties may choose to meet and otherwise conduct the arbitration anywhere in the world (default rule 29 – the concept of venue as the place of the hearing as opposed to the juristic seat). The English courts have on occasions interpreted purposively references to 'seat' and 'venue'. In *Process & Industrial Developments Ltd v Nigeria* [2019] EWHC 2241 (Comm) the court equated a reference to a venue in London as meaning the arbitration was seated there, rather than in Nigeria, despite the subject of the dispute being in Nigeria, and the contract being subject to Nigerian law and neither party being English. The case was important to the parties as the case related to enforcement of the award which was for $6.6 billion, or about 1 per cent of Nigerian GDP. While this decision conflates 'venue' and 'seat', it is consistent with earlier decisions such as *Shagang South-Asia (Hong Kong) Trading Co Ltd v Daewoo Logistics* [2015] EWHC 194 (Comm), [2015] 1 All ER (Comm) 545 where it was held that, *prima facie*, the selection of the place of arbitration (ie the venue) would determine the applicable curial law unless an agreement to the contrary was established. This applied *Braes of Doune Wind Farm (Scotland) Ltd v Alfred McAlpine Business Services Ltd* [2008] EWHC 426 (TCC) where the arbitration agreement was subject to English law and provided that the seat of the arbitration was to be Glasgow, Scotland. The English High Court (TCC) held that although the agreement stated that the seat of the arbitration was to be Glasgow, the parties had meant that that was the place where the hearings should take place (ie venue), and the seat was, therefore, in England. It is fair to say that many contract clauses use terms such as 'seat' and 'venue' fairly loosely, but it also has to be said that *Process & Industrial Developments* holds that venue means seat, and *Braes of Doune* that seat means venue. It can be speculated that, were *Braes of Doune* to come before a Scottish court with the 2010 Act now in force, a different decision might be reached, on the basis that, as Scotland is stated as the seat, s 3(1)(a) makes it clear that, where so designated by the parties, the 'seat' is in Scotland. Default rules 30–40 include more provisions which can be used by the parties. By employing such of the default provisions as they see fit, and coupled with the mandatory rules, the parties themselves should be able to determine the speed and cost of their arbitration subject to the overriding principles in s 1.

It is worth noting that the Act has followed a different approach to that in the Arbitration Act 1996 of allowing the tribunal to determine evidence and procedure 'subject to the right of the parties to agree any matter' (1996 Act s 34). While default rule 28 limits the parties' autonomy to choose its procedure and methods of evidence by giving this right to the tribunal, the parties can decide to delete the rule in the first place and, thus, autonomy is maintained.

The same point has recently come before the Indian Supreme Court in the case of *BGS SGS SOMA JV v NHPC Ltd* Civil Appeals 9307/9308/9309 of 2019. While this relates to the provisions of the Indian Arbitration and Conciliation Act 1996, the court ruled that, in international arbitrations, reference must also be had to the UNCITRAL Rules (although the Act would prevail in case of conflict between these). While part of the appeal related to Indian procedural issues, the court also ruled that the designation of a seat confers exclusive jurisdiction on the courts of such seat and where a place of arbitration was stated this would be the seat, whether designated as seat, venue or place, unless there was evidence to the contrary. This seems consistent with the English approach on *Process & Industrial Developments* and seems to reflect a trend that distinctions of language between seat and venue will only apply if there is a clear intent that the two should be separate and distinct (eg 'Seated in Edinburgh, but with hearings to be held in Dublin').

Clarity of language

Lastly, to assist party autonomy, the Act is drafted in simple language wherever possible, which is part of the stated commitment of the Scottish Government to the greater use of plain English to make legislation readable (Plain English and Legislation booklet: www.scotland.gov.uk/Publications/2006/02/17093804/0). In addition, the Scottish Government prepared its own Notes on the Arbitration (Scotland) Bill and subsequently also on the 2010 Act and these are available online at the Office of Public Sector Information website (www.legislation.gov.uk). This approach to making the Act available in a reasonably accessible form is helpful, not least because non-lawyers (and indeed lawyers who are not trained in the law of Scotland) may be making use of the legislation, and it is anyway a sensible goal to ensure that the law is as understandable as possible.

Court intervention

The third principle (s 1(c)) addresses the role of the court and when it should intervene. At the outset of the Act it was hoped that the Scottish courts would not take an overly 'interventionist' approach and in the cases brought before them, they have not done so. In international and domestic arbitration, the role of the domestic or national court should be seen as supporting or assisting the arbitral tribunal. It should not intervene unless it is called upon to do so and should be reluctant to involve itself in the arbitration unless that is really necessary. As Blackaby and Partasides comment: 'The relationship between national courts and arbitral tribunals swings between forced cohabitation and true partnership. Arbitration is dependent on the underlying support of the courts, which alone have the power to rescue the system when one party seeks to sabotage it' (*Redfern and Hunter on International Arbitration* (6th edn) para 7.01).

The principle here follows the wording in the Arbitration Act 1996 which itself followed the Model Law. The Model Law, Art 5 provides: 'In matters governed by this Law, no court shall intervene except where so provided in this Law.' But this must be read in conjunction with Art 6 which provides for a 'competent court or other authority' (as specified by each state). This is the court or authority competent to perform the functions entrusted to it by the Model Law. These courts or other competent authorities are required by the Model Law to 'perform certain functions of arbitration and assistance'. Thereafter, throughout the Model Law, provision is made in many of the Articles for the competent court or other competent authority to, for example, decide upon a challenge to the arbitrator if there are 'justifiable doubts' as to his impartiality or independence. (Cf the language of rule 77 of the Scottish Arbitration Rules.)

The 2010 Act here adopts a similar method of stating the founding principle and then making provision for court intervention beyond which the court should not stray. Most of these provisions are in connection with the 'support' of the tribunal. For example, s 10 provides for where the court must 'sist' (ie suspend) proceedings; s 13 provides for when a court may 'intervene' in arbitrations; mandatory rules 12–14 provide for removal of arbitrators and dismissal of tribunals by the court; mandatory rule 21 provides for an appeal to the court against a tribunal's ruling on jurisdictional objection, and so on. Certain parts of the Rules provide the explicit powers given to the court in respect of certain aspects of arbitration: see, eg, mandatory rules in Part 5 (powers of court in relation to arbitral proceedings) and in Part 8 (challenging awards).

As to the general predisposition of courts to intervene in arbitrations, the Commercial Court of the Queen's Bench Division in England gave guidance on this topic in *Emmott v Michael Wilson & Partners Ltd* [2008] EWCA Civ 184 (which also deals with confidentiality in arbitration). In this case the court reiterated that judicial interference in the arbitral process should be kept to a minimum, and that the proper role of the court was to support the arbitral process rather than review it. It considered that the circumstances in which the court could properly interfere with or review the arbitral process were limited and that it was not for the court in every case to review the decision made by the tribunal and consider whether it ought to have been made. It considered that would be inconsistent with the general principle in s 1(c) (the analogous English provision) that the court should not intervene except where the Act so provided. The Scottish courts had indicated at the time the Act came into effect that they were likely to follow a similar non-interventionist approach, and this has proved to be the case in the relatively limited number of appeals that have reached the courts. (For a recent example, and where the court reiterated the very high hurdle that appeals must cross to bring an award before the courts for review, see *Arbitration Appeal No 1 of 2019* [2019] CSOH 60.) Indeed, the small number of cases may itself represent a recognition, by those minded to appeal, that the courts are unlikely to intervene.

The House of Lords in the *Fiona Trust* litigation [2007] UKHL 40 (*sub nom Premium Nafta Products Ltd v Fili Shipping Co Ltd*) gave strong support to a 'liberal' interpretation of arbitration clauses in commercial agreements, on the (reasonable, in our opinion) view that business people were more interested in the intent of the clause than in fine legal meanings. This view appears not only in the leading speech of Lord Hoffmann (paras 13 ff) but also, for present purposes perhaps more importantly, in the speech of the leading Scottish judge in the case, Lord Hope (at paras 29 ff).

Similar approaches have been taken in other common law jurisdictions. As an example, in the case of *Arnwell Pty Ltd v Teilaboot Pty Ltd* [2010] VSC 123 the Supreme Court of Victoria, applying Australian domestic arbitration law, refused to order an adjournment of an arbitration hearing, which the arbitrator had failed to grant. The court expressed a reluctance to get involved in interlocutory issues, save in extreme circumstances.

This overall approach is likely to be welcomed by users of arbitration. As noted above, the now-abandoned 'stated case' procedure (under the Administration of Justice (Scotland) Act 1972 s 3) appeared to many observers to make it simply too easy to re-run a lost argument in the arbitration before the civil courts. This had the dual effects of increasing delay and expense, often to a considerable extent, but also effectively breaching the hoped-for confidentiality and privacy of the arbitral process. The response of the English courts to the 1996 Act has been very positive in this respect, with a clear desire only to intervene when not to do so would lead to an obvious miscarriage of justice.

Human rights compliance

As to whether s 1 is subject to the ECHR as a result of the Human Rights Act 1998 s 3, some guidance is provided by the Commercial Court of the Queen's Bench Division in the case of *Nurdin Jivraj v Sadruddin Hashwani* [2009] EWHC 1364 (Comm), the facts of which are discussed further below. At para 66 Steel J stated:

> It was the submission of Mr H that the effect of this provision was that Section 1 of the Arbitration Act [ie 1996 Act] should be read as subject to the proviso that the relevant agreement does not unjustifiably violate the parties' convention rights. This is not a process of interpretation but a proposal to give direct effect to the rights under the Human Rights Act as between private parties. It is no more legitimate than incorporation of such a proviso in all statutes or statutory instruments. Mr J is relying on his contractual right to enforce the arbitration agreement.

The decision of Steel J was partially reversed by the Court of Appeal ([2010] EWCA Civ 712) and that decision was itself reversed by the Supreme Court ([2011] UKSC 40), not in relation to this point, but rather on the basis that arbitrators are not 'employees', and so the issue of employment discrimination never arose.

Article 6 of the European Convention on Human Rights

The relevant provision of the ECHR, incorporated into UK law by the Human Rights Act 1998 s 1(2), is Art 6(1):

> In the determination of his civil rights and obligations or of any criminal charge against him, everyone is entitled to a fair and public hearing within a reasonable time by an independent and impartial tribunal established by law. Judgement shall be pronounced publicly by the press and public may be excluded from all or part of the trial in the interest of morals, public order or national security in a democratic society, where the interests of juveniles or the protection of the private life of the parties so require, or the extent strictly necessary in the opinion of the court in special circumstances where publicity would prejudice the interests of justice.

In the *Fiona Trust* litigation at para 20 Lord Hoffmann commented:

> Mr Butcher submitted that the approach to construction and separability adopted by the Court of Appeal infringed the owners' right of access to a court for the resolution of their civil disputes, contrary to article 6 of the European Convention on Human Rights. I do not think there is anything in this point. The European Convention was not intended to destroy arbitration. Arbitration is based upon agreement and the parties can by agreement waive the right to a court. If it appears upon a fair construction of the charter that they have agreed to the arbitration of a particular dispute, there is no infringement of their Convention right.

In *BLCT (13096) Ltd v J Sainsbury plc* [2003] EWCA Civ 884, the Court of Appeal held that statutory provisions limiting the right of appeal from an arbitral award did not offend Art 6. It decided that although the court had a residual jurisdiction to intervene in the event of unfairness, the parties had already had a full hearing before the arbitrator and had had the opportunity of putting their case which did not offend Art 6 considerations: see further *North Range Shipping Ltd v Seatrans Shipping Corpn (The Western Triumph)* [2002] EWCA Civ 405. The court also decided that although the proceedings were in private, the parties had waived their right to assert that this violated Art 6 by virtue of their agreement to go to arbitration.

In another case on the privacy aspect, as to whether the fact that a hearing is conducted in private affects the compatibility of it with the Convention, in *Department of Economic Policy and Development of the City of Moscow v Bankers Trust Co* [2004] EWCA Civ 314, the fact that an arbitration claim was heard in private pursuant to the Civil Procedure Rules 1998, Part 62, r 62.10 (the part of the Rules dealing with arbitration claims and in particular court orders in respect of hearings), did not mean that the judgment was automatically immune from being 'published'. Where the court had made an order prohibiting publication on account of the sensitive content of the case, any subsequent report of the legal principles arising from the case would not be in breach of such an order if it was 'brief, neutral and did not disclose any private or confidential information'. This decision has been followed in the case of *Kazeminy v Siddiqi* [2010] EWHC 201 (Comm).

In English law, the main concern of the courts has been whether the procedure has been 'fair' (see eg *English v Emery Reimbold & Strick Ltd* [2002] EWCA Civ 605) but where there has been consideration of human rights law compliance, it has been held that there is no overarching principle laid down by the Human Rights Act 1998 that an award tainted by apparent bias has to be set aside: see *ASM Shipping Ltd of India v TTMI Ltd of England* [2006] EWCA Civ 1341.

As to arbitral procedure and the 1996 Act, the restriction of rights of appeal under s 67(4) of the Act has been held to be compatible with the ECHR Art 6: *Kazakhstan v Istil Group Inc* [2007] EWCA Civ 471. The Article 6 issue has recently been before the European Court of Human rights in

Apollo Engineering Ltd v United Kingdom (2019) 69 EHRR SE12, which related to the very lengthy Scottish arbitration case mentioned in the Introduction. The court did not consider that arbitration *per se* caused any issues under Art 6 and cited its own 2018 decision in *Mutu and Pechstein v Switzerland* (Applications 40575/10 and 67474/10) which related to a sports arbitration, freely entered into by the parties. The court also referred to the case of *Hamlyn & Co v Talisker Distillery* (1894) 21 R (HL) 21 as authority for the validity of arbitration clauses under the law of Scotland, and seemed to view the supervisory role of the Scottish courts as preventing any argument that Art 6 would be engaged. This case was under the pre-2010 Act law, but it seems unlikely that, given the much clearer structure in the 2010 Act, the decision would be any different on a case relating to an arbitration under the Act.

A linked issue – identity of arbitrators

While not strictly a human rights point, the case of *Nurdin Jivraj v Sadruddin Hashwani*, already cited, turned on the ability of the parties to impose conditions on the backgrounds of the arbitrators appointed which were not directly relevant to the issue in dispute. In this case, which related to a joint venture between two members of the Ismaili community, the arbitration clause included the requirement that the arbitrators should be 'respected members of the Ismaili community and holders of high office within the community' and that the chairman of the tribunal should be 'the President of the HH Aga Khan National Council for the United Kingdom for the time being'. The Ismaili community was held to be a religious group within the meaning of the Employment Equality (Religion or Belief) Regulations 2003 (SI 2003/1660), now subsumed into the Equality Act 2010. Accordingly, it was initially held that the arbitration clause was discriminatory and could not stand. The decisions of both Steel J at first instance and the Court of Appeal held, perhaps surprisingly, that arbitrators were 'employees' because of the very wide definition of the term in the 2003 Regulations. Whereas Steel J then supported the appointment of Sir Anthony Colman – a well-known arbitrator, but not an Ismaili Muslim – as arbitrator (as proposed by one of the parties), the Court of Appeal took the logical further step that, if the arbitration clause was discriminatory, it was void, and struck down this appointment as well, leaving the parties with a wholly ineffective clause.

The Court of Appeal ruling in *Jivraj* was seen as an unhelpful restriction on party autonomy and was a prime example of the law of unintended consequences in relation to the Equality Regulations. It was, however, primarily based on employment and equality law, rather than the law of arbitration, although its effect on the latter was both significant and unwelcome. However, the Supreme Court unanimously reversed the Court of Appeal (see [2011] UKSC 40) and ruled that the 2003 Regulations did not apply to arbitrators. While welcome, this may not be the end of the story. The 2003

Regulations were based on EU Directive requirements, which extended to the self-employed, and there was criticism in some other European jurisdictions that the Supreme Court focused on entry to the profession of arbitrator being non-discriminatory, rather than the ability to obtain individual appointments.

It is suggested that there are also other potential issues thrown up by the arguments in *Jivray*: for example, whether the Jewish *Beth Din* arbitration courts, whose awards have been routinely accepted as valid arbitration awards (see, eg, *Saloman v A Saloman and Company Ltd* [1897] AC 22), could be open to challenge on similar grounds. Further, *Shari'a* courts are understood to have been established to hear civil claims, stating that their authority is based on the Arbitration Act 1996, and, indeed, calling the organisation the Muslim Arbitration Tribunal. It was reported at one stage (*The Scotsman*, 8 October 2008) that one was to be in Glasgow where, if that was considered the seat, the 2010 Act would actually apply, given s 3 of the Act. However, current indications are that the Glasgow centre may not yet have been established. In these cases, the religious beliefs of the arbitrators would be critical to their acceptance by the parties and, it is suggested, there is nothing inherently wrong with this if one accepts the concept of party autonomy. This is particularly the case where the arbitrators need to be skilled in interpreting religious-based laws, where conventional legal training may be less relevant.

Arbitration in consumer matters

It should be noted that there has been some reluctance to force private individuals to be required to accept arbitration as a dispute resolution process in consumer matters. This has not necessarily been on human rights grounds but, for example, under the Unfair Terms in Consumer Contracts Regulations 1999 (SI 1999/2083) and the Unfair Arbitration Agreements (Specified Amount) Order 1996 (SI 1996/3211) and also ss 89–91 of the Arbitration Act 1996, which, unlike the bulk of that Act, apply in Scotland as well as the rest of the UK: see, eg, the English case of *Mylcrist Builders Ltd v Buck* [2002] EWHC 2172 relating to a building dispute with a private occupier. This can be contrasted with *Heifer International Inc v Christiansen* [2007] EWHC 3015 (TCC) where the arbitration clause was upheld, notwithstanding the fact that the arbitration was to take place in Denmark, as the parties had received legal advice before agreeing to the provision (this did not seem to have been the case in *Mylcrist*). This issue is also addressed under European law, for example *Asturcom Telecomunicaciones SL v Rodriguez Nogueira* (Case C-40/08) [2009] ECR I-9579 where the European Court of Justice (First Chamber) held that national courts were required, where possible, to evaluate whether an arbitration award in consumer matters, made in the absence of the consumer, arose from an unfair arbitration clause within the meaning of Council Directive 93/13/EEC. This obligation also arises even where the consumer has participated in the arbitration, and not raised the issue of unfairness (*Mostaza Claro v Centro Móvil Milenium* SL (Case C-168/05) [2006] ECR I-1421)

Key terms

The fact that s 2 of the Act includes a number of basic definitions has been mentioned already, including that the definition of arbitration includes international, cross-border in the UK and Scottish domestic arbitration.

'Arbitrator' is now the term to be used instead of the old Scottish terminology of 'arbiter'.

As the Scottish Government recognised in the Explanatory Notes to the Bill:

> In Scots common law there is a technical difference between the term 'arbiter', more commonly used, and the term 'arbitrator', where an arbiter decides in accordance with the law while an arbitrator can decide in terms of general equitable considerations (known as *'ex aequo et bono'*). The term 'arbitrator' is however employed throughout the regime established by the Bill following modern international arbitral practice.

It is suggested that this decision was a good one, since the distinction between arbiter and arbitrator would not be well-understood by the general public or by commercial parties from outside Scotland, since the term in international use is 'arbitrator' in both cases. This therefore makes Scotland consistent with international practice, which will be important if Scotland is to become an attractive seat for international disputes.

Where the parties do not specify the number of arbitrators in their agreement, and if they have not disapplied default rule 5, the tribunal will consist of a sole arbitrator. Note also that the rules still envisage the possibility of having an even number of arbitrators, which is unusual in an international context, and potentially problematic. This might reflect older Scottish practice, but it may be wiser to appoint odd numbers to prevent the possibility of deadlock and the need to go through a second stage process to resolve the issue. In most cases a single arbitrator will likely be appointed.

Dispute

'Dispute' is defined widely and avoids the previous problems in English jurisprudence under the 1996 Act whereby the courts took a strict line on the construction of words such as 'disputes' or 'differences', 'arising under the contract' and 'arising out of the contract'. Thus, historically some contractual disputes could be arbitrated in terms of the arbitration clause but other 'disputes' – say those based in delict or tort – could not.

Following the decision in *Fiona Trust & Holding Corpn v Privalov* [2007] EWCA Civ 20 (affirmed on appeal [2007] UKHL 40; see Lord Hoffmann at para 12) it is now the position in England and Wales that the courts will very likely hold that any jurisdiction or arbitration clause in an international commercial contract should be liberally construed.

The definition in this Act avoids any ambiguity by stating that 'disputes' will encompass 'any other difference (whether contractual or not)'. This is a sensible solution to a problem that was often greeted with incredulity by users of arbitration.

The *Fiona Trust* approach has been followed in later cases, for example *Uttam Galva Steels Ltd v Gunvor Singapore Pte Ltd* [2018] EWHC 1098 (Comm) where the terms of the arbitration agreement were agreed to extend to bills of exchange relating to the transaction, despite this being contrary to the decision in the pre-*Fiona Trust* case of *Nova (Jersey) Knit v Kammgarn Spinnerei* [1977] 1 WLR 713, which was on the same point, although relating to a dispute under West German law.

However, it should not be assumed that *Fiona Trust* means that any dispute can be shoe-horned into an arbitration agreement, irrespective of the actual wording used. The English cases of *Michael Wilson & Partners v John Emmott* [2018] EWCA Civ 51 and *Dreymoor Fertilizers PTE Ltd v Eurochem Trading GmbH* [2018] EWHC 909 (Comm) show the need to analyse what has actually been agreed and not to assume that, if there is an arbitration clause relating to some of the relationships between the parties, this will automatically allow any dispute to be sent to arbitration. The courts have emphasised that the *Fiona Trust* test is what a reasonable business person would do, which would not always necessarily be to combine disputes in one method of dispute resolution.

The Australian courts do not seem to have been as keen to embrace the *Fiona Trust* approach, and in *Rinehart v Hancock Prospecting Pty Ltd* [2019] HCA 13 the Australian High Court held that an arbitration clause relating to disputes 'under' three Deeds did not catch a dispute as to whether the Deeds themselves had been procured by misconduct.

Seat of arbitration

Place of the seat

Section 3 defines the 'juridical' seat of the arbitration. It is well established in international arbitration that an arbitration process is normally governed by the law of the place in which it is held, ie the 'seat' (sometimes called *'forum'* or *'locus arbitri'*). This is not necessarily the same as the law governing the dispute itself (eg the governing law of the contract in issue.)

It is not a simple matter of geography, however. The juristic place of the arbitration will largely determine the law that is to apply to the arbitration, ie the *lex arbitri*. The seat provides the arbitration's 'centre of gravity' which will normally dictate the law regulating the arbitration.

Thus, the 'seat' is a concept independent of the place where the arbitral hearings or the other parts of the arbitration take place. As per this section, it can be designated (as agreed between the parties) or can be determined by the tribunal itself or by the court. The determination or designation of the 'seat' of the arbitration is crucially important as it will have consequences for the operation of the arbitration (particularly in enforcement). In an international arbitration, the award should contain reference to the 'seat', ie at the end where the tribunal will state that the award has been made at the seat.

This section therefore makes provision for a constant Scottish juridical seat, no matter where the arbitration physically takes place. As stated above, this does not affect the substantive law that will be applied in the determination of the dispute that has been referred to arbitration. That should have already been provided for in the contract or other agreement between the parties or, if not, will be determined in a similar way by the tribunal. This is clearly stated in s 3(2).

Obviously where the seat is designated or determined to be Scotland, the mandatory rules under the Act will apply.

Comparison with English position

Section 3 follows closely the terms of the 1996 Act s 3. A comparison is worthwhile in that there is a substantial body of case law on these analogous provisions. The 1996 Act s 3 provides that:

> … 'the seat of the arbitration' means the juridical seat of the arbitration designated –
>
> (a) by the parties to the arbitration agreement,
> (b) by any arbitral or other institution or person vested by the parties with powers in that regard, or
> (c) by the arbitral tribunal if so authorised by the parties, or determined, in the absence of (a) by the parties to the arbitration agreement, or
>
> any such designation, having regard to the parties' agreement and all the relevant circumstances.

The phrase 'juridical seat of the arbitration' has been interpreted judicially in England and Wales in *Dubai Islamic Bank PJSC v Paymentech Merchant Services Inc* [2001] 1 Lloyd's Rep 65. The court held that English law demanded that an arbitration had to have a juridical seat before it began and the requirement imposed upon the court by s 3 of the Act, namely to consider the 'relevant circumstances' in the determination of the appropriate jurisdiction of the seat, was one which involved consideration of the pre-arbitration circumstances, not those subsequently arising. This is logical, since the whole basis of arbitration is a consensual contractual commitment at a particular moment (ie the signing of the contract or agreement), and the selection of a juridical seat needs to be looked at in that context.

Sometimes the provision of a venue can be tantamount to designation of the juridical seat (see eg *Shashoua v Sharma* [2009] EWHC 957 (Comm)). Where there is an agreement as to the seat of an arbitration that will bring in the law of that country as the curial law and is analogous to an exclusive jurisdiction clause (*Shashoua v Sharma*). The English courts have also held that where there is agreement as to the 'curial law' of the seat, but also as to the courts of the seat having supervisory jurisdiction over the arbitration, then by virtue of that agreement as to the seat, the parties are deemed to have agreed that any challenge to an interim or final award can be made only in the courts of the place designated as the seat of the arbitration: see *C v D* [2007] EWCA Civ 1282.

Braes of Doune Wind Farm (Scotland) Ltd v Alfred McAlpine Business Services Ltd [2008] EWHC 426 (TCC) has been referred to above. The facts of the case were that the claimant (Braes of Doune) was the employer under an engineering, procurement and construction (EPC) contract whereby the respondent contractor (McAlpine) undertook to carry out works in connection with the provision of 36 wind turbine generators at a site in Scotland. The contract provided for liquidated damages for delay. The contract was governed by English law and conferred exclusive jurisdiction on the English courts subject to arbitration in accordance with the Construction Industry Model Arbitration Rules. The arbitration agreement was subject to English law and provided that the seat of the arbitration was to be Glasgow, Scotland and that any reference to arbitration was deemed to be a reference to arbitration within the meaning of the Arbitration Act 1996. It was held that the parties had agreed that the curial law or law which governed the arbitral proceedings would be that of England. Further, where 'in substance' the parties agreed that the laws of one country would govern and control a given arbitration, the place where the arbitration was to be heard would not dictate what the governing or controlling law would be. Were the same facts to arise again, it is suggested that by virtue of the provisions of the 2010 Act, if the arbitration were stated to be seated in Scotland, that Act and its rules would apply, save where the 1996 Act provided different rules that could displace any of the default rules in the 2010 Act.

This line of reasoning, however, leads to the case of *Process & Industrial Developments Ltd v Nigeria* [2019] EWHC 2241 (Comm) also mentioned above. In this case the arbitration clause stated that the 'venue' was to be London. The dispute involved a proposed gas processing development in Nigeria, which was governed by Nigerian law, and where the Nigerian Government was a party. Whether the award of $6.6 billion was valid and enforceable depended on where the arbitration was seated (in the sense already discussed), as the award had been struck down in the Nigerian courts. The English court held that 'venue' meant 'seat' and therefore the arbitration was seated in London, and the Nigerian courts did not have jurisdiction. This decision reached a different conclusion from the *Braes of Doune* case discussed earlier (where 'seat' was held to mean 'venue'), but does, however, follow on from the earlier case of *Atlas Power Ltd v National Transmission and Despatch Co Ltd* [2018] EWHC 1052 (Comm). Here again, the word 'seat' was not used, but Phillips J found that the arbitration was seated in London. Further, while the contract initially provided that arbitrations should be conducted in Lahore, Pakistan, there were also provisions requiring the arbitration to be held in London: if certain value thresholds were reached; if certain issues were involved; or if the party requiring the transfer to London paid the additional costs incurred as a result. The thresholds in question had been exceeded, so one of the parties designated London, rather than Lahore. This appears to have been taken to amount to a designation of the seat after the agreement was already in existence, which makes sense on the facts, but it is suggested that, in both of these cases, a little careful drafting, merely adding the actual word 'seat' (as appears in many contracts), would have saved a great deal of delay, cost and uncertainty. It should also be noted that, had the designated seat been in Scotland, it would appear that s 3 of the Act would have come into play once the designation was made and, thus, the Act and the mandatory rules (and any default rules not displaced) would have come into effect from that moment, and not from the date of the arbitration agreement itself. The position in England is now also that, where the arbitration agreement is silent, the law governing that agreement will be the law of the seat (*Enka Insaat Ve Sanayi AS v OOO Insurance Company Chubb* [2020] UKSC 38).

Designation

Designation of the juridical seat should be made by the parties either in the arbitration agreement or, as in *Atlas Power* mentioned above, by a subsequent decision. In default it can be made by any third party to whom the parties give power (including an arbitral appointments referee, but only if specifically given such powers by the parties, as they do not appear to have this power under s 24), or, where the parties fail to designate or fail to authorise a third party, by the tribunal or by the court. The third party might be an institution such as the Chartered Institute of Arbitrators (Scottish Branch) or the Law Society of Scotland or the Faculty of Advocates or RICS etc. It is very simple to include the seat in the agreement to arbitrate, and it should be standard practice to do so, failing which the decision may turn out to be something that at least one of the parties neither intended nor finds attractive.

Designation by the court

The ultimate power to designate rests with the court. In the absence of designation, the court will be called upon to determine whether Scotland is to be the juridical seat of the arbitration. Some of the guidance from the English case law mentioned above may be persuasive, but not necessarily decisive. It is right to point out that the *Braes of Doune* case was heard in

England, but it is always possible that a Scottish court might have taken a different view to handing over control of a Glasgow-seated arbitration to another jurisdiction. Another English case on this point is *Chalbury McCouat International Ltd v PG Foils Ltd* [2010] EWHC 2050 (TCC) where the court was left to decide the seat of an arbitration between an English company and an Indian one for the demolition of an industrial plant in the Netherlands. There was a separate agreement to reassemble the plant in India, but the arbitration was under the first agreement. There was no proper law clause in the contract (had there been, and had it been English law, this would be sufficient connection with England, following *International Tank & Pipe SAK v Kuwait Aviation Fuelling Co KSC* [1975] 1 Lloyd's Rep 8) and the parties were not both from the European Union where the Rome Convention would have assisted. In this case, Ramsey J agreed that there was sufficient connection with England, and used powers under s 18 of the 1996 Act to instruct the President of the LCIA to appoint a sole arbitrator.

As a final point, it is worth repeating that designating the legal seat does not necessarily require that hearings or meetings take place in that location (although this will often be the case). It is important that the decision on the seat is arrived at on the basis of sound legal advice.

Arbitration agreement

Arbitration agreement

Section 4 of the Act defines an 'arbitration agreement' as 'an agreement to submit a present or future dispute to arbitration (including any agreement which provides for arbitration in accordance with arbitration provisions contained in a separate document).'

Agreement to arbitrate

The agreement to arbitrate will be the cornerstone of the arbitration. It is a record of the parties' consent to arbitrate. There are two types of arbitration agreement: namely the 'arbitration clause' and the 'submission agreement'. The clause will be inserted into the parties' contract and make provision for any future differences or disputes to be determined by arbitration. An arbitration agreement, on the other hand, will generally be drawn up between the parties after the difference or dispute has arisen – ie when it is already an existing dispute. The most common method is for an arbitration clause to be inserted into the principal agreement between the parties. It is also, generally, the most desirable, not least because it is negotiated at a time when the parties have a common objective, rather than when they are already in dispute.

Written and oral agreements

As phrased, the agreement could be made orally or in writing. The Explanatory Notes to the Bill stated that 'Arbitration agreements are recognised by the Bill whether they are concluded orally or in writing. Accordingly, all arbitrations in Scotland may in principle be subject to the [Bill]'.

Historically, Scots law recognised both oral and written arbitration agreements and, if the Act did not extend specifically to oral agreements, such agreements would presumably continue to be subject to the common law and would not benefit from the provisions in the Act and, perhaps, permit a disparate approach to arbitration in Scotland, one of the mischiefs the Act seeks to address. It would, of course, have been possible to merely say that oral agreements to arbitrate would no longer be recognised, and thus eliminate what is a slightly unusual provision in the law of Scotland, and one that may still give rise to problems.

The approach actually adopted is in contrast with the analogous provisions of the Arbitration Act 1996 s 5 which state categorically that an agreement must be in writing (as must any variations thereto), albeit that Act also recognises a 'non-written agreement' that incorporates by reference the terms of a written form of agreement containing an arbitration clause as an 'arbitration agreement in writing' (s 5(3)); see, for example, the terms of the London Maritime Arbitrators Association (LMAA). Other jurisdictions have also taken the view that arbitration agreements must be in writing: for example, the Malaysian Arbitration Act 2005 s 9(4), although, interestingly, a claim in a court pleading that an arbitration agreement exists, which is not denied by the other party, is treated as a valid agreement (s 9(4)(c)).

Problems with oral agreement awards

It is usual practice in other jurisdictions for agreements to be in writing, or at least evidenced in writing (see, eg, s 5 of the 1996 Act); and writing is, as will be discussed below, a requirement for enforcement under the New York Convention. As to whether the award requires to be in writing, section 1(2) of the Requirements of Writing (Scotland) Act 1995 does not include awards as documents requiring to be in writing. However, if the award related to heritable property and the 'creation, transfer, variation or extinction of an interest in land otherwise than by operation of a court decree, enactment or rule of law' (s 1(2)(b)) then the award would likely have to meet the formalities required by the Act. The point has not been tested in any case law to date. Note that the 2010 Act also impliedly requires an agreement to be in writing if under s 12 of the 1995 Act the tribunal's award is registered for execution in the Books of Council and Session or in the sheriff court books 'provided that the arbitration agreement is itself so registered'. It is probably the case, though, that an agreement which is in writing or meets the requirements of Art II(2) of the New York Convention could still be varied verbally by the parties under the Act without, it is suggested, altering the validity or enforceability of the original agreement under the Act.

This is particularly relevant to the enforcement of any award. As just touched upon, the New York Convention Art II(1) and II(3) regulates the recognition and enforcement of arbitration agreements. It provides in Art II the requirements to be fulfilled before contracting states are required to recognise and enforce awards. These are that the agreement is 'in writing'; it deals with existing or future disputes; these disputes arise in respect of a defined legal relationship (whether contractual or not) and they concern a subject-matter capable of settlement by arbitration (Art II(1)). Therefore, to have an enforceable award under the Convention, there has to have been an arbitration agreement (arbitration clause or submission agreement) 'in writing'.

The Convention defines 'in writing' as including 'an arbitral clause in a contract or an arbitration agreement, signed by the parties or contained in an exchange of letters or telegrams'. The Convention was prepared in 1958 prior to the proliferation of electronic communications (but when telegrams were still in use) and, given the number of countries which have ratified it, it would be a monumental task to draft new provisions to meet the modern era and then to get them re-ratified by all those countries.

It may be that the exchange of emails might constitute an agreement in writing and the 2006 revisions to the Model Law reflect this in long and short form, making provision for the recognition of 'electronic communication' (Art 7, Options I and II). Article 7(2) of the original Model Law requires arbitration agreements to be in writing which may include 'an exchange of letters, telex, telegrams or other means of telecommunications which provide a record of the agreement, or an exchange of statements of claim and defence in which the existence of an agreement is alleged by one party and not denied by another'.

The real difficulty is that the provisions have not kept pace or do not easily fit with modern methods of communication. Although email and scanning documents into pdf files is normally done now in international commercial business, this method, like the telex and fax before it, will no doubt in future fall out of use and possibly be replaced by blockchain or similar concepts.

Some states have tried to keep up. As an example, Singapore has recently amended its International Arbitration Act specifically to include the electronic communications terms of the 2006 Model Law revision and LCIA (Art 4) and ICC (Art 3) have both amended their rules to cover electronic communications. It is suggested that this could be an opportunity for Scottish courts to take the same view, particularly where the parties routinely communicate by email or other electronic means.

What if the arbitration agreement required any notice of arbitration to be served in defined ways – referencing, for example, fax but not email? The simple answer would be to say that the parties are entitled to agree a specific requirement as a matter of contract.

Were the issue to arise, there should be no reason to distinguish fax from email, as Parliament has to be taken as having legislated against that background when enacting the Electronic Communications Act 2000.

In another case *Neocleous and another v Rees* [2019] EWHC 2462 (Ch) an automatically generated email footer containing the name, role and contact details of the sender rendered the document 'signed' for the purposes of the Law of Property (Miscellaneous Provisions) Act 1989 s 2(3) as the inclusion of the name was for the purpose of giving authenticity to the document. This matter is also discussed in *Chitty on Contracts* (33rd edn), which states at para 32-023: 'In view of rapidly evolving means of recording, "writing" includes recording by any means.' See also Fraser Davidson, *Arbitration* (2nd edn) para 5.56 re Model Law and 'other means of communications which provide a record of the agreement', which the author thinks would include email and voicemail. The latter may be an issue of debate, but rapidly moving technology may mean that the courts will be required to look at the methods by which people and businesses conduct what would be considered 'written' communications, and that the purpose of the requirement is certainty as to the content of such communications, which can be achieved just as well by an email as by a typed letter.

Undoubtedly the courts will need to consider the impact of the Internet. The US Second Circuit Court of Appeals in *Hines v Overstock.com Inc* [2010] US App LEXIS 11265 (2nd Cir, June 3, 2010) refused to enforce an arbitration clause which was found only on a scroll-down of terms and conditions on a website. (This may, however, have been influenced by the fact that perhaps few people scroll down such documents unless there is a compelling reason to do so, and may also be related to the reluctance to enforce binding arbitration on consumers that we address under s 1.) It should be noted, however, that there are a number of other US decisions which take a more liberal approach, and the decisions seem often to be fact-specific.

Caution required in drafting agreements 'in writing'

Although the Act recognises verbal agreements (whether made by reference to another document or not) it is suggested that caution is required as some countries au fait with international arbitration may still refuse to recognise agreements that are not in a 'written document signed by the parties' or contained in 'an exchange of letters or telegrams' (see *Redfern and Hunter on International Arbitration* (6th edn) para 2.23 and the cases cited therein). In *Charterer (Norway) v Shipowner (Russian Federation)* 16 August 1999 (2002) XXVII Ybk Comm Arb 519–22 (Norway No 1), the Norwegian Court of Appeal refused to recognise a London rendered award on the basis that the exchange of emails constituting the agreement did not in its view satisfy the requirements of Art II(2) of the Convention.

Recognising these issues, the 2010 Act makes specific provision in ss

18–22 for what are termed 'Convention awards', ie an award made in pursuance of a written arbitration agreement in the territory of a state (other than the UK) which is a party to the New York Convention. Note that a person seeking recognition and enforcement of a Convention award must produce 'the original arbitration agreement' or a 'duly certified copy of it' (s 21(2)). There is no definition there of 'in writing' although the Scotland Act 1998 (Transitory and Transitional Provisions) (Publication and Interpretation etc of Acts of the Scottish Parliament) Order 1999 (SSI 1999/1379) Sch 2 provides that 'writing' includes 'typing, printing, lithography, photography and other modes of representing or reproducing words in a visible form', and expressions referring to writing are construed accordingly; and the general law is moving towards recognising many non-traditional media as being 'writing' for this purpose.

In summary, however, it is difficult to see that an oral arbitration agreement, even if legally valid under the Act, can ever be the optimal method of proceeding, and the terms of such agreement should prudently always be reduced to 'writing' (giving the word a possibly extended meaning) both for certainty and to ensure the risk of challenges on enforcement are reduced. It is suggested that the retention of the right for oral arbitration agreements in the Act was unnecessary, and inconsistent with general practice in the commercial world, and might be a matter for review if and when the Act is amended.

The arbitration agreement, if in writing, will usually be signed by the parties, and the only issue tends to be whether those signing had the authority to bind the corporate bodies they represent, or whether the actual method of execution is valid in the jurisdiction concerned (eg one or two signatures, are witnesses required, etc). The 1996 Act removes any issue on signatures by making it clear that, while an arbitration agreement has to be in writing, it does not have to be signed (s 5(2)(a)). However, the Indian Supreme Court has recently had to consider whether signatures are required under Indian law, in the case of *Caravel Shipping Services Private Ltd v Premier Sea Foods Exim Private Ltd* MANU/SC/1252/2018. The case allowed arbitration despite the lack of signatures, but clearly turns on the requirements of Indian law (which required an arbitration agreement to be in a document signed by the parties – s 7(4) Arbitration and Conciliation Act, 1996), and this highlights that any arbitration agreement needs to meet the requirements for legal validity in the country concerned. The fact that the Act allows oral agreements to arbitrate would, it is argued, allow an unsigned arbitration agreement to be valid in Scotland, provided there was evidence that the parties had reached agreement on the submission to arbitration, and possibly on the basis that it was an oral agreement evidenced in writing. Putting everything in writing and getting it properly signed is, however, clearly best practice.

Commercial element in addition

At an international level there must also be a 'commercial' element – as considered by the national law of the state making such declaration (New York Convention Art I(3); see *Redfern and Hunter on International Arbitration* (6th edn) paras 11.46 ff). This is unlikely to be a major issue, but does emphasise that international arbitration is generally not available for non-commercial disputes such as family matters.

An arbitration agreement with no mention of arbitration?

There may be an arbitration agreement even where there is no mention of 'arbitration' or 'arbitrator'. This would be so where the intent of the parties is reasonably clear. See the analogous provisions of s 6 of the 1996 Act and the case of *David Wilson Homes Ltd v Survey Services Ltd (now in liquidation)* [2001] EWCA Civ 34, for an example, although where reference was made to mediation in preference to arbitration that was not enough to establish an arbitration agreement (*Flight Training International Inc v International Fire Training Equipment Ltd* [2004] EWHC 721 (Comm)).

These cases fall into the general category of 'pathological' clauses – those that are so uncertain or contradictory as to be unenforceable. However, the English courts in particular have, on a number of occasions, managed to salvage an arbitration agreement out of something that looked fairly hopeless. In *Paul Smith Ltd v H&S International Holding Co Inc* [1991] 2 Lloyd's Rep 127, the contract included clause 13 referring disputes to ICC arbitration and the following clause 14 giving the English courts exclusive jurisdiction. The courts interpreted this as a submission to arbitration, with clause 14 meaning that English law governed the arbitration agreement. Possibly a slight stretch, but it may well reflect what was intended. A similar approach was adopted in *Hiscox Dedicated Corporate Member v Weyerhaeuser* [2019] EWHC 2671 (Comm), which is examined more closely later in the text.

However, in *ERJ Lovelock v Exportles* [1968] 1 Lloyd's Rep 163, even Lord Denning had found himself unable to give meaning to clauses that referred 'any dispute and/or claim' to arbitration in England and 'any other dispute' to arbitration in Moscow under USSR Chamber of Commerce Foreign Trade Arbitration Commission rules. Other decisions include *Mangistaumunaigaz Oil Production Association v United World Trade Inc* [1995] 1 Lloyd's Rep 617 where a clause referring disputes to 'arbitration, if any, by ICC Rules in London' was interpreted to either exclude the 'if any' or to read it as 'if any dispute arises', whereas in *Kruppa v Benedetti* [2014] EWHC 1887 (Comm) the court found itself unable to salvage a clause requiring the parties to first seek to resolve the matter through Swiss arbitration, and if that did not, in fact, lead to resolution, to go to the English courts.

There is a common thread running through many of these cases, which is that it seems probable that either the arbitration provisions were not read or, if they were, they were not really understood. A few minutes' thought can probably save a significant sum in disputes if the issue ever arises. The problem is that, when negotiating a contract, parties tend to be in a positive frame of mind, and disputes going to courts or arbitration are not a real concern. By the time they are, it is too late. This is not a peculiarly English or a Scottish problem – there are pathological clause cases in a number of countries.

Incorporation of arbitration provisions by reference

There can be incorporation of arbitration provisions by reference or, in the words of the Act, 'any agreement which provides for arbitration in accordance with arbitration provisions contained in a separate document' (s 4). This approach is similar to that of s 6(2) of the 1996 Act which provides that 'the reference in an agreement to a written form of arbitration clause or to a document containing an arbitration clause constitutes an arbitration agreement if the reference is such as to make that clause part of the agreement'.

Presumably, in order for there to be an 'incorporation by reference' there would have to be an 'agreement which provides for arbitration' (whether oral or written). In England, an arbitration clause contained in standard conditions of contract that was incorporated by reference into the contract was binding even though the incorporating clause was silent on the matter: see *Secretary of State for the Foreign and Commonwealth Office v Percy Thomas Partnership* (1998) 65 Con LR 11, and more recently *Habas Sinai Ve Tibbi Gazlar Isthisal Endustri AS v Sometal Sal* [2010] EWHC 29 (Comm). Where, however, there was no clear incorporation of a 'jurisdiction and arbitration clause' into the parties' contract then the court had no jurisdiction to entertain any claims under that clause (*Africa Express Line Ltd v Socofi SA* [2009] EWHC 3223 (Comm)). The issue came before the English courts in *Stellar Shipping Co LLC v Hudson Shipping Lines* [2010] EWHC 2985, where it was held that, by guaranteeing the performance of subsidiaries' obligations under a contract of affreightment, by endorsing the contract the guarantor had accepted that disputes should be dealt with in accordance with the arbitration agreement included in such contract. This point also arose in the Indian case of *Caravel Shipping Services Private Ltd v Premier Sea Foods Exim Private Ltd* MANU/SC/1252/2018 mentioned earlier, but the decision appears to have focused on whether a signed agreement was necessary.

'One-stopness'

An issue sometimes arises as to whether an arbitration agreement incorporated into one contract allows linked issues not strictly within the ambit of that contract to be arbitrated at the same time. This has been described in the English courts as 'one-stopness'. While perhaps not the most elegant phrase in legal English, it does, nonetheless, describe a desire to simplify the dispute resolution process.

In *Norscot Rig Management PVT Ltd v Essar Oilfields Services* [2010] EWHC 195 (Comm), a dispute concerning an operations management agreement had been referred to a sole arbitrator. As part of its defence and counterclaims, Essar raised issues that arose from a different contract (the blow out preventer stack contract). The latter contract did not include an arbitration clause. Norscot argued that, as a result, the counterclaims should be litigated separately. The court ruled that the matters either 'arose out of' or were related to the operations management agreement and, therefore, should be included in the arbitration. The court was influenced by the decision in *UBS AG v HSH Nordbank AG* [2009] EWCA Civ 585, where the Court of Appeal had expressed a desire to encourage a 'one-stop' approach to allow disputes arising from the same commercial relationship to be determined in the same proceedings, and this also sits comfortably with the decision in *Fiona Trust* already discussed in relation to taking a pragmatic view of the general intentions of business people to avoid a multiplicity of actions. This issue arose in *Sonact Group Ltd v Premuda SpA (The Four Island)* [2018] EWHC 3820 (Comm) relating to a charterparty which contained an arbitration clause, with the arbitration to be seated in London. A dispute arising from this charterparty was settled by a Settlement Agreement which had no arbitration clause (or any other method of dispute resolution). The English court held that the parties had intended that any disputes under the Settlement Agreement should also be covered by the arbitration terms from the original charterparty, and, therefore, refused to interfere in the tribunal's decision to accept jurisdiction. A similar issue arose in *Etihad Airways PJSC v Flother* [2019] EWHC 3107 (Comm), where the court interpreted a jurisdiction clause on the basis that the parties had likely intended that any dispute arising out of the relationship into which they had entered would be decided by the same tribunal, applying *Fiona Trust & Holding Corpn v Privalov*. See also the Scottish case of *BN Rendering Ltd v Everwarm Ltd* [2018] CSOH 45, where one clause of the terms and conditions provided that any dispute be referred to arbitration and any awards made thereunder could be enforced through the courts, and another provided that the contract was governed by, and construed in accordance with, the laws of England, and that the parties submitted to the exclusive jurisdiction of the English courts. Lord Bannatyne ruled (at para [69]):

> Some support for Mr Tariq's construction can be obtained from the presumed intention of parties in respect to such clauses to have 'a one-stop shop' rather than fragmentation of the resolution of disputes. I accept that this must be a weak presumption, given it is contained in the defender's standard terms, nevertheless it is I believe a factor to which I am entitled to have regard and reinforces the view which I have formed on the clear wording of the clause itself that the true construction is that all court proceedings are referred to the English courts.

It has to be said that contractual provisions of this type are very common, and are usually understood, in the way Lord Bannatyne decided, to be a reference to arbitration, but with an exclusive jurisdiction clause for any matters that, nonetheless, did have to go to court. These cases do, however, emphasise the importance of addressing boilerplate issues, such as governing law and dispute resolution, even in settlement agreements (see *Sonact*). Parties may assume this is irrelevant as the dispute is now settled and nothing can go wrong, but this is not always a correct assumption.

The courts in Alberta have recently addressed this issue in *Canadian Natural Resources Ltd v Flatiron Constructors Canada Ltd* 2018 ABQB 613. Here complex litigation and arbitration had been commenced on different issues under a single project. The court decided that it was most expedient that the court case proceeded first, and so the arbitration was stayed. The Alberta Arbitration Act 2000 provides in s 6 that no court may intervene in arbitrations but one of the exceptions is 'to prevent manifestly unfair or unequal treatment of a party to an arbitration agreement'. In this case, that was held to involve staying (sisting in Scottish terms) the arbitration while the court case proceeded.

These cases may follow the approach in the English courts following the 1996 Woolf Review reforms of civil litigation in England and Wales to reduce multiplication of litigation, and associated delays and costs. In Scotland, Lord Gill's 2009 Scottish Civil Courts Review advocated a similar approach. However, the 2010 Act did not specifically address the point, and it is interesting to note the *obiter* comments of Lady Wolffe in *Autauric Ltd v Glasgow Stage Crew Ltd* [2019] CSOH 111 (at para [17]):

> In contrast to the Civil Procedure Rules ('the CPR') in England, our Rules do not articulate an overriding objective of civil litigation or an acknowledgement of considerations of efficiency, effectiveness or the proportionate use of resources (including court resources). Again in contrast to the CPR, our Rules do not impose a positive obligation on litigants to assist the court in achieving that overriding objective. Maybe they should.

This does, of course, contrast with the position in arbitration, where such a positive duty is imposed on the parties by mandatory rule 25, to which we return later.

It would, of course, be possible for parties to say that only a specific range of issues could be referred to arbitration, or even that different arbitration processes were required for different issues or contracts. However, to avoid a multiplicity of proceedings, any such provisions will need to be drafted with precision and clarity.

End of the right to arbitrate

While most arbitration clauses are wide enough to allow disputes after termination to be arbitrated, there may be doubt as to whether this is correct once all of the obligations under the contract containing the arbitration clause have been discharged. This matter came before the Indian Supreme Court in *Union of India v Hari Singh* Civil Appeal 7970/2010, where the court ruled that principles of 'accord and satisfaction' meant that, once a final payment had been made under the contract, the right to arbitrate was lost. This is, perhaps, an exceptional position, but does emphasise that, as the agreement to arbitrate is contractual, it must come to an end at some stage, just as with any other contract.

It should also be noted that not every binding decision on a dispute made outside the courts is necessarily an arbitration award. For example, in *Berkeley Burke SIPP Administration LLP v Charlton* [2017] EWHC 2396 (Comm) the English courts held that an ombudsman's decision was not an arbitration award capable of founding an appeal under s 69 of the 1996 Act.

Separability

Section 5 deals with the separability (sometimes referred to as the severability) of the arbitration clause. It means that the clause is treated as being separate and independent from the overall or main contract in which it is found – ie it is hived off and treated as a separate entity.

If the contract itself is found to be void, voidable or unenforceable the clause within it still lives on unaffected. These terms are slightly different from s 10, which, in relation to the arbitration agreement, uses 'void, inoperative or incapable of being performed' in a similar context.

So, for example, the arbitration clause could still be used even where one party claims the contract itself is void, ie to resolve the very issue of whether this claim is correct.

The wording used here is similar to other wording found in some of the institutional rules and in the Arbitration Act 1996. An example can be found in the current UNCITRAL Rules which specify that 'an arbitration clause … shall be treated as an agreement independent of the other terms of the contract' (Art 23.1).

But what if the main contract was void *ab initio* – ie from the very beginning? The Act here specifies that the fact that the other agreement is *void* (emphasis added) does not in itself affect the arbitration agreement. So, on one interpretation, the fact that the original contract containing the arbitration clause was void from the very start and did not 'legally get off the ground' would not prevent validity being given to the arbitration clause found in it. But that is not to say that the arbitration clause cannot be attacked on the same basis as that rendering the main contract void – in other words it will not necessarily be valid in all circumstances.

Section 5(3) means that a tribunal can rule on whether an agreement that includes an arbitration clause is valid in accordance with that arbitration agreement. It follows that, if the tribunal determined that it was not, then that would not affect the tribunal's ability to have made such a determination. The word 'includes' must mean that it is a ruling on the contract or agreement which itself includes the arbitration agreement. Note, however, that it may not be possible to avoid laws that have mandatory effect on a transaction by simply choosing a different law to govern the arbitration. The English case of *Accentuate Ltd v Asigra Inc* [2009] EWHC 2655 concerned an agreement specifying that any arbitration was subject to Canadian law (law of Ontario and Canadian Federal Law). The dispute related to a commercial agency agreement, which was subject to mandatory European Union laws (Commercial Agents (Council Directive) Regulations 1993 (SI 1993/3053)). The effect of a Canadian arbitration would be that these Regulations would be ignored. The court held that the arbitration provisions were 'null and void' and 'inoperative', and allowed litigation to commence without a stay of arbitration. While this case was specifically about the Commercial Agents Regulations, it appears to have general application, following *Ingmar GB Ltd v Eaton Leonard Technologies Ltd* (Case C-381/98) [2000] EUECJ in which the European Court made it clear that all European Union laws were mandatory, notwithstanding a choice of law provision to the contrary. This argument is developed further in the case of *Slovak Republic v Achmea BV* (Case C-284/16) EU:C:2018:158 where the European Court of Justice ruled that the arbitration provisions in a Bilateral Investment Treaty between the Netherlands and Slovakia were invalid because they could allow a tribunal (in this case seated in Frankfurt) to rule on the law of the European Union, and this was inconsistent with the Treaty on the Functioning of the European Union (originally the Treaty of Rome). This casts considerable doubt on the common use of arbitration to resolve investment treaty disputes, at least where European Union parties are involved. The issue of the interaction between investment arbitrations and European Union law has recently come before the UK Supreme Court in *Micula and others v Romania* [2020] UKSC 5, but the court removed a stay on enforcement as the General Court of the European Union had struck down a Commission decision that Romania's payments were unlawful state aid, and, in any event, they were agreed to before Romania joined the European Union, but the Commission's investigations were continuing. The arguments relate to specific rules on investment arbitrations, and it does not seem to take the issue of how the UK courts will apply *Achmea* much further, although it does suggest a willingness to make decisions under English (in this case) law in circumstances where the European Courts have not made a binding decision. It is unclear how this will be impacted by Brexit, to which we now turn. The result of Brexit will change the basis of enforcement, and this is a developing area of law.

At the time of writing this edition, the full impact of the Brexit settlement, particularly in relation to the future application of European Union law and/or rulings of the European Court remains uncertain, and it is therefore unclear whether *Achmea*, *Ingmar*, or, indeed the specific facts of *Accentuate*, will continue to be relevant, but the general principle remains that arbitration under one law is unlikely to be a method of evading mandatory applicable provisions of another legal system. However, it seems probable that at least *Achmea* will have some impact on UK parties involved in investments in the European Union.

The English position

The analogous provision of the Arbitration Act 1996 (s 7) refers to an arbitration agreement not being regarded as 'invalid, non-existent or ineffective because that other agreement is invalid, or did not come into existence or has become ineffective', which can be read as 'void'. There have been a number of cases on this subject-matter. In the *Fiona Trust* litigation [2007] UKHL 40, the House of Lords held that arbitrators and not the courts should determine whether the underlying contract was void for illegality unless that illegality was directed at the arbitration clause itself (per Lord Hoffmann at paras [12] and [13]).

Law governing arbitration agreement

If the parties agree to seat their arbitration in Scotland, but do not specify a law to govern the arbitration agreement, s 6 of the Act states that Scots law shall apply. As detailed under s 4, normally the arbitration agreement may be in a submission agreement or, more usually, in an arbitration clause in the main contract.

As seen in the discussions relating to 'seat' under s 3 above, the law which governs that agreement is not necessarily the same as the substantive law chosen by the parties to govern their main contract.

In *Tamil Nadu Electricity Board v ST-CMS Electric Co Private Ltd* [2007] EWHC 1713 (Comm), where an agreement, governed by the law of India, provided for the settling of disputes arising out of that agreement by arbitration according to the laws of England, it was held that the intention was that English law should prevail over Indian law in determining the ambit or scope of the arbitration agreement, whatever Indian law might itself provide. Note here that the 'agreement' or main contract provided for the parties' obligations to be governed by the law of India, which makes the decision somewhat surprising.

Section 6 avoids the problem existing in international arbitration of having to 'divine' the law applicable to the arbitration in accordance with a range of factors by imposing on the parties by implication that Scots law (by virtue of the seat – see s 3) will govern the arbitration agreement unless the parties by agreement dictate otherwise. This is a sensible and practical solution; and if the parties desire something different, they need to provide for it in the arbitration agreement. Were it not for this provision, the general law could still determine the governing law (eg Rome I Regulation while this still applies to the UK), but this provides a simple and understandable solution, without the need for lengthy and expensive court proceedings.

Scottish Arbitration Rules – Mandatory and Default Rules

Section 7 of the Act states, with admirable brevity, 'The Scottish Arbitration Rules set out in schedule 1 are to govern every arbitration seated in Scotland (unless, in the case of a default rule, the parties otherwise agree).'

Given the passage of time since the 2010 Act came into force, it may now be assumed that references by parties in arbitration agreements to the 'Scottish Rules' will be taken to mean the Rules as encapsulated in schedule 1 to the Act, as noted above. Indeed s 31(1) provides for that where the phrase 'Scottish Arbitration Rules' is used. The schedule sets out the Rules in the form of a single code and they (together with the sections) will govern every arbitration seated in Scotland as a matter of Scots law, and not as a matter of contract between the parties. This, of course, is subject to such of those default provisions as are modified or disapplied by the agreement of the parties. For example, if the parties adopt a different set of rules (eg LCIA) then those rules will apply, but only to the extent that they do not conflict with the mandatory rules. In addition, the default rules will continue to apply to the extent that they are not modified by the institutional rules or unless they have been specifically excluded. It will, of course, also be open to parties to adopt the Scottish Rules for arbitrations seated outside Scotland, subject to this being allowed under local law, but this will be by operation of contract, not the Act itself.

Accordingly, when including well-known institutional rules in their arbitration agreement, parties need to take care that these do not conflict with mandatory rules, or that the impact of such a conflict is understood.

Mandatory rules

Section 8 of the Act states:

> The following rules, called 'mandatory rules', cannot be modified or disapplied (by an arbitration agreement, by any other agreement between the parties or by any other means) in relation to any arbitration seated in Scotland –
>   rule 3 (arbitrator to be an individual)
>   rule 4 (eligibility to act as an arbitrator)
>   rule 7 (failure of appointment procedure)
>   rule 8 (duty to disclose any conflict of interests)
>   rules 12 to 16 (removal or resignation of arbitrator or dismissal of tribunal)
>   rules 19 to 21 and 23 (jurisdiction of tribunal)
>   rules 24 and 25 (general duties of tribunal and parties)
>   rule 42 (point of law referral: procedure etc.)
>   rule 44 (time limit variation: procedure etc.)
>   rule 45 (securing attendance of witnesses and disclosure of evidence)
>   rule 48 (power to award payment and damages)
>   rule 50 (interest)

rule 54 (part awards)
rule 56 (power to withhold award if fees or expenses not paid)
rule 60 (arbitrators' fees and expenses)
rule 63 (ban on pre-dispute agreements about liability for arbitration expenses)
rules 67, 68, 70, 71 and 72 (challenging awards)
rules 73 to 75 (immunity)
rule 76 (loss of right to object)
rule 77 (independence of arbitrator)
rule 79 (death of arbitrator)
rule 82 (rules applicable to umpires).

The structure of the Act follows the design of the English model in part. There are mandatory provisions which cannot be removed or taken out, even by the agreement of the parties, while leaving other parts as 'non-mandatory' or, in the language of the Act, 'default'.

As noted above, although the Act gives effect to party autonomy both in principle (s 1) and in a large measure by the operation of default rules, there has to be some measure of fettering of autonomy to ensure the successful operation of arbitrations in Scotland under the Rules.

Mandatory rule 3 makes it clear that the arbitrator must be an individual, and it is not open to appoint a body corporate or an institution to act as arbitrator. This is in line with practice elsewhere and is not the same as having a body acting to appoint an arbitrator, which is not prohibited – see eg s 24 (arbitral appointments referee).

Obviously the rules are not just mandatory for the parties. An arbitrator who departs from them will be in breach and give the parties the option of seeking their removal. Mandatory rule 12(e) provides a ground of removal of an arbitrator by the Outer House on the basis that 'substantial injustice has been or will be caused to that party because the arbitrator has failed to conduct the arbitration in accordance with ... these rules (in so far as they apply)'.

Likewise, any award issued in pursuance of such a breach would be open to challenge. Mandatory rule 68(2)(a)(ii) permits a challenge to an award by appeal to the Outer House on the ground of serious irregularity which has caused or will cause substantial injustice to the appellant such as the tribunal 'failing to conduct the arbitration in accordance with the arbitration agreement or these rules (in so far as they apply)'.

The provision in mandatory rule 63 prohibiting pre-agreement of liability for arbitration expenses mirrors problems in the field of construction adjudication in England where the growth of so-called 'Tolent clauses' to this effect (after the decision in *Bridgeway Construction Ltd v Tolent Construction Ltd* [2000] CILL 1662 (TCC)) was brought to an end by the decision in *Yuanda (UK) Co Ltd v WW Gear Construction Ltd* [2010] EWHC 720 (TCC), that such clauses conflict with the provisions of the Housing Grants,

Construction and Regeneration Act 1996 s 108, as amended by Part 8 of the Local Democracy, Economic Development and Construction Act 2009. Unfortunately, the Scottish courts declined to follow the lead in *Yuanda*, and in *Profile Projects Ltd v Elmwood (Glasgow) Ltd* [2011] CSOH 64, Lord Menzies allowed what amounted to a Tolent clause, partially on the basis that requiring the referring party to pay the costs of an adjudication in any event would not disable it from making the application. This decision was criticised, not least because, while it might be the case that this did not disable access to adjudication in many cases, it was a substantial deterrent running contrary to the point of the legislation, and was seen as being somewhat divorced from commercial reality. But this issue does not arise in arbitration, where mandatory rule 63 effectively makes *Yuanda* the law of Scotland in this area.

The approaches in both *Yuanda* and the mandatory rules are, it is suggested, sensible. In practice, these clauses had reached the stage where the contractor or subcontractor was required to be always liable for adjudication costs and expenses, even where the client/main contractor commenced the adjudication, and lost. Mandatory rule 63 obviates this.

Default rules

Section 9 provides that all non-mandatory rules are called default rules. In respect of the default non-mandatory provisions, consistent with the concept of party autonomy, the parties to an arbitration seated in Scotland may modify or disapply any of the default rules (or any *part* of them) in relation to that arbitration. If they have not done so then the default rules will apply. This illustrates the point made above concerning default rules, although it should be noted that the modification or disapplication can either be specific or, say, by adopting institutional rules or by applying a law other than the law of Scotland to cover a particular issue (see below).

In line with party autonomy, the parties are properly given a very wide latitude in respect of this, and may agree to delete default clauses in the agreement or to do so by any means at any other time before or after the arbitration has begun, albeit this might foreseeably cause procedural problems and result in additional expenses considerations. In practice, it is suggested that the frequency of parties seeking to modify the default rules after arbitration has commenced will be very limited. In such circumstances, all of the parties would have to consent to such a modification and are unlikely to do so unless the parties' mutual interests coincide. An example might be to remove the confidentiality obligations in default rule 26 because the parties wish to have the results of the arbitration widely known. An example could be in the field of rent review arbitration, where it is understood that parties wish general levels of rents for comparable properties to be in the public domain; or a government body that wished to be shown to be being transparent for political reasons.

It is probably fair to say that most arbitration clauses in contracts have very short provisions as to the applicable rules, and do not include any modifications or deletions. For example, the Scottish Arbitration Centre publishes a number of useful standard clauses, but none of these modify any of the default rules (see www.scottisharbitrationcentre.org). The general approach may reflect the fact that, when parties agree any type of dispute resolution clause, they are not contemplating at the start of the contract that a dispute will indeed arise.

Scottish seat and the *lex arbitri*

Under s 6 (law governing an arbitration agreement), where the parties agree that an arbitration is to be seated in Scotland and the arbitration agreement does not specify the law governing the arbitration agreement, then, subject to agreement otherwise, it is governed by Scots law. It follows therefore that the parties can choose a Scottish seat but make provision for the applicable law (*lex arbitri*) to apply to certain subjects (even down to the applicable law for the subject-matter of a particular rule). So, to take a simple example, where the parties are based in Ireland and, although happy to use the Scottish seat and the Act and default rules, they wish to modify default rule 36 under the 2010 Act in connection with the administration of oaths or affirmations to witnesses and parties and to substitute in that context the provisions of the Irish Arbitration Act 2010 s 14 which makes similar provision, they would be entitled to do so and Irish law would then regulate this subject-matter albeit that the rest of the procedure was applying all the other Scottish default rules and of course the mandatory ones as well.

So, in general, one can envisage various permutations in the application or modification or disapplication of these default rules.

For example, assuming a Scottish seat:

- If the parties' agreement is a bare arbitration agreement in a main contract and it is silent on the default rules, then they will all apply unless the parties subsequently agree before or during the arbitration to modify or disapply them.
- If they put provisions into the arbitration agreement as to the default rules, those provisions will apply unless again the parties make alternative provision by other means before or during the arbitration.
- If they do not put provisions in the agreement but agree, say, that the LCIA Rules will apply to their arbitration, then the default rules will be treated as having been modified or disapplied to the extent that they are inconsistent with or disapplied by those Rules, but will continue to apply to the extent that the point is not addressed in the incorporated institutional or other rules.
- If they choose a law other than the law of Scotland as the applicable law to the arbitration (*lex arbitri*), or to a specific issue (such as the Irish

oaths example above), then that law will apply to the extent that it includes rules which are inconsistent with the default rules under the Act. Again, the remaining default rules will continue in full effect. But note that the mandatory rules will continue to apply to an arbitration seated in Scotland and governed by the Act, even where inconsistent with an agreed *lex arbitri*.

- Lastly, if there is already agreement in place regarding the default rules, this agreement may nevertheless be modified by subsequent agreement of the parties.

As Harris, Planterose and Tecks have remarked in connection with the 1996 Act's division of mandatory and non-mandatory rules: it was 'originally thought that this system was, at least initially, likely to present considerable difficulty for lay parties, and considerable scope for lawyers', and they continue that they have seen 'no evidence that this has in fact been the case' (*The Arbitration Act 1996: A Commentary* (5th edn) p 42). With the dearth of case law in Scotland, it is not yet known whether these observations would have an equal application.

Suspension of legal proceedings

Suspension of legal proceedings

Procedural considerations

The wording of s 10, which provides for the suspension of legal proceedings when matters have been referred to arbitration, appears to have been influenced by the similar provisions in s 9 of the 1996 Act, relating to a 'stay of proceedings' to use the English terminology. It was, therefore, anticipated that 'applications' under this section would require to be made by way of motion in the legal proceedings in question. The Rules of Court, however, have adopted the petition procedure under RCS Chapter 14 instead, with the disapplication of some of the procedural rules (RCS 100.5).

This, when taken together with s 10(1)(d)(i), could, on one construction, lead to potential practical difficulties for the defender/respondent in any such proceedings. The concern is that the petition to sist for arbitration will be separate from the court action that is being challenged. If the petition succeeds, the action is sisted. If, however, it fails (for example because there is held to be no valid arbitration agreement), then the proceedings will go ahead, and the defender may be exposed if he has failed to lodge defences in time under the rules relating to the commercial court/ordinary actions.

If, however, the defender decides to lodge defences denying liability (perhaps as a simple denial as an alternative to a claim that the matter should proceed to arbitration, and, therefore, that the court has no jurisdiction), then it is arguable that this could amount to taking a 'step in the legal proceedings to answer any substantive claim against the applicant', which would remove the right to a mandatory sist under s 10. It is arguable that the court would retain an inherent jurisdiction within the proceedings to sist in any event, but this would not be under s 10, and might well be met with the response that the correct remedy is established by the Act, and that a claim for a 'second bite' is incompetent.

It should also be noted that it does not appear possible to conjoin an action and a petition.

However, such reported cases as have arisen since the Act came into force have concentrated on appeals after awards have been made, and it does not seem that the concern expressed in the First Edition of this book that the rules could cause practical problems has come to pass; a sensible and robust approach is being adopted here as elsewhere in relation to arbitration and sisting of court proceedings, and any difficulty remains theoretical rather than practical.

Court

Interestingly, 'court' is generally defined in s 31(1) as the Outer House or the sheriff court, but, for s 10, among others, it means 'any court', and so the sheriff court would also sensibly be included here. It should be noted that, while rules in relation to arbitrations are contained in the Sheriff Court Rules, they are not as detailed and, it is suggested, as clear as those for the Court of Session, which may result in many applications under the Act being dealt with in the Outer House, even where the Sheriff Court might have concurrent jurisdiction. One may also note that there are specialist arbitration judges assigned to the Outer House.

Underlying considerations

When parties agree in an arbitration agreement to resolve their differences or disputes by arbitration then what happens if one party seeks instead to raise or participate in proceedings before a court? As Lord Dunedin observed in 1922 in *Sanderson & Son v Armour & Co Ltd*: 'If the parties have contracted to arbitrate, to arbitration they must go' (1922 SC (HL) 117 at 126). This has been the common policy of courts in both Scotland and England. Courts in Continental Europe and elsewhere sometimes take a less robust line.

It follows therefore that national or domestic courts should not entertain proceedings in those courts at the instance of one of the parties in respect of a matter that is the subject of an arbitration agreement. This is part of the general duty on the courts imposed by, for example, the New York Convention, to support arbitrations, and prevents one party from breaching what was an obligation to the other, and then seeking the support of the courts to make its breach effective. It is also analogous with the English decisions in *Cable &*

Wireless v IBM United Kingdom Ltd [2002] EWHC 2059 (Comm), where the parties were required to try alternative dispute resolution (in this case effectively mediation) before coming to court, as this was what they had agreed in the contract; and *Emirates Trading Agency LLC v Prime Mineral Exports Private Ltd* [2014] EWHC 2104 (Comm), where it was held that a requirement for 'friendly discussion' was a valid and enforceable condition precedent before invoking an arbitration clause. This general approach in relation to different types of alternative dispute resolution included in contracts has also been followed in later decisions, but only where the wording is clear as to what is actually required (for example, the enforcement of a tiered dispute resolution clause in *Ohpen Operations UK Ltd v Invesco Fund Managers Ltd* [2019] EWHC 2246 (TCC)).

It is, of course, right to say that if both parties agree to proceed to court, rather than arbitration (ie on the principle of waiver) there can be no objection to such a course of action.

Meaning of sist

The concept of a 'sist' is part of Scottish civil procedure and means to stop the legal case (or 'cause'). Everything is put 'on ice' until the sist is 'recalled'. Normally either party to the proceedings can apply for it although traditionally the court itself on its own motion (what is termed *ex proprio motu*) could not impose a sist (it was a decision for the party/ies). If the parties do apply, note therefore that there is no automatic entitlement. The court is said to be 'vested with a discretion' whether to grant it or not. This is because once an action or cause is commenced, the parties as a matter of right can insist on it carrying on (*Connell v Grierson* (1865) 3 M 1166 at 1167). This is not the position with s 10, which makes provision for a mandatory sist.

At common law, Scots law always recognised that a court action could be sisted to enable a question to be decided by arbitration on the basis that the parties, by agreeing to refer a dispute to arbitration, had voluntarily limited or excluded recourse to the court. The court's jurisdiction was not considered to be wholly ousted (*Hamlyn & Co v Talisker Distillery* (1894) 21 R (HL) 21 at 25, 27 per Lord Watson) but it was deprived of jurisdiction to enquire into and decide the merits of the case. (Note that Lord Watson in that case used the language of 'staying procedure' (p 25) which was followed by Lord Dunedin in the case of *Sanderson* above.)

In the event of the arbitral proceedings being abortive, then the court process can be revived by the recalling of the sist.

Section 10 incorporates elements of this common law position into statute, subject to certain qualifications, the main one being the recognition of a 'mandatory sist', albeit that the Rules of the Court of Session had recognised mandatory sists in certain other circumstances (see eg RCS 65.4 where there is a reference to the European Court – 'the cause ... shall be sisted'). It is, therefore, important that when a party to what they consider to be a valid arbitration agreement finds that legal proceedings have been issued by the other party, they take prompt legal advice. Such advice will enable determination of whether it is possible to sist the proceedings if they are in Scotland and to consider what other options are available in other jurisdictions, such as anti-suit injunctions or interdicts. These effectively became inapplicable within the European Union following the decision in *West Tankers Inc v RAS Riunione Adriatica di Sicurta SpA (The Front Comor)* [2007] UKHL 4 (on appeal from [2005] EWHC 454 (Comm) and the subsequent European Court decision [2009] EUECJ C-185/07 *sub nom Allianz SpA v West Tankers Inc*, and *National Navigation Co v Endesa Generacion SA (The Wadi Sudr)* [2009] EWCA Civ 1397). The European Parliament subsequently took steps to reduce the impact of *West Tankers*, through the Brussels I (Recast) Regulation EU 1215/2012. However, the English courts took the view in *Nori Holdings Ltd and others v Bank Okritie Financial Corporation PJSC [2018] EWHC 1343 (Comm)* that the Recast Regulations did not have the effect intended, and Males J refused to issue an anti-suit injunction against proceedings in Cyprus, although an injunction was issued against other proceedings in Russia (which is, of course, not a European Union State, and to which *West Tankers* could never apply). Accordingly, *West Tankers* would appear still to be good law in England and, coupled with the detailed reasoning, would seem likely to be followed should the same issue arise in Scotland. However, there is a conflict in that the Advocate General's Opinion in the European Court of Justice case of *Gazprom OAO v Lietuvos Respublika* (Case C-536/13) recommended that the European Court should find that the Brussels 1 (Recast) Regulation allowed the recognition of what amounted to an anti-suit injunction in an arbitral award. While not exactly on the point, this was seen as potentially having the effect of solving the *West Tankers* problem. However, the final decision of the Court decided the Recast Regulation did not apply, on timing grounds, and seems to still take a view against the concept of anti-suit injunctions. For the moment, the jurisprudence of the European and English courts appears to reach the same decision, but not necessarily for the same reasons, and the issue has yet to arise in Scotland.

While the English courts seem ready to issue anti-suit injunctions in appropriate cases, there are no Scottish cases on this specific issue, and there is no indication that the Scottish courts have been asked to grant interdict in such circumstances. It therefore remains to be seen whether the Scottish courts will, as and when the issue arises, follow the English authorities cited, or take a more restrictive position, particularly to the extent that decisions of the European Court of Justice continue to have relevance after Brexit.

While the final impact of the Brexit settlement is uncertain, it is speculated that there will be no great pressure to retain compliance with European Union law in the fairly esoteric area of anti-suit injunctions/interdicts in support of arbitration, and it might be the case that *West Tankers* will cease to be good authority, and the practice will revert to the earlier position when there was no distinction as to the jurisdiction concerned.

An interesting variation on anti-suit injunctions relating to proceedings outside the European Union is found in *AES Ust-Kamenogorsk Hydropower Plant LLP v Ust-Kamenogorsk Hydropower Plant JSC* [2011] EWCA Civ 647. Here the English courts were asked to restrain proceedings in Kazakhstan. However, the party seeking the injunction had no intention of commencing arbitration proceedings itself. It was refused an injunction under s 44 of the 1996 Act, on the basis that arbitration proceedings must have been commenced, or at least contemplated. However, it was entitled to an injunction under s 37 of the Senior Courts Act 1981 (previously the Supreme Court Act 1981) to protect a contractual right. The initial ruling was appealed, partially on the basis that the respondent had submitted to the Kazakhstan courts, but the appeal was dismissed. The Appeal Court also held it was not bound by what it considered a misconstruction of the English arbitration clause by the Kazakhstan courts. This contrasts with the position in *Dallah Estate and Tourism Holding Co v Ministry of Religious Affairs of the Government of Pakistan* [2010] UKSC 46, where the English courts felt themselves quite able to construe French law (although the French courts have subsequently ruled that this was also a misconstruction).

An interesting development in the anti-suit injunction field was the decision in *Aqaba Container Terminal (PVT) Co v Soletanche Bachy France SAS* [2019] EWHC 471 (Comm) where a permanent injunction was granted to prevent the defendant from pursuing court proceedings in Jordan in an effort to get the construction contract containing the arbitration agreement declared void, when they had already participated in the arbitration, and where the issue on the validity of the contract was, itself, arbitrable. The courts are clearly prepared to prevent a party seeking to circumvent the arbitration agreement in this way. In *Evison Holdings Ltd v International Co Finvision Holdings* [2019] EWHC 3057 (Comm) an anti-suit injunction restraining a Russian company from pursuing proceedings in Russia concerning the claimant's alleged wrongdoing while in control of the company was discontinued on the basis that the claimant had not made out its case that the Russian proceedings were designed to impede arbitration proceedings in London involving the same issues.

As stated above, outside the European Union, the position as to whether Scottish courts would grant an anti-suit interdict (the Scottish equivalent of an English injunction) in support of arbitration has never been clear. However, under the new clearer statutory regime, it is suggested that, as mentioned above, there is no reason why such a remedy should not be available.

There is a danger in trying to raise multiple proceedings, as was illustrated in *Excalibur Ventures LLC v Texas Keystone Inc* [2011] EWHC 1624 (Comm) where the claimant commenced simultaneous court proceedings in England and an ICC arbitration in New York, against four defendants, three of whom had no real connection to the arbitration agreement. The English High Court granted an injunction to restrain the claimant from pursuing the New York arbitration proceedings, partially on the basis that the defendants had never been party to the claimed arbitration agreement (a similar point to *Dallah*).

However, the judge (Mrs Justice Gloster) also decided that the matter should be determined by the English courts, and not by the arbitrators in New York. At least part of the reason may have been the decision to launch the English proceedings, and seeking (unsuccessfully) a worldwide freezing injunction (sometimes referred to as a *Mareva* injunction) was broadly inconsistent with the claimant's claim that there was an arbitration agreement in force. The courts may also restrain a foreign arbitration if they consider the correct jurisdiction is the courts (see *Sabbagh v Khoury* [2018] EWHC 1330 (Comm) discussed further below where a Lebanese arbitration was restrained), and will not always restrain foreign court proceedings in support of arbitration where there are legitimate motives for such proceedings, other than frustrating the arbitration (see *A v OOO 'Insurance Company Chubb' and other companies* [2019] EWHC 2729 (Comm), also discussed below, where the English courts refused to restrain Russian proceedings, notwithstanding the fact that it could cause issues for an arbitration seated in London) and *IS Prime Ltd v TF Global Markets (UK) Ltd* [2020] EWHC 3375 (Comm) where an agreement to submit to non-binding arbitration was held not to amount to an arbitration agreement, and English court proceedings would not be stayed.

There are other examples of the English courts continuing the practice of issuing anti-suit injunctions in support of arbitration, where the other jurisdiction is outside the European Union. In *Star Reefers Pool Inc v JFC Group Co Ltd* [2010] EWHC 3003 (Comm), an anti-suit injunction was granted to restrain Russian litigation where the parties were already involved in arbitration in London. The basis for this injunction was, first, that it was reasonably certain that the parties had selected English law as the governing law of the guarantees (or, possibly, purported guarantees) in question, and, secondly, that it was believed the Russian proceedings had been commenced to seek to frustrate the London arbitration and were therefore 'vexatious and oppressive'. However, another English case (*Louis Dreyfus Commodities Kenya Ltd v Bolster Shipping Company Ltd* [2010] EWHC 1732) makes it clear that the similar provisions in the 1996 Act do not prevent *any* other legal proceedings where a valid arbitration clause exists. Here Mexican proceedings existed where Louis Dreyfus had been joined as a third party. In the context of Mexican practice, it was stated to have been joined to assist the court in determining the truth, rather than being exposed to having a judgment rendered against it. The Mexican proceedings themselves were between different parties from those in the English arbitration. A possible effect of the Mexican judgment could be to determine that Louis Dreyfus was liable in relation to the subject-matter of the arbitration. Despite this, the High Court refused to grant an anti-suit injunction as the same parties were not involved, and the issues were also not identical.

An interesting reversal of the usual arguments arose in *Noble Denton Middle East v Noble Denton International Ltd* [2010] EWHC 2574. In this case two applications were made to the English High Court, the first to appoint an arbitrator under s 18 of the 1996 Act, and the second to stay the arbitration proceedings in favour of proceedings in Texas. The responding party acknowledged that there was a good arguable case that the dispute was governed by an English arbitration clause, and the claimants also conceded that their case was arguable, not certain. Burton J had no difficulty in appointing the proposed arbitrator, and leaving the tribunal to determine its jurisdiction. The more interesting part of the decision for present purposes is that the judge declined to restrain the arbitration in favour of the Texas proceedings. While this is perhaps unsurprising as he had only just appointed the arbitrator, the reasoning was that signing an English arbitration clause amounted to an exclusive jurisdiction agreement, even though the contract did not state this in terms. This does, therefore, put arbitration in a slightly different position from litigation on this issue, in that it seems to be the position that an arbitration clause is at least as strong as, and possibly stronger than, a conventional exclusive jurisdiction clause in relation to court proceedings. On this basis, there would have to be very strong grounds for overriding the exclusive arrangements. The court cited *Deutsche Bank AG v Sebastian Holdings Inc* [2009] EWHC 3069 (Comm) on this point.

It should not, however, be assumed that the English courts will automatically grant anti-suit injunctions. In *Evison Holdings Limited v International Company Finvision Holdings and another* [2019] EWHC 3057 (Comm) mentioned above, the court refused to grant an injunction against a non-party to the arbitration agreement who had commenced proceedings in Russia on substantially the same issues. Evison's counsel relied on earlier cases where injunctions had been granted against non-parties, namely *BNP Paribas SA v Open Joint Stock Company Russian Machines and another* [2011] EWHC 308 (Comm) and *Mace (Russia) Ltd v Retansel Enterprises Ltd* [2016] EWHC 1209 (Comm). However, in those cases the non-party had been in common control with the party to the arbitration, and the action was seen as an attempt to frustrate the arbitration process. In *Evison* this was not the case, but it was claimed that Finvision were colluding with the non-party. The court held that the non party was pursuing its own legitimate aims, and, therefore, the injunction was refused. There may be an issue with whether a party is indeed a 'party' or a 'non-party'. A question of whether the law governing the validity of the arbitration agreement also governed the question of whether the award debtor became a party to it was held to be decided in accordance with s. 103(2)(b) of the 1996 Act. The issue arose from the majority of the tribunal forming the view that French law determined this point (the arbitration was seated in Paris, and this was thus the *lex arbitri*), whereas the court took the view that the relevant law was the governing law of the underlying contract (English), which produced a different result, as a purported novation agreement was not effective as a matter of English law. The award could not, therefore, be enforced against the award debtor under the New York Convention (*J (Lebanon) v K (Kuwait)* [2019] EWHC 899 (Comm)). The case was appealed as *Kabab-Ji SAL (Lebanon) v Kout Food Group (Kuwait)* [2020] EWCA Civ 6, where the Court of Appeal held that the express choice of English law as the governing law of the contract meant that this law also governed the arbitration agreement. The choice of Paris as a seat did not change this, and English law should be used to determine the issue; and it was confirmed that the purported novation was invalid. The Paris Court of Appeal subsequently reached a different decision, so the issue rumbles on.

Structure of section 10

In the First Edition of this book, it had been anticipated that s 10 would be a source of a number of reported decisions, but this has not proved to be the case. By way of comparison, the Arbitration Act 1996 s 9 makes provision for the 'stay of legal proceedings' (ie the same concept) and has resulted in a large body of English case law, particularly in an international context. The lack of similar litigation in Scotland may reflect the fact that a return to the international arbitration market is in its early stages.

The UNCITRAL Model Law (as amended), Art 8 makes provision for arbitration agreements and substantive claims before a court. It states:

> (1) A court before which an action is brought in a matter which is the subject of an arbitration agreement shall, if a party so requests not later than when submitting his first statement on the substance of the dispute, refer the parties to arbitration unless it finds that the agreement is null and void, inoperative or incapable of being performed.
> (2) Where an action referred to in paragraph (1) of this article has been brought, arbitral proceedings may nevertheless be commenced or continued, and an award may be made, while the issue is pending before the court.

The New York Convention addresses this point in Art II(3):

> The court of a Contracting State, when seized of an action in a matter in respect of which the parties have made an agreement within the meaning of this article, shall, at the request of one of the parties, refer the parties to arbitration, unless it finds that the said agreement is null and void, inoperative or incapable of being performed.

As detailed above, the Scottish approach here is an amalgam of the two. It adopts the imperative non-discretionary element for the court, in that it *must* sist (similar to the 'shall' imperative in the Model Law and in the 1996 Act s 9(4)).

The 1996 Act approaches it slightly differently, giving a party against whom legal proceedings are brought in respect of a matter to be referred to arbitration an entitlement to apply, upon notice to the other parties in the legal proceedings, for a stay of those proceedings in so far as they concern that matter. Under the English provisions, subject to a number of safeguards, on an application under s 9 the court shall grant a stay unless satisfied that the arbitration agreement is 'null and void, inoperative or incapable of being performed' (s 9(4)), reflecting the language of Art II(3) of the New York Convention. That is also the same wording as used in s 10(1)(e) of the 2010 Act.

The same issue was considered by the Irish High Court in *Barnmore Demolition and Civil Engineering Ltd v Alandale Logistics* (No 5910P) 11 November 2010; unreported. In this case, Mr Justice Feeney reviewed the obligations of the court under the UNCITRAL Model Law, which uses identical language and has also now been further adopted into Irish law by that country's Arbitration Act 2010. The judgment makes it clear that the party seeking a stay of legal proceedings must demonstrate that there is a valid arbitration agreement in existence. It also indicates that the Irish courts will be prepared to conduct a full investigation as to whether a valid agreement exists, and not merely a consideration as to whether there is *prima facie* evidence of such an agreement.

Paragraphs (a)–(e) within s 10(1) of the Scottish Arbitration Act 2010 have to be read conjunctively by virtue of the words 'if' in s 10(1) and 'and' in s 10(1)(d)(ii), so all these elements have to be present before a party to legal proceedings can make an 'application', whereupon the court must grant a sist. Also it seems that, on a proper construction of the section, they must be read together as at s 10(1)(c) the only requirement is that notice be given to the 'other parties to the legal proceedings'.

The arbitration agreement

Section 10 requires the court on application to sist the legal proceedings if 'an arbitration agreement provides that a dispute on the matter is to be resolved by arbitration (immediately or after the exhaustion of other dispute resolution procedures)'. This implements the *dicta* of Lord Dunedin above: 'If the parties have contracted to arbitrate, to arbitration they must go.' This latter proviso envisages the operation of 'stepped', 'escalation', or 'tiered' resolution clauses in contracts whereby the parties agree to attempt to resolve their differences or disputes progressively by trying one process before moving onto another. The most common type is a series of formal negotiations at different levels within the party organisations, possibly followed by mediation, failing which the dispute or difference will then progress to the arbitration stage. The English courts have been prepared to enforce such clauses: see *Cable & Wireless v IBM United Kingdom Ltd* [2002] EWHC 2059 (Comm). The *Cable & Wireless* case related to an agreement to use unspecified alternative dispute resolution, to be recommended by the Centre for Effective Dispute Resolution (CEDR). In practice, this was mediation. While the case did not specifically address a stepped negotiation approach, the logic would appear to be the same, and the English courts have been prepared to enforce tiered dispute resolution, so long as the meaning of the clause is clear, as discussed in cases mentioned above.

Unfortunately, the wording of dispute resolution clauses is not always clear, particularly when both arbitration and the courts are mentioned. This produced considerable difficulties in *Hiscox Dedicated Corporate Member v Weyerhaeuser* [2019] EWHC 2671 (Comm), where an anti-suit injunction in the English courts was met by an injunction in the US courts restraining other insurers in the same dispute from seeking anti-suit injunctions in London (an anti-anti-suit injunction injunction). The English court ruled that arbitration would be the route, and the references to the courts only applied to the extent of enforcement and 'effectuating arbitration'. It is unclear what effect this order would have on the US injunction, since the principle of comity does not appear to have been observed in making the original order.

'Concerning any matter under dispute'

This has already been addressed and must be taken to mean that the 'matter' must be one which is 'under dispute' under an arbitration agreement in terms of s 10(1)(a). However, s 10(1) states that these are legal proceedings 'concerning' any such matter and accordingly the proceedings may not have to be identical. Indeed, it seems possible to sist part only of the proceedings where the bases of action are separable. It does not seem possible for the court to require all matters to be heard together for the sake of convenience, since it cannot compel arbitration of matters not covered by an agreement, and must sist where the matter is subject to arbitration, even if this appears to conflict with the founding principle in s 1(a) (unnecessary delay or expense).

The English courts have considered whether the point is or is not 'disputable': see *Halki Shipping Corpn v Sopex Oils Ltd* [1997] EWCA Civ 3062. Section 9(1) of the 1996 Act deals with a 'matter to be referred to arbitration' and thus the English courts have construed this as meaning that the court has only to consider whether there is a dispute within the meaning of the arbitration agreement, not whether there is a dispute between the parties (*Halki Shipping Corpn v Sopex Oils Ltd*). Making a claim is not a 'dispute': see *Collins (Contractors) Ltd v Baltic Quay Management (1994) Ltd* [2004] EWCA Civ 1757; *Beck Peppiatt Ltd v Norwest Holst Construction Ltd* [2003] EWHC 822 (TCC); *CIB Properties Ltd v Birse Construction Ltd* [2004] EWHC 2365 (TCC).

Lord Glennie in *Norwest Holst v Carfin Developments Ltd* [2008] CSOH 138 noted that there was a 'logical puzzle' inherent in the approach to 'disputability', which was previously highlighted by Lord Hamilton in para [11] of his Opinion in *Strathmore Building Services v Greig (t/a Hestia Fireside Design)* 2000 SLT 815. Although the existence of an arbitration clause has the effect of requiring the Scottish court to abjure any enquiry into the merits of the case, the court must, if so requested, enquire into the merits of the case, at least to some extent, in order to decide whether there is a dispute requiring to be referred to arbitration. Only if it was 'readily and immediately demonstrable', to borrow an expression from the judgment of Saville J in *Hayter v Nelson Home Insurance* [1990] 2 Lloyd's Rep 265 at 271, that the defender has no good grounds for defending the claim should a sist for arbitration be refused. The court noticed that the formulation adopted by Lord Johnston in *Orkney Islands Council v Charles Brand* 2002 SLT 100 at para [14] was this:

The jurisdiction of the arbiter should only be ousted by the Court if there is no basis upon which a two sided dispute can be identified.

In *Sodzawiczny v Ruhan and others* [2018] EWHC 1908 (Comm), the English Commercial Court addressed the meaning of 'matter' in s 9(1) of the 1996 Act. The same word is used in s 10(1) of the Scottish legislation. The ruling includes a finding that a 'matter' is anything capable of constituting a dispute or difference, and thus the use of 'matter' does not alter the rulings on 'dispute of difference' mentioned above.

There is a practical issue here as to how long to wait before a claim converts into a dispute. While it is trite law that the mere presentation of a claim is insufficient to create a dispute, it is equally correct that merely ignoring a claim cannot prevent the commencement of an arbitration forever. It is good drafting practice to include a provision in a contract to the effect that the party receiving any claim has a set period of time to respond one way or the other. This will have the effect of pre-determining a 'reasonable time' for a response in such circumstances, and preventing the need for lengthy and expensive litigation to determine whether there is anything to arbitrate, before even starting the arbitration itself.

It is suggested that the law may have over-complicated this issue. The arbitrator should be able to determine if there is a dispute, since they have power to determine whether they have jurisdiction. If there is none, they can (indeed, must) decline jurisdiction, since there is nothing to arbitrate. Only if they fail to do so, and purport to commence to arbitrate a non-issue, should the parties go to court to prevent that.

Legal proceedings: further discussion

From the wording it is suggested that the sist might only be in connection with part of the legal proceedings – ie one could envisage an action brought in the Court of Session with various heads of claim (or what are called 'conclusions') only some of which might be subject to the arbitration agreement.

As discussed above, there is some guidance given on what constitutes 'legal proceedings' from the English cases. A statutory demand has been held not to be 'legal proceedings' for the purposes of the analogous s 9 of the 1996 Act (*Shalson v DF Keane Ltd* [2003] EWHC 599 (Ch)). 'Pre-action disclosure' has been held not to constitute 'legal proceedings' (*EDO Corpn v Ultra Electronics Ltd* [2009] EWHC 682 (Ch)). A petition under the Companies Act 1985 s 459 (now Companies Act 2006 ss 994–996) for unfair prejudice on the minority shareholders was held not to constitute 'legal proceedings' in *Exeter City AFC Ltd v Football Conference Ltd* [2004] 1 WLR 2901, but in another later football case (*Fulham Football Club (1987) Ltd v Sir David Richards and another* [2010] EWHC 3111 (Ch)) the court held that a stay could be granted where the dispute fell squarely within the terms of the arbitration agreement. This resolved a conflict between the *Exeter City* case and *In re Magi*

Capital Partners LLP [2003] EWHC 2790 (Ch) where a stay to arbitration was allowed in relation to the winding up of a limited liability partnership and *Bridgehouse (Bradford No. 2) Ltd v BAE Systems PLC* [2020] EWCA Civ. 759 relating to the impact of a striking off of a company.

In *Bilta (in liquidation) v Nazir* [2010] EWHC 1086 (Ch) the English High Court held that the quality of any procedural step taken by an applicant under the equivalent provision of the 1996 Act (s 9) in court proceedings must be examined objectively in the light of the whole context known to both parties. Interestingly, while the court declined a stay in this case, this was because the court was bound by the earlier decisions in *Patel v Patel* [1999] 1 All ER (Comm) 923 and *Capital Trust Investment Ltd v Radio Design AB* [2002] EWCA Civ 135. Had it not been for these decisions, Sales LJ indicated he would have held that the service of a defence might be required before the right to a stay was lost.

A useful Scottish case on this point (albeit under the previous law) is the decision of Lord Glennie in *UBC Group Ltd v Atholl Developments (Slackbuie) Ltd* [2010] CSOH 21. Here UBC started legal proceedings and then, when a counterclaim was lodged, attempted to have the matter sisted for arbitration. Lord Glennie appears to have taken the view that, having taken the active step of choosing litigation (notwithstanding the arbitration agreement), UBC could not benefit from initiating the litigation then choosing thereafter to attempt to resort to arbitration. There seems no reason why the same result would not be achieved under the Act.

'Legal proceedings' are not defined in the interpretation section (s 31(1)) but, as already stated, will, presumably, have the meaning of any 'legal proceedings' anywhere in the world. One can envisage having an arbitration in Scotland, but with legal proceedings in, say, India.

Arbitration agreement 'provides that a dispute is to be resolved by arbitration'

Section 10(1)(a) requires that there be an arbitration agreement, and s 10(1)(b) additionally requires that the applicant (in the petition under s 10) must be a party to such an arbitration agreement, or claiming 'through or under' such party – see discussion on this matter under s 11 below. What happens, though, if the party argues that there is no arbitration agreement and therefore it was correct to raise the legal proceedings? As already discussed, a tribunal is empowered to determine its own jurisdiction and will be held to have jurisdiction even if the contract containing the arbitration agreement is 'void, voidable or otherwise unenforceable' – part of the important concept of separability contained in s 5 and also discussed above. The issue remains as to which body determines whether there is a valid arbitration agreement.

In *Fiona Trust & Holding Corpn v Privalov* [2007] EWCA Civ 20, the Court of Appeal stated:

One of the reasons given in the cases for a liberal construction of an arbitration clause is the presumption in favour of one-stop arbitration. It is not to be expected that any commercial man would knowingly create a system which required that the court should first decide whether the contract should be rectified or avoided or rescinded (as the case might be) and then, if the contract is held to be valid, required the arbitrator to resolve the issues that have arisen. This is indeed a powerful reason for a liberal construction.

(As this case has been cited several times already, and will appear again, it is worth mentioning that the dispute which led to the House of Lords' decision came back before Andrew Smith J and his, very extensive, decision that appears at [2010] EWHC 3199 (Comm) deals with the factual background, and some other claims, including some alleging dishonesty, that were brought between various of the parties.)

This statement, it is suggested, is a very fair summary of the attitude of 'commercial men' in these situations. The court considered that the case was one in which court proceedings had been instituted and an application had been made to stay (some part of) those proceedings. It considered that s 9 governed the position and for that section to apply there had to be an arbitration agreement. If the existence of an arbitration agreement was in issue, that question was initially to be decided by the tribunal under s 9 and not by the court (para 36).

The court in *Fiona Trust* considered that it was contemplated by the Act that 'it will, in general, be right for the arbitrators to be the first tribunal to consider whether they have jurisdiction to determine the dispute' (at para [34]) and went on (at para [36]):

> We would go further than this and say that, if the party who denies the existence of a valid arbitration agreement has himself (as the owners have here) instituted court proceedings and the party who relies on the arbitration clause has applied for a stay, the application for a stay is the primary matter which needs to be decided. It would only be if a stay were never applied for or were refused, but for some reason the party relying on the arbitration clause insisted on continuing with the arbitration that any question of an injunction should arise.

The court endorsed the approach that had been taken by HHJ Humphrey Lloyd in *Birse Construction v St David* [1999] BLR 194 in which he pointed out that there were four possible approaches to deciding whether an arbitration agreement exists to which s 9 applied:

(1) to determine on the evidence before the court that such an agreement does exist, in which case (if the disputes fall within the terms of that agreement) a stay must be granted, in the light of the mandatory 'shall' in s 9(4). It is this mandatory provision that is the statutory enactment of the relevant Article of the New York Convention, to which the UK is a party;

(2) to stay the proceedings on the basis that it will be left to the arbitrators to determine their own jurisdiction pursuant to s 30 of the 1996 Act,

taking into account the subsequent provisions in the 1996 Act for challenge to any decision eventually made by the arbitrators;

(3) not to decide the issue but to make directions pursuant to what is now Civil Procedure Rules Part 62.8 for an issue to be tried as to whether an arbitration agreement does indeed exist; or

(4) to decide that no arbitration agreement exists and to dismiss the application to stay.

In *Albon (t/a NA Carriage Co) v Naza Motor Trading Sdn Bhd* [2007] EWHC 665 (Ch), on an application under s 9(1) it was held that the court could and should decide whether the arbitration agreement was concluded, except where there was insufficient evidence for it to resolve the issue on the application. If that were the case, then it could stay the proceedings under its inherent jurisdiction for the matter to be determined by the arbitrators. The reasoning in *Al-Naimi (t/a Buildmaster Construction Services) v Islamic Press Agency Inc* [2000] 1 Lloyd's Rep 522 was applied by the court.

A similar pragmatic approach was taken in another English case, *A v B* [2018] EWHC 1370 (Comm) where an arbitration clause was upheld, despite being uncertain (for example, it said the arbitration should be conducted by the non-existent 'London International Arbitration Court'). It was suggested that this may have been a mistranslation from Russian, and intended to refer to the LCIA – same words, different order. The problem was that the tribunal was constituted under LMAA rules. This made sense considering it was a shipping dispute. The court (Phillips J) decided that the clause really intended to refer to some sort of *ad hoc* arbitration, seated in London, so use of LMAA rules was fine. With respect, this seems to stretch the wording somewhat, but it gave effect to the desire of the parties to arbitrate in London, and produced a practical result without requiring the parties to re-start the arbitration.

The examples quoted might be thought to suggest that, where there is any issue, the courts will always send the case to arbitration, but that is not necessarily the case. One example is the English Court of Appeal's decision in *Airbus SAS v Generali Italia SpA and others* [2019] EWCA Civ 805. In this case there were contractual agreements with conflicting clauses (ICC Geneva arbitration or English courts) and one party had commenced court proceedings in Italy. On the facts of the case, the court decided that the English courts were the correct venue.

This can be taken further, and the courts will, occasionally, restrain an arbitration in favour of litigation. Recent examples include *Sabbagh v Khoury and others* [2019] EWCA Civ 1219 in the English courts, restraining arbitration in Lebanon on the basis that the disputes in question did not fall within the arbitration agreement, and *Jaya Sudhir a/l Jayaram v Nautical Supreme Sdn Bhd and others* (Federal Court Civil Appeal No 02(i)-83-09/2018(W)) in the Malaysian courts, where a third party was able to restrain an arbitration which was believed likely to affect its interests. This latter case is somewhat unusual, and depends on Malaysian law provisions, but is included to show that anti-suit injunctions are a peculiarly English phenomenon.

A further case which touches on this issue is *Midgulf International Ltd v Groupe Chimique Tunisien* [2010] EWCA Civ 66. Here there were two contracts for the sale of sulphur. The first was in writing, and clearly included a London arbitration clause. The second was oral, but Midgulf claimed that it was on the same terms as the first contract. Groupe Chimique commenced litigation in Tunis under the second agreement (on the basis that it did not incorporate the arbitration clause), while accepting that the dispute under the first agreement was validly arbitrated in London. The English Court of Appeal eventually sorted this out, and issued an order restraining the Tunisian proceedings, and staying all matters to arbitration in London. This issue did, however, take a considerable period of time and the intervention of the Court of Appeal to resolve. Costs would presumably also have been considerable for both parties and, further, the whole dispute resolution process was, presumably, put on hold during the course of this litigation.

UK Supreme Court decision on international commercial arbitration

In its first decision on an international arbitration case, the UK Supreme Court held in *Dallah Estate and Tourism Holding Co v Ministry of Religious Affairs of the Government of Pakistan* [2010] UKSC 46 that it would not enforce a French arbitral award under the New York Convention. The basis of this refusal was that the relevant Pakistani Ministry was not a party to the arbitration agreement. The ICC tribunal in question had purported to determine its jurisdiction, but the Supreme Court upheld the view of the lower courts that it simply could not do this where the party concerned was not a party to a valid agreement to arbitrate. The matter is complicated by the application of French and Pakistani law, but the decision does appear to suggest that the courts will intervene where a basic flaw in the claim to jurisdiction exists.

It should be remembered that the refusal of the English courts to enforce the French award does not reverse that award. The case was appealed to the Paris Court of Appeal, and the award against the Government of Pakistan was upheld, notwithstanding the ruling of the Supreme Court, of which the court was aware. This means that the Supreme Court has ruled that the tribunal got French law wrong, and the French courts have said that they did not. It will be interesting to see what happens if and when Dallah seeks to enforce the award in another New York Convention state.

Who can apply?

Under s 10(1)(b) the applicant for a sist can be any party to legal proceedings if the applicant is also a party to the arbitration agreement (and conceivably therefore the claimant, although this seems somewhat improbable) or any party claiming through or under such a party.

Notice of application

Under s 10(1)(c) it is a requirement that notice of the application to sist under the section and RCS 100.5(1) must be given to the other party or parties to the legal proceedings. Note that there is no requirement in the Act to advise the tribunal. However, it is suggested that there is no obvious reason not to do so, and it may be good practice to give at least informal notice, if only to prevent the tribunal wasting time and expenses.

The period of such notice is not specified, but RCS 100.4 disapplies the existing periods of notice under RCS 14.6. However, RCS 100.3 envisages a wide discretion vested in the judge dealing with the cause, which in most cases will be one of the arbitration judges nominated by the Lord President under RCS 100.2 (or any other judge or the vacation judge if the arbitration judges are unavailable).

The terms of RCS 100.3 and 100.5 taken together would appear to be wide enough to allow for more unusual methods of service in appropriate cases. Courts in other jurisdictions have allowed service by Twitter and Facebook and other internet media (eg litigation between the Dutch anti-piracy coalition BREIN and the Pirate Bay website where both Twitter and Facebook service was ordered) and a Scottish arbitration judge would appear to have similar powers.

Intimation of petitions is currently governed by RCS 14.7, but it is unclear whether Chapter 14 will apply to petitions under s 10 for this purpose, or if provision is made separately under the powers in RCS 100.3. It is probable that RCS 14.7 will apply, at least in the interim, since RCS 100.4 specifically disapplies the rules on either side of RCS 14.7, but does not mention the latter rule.

It is also to be noted that as RCS 14.6 and 14.8 are disapplied by RCS 100.4, and this might suggest that it is not envisaged that answers to the petition will be required. The requirement for notice in s 10(1)(c) would seem to imply that there is a right to be heard, which would also be consistent with general principles of natural justice, as a party should not be deprived of the right to a trial without due process. The current procedures in Chapter 14 do not provide a full answer as to the procedure to be adopted, and therefore such answer may lie in the wide powers given to the judge in RCS 100.3 to fix procedure 'as he shall determine'.

Failure to observe the requirement for notice would appear to prevent the court granting a mandatory sist. It is suggested therefore that care needs to be taken to ensure that the arbitration judge, or other judge, has not set special rules for notices in the particular case as provided for in RCS 100.3.

Losing entitlement to a sist

As mentioned above, there is a possible trap in s 10(1)(d)(i) and (ii). The provisions of (i) include the relatively non-controversial statement that by taking steps in the legal proceedings a party may lose the right to apply for a sist. However, the difficulty is that, as discussed above, a 'step' is not fully defined. The only test is that the step must be 'to answer any substantive claim against the applicant'. As discussed above, it is at least arguable that lodging 'holding defences' including a bare denial would meet this test. This would seem to result in the applicant losing the right to a mandatory sist, since the provisions of the various sub-clauses of s 10(1) are conjunctive. There may be an inherent common law power vested in the judge to sist in any event.

In *Heart of Midlothian Football Club Plc v Scottish Professional Football League Ltd* [2020] CSOH 68 it was held that each of the conditions in terms of s 10(1) were satisfied and the terms of the statute required the grant of the application to sist the proceedings: regarding s 10(1)(d)(i), the respondents had taken steps to answer the petitioners' substantive claims but that was not a bar to having the action sisted where any responses given to substantive claims were subject to the clear qualification that a sist for arbitration was requested, then no step had been taken which should bar the request for arbitration.

The court examined the wording of section 10(1)(d)(ii) and considered that it must have been Parliament's intention to incorporate the common law test for waiver into the statutory scheme. It concluded that 'legal proceedings' had to mean not just the proceedings before the court but also those proceedings which had been before it previously in the prior case, as these were legal proceedings concerning the same matter under dispute. The court concluded that it would 'be highly artificial to disregard what has gone before in construing the provisions of section 10'. As the party seeking to sist had had previous knowledge of its rights and remedies, had elected not to vindicate them, and had thereby waived its right to arbitrate, the motion was refused.

The wording in s 10(1)(d)(ii) presumably should be read as 'since the bringing of the legal proceedings', since the applicant under s 10 will inevitably be the defender under the legal proceedings and will not therefore 'bring' such proceedings. This terminology appears in other legislation and the Model Law, as already mentioned, and it is anticipated that decisions in other jurisdictions on this point will be of some assistance. It is suggested that it will, however, be necessary for the respondent to the petition to demonstrate some positive act on the part of the applicant so as to meet the requirement to show a 'manner indicating a desire' for the legal process to be used. It is arguable that inaction could meet this test, but this will be difficult where arbitration has been commenced, and particularly where active steps have been taken to pursue such arbitration.

Void, inoperative or incapable of being performed

Under s 10(1)(e), where a court is 'satisfied' that the arbitration agreement itself is 'void, inoperative or incapable of being performed' (mirroring the language of Art II(3) of the New York Convention) it shall not impose a mandatory sist.

As discussed above under 'concerning matter under dispute', this can give rise to what Lord Glennie and Lord Hamilton agreed was a 'logical puzzle'. The court should not be enquiring into the merits of the case, but cannot fail to do so if this issue is raised. The same logic applies to this sub-clause, albeit restricted to the operability etc of the arbitration agreement.

It should be understood that, even if all other practical steps are taken, and criteria met by the applicant, failure at this stage is fatal to the petition for a mandatory sist.

While it is probable that 'satisfied' in this context means that the civil test of 'balance of probabilities' needs to be met, it is suggested that the court may wish to apply the higher end of that standard where it is suggested that, for example, an agreement is void. The potential problem is what happens if the arbitrators consider that they have jurisdiction (which they are entitled to do) and the court disagrees. In an international context, this is the issue in *National Navigation Co v Endesa Generacion SA (The Wadi Sudr)* [2009] EWCA Civ 1397, although the issue fell to be determined on questions of European law, and also *Dallah* (see above). This is an area of potential conflict between arbitrators and the courts.

In summary, where it appears possible that one party will raise the issue of the validity of the arbitration agreement, it may be worth seeking a ruling from the tribunal before the court is seized of the matter. Once the issue is before the courts, then, whatever the strict law, it would be a bold arbitrator who sought to oust the jurisdiction of the judge by a rapid interim award.

Multiple applications

While the Act is silent on the point, it would appear to be possible to make more than one application for a mandatory sist, subject to general principles of *res judicata*, in effect, not allowing the reopening of previous decisions unless there has been a change in material facts. (On this see also the commentary to the following section.) The provisions of s 10 allow only for a sist of the proceedings. It must be the case that the pursuer in the proceedings could seek to recall the sist in the event, for example, that the arbitration became inoperative at a later date as a result of some factor not in the contemplation of the parties when the sist was granted.

The reason for this is that had the Act intended to mean that the sist was of permanent effect, then the section would, presumably, have referred to dismissal, not sisting. Whilst there is no procedure for recalling a sist in the Act, it is assumed that the general procedures in this area would apply, subject to any special requirements set by the arbitration judge under RCS 100.3.

No contracting out

Section 10(2) means that a provision in an arbitration agreement that purports to prevent bringing legal proceedings is void in the event that such proceedings are commenced nonetheless, and the court refuses a mandatory sist under s 10. It is, however, suggested that while the effect of such a clause might be void, the very existence of the clause would support an application to sist, and possibly defeat a challenge under s 10(1)(d)(ii).

While the meaning is not fully clear, it is suggested that the main effect would be where a contract included a provision of the type envisaged by this section, but the arbitration agreement was void, inoperative, or otherwise incapable of being performed. In such a case, it is suggested that the arbitration could not proceed, and a sist would likely be refused under s 10(1)(e). The provisions of s 10(2) would prevent a party seeking to defend litigation on the basis of the contractual clause, and thus leaving the other party with no legal remedy.

This clause does not apply to statutory arbitrations.

Seated in Scotland

Section 10 envisages the court granting a sist of Scottish legal proceedings irrespective of where the seat of the arbitration is situated. This would, therefore, support foreign arbitrations, and is consistent with Scotland taking its proper place in the world of international arbitration, and would support the concept of comity in that it would be expected that foreign courts would stay their *proceedings* in support of a valid arbitration seated in Scotland (s 10(3)).

Enforcing and challenging arbitral awards etc

Arbitral award to be final and binding on parties

Section 11(1) makes the clear statement that 'A tribunal's award is final and binding on the parties and any person claiming through or under them (but does not of itself bind any third party)'. This language mirrors what is often seen in arbitration clauses that the process should be 'final and binding', and fits with the goal of arbitration as a process to provide quick and effective dispute resolution, without difficulties in enforcement, or scope for lengthy appeals.

The term 'final and binding' tends to be considered as a single unit, but it does contain two distinct concepts. This was illustrated in the recent Irish case of *K&J Townmore Construction Ltd v Kildare & Wicklow Education and*

Training Board [2019] IEHC 666, where the court had to interpret an expert determination agreement which used 'binding' rather than 'final and binding'. On the facts, the court held that, as 'final' was used elsewhere in the agreement, the intention of the parties was that the determination should be both final and binding.

While expert determination can (like construction adjudication) be binding on an interim basis, not final, the Act rightly makes an arbitration award both final and binding, thus removing any doubt.

It follows from s 11 that matters determined in the arbitration award will be binding upon the parties to it, such that neither can reopen the same issue so decided at a later stage, either in the courts or in a further arbitration. (This was touched upon under s 10.) The matter will be what in Scots law is called *res judicata* – the point has already been decided.

But this will only be as between the same parties and as to the same subject-matter and will not affect third parties. As s 11 makes clear, the award will not bind third parties because these third parties were not part of the arbitration, and so it follows that their interests should not be adversely affected by that award. So, if the parties give the tribunal the power to rectify (ie correct) a document or deed or to 'reduce' it (ie quash), then, if the tribunal chooses to do so, that will have no adverse effect against the interests of any third parties acting in good faith (s 11(2)).

It should be noted that s 11(4) says that s 11 does not apply to provisional awards made under default rule 53 (assuming it has not been displaced). Rule 53 provides that such an award can only be made where the tribunal would have the power to grant the same on a permanent basis. Section 11(4) then provides that such an award is not final and is binding only to the extent specified in such award, or until superseded by a subsequent award. The position is therefore analogous to construction adjudication, where an adjudication award is binding on the parties in the interim, but can be challenged in court or arbitration later when a final (and fully binding) determination will be made.

Unlike in England where the provision is non-mandatory, s 11 will have universal effect and so would preclude parties from, for example, arbitrating before a sole arbitrator with an agreement to thereafter bring the same dispute before a panel on condition of the losing party paying a proportion of the costs of the originating (non-binding) provisional award. It will also have the effect of turning all arbitration agreements or clauses to which it applies into final and binding arbitration agreements. The issue arises as to whether this can be changed if, for example, specific provision is made in the agreement or any incorporated rules. However, s 11 is part of the Act, and if the arbitration is governed by the Act (eg if it is seated in Scotland), it is suggested that the parties would not necessarily have power to override the statutory provision.

For a court case following matters determined in arbitration, see *Michael Wilson & Partners Ltd v Sinclair and others* [2017] EWCA Civ 3. The court was not precluded from finding that a court claim which had already been determined in a prior arbitration was an abuse of process, but should be cautious about doing so. The facts in this case were that the parties were not the same in both sets of proceedings; the defendant to the court proceedings had declined to be a party to the arbitration. He could not therefore claim that he was being subject to multiple proceedings and could not seek to take the benefit of the arbitration award.

Through and under

The Act does not define the phrase 'through and under', which seems to be borrowed and adapted from s 82(2) of the 1996 Act (which makes reference to 'claiming under or through a party'). An example might be a party having 'rights of subrogation', which is a term mainly used in the field of insurance whereby an insurer steps into the shoes of the insured to pursue a claim in the insured's name to recover sums paid out on an insurance claim. Since such a party has only the same rights as the insured, it would be bound by any arbitration agreement entered into by the insured in respect of the matters in dispute in so far as they relate to a claim under a contract.

Interestingly, the Chinese Supreme People's Court issued a decree in March 2009 to the effect that an arbitration clause in a contract for the carriage of goods by sea was not binding on an insurer who had taken over the rights of the consignee by way of subrogation (*China Pacific Property Insurance Corpn v Beijing COSCO Logistics Co Ltd*). This is not, of course, authority in Scotland, and it is unclear whether the insurer would have been allowed to enforce the arbitration clause under its subrogation rights had it wished to do so. The case does illustrate the fact that arbitration law is not the same in all parts of the world.

The issue of subrogation also arose in the recent English case of *A v OOO Insurance Company Chubb and other companies* [2019] EWHC 2729 (Comm) where the insurer who had paid out $400 million under a claim relating to a fire at a power plant in Russia issued proceedings in Russia, but was met with an application for an anti-suit injunction on the basis that any subrogation rights arose from the contractual relationship between the defendant in the Russian proceedings and the insured, and that contract contained an arbitration clause. The injunction application was dismissed on a range of technical and evidentiary grounds, but the factual matrix illustrates that a subrogation claim would usually be the same as the original party's, which might then bind the insurer to the dispute resolution clause in the underlying contract. The reasons for the dismissal of the application also illustrate the need to prepare any such claim fully, and to take care that the right procedures are utilised. Among the criticisms levelled were the use of an *ex parte* application when an application on notice would have been appropriate, a delay in the application after 'A' knew of the Russian proceedings, and the failure of either side to be clear about Russian law. These applications are unlikely to be treated as a mere formality in either Scotland or England.

Likewise, where interests have been validly assigned, similar considerations apply.

However, in another foreign case, the Indian Supreme Court (*SN Prasad v Monnet Finance Ltd* Civil Appeals 9224/2010 and 9225/2010) ruled that an arbitration clause in two loan agreements did not bind the guarantor of those agreements, whose guarantee was in a distinct document. It is suggested that seems correct, but does perhaps illustrate the limitations of 'through' in this context.

Another example may be via the creation of what was previously called a *jus quaesitum tertio*, whereby two parties contract for the benefit of a third party. The Scottish courts could allow that third party to enforce the contractual right. In the past this was permitted only where the contractual provision was clear. Thus, for example, where an employer and a contractor put a clause into a main contract giving the subcontractor a right to arbitrate any dispute, Scots law would probably recognise a right but not an obligation to arbitrate. However, if a subcontract purported to give the right to the subcontractor to arbitrate against the employer using the name of the main contractor, this would not seem to have worked under Scots law although it was accepted under English law: see *Northern Regional Health Authority v Derek Crouch Construction Co Ltd* [1984] 2 All ER 175. (Note this was overruled later, but on a different point.) This has all now been placed on a statutory footing by the Contracts (Third Party Rights) (Scotland) Act 2017. In terms of s 9(1) of the 2017 Act, third-party rights are provided in connection with arbitration agreements in relation to a 'dispute' as referenced in subsections (2) or (3). The 'person who has the third-party right mentioned in subsection (2) or (as the case may be) (3) is to be regarded as a party to the arbitration agreement mentioned in that subsection'.

The third party will not be deemed to have renounced a third-party right to enforce or otherwise invoke an undertaking to resolve a dispute by arbitration by bringing legal proceedings in relation to the dispute, and in the absence of an arbitration agreement a third party cannot participate in an arbitration (against the wishes of the existing parties) and cannot be ordered to be joined to the proceedings by a tribunal.

Where a party alleged to be a party to an arbitration chooses to take no part in the arbitration (the 'empty chair'), then, by s 14 of the 2010 Act, they are still entitled in a court action to question the validity of the arbitration agreement, the constitution of the tribunal or the scope of the matters submitted to arbitration with the rights as undisputed parties. Likewise, a third party will also have the same right as a party who participates, to appeal against any award under the challenge rules.

The position in the rest of the UK under the Contracts (Rights of Third Parties) Act 1999 makes third parties who have been clearly granted such rights, parties to the arbitration but again this is only a right and cannot create an obligation to arbitrate where there has not been any consent. Since the Scottish 2017 Act shares features with the English 1999 Act (which itself arguably brought the law of England, Wales and Northern Ireland roughly into line with what was then the law of Scotland), it is anticipated that the same position would apply in Scotland, thus leaving the law effectively unchanged on this specific point.

In the event that the parties wish to confer rights on a third party either arising from an arbitration or to participate in such an arbitration, these should be clearly stated. This clarity should extend to exactly which third party or parties are to benefit.

Final and binding

Section 11(3) makes it clear that while the award is 'final and binding' it is still subject to challenge to the limited extent provided under Part 8 of the Scottish Arbitration Rules or by any available appeal or review process (presumably in accordance with the arbitration agreement or any institutional rules).

As mentioned above, s 11(4) further makes it clear that provisional awards are not final and are only binding to the extent specified in the award or until superseded by a subsequent award.

Enforcement of arbitral awards

As noted previously, the function of the national or domestic court is to support the arbitration and the arbitration process and s 12 is a good example of the application of that concept. Obviously, arbitral tribunals are vested with powers and jurisdiction but only to the extent that the parties vest them with such power and jurisdiction, and this does not extend to enforcement of their awards outwith the tribunal. At the point of enforcement the tribunal no longer has any locus (and, indeed, is no longer possessed of any practical powers) and if the parties seek to enforce the award (or more likely the winning party seeks unsuccessfully to enforce the award against the losing party) then they have to go to the court for assistance.

Section 12 provides the basis upon which the award may be enforced. Under the Act, 'court' is defined as (any) sheriff court or the Court of Session (which must be taken to mean the Outer House construing the content of s 31(1)). In terms of s 12(1) the party must make an application whereupon the court has discretion (it 'may') to enforce the award as if it were an extract registered decree bearing a warrant for execution. This means it is equivalent to a decree or judgment on which all methods of enforcement in Scotland are available.

It should be noted that the word 'may' gives the court that discretion which it might decline to exercise even if all procedural matters were satisfied where, for example, the award was seen to be an attempt to breach the various money laundering regulations or was otherwise contrary to public policy. The English decision of *Soleimany v Soleimany* [1998] EWCA Civ 285 is illustrative here. A procedurally valid award of the London Beth Din was refused enforcement as Jewish law had ignored the fact that the purpose of the underlying contract was illegal. The contract related to export of Iranian carpets in deliberate breach of Iranian law and export controls. While this decision was under the Arbitration Act 1950 s 26, there is no reason to suppose that it does not remain good law today.

Some guidance as to what may be covered by the concept of 'public policy' in this context may be found in the Swiss decision in relation to a slightly unusual series of events arising from FIFA regulations on football transfer fees. The Swiss courts had held that FIFA's Regulations on the Status and Transfer of Players 1997 were void as breaching both Swiss and European Union competition law. After this decision, the Portuguese club Benfica made a fresh application for compensation in respect of the same player whose transfer to Atlético Madrid had produced the first decision. This was refused by FIFA, but Benfica appealed to the Court of Arbitration for Sport, seated in Lausanne, Switzerland, which proceeded to find for Benfica, notwithstanding the earlier court ruling on the same facts (and the same player). The Swiss courts had no difficulty in refusing enforcement and striking down the decision, although this is understood to be the first occasion on which they have taken such a step on public policy grounds (Swiss Supreme Court's decision 4A_490/2009, of 13 April 2010, in *Club Atlético de Madrid SAD v Sport Lisboa E Benfica – Futebol SAD and Fédération Internationale de Football Association (FIFA)*).

Procedural issues

Section 12(2) provides that the order cannot be made where appeal or correction processes are pending. Further, s 12(3) and (4) provide that enforcement may be refused to the extent that the tribunal did not have jurisdiction.

Under RCS 100.5(1) an application under the Act is to be made by petition.

In relation to applications under s 12, the procedure is set out in RCS 100.10 as follows:

Applications for enforcement of a tribunal's award under the 2010 Act
(1) A petition or note under section 12 of the 2010 Act for enforcement of a tribunal's award shall –
    (a) identify the parties to the cause and the arbitration process from which the cause arises;
    (b) specify that the award is not currently the subject of –
        (i) an appeal under Part 8 of the Scottish Arbitration Rules (challenging awards);
        (ii) any arbitral process of appeal or review; or

      (iii) a process of correction under rule 58 of the Scottish Arbitration Rules; and

  (c) specify the basis on which the tribunal had jurisdiction to make the award.

(2) There shall be produced with such a petition or note –

  (a) the original tribunal's award or a certified copy of it; and

  (b) the documents founded upon or adopted as incorporated in the petition or note.

This follows the requirements of s 12 but additionally RCS 100.10(2) requires the production of the original or a certified copy of the award and any documents founded upon or 'adopted as incorporated' (a formal pleading phrase meaning that the documents have been made part of the pleadings) in the petition or note. In this context this could include evidence to support the statement under RCS 100.10(1)(b) that any appeal or correction process has been concluded.

It should be observed that RCS 100.10(1) provides that the application will be by petition under RCS 100.5(1) but if proceedings are already pending before the court in terms of that subsection, the application is made by a 'note' in the process of the petition (ie entering the petition process which is already ongoing).

Ordinary action procedure

In an ordinary court action, where the court makes a determination in favour of one party over the other, it will grant a decree in favour of that successful party. In essence it will be what is called an 'interlocutor', expressing the decision of the Court. Once this is 'extracted', ie formalised in the court procedure, it is then enforceable against any party subject to it.

Section 12 provides for something similar. Where the court grants an order under this section, the tribunal's award can be enforced by executing diligence (enforcement) in the same way as a court decree may be enforced (without a further warrant). This does not prevent the award from having effect as if it were a court order.

The provisions within s 12(2) all relate to arbitral appeals, but where appeals in a foreign jurisdiction would be heard in the courts, it is suggested that the same rules would apply, and enforcement should be declined until the end of the judicial appeal process. An example in England and Wales can be seen in the English court's refusal to enforce in these circumstances in *Continental Transfert Technique Ltd v Federal Government of Nigeria* [2010] All ER (D) 184 where an appeal was proceeding in the Nigerian courts.

Lack of jurisdiction and s 12(3) and (4)

The party against whom the decree arbitral is made can object to the application for an order, particularly on the basis that the arbitrator had no jurisdiction, but this is only when the party has not lost the right to object under rule 76 (see below). (Cf Arbitration Act 1996 s 66(3) where a party which does not participate in the arbitration can still raise a passive defence by opposing leave sought to enforce the award as a judgment on the ground that the tribunal lacked substantive jurisdiction to make the award.)

It should be added that there are other grounds on which enforcement of an award may be rejected, even if it is final and binding. As an example, see the decision in *Dallah Estate and Tourism Holding Co v Ministry of Religious Affairs of the Government of Pakistan* [2010] UKSC 46 where the arbitration had been pursued against the wrong defendant.

The best advice must be that, if there are issues relating to the jurisdiction of the tribunal, these should be taken early, and before substantive steps have occurred.

Registration of awards in the Books of Council and Session

The Books of Council and Session are simply a repository in Edinburgh for registration and preservation of important documents. Section 12(5) permits the award to be registered there (or in the Sheriff Court Books, which is a similar sheriff court based facility) unless the parties have agreed otherwise. This is therefore the default position. It is also a requirement that the arbitration agreement itself must also be so registered. Presumably this can have taken place at the time it was executed and, if not, must be simultaneous with registration of the award.

Unless agreed otherwise, it may therefore be prudent to register both the arbitration agreement and any award. Note that if the arbitration agreement states that the parties do not agree to register, it will be impossible to register the award under s 12. Although an oral arbitration agreement is permitted by the Act, it is impossible to see how it could be registered and so it would seem to follow that even a written award under such an agreement cannot be registered under this section. This is a further reason to avoid oral arbitration agreements.

Also note that at enforcement stages the original agreement or a certified copy thereof will be needed and thus getting a copy from the Books of Council and Session may simplify the process.

Foreign seats

Section 12(6) states that s 12 applies regardless of the seat. This allows the potential of enforcement of awards outwith the New York Convention where enforcement is covered by ss 18–22 and s 12(7) makes it clear that such rights are not affected by s 12 or 13, nor are any rights of enforcement under any other enactment or rule of law.

As mentioned above, the parties may continue to register awards for execution in the Books of Council and Session or the Sheriff Court Books, unless they agree otherwise.

New York Convention requirements

In terms of enforcement under the New York Convention Art V(1)(e), recognition and enforcement of the award may be refused, at the request of the party against whom it is invoked, only if that party furnishes, to the competent authority where the recognition and enforcement is sought, proof that: 'The award has not yet become binding on the parties, or has been set aside or suspended by a competent authority of the country in which, or under the law of which, that award was made.'

So the award has to be final and binding before there can be recognition and enforcement under the Convention, but once this is the case, the courts will be reluctant to prevent enforcement. A recent example is *RBRG Trading (UK) Ltd v Sinocore International Co Ltd* [2018] EWCA Civ 838, where a Chinese CIETAC arbitration award was enforced, notwithstanding allegations of attempted fraud by altering dates on bills of lading, but which did not deceive the other party, and which had been dealt with by the tribunal.

Court intervention in arbitrations

Section 13 prevents the raising of legal proceedings in respect of the tribunal's award or any other act or omission of the tribunal other than in accordance with the Act. It particularly eludes judicial review or other types of review or appeal of arbitral awards. Ordinarily the Court of Session is seized of a supervisory jurisdiction to review the acts and conduct of certain categories of natural and legal persons, where it exercises a jurisdiction in furtherance of which a decision is made by it. If that decision is challenged, the court is empowered in certain circumstances to quash the decision and to order that matters are reconsidered anew.

The remedy of judicial review is available only in the Court of Session and proceeds by way of petition in terms of RCS Chapter 58. (See *Tor Corporate v Sinopec Group Star Petroleum Corpn Ltd* 2008 SC 303 for an example under the old Model Law provisions.)

Prior to the coming into force of this Act, it was clear that the conduct of (then) 'arbiters' was reviewable notwithstanding the (then) power under s 3 of the Administration of Justice (Scotland) Act 1972 to 'state a case on a question of law' to the Court of Session: see eg *Kyle & Carrick District Council v A R Kerr and Sons* 1992 SLT 629; *Shanks & McEwan (Contractors) Ltd v Mifflin Construction Ltd* 1993 SLT 1124. An arbiter's acceptance of appointment was also reviewable: *Haden Young Ltd v William McCrindle & Son Ltd* 1994 SLT 221.

Section 13 removes that right as any petition for review of a decision of an arbitral tribunal would, it is submitted, fall into the category of 'legal proceedings' as used in the Act. Appeals to the Court of Session are allowed but only under and in terms of the mandatory provisions of Part 8 of the Scottish Arbitration Rules. For guidance see Opinion of Lord Glennie in *Arbitration Application No 3 of 2011* [2011] CSOH 164.

Objection to a tribunal's jurisdiction by way of application to the court is also tightly controlled, being limited to an order under s 12 for enforcement or using the procedures available in the Rules – namely appealing against a tribunal's ruling on an objection to jurisdiction under mandatory rule 21; making an application to the Outer House for determination of any question as to the tribunal's jurisdiction under mandatory rule 22; or challenging an award on the grounds that the tribunal did not have jurisdiction under mandatory rule 67. This approach is wholly consistent with the desire to limit the involvement of the courts, and to move away from the stated case approach.

Where UNCITRAL applies

Party autonomy (see s 1) is the key to arbitration and it is possible under the Act for the parties to agree that rules or codes other than the Scottish Arbitration Rules will apply to regulate the arbitration albeit that it is seated in Scotland. One of the codes available is the UNCITRAL Model Law on International Commercial Arbitration 1985 with amendments as adopted in 2006, which can be found online at www.uncitral.org.

Section 13(4) provides that, where the parties agree that the Model Law is to apply, Articles 6 and 11(2)–(5) are to have the force of law in Scotland in relation to that arbitration. The Model Law was, of course, part of the law of Scotland (but not of the rest of the UK) until the Act came into force. It appears that the purpose of s 13(4) is to ensure the effectiveness of these provisions in relation to default rules under the 2010 Act.

As the preamble to the Model Law states:

> It covers all stages of the arbitral process from the arbitration agreement, the composition and jurisdiction of the arbitral tribunal and the extent of court intervention through to the recognition and enforcement of the arbitral award. It reflects worldwide consensus on key aspects of international arbitration practice having been accepted by States of all regions and the different legal or economic systems of the world.

As stated above, if the parties choose the Model Law to apply to their arbitration seated in Scotland, then s 13 gives force of law to Arts 6 and 11(2)–(5) of the Model Law. Article 6 provides:

> **Court or other authority for certain functions of arbitration assistance and supervision**
> The functions referred to in articles 11(3), 11(4), 13(3), 14, 16(3) and 34(2) shall be performed by … [*each State enacting this model law specifies the court,*

courts or, where referred to therein, other authority competent to perform these functions].

The words in square brackets, by virtue of s 13(4) of the 2010 Act, will read 'the Court of Session and any sheriff court having jurisdiction'.
   Article 11(2)–(5) of the Model Law provides:

(2)   The parties are free to agree on a procedure of appointing the arbitrator or arbitrators, subject to the provisions of paragraphs (4) and (5) of this article.
(3)   Failing such agreement,
   (a)   in an arbitration with three arbitrators, each party shall appoint one arbitrator, and the two arbitrators thus appointed shall appoint the third arbitrator; if a party fails to appoint the arbitrator within thirty days of receipt of a request to do so from the other party, or if the two arbitrators fail to agree on the third arbitrator within thirty days of their appointment, the appointment shall be made, upon request of a party, by the court or other authority specified in article 6;
   (b)   in an arbitration with a sole arbitrator, if the parties are unable to agree on the arbitrator, he shall be appointed, upon request of a party, by the court or other authority specified in article 6.
(4)   Where, under an appointment procedure agreed upon by the parties,
   (a)   a party fails to act as required under such procedure, or
   (b)   the parties, or two arbitrators, are unable to reach an agreement expected of them under such procedure, or
   (c)   a third party, including an institution, fails to perform any function entrusted to it under such procedure, any party may request the court or other authority specified in article 6 to take the necessary measure, unless the agreement on the appointment procedure provides other means for securing the appointment.
(5)   A decision on a matter entrusted by paragraph (3) or (4) of this article to the court or other authority specified in article 6 shall be subject to no appeal.
   The court or other authority, in appointing an arbitrator, shall have due regard to any qualifications required of the arbitrator by the agreement of the parties and to such considerations as are likely to secure the appointment of an independent and impartial arbitrator and, in the case of a sole or third arbitrator, shall take into account as well the advisability of appointing an arbitrator of a nationality other than those of the parties.

It should be noted that these references are to the Model Law as at the date of the 2010 Act (see s 31 where it is defined as the 1985 version, as amended in 2006), and so if the wording and/or numbering of the Model Law were to be changed in a later version, the Act might require amendment accordingly.
   Section 13 therefore allows parties who have incorporated the UNCITRAL Model Law into their arbitration to go to court (the Outer House of the Court of Session or the appropriate sheriff court having jurisdiction) to get the appointment of their arbitrators finalised or selected.

Persons who take no part in arbitral proceedings – the 'empty chair' defence

Section 14 protects the rights of those who are alleged to be a party to the arbitral proceedings, but who do not, for whatever reason, participate in the arbitration and do not wish to be coerced into entering the arbitration, to dispute that there is a valid arbitration agreement or the other practical matters in s 14(1)(a) and (b) affecting the validity of the tribunal's constitution, or that the issues in dispute should have been referred to arbitration. It has been suggested that this section may also be used by a party who merely declines to participate in the arbitration while not denying the validity of the arbitration agreement itself. Although this may be theoretically correct, it is difficult to see how such a party would have any argument which falls within s 14(1) and, in any event, it would be extremely dangerous to decline to participate when the validity of the arbitration is not in dispute.

Section 14 should be used only where there is a clear dispute as to the validity of the arbitration itself and not merely to seek to delay the process. Where the arbitration is properly constituted, there is a risk that the tribunal may have made interim awards binding on the party who has raised the objection.

If a party is going to employ this section, then obviously it cannot participate in any way in the arbitration and maintain this argument. Such a party is, however, permitted to state simply its objection without being held to have participated by doing so (*Caparo Group Ltd v Fagor Arrasate Sociedad Cooperativa* [2000] ADRLJ 254). It may walk a fine line between protesting the jurisdiction of the tribunal and asserting that it should decline jurisdiction whilst not recognising that the tribunal has jurisdiction, nor inviting the tribunal to consider or determine the issue of jurisdiction. (See *Sovarex SA v Romero Alvarez SA* [2011] EWHC 1661 (Comm) on the analogous s 72 provisions of the 1996 Act.) (See also *Caparo Group Ltd v Fagor Arrasate Sociedad Cooperativa* [1998] 8 WLUK 75 and *Law Debenture Trust Corp Plc v Elektrim Finance BV* [2005] EWHC 1412 (Ch).)

It is not clear whether the tribunal itself should await a decision from the court. If it is confident in its jurisdiction, it is arguable that the tribunal may elect to proceed in the absence of any declaration (which would be the remedy of a 'declarator' in Scotland) or interdict under s 14(1) even in the face of a challenge in the court.

Section 14 provides three possible courses for the 'alleged' party: (1) he may do nothing; (2) he may go to the court; or (3) he may decide to participate despite his objections. If he takes the last course of action, he will lose the right to challenge the arbitration under s 14.

So, subsection (1) allows someone to challenge the jurisdiction of the tribunal on the same grounds as a party, by court proceedings. Thus, he can dispute that he is a party but need not actually participate in the proceedings (with the cost implications of such participation).

Subsection (2) gives him the same rights as an actual party to the proceedings to appeal against any award made in the arbitration under mandatory rule 67 (substantive jurisdictional challenges) and mandatory rule 68 (serious irregularity challenges), but relieves him of any duty to exhaust available arbitral procedures (as required in mandatory rule 71(2)).

So, where an award had been made which purportedly affects him, then he has the rights contained in this subsection to challenge the award.

A constant problem for tribunals in arbitrations, particularly in an international context, is what to do with a non-participating party. A respondent to an arbitration need not participate in the arbitration and it is not like court processes whereby a defendant/defender must enter the process or else risk decree or judgment passing against him, there being no defence disclosed or advanced. In Scotland this is called 'summary decree' and in England 'summary judgment'.

In arbitration, to do so would be to improperly prefer the claimant's case over the respondent without enquiry, thereby not treating the parties equally. Therefore, normally, the tribunal has to 'run' matters to the end to give rise to a valid enforceable award including, if necessary, permitting the claimant to lead evidence and make submissions in a hearing and then to weigh the evidence and make a determination – all in the absence of the respondent. The risk for a respondent who simply wants to delay is that there will at some point be an award which can be enforced against it. The risk for a non-participating respondent which contests the jurisdiction of the tribunal is that the respondent is actually wrong, and in the final analysis finds that there is an award against it which could be enforced. If the 'winning' party then sought to enforce the award by applying to the court under s 12 (enforcement of arbitral awards) the respondent could technically make an objection to that on the basis that there was no jurisdiction (s 12(3)) to make the award unless there has been 'participation' such as to give rise to the loss of the right to object in terms of mandatory rule 76. (See the Supreme Court's decision on the equivalent English position in *Dallah Estate and Tourism Holding Co v Ministry of Religious Affairs of the Government of Pakistan* [2010] UKSC 46, referred to again below.) Section 14 allows the respondent not to participate in the arbitration, but at its own risk.

Interpretation of similar provisions in 1996 Act

Section 14 is almost identical to s 72 of the 1996 Act, which is entitled 'Saving for rights of person who takes no part in proceedings'. It is suggested that the principles to be extrapolated from the English cases on s 72 may be instructive. In *Zaporozhye Production Aluminium Plan Open Shareholders Society v Ashly Ltd* [2002] EWHC 1410 (Comm), the court considered granting an interim injunction to restrain the continuation of arbitration proceedings due to be heard the next day where the application was made by the respondents who now alleged (for the first time) that they had a defence on the basis that they had a potential challenge to the jurisdiction of the tribunal as their agent had entered the contract without authority. The court determined it was not appropriate to grant the relief at that late stage.

In *Arab National Bank v El-Abdali* [2004] EWHC 2381 (Comm), where an arbitration award had been obtained against an international bank by fraud, the court held that the bank had been entitled to relief under the Arbitration Act 1996 s 72 to prevent enforcement of the award and to protect its reputation by restraining publication of the award.

In *Law Debenture Trust Corpn plc v Elektrim Finance BV* [2005] EWHC 1412 (Ch), the court held that where in arbitral proceedings those proceedings were not, or were no longer, capable of encompassing the dispute between the parties, the defendant was then an 'alleged party' to those alleged proceedings and could seek a determination under the Arbitration Act 1996 s 72 that there was no valid arbitration agreement between the parties. In this case the applicant had been a *prima facie* party in a validly constituted arbitration but not an arbitration empowered to determine *these* issues.

In the important decision of *Fiona Trust & Holding Corpn v Privalov* [2007] EWCA 20, shipowners had made an application under the Arbitration Act 1996 s 72 seeking to restrain the arbitration proceedings on the basis that they had rescinded both the charters and the arbitration agreements in them. The defendant then sought a stay of the claimant's rescission claims under s 9 of the Act. The judge declined to stay the claims for rescission and restrained the arbitration proceedings pending the trial of the action. The defendant submitted that 'out of' was a wider phrase than 'under' and that the parties therefore intended a wide meaning to be given to the arbitration clause. Whilst the court noted that s 72 had no application to the instant case, it commented that:

> For our part, we would go further than this and say that, if the party who denies the existence of a valid arbitration agreement has himself (as the owners have here) instituted court proceedings and the party who relies on the arbitration clause has applied for a stay, the application for a stay is the primary matter which needs to be decided. It would only be if a stay were never applied for or were refused, but for some reason the party relying on the arbitration clause insisted on continuing with the arbitration that any question of an injunction should arise. Of course section 72 might well be applicable if the party denying the existence of an arbitration agreement had not started English proceedings and did not wish to do so. Such a party would then be entitled to apply under section 72 for a declaration that there was no valid arbitration agreement; even then an injunction would usually be necessary only if there was some indication that the other party was intending not to comply with any declaration which the court might make. This is all a long way from the present case in which court proceedings have been instituted and an application has been made to stay (some part of) those proceedings. Section 9 governs the position and for that section to apply there must be an arbitration agreement. If the existence of an arbitration agreement is in issue, that question will have to be

decided under section 9 and there is no reason, at the moment at any rate, for any invocation of section 72 at all. (para 36)

In the Supreme Court decision in *Dallah* (cited above) the arbitration was commenced in France under ICC Rules against the Pakistani Ministry of Religious Affairs, who refused to take part on the basis that the correct defendant was a trust involved in the management of a *madrassa* in Pakistan, sponsored by the Ministry, but not owned by it, and which had ceased to exist as a legal entity. The court agreed and refused to enforce the French award under the New York Convention. This decision has been the subject of some criticism, on the basis that it appears to interfere with the arbitrators' exercise of their own determination of their jurisdiction. It is suggested, however, that this criticism is misplaced. The powers of the arbitrators derive solely from a consensual contractual agreement between the parties. Within that scope, they have the ability to determine their own jurisdiction. However, the position here was that the respondent was held never to have been a party to any such agreement. On that basis, the arbitrators never had any power to determine anything in relation to the Ministry. As discussed earlier, the position in *Dallah* was, however, made more complicated by the French courts subsequently disagreeing with the Supreme Court and allowing enforcement of the award in France.

Interestingly, the New York courts have made a similar ruling in *Dedon GmbH v Janus et Cie* 2010 US Dist LEXIS 112131 where an arbitration had been commenced in London under ICC Rules, but the agreement purporting to include the arbitration clause had never been signed by the parties. It was asserted that the contract had not been adopted by performance. On this basis the court refused to compel arbitration in London, or to wait for the London tribunal to rule on its own jurisdiction. The logic is similar to that in *Dallah*. There is no power to rule on your own jurisdiction if there is no agreement to arbitrate.

On a similar point, the British Columbia Supreme Court refused to enforce an award where the tribunal had applied an *alter ego* doctrine to make an award against a party other than the party to the arbitration agreement, when such a doctrine was not recognised in British Columbia provincial law (*Javor v Francoeur* [2003] BCSC 350).

However, the scope of appeals in this area is not limitless. In the English case of *Broda Agro Trade (Cyprus) Ltd v Alfred C Toepfer International GmbH* [2010] EWCA Civ 100 relating to a GAFTA arbitration, the respondent denied there was a valid arbitration agreement, but the tribunal ruled that one existed, and ordered delivery of submissions. The respondent made submissions on the merits, and, when an award was made against it, applied to the court under s 72 of the 1996 Act on the somewhat hopeful basis that making submissions on the merits did not amount to 'taking part' in the proceedings. Both the High Court and Court of Appeal disagreed, and indicated that any application should have been made under s 67 on the grounds of lack of substantive jurisdiction or s 68 on the grounds of serious irregularity. The respondent's problem was that it was out of time for such applications, and the court declined to extend the time limits.

It bears repeating that, if there is doubt as to the jurisdiction of the tribunal, best practice may be to resolve the matter then, and not rely later on a challenge to a contrary award.

Effect of an unsuccessful challenge

The court in *Hackwood Ltd v Areen Design Services Ltd* [2005] EWHC 2322 (TCC) considered the circumstances where a party does not participate and then unsuccessfully applies under s 72. The applicant in that case had applied under the Arbitration Act 1996 s 72 for declarations that it was not party to any arbitration agreement with the respondent and that therefore arbitration proceedings started by the other side were a nullity. The court considered the documents and held that the arbitration was properly constituted, and that the applicant was a party to the arbitration agreement. It considered it was clear that s 72 required that an applicant should not take part in the arbitral proceedings down to the determination of his own application. If it had been the intention to debar an unsuccessful applicant from subsequent participation in the proceedings, the Act would have spelt that out in clear terms as the applicant would be denied a contractual right. It was for the arbitral tribunal to decide whether it was appropriate for an unsuccessful s 72 applicant to be allowed to participate in the arbitration.

The message must remain that it is very risky to simply refuse to participate where there are real doubts as to jurisdiction. *Hackwood* makes it clear that the tribunal has wide discretion, and might well take the view that, where the defendant has been given clear notice and ample opportunity to participate, and the tribunal has carried out a full review of the evidence, it is bound by the decision reached. No party is compelled to participate in an arbitration but it must take its chances if it declines to do so.

Finally, sometimes the 'empty chair' is not a tactic. In the English case of *Glencore Agriculture BV v Conqueror Holdings Ltd* [2017] EWHC 2893 (Comm) Glencore applied to set aside an award on the basis that the first time they knew the arbitration was taking place was when they received the award itself. The dispute related to a charterparty. The notice of arbitration had been served on an email address of an employee the claimant had been dealing with, but who appears to have left Glencore. It was held that the employee in question did not have authority to accept service, and so the arbitration was a nullity, and the award was set aside. The issue of proper service has arisen in a number of cases, and emphasises the need to check the correct method for service, either in the contract, or under the general law of the jurisdiction concerned.

Anonymity in legal proceedings

Section 15 states:

(1) A party to any civil proceedings relating to an arbitration (other than proceedings under section 12) may apply to the court for an order prohibiting the disclosure of the identity of a party to the arbitration in any report of the proceedings.

(2) On such an application, the court must grant the order unless satisfied that disclosure –

    (a) is required –

        (i) for the proper performance of the discloser's public functions, or

        (ii) in order to enable any public body or office-holder to perform public functions properly,

    (b) can reasonably be considered as being needed to protect a party's lawful interests,

    (c) would be in the public interest, or

    (d) would be necessary in the interests of justice.

(3) The court's determination of an application for an order is final.

Section 15 seeks to protect the identity of any party who raises legal proceedings 'relating to an arbitration' other than those proceedings under s 12 in respect of enforcement of arbitral awards. It is the reason why Scottish arbitration cases have almost always been cited as '*Arbitration Application No x of 201x or Arbitration Appeal No x of 201x*'. This contrasts with the English position whereby, while some anonymous reporting has taken place (using the *A v B* convention), many cases quote the names of the parties.

Generally, arbitral proceedings are private and confidential. This is one of arbitration's great strengths for parties in dispute who can resolve their disputes without having to disclose to the outside world, first, that they are in dispute and, secondly, the nature of that dispute. Unlike courts, 'justice' need not be 'seen' to be done. (See also default rule 26 as to confidentiality in arbitrations.)

At both international and domestic level this protects all parties from, for example, share price fluctuations (although in some circumstances the existence of the dispute will need to be disclosed under Stock Exchange rules); trade secrets being disseminated; adverse publicity; bad commercial decisions being disclosed; competitors seeking to take advantage of the dispute that has arisen etc.

There is a clear correlation between the concepts of anonymity and confidentiality. The latter is discussed under rule 26. This section provides a mechanism for a party seeking an order prohibiting the disclosure of the identity of a party to the arbitration.

The concept of anonymity is not unusual in international arbitrations. In the current UNCITRAL Rules, Art 28.3 requires that:

> Hearings shall be held *in camera* unless the parties agree otherwise. The arbitral tribunal may require the retirement of any witness or witnesses during the

testimony of other witnesses. The arbitral tribunal is free to determine the manner in which witnesses are examined.

The ICDR, ICC, LCIA, WIPO and CIETAC all have similar provisions. However, there have been some moves away from this general principle (eg *Esso Australia Resources Ltd v Plowman* (1995) 183 CLR 10 in Australia and *United States v Panhandle Eastern Corpn* 119 FRD 346 (D Del 1988) in the United States).

Under the Act, a party may apply for the order prohibiting disclosure in any 'report' of the proceedings. On application the court has to grant the order unless it is 'satisfied' that one of four categories in s 15(2)(a)–(d) has been met. As elsewhere in the Act there is no appeal from this determination. It should be noted that s 15(1) would allow a party to seek anonymity only for itself or indeed only for another party. The circumstances in which this is likely to arise are limited but it is conceivable that, for example, a government body might be anxious to preserve the anonymity of private individuals with whom it is in dispute. However, it should not be assumed that the grant of anonymity is automatic. In the case of *North Lanarkshire Council v Stewart and Shields Ltd* [2017] CSOH 76, the application for anonymity by the Council was rejected, as is clear from the unredacted citation. The Council had included a note concerning the outcome of the arbitration in their annual accounts, and were then obliged to publish these accounts as a matter of Local Government Law. However, they probably went further than was needed. One of the notes to the accounts stated:

> Arbitration proceedings between the Council and Stewart and Shields Limited for construction of the Antonine Day Care Centre which took place within the 2015/16 financial year found in favour of the contractor due to the Council not being entitled to terminate the contractor's employment. The above provision has been made in the accounts on a best estimate basis for claims quantified to date by the above parties.

Counsel for the Council fairly conceded that they might do things differently in the future. The court refused anonymity on the basis that, in effect, the horse was already out of the stable, and it was unreasonable to seek to anonymise something that was already public knowledge (ie the identities of the parties to the arbitration) and would remain public knowledge whatever order was made. This was, of course, an application under s 15, but the disclosure, or rather the extent of the same, would also seem to fall foul of the confidentiality obligations in rule 26 which, while a default rule, does not seem to have been excluded in the case. The case is discussed further when we deal with rule 26 below.

There is no entitlement to anonymity in civil proceedings relating to an arbitration unless and until at least one party makes an application to the court for the order. RCS 100.9 now specifies the procedure to be adopted in seeking such an order in the Court of Session. This includes a requirement that any petition or note be referred to publicly by number and year pending the court's determination of the application under s 15. It also requires that the proceedings under s 15 shall be heard in private. If the court does not grant the application, then by operation of RCS 100.9(3) all applications and appeals made under the Act shall be heard in public and by implication the names of the parties will be revealed.

An application for anonymity must be lodged 'not later' than the hearing of a motion for further procedure under RCS 100.5(5) (after the period of notice following intimation and service).

Anonymity and the Rules of Court

There is a real issue in the interface between the operation of the Rules of Court and the requirements under the Act. It appears to have been assumed that the petitioner will seek anonymity. If, however, the petitioner fails to do so, then no anonymity will apply unless and until the respondent lodges an application under s 15. In the interim the protection under RCS 100.9(2) does not exist and the existence of the dispute and the names of the parties will be a matter of public record. It is envisaged that this might arise where, for example, the petitioner is alleging that the tribunal has no jurisdiction and is seeking an order to restrain the arbitration and refer the matter to the courts, but could also be deployed for tactical reasons to embarrass the other party. What the respondent will have to do to secure anonymity is to also be ready to lodge a request for anonymity prior to the 'hearing on further procedure' and should give as much notice to the other party as possible so as to prevent any continuation of that hearing. (See *Arbitration Application No 3 of 2011* [2011] CSOH 164 at paras [21], [22].) In practice, the fact that virtually all arbitration cases under the Act have been anonymised suggests the process is working satisfactorily.

Statutory arbitration

Statutory arbitration

Statutory arbitrations are those arbitrations which arise not by the consensual agreement of the parties to resolve their dispute by arbitration but by the operation of an Act or other piece of legislation which provides that certain types of dispute arising within its remit should be referred to statutory arbitration. The Act provides specific provisions in ss 16–17 in relation to statutory arbitrations but, at the time of writing this edition, and some ten years after the Act was passed, these provisions have yet to be brought into effect. This failure runs counter to the genuine efforts made by the Scottish Government to promote arbitration and other methods of alternative dispute resolution and remains unexplained. This section is, therefore, included on the basis that ss 16–17 will be brought into effect at some stage. It is also possible that the parties to a statutory arbitration could, as a matter of party autonomy, agree that the arbitration should be conducted as if the sections were in effect.

As the Explanatory Notes to the Act explain, the provisions here interact with various other Acts (and subordinate legislation) which provide for particular arbitration procedures for particular statutory purposes. Once the sections are in force, the 2010 Act will allow parties to those arbitrations the benefits of the procedures set out in the Act where appropriate. The effect of s 16 is that the enactment is to be treated as if it were an arbitration agreement between the parties.

Section 16(3) provides, however, that if the other legislation makes provision which is inconsistent with the Act, that other legislation prevails.

Again, as the Notes explain, subsection (4) provides that every statutory arbitration is to be seated in Scotland. It is, thus, implicit that this is a reference to only statutory arbitrations under Scottish legislation. This is not, however, stated in s 16(1) which refers only to an 'enactment'. It is suggested that the word 'Scottish' is to be implied, and that such a *lacuna*, if it is a *lacuna*, is unlikely to lead to any practical problems. In the case of domestic arbitration, the effect is to prevent parties to a statutory arbitration from agreeing to seat the arbitration outwith Scotland. This is, however, subject to conflict of law rules (for instance on the interaction with the equivalent s 95(2) of the Arbitration Act 1996 for the other jurisdictions of the UK).

Subsection (5) identifies the rules that do not apply to statutory arbitrations and subsection (6) limits the circumstances in which statutory arbitrations covering different matters can be consolidated (permitted by rule 39 where parties so agree). There are other Acts and pieces of subordinate legislation beyond the 2010 Act which provide for particular arbitration procedures for particular statutory purposes. The Notes explain that it was decided policy that the Act would not interfere with this specific legislation but equally it was considered that parties to those arbitrations could benefit from the procedures set out in the Act if they augmented and enhanced the statutory provisions. Thus, this section provides that where a dispute on a particular matter is referred to arbitration under such legislation, the Act will apply to any arbitration under that other legislation, as if the reference to arbitration was as a result of an agreement between the parties. But if the other legislation makes provision which is inconsistent and/or incompatible with the Act, that other legislation should prevail.

Arbitration provisions in Scottish statutes are now relatively rare. In its heyday, the legislation pre the Agricultural Holdings (Scotland) Act 2003 made provision for arbitration in connection with agricultural tenancies (now replaced by applications to the Land Court). The Scottish Government has expressed an intention to insert more statutory arbitration provisions into future Acts of the Scottish Parliament, which is consistent with a general approach to seek to resolve disputes outwith the court system where possible, but, as already noted, this intention sits uneasily with the failure to bring this part of the 2010 Act into effect. Interestingly, in England, statutory arbitration under the Agricultural Holdings Act 1986 is covered by the Arbitration Act 1996, even though such arbitrations are not necessarily consensual (see *Peel v Coln Park LLP* (2010) 154 Sol Jo 38).

The Explanatory Notes to the Act also make clear that the subordinate legislation powers in s 17(a) allow the Scottish Ministers by order to modify the Rules (and other Act provisions) as they apply to statutory arbitrations and, in paragraph (b), to amend any enactment which provides for arbitration to satisfactorily apply the rules (or other Act provisions) to arbitrations conducted under that specific legislation. The statutory instrument procedure requiring affirmative approval by the Scottish Parliament applies where primary legislation is amended.

It has been suggested that s 17(b) purports to give Scottish Ministers the power to amend non-devolved legislation. It is probably better to consider that the whole section has to be read as only allowing Ministers to act within their powers, since the Scottish Parliament does not have power under the Scotland Act 1998 to amend the extent to which powers are devolved under that Act.

Supplementary

Prescription and limitation

Section 23 amends ss 4, 9 and 22A of the Prescription and Limitation (Scotland) Act 1973 and inserts ss 19D and 22CA into that Act.

As the Explanatory Notes to the Bill observed, both positive and negative prescriptive periods whereby rights are created or expire are interrupted by arbitration. By amending the Prescription and Limitation (Scotland) Act 1973, s 23(2) and (3) align the date deemed to be the date of judicial interruption with the 'commencement' date when the arbitration begins. The 1973 Act has been amended by the Prescription (Scotland) Act 2018 and will be further amended as the provisions of the 2018 Act come into force, but the changes relate in the main to negative prescription periods, and the principles by which the 1973 Act applies to arbitration following the 2010 Act are not changed.

Changes to positive prescription provisions

Section 1 of the 1973 Act makes provision for land that has been possessed by any person, or by any person and his successors, for a continuous period of 10 years 'openly, peaceably and without any judicial interruption'. Section 2 provides for special cases of possession for 20 years and s 3 provides for positive servitudes over land possessed for a continuous period of 20 years 'openly, peaceably and without any judicial interruption'.

Section 4(2) provides that, in respect of the positive prescriptive periods, 'appropriate proceedings' causing judicial interruption mean:

(a) any proceedings in a court of competent jurisdiction in Scotland or elsewhere, except proceedings in the Court of Session initiated by a summons which is not subsequently called; and

(b) any arbitration in Scotland in respect of which an arbitrator (or panel of arbitrators) has been appointed;

(c) any arbitration in a country other than Scotland, being an arbitration an award in which would be enforceable in Scotland.

These provisions are now amended by s 23 of the 2010 Act so that under s 4(3) of the 1973 Act, the date of a 'judicial interruption' in Scottish seated arbitration will be 'when the claim has been made in an arbitration, the date when the arbitration begins'. The new subsection (4) provides that the date that the arbitration begins will be either the date when the parties to the arbitration agree that it begins or, in the absence of such agreement, when it begins in accordance with rule 1 of the Scottish Arbitration Rules. Section 4(2)(c) of the 1973 Act continues unamended to regulate arbitrations in countries other than Scotland.

Changes to negative prescription provisions

Section 9 of the 1973 Act makes provision for negative prescription and the making of a 'relevant claim' to interrupt the running of prescriptive periods. Sections 6, 7, 8 and 8A of the 1973 Act make provision for the extinction of obligations by periods of five and 20 years, the extinction of property rights by a period of 20 years and the extinction of obligations to make contributions between wrongdoers, respectively. As the titles suggest, after the running of these periods in respect of these obligations and rights there is no remedy for the creditor or aggrieved party unless that period is 'interrupted' by a 'relevant claim'.

As stated above, there have been and will be modifications in this area under the Prescription (Scotland) Act 2018, but the negative prescription periods remain at five and 20 years.

Section 9(3) of the 1973 Act (which is unamended by the 2018 Act) provided that:

> Where a claim which, in accordance with the foregoing provisions of this section, is a relevant claim for the purposes of section 6, 7, 8 or 8A of this Act is made in an arbitration, [and the nature of the claim has been stated in a preliminary notice relating to that arbitration, the date when the notice was served] shall be taken for those purposes to be the date of the making of the claim.

Section 23(3) of the 2010 Act repeals the words in square brackets and substitutes 'the date when the arbitration begins'. This date will be the same as defined in the amended s 4, ie either the date when the parties to the arbitration agree that it begins or, in the absence of such agreement, when it begins in accordance with rule 1 of the Scottish Arbitration Rules.

An issue could arise where there is no agreement between the parties as to when the arbitration began and where the arbitration is not seated in Scotland and thus not subject to the Scottish Arbitration Rules, rule 1. In that scenario, it is suggested that the pleadings in any subsequent action contain full details of when the claim was made, given that the whole section defines and regulates 'relevant claims' made by or on behalf of creditors in implement or part implement of the obligations. We consider that an argument could be sustained before the court that that should be the relevant date in the absence of any agreement between the parties as to when the arbitration began or and in the absence of any assistance from rule 1.

Limitation period interruption by arbitration proceedings

Section 23(4) inserts a new s 19D into the 1973 Act. Under the 1973 Act s 17(2) (actions in respect of personal injuries not resulting in death), s 18(2) (actions where death has resulted from personal injuries), s 18A(1) (limitation of defamation and other actions) and s 18B(2) (actions of harassment), all have limitation periods of three years (all unamended by the 2018 Act). By virtue of the new s 19D, these periods will now be interrupted for 'any period during which an arbitration is ongoing'. This may cause problems where the arbitration becomes moribund, but has not actually been brought to an end. However, this provision removes any doubt as to whether the commencement of arbitration stops the time bar taking effect on personal injury cases, which has been stated as a concern in respect of proposals to use arbitration in this area.

If an arbitration has stopped being an effective process, it may be appropriate for a party who might otherwise have the benefit of a prescription or limitation period to take formal steps to bring the arbitration to an end, so as to allow the period to start running again. This may be particularly attractive where the reason for the ineffectiveness of the arbitration islack of action by the other party, which, it may be supposed, is likely to continue. The arbitration can be in Scotland or outwith Scotland (so long as the award is enforceable in Scotland).

Note that it is only the commencement of arbitration itself that stops time running. In a case in the Court of Queen's Bench in Alberta (*Suncor Energy Products Inc v Howe Baker Engineers Ltd* [2010] AJ No 618), the parties had included a staged dispute resolution process of the type often used in oil and gas contracts. The notice of dispute triggering the first stage of the process was served within the two-year limitation period under Alberta law, but the notice to arbitrate commencing the arbitration process was out of time. The court held that only the latter document could interrupt the limitation period. It is suggested that a similar decision would be reached in Scotland on an application under the Act.

Amendments to consumer protection provisions

Section 23 also amends the 1973 Act s 22A and s 22C which provide for a 10-year prescriptive period in defective product liability cases and actions under the Consumer Protection Act 1987 where death has resulted from personal injuries; and s 23(6) inserts a new '22CA Interruption of limitation period for 1987 Act actions: arbitration'. With s 22A, again there is a provision for interruption by making a 'relevant claim' and s 22A(4) is amended in a similar manner to the examples above so that a claim will be deemed to have been made at 'the date when the arbitration begins'. (Note that s 22A has been amended by the Prescription (Scotland) Act 2018, but in respect to the appointment of receivers or administrators.)

Section 22C of the 1973 Act covers liability under s 2 of the 1987 Act for reparation for damage caused wholly or partly by a defect in a product where the person has died from personal injuries and the damages claimed include damages for those personal injuries for that death. The three-year limitation period is calculated in relation to *inter alia* the date of death, or the earliest date on which the person was aware, or could reasonably practicably be aware, of the defect in the product. The Act allowed the start of the limitation period to be postponed or the running of it to be suspended in defined circumstances. For those injured, the period was disregarded where that claimant was of legal disability by virtue of unsound mind, or nonage (not having reached the age of legal capacity) (s 22B(4)). For classes of relatives of a deceased the same disregard is permitted for relatives with legal disability by virtue of nonage or unsoundness of mind.

The 2010 Act now adds a following section, s 22CA, which provides that any period under ss 22B(2) and 22C(2) will be interrupted by the ongoing period of an arbitration relating to a matter relating thereto. Again this may be a Scottish seated arbitration or an arbitration seated outside Scotland so long as the award is capable of being enforced in Scotland.

While the commencement of arbitration will prevent time running, the law of Scotland is clear that other methods of dispute resolution are not effective for this purpose: see *Diamond v PJW Enterprises Ltd* 2004 SC 430 (adjudicator); *MacDonald Estates plc v NCP Ltd* 2010 SC 250 (expert); and *David Clark v Argyle Consulting Ltd* [2010] CSOH 154 (financial ombudsman). It is important to remember that consensual dispute resolution techniques, such as mediation, will not stop time running. While such methods are to be encouraged, the parties and their advisers need to ensure that legal rights have not been lost in the event that the mediation or other dispute resolution technique fails.

On this subject, it is also worth remembering that the contract may impose its own time bars outwith anything contained in statute. This can include a time limit as to when the parties can commence arbitration. An example can be found in the recent English case of *Haven Insurance Company Ltd v EUI Ltd (T/A Elephant Insurance)* [2018] EWCA Civ 2494, where the Court of Appeal upheld an extension of time to commence an arbitration. In this case, which arises from the rules of the Motor Insurers Bureau, the period was a very short 30 days. An arbitrator was appointed, but the appointment was challenged as being out of time. The arbitrator rejected the challenge, and the High Court ruled the appointment was late, but allowed an extension of time under s 12(3) of the 1996 Act. The reasons included a lack of clarity in the rules, and the circumstances were outside the contemplation of the parties when they agreed to the time bar provision. This does, however, emphasise the need to comply with limitation provisions, whether statutory or contractual, since it took applications to the arbitrator, the High Court and the Court of Appeal to resolve this.

Arbitral appointments referee

The Explanatory Notes on s 24 are short and simply state that Scottish Ministers are given the power to authorise by order who is to be an arbitral appointments referee able to appoint an arbitrator in default of the parties making provision for this (see rule 7 of the Scottish Arbitration Rules). The Scottish Ministers must have regard to the criteria for appointment laid out in s 24(2).

The wording of s 24(3) is therefore surprising. It seems that s 24(2)(b) was intended to achieve the goal of ensuring that referees would have power to discipline arbitrators who fell below acceptable standards. However, s 24(3) specifically allows the appointment of arbitrators over whom the referee enjoys no such disciplinary control. It is suggested that such an appointment should only be made where some other body could exercise such control (eg the Dean of the Faculty appointing a solicitor, which solicitor was subject to the disciplinary rules of The Law Society of Scotland).

Under mandatory rule 7 of the Scottish Arbitration Rules there are provisions for the failure of the arbitral tribunal appointment process. Under rule 7(2) either party may refer the matter of the appointment of an arbitrator to an 'arbitral appointments referee' and this section provides for those who may act as a referee.

By the Arbitral Appointments Referee (Scotland) Order 2010 (SSI 2010/196), the first list of referees were:

- Agricultural Industries Confederation Limited
- Chartered Institute of Arbitrators
- The Dean of the Faculty of Advocates
- Institution of Civil Engineers

- Law Society of Scotland
- Royal Incorporation of Architects in Scotland
- Royal Institution of Chartered Surveyors
- Scottish Agricultural Arbiters and Valuers Association.

Under rule 7(8) the referee must, before making an appointment, have regard to the nature and subject-matter of the dispute and the terms of the arbitration agreement (including any term relating to the appointment of arbitrators) and the skills, qualifications, knowledge and experience which would make an individual suitable to determine the dispute.

In terms of rule 7(5) the referee makes the necessary appointment. There is interesting Malaysian authority on this point in the Kuala Lumpur High Court decision in *PT Permata Hijau Sawit v Pacific Inter-Link Sdn Bhd* [2011] 6AMR 343, where an arbitrator appointed by the Palm Oil Refiners Association of Malaysia (PORAM), who was a member of its panel, was held not to have the requisite experience in the palm oil trade to arbitrate under PORAM rules. This line of reasoning would suggest that a similar challenge could be raised in Scotland even where a referee appointed an arbitrator under this section. It is therefore not like the situation whereby the parties resort to a body or individual to nominate arbitrators with whom the parties themselves then make arrangements. However, a slightly different approach was taken by the English Court of Appeal in *Allianz Insurance PLC and another v Tonicstar Ltd and others* [2018] EWCA Civ 434 where it was held that a requirement that arbitrators had 'not less than ten years' experience of insurance or reinsurance' could be met by a barrister practising in those fields for the requisite period. (This reversed the earlier decision in *Company X v Company Y* 17/7/00 Morison J (unreported) which had held that experience in a field required being active in that field, not advising those in it.) It has to be said that different clients might take different views as to whether the Court of Appeal was correct, and when seeking the appointment of an arbitrator, the precise requirements should be set out clearly – it is suggested that if parties want someone who has worked at the relevant coal face, it is as well for them to stipulate that.

Where s 24 applies, the referee actually appoints the arbitrator. The referee might incur liability to the parties for failing to take proper account of the requirements of rule 7(8) or for the appointment of an individual who failed to have the skills, qualifications, knowledge and experience such as to be 'suitable' as required by s 24. However, rule 74 would appear to give the referee complete immunity, save only where the decision was made in bad faith.

The parties are free to select an appointment or nomination body which is not an approved referee. As an example, the Scottish Arbitration Centre offers an appointment service, but is not a nominated referee under s 24. Equally the parties are free to specify a referee as a nominating body. Here the distinction can be drawn between appointment (meaning specifying an arbitrator) and nomination (meaning suggesting a name or names for agreement by the parties themselves). This distinction is not dealt with in s 24.

Power of judge to act as arbitrator or umpire

Section 25 makes provision for a judge of the Court of Session to accept appointment as an arbitrator or an umpire in a dispute of a 'commercial character'. This is permitted only where the Lord President, 'having considered the state of Court of Session business', has authorised it.

As the Policy Memorandum prepared by the Scottish Government in relation to the Bill made clear at para 115, pressure on resources of the Court of Session and High Court meant that there would be no scope for the use of a judge as arbitrator or umpire at that time. As the resources of the Court of Session are still not over-abundant and judicial time remains a keenly protected resource, this position is unlikely to have changed.

The Act does not provide the Lord President with any guidance in his consideration of the state of Court of Session business and it is respectfully suggested that he must hold therefore an overall discretion as to whether to permit a Lord Ordinary to act as arbitrator or umpire.

Why would the parties choose to select a judge as arbitrator? There may be many reasons but, in particular, where the dispute is centred on a pure point of law and the arbitration is a test case for other similar disputes between the parties, then a careful and reasoned determination by the judge without the necessity for actually going to court could be an attractive one. The fee will be such as Ministers may prescribe by order and is payable to the Court of Session. It is assumed that this would have followed the previous model of appointment fee plus daily rate. It will, presumably, require to cover the full cost of the judge's time and all necessary support staff to prevent any subsidy from the public purse. Prior to the Act, this was governed by the model of an appointment fee plus a daily rate under the Appointment of Judges as Arbiters (Fees) Order 1993 (SI 1993/3125). No new Order appears to have been made since the Act was passed but, since the principles are unlikely to have changed, this may not be surprising (although the Order uses the now defunct term of 'arbiter'). However, it appears possible that the 1993 Order itself may have lapsed when the 2010 Act repealed the underlying provisions in the Law Reform (Miscellaneous Provisions) Act 1980. This is save in respect of statutory arbitrations, the provisions for which, as discussed elsewhere, have yet to be brought into effect. This leaves the position in limbo, but is consistent with the indication that the use of judges as arbitrators is unlikely to be sanctioned with any frequency, if at all.

Where there is an appointment of the judge to a tribunal then the jurisdiction of the Outer House under the Act and the Rules is supplanted by that of the Inner House (s 25(3)). It is to be seen how this operates in practice.

The judicial resources of the Inner House are at a greater premium. The procedures are not easily comprehended by the non-practitioner and are also necessarily much slower than those of the Outer House. Note also that the Inner House has jurisdiction even where the tribunal consists of three members, only one of whom is a judge of the Court of Session. While this provision obviously protects against allegations of partiality or bias, it will have a knock-on effect in terms of delay and cost.

On the issue of delay, given the fact that judges are also likely to be engaged in discharging their judicial function, and that s 25 does not permit the Lord President to relieve a judge from that function, it is likely that judicial arbitrations on any matter of complexity may take some time as a result. This problem can, of course, arise with very busy arbitrators in other fields. On balance we would recommend only following this route if there are compelling reasons to do so.

Finally, the cautionary tale of *Equitas Insurance Ltd v Municipal Mutual Insurance Ltd* [2019] EWCA Civ 718, where the English Court of Appeal allowed an appeal on a point of law under s 69 of the 1996 Act against an award by a judge-arbitrator. The arbitrator in question was Lord Justice Flaux, which may have made for an interesting first instance hearing for the party seeking to overturn the legal reasoning of a judge of the Court of Appeal. Even senior judge arbitrators are not immune from making mistakes.

Arbitrability of disputes

Section 30 states that 'Nothing in this Act makes any dispute capable of being arbitrated if, because of its subject-matter, it would not otherwise be capable of being arbitrated'. This makes clear that if a dispute was not capable of being arbitrated before, it is not rendered arbitrable by the Act.

What is not capable of being arbitrated? For example, matters which affect public rights or the status of parties in law may not be referred to arbitration. Criminal liability cannot be arbitrated. There may be associated issues of capacity of parties to contract to arbitrate, eg a company which is not empowered to do so.

It should be remembered that Art V(2)(a) of the New York Convention permits a court to decline to enforce an award on the basis that the dispute is not arbitrable under the law of that state. (Cf 2010 Act s 20(4)(a).) It should also be borne in mind that there can be refusal of recognition and enforcement under Art V(1)(a) and s 20(2)(b) on the ground that the arbitration agreement was invalid under the law which the parties agree should govern it, which failing, the law of the country where the award was made.

Different countries may, of course, take different views. As an example, Chinese law does not allow arbitration of inheritance disputes: see the 2010 decision of the Supreme People's Court in *Wu Chunying v Zhang Guiwen* refusing enforcement of an arbitration award from Mongolia, where, it appears, such disputes are arbitrable. In another case, the Supreme People's

Court ruled in 2017 in *Dalian Huarui Heavy Industry Group Co Ltd v Forge Group Constructions Pty Ltd* that while the underlying contract contained an Australian arbitration clause, this would not apply to a dispute relating to claims of fraud in a letter of guarantee on the same contract, primarily on the basis that the letter of guarantee was a distinct stand-alone document and did not contain an arbitration clause. The Turkish courts have also ruled that disputes relating to liens over ships and associated disputes were governed by Art 23 of the International Private and Procedural Law, and such matters were reserved to the courts: *Decision of the 11th Civil Chamber of the Turkish Court of Appeals, 10 December 2009* E2008/7283, K2009/12746. On the other side, the English courts have ruled that issues that might also be the subject of an unfair prejudice petition under the Companies Act 2006 were capable of being referred to arbitration: *Fulham Football Club (1987) Ltd v Sir David Richards and The Football Association Premier League Ltd* [2010] EWHC 3111 (Ch). However, the Singapore Supreme Court in *Larsen Oil and Gas Pte Ltd v Petroprod Ltd* [2011] SGCA 21 has allowed arbitration on issues between an insolvent company and third parties, but not in relation to the insolvency proceedings themselves, and associated avoidance claims. Also, the United States Supreme Court held in the case of *Henry Schein, Inc v Archer & White Sales, Inc* 586 US_139 S Ct 524 (2019) that the court would not enquire into the arbitrability of a dispute (in this case the issue of whether the dispute was arbitrable as it contained a claim for injunctive relief) as that matter was clearly reserved to the arbitrator by the rules in question (American Arbitration Association). The continued support for arbitration in this case is illustrated by the fact that the decision was 9– 0 and the decision in *Heart of Midlothian Football Club Plc v Scottish Professional Football League Ltd* [2020] CSOH 68 shows similar support in Scotland.

This may, however, be an area where the law will develop in coming years. It was, for example, traditionally assumed that matrimonial law was not a suitable area for arbitration, and that remains the case in respect of matters such the granting of a divorce or the legal custody of children, on sensible public policy grounds. However, matters such as financial and property disputes are seen to be capable of being resolved by arbitration, and the use of this method of resolving disputes is (along with mediation) understood to be on the increase in Scotland and elsewhere. In England, the Family Law Arbitration Scheme was launched in February 2012, and courts have been supportive of the scheme, (see *BC v BG* [2019] EWFC 7). Although in *Haley v Haley* [2020] EWCA Civ 1369 it was held that arbitration awards could be set aside if they were considered wrong, on what amounts to a lower test than under the 1996 Act. Scotland has also developed family law arbitration, notably through the Family Law Arbitration Group Scotland ('FLAGS'), which seems to have wide support. It is anticipated that, if matters come before the courts, a similar line will be taken to that in England to promote and support the use of arbitration in appropriate cases.

Another area where arbitration may be useful is in personal injury cases, where the amendments to the Prescription and Limitation (Scotland) Act 1973 introduced by s 23 of the 2010 Act make it clear that arbitration will act just as effectively as litigation in preventing the three-year time bar taking effect.

Finally, there may be benefits in resolving disputes by arbitration where confidentiality (even as to the existence of a dispute) may be important to the parties. Professional negligence and intellectual property are two of the fields where this issue may well arise.

Certain matters are not arbitrable as a matter of statute. For example, the Employment Rights Act 2006 s 203 and the Equality Act 2010 s 144 both render void any agreement to arbitrate claims under those pieces of legislation, unless certain pre-conditions are satisfied. This matter came before the courts in *Clyde & Co LLP v Krista Bates van Winkelhof* [2011] EWHC 668 (QB). This related to a claim for sex discrimination proceeding before an employment tribunal. The claimants in the case (a well-known law firm) tried to get round the difficulty with anti-suit injunctions within the European Union following *West Tankers* (*Allianz SpA v West Tankers Inc* [2009] EUECJ C-185/07) by the ingenious device of seeking a mandatory injunction (available under English law) requiring the defendant partner to consent to staying her employment tribunal case as the partnership agreement included internal procedures, including arbitration. The court refused this application, and considered that the agreement was rendered void by s 144, and the court could not exercise any inherent jurisdiction through a mandatory injunction to defeat the legislation and circumvent *West Tankers*.

To avoid any doubt, disputes with the Crown are still potentially arbitrable as s 34(1) states that the Act binds the Crown. In addition, the Queen (s 34(2)) and the Prince and Steward of Scotland (s 34(3)) (currently Prince Charles, Duke of Rothesay) can also authorise persons to represent them in arbitrations in a personal capacity, and not in right of the Crown.

It should, therefore, be understood that, while the Act did not specifically make anything arbitrable that would not otherwise have been so, it does not preclude anything from being arbitrable either, if the wider law and public policy allow the same.

Finally, a cautionary tale from Canada: *Federal Electric (1976) Ltd v McDonald Brothers Construction* [2019] ONSC 496, in the Ontario Supreme Court. In this case Federal Electric had a dispute with their client Public Works and Government Services Canada – in effect the Federal Government – and another with their subcontractor, McDonalds. The subcontract included an arbitration clause, but the main contract did not, and specifically referred matters to the courts. The facts in the two disputes were basically the same. The subcontract also included a clause in common form in construction and other contracts to the effect that, where a dispute under the subcontract was on the same issues as one under the main contract, the former dispute could be consolidated into the main contract proceedings to be resolved at the same time. The court upheld this view and consolidated the actions, even though the effect was to require McDonalds to litigate when they had contracted to arbitrate. The consolidation clause was clear. It is suggested that this is consistent with the approach in *Fiona Trust* and a similar approach seems likely to be taken in England and Scotland. It does emphasise that, where such a clause exists, the subcontractor needs to actually check the dispute resolution provisions in the main contract, and ensure that they are consistent with those in the subcontract, or, if not, that they are acceptable to the subcontractor.

Schedule 1 to the Arbitration (Scotland) Act 2010 – Scottish Arbitration Rules

COMMENCEMENT, CONSTITUTION AND IMMUNITY OF TRIBUNAL (PART 1)

From this point forward, we move out of the sections of the Act itself, and into the Scottish Arbitration Rules set out in Schedule 1 to the Act. As already explained, these split into Mandatory rules which cannot be changed, and Default rules which are subject to exclusion or amendment by the parties.

At Stage 1 of the consideration of the Arbitration (Scotland) Bill in the Scottish Parliament the then Minister for Enterprise, Energy and Tourism (Jim Mather) said:

> The Scottish arbitration rules that will govern the conduct of arbitration are set out in schedule 1. We deliberately put the procedural rules in one place. During the consultation process, many consultees commented favourably on the fact that the rules were set out separately from the main body of the bill. That approach means that the rules can be read as a relatively self-standing code that can be used as a guide by practitioners and users. It also makes it easier to compare the rules with those of arbitral institutions and those that are agreed between parties. The rules are designed to be as accessible as possible to anyone who finds themselves involved in arbitration or who is considering using it. (SP Official Report, 25 June 2009, col 18955)

This approach is to be endorsed, which provides a complete range of Rules covering most areas.

Commencement of arbitration

Rule 1 states that 'An arbitration begins when a party to an arbitration agreement (or any person claiming through or under such a party) gives the other party notice submitting a dispute to arbitration in accordance with the agreement.' Rule 1 is a default rule, which applies if the parties have not agreed to modify it or disapply it.

The parties may have a contract between them and a 'dispute or difference' has arisen in connection with provisions of that contract. Within that contract there may be dispute resolution provisions including an arbitration clause. One party may wish to invoke the arbitration agreement. This rule provides for how that party should begin the arbitral proceedings using the clause or agreement contained within the contract. Alternatively, the parties may simply agree to the submission of the dispute to arbitration under a new agreement (a 'submission agreement') unrelated to the original dispute resolution clause as an *ad hoc* arbitration.

The commencement of arbitration is important for a number of reasons. An arbitration which has not commenced properly may lead to any subsequent award being challenged on the basis that the arbitral tribunal lacked substantive jurisdiction, with resulting associated waste of time, effort and cost.

Also, the commencement of arbitration may have consequences for the running of periods of limitation and prescription. This has already been discussed in connection with s 23 of the Act. Note that s 4(4)(b) of the Prescription and Limitation (Scotland) Act 1973, as amended, states that where the parties do not agree as to the date of commencement of the arbitration, it is decided in terms of this rule. In addition, although the rule is a default rule and so will not apply when the parties remove it, the date may, in fact, be the same if the parties defined their commencement date in similar terms.

Giving notice

There are two initial points to consider. First, the arbitration does not commence with a submission document or a statement of the aggrieved party's claim. It is the giving of notice of the intention to submit the matter to arbitration which is important for the purposes of establishing the commencement date. Secondly, the wording used in this rule is that the one party 'gives' the other notice. In the Notes to the Bill it stated that 'An arbitration begins when a party to an arbitration agreement (or any person claiming through or under such a party) gives the other party notice' but the Notes to the Act state that the arbitration will begin 'on service of notice'. Service is not in the wording nor defined in the Act. Nor is the word 'gives' defined so as to determine what steps are required for adequate notice in this context.

The arbitration agreement, or the contract of which it is part, may contain provisions as to service and notice but, in the absence of that, would delivery be required in either or both cases to make service effective? What constitutes the giving of notice? Is 'service' in the sense of (effective) delivery required? This is unclear from the rule. While this may appear to be a distinction without a difference, many commercial contracts include quite precise requirements for the service of formal notices. There is no common provision, and many older drafts still include telex, and many do not allow for the use of email, but the point is that it is possible for a party to have 'given' a notice (ie sent it to the other party) but not have 'served' the same as required by the contract (eg sent by email, not registered post). Rule 1 only requires 'giving', but this, it is submitted, cannot be correct where the document which amounts to the arbitration agreement provides for specific requirements to be observed, and, as rule 1 is a default rule, this could be seen to amend the rule accordingly. However, see the discussion above on the service of notices generally and, for example, the decision of the English courts in *Jawaby Property Investment Ltd v The Interiors Group* [2016] EWHC 557 (TCC) where a payment application was allowed to be served by email, although the contract specified service by hand, fax or post. Decisions on these issues in recent years have not been wholly consistent, and the advice must always be to follow the requirements of the contract (including an arbitration agreement) wherever possible.

However, there is also assistance in default rule 83, which provides the rules for intimating certain formal notices or documents under the arbitration agreement or in the course of arbitral proceedings, all in the event that this is not already agreed between the parties (as this is a default rule). Rule 83(1) defines 'a formal communication' as including 'a notice' which is 'made or given … in pursuance of an arbitration agreement' and 'for the purposes of the rules' (rule 83(1)(a) and (b)). A formal communication must be in writing (rule 83(2)) and it is deemed to be 'made, given or served' if hand delivered (rule 83(3)(a)) or sent by first class post to (if an individual) their principal place of business or last-known abode (rule 83(3)(b)(i)) or, with a body corporate, to its principal or registered office (rule 83(3)(b)(ii)) or in *either* case to any postal address designated for the purpose by the intended recipient (rule 83(3)(b)(iii)).

Electronic communication is also permitted. A 'formal communication' can be sent 'in some other way' which includes 'email, fax or other electronic means' (rule 83(3)(c)). However, any electronic communication will be treated as being in writing only if 'it is legible and capable of being used for subsequent reference' (rule 83(4)).

Rule 83(5) provides for the situation where formal communication is to be deemed to have been made, given or served. Rule 83(6) provides that the tribunal may determine that a formal communication may be delivered in another manner (presumably including Facebook and Twitter if they are not considered to be 'electronic means'), or need not be delivered at all. Lastly, rule 83(7) simply states that rule 83 is not applicable to legal proceedings.

While rule 83 gives a comprehensive set of methods by which service can be effected, this still leaves the problem already addressed that the contract containing the arbitration clause, or the stand-alone arbitration agreement, may contain specific provisions amending these requirements. Rule 83 is a default rule, so the contractual arrangements would again override the rule 83 provisions, as they would with rule 1.

The answer may lie, as in many situations, in a careful reading of the contract.

When is the communication 'made, given or served'?

Rule 83(5) provides assistance again. The communication is – unless the contrary is proved – to be treated as having been made, given or served:

- where hand delivered, on the day of that delivery;
- where posted, on the day that it would be delivered in the ordinary course of post (which would presumably take account of postal strikes, losses in the post etc); and
- where sent in any other way on the day *after* it was sent.

Again, this is subject to nothing different being stated in the contract or arbitration agreement, which would then override the rule.

Equivalent notice procedure in England

In the English case of *Villa Denizcilik Sanayi Ve Ticaret AS v Longen SA (The Villa)* [1998] 1 Lloyd's Rep 195, the court found the following facts established. By letter dated 13 March 1997, the applicants advised the respondents, *inter alia*, that:

> In view of your refusal to pay hire under the ... Charterparty we hereby give you formal notice of our commencement of arbitration against you under the terms of the ... Charterparty which requires the appointment of a sole arbitrator. As indicated to your solicitors we propose the appointment of one of the following three arbitrators.

Mance J held that the letter of 13 March was sufficient to commence arbitration proceedings.

In England it has been held that a broad and flexible approach to the equivalent provisions in the 1996 Act s 14(4) is required, concentrating on substance rather than form (*Nea Agrex SA v Baltic Shipping Co Ltd (The Agios Lazarus)* [1976] QB 933).

Section 16(3) of the 1996 Act states that: 'If the tribunal is to consist of a sole arbitrator, the parties shall jointly appoint the arbitrator not later than 28 days after service of a request in writing by either party to do so.' For an effective notice of arbitration to have been given, pursuant to the 1996 Act s 16(3), all that was required was that the notice identified the dispute to which it related with sufficient particularity and made it clear that the person giving it was intending to refer the dispute to arbitration, and not as a threat that they would do so if their requests were not met. A notice would not necessarily be ineffective simply because the sender had identified wrongly the document containing or evidencing the contract where the dispute was otherwise sufficiently identified. (See eg *Atlanska Plovidba v Consignaciones Asturianas SA (The Lapad)* [2004] EWHC 1273 (Admlty).)

For an example of where a letter was not a sufficient notice to commence arbitration proceedings for the purposes of s 14(4) (commencement of arbitral proceedings where the arbitrator is to be appointed by the parties) see *Taylor Woodrow Construction Ltd v RMD Kwikform Ltd* [2008] EWHC 825 (TCC).

It will be seen from these cases that the English courts have generally taken a fairly robust line with arguments based on the technicalities of notices. If the other party knew that an arbitration had started, that was really enough. It is unclear how the Scottish courts will approach this issue. It remains good practice to make every effort to get all the notices correctly worded and delivered in accordance with the contract or other agreement or the Rules, rather than relying on any available avenues of appeal. In summary, and as best practice, state in terms that the notice is intended to commence the arbitration.

It is good practice to ensure that the contract itself is drafted initially so as to have an adequate and up-to-date clause on the service of notices. But even if this is not the case, care should be taken to ensure that the method of service is compliant with the terms of the notices provision of the contract and also that it is possible to prove delivery to the other party in accordance with the contract or the Rules.

There are Scottish cases which advocate a strict approach to the giving of notice, particularly in connection with commercial lease cases: see eg *Batt Cables plc v Spencer Business Parks Ltd* [2010] CSOH 81 and *Ben Cleuch Estates Ltd v Scottish Enterprise* [2006] CSOH 35; [2008] CSIH 1 (although see *Hoe International v Anderson* 2017 SC 313).

If the Scottish courts are minded to ensure that the 2010 Act is applied as intended for use by laymen and written in clear language, a broad construction may be preferred, in line with English practice set out above. Presumably some evidence of actual delivery or receipt would be required but the form of words and the method of intimation may not be as important, either in accordance with the agreement or in the absence thereof.

The courts might endorse Thomas J's view in respect of the corresponding English provision (s 14) in *Seabridge Shipping AB v AC Orsleff's Eftf's A/S* [1999] 2 Lloyd's Rep 685 that a 'strict and technical approach to this section has no place in the scheme of the 1996 Act'.

'In accordance with the agreement'

Another issue which arises is how to read the wording 'in accordance with the agreement'. One could envisage an arbitration agreement which did not make provision as to the commencement of arbitration under it; indeed many arbitration clauses are extremely short, some merely make reference for the Act to apply, and many not even that, and possibly to the seat, or often location of venue, of the arbitration and to a set of institutional rules. Is it the notice which is to be in accordance with the agreement, or the intention to submit or the dispute? It would seem correct that, where the agreement itself or any rules incorporated are silent, what is needed is some communication that 'fires the starting gun' and makes it clear that the arbitration has commenced.

'Claiming through and under'

The Notes to the Act make clear that the use of the phrase 'claiming through and under' permits a third party to commence the arbitration through or under a party to that arbitration agreement. Thus, where a party to that agreement assigned or novated (legally transferred) the rights under the agreement to a third party then such third party would be entitled to commence the arbitration in furtherance of that assignation – in other words, the right to commence had been transmitted by the assignation.

Appointment of tribunal

This is covered in Default rule 2.

The Explanatory Notes to the Act state that:

> Arbitration agreements only take effect when a dispute arises. If the parties have included provision in the arbitration agreement about the appointment of an arbitrator or arbitrators then those provisions will apply. If, however, no provision has been made in the arbitration agreement for the appointment of an arbitrator, if there are gaps in the provisions on appointment, or if the parties fail to carry out those provisions, then the Act provides default rules to allow for the appointment of an arbitrator to take the arbitration forward. This changes the common law position in Scots law and rule 2 makes clear how the structure of the appointment provisions in the rules apply. An arbitrator's appointment may take effect on the appointment being made or at such time as may be agreed between the parties.

It is part of the fundamental principle or doctrine of 'party autonomy' that parties are free to agree how to resolve their disputes subject only to such safeguards as are necessary in the public interest. (This is enshrined in the founding principles contained in s 1(b) of the Act.)

As part of that, and as explained above, essentially the parties are entitled to decide the procedure for the appointment of the tribunal whether by reference to institutional rules or provisions inserted into the arbitration agreement or whether they agree these provisions at the time of the contract or later, sometimes even at or about the time that the dispute arises.

This rule applies in the default situation where there is no agreed provision or rules set down for appointment, and it then allows the agreement to set out that the tribunal is (a) a named individual or individuals, (b) appointed by the parties themselves, (c) appointed by another person, or (d) appointed 'in any other way'. It is unusual for such a clause in an agreement to stipulate a specific individual or individuals to act as arbitrator(s) in the event of a dispute for the simple reason that that could lead to potential uncertainty at a future point when the dispute arose as to whether the arbitrator or tribunal would or could act, and also restricts the ability to select a person with particular skills once the nature of the dispute is known. More common is the stipulation of a nominating or appointing body. (See also the commentary to s 24 in relation to the new office of arbitral appointments referee ('AAR') to assist parties in the appointment of the tribunal.)

It is fair to say that, since the rule does not contain any mandatory provisions, and merely states what the arbitration agreement 'may' do, with a final provision (rule 2(d)) allowing appointment 'any other way', if it is excluded, this can only presumably be by stating that there is no appointment procedure, and leaving matters to the default powers of the court. However, since that would itself be appointment 'any other way', it is arguable that this should have been a mandatory rule, although nothing may really turn on the point.

Once the parties are in dispute, it is essential that a system is in place to facilitate the swift appointment of the arbitral tribunal to allow the arbitration to proceed quickly and efficiently 'without unnecessary delay and expense' (as it is required to do as per s 1(a)).

The Act aims to provide the rules to allow for the swift and effective appointment of an arbitrator. An arbitrator's appointment takes effect immediately on the appointment being made (or at such time as may be agreed between the parties).

If parties agree, rule 2 will be operated in conjunction with rules 6 (method of appointment) and 7 (failure of appointment procedure).

It is best practice to ensure that the contract includes a method for appointing the tribunal, and the usual procedure is to select a set of institutional rules, and then provide that, if the parties cannot agree within a set period, the president, chairman or similar person within the relevant institution shall make the appointment. Within the context of the Act, it may well be that parties will nominate a body which is also an AAR (see s 24) for this purpose, although it should be noted that it is not a requirement that an appointing body nominated in a contract be an AAR.

Identity of and eligibility to act as an Arbitrator

Mandatory rule 3 provides that 'Only an individual may act as an arbitrator'. Accordingly, the arbitrator appointed must be a natural person (see comments in relation to s 13). The reason for this rule is that, historically, it was possible to appoint an unincorporated body to act as arbitrator. Thus, the parties could appoint a solicitor firm's partnership or an LLP.

This brings Scotland into line with what is the common practice in many other jurisdictions, and states the position clearly and removes any ambiguity. It also removes the risk that the role of arbitrator can, in effect, be delegated to a firm; so it is not possible to appoint a firm of solicitors to act as arbitrator.

It is considered that this is a small price to pay for the clarity of this very short rule.

Mandatory rule 4 expands this point by providing that:

An individual is ineligible to act as an arbitrator if the individual is –

(a) aged under 16, or

(b) an incapable adult (within the meaning of section 1(6) of the Adults with Incapacity (Scotland) Act 2000 (asp 4)).

Legal capacity

In the first place, to be entitled to act an arbitrator must have *legal* capacity in the sense of being over a certain age. The Adults with Incapacity (Scotland) Act 2000 also provides that that age is 16. Section 1(6) of the 2000 Act provides:

> For the purposes of this Act, and unless the context otherwise requires – 'adult' means a person who has attained the age of 16 years.

In the second place, someone who is over that age but lacks legal capacity for some other reason will not be entitled to act as an arbitrator. Again s 1(6) of the 2000 Act provides guidance:

> 'incapable' means incapable of –
>
> (a) acting; or
> (b) making decisions; or
> (c) communicating decisions; or
> (d) understanding decisions; or
> (e) retaining the memory of decisions,
>
> as mentioned in any provision of this Act, by reason of mental disorder or of inability to communicate because of physical disability; but a person shall not fall within this definition by reason only of a lack or deficiency in a faculty of communication if that lack or deficiency can be made good by human or mechanical aid (whether of an interpretative nature or otherwise); and 'incapacity' shall be construed accordingly.

In England the age of capacity is 18 (Family Law Reform Act 1969 s 1).

In the first edition of this work, it was stated that it was 'a little bizarre that a 16-year-old can arbitrate a major dispute but not vote in a local council election'. However, in the interim period voting at the age of 16 has been allowed in some elections in Scotland, and this rule would, therefore, seem to reflect a general trend. However, it seems unlikely that huge numbers of 16-year-olds will be appointed under the Act and, if they are, the parties will, presumably, have been happy with the arrangements.

It is notable that, while the arbitrator has to be 'eligible' (see below), there is no provision for any formal qualification, or compliance with a code of practice. There are some voluntary bodies which regulate their members (eg Chartered Institute of Arbitrators, which has four categories of membership depending on experience and having passed examinations: namely, the Associate (ACIArb), the Member (MCIArb), the Fellow (FCIArb) and the Chartered Arbitrator).

This is in marked contrast with the approach to, for example, mediation in the European Union, particularly considering that an arbitrator makes a final and binding decision, and the mediator does not. It may be that this will be an area where further legislation or a voluntary code will be needed. The matter can be addressed by the parties through specifying the required qualifications, or by using one of the reputable appointing bodies such as the AARs in s 24. It is suggested that these considerations are taken into account at the point of the appointment. However, care needs to be taken that any 'requirements' do not fall foul of equality legislation as outlined under s 24. In particular, there may be issues as to whether it is possible to require that, for example, an arbitrator be aged over 25 when the Act has provided that anyone over the age of 16 may be the arbitrator, and this could be construed as age discrimination, unless justified. A better approach might be to use the common form that the arbitrator needs to have '10 years' experience' in the relevant field, rather than specifying an age.

Bankruptcy and capacity

It is not the case in England that the bankruptcy of a *party* necessarily brings to an end its capacity to arbitrate. In *Syska v Vivendi Universal SA* [2009] EWCA Civ 677, the English Court of Appeal held that where an entity was involved in an arbitration in London prior to the foreign (here Polish) insolvency proceedings being commenced, it was the law of England which would determine the effect of the insolvency proceedings on the pending London arbitration, and held that the London arbitration could proceed. See also *Re Exchange and Commodities Ltd* [1983] BCLC 186 and *A Straume (UK) Ltd v Bradlor Developments Ltd* [2000] BCC 333 (for further assistance see Hargrave and Libero, 'Arbitration and Insolvency: English and Swiss Perspectives' (2009) 75 *Arbitration* 47 at 47–52). This would also be the case now in Scotland under this rule.

In Scotland, prior to the 2010 Act, if the potential arbitrator was an undischarged bankrupt then he fell into the category of an individual who as such was ineligible to act as a tribunal member.

Number of arbitrators

Default rule 5 provides that 'Where there is no agreement as to the number of arbitrators, the tribunal is to consist of a sole arbitrator.'

If the arbitration agreement is silent on the number of arbitrators to be appointed, the Act provides a default rule that the arbitration is conducted by a single arbitrator. This is consistent with the founding principles to resolve disputes without unnecessary expense (s 1(a)). While it is a default rule, it is suggested that here this really means that the agreement can provide a different number, since if the rule were merely to be excluded and nothing else were to be stated, the agreement would be unworkable.

It is suggested that the rule could have been mandatory with no adverse effect.

This rule follows (in part) the Model Law Art 10 which provides:

Number of arbitrators
(1) The parties are free to determine the number of arbitrators.
(2) Failing such determination, the number of arbitrators shall be three,

and the provisions in s 15 of the 1996 Act which provide:

(1) The parties are free to agree on the number of arbitrators to form the tribunal and whether there is to be a chairman or umpire.
(2) Unless otherwise agreed by the parties, an agreement that the number of arbitrators shall be two or any other even number shall be understood as requiring the appointment of an additional arbitrator as chairman of the tribunal.
(3) If there is no agreement as to the number of arbitrators, the tribunal shall consist of a sole arbitrator.

Agreement

Again as part of the principle of party autonomy, the parties are free to agree as to the number of arbitrators they wish to appoint for their arbitration.

For the most part the arbitration agreement will dictate the composition of the tribunal and may do so by reference to institutional rules (eg UNCITRAL Arbitration Rules Art 7; LCIA Rules 2020 Art 5; ICC Rules 2021 Art 12). This agreement could conceivably be verbal, although see the point made under s 4 concerning the New York Convention and enforcement and the further point that there could be an oral addition or variation to an already written arbitration agreement (cf 1996 Act s 5).

Odd numbers not required

Note that there need not be an uneven number of arbitrators. As noted above, this rule leaves it open for the parties to agree two-person arbitral tribunals which may run into trouble in the event that the tribunal is divided. The English provisions in the 1996 Act overcome this via s 15(2) which provides that where an arbitral tribunal is comprised of two or an even number that is understood as requiring the appointment of another arbitrator as chairman. There is no such implication in Scotland that the appointment of a further arbitrator as chairman is required (cf rule 6(b)) or that the former practice of appointing an umpire is retained. It may be that the history of this practice is the reason why the Act and the rules do not seek to require an odd number of arbitrators. If so, it must be questioned whether this was necessary, or sensible.

Although consistent with the founding principles in s 1 of party autonomy and the object of arbitration being to resolve disputes without unnecessary delay or expense, it might be questioned to what extent a two-, or indeed four-, person arbitration which is deadlocked could achieve that aim or principle. Best practice would seem to dictate the creation of a panel with an uneven number of members to avoid this result, that is, agree the number without having to rely on this default rule. Although three-person panels are common in international arbitration, the Act does seem to encourage single arbitrators, and the reduction in delay and expense that this can produce should be taken into account before deciding on the standard default reaction of a three-person tribunal. It should also be noted that, where default rule 6 applies, the parties actually lose an element of control in the appointment of the 'remaining arbitrator(s)' over and above the one they each appoint. This will usually be the chairman of the tribunal. This is not uncommon in international arbitration, but is a factor to consider when determining the size of the tribunal.

No requirement for a clerk

Finally, note also that there is no requirement to appoint a clerk. Historically, the appointment of a clerk to the arbitration was part of the 'arbitration furniture' in Scotland – it was nearly always done. The clerk tended to be a lawyer with arbitration experience and/or knowledge of Scots arbitral law and would sit with the 'arbiter' at the hearing. It was of course an additional cost to the parties and therefore could act as a deterrent to them resolving their disputes by arbitration. The Act makes no requirement for the appointment of a clerk although default rule 32 gives the tribunal the power to appoint one 'to assist it in conducting the arbitration', but if 'significant expense' is likely to arise by virtue of such an appointment, the parties' consent is then required.

On one view there is less need to appoint clerks in that the law is now all stated in one place and is easily viewed, understood and applied. Against that background the tribunal may consider that it is an unnecessary expense in the arbitration. On the other hand, the parties are free to agree that the tribunal should be entitled to appoint a clerk or may themselves do so. This may be particularly the case where the parties have appointed a tribunal with practical rather than legal expertise. See also the discussion on tribunal secretaries on page 213.

Method of appointment

Default rule 6 provides:

> The tribunal is to be appointed as follows –
> (a) where there is to be a sole arbitrator, the parties must appoint an eligible individual jointly (and must do so within 28 days of either party requesting the other to do so),

(b) where there is to be a tribunal consisting of two or more arbitrators –
   (i) each party must appoint an eligible individual as an arbitrator (and must do so within 28 days of the other party requesting it to do so), and
   (ii) where more arbitrators are to be appointed, the arbitrators appointed by the parties must appoint eligible individuals as the remaining arbitrators.

Rules 6 and 7 will operate together as discussed in the commentary to rule 2 above. Rule 6 is a default rule so that parties can avoid its provision by disapplying it or making a different provision in their agreement or later. However, where the rule does operate as a default rule, then the provisions of rule 7 will apply as a mandatory provision in any event, since rule 7 applies whatever method of appointment is selected, where such method fails. Put simply, if the parties choose rule 6 then they will also get the safety net of rule 7.

For a sole arbitrator, the parties can appoint that person if he is an eligible person (mandatory rule 4) and they do so jointly. Where there are to be two arbitrators, each party may appoint an arbitrator albeit that these arbitrators have to be independent of the parties appointing them (see rule 77). Where there are to be three (or more) arbitrators, the two arbitrators appointed by the parties then appoint the third person (possibly the chairman, although this is not specifically stated) or any additional members. There is a 28-day time limit imposed.

If this does not work for any reason, then the provisions of rule 7 will come into play.

While 28 days is longer than is sometimes the case under institutional rules, it is a relatively short period in practice, and, if it is not complied with, the appointment can move out of the control of the party concerned (or the first two arbitrators appointed by the parties). Accordingly, best practice is to get on with the appointment process without delay. A party commencing an arbitration should already have its arbitrator(s) to be nominated in mind and, ideally, have confirmed that they are available, before commencing the process.

Of course as a default rule it is open for the parties to provide the procedure for the appointment of the arbitral tribunal and often this will be by reference to institutional rules (eg UNCITRAL Model Law Art 11(2) and (3); CIArb Rules Arts 2 and 4; LCIA Rules 2020 Art 7; ICC Rules 2021 Art 12). The provision in the Act is analogous to the 1996 Act s 16 (procedure for appointment of arbitrators). Section 16 requires the appointment of arbitrator(s) within certain time periods (14 days and 28 days) of the 'service of a request in writing by either party to do so'.

Who should be appointed?

Conventional advice is that the party should first ask for CVs and check the credentials and availability of prospective arbitrators and thereafter (certainly in larger cases) interview them. Interviewing arbitrators may be an alien concept to some of those charged with advising on parties' cases and it is certainly something which may make many lawyers uncomfortable. However, in the international context it is quite normal. Some assistance in how to proceed is provided by a Practice and Standards Sub-Committee of the Chartered Institute of Arbitrators on the List of Guidelines, Protocols and Rules page of the website (www.ciarb.org). There are also useful provisions in relation to disclosure of conflicts of interest in mandatory rule 8, which are discussed below. Note that the new LCIA and ICC Rules provide steps to be taken for the appointment of the Tribunal.

Failure of appointment procedure

As stated in the previous section, rule 7 is a mandatory rule, which applies whether or not rule 6 is the default method of appointment.

As referred to in the commentary to rule 6, this provision will come to operate where the parties have attempted an appointment, whether under rule 6 or otherwise, which has failed. The rule provides a step-by-step process to resolve the issue and ensure that the tribunal is appointed, and the arbitration can proceed.

Problems may be caused by a party not participating in the appointment process, possibly for tactical reasons. Such non-participation can cause difficulties for the remaining tribunal member(s) and also for the smooth running of the arbitration. This rule allows the arbitral appointments referee ('AAR') (as opposed to the court) to step in to assist in the appointment. The court only acts as a back-stop if the AAR process also fails (see rule 7(6)).

Arbitral appointments referee

Section 24 creates the office of arbitral appointment referee and this has been discussed in the commentary to rule 2.

Note that the AAR or, in default, the court *must* have regard to: (a) the nature and subject-matter of the dispute; (b) the terms of the agreement; and (c) 'the skills, qualifications, knowledge and experience which would make an individual suitable to determine the dispute' (rule 7(8)). The parties do not, of course, have any such obligations, other than to comply with any specific terms of the agreement. However, the AAR is protected from liability (other than when acting in bad faith) by mandatory rule 74. Section 24 simply sets up the office of the AAR and states what is required to be on the approved list. This mandatory rule goes much further and requires the

AAR (and the court) to take cognisance of the factors stated above when making the appointment. The first two are unlikely to be problematic. The third criterion will require the AAR to be very careful in selecting the person whom it will appoint. It is to be recollected that this is an appointment and not a nomination. An arbitrator appointed under rule 7 is required, in effect, to have skills, qualifications, knowledge and experience not required to be considered for eligibility to act as an arbitrator under rule 4.

Rule 7(6) is also slightly unusual, in that, having created a mandatory requirement to use AARs, a party is entitled to refuse to use such a body, and then the matter goes to the court. The court also has default jurisdiction where the AAR fails to make the appointment within the set time, or where a party objects to this appointment. It is not stated whether such objection has to be on 'reasonable grounds'. It may be the case that the courts will need to take a robust line with objections under rule 7(6)(a) where the objection appears to be raised purely to delay the process.

It has been noted that Scottish courts are relatively unused to appointing arbitrators. While court default appointments are possible in many other jurisdictions, it is not thought this power had been widely used prior to the Act coming into effect. There is limited anecdotal evidence of its subsequent use but some fall-back position is needed, notwithstanding the possible difficulties. Again on an anecdotal basis, it is understood that, in such cases as have arisen, the tendency has been to refer the matter to an appointing body such the Faculty of Advocates or The Law Society.

Where rule 7 comes into play, the time limits are short (sometimes as little as seven days), and this, therefore, re-emphasises the need to keep on top of the process, and to be well prepared for commencing arbitration, or to take early steps to prepare if an arbitration notice is received.

Duty to disclose any conflict of interests

The Supreme Court decision in *Halliburton v Chubb Insurance* [2020] UKSC 48 makes it clear this is a very live issue.

(1) This rule applies to –
  (a) arbitrators, and
  (b) individuals who have been asked to be an arbitrator but who have not yet been appointed.
(2) An individual to whom this rule applies must, without delay disclose –
  (a) to the parties, and
  (b) in the case of an individual not yet appointed as an arbitrator, to any arbitral appointments referee, other third party or court considering whether to appoint the individual as an arbitrator,
  any circumstances known to the individual (or which become known to the individual before the arbitration ends) which might reasonably be considered relevant when considering whether the individual is impartial and independent.

The Explanatory Notes to the Act state:

> Rule 8 requires an arbitrator (and any umpire, see rule 82) – including when
> asked to act but not yet appointed – to disclose, without delay, to the parties
> any circumstances which might reasonably be considered relevant when con-
> sidering if he or she is impartial or independent. The obligation to disclose
> continues throughout the arbitral proceedings. If an arbitrator fails to disclose,
> the court can take that into account as regards his or her expenses in removing
> them (rule 78).

Paragraph 8(2)(b) extends this duty of disclosure as it applies to a prospective arbitrator (ie before appointment), so that they must also make
disclosure to any arbitral appointments referee, other third party or court
whom the parties have asked to appoint an arbitrator.

The mandatory effect of the rule requires disclosure only. The parties
could, for example, ignore disclosure and appoint a non-independent arbitrator if satisfied that he or she will nevertheless act impartially. A challenge to that arbitrator or an award would only be successful if substantial
injustice is shown to have resulted in lack of impartiality, independence or
fairness, which may be unlikely in the event of disclosure where the parties
have agreed to proceed.

The onus of disclosure is on the arbitrator. He or she must disclose to
the parties any circumstances reasonably considered relevant as to his or
her impartiality. If the arbitrator fails to do so, there can be consequences
(eg the court can remove them, and take that into account as regards their
fees and expenses (rule 68(4)(b)). The test is objective, not subjective, but,
it is suggested, should amount to a matter likely to give rise to a justifiable doubt as to the arbitrator's impartiality. For example, being in a long-
term business partnership with a party is clearly something that would
have to be disclosed, but it might be questioned whether the fact that an
arbitrator and one of the parties had both been invited to the same event
with 500 other guests, and never spoken, would be considered a 'relevant'
consideration.

The reason for requiring disclosure by the arbitrators is that a later discovery as to a potential or perceived partiality could prevent the smooth
operation of the tribunal and lead to complications. Indeed, it could render
the entire process null and void, with huge waste of time and money.

In Scots law, at common law, it is well established that a party acting
in the role of judge, adjudicator or arbitrator should act without bias. The
Latin tag *nemo judex in sua causa* ('no one may be a judge in his own cause')
is often used. This freedom from bias was analysed by Lord Clyde in *Millar
v Dickson* [2001] UKPC D4, where he noted that there were 'distinct considerations of structural independence and objective impartiality, but the
two concepts are closely linked and it may be sufficient to speak simply of
independence. Judicial independence … is an indispensible condition for the
preservation of the rule of law.'

Of course the issue is not restricted to Scotland or the UK. This matter has come before the Swedish Supreme Court in *Korsnäs Aktiebolag v AB Fortum Värme* (Case T 156-09). Here the complaint was that the arbitrator had been appointed frequently by lawyers from the same law firm. The court looked at the appointments of someone who was clearly a leading arbitrator, and found that, viewed objectively, the number of appointments accepted from the firm in question (about 10 per cent of his total appointments) was unlikely to lead to any bias. Whilst a favourable ruling was obtained, this case sounds a cautionary note where lawyers have their favourite arbitrators (as is often the case), and it makes disclosure as required by the Act all the more important.

The *Halliburton* case brought this issue into sharp focus in the UK, particularly because the particular field (marine insurance) has long relied on a relatively small pool of expert arbitrators. However, the issue related not so much to the fact that the arbitrator in question took multiple appointments from the same party on different aspects of the same dispute, but rather that later appointments, after the arbitration in question had commenced, were not disclosed. It is suggested that rule 8 makes it absolutely clear that the position in Scotland is that, if a matter was disclosable at the start of the arbitration, it remains disclosable as the arbitration progresses. In *Halliburton* the arbitrator had declared previous appointments at the start of the arbitration, but failed to disclose new ones he received later. That, it is suggested, falls within the clear wording of the final paragraph of rule 8, and should be disclosed in an arbitration in Scotland and the Court's decision that the disclosure was required is, therefore, consistent with the law in Scotland.

As will be seen in the rules regulating the arbitrator's tenure as well as those relating to removal of the arbitrator (rules 9–13), impartiality, or rather the lack thereof, will be a basis for challenging the jurisdiction of the tribunal and can lead ultimately to removal by the court and consequences in relation to fees and expenses.

An extreme example of lack of independence appears in the Indian Supreme Court case of *Denel (Proprietary) Ltd v Bharat Electronics Ltd* (2010) 6 SCC 394, where the contract required an employee of one of the parties to act as arbitrator. In this case, the court set this aside and appointed an independent arbitrator. It should be added that this practice, or the related approach of having an employee appoint the arbitrator, seems to be relatively common in India. In the recent Indian Supreme Court case of *Union of India v Pradeep Vinod Construction Co SC* [2019] Civil Appeal No 6400/2016, the requirement was that the arbitrator be a railway official, when the railway company was a party. The Indian Supreme Court did, however, hold that it was not fatal that the arbitrator was a former employee of a party (*Government of Haryana PWD Haryana (B and R) Branch v M/s G F Toll Road Pvt Ltd and others* ([2019] Civil Appeal No 27/2019 in SLP (C) No 20201 of 2018)). It is suggested that none of these practices is likely to fare well in the event of a challenge in Scotland, and, wherever an arbitration is to take place, parties would be well advised not to agree to such clauses.

Arbitrators and bias

There have been problems in England with counsel and arbitrators coming from the same set of barristers' chambers: for example, *Hrvatska Elektroprivreda v Republic of Slovenia* (ICSID Case No ARB/05/24). This presented a challenge, because non-English parties had difficulty in understanding the chambers concept as being a collection of unconnected individuals working in a single building, with a shared set of administrators and sharing overhead costs (and looking very like a partnership). Many chambers in England have now separated their arbitrator members away from practising barristers on the chambers' websites. The position of Scottish advocates is not the same, and it is difficult to see that mere common membership of the Faculty of Advocates would give rise to a challenge. The case may be different with specialised commercial stables or chambers, particularly those which have devolved from overall control by the Faculty's service company. This is yet to be tested. It is suggested that it is likely, by analogy with the position in English case law, that solicitors in partnership or in LLPs will be prevented (on the basis of conflict of interest) from representing a party if a partner in the firm or partnership has had or has dealings with the other party to the arbitration.

In another ICSID case, *The Rompetrol Group NV v Romania* (ICSID Case No ARB/06/3) (Decision of the Tribunal on the Participation of a Counsel) the tribunal, composed of Sir Franklin Berman, Mr Donald Donovan and Mr Marc Lalonde, determined that Mr Barton Legum, a partner with Salans & Associés, could continue to represent Rompetrol in its arbitration against Romania. Mr Legum formally took over as counsel for Rompetrol in the summer of 2009 after his colleague, Ms François-Poncet, announced her departure from private practice. On learning of this proposed change of counsel, Romania sought 'to remove Mr Legum from the case and to forbid him from participating in it in any way' after learning that Mr Legum and Mr Donald Donovan, a member of the tribunal, had both worked at Debevoise & Plimpton LLP from 2004 to 2008. This application was unsuccessful.

Nationality *per se* is not a consideration unless institutional rules make it so. It was recognised in *ASM Shipping Ltd of India v TTMI Ltd of England* [2005] EWHC 2238 (Comm) that it was not necessary to draw a distinction between cases where there was a foreign party and those cases where there was not. The test is what an objective and independent observer would think. There should be an even-handed approach to apparent bias no matter the nationality of the parties: *Lawal v Northern Spirit Ltd* [2003] UKHL 35. In the facts of the *ASM* case, one of the three arbitrators was a QC who had 'close connections' with one of the parties' solicitors. The court recognised that in specialist arbitrations 'prior contact between parties and their lawyers and arbitrators was to be expected' but here it was thought that there was a real *possibility* of bias (ie not actual), following *Porter v Magill* [2001] UKHL 67.

Another example might be the situation where the arbitrator contacted the witnesses but did not tell the parties or their advisers or keep a record of what was said. In addition to this being very poor practice, it would also perhaps create a real possibility of bias in the mind of the fair-minded and informed observer as it was considered to be by the court in *Norbrook Laboratories Ltd v Tank* [2006] EWHC 1055 (Comm). A similar point arose in *Fleetwood Wanderers Ltd (t/a Fleetwood Town Football Club) v AFC Fylde Ltd* [2018] EWHC 3318 (Comm), where the arbitrator made his own enquiries as to whether a particular Article from FIFA Regulations on player transfers had been incorporated into the Rules of the English Football Association. This research was not discussed with, or disclosed to, the parties. This was held to be an 'irregularity', but the discrete part of the award affected by this irregularity was remitted to the arbitrator under s 68(3) of the 1996 Act to allow the parties to make representations, and for the arbitrator to reconsider the issue, rather than setting aside the whole award. This decision was at least in part on the basis that there was no evidence of bias. There is another example in the Scottish case of *Partners of Dallas McMillan, Petitioners* [2015] CSOH 136 where, in a partnership dispute arbitration, the arbitrator had *ultra vires* instructed her own firm as valuers; had given no indication during the course of the arbitration that she had intended to take legal advice or to obtain advice from an expert in valuation, and afforded the parties no opportunity to comment on the advice given and the basis of fact on which it had been sought, all contrary to the arbitration agreement itself and contrary to natural justice in obtaining such advice without informing the parties; acted in other ways which the court held were *ultra vires*, and was considered by it to have 'misunderstood her role'. But see *Field v Network Rail Infrastructure Ltd* [2020] EWHC 3440 (Ch) where the arbitrator's use of his own expertise was not considered to be problematic.

The main concern is that a partial or non-independent arbitrator will favour one of the parties over the other, whether deliberately or not, and will thus be biased. The courts' approach to bias is now found in the House of Lords' decision of *Porter v Magill* (above) in which Lord Hope gave the leading judgment. The test was formulated as 'whether the fair-minded and informed observer, having considered the facts, would conclude that there was a real possibility that the tribunal was biased'.

Lord Hope also gave guidance in connection with Scottish arbitration under the pre-existing law in *ERDC Construction Ltd v HM Love & Co (No 2)* 1996 SC 523 at 529 ff:

> It is an implied condition of an arbiter's appointment that he should be in a position to approach with an open mind the question which has been submitted to him for his decision. As Lord Dunpark said in *Grahame House Investments Ltd v Secretary of State for the Environment* [1985 SC 201, 1985 SLT 502] at 508:
>
>> 'As it is a judicial function which an arbiter is called upon to perform, it must be presumed that every arbiter will approach the question for his decision with an open mind unless by prior word or deed an arbiter has precluded himself from acting judicially as arbiter. He may so preclude himself if his

prior actings indicate that he is biased or he has necessarily prejudged the
issue to be determined by him.'

As the last sentence of that passage indicates, an arbiter may disqualify himself from acting by something which he does prior to, or outwith, the arbitration proceedings which indicates that he has prejudged the issue which he
was appointed to decide. In *Dickson v Grant*, (1870) 8 March 566 for example,
an architect was held to be disqualified from acting as arbiter where he had
been examined as a witness for one of the parties in regard to some of the
matters in dispute. The court was careful to make it clear that the fact that he
was, to the knowledge of both parties, architect under the contract did not
invalidate his nomination as arbiter: see also *Crawford Bros v Commissioners
of Northern Lighthouses* [1925 SC (HL) 22, 1925 SLT 341]. But, as Lord Neaves
said at p 569, he must be careful not to prejudge the question which may
ultimately come before him and he should refrain from taking active steps
on either side. In *Halliday v Duke of Hamilton's Trs* [(1903) 5 F 800] a similar
problem arose, because the arbiter named in the arbitration clause was the
engineer to the employers under the engineering contract. In the course of
his duties as engineer he had written letters to the employers expressing his
opinion on some of the matters in dispute. It was held however that there
was nothing in his letters to show that he would not, as arbiter, regard the
question in dispute with an open mind. The point was put by Lord Trayner
at p 810 in these words:

> 'I should certainly be disposed to exclude from the office of arbiter anyone
> who had put himself in the position of having already decided the question
> in dispute before the reference had been finally made, but in this case I think
> there is no reasonable ground whatever for excluding the Messrs Stevenson.
> I do not think that anything in their letters indicates a want of open mind on
> their part ...'

> I have reached the same opinion, without any difficulty, in the present case.'

It should be remembered that if the 'fair-minded, informed observer'
(*Porter*) would have considered that there was bias then that would probably
fall into the category of 'serious irregularity' and thus also be sufficient for an
appeal under rule 68 (see below).

In Scotland, prior contact or dealings or relationships with parties and
lawyers and arbitrators is to be expected and we do not consider that the
mere fact that one is known to the other is sufficient on its own to set up an
objection.

However, parties and potential arbitrators need to take care to avoid
the impression of possible impropriety, even where none exists. There are
reported to be instances where searches of social networking sites such
as Facebook and LinkedIn have revealed that parties are linked (possibly
with a title such as 'Friends' on Facebook), which can create problems. If
in doubt, such matters should be disclosed and explained. It is interesting

to speculate whether, having not objected to the previous appointments disclosed in *Halliburton*, there would have been an objection if the later appointments had also been disclosed. The advice to arbitrators or potential arbitrators, must be that sunlight is the best antiseptic, and, if in doubt, disclosure is usually the best course of action. While there may be temptations not to disclose on the basis that there is no 'real' bias, and the arbitrator has to make a living, the threat of an application to be removed for non-disclosure (as in *Halliburton*) should suggest the need to err on the side of caution. If the position is not clear cut, guidance may be obtained from the IBA Guidelines, to which we turn.

IBA Guidelines on Conflicts of Interest in International Arbitration

All parties may derive some assistance from the *IBA Guidelines on Conflicts of Interest* (2004) which help parties and arbitrators identify those factors which might be disclosed. See http://www.ibanet.org where the Guidelines can be found in the Publications section. The Guidelines suggest approaching the issue by classifying the conflicts of interest like traffic lights.

The Red List

Red category (waivable and non-waivable) consists of two parts: 'a non-waivable Red List' and 'a waivable Red List'.
    As the Guidelines explain:

> These lists are a non-exhaustive enumeration of specific situations which, depending on the facts of a given case, give rise to justifiable doubts as to the arbitrator's impartiality and independence; ie, in these circumstances an objective conflict of interest exists from the point of view of a reasonable third person having knowledge of the relevant facts. The non-waivable Red List includes situations deriving from the overriding principle that no person can be his or her own judge. Therefore, disclosure of such a situation cannot cure the conflict. The waivable Red List encompasses situations that are serious but not as severe. Because of their seriousness, unlike circumstances described in the Orange List, these situations should be considered waivable only if and when the parties, being aware of the conflict of interest situation, nevertheless expressly state their willingness to have such a person act as arbitrator.

One of the non-waivable examples given is of an arbitrator who has a significant financial interest in one of the parties or the outcome of the case. An example given of a waivable Red List consideration is where the arbitrator has given legal advice or provided an expert opinion on the dispute to a party or an affiliate of one of the parties. That would have to be disclosed but the parties *could* waive it.

The Orange List

The Orange List is a non-exhaustive enumeration of 'specific situations which (depending on the facts of a given case) in the eyes of the parties may give rise to justifiable doubts as to the arbitrator's impartiality or independence'.

An example given is where the arbitrator has within the past three years served as counsel for one of the parties or an affiliate of one of the parties or has previously advised or been consulted by the party or an affiliate of the party making the appointment in an unrelated matter, but the arbitrator and the party or the affiliate of the party have no ongoing relationship. Another is where the arbitrator has within the past three years served as counsel against one of the parties or an affiliate of one of the parties in an unrelated matter.

The Green List

The Green List contains a non-exhaustive 'enumeration of specific situations where no appearance of, and no actual, conflict of interest exists from the relevant objective point of view. Thus, the arbitrator has no duty to disclose situations falling within the Green List.'

An example given is where the arbitrator has previously published a general opinion (such as in a law review article or public lecture) concerning an issue which also arises in the arbitration (but this opinion is not focused on the case that is being arbitrated).

While the guidelines are not decisive, they are often the first port of call for arbitrators, parties or their solicitors with concerns about conflicts of interest in the appointments. In *ASM Shipping Ltd of India v TTMI Ltd of England* [2005] EWHC 2238 (Comm) Morrison J (at para 39(4)) stated that the IBA Guidelines do not purport to be comprehensive and as the Working Party added 'nor could they be'. He considered that the Guidelines should be 'applied with robust common sense and without pedantic and unduly formulaic interpretation'. However, in *W Ltd v M Sdn Bhd* [2016] EWHC 422 (Comm) the Court held that the IBA Guidelines were not binding on the court but they made a distinguished contribution in the field of international arbitration. Their objective of assisting in assessing impartiality and independence was commendable. However, the Court considered that there were weaknesses in the 2014 version which meant that the Guidelines could not yet be quite correct. It identified what it considered to be the 'weaknesses' in the Guidelines and saw a tension between some of the 'general standards' dealing with independence and impartiality, and inconsistency between the situations included or not included in the non-waivable list.

Arbitrator's tenure

Default rule 9 provides:

> An arbitrator's tenure ends if –
> (a) the arbitrator becomes ineligible to act as an arbitrator (see rule 4),
> (b) the tribunal revokes the arbitrator's appointment (see rule 10),
> (c) the arbitrator is removed by the parties, a third party or the Outer House (see rules 11 and 12),
> (d) the Outer House dismisses the tribunal of which the arbitrator forms part (see rule 13), or
> (e) the arbitrator resigns (see rule 15) or dies (see rule 79).

This is fairly self-explanatory, and eligibility has been discussed in connection with rule 4 and revocation is discussed below in connection with rules 9 and 10. Removal by the Outer House is discussed in the commentary to rules 11 and 12 as well as dismissal by it under rule 13. Finally, resignation and death of the arbitrator is discussed in the commentaries to rules 15 and 79 respectively.

Challenge to appointment of arbitrator

Default rule 10 states:

> (1) A party may object to the tribunal about the appointment of an arbitrator.
> (2) An objection is competent only if –
>   (a) it is made on the ground that the arbitrator –
>   (i) is not impartial and independent,
>   (ii) has not treated the parties fairly, or
>   (iii) does not have a qualification which the parties agreed (before the arbitrator's appointment) that the arbitrator must have,
>   (b) it states the facts on which it is based,
>   (c) it is made within 14 days of the objector becoming aware of those facts, and
>   (d) notice of it is given to the other party.
> (3) The tribunal may deal with an objection by confirming or revoking the appointment.
> (4) If the tribunal fails to make a decision within 14 days of a competent objection being made, the appointment is revoked.

Rule 10 is a default rule. This and the following four rules can be considered to be the rules relevant to objection and removal of the arbitrator (or umpire).

Under rule 10 it is only an *objection* which can be made and it would be left to the tribunal to consider whether it was a 'competent' objection and thereafter whether there was sufficient in that objection to revoke the appointment. It is not an absolute right to *require* removal.

Grounds for objection

The *only* grounds for 'a party' to object about an arbitrator are that he or she:

(a) is not impartial or independent,

(b) has not treated the parties fairly, or

(c) does not have a qualification which the parties agreed (before the appointment) the arbitrator should have.

The use of the present tense 'is' (at rule 10(2)(a)(i)) might connote that the arbitrator has to be continuously not impartial or independent for the objection to be competent but this is not the case. Isolated incidents could be enough.

An objection must be based on facts from which the tribunal is invited to infer that there is a lack of independence and impartiality. What if there were to be evidence of prior lack of impartiality which had now been resolved? It is suggested that in this unlikely event, there could still be said to have been sufficient lack of independence and impartiality to object to the arbitrator, and that there is not a need to prove the matter complained of is still existing at the time of the objection.

Independence and impartiality

While the Act uses both independence and impartiality, it may be that these two elements are simply so closely related that they should be seen collectively and not separated out. *Redfern and Hunter on International Arbitration* on the other hand describe questions of 'independence' as arising out of 'the relationship between an arbitrator and one of the parties, whether financial or otherwise' which is susceptible to an objective test (unrelated to the arbitrator's state of mind) (6th edn, para 4.77) whereas 'impartiality' is considered to be 'connected with actual or apparent bias of an arbitrator – either in favour of one of the parties, or in relation to the issues in dispute' and is thus a 'subjective and more abstract concept than independence involving primarily a state of mind' (para 4.78). (See also the discussion below in connection with rule 77.)

Qualifications

The final ground based on the qualifications of the arbitrator can lead to a challenge and this issue has been discussed already in relation to rule 7, and is discussed further in the commentary to rule 68 (appeal on a serious irregularity). It is an extension of the principle of party autonomy – it is for the parties to select their arbitrators and require of them whatever qualifications they wish. So they may specify in the arbitration agreement that the arbitrator will be an individual with, for example, a law degree, or be a member of the Faculty of Advocates or a Fellow of the Chartered Institute of

Arbitrators or a Fellow of the Royal Institution of Chartered Surveyors, or a Fellow of the Chartered Institute of Arbitrators etc.

As already discussed, there has been doubt as to whether it would now be permissible to require that the arbitrators must be, for example, of a particular gender, or a particular religion or sect, but this is not addressed in the Act. In *Virdee v Virdi* [2003] EWHC Civ 41 there was a successful application that new arbitrators had to be of the Sikh religion, and, in the case of *Nurdin Jivraj v Sadruddin Hashwani* [2011] UKSC 40 (as discussed under ss 1 and 24), which was heard after the Act was passed, the Supreme Court upheld the objection to the appointment of an arbitrator who was not, as the parties had agreed, a member of the Ismaili community, where this was not directly relevant to the dispute. This matter is discussed in further detail in rule 68(2)(j).

It is suggested that, as a matter of good practice, restriction on the background of arbitrators should be included only where such restrictions are truly necessary to enable the determination of the dispute, or for the parties to have confidence in the decision. A practical example would be a contract to be arbitrated in Scotland, but with English governing law (common in the oil and gas industry). This might provide that the arbitrator be a member of the Faculty of Advocates or Law Society of Scotland because the dispute was likely to turn on legal interpretation, but that the arbitrator should also be dual-qualified in English law, because of the governing law of the contract.

Facts not allegations

The objection must be made on the basis of fact and not on spurious or ill-advised or unprovable allegations or insinuations. 'Facts', we suggest, will be those that are capable of being proved by evidence and the arbitrator should if necessary request sight of any such evidence available to substantiate or corroborate that fact supporting the grounds of objection.

Where an objection is made on the ground of any improper act or omission on the part of an arbitrator, this should only be put forward if the party making the allegation is satisfied that it would be able to prove the same. The standard of proof is likely to increase in proportion to the nature of the alleged offence, with, we suggest, the full criminal standard of beyond reasonable doubt being required where, for example, fraud or dishonesty is alleged.

Time limits

The time limit for raising an objection is only 14 days from the date of the objector becoming aware of the relevant fact. It is suggested that the test of that is likely to be when the objector had all the relevant facts, even if he did not appreciate that this might be grounds for an objection. This would be consistent with the Supreme Court decision in *David T Morrison & Co Ltd v ICL*

Plastics Ltd and others [2014] UKSC 48 arising from the ICL Plastics explosion in Glasgow. This decision, which was on a 3 to 2 basis, was seen as changing Scots law on limitation and prescription, and has been the subject of considerable criticism, but remains good law at the date of this edition. However, the implementation of the Prescription (Scotland) Act 2018 will change this with new subsections at s 5(4) and (5) replacing the existing discoverability formula for determining the knowledge which a pursuer must have before the prescriptive period begins to run once those sections come into force.

Once the objection is received, the tribunal has only a further 14 days to make a decision, failing which, the appointment is automatically revoked. This is obviously intended to bring matters to a head as quickly as possible and to prevent these procedural arguments dragging on during the arbitration.

If the arbitrator's appointment is revoked under this rule then his tenure is considered to be at an end in terms of default rule 9 (if not disapplied).

Removal of arbitrator by parties

Default rule 11 provides:

(1) An arbitrator may be removed –
   (a) by the parties acting jointly, or
   (b) by any third party to whom the parties give power to remove an arbitrator.
(2) A removal is effected by notifying the arbitrator.

This rule allows the parties to get together jointly to remove the arbitrator. If the rule applies, they have to do the removal jointly or together empower a third party to do so. The arbitrator is removed by 'notifying' him or her. Notice procedure is provided for in rule 83 (formal communications).

If arbitration is a 'creature of consent', like many other provisions throughout the Act, where all the parties come together and agree to do something, it is difficult if not impossible for the arbitral tribunal to refuse to do it. This rule, it is suggested, is akin to a summary termination provision without the option to make representations or to appeal!

If the tribunal is composed of a single arbitrator then he or she will be removed and the parties will have to once again take whatever steps are required in the appointment of a new tribunal. If the tribunal consists of two or more arbitrators then, as the Act is silent on this, on one view the tribunal can continue (authority tacitly being given by the parties to do so) albeit that on a strict construction the tribunal may not be constituted in the form that was required by the agreement (see rule 2 above and rule 68 below). As seen throughout the Act and the Rules, one can envisage the operation of the doctrine of personal bar or there being considerations of acquiescence, both or either of which may apply in the event of later challenge. Alternatively, it might be argued that the parties could be said to have 'novated' or 'amended' the original agreement so that the truncated tribunal is in compliance with that new or amended agreement. If, as is likely, this creates a tribunal with an even number of arbitrators, this creates problems, which were addressed earlier. On balance it seems more sensible to appoint a new arbitrator to fill the vacancy, but all options will be open to the parties.

If the parties decide to remove one arbitrator from a multi-arbitrator tribunal, they should agree in writing whether the remaining arbitrator or arbitrators should continue, or whether a new arbitrator is to be appointed.

It seems that the parties can also give express power to the arbitral appointments referee (see s 24) or any other body or person to remove the arbitrator, although it is not clear on what grounds other than those above that the parties have lost confidence etc and simply wish the tribunal to be removed. While the purpose of this provision is not totally clear, the reference in rule 14(1)(b)(ii) suggests that the intention is to allow an AAR or other institution to use an appeal process before removal, since it is a requirement that such a process should be exhausted before the court has power to remove an arbitrator or dismiss a tribunal under rules 12 and 13 respectively.

Although the Act does not provide an opportunity for the arbitral tribunal to make representations in respect of the projected removal, it can be noticed that where the court is being requested to do so under rules 12 or 13, then rule 14 comes into operation to the extent that the arbitrator or the tribunal is 'notified' and 'given the opportunity to make representations'. By analogy, the parties may consider agreeing to afford the arbitrator the same opportunity under this rule, although they are not obliged to do so.

For the arbitrator it may be possible to request that opportunity by analogy with those other rules, although by this stage the arbitrator would have lost the confidence of both parties, and this may be a fairly hopeless cause.

If the arbitrator is removed by the parties or a third party empowered to do so then in terms of rule 9 (if not disapplied) his tenure is at an end.

Finally, there remains an unsettling possibility that an arbitrator is removed to allow the parties to proceed with an unlawful act (for example, money laundering, breach of tax or VAT rules or local laws, concealing assets through purported arbitral proceedings, hiding monies through purported payment of fees and expenses of an arbitration, etc). This is a very difficult area, particularly for the arbitrator. The arbitrator cannot just turn a 'blind eye' to events, but it is difficult to see what he or she can do under the Act, since the notification means he or she has been removed and, as already stated, no longer has any role as an arbitrator. The extent to which arbitrators can report their suspicions to the relevant authorities is connected with duties of confidentiality, and the 'tipping' rules in the UK and other national money laundering regulations, but there is an obvious potential clash with duties of confidentiality under default rule 26, if it applies. The arbitrator could, conceivably, apply to the court for guidance where such a move was threatened, but once the notification has been received, he or she has no role in the arbitration, and no right to apply to the court.

Removal or dismissal of arbitrator by court

Rule 12 provides:

> The Outer House may remove an arbitrator if satisfied on the application by
> any party –
> (a) that the arbitrator is not impartial and independent,
> (b) that the arbitrator has not treated the parties fairly,
> (c) that the arbitrator is incapable of acting as an arbitrator in the arbitration
>   (or that there are justifiable doubts about the arbitrator's ability to so act),
> (d) that the arbitrator does not have a qualification which the parties agreed
>   (before the arbitrator's appointment) that the arbitrator must have,
> (e) that substantial injustice has been or will be caused to that party because
>   the arbitrator has failed to conduct the arbitration in accordance with –
>   (i)   the arbitration agreement,
>   (ii) these rules (in so far as they apply), or
>   (iii) any other agreement by the parties relating to conduct of the arbitration.

This rule is mandatory, unlike the power of the parties to remove an arbitrator under rule 11. The Notes to the Act state in relation to this mandatory rule that:

> Rule 12 makes mandatory provision for removal of an arbitrator or umpire by
> the court because of lack of impartiality, independence, fairness or lack of qual-
> ifications, as opposed to by the parties and any other arbitrators or umpires
> on application by any party. The court can also judge under rule 12(c) that the
> arbitrator is incapable (or there are doubts about capacity) of acting, which
> includes the eligibility requirement on capability in rule 4 – someone may be
> capable under the Adults with Incapacity (Scotland) Act 2000 (asp 4), but may
> still be incapable of acting as an arbitrator under this provision.

Rule 12 picks up on a number of the considerations already canvassed above in connection with 'impartiality and independence' (s 1, rules 8, 10, 24, 68–77); 'fairness' (s 1, rules 1, 10, 68); 'eligibility' (rules 4, 9, 10, 69); 'capability' (rules 4, 68); 'qualifications' (rules 10, 68); and 'substantial injustice'.

Rule 12(e) allows individual arbitrators to be challenged on grounds of failure to conduct the arbitration in accordance with the arbitration agreement (subject to any contrary mandatory rule) where there has been or will be substantial injustice caused to a party. The 'substantial injustice' test means that minor procedural breaches will not permit removal or dismissal or challenge of an award. This will, for example, cover failure to take reasonable steps to prevent unauthorised disclosure of confidential information under rule 26(2) – if that default rule applies – but only if any breach of confidence thereunder has caused substantial injustice. The possibility canvassed in the previous section of an arbitrator being obliged to tip off the authorities about money laundering concerns is interesting, as the impact on the parties could be very serious (including criminal sanctions), but, arguably, there is no 'injustice' (serious or otherwise) to the parties in reporting a breach of law.

The issue may, therefore, turn on whether the notification was correct, or at least reasonable in the circumstances, which may produce difficult decisions on whether the test of the arbitrator's decision is objective or subjective, given the consequences for an arbitrator of getting the decision to report wrong.

This rule limits the grounds upon which an arbitrator may be removed. Any party may apply but the decision is wholly within the discretion of the court and the court must be 'satisfied' that one of the grounds applies before granting the application. It is suggested that the court may approach this in a similar manner to the 1996 Act s 24 which lays down an objective test that reflects the common law: *Laker Airways Inc v FLS Aerospace Ltd* [1999] 2 Lloyd's Rep 45 at 48 and *Rustal Trading Ltd v Gill & Duffus SA* [2000] 1 Lloyd's Rep 14 at 18.

Thus a Scottish court might look at some of the cases already discussed above, such as *Porter v Magill* [2002] 2 AC 357 at 494 in which Lord Hope expressed the test for apparent bias as endorsed by the Supreme Court in *Halliburton*. This test was considered again by the Court of Appeal in *Flaherty v National Greyhound Racing Club Ltd* [2005] EWCA Civ 1117, where at para [27] Scott Baker LJ observed that:

> The test for apparent bias involves a two-stage process: the court must first ascertain all the circumstances which have a bearing on the suggestion that the tribunal was biased. Then it must ask itself whether the circumstance would lead a fair minded and informed observer to conclude that there was a real possibility that the tribunal was biased.

It is suggested that it will be in only the most serious of cases that the court will remove the arbitrator. An example of the kind of conduct which may give rise to removal might be the facts of *Norbrook Laboratories Ltd v Tank* [2006] EWHC 1055 (Comm) where the arbitrator communicated with the parties' witnesses but did not keep a record and did not disclose the fact that he had done this to the parties or their advisers.

The most recent guidance from the Supreme Court is in the *Halliburton* case already mentioned where the arbitrator was not removed, despite having breached a duty of disclosure.

'Application by any party'

In terms of RCS 100.5(1), all applications have to be made to the court by petition and, in terms of RCS 100.7(1), the petitioner must set out the facts and circumstances on which the petition is founded and the relief claimed.

In applications under rules 22, 41, 67, 68 and 69 particular matters should be identified (RCS 100.7(3)). These are:

(a) the parties to the cause and the arbitration from which the cause arises;

(b) the relevant rule of the Scottish Arbitration Rules or other provision of the 2010 Act under which the petition or note has been lodged;

(c) any special capacity in which the petitioner or noter is acting or any special capacity in which any other party to the proceedings is acting;

(d) a summary of the circumstances out of which the application or appeal arises;

(e) the grounds on which the application or appeal proceeds;

(f) in the case of an appeal under rule 67(1), whether the appellant seeks the variation or the setting aside of an award (or part of it);

(g) in the case of an appeal under rule 69(1), whether the appeal is made with the agreement of the parties to the arbitration; and

(h) any relevant requirements of the Scottish Arbitration Rules which have been met.

It is suggested that these matters are a helpful reminder of what to put into a 'general petition' under RCS 100.7(1).

The limited grounds for removal are set out in the rule, but the same issues on these points will arise as discussed in the earlier rules mentioned above. It should be noted that rule 12(b) (reflecting the duties imposed by rule 24) allows removal of the arbitrator for failing to treat the *parties* fairly. It is arguable that this requires unfairness to both parties, but this is an entirely academic point, since if the arbitrator was fair to one party, but not the other, he would appear to breach the duty of impartiality and independence, and thus could be removed under rule 12(a).

If the court removes the arbitrator then, in terms of default rule 9 (if not disapplied), the arbitrator's tenure is at an end. However, if there is more than one arbitrator, the other arbitrator(s) remain(s) in office. In practice, it is likely that a new arbitrator will be appointed, but the parties could agree to allow the remaining arbitrators to proceed.

Where an arbitrator has been removed, a positive decision is needed as to whether a new arbitrator is to be appointed, and this should be discussed with the other party where relevant.

Dismissal of tribunal

Mandatory rule 13 covers the power of the court to dismiss a tribunal (as opposed to an individual arbitrator), stating as follows:

> The Outer House may dismiss the tribunal if satisfied on the application by a party that substantial injustice has been or will be caused to that party because the tribunal has failed to conduct the arbitration in accordance with –
> (a) the arbitration agreement,
> (b) these rules (in so far as they apply), or
> (c) any other agreement by the parties relating to conduct of the arbitration.

Rule 13 sets up an option for any of the parties to apply to the Outer House for dismissal of the whole tribunal (and presumably it is the whole tribunal consisting of two or more arbitrators otherwise the court would exercise the power to remove 'an arbitrator' under rule 12 albeit on these but also additional grounds). In the latter case, under rule 12, the remaining members of the tribunal would remain in office. It is suggested that, where a single arbitrator is involved, rule 12 is the appropriate route, rather than 13.

It is for the court to decide. It has a discretion to do so by the use of the word 'may' and will do so only if 'satisfied' that there has been 'substantial injustice' which is not defined in the Act. The question of 'substantial injustice' is considered below in connection with serious irregularity appeals under rule 68.

If the tribunal is dismissed by the court, then its tenure is at an end under default rule 10. In practice this is the case whether or not this rule is disapplied.

'Application by a party'

As before, in terms of RCS 100.5(1), all applications have to be made to the court by petition and, in terms of RCS 100.7(1), the petitioner must set out the facts and circumstances on which the petition is founded and the relief claimed.

In applications under rules 22, 41, 67, 68 and 69 particular matters should be identified. Like applications under rule 13 above, it is suggested that these matters are a helpful reminder of what to put into a 'general petition' under RCS 100.7(1). The relevant matters as set out in RCS 100.7(3) are listed under rule 12 above.

'Dismissal' and removal

There is no definition of 'dismissal' – is this the same as 'removal' in terms of rules 11 and 12 and of the 1996 Act s 24? It is probable that the explanation lies in dismissal applying to the whole tribunal – it being relieved of its duties and thus 'dismissed' (see also mandatory rule 14 for support)   whereas 'removal' applies to an individual arbitrator (again see rule 14 for support).

Failure to conduct the proceedings

A failure to conduct the proceedings properly is probably sourced from the 1996 Act s 24(1)(d)(i) which refers to the arbitrator having 'refused or failed properly to conduct the proceedings ... and that a substantial injustice has been or will be caused to the applicant'. As was noted in *Benaim (UK) Ltd v Davies Middleton Ltd (No 2)* [2005] EWHC 1370 (TCC), although 'failure to conduct the proceedings properly' was not defined in the Act, it would include a failure to comply with the arbitrator's general duties imposed in the other provisions of the 1996 Act (ss 33 and 68(2)(a), (b) and (c)). Given the increasing emphasis on efficient case management in the courts in both

Scotland and England as referred to earlier, it may be that use will be made of this rule to dismiss tribunals which simply do not progress with the arbitration in an efficient manner.

These rules are supplemented by mandatory rule 14 which states that:

(1) The Outer House may remove an arbitrator, or dismiss the tribunal, only if –
    (a) the arbitrator or, as the case may be, tribunal has been –
        (i) notified of the application for removal or dismissal, and
        (ii) given the opportunity to make representations, and
    (b) the Outer House is satisfied –
        (i) that any recourse available under rule 10 has been exhausted, and
        (ii) that any available recourse to a third party who the parties have agreed is to have power to remove an arbitrator (or dismiss the tribunal) has been exhausted.
(2) A decision of the Outer House under rule 12 or 13 is final.
(3) The tribunal may continue with the arbitration pending the Outer House's decision under rule 12 or 13.

Where dismissal or removal is being considered, this mandatory rule 14 provides some protection for the tribunal or arbitrator. It also supports the fact that a rule 12 application covers a single arbitrator being 'removed', whereas a rule 13 application is to 'dismiss' an entire tribunal.

Notification

There must be notification (the Rules of the Court of Session refer to 'intimation' and the Act refers to 'notification') of the application. In practical terms this will always be the case as an application must be made by petition or note (RCS 100.5) and that petitioner or noter has to 'enrol a motion' (ie put a request before the court) for 'intimation and service of the petition or note and the court may make such order as is appropriate in the circumstances of the case' (RCS 100.5(3)).

At the end of the period of notice, following intimation and service, the party will enrol a motion for further procedure and the court may make 'such order as is appropriate in the circumstances of the case, including where appropriate an order disposing of the petition or note' (RCS 100.5(5)). Note, though, that the arbitration judge has a wide discretion as to how the proceedings will be conducted (see RCS 100.2).

Representations

Once notified the arbitrator or tribunal is entitled to have the opportunity to make representations. This will presumably be to the court, although on one interpretation it could be to the parties in the first instance and then the court under the court's rules. In practical terms, it is suggested that any representation is copied to the parties or their representatives and the court.

The court will allow those representations either under RCS 100.5(3) after the motion for intimation and service when the 'court may make such order as is appropriate in the circumstances of the case', or perhaps 'upon expiry of any period of notice' and, when the petitioner or noter enrols a motion for further procedure, the 'court may make such order as is appropriate in the circumstances of the case'.

In most cases, if the arbitrator or tribunal wishes to make representations, those representations must relate to the grounds for the application, and to the reasons why the arbitrator or the arbitral tribunal should not be removed or dismissed as the case may be.

Court must be satisfied

The other safeguard for the tribunal or arbitrator is that before removal or dismissal, the court, in the exercise of its discretion, must be satisfied that any recourse available under rule 10 has been exhausted and that any available recourse to an empowered third party to remove or dismiss has been exhausted.

Rule 10 is a default rule so if it has been excluded by the parties the court will not have to consider that issue, since there is no such recourse to be exhausted. If it has not been excluded, the recourse under this rule will be that of the tribunal confirming or revoking the individual arbitrator's appointment. Likewise, if there is no empowered third party in the arbitration then the court need not take account of that.

Like other provisions of the Act, the decision of the arbitration judge in the Outer House is final and there will be no reclaiming motion (ie an appeal from the Outer House to the Inner House of the Court of Session) permitted.

The continuing arbitration

Under rule 14(3), while the question of removal or dismissal is before the court under rules 12 or 13, the tribunal is specifically empowered to continue acting. One could envisage loss of confidence on both sides and difficulty in so continuing at a practical level but the important point is that the progress of the proceedings cannot be waylaid, delayed, frustrated or hampered simply by one party deciding to bring an application under rules 12 and 13. Of course, if both parties lose confidence, the better route is rule 11, when the issue of the continuing arbitration is moot since the arbitrator has been removed by simple notice. This also supports the founding principle of resolving disputes without unnecessary delay or expense in s 1(a), and the duty imposed on the tribunal to conduct arbitrations without unnecessary delay (mandatory rule 24(1)(c)(i)).

Although the use of the word 'may' confers on the arbitrator or the tribunal a discretion to proceed or not in the face of an application to remove or dismiss, it is suggested that arbitrators should, particularly where the basis of the challenge is not obviously correct, proceed with their duties until ordered to stop. If an individual arbitrator considers the application correct, they could use the power to resign under rule 15 (see below), but this cannot apply to a tribunal as a body, merely each individual, since, as we will see, rule 15 does not apply to applications under rule 13, and in this case the arbitrator would require some other grounds for resignation under rule 15. Failure to proceed where the basis of the application is not obviously correct allows the complaining party the ability to secure a procedural advantage at a relatively small cost, even if the claim itself fails. If the matter complained of is sufficiently egregious, the court would no doubt be prepared to issue an interim interdict to restrain the arbitrator from proceeding pending a full hearing.

If the Outer House decides that there should be dismissal or removal then the parties will, as already mentioned, have to decide how they wish to continue. Removal of one arbitrator from a multi-person panel may not require matters to be restarted from the beginning. Removal of a sole arbitrator or dismissal of the whole tribunal is likely to require that measure. If the parties have incorporated rules 9 and 17, the arbitrator's 'tenure' will have come to an end in terms of default rule 9, and, in terms of default rule 17, the tribunal must be reconstituted in accordance with the original tribunal appointing procedure or by using rules 6 and 7.

Resignation of arbitrator

Mandatory rule 15 allows an arbitrator to give notice of resignation to the parties and any other arbitrators, but only in limited circumstances, namely:

(1) ...
    (a) the parties consent to the resignation,
    (b) the arbitrator has a contractual right to resign in the circumstances,
    (c) the arbitrator's appointment is challenged under rule 10 or 12,
    (d) the parties disapply or modify rule 34(1) (expert opinions) after the arbitrator is appointed, or
    (e) the Outer House has authorised the resignation.
(2) The Outer House may authorise a resignation only if satisfied, on an application by the arbitrator, that it is reasonable for the arbitrator to resign.
(3) The Outer House's determination of an application for resignation is final.

If there is consent of the parties, then there is no problem, although it is suggested that the arbitrator should have a good reason to resign rather than on their own whim or for their own convenience.

If there is a contractual right vested in the arbitrator permitting them unilaterally (ie without consent but probably only in prescribed circumstances) to resign then again that is permitted.

If there is a challenge to their appointment (as opposed to their continued acting) in terms of rule 10 (challenge to appointment of arbitrator) or 12 (removal of arbitrator by court), they may resign to avoid the necessity of proceedings. As mentioned already, this does not cover an application to dismiss the entire tribunal under rule 13. This produces a slightly strange result that individual arbitrators can pre-empt a removal application under rules 10 or 12, but an entire tribunal cannot do the same in respect of an application under rule 13. It is anticipated that this issue is theoretical rather than practical, in that the number of removal or dismissal applications will, hopefully, be limited, and where everyone agrees that the tribunal cannot proceed, common sense and party autonomy is likely to mean that the courts will not need be involved.

If the parties have modified or disapplied rule 34(1) (expert witnesses: see commentary below) after their appointment, then this entitles the arbitrator to resign. Default rule 34 permits the tribunal to take expert evidence on any matter arising in the arbitration. If the rule is removed by the parties, then the arbitrator may have to exercise caution in taking an appointment if they feel that they are not capable of discharging the function without expert evidence. If rule 34 is left in by default but thereafter modified or disapplied by the parties, then this permits the arbitrator to resign in terms of rule 15 since it may be that they would have declined the appointment without this power.

Where the Outer House has authorised a resignation the arbitrator may resign but that may only happen on the Outer House being 'satisfied' on an application by the arbitrator himself that it is 'reasonable' for him to resign. That decision of the Outer House is final.

If an arbitrator therefore finds themself in an intolerable position created by the parties (say being required to take particular actions because the parties have come together to try to frustrate the conduct of the arbitration or have asked the arbitrator to do something contrary to the duties imposed), then it may be open to the arbitrator to tell the parties that they are minded to resign; and if thereafter they elect to do so, it might be best to use the provisions of rule 15(1)(e) and (2) and thereby obtain the authorisation of the Outer House. This may be the way to resolve, for example, an issue on money laundering etc raised under rule 11.

Note also that it is the arbitrator who has to make the application, and therefore incur the expenses of the application (petition procedure) before the arbitration judge. If opposed by the parties, this could result in considerable expenses (ie court costs). These will probably not be covered as part of the 'arbitration expenses' in terms of rules 59 and 60, unless specifically referred to in the arbitration agreement (which is unlikely). The judge, in his discretion, may however award expenses in favour of the arbitrator applicant either in terms of a discretion at common law exercised by a judge of the Outer House in connection with the award of expenses or under RCS 100.5(5) which states that he 'may make such order as is appropriate in the circumstances of the case'.

This rule is tied in with mandatory rule 16 to some extent as a resignation will bring the arbitrator's tenure to an end (see also above) but there may be liability for their actions as well as questions about whether they are entitled to any fees and expenses. By implication it is also tied in with mandatory rule 73 (immunity of tribunal etc). The arbitrator is immune for anything done or omitted to be done by them in the performance of their or the tribunal's functions, but this does not apply where there is any liability arising from an arbitrator's resignation (rule 73(2)(b)). The only exception to this is under rule 16(1)(c) where the Outer House makes an order in respect of that liability as arbitrator.

Arbitrators should take great care before resigning and may need to consider independent legal advice in appropriate cases, to ensure they understand the full consequences of their action.

Liability etc of arbitrator when tenure ends

Mandatory rule 16 covers the liability of the arbitrator when their tenure comes to an end. The rule gives wide powers to the Outer House in the following terms:

(1) Where an arbitrator's tenure ends, the Outer House may, on an application by any party or the arbitrator concerned, make such order as it thinks fit –
   (a) about the arbitrator's entitlement (if any) to fees and expenses,
   (b) about the repaying of fees or expenses already paid to the arbitrator,
   (c) where the arbitrator has resigned, about the arbitrator's liability in respect of acting as an arbitrator.
(2) The Outer House must, when considering whether to make an order in relation to an arbitrator who has resigned, have particular regard to whether the resignation was made in accordance with rule 15.
(3) The Outer House's determination of an application for an order is final.

Under this rule, when the arbitrator's tenure comes to an end, any party as well as the arbitrator can apply to the court for an order from the Outer House (as it thinks fit) in respect of the arbitrator's entitlement to fees and expenses due as well as those already paid, and, if the arbitrator has resigned, his liability (if any) following that resignation. Where the court is considering an order in connection with resignation it has to have regard to whether it was within the terms of rule 15.

Tenure ends

The tenure of the arbitrator or tribunal will end: (1) when the parties or a third party appointed and empowered by them removes or dismisses him or it; (2) when the court does so; (3) when the arbitrator or the tribunal resigns (in terms of the five grounds in rule 15); (4) on the death of the arbitrator; and (5) when the tribunal or arbitrator has performed all of its or his obligations under the arbitration agreement and has issued the final award, thereafter being *'functus officio'* (ie tenure is at an end).

Repayment

Repayment entails not just a repayment of fees and expenses but, where there was a removal or dismissal and the arbitrator or tribunal had taken a sum of money on deposit at the beginning of the arbitration as a security for their/its future fees, which is commonplace in international arbitrations, then that portion of security in respect of fees not earned would have to be returned or repaid.

Liability

The liability of the arbitrator is uncapped under this rule and thus the court could make an order imposing a considerable liability for expenses directly on the arbitrator. Indeed, the arbitrator could conceivably find that his liability exceeds any fees earned by him

In England and Wales there is the concept of wasted costs orders which have influenced this area of law in that jurisdiction. There is no identical concept in Scots law, although awards have been made against solicitors (but not counsel) for expenses occasioned by their own fault (see *Stewart v Stewart* 1984 SLT (Sh Ct) 58 and *Bremner v Bremner* 1988 SLT 844); but as the provision for uncapped liability is provided for in rule 16(1)(c), it should not be assumed that the Outer House would not use it. Arbitrators could seek indemnity from the parties in the arbitration agreement, but such indemnity is unlikely to assist if the arbitrator has behaved improperly in a material way.

Finality

As with other court provisions under the Act, there is a 'finality' provision to the rule to prevent using reclaiming motions (appeals) as a vehicle for engineering delay and preventing the smooth running of the arbitration.

Where the arbitrator is removed under rule 12 or the tribunal is dismissed under rule 13 application procedure, as the case may be, as the application proceeds by petition (RCS 100.5(1)), they should carefully consider whether they wish to enter the process, ie lodge answers to the petition. They should also in any event carefully consider whether they wish to enter the procedure before the court by note. This would seem sensible, given the potentially serious consequences of an order under rule 15, and the inability to appeal such a decision.

Under RCS 100.5(2), where there are proceedings depending before the court (ie proceedings have been raised already and are waiting for a decision before the court) then a party seeking to make an application has to proceed by note. That note would be the arbitrator's/tribunal's application in terms of rule 16 for an order in connection with their/its own liability. (It seems that the arbitrator would have a sufficient title and interest to make the application by note as its/their dismissal/removal and its/their interest in obtaining an order from the court.)

Reconstitution of tribunal

Where the arbitrator's tenure ends by any of the methods discussed above, default rule 17 provides a process for reconstituting the tribunal. Rule 17(1) effectively requires the use of the process set out in the original arbitration agreement, and, if that fails, the use of rules 6 and 7. It is submitted that this is sensible, and what one might assume to happen.

Rule 17 is a default rule, and so if, for example, institutional rules have been used which provide a different solution, it may be ousted. If the parties do choose to modify this rule or disapply it, they should be careful to make sure that some alternative provisions apply for reconstitution to permit the proceedings to continue.

The rule goes on to say that it is for the reconstituted tribunal to determine whether, and if so how much of, the work done by the previous tribunal should still be used. This includes awards, appointments or any acts. It will be seen in rules 24 and 25 below that the tribunal and the parties have general duties imposed on them by the rules to ensure that there is no unnecessary delay and expense, as well as the founding principles reflecting the same in s 1.

It should only be in extreme situations that a reconstituted tribunal elects to start again right from the beginning and to incur for the parties the inevitable cost and delay in doing so. The tribunal should try to make use of as much of what has already been done as is possible and try to provide continuity for the parties and, also, for the witnesses and experts who have not yet given evidence.

The previous tribunal, which has had the benefit of hearing evidence first hand, is in a much better position to assess the credibility and reliability of that evidence which may otherwise be lost to the reconstituted tribunal. This would not apply of course where witness statements as evidence had been agreed and lodged. That consideration in connection with credibility and reliability may inform the decision of the reconstituted tribunal whether to hear those portions of oral evidence again. If that is impossible then a transcript of the evidence should be used. If that is also unavailable, again that may influence the reconstituted tribunal as to whether to rehear the oral evidence.

Objection or appeal not removed

Note that a party can still object and appeal on any ground which arose *before* the tribunal made its decision.

Arbitrators nominated in arbitration agreements

Default rule 18 provides that, in the absence of the parties' agreement to do something different, any provision of the agreement which nominated an individual as a tribunal member has no effect when his tenure (under rule 9) comes to an end. Note, though, that any further disputes under the original agreement which are referred to arbitration could permit that individual to be appointed (note not reappointed) in respect of those disputes.

However, in relation to the initial arbitration, if the arbitration agreement does not contain any alternative, the question of reconstitution of the tribunal will fall to be dealt with as if there were no provision for appointment, and the parties will have to fall back on either any incorporated institutional rules, an arbitral appointments referee, or the court.

Immunity of tribunal etc

Mandatory rule 73 is in the part of the rules titled 'Miscellaneous', yet it contains the important rule both granting immunity to the tribunal, but also stating the circumstances in which such immunity may be lost. The rule reads as follows:

(1) Neither the tribunal nor any arbitrator is liable for anything done or omitted in the performance, or purported performance, of the tribunal's functions.
(2) This rule does not apply –
    (a) if the act or omission is shown to have been in bad faith, or
    (b) to any liability arising from an arbitrator's resignation (but see rule 16(1) (c)).
(3) This rule applies to any clerk, agent, employee or other person assisting the tribunal to perform its functions as it applies to the tribunal.

It should be noted that, as this is a mandatory rule, it is not possible to constitute a tribunal governed by the Act that has either greater, or lesser, immunity than that stated.

An obvious way to compromise the tribunal would be to allege misconduct or negligence (or breach of contract) coupled with a threat to raise an action of damages in the court. Thus, an unscrupulous claimant or respondent could derail the arbitration process leaving the arbitrators compromised by a pending action in the court. It would be a 'back-door' method of trying to get the decisions and awards of the tribunal reviewed or reopened. Such a course is prevented, in part, by giving the arbitrator and the tribunal limited immunity. It will also apply to those who assist the arbitrator, namely any 'clerk, agent, employee or other person assisting'.

The rule follows the 1996 Act s 29, there being no liability for 'anything done or omitted' in the performance or purported performance of the tribunal's functions. Similar provisions appear in other jurisdictions (eg International Arbitration Act 1974 s 28 in Australia).

If such immunity did not exist, it could be difficult to persuade individuals to act as arbitrators in high-value disputes, particularly with adversarial parties, if they risked personal ruin in the event of an actual or perceived error of judgment.

Finally, this provision is consistent with the immunity offered to others acting in a judicial or quasi-judicial capacity.

Limited immunity?

The immunity is limited because bad faith on the part of the tribunal will disapply the rule. This is consistent with general principles that a person should not be able to hide behind statutory or contractual immunities when they have acted dishonestly or otherwise in bad faith. Equally, subject to rule 16(1)(c) any liability arising from an arbitrator's resignation may also disapply the rule. 'Bad faith' is not defined. There have not been any decisions in respect of the 1996 Act s 29 that provide any guidance. There have been some earlier English cases under the common law, such as *Sutcliffe v Thackrah* [1974] AC 727 relating to construction contracts where it was held that an architect had to act in a 'fair and unbiased manner' in applying the contract. While not a case on arbitration, the analogy is clear, and genuine bias (as opposed to a party's perception of the same) could be argued as amounting to bad faith. It is suggested, however, that the courts would be likely to require that an arbitrator had acted in a way that was more than unwitting bias before depriving him of this statutory immunity. In *Arenson v Casson Beckman Rutley & Co* [1977] AC 405 it was held that a party acting as what might be thought of as a 'quasi-arbitrator', resolving a dispute but not formally appointed as arbitrator, still had immunity for his actions 'although not for fraud or collusion' (Lord Simon of Glaisdale considered that the 'essential prerequisite ... to claim immunity as an arbitrator is that, by the time the matter is submitted to him for decision, there should be a formulated dispute between at least two parties which the decision is required to resolve' (at 424). Note that the Scottish judges also expressed views on the immunity of the arbitrator. Lord Kilbrandon considered under the then common law, and the then applying Arbitration Acts that arbitrators did not have full immunity (at 431A–B and 432D) and Lord Fraser of Tullybelton considered that 'it may be that a person, even if formally appointed as an arbitrator, ought not in all cases to be accorded immunity' (at 442D).

In England, in the context of the tort of misfeasance in public office, or, as it is sometimes called, deliberate abuse of power, the term 'bad faith' has had a restricted meaning. Traditionally, a moral element has been an essential ingredient. Lack of good faith connotes either (a) malice in the sense of personal spite or a desire to injure for improper reasons, or (b) knowing that one does not actually have the power to make the decision in question. It remains to be seen whether 'bad faith' under the Arbitration Act

1996 and Construction Acts will be interpreted more widely by the courts, but it is suggested the courts should be cautious about removing immunity, save in the most egregious cases. (See also the discussion under rule 75 in connection with *Jones v Kaney* [2011] UKSC 13.)

If the arbitrator has resigned, then he is not protected from any claims in breach of contract. Rule 16(1)(c) provides that where an arbitrator has resigned, the Outer House may on an application by any party or the arbitrator concerned make such order as it thinks fit about the arbitrator's liability in respect of acting as an arbitrator. That could encompass an order from the court finding that he was entitled to relief from liability together with an order regarding his entitlement to fees and expenses. The parties could, of course, agree to extend the immunity on a contractual basis where the resignation was consensual. The wording of rule 73(2)(b) is slightly strange, in that the text says the immunity protection does not apply on resignation, but the text in brackets then seems to make this subject to rule 16(1)(c), but that provision merely gives the power to the court to make an order in such circumstances. It would, therefore, appear that, while a resigning arbitrator loses immunity as a result of their resignation, if the parties wish to pursue any claim against the arbitrator, this must be under rule 16, and requires a court order.

Accordingly, an arbitrator considering resignation should either get the parties to agree that they should continue to enjoy immunity, or, if they do resign, consider applying to the court to grant them immunity, rather than exposing themself to potentially ruinous litigation.

Immunity of appointing arbitral institution etc

Rule 74 provides immunity likewise for appointing institutions and will apply in all cases, being mandatory. Such immunity is standard in international arbitration, and it is unlikely that any institution would be involved in appointments without such protection. Similar considerations apply as to the reasons why immunity is granted to arbitrators, and there can be no attempt to reopen or revisit an arbitral award by alleging vicarious liability on the part of the appointing institution.

This has relevance as there may be situations (eg under rule 7 (failure of appointment procedure)) where the arbitrator is appointed by an appointing body (eg under s 24). Such body will actually appoint the arbitrator and thereby might be taken to be warranting or in some way vouching for the performance of the arbitrator or tribunal. This is in contrast to a nominating body which simply recommends names for the parties themselves to then appoint.

For similar considerations as under rule 73, as a matter of policy such institutions, including an arbitration appointments referee, other third parties, agents and employees as it applies to the referee or other third party, shall be immune.

Note that if the referee or institution were to have an administrative function beyond the appointment then rule 74 would not provide immunity for that function, although they might be treated as a 'person assisting the tribunal' under rule 73(3), and therefore obtain immunity under that provision.

Immunity of experts, witnesses and legal representatives

Mandatory rule 75 provides:

> Every person who participates in an arbitration as an expert, witness or legal representative has the same immunity in respect of acts or omissions as the person would have if the arbitration were civil proceedings.

The Explanatory Notes to the Arbitration (Scotland) Bill provide:

> As arbitration is a private version of judicial proceedings, the Bill places experts, witnesses and legal representatives in no more vulnerable a position if they are taking part in arbitration proceedings than if they are taking part in civil court proceedings.

Rule 75 makes mandatory provision for immunity for experts, witnesses and legal representatives in arbitration as traditionally set out in *Karling v Purdue* 2004 SLT 1067. When a witness gives evidence before a court, he will have immunity from any civil action in negligence in respect of the things said or done by him during those proceedings.

The position on immunity for expert witnesses is currently in flux, at least in England. The established law was the decision in *Stanton v Callaghan* [2000] QB 75, which provided blanket immunity. However, following the removal of blanket immunity for advocates under *Arthur J S Hall & Co v Simons* [2003] 3 WLR 543, the Supreme Court was asked to reconsider the extent of immunity in *Jones v Kaney* [2011] UKSC 13. The decision has, in effect, reversed the *Stanton v Callaghan* ruling. This was on the basis that the logic was the same as the removal of advocates' immunity, but two justices disagreed, and it must be said that it is not clear that the position of advocates and expert witnesses is necessarily identical. However, since the rule restricts the immunity of expert witnesses to that enjoyed in legal proceedings, this ruling would appear to restrict such immunity to protection from defamation proceedings (which is understood to remain). The Supreme Court stated that advocates had not been deterred by the decision in *Arthur J S Hall & Co v Simons*, but time will tell if the same is true for expert witnesses. It should be remembered that advocates appear in court for their living, whereas many expert witnesses only appear infrequently, and may well be deterred by the prospect of getting dragged into satellite litigation by losing parties. It is anticipated that they will either seek indemnities or insurance (or both), and the impact of this decision on the willingness of expert witnesses to participate in arbitration was uncertain, although the passage of time has suggested that the impact has not been as severe as had been feared. However, rule 75 only grants expert witnesses the same protection as they have in court proceedings, and *Jones v Kaney* would appear to have removed the bulk of such protection.

Interestingly, the position in Canada has not moved as far, and the Ontario courts ruled in *Reynolds v Kingston (City) Police Services Board* (2007), 84 OR (3d) 738 (Ont CA) that a party cannot sue their own expert witness. It is, therefore, presumably the case that nor can the other party, as there would, presumably, be no duty of care in tort/delict.

Loss of right to object

Mandatory rule 76 states:

(1) A party who participates in an arbitration without making a timeous objection on the ground –
  (a) that an arbitrator is ineligible to act as an arbitrator,
  (b) that an arbitrator is not impartial and independent,
  (c) that an arbitrator has not treated the parties fairly,
  (d) that the tribunal does not have jurisdiction,
  (e) that the arbitration has not been conducted in accordance with –
    (i) the arbitration agreement,
    (ii) these rules (in so far as they apply), or
    (iii) any other agreement by the parties relating to conduct of the arbitration,
  (f) that the arbitration has been affected by any other serious irregularity, may not raise the objection later before the tribunal or the court.
(2) An objection is timeous if it is made –
  (a) as soon as reasonably practicable after the circumstances giving rise to the ground for objection first arose,
  (b) by such later date as may be allowed by –
    (i) the arbitration agreement,
    (ii) these rules (in so far as they apply),
    (iii) the other party, or
  (c) where the tribunal considers that circumstances justify a later objection, by such later date as it may allow.
(3) This rule does not apply where the party shows that it did not object timeously because it –
  (a) did not know of the ground for objection, and
  (b) could not with reasonable diligence have discovered that ground.
(4) This rule does not allow a party to raise an objection which it is barred from raising for any reason other than failure to object timeously.

Rule 76 is directed towards supporting the founding principle in s 1(a) of avoiding unnecessary delay and expense, and preventing parties seeking to delay proceedings or avoid the effect of an award by objecting on the basis of lack of jurisdiction or irregularity but doing so late in the day.

The rules set up the concept of a 'timeous objection' defined in sub-paragraph (2) as being 'as soon as reasonably practicable'. Reasonable practicability is not defined in the Act, but guidance can be obtained from the English Court of Appeal decision in *Edwards v National Coal Board* [1949] 1 KB 704 which stated that 'reasonably practicable' is a narrower term than 'physically possible'. (*Edwards* was followed in *Austin Rover Group Ltd v HM Inspector of Factories* [1990] 1 AC 619, and thereafter in *Baker v Quantum Clothing Group* [2009] EWCA Civ 499, which was reversed by the Supreme Court [2011] UKSC 17, but not on this point.) For Scottish dicta see *Mains v Uniroyal Englebert Tyres Ltd (No 1)* 1995 SC 518 and *Beggs v Motherwell Bridge Fabricators Ltd* 1998 SLT 1215.

Those failing to take timeous action to object and participating lose the right to object. Making a timeous objection will be a question of fact.

Rule 76(1) makes the rule applicable to a party who 'participates in an arbitration'. One could envisage a party being involved in the arbitration nominally and thereby 'participating' within the meaning of the rule but thereafter losing the right to object. Thus, if a respondent had a problem with the arbitrator for one of the grounds in sub-paragraph (1) and did nothing about it, then it seems that from the time of the appointment of the arbitrator the clock would start ticking on the timeous element of any potential objection. If a party did not participate at all and the final award was made, that party would have lost the right to object as any objection at that point would not be timeous as it would not have been made 'as soon as reasonably practicable after the circumstances giving rise to the ground for objection first arose' – ie here the appointment. The right would be reacquired only if provision is made in the arbitration agreement or if allowed by the other party (or the rules) or where the tribunal itself considers that there is justification and allows a late objection under rule 76(2)(c) (cf *Rustal Trading Ltd v Gill & Duffus SA* [2001] 1 Lloyd's Rep 14).

It is suggested that a party should, therefore, raise any relevant issue as soon as it is or reasonably ought to be, aware of the objection and the rule will not apply only where that party shows (ie bearing the burden of proof) that it did not know of the ground for objection and could not with reasonable diligence have discovered the ground.

The time bar will not, however, fall where the party was unaware of the ground for the objection, and could not have become aware with reasonable diligence (rule 76(3)). It should be noted that this relates to lack of knowledge of the ground of objection, not, for example, failure to appreciate the legal position. It may, however, be that a tribunal would exercise its discretion under rule 76(2)(c) where an unrepresented party was unaware of the legal significance of a potential ground for objection. The Supreme Court decision in *David T Morrison & Co Ltd v ICL Plastics Ltd and others* [2014] UKSC 48 discussed earlier would seem to support this approach, albeit that it was concerned with the issue of limitation and prescription.

English provisions

Section 73 of the 1996 Act provides for objections being made 'forthwith' or 'within the prescribed period of time'. The body of case law on the meaning of 'forthwith' is considered not to be totally helpful to a definition or guidance towards 'reasonable practicability' under rule 76(2)(a).

Independence of arbitrator

Rule 77 is another important, mandatory, rule, which provides:

> For the purposes of these rules, an arbitrator is not independent in relation to an arbitration if –
> (a) the arbitrator's relationship with any party,
> (b) the arbitrator's financial or other commercial interests, or
> (c) anything else,
> gives rise to justifiable doubts as to the arbitrator's impartiality.

As already mentioned, it is rather strange that these very important mandatory provisions find themselves in the miscellaneous part at the back of the Rules, particularly as the themes such as impartiality run throughout the entire Act (eg rules 8(2), 10(2)(a), 12(a), 24(1)(a)). Indeed, there has been quite a bit of reference to them throughout the commentary. Rule 77 sets out when an arbitrator will not be taken to be independent in relation to an arbitration. The key is whether his relationship with any party, his financial or other commercial interests or anything else gives rise to justifiable doubts as to his impartiality.

It should be noted that it is not whether he actually *is* impartial, but whether the relationship gives rise to justifiable doubts. This issue has already been considered in relation to rule 24(1)(a) which introduces the obligation of impartiality, which these rules then explain.

It should be noted that rule 77 equates lack of impartiality with lack of independence. In reality an arbitrator could be impartial while not being independent, and could be partial while being independent. They are really distinct concepts, but the purpose of this rule is to prevent an arbitrator acting where there must be doubts as to whether he can make a fair decision between the parties. Accordingly, the distinction may be academic.

The decision in the leading case of *Halliburton* has already been discussed, and touches on the extent to which disclosure may remove concerns about impartiality and also that the test of whether the concerns justify removal is at the date of the first court hearing in an application to remove the arbitrator.

Consideration where arbitrator judged not to be impartial and independent

The consequences where an arbitrator fails to act independently or impartially, are set out in Default rule 78, which provides:

(1) This rule applies where –
- (a) an arbitrator is removed by the Outer House under rule 12 on the ground that the arbitrator is not impartial and independent,
- (b) the tribunal is dismissed by the Outer House under rule 13 on the ground that it has failed to comply with its duty to be impartial and independent, or
- (c) the tribunal's award (or any part of it) is returned to the tribunal for reconsideration, or is set aside, on either of those grounds (see rule 68).

(2) Where this rule applies, the Outer House must have particular regard to whether an arbitrator has complied with rule 8 when it is considering whether to make an order under rule 16(1) or 68(4) about –
- (a) the arbitrator's entitlement (if any) to fees or expenses,
- (b) repaying fees or expenses already paid to the arbitrator.

Mandatory rule 24 requires the arbitrator to act independently, and rule 77 lays down the requirements for such independence. Default rule 78 provides for what happens if an arbitrator has been removed under rule 12 for lack of impartiality and independence; when the entire tribunal has been dismissed under rule 13 for failure to comply with its duty to be impartial and independent; or where the tribunal's award (or part of it) is returned for reconsideration or is set aside or either under rule 68.

In those circumstances the Outer House (and only the Outer House) can consider whether an arbitrator has complied with rule 8 when considering whether to make an order under rules 16(1) or 68(4) about the arbitrator's entitlement to fees or expenses and whether there should be a repaying of fees or expenses already paid to an arbitrator.

It is interesting that rule 78 implies that there are two distinct tests to be passed, namely lack of independence *and* lack of impartiality, whereas rule 77 defines lack of independence as lack of impartiality. Rule 78 could, therefore, have merely used 'independence'.

It will be recalled that mandatory rule 8 provides that an arbitrator is under a duty to disclose any conflict of interest, rule 8(2) requiring the disclosure 'without delay'. Mandatory rule 16 deals with the liability of the arbitrator when his tenure is at an end and rule 16(1) in particular provides that the Outer House (and only the Outer House) may, on an application by any party or the arbitrator, make an order as it thinks fit about the arbitrator's entitlement to fees and expenses, about the repaying of fees or expenses already paid and, where the arbitrator has resigned, about the arbitrator's liability in respect of acting as an arbitrator.

Mandatory rule 68(4) provides that in a 'serious irregularity' appeal the Outer House may make such orders as it thinks fit about any arbitrator's entitlement (if any) to fees and expenses and such an order may provide for the repayment of fees or expenses already paid to the arbitrator. This is considered further later.

Death of arbitrator

Mandatory rule 79 makes the simple statement that 'An arbitrator's authority is personal and ceases on death.'

Sometimes in law rights vested in a party at death can transmit to his executors (ie those persons administering his estate). Mandatory rule 79 makes clear that an arbitrator's authority ceases on his death, which is consistent with the role of arbitrator being a personal appointment. The fact that bodies corporate cannot be arbitrators is also consistent with this approach. This is a mandatory rule and applies in all cases.

Rule 79 complements the following rule which provides for whether an arbitration agreement is discharged by the death of a party. It also complements the fact that an arbitrator must be a natural person under mandatory rule 3, and can no longer be, for example, a partnership.

This provision is similar (in part) to the 1996 Act s 26.

In long-running arbitrations with a single arbitrator, particularly when significant sums are involved, it is sometimes the practice to insure the arbitrator's life. While this does not solve the problem of having to restart the arbitration, it can, at least, prevent the duplication of costs. It is, however, a matter to be handled with some delicacy when asking the arbitrator to submit to an insurance medical …

Death of party

As a corollary to rule 79 above, on the death of one of the parties, default rule 80 provides that the arbitration agreement is not discharged and his interests in the arbitration will transmit to his executors or personal representatives on death. It will be for the executors or representatives then to determine whether to continue in it. If a party dies and is either intestate and his next of kin do not seek to be appointed as executors or personal representatives under the relevant law, or his executors named in a will decline to confirm to the estate of the deceased, the matter could still grind to a halt unless the other party sought appointment as an executor-creditor, and would then be in the slightly bizarre position of being on both sides of the arbitration.

This is a default rule, and it could be amended where, for example, the arbitration related to a matter which ceased to be relevant if a party died (for example, a personal right to occupy property).

While not on the issue of the death of a party, in England under the 1996 Act s 8 where a corporate body ceases to exist, any arbitration in which it was involved will fall (*Morris v Harris* [1927] AC 252) and cannot be revived, unless the company is restored to the register having been struck off rather than being dissolved.

The 2010 Act employs almost identical wording and a similar case for this might be argued here.

Likewise, presumably in bankruptcy if the trustee adopts a contract containing the agreement then it will be enforceable by or against him on the basis that he is stepping into the shoes of the bankrupt. If, however, the trustee declines to adopt the contract, then it will fall.

Unfair treatment

Default rule 81 is another brief provision, to the following effect:

> A tribunal (or arbitrator) who treats any party unfairly is, for the purposes of these rules, to be deemed not to have treated the parties fairly.

Default rule 81 provides that, subject to the agreement of the parties, the unfair treatment of any party by the tribunal will be deemed to be unfair treatment of the parties which may resonate with the other provisions in the Act. It is difficult to see why this is a default rule, as the only reason for a party not to want it included would seem to be if it was certain it was only the other party who would be treated unfairly. Further, since treating one party unfairly would seem likely to amount to evidence of impartiality, it is difficult to see why this rule is required at all.

Rules applicable to umpires

Mandatory rule 82 clarifies the application of certain specific rules to umpires. Sub-paragraph (2) clarifies that the parties cannot choose to disapply mandatory rules in relation to umpires, but can modify or disapply the default rules. It is suggested that the use of umpires is likely to be limited under the present legislation, but this rules clarifies the position should their use be required.

Formal communications

Default rule 83 provides for the mundane but often crucially important area of the means of intimating certain formal notices or documents under the arbitration agreement or in the course of arbitral proceedings, in the event that this is not already agreed between the parties.

Rule 83(1) provides the definition for 'formal communication'; sub-paragraph (2) requires it to be in writing; sub-paragraph (3) makes provision for the delivery of a formal communication, but seems to assume that all such communications will take place within the UK (eg the reference to first class mail, and the implied assumption that letters will arrive the next day); and rule 83(4) provides that any electronic communication will be treated as being in writing only if it gets to its destination in a readable state and can be used as a record. This is fine in practice, but how can a sender prove, for example, that a fax or email received by the other party was in a readable form? This provision appears not to take full account of current practices in communications, and might also have benefited from including a definition of 'writing', failing which the general law will apply to the interpretation of this word.

It makes sense to agree the method for serving notices, and it may be advisable to amend this default rule to reflect the method by which the parties communicate, and the realities, particularly where the communications will be international, and where the usual mode of communication is by email.

While rule 83 requires communications to be in writing, it does not say they should be signed (whereas the 1996 Act specifically provides that no signature is required – s 5(2)(a)). This is, however, good practice for formal communications, and may give rise to a further requirement to agree methods of verified electronic signatures that may be acceptable, or whether faxed or scanned copies of signed documents will be enough. As with our understanding of what 'written' means, the law on what constitutes a 'signature' is also developing. As an example, the recent English case of *Neocleous and another v Rees* [2019] EWHC 2462 (Ch) mentioned above, it was held that an email sign off could constitute a signature for the purposes of a property transaction, where the name in the sign off was clearly intended to identify an individual and indicate their consent to the contents of the email.

Rule 83(5) provides for where formal communication is to be deemed to have been made, given or served; rule 83(6) provides that where it is not reasonably practicable for formal communication to be made, given or served, the arbitrator will have the power to determine that another means of intimation is used or may dispense with intimation which will allow the arbitrator to expedite the process while also reducing court involvement.

Specific provision for review by the court on this matter has not been made but in some cases the general provisions on challenging the decision of an arbitrator might be relevant.

Rule 83(7) means that the rule only applies to documents which are being produced under the arbitration agreement or as part of the arbitration proceedings. If the documents relate to proceedings of the court, then the rules of court in relation to delivery and service of documents will apply.

Notices, and the method of communicating them to the other party, are important – much can depend on them. In *Muir Construction Ltd v Hambly Ltd* 1990 SLT 830 the court held that a notice (in this case of termination) was invalid because it had been delivered by hand, and not by registered or recorded delivery post as required in the contract. In *Ben Cleuch Estates Ltd v Scottish Enterprise* [2008] CSIH 1, 2008 SC 252 a key issue related to the service of a notice in the exercise of a break option in a commercial lease. The tenant was held not to have validly exercised the option when it had served the notice on the landlord's agents (a surveyors' firm) and not at the address of the landlord which was required under the lease. There is, however, a competing Inner House decision on this point in *Hoe International Ltd v Andersen* [2017] CSIH 9, where the court held that contractual notices ought to be construed in the manner of a reasonable commercial person. The interpretation of the contractual requirements for the sending of a valid notice also required to be determined in accordance with the ordinary principles of contractual construction. The court held there is a requirement for a purposive construction and held that a court ought to be slow to adopt a strict approach to contractual requirements governing the sending of notices.

Periods of time

Default rule 84 concludes the rules, and provides as follows:

> Periods of time are to be calculated for the purposes of an arbitration as follows –
> (a) where any act requires to be done within a specified period after or from a specified date or event, the period begins immediately after that date or, as the case may be, the date of that event, and
> (b) where the period is a period of 7 days or less, the following days are to be ignored –
>   (i)   Saturdays and Sundays, and
>   (ii) any public holidays in the place where the act concerned is to be done.

The Explanatory Notes to the Arbitration (Scotland) Bill stated that this rule 'provides default provisions for calculating time periods in the absence of agreement between the parties'.

JURISDICTION OF TRIBUNAL (PART 2)

Jurisdiction of the tribunal

Mandatory rule 19 provides for the tribunal to make a ruling in connection with its own jurisdiction. This is a common feature in *lex arbitri* and institutional rules in global practice. By virtue of the fact that an arbitral tribunal is not a court in the conventional sense, there are no 'conventional' rules as to whether it, as a body, has jurisdiction to determine any dispute being placed before it. Without jurisdiction, it would not be empowered to determine the dispute between the parties.

This rule provides for a clear power for the arbitrator to decide their own jurisdiction as part of the international doctrine of *'competence/competence'*. This has a relationship with 'separability' (see section 5). Both are directed towards determining the tribunal's jurisdiction. With separability, the existence and operability of the main contract does not affect the validity of the arbitration agreement and, indeed, a question of the validity of the arbitration agreement may itself be the subject of the arbitration. With *'competence/competence'* the tribunal is empowered to determine whether the arbitration agreement itself is valid and to rule on its own jurisdiction (mandatory rule 9(a)) and it will be important that the tribunal has been constituted in accordance with the arbitration agreement (rule 19(b)).

The other key element of the rule is that, as the Explanatory Notes comment (rule 19(c)), 'The extent of an arbitrator's jurisdiction and his or her power to decide his or her own jurisdiction is important in arbitration since it determines exactly what issues the arbitrator is to decide.'

One might question why this is a mandatory rule as another doctrine of international arbitration – that of party autonomy – holds that the parties should be free to determine how their dispute should be decided, including whether their tribunal should have the power in the first place. It is suggested that this is not as controversial as it might first appear, since the parties must have actually created the tribunal by some form of agreement, and, therefore, it makes sense to allow the body thus created to decide whether what is before it is a matter envisaged by that agreement. The background to making this mandatory was that at common law, as the Scottish Government Policy Memorandum noted, there was 'uncertainty about the extent to which an arbitrator can rule on his or her own jurisdiction [leading] arbitrators to be cautious for fear of not having immunity in relation to a decision on jurisdiction. In those circumstances arbitrators may decline to rule on their own jurisdiction, which may result in unnecessary referrals to the courts' (para 135) and by making the power mandatory, Scots law was brought 'into line with international arbitral practice by providing a clear power for the arbitrator to decide his or her own jurisdiction'.

As a mandatory provision it was designed deliberately to prevent the parties excluding the arbitrator from ruling on jurisdiction, which was thought would 'save a great deal of time and therefore expense' (Policy Memorandum para 136).

Any early challenge to jurisdiction will likely be in terms of this rule and the tribunal may either dispose of it at that point or postpone it to a later award (see rule 20).

Competence/competence generally

This doctrine of *competence/competence* is an internationally accepted principle which is incorporated into the Scottish provisions so that arbitrators are competent to determine whether they actually have the power to decide the issue before them (their 'competence').

It is not mandatory in all systems of arbitration law and does not necessarily apply in other jurisdictions. A criticism often voiced of this is that the arbitrators will likely decide that they have jurisdiction and they do not wish to voluntarily remove themselves from a potentially remunerative appointment. That is perhaps unfair, and the contrary view is that the parties have appointed the tribunal to determine *all* aspects of the dispute arising from the contract etc, including the jurisdictional ones, and so have impliedly empowered the tribunal in any event. As stated above, the tribunal is a creature that comes into existence only as a result of a contractual decision by the parties, and at least one of them must have referred the issue to arbitration – it is not a case of seeking to seize jurisdiction over a matter against the wishes of the parties.

In some jurisdictions, competence/competence is deeply rooted. In others it is recognised, but left to the parties to determine whether the tribunal should be vested with the power.

The position in England under the Arbitration Act 1996 s 30 is that the tribunal will have the power to determine its own jurisdiction but a final decision on substantive jurisdiction will be for the courts (*Dallah Real Estate & Tourism Co v Ministry of Religious Affairs of the Government of Pakistan* [2010] UKSC 46). The section also leaves open the possibility that the parties can agree that the tribunal should not and will not decide questions of its own jurisdiction.

Where that is not agreed, the English courts have held that s 30 likely contains an exhaustive definition of jurisdictional matters (*Union Marine Classification Services LLC v Comoros* [2015] EWHC 508 (Comm); *C v D1* [2015] EWHC 2126 (Comm)).

In *Excalibur Ventures LLC v Texas Keystone Inc* [2011] EWHC 1624 (Comm), the English courts declined to allow the New York arbitrators to determine whether they had jurisdiction, but this was at least in part because the claimants had also started simultaneous court proceedings in England and sought injunctive relief, which course was inconsistent with their claim that an arbitration agreement existed with the defendants.

The English courts have also held that the exercise of determining whether a dispute falls within an arbitration clause requires a careful and commercially minded construction (*AmTrust Europe Ltd v Trust Risk Group SpA* [2015] EWCA Civ 437) and a broad and purposive construction should be followed. Some guidance on the issue in England and Wales can be found in the Chartered Institute of Arbitrators: Guidelines for Arbitrators dealing with Jurisdictional Problems (2011).

Some jurisdictions do not recognise the doctrine at all (eg law of the People's Republic of China).

It will be recalled that the court cannot interfere with the arbitration unless certain grounds have been established (see section 10). This is because of the principle of party autonomy – as explained above, it is for the parties to decide how to resolve their dispute as well as the principle that the court should not get involved in that unless invited to do so or, in the interests of justice, has to do so.

Thus, where there is a jurisdictional point, in the first instance the tribunal is permitted to decide its own jurisdiction. The court will only become involved if invited to do so by the tribunal or the parties or where there is a valid appeal under the limited grounds set out in the Act and the Rules. There is probably one exception to that and that is where a court, on an application to sist legal proceedings under s 10, considers that the whole arbitration agreement is void, inoperative or incapable of being performed (s 10(1)(e)). If the court has made that determination already, then the tribunal will have to accept that it is without jurisdiction and therefore *functus officio* and not able to make any decision in relation to its own jurisdiction.

Types of challenge

There are many types of challenge, but common ones include a challenge to the constitution of the tribunal in respect of some flaw or error in the principal contract which contained the dispute resolution clause setting up the arbitral tribunal. (As noted above, s 5 arbitration agreement clauses are 'severable' from the main contract: see *dicta* in *Vee Networks Ltd v Econet Wireless Ltd* [2005] 1 Lloyd's Rep 192.)

Other challenges include that one party did not enter into the main contract in the first place (eg did not have power or capacity to do so), or it was misled and induced to contract by a misrepresentation, or that it was in error as to the key terms when it entered the contract and thus should not be held to it, etc. Another frequent challenge is that the other party has in some way departed from the agreement to arbitrate by its actings, thus setting up, for example, a plea of personal bar in law (similar to English estoppel), or that the actings demonstrate that the other party has 'acquiesced' in not going to arbitration or has 'waived' its right to insist in arbitration.

There may also be challenges based on the legal doctrine of 'frustration', or a contractual *force majeure* event beyond control of the parties which suspends or extinguishes the obligations of the parties under the contract, including the obligation to arbitrate any dispute.

Another situation is where Party A assigns his rights under a contract with Party B in favour of Party C. An issue can arise as to whether C is entitled to or bound by the arbitration agreement originally constituted between A and B. The English courts have held that where an arbitration agreement is contained within a contract and a person who claimed to be an assignee of that contract wishes to arbitrate a claim under the contract, that is a dispute as to whether there was a valid arbitration agreement within the meaning of s 30 and s 67 (*A v B* [2016] EWHC 3003 (Comm)).

Issues therefore can arise as to whether the assignee has the right to arbitrate. In *Cockett Marine Oil DMCC v ING Bank NV and another* [2019] EWHC 1533 (Comm), the claimants had entered a supply contract with the second defendants, which were made by way of an exchange of emails. The claim was assigned to a third-party bank. A dispute arose in respect of the agreement and the second defendants claimed payment of the price of the bunkers. An arbitration was commenced by them and the bank as assignee.

In the arbitration, the tribunal's jurisdiction was challenged by the claimants, who argued that an arbitration agreement had not been incorporated into the contracts and that the assignment of claims to the bank was invalid. The court confirmed that the tribunal's ruling that the contracts included the second defendants' standard terms and conditions, which contained a London arbitration clause, was correct. Therefore, the assignment was valid, with the result that the tribunal had had jurisdiction to determine claims brought by the assignee.

As with assignation, so with novation. Care should be taken where existing obligations (including arbitration agreements) are novated into a new contract. Failure by a party to challenge a tribunal's jurisdiction in connection with the pre-novated arbitration provisions may result in that right being lost (*C v D1* [2015] EWHC 2126 (Comm)).

Lastly in this list of examples, contracts are often interrelated and for the sake of economy and brevity sometimes clauses are inserted into one contract and 'incorporated by reference' into another. The English courts have held that where there are multiple related agreements, the presumption that the parties did not intend disputes to be determined by different tribunals might apply (*Fiona Trust & Holding Corpn v Privalov* [2007] UKHL 40); and where there are inconsistent arbitration agreements, it might be necessary to identify the centre of gravity and determine which agreement lay at the commercial centre of the transaction (*UBS AG v HSH Nordbank AG* [2009] EWCA Civ 585).

With arbitration clauses, disputes can arise where the clause is in one contract and has been omitted in another or where the incorporation is flawed in some way. The English courts have held that there are no special rules about the incorporation of an arbitration clause in a contract. In *Habas Sinai Ve Tibbi Gazlar Isthisal Endustri AS v Sometal Sal* [2010] EWHC 29 (Comm), an English case involving a Turkish dispute, it was held that an arbitration clause had been validly incorporated into a contract when it had been signed by agents who had ostensible authority to enter the contract, notwithstanding the principal's insistence on arbitration in Turkey. The contract did not refer to an arbitration clause but said that 'all the rest will be the same as our previous contracts'. One party asserted this meant that arbitration under the London Court of International Arbitration ('LCIA') Rules was incorporated. Unfortunately, while LCIA was referred to in the earlier contracts, so were UNCITRAL and the Court of Arbitration in Istanbul. On the facts, the court held that the LCIA Rules had been validly incorporated as the agents who arranged for that had jurisdiction, and that the parties had submitted to arbitration. This can be important for how any disputes arising might be determined, as to whether the arbitration provisions are carried through from another contract (sometimes even without reference to arbitration) or whether the disputes must properly be litigated. (See for another example *Hiscox Dedicated Corporate Member Ltd v Weyerhaeuser Co* [2019] EWHC 2671 (Comm).)

What if an agreement has terminated the commercial relationship created by an earlier agreement? The English courts have held that the presumption that the parties did not intend disputes to be determined by different tribunals might apply with 'particular potency' (*Monde Petroleum SA v Westernzagros Ltd* [2015] EWHC 67 (Comm)).

In making decisions in relation to such points, it is to be remembered that the law to be applied is not necessarily Scots law. It will depend on the law governing the contract or the law governing the creation of the contract (including questions of capacity and formality) or the law the parties agreed would cover arbitrability of their disputes. If the issue is not arbitrable under Scots law, then it would seem that the tribunal could not decide the point, since it cannot give itself power to arbitrate something which Scots law says is incapable of being arbitrated. (See also the commentary to s 30 above.)

'May rule'?

It is suggested that the use of 'may' (ie that it is discretionary) should be read as meaning that when the parties challenge the jurisdiction the tribunal can make this ruling; or, the tribunal could, of course, decline to rule on the point at the point of challenge and reserve the question to the final award on the merits.

Power to 'rule' on jurisdiction only

The arbitral tribunal may rule on whether there is a valid arbitration agreement (rule 19(a)); whether the tribunal is properly constituted (rule 19(b)); and what matters have been submitted to arbitration in accordance with the arbitration agreement (rule 19(c)). Note that this is not necessarily a final jurisdictional determination as it is always open to a party later to challenge an award on the basis that the tribunal did not have jurisdiction. The question of substantive jurisdiction could still be finally disposed of at that later stage by the court in terms of mandatory rule 67 which gives the court the power to confirm the award or vary/set aside the award in whole or in part. (See the discussion in the commentary to rule 67 below.)

The rationale for the wording of this rule was that the previous law considered that this power was only exercised to decide the matter on a *preliminary* basis and the ultimate determination was always to be made by the court (cf the position in England and Wales). This caused uncertainty with tribunals as to the extent to which they could rule on jurisdiction, which in turn, in the words of the Policy Memorandum, 'led arbitrators to be cautious for fear of not having immunity in relation to a decision on jurisdiction' (para 135). (See also comments above about 'due process paranoia'.) The result was that there were many unnecessary referrals to the courts.

It is also presumably for this reason, or at least in contemplation of this issue, that the Act makes provision for the parties to refer a point of jurisdiction to the Outer House for determination under rule 22 (if they have agreed to include it – it is a default rule) and the procedure for doing so is provided for in mandatory rule 23.

What does the tribunal do if there is no jurisdiction?

The tribunal may decide that, for example, the respondent is not a party to the arbitration agreement. What does it do then? Mandatory rule 20(3) is examined below but basically there will be no valid arbitration agreement as there is no agreement that that party would be subject to its jurisdiction. At the same time the claimant has his case prepared and presented. The tribunal should be careful not to express any view on the merits of the case, eg as to liability or quantum, or uphold or dismiss any aspect of the claim. It should simply issue its determination or ruling that there is no substantive jurisdiction. It would be good practice to also issue reasons for that ruling. For an example in England, see *LG Caltex Gas Co v China National Petroleum Corpn* [2001] EWCA Civ 788.

Matters submitted to the arbitration

The tribunal is empowered to determine the extent or scope of the subject that has referred to it for a decision (see guidance in the English case of *Al Naimi v Islamic Press Agency Inc* [2000] 1 Lloyd's Rep 522) and whether the matter has been brought to the arbitration in the correct manner (*Lafarge (Aggregates) Ltd v London Borough of Newham* [2005] EWHC 1337 (Comm)). In respect of rule 19(c), the matters submitted to the arbitration as *per* the agreement, the jurisdiction of the tribunal depends on the scope of the arbitration agreement. The tribunal will have to make a determination on a true construction of the arbitration agreement. Thus, for example, if there is a claim and a counterclaim as set-off/compensation, it is for the tribunal to decide whether it has jurisdiction to determine all parts of the dispute between the parties.

Tribunal properly constituted (rule 19(b))

Whether the tribunal is properly constituted would include requirements imposed by the Act, eg rule 4 (eligibility to act); rule 5 (number of arbitrators); rule 6 (method of appointment), rule 10(2)(iii) (whether it has the qualifications required etc); as well as the parties' express agreement and any default or other incorporated provisions applying (eg institutional requirements). For an example, see the English case of *Minermet SpA Milan v Luckyfield Shipping Corpn* [2004] 2 Lloyd's Rep 348.

Objections to the tribunal's jurisdiction

Mandatory rule 20 provides the mechanism for 'a party' to make an objection to the tribunal about the jurisdiction of the tribunal itself (perhaps on one of the grounds mentioned above). The rule refers to 'any party' (r 20(1)), which is in keeping with the interpretation of the rest of the Act. This must be deemed to mean the 'parties to the arbitration' and whilst one could envisage the tribunal raising an issue of jurisdiction this rule would not apply in the sense of objection.

The party is given the power to 'object', on the basis that it lacks jurisdiction, or that it has exceeded its jurisdiction.

It is also open to a party to bring its 'objection' to the tribunal's jurisdiction directly to the Outer House to determine any question as to the tribunal's jurisdiction using default rule 22 (if not disapplied) thus bypassing the tribunal if the parties are in agreement or if the tribunal consents. See comments below and the commentary to that rule as to the timing and order of such a challenge.

Rule 20 is clearly influenced by the Model Law Art 16(2) and (3) and the 1996 Act s 31 (cf rule 20(2) and (4) with Art 16(2) and (3) of the Model Law and s 31(4) of the 1996 Act).

One clear difference though is in connection with the tribunal's response to the objection. At this point rule 20 should be noted, that if the tribunal considers that the objection is well founded and it has no jurisdiction, or has exceeded its jurisdiction, it *must* end the arbitration so far as it relates to a matter over which it has ruled that it does not have jurisdiction, whether because no such jurisdiction existed at all, or because such jurisdiction as does exist has been exceeded (rule 20(2)). The 1996 Act and the Model Law both provide power to the tribunal to make an award on jurisdiction at that time or to postpone or delay it to the award on the merits at the end of proceedings as does rule 20(4).

Making an objection

The objection under this rule is made to the tribunal itself rather than to a court, thus avoiding spurious delaying objections being made to the latter (which now can be made only after the final award or after the tribunal rules on the objection under this rule) by parties in agreement or with the tribunal's consent (mandatory rule 23).

'May'

The permissive 'may' again appears. While this makes clear that a party is not compelled to object, it raises a question as to whether a failure to object to jurisdiction of the tribunal be later considered as a waiver of the right to raise such an objection? The timing provisions in rule 20(2) go a long way to resolving this matter, but the possibility of later challenges under rule 20(2)(b) (albeit prior to any award – see the final sentence of rule 20(2) and cf *Five Oceans Salvage Ltd v Wenzhou Timber Group Co* [2011] EWHC 3282 (Comm)) might be argued as opening up the ability to 'keep the powder dry' on such an objection. It must be considered best practice for a party with a *bona fide* objection to jurisdiction, within its knowledge, to make it timeously to avoid issues later under rule 76 and that must mean, in the words of the rule 20(2)(a) 'before, or as soon as is reasonably practicable after, the matter to which the objection relates is first raised in the arbitration'.

In arbitral practice generally, a right to object to the jurisdiction of the tribunal is *not* normally held to have been waived or given up just because that party participated in the appointment process (cf 1996 Act s 31(2)). As matters progress, the party may come to the view that the tribunal does not, in fact, have the jurisdiction that had been assumed and will therefore have to object as soon as 'reasonably practicable' after coming to this conclusion. On the other hand, if that party considers that the tribunal has no jurisdiction right from the start (eg that the whole contract is void) then that objection should be made immediately.

The arbitrator's appointment can be challenged under default rule 10 but only if they have not been impartial, independent, not treated the parties fairly or the arbitrator does not have a qualification which the parties agreed upon. These issues do not go to the question of jurisdiction.

What about the 'non-participating party', ie the party which refuses to have anything to do with the process? That party will still retain a right to challenge under a rule 67 appeal even though the challenge was not made at the start or when reasonably practicable, but note that institutional rules may restrict this, such as LCIA 2020 article 23.3 where there can be no objection to jurisdiction later than the time for the statement of defence.

Timing of the objection

There is an implicit, albeit somewhat elastic, time element for successful challenge – that of 'as soon as reasonably practicable', ie as soon as is practicable after first raised or later if the tribunal permits it as justified according to the circumstances. (Cf in England and Wales, and the comments of the High Court in *Republic of Serbia v ImageSat International NV* [2009] EWHC 2853 (Comm).)

In law, the test of reasonable practicability can be found in *Edwards v National Coal Board* [1949] 1 KB 704 at 712 *per* Asquith LJ, endorsed by Lord Reid in *Marshall v Gotham* [1954] AC 360 at 373. See also the discussion above under the commentary to rule 20 and below in relation to rule 76. The end stop for objection is up until the date of the final award.

This is a different approach from s 31(1) of the 1996 Act which provides that 'An objection that the arbitral tribunal lacks substantive jurisdiction at the outset of the proceedings must be raised by a party not later than the time he takes the first step in the proceedings to contest the merits of any matter in relation to which he challenges the tribunal's jurisdiction.'

It also varies from Art 16(2) of the Model Law which provides that 'a plea that the arbitral tribunal does not have jurisdiction shall be raised not later than the submission of the statement of defence.' (Although power is given to admit a later plea if it considers the delay justified.) Note that the Model Law also limits the time for making an objection to a particular stage in the procedure.

Objection to the tribunal

The right of objection to the 'tribunal' suggests that the tribunal has already been appointed and established and is 'extant' as opposed to being 'about to be created' or 'appointed'. Accordingly, the objection can only come *after* the tribunal has been constituted.

Options open to the tribunal

As noted above, if the objection to jurisdiction (in whole or in part) is upheld, then the arbitration in connection with it *must* end, either completely, or in relation to the part in respect of which the objection has been upheld. There is no definition of 'end' (the Explanatory Notes mention 'terminate') but it must mean that the tribunal is *functus officio* and no longer has the power vested in it by virtue of the agreement. Presumably before it 'ends' the arbitration, the tribunal should '"set-aside" any provisional or part awards already made in so far as the award relates to such a matter'.

Any such orders or awards would seem generally to be void *ab initio* for lack of jurisdiction, but the provision to set them aside is a sensible practical provision. It also allows for the unlikely possibility that the tribunal did have jurisdiction (and the awards etc were valid) but that this is no longer the case, making the awards voidable rather than void. It is, presumably, to be understood that any purported effect they may have had in the past is at an end, and any money paid under an interim award would have to be returned. There is no mention as to what would happen in relation to interest on such sums, but one could envisage arguments based on 'error', and liability might turn on the extent to which one or both of the parties was genuinely, albeit mistakenly, of the opinion that jurisdiction existed.

Like the English and Model Law procedures the tribunal can postpone this by delaying the ruling until it makes an award on the merits which then includes that ruling on jurisdiction (rule 20(4)(b)) or it can rule on the objection independently. However, where the parties agree on which course to take, they can force the tribunal's hand and it must take that course (similar to Model Law and the 1996 Act).

When can the arbitrator make a determination?

The English courts have held that an arbitrator is entitled to make the determination on jurisdiction right at the outset: *Aoot Kalmneft JSC v Glencore*

International AG [2001] 2 All ER (Comm) 577. In that case, the court held it was not appropriate to challenge a decision made pursuant to the 1996 Act s 31(4) by way of an application under s 67 of that Act (similar to the provisions in rule 67). Once a ruling had been made under s 31(4), a challenge under s 67 could only be made in relation to the arbitrator's conclusion that he had jurisdiction or not. It held that there was no power to set aside a ruling on the ground that it would be more appropriate to reconsider the issue with the benefit of more evidence. The court there took account of the underlying philosophy of the Arbitration Act 1996 and its principles of party autonomy and finality of awards, and of the public policy factor of avoiding delays, while making allowance for the potential inexperience of foreign parties in dealing with English arbitration procedures. The Courts have also highlighted that there are material differences between the English Civil Procedure Rules (CPR) and the Arbitration Act and its underlying philosophy (see for example *Merthyr (South Wales) Ltd v Cwmbargoed Estates Ltd* [2019] EWHC 704 (Ch)).

This is a point to consider, and, while prompt action is desirable, arbitrators (and the courts) will, presumably, allow some leeway where it has been difficult for a party to ascertain whether a jurisdictional point exists or not.

Therefore, considerations likely to be relevant to applications for extension of time might include:

- the extent of the delay;
- whether a party had acted reasonably in letting a time limit expire and accruing subsequent delay;
- whether the respondent to the application or the arbitrator had caused or contributed to the delay;
- whether irremediable prejudice would be caused to the respondent because of delay if the application was permitted to proceed;
- whether the arbitration had continued in the interim and, if so, what impact determination of the application would have upon it;
- the strength of the application, and whether, in all the circumstances, it would be unfair to refuse the applicant the opportunity of a determination.

Provisional, part and final awards and the operation of the arbitral proceedings

As the tribunal establishes its jurisdiction and begins the arbitration process, it may determine to make provisional awards (if empowered) or part awards before making its final award after ventilation of the merits.

'Provisional awards' are defined and dealt with in default rule 53 (note there will thus only be power to make a 'provisional award' if the parties have not modified or disapplied this rule). A 'provisional award' is an award 'granting any relief on a provisional basis which [the tribunal] has the power to grant permanently' (rule 53).

'Part awards' are dealt with in mandatory rule 54. These are awards which decide 'some (but not all) of the matters which the tribunal is to decide in the arbitration' (rule 54(2)). The rationale is obviously that if the tribunal did not have the jurisdiction in the first place it should recall or set aside the awards it has made so far in the proceedings. There is no mention of final award – because the objection has to precede a final award and also there are procedures under mandatory rule 67 in Part 8.

There is no definition of 'award' nor of 'final award'. Presumably this is intended so as to give the widest definition as to what constitutes an 'award'.

In England, the decision in *Ranko v Antarctic Maritime SA* (1998) LMLN 492 held that a letter from an arbitrator, finding and declaring that there was a contract between parties which included a written arbitration agreement and that all disputes under the contract had been referred to arbitration, was an award as to the arbitrator's substantive jurisdiction even though it did not comply with the requirements of s 52 in that it did not state the seat of the arbitration or the arbitrator's reasons.

Time limits

In the Model Law, Art 16 requires the tribunal to make a ruling, and it is final unless challenged within 30 days. Under the 1996 Act, appeals must be brought within 28 days (ss 67(1) and 70(3)) unless there is reasonable excuse (see eg *PEC Ltd v Asia Golden Rice Ltd* [2012] EWHC 846 (Comm)). Under the 2010 Act, a party may appeal to the Outer House (see mandatory rule 21) 'no later than 14 days after the tribunal's decision on an objection under rule 20' (ie an objection on jurisdiction).

Conflicts between tribunal and parties

Rule 20(4) provides for a situation whereby the parties acting in concert can 'control' the tribunal with the wording 'but, where the parties agree which of these courses the tribunal should take, the tribunal must proceed accordingly'.

Feasibly a tribunal could find itself in conflict with its obligations under mandatory rule 24 (general duty of tribunal) as it would be wary of making any order conflicting with the joint will of the parties.

It is, of course, implicit that the parties cannot order the tribunal to do something unlawful. While this is an unexceptional proposition, the wide range of activities which may, for example, breach the various money laundering regulations could lead to conflict if the tribunal thought it was being asked to give a cloak of arbitral respectability to an otherwise problematic transaction.

What does 'setting aside' mean?

Setting aside is not defined in the Act. It does not appear in other provisions and there are no relevant notes. Normally if a court or tribunal 'sets something aside', this means that it puts it literally to one side (and therefore gives it no effect) for the purposes of that hearing or that court action. This contrasts with the concept of 'reduction', which is a remedy that is available only in the Court of Session whereby the court determines that something (decision, judgment, decree, etc) should be quashed as if it was never in existence.

If something is 'set aside' it still exists – it just has no effect for those present proceedings. The term is not without difficulty and setting aside *ope exceptionis* in court proceedings, 'setting aside' in arbitral proceedings and reduction in Court of Session proceedings are not always clearly understood. (See Lord Clarke's decision in *Vaughan Engineering Ltd v Hinkin and Frewin* 2003 SLT 428 for a helpful discussion of the different concepts and the meaning of setting aside '*ope exceptionis*'.)

In the context of arbitration proceedings, one could argue that the setting aside is tantamount to or has the equivalent effect of reduction. See the *obiter* comments of Lord Glennie in *SGL Carbon Fibres Ltd v RBG Ltd* [2011] CSOH 62 at para [47]: 'To my mind the concept of a decision which is binding but unenforceable, having been set aside but not reduced, is, in this context at least, conceptually nonsensical.'

Further, 'setting aside or varying a judgment' is also part of *English* court procedure (Civil Procedure Rules (SI 1998/3132) Part 13), and the language appears to have crept into the Act.

Entertaining a late objection

It is clear that the tribunal may entertain a late objection if it considers that circumstances justify it. If 'justified' in the discretion of the tribunal it may permit the objection by such later time as it shall 'allow'.

It follows that the tribunal is vested with a discretion to determine late objections to jurisdiction (which will be late by virtue of being beyond the 'as soon as reasonably practicable' period). So, it can accept or reject those circumstances as justification and it is suggested that this exercise of discretion would not be appealable to the Outer House, since it is, as stated, a discretion. (That is not to say that where a party submits that a timeous objection *has* been made in terms of the practicability argument, the tribunal's decision on that aspect may not still be subject to review by the court.)

Under s 31(2) of the 1996 Act, any objection should be made 'as soon as possible after the matter alleged to be beyond its jurisdiction is raised', although again it may admit a later objection if the delay is 'justified' (s 31(3) and see also the comments of the court in *Republic of Serbia v ImageSat International NV* [2009] EWHC 2853 (Comm)).

Losing the right to object

The wording of mandatory rule 76(1)(d) states that: 'A party who participates in an arbitration without making a timeous objection on the ground ... that the tribunal does not have jurisdiction ... may not raise the objection later before the tribunal or the court.' However, the rule will not apply where the party can show that it did not object timeously because 'it did not know of the ground for objection and could not with reasonable diligence have discovered that ground' (mandatory rule 76(3) and cf 1996 Act s 73(1); *Hussmann (Europe) Ltd v Al Ameen Development & Trade Co* [2002] 2 Lloyd's Rep 83).

Under some arbitration rules and codes, a party can employ an 'empty chair' strategy of simply not turning up and not participating in the tribunal. Unlike a court, the tribunal must go through the motions of determining the case and cannot grant summary judgment or decree in default of stateable defence as a court is empowered to do so. Thus the other party who is participating has to incur the costs – even of leading the evidence in support of its claim – in order to be entitled to its award as any other course would lay open a challenge at a later date under the New York Convention.

As discussed below, once an 'award' is made then the avenue for jurisdictional challenge will be rule 67 (see commentary to that rule below).

Termination of tribunal or setting aside for no or exceeded jurisdiction

If the tribunal upholds the objection, it is required to ('must') end the arbitration and set aside any provisional or part awards made already in so far as the award relates to such a matter.

Delay ruling on objection

The tribunal can postpone the whole issue of jurisdiction until its final award. This aspect may be frustrating to those used to litigation whereby jurisdictional challenges are disposed of in early course and certainly never held over or postponed to the point of the judgment on the basis that it could result in wasted expenses to do so. Indeed, as the Policy Memorandum to the Bill noted, the tribunal is empowered to 'delay and rule [on jurisdiction] in the award on the merits of the dispute' which will 'allow the tribunal to ignore its general duty to conduct the arbitration without unnecessary delay and efficiently and to delay deciding on jurisdiction until it decides the dispute' (para 138). But in arbitration practice this is recognised procedure (cf Model Law Art 16(3) and 1996 Act s 31(4)).

Any Scottish arbitral tribunal considering postponement will have to do so taking cognisance of its duties of expedition and reduction of cost and will have to take account of this course of action thereby postponing at the beginning of an arbitration for its duration the question of jurisdiction.

Appeal against tribunal's ruling on jurisdictional objection

This mandatory rule gives a right of appeal from a ruling by the tribunal on an objection by a party in respect of jurisdiction. Rule 21(1) ensures that the appeal has to be commenced no later than 14 days after the tribunal's decision on the objection. Like elsewhere, the appeal will be by application and, in practical terms, will be by petition to the Outer House. For the purposes of the time limits here, the appeal will be made when the party has lodged the petition with the Petition Department in the Court of Session (see *Tor Corporate AS v Sinopec Group Star Petroleum Corpn Ltd* [2008] CSIH 9).

Appeal by petition

Whereas elsewhere in the Act the recourse to the Outer House is expressed as making an 'application', this is an appeal in a similar sense to rules 67–71 and in terms of RCS 100.5 'an appeal under the 2010 Act shall be made by petition' (RCS 100.591)). (Cf the abbreviated form of petition for applications in respect of the recognition and enforcement of foreign judgments (Form 62.28) and the discussion by the Inner House in *Drika BVBA v Giles* [2018] CSIH 42.)

The appeal will be to the Outer House unless the tribunal contains or consists of an Outer House judge as arbitrator under rule 25, in which case it will be to a Division of the Inner House.

It is important to note at the outset that the Outer House judge has a discretion as to procedure in a cause brought under the Scottish Arbitration Rules (RCS 100.3).

Petitions to the Court of Session are in a prescribed form (Form 14.4). RCS 14.4 provides that a petition shall include: (a) a statement of facts in numbered paragraphs setting out the facts and circumstances on which the petition is founded; (b) a prayer setting out the orders sought; and (c) the name, designation and address of the petitioner and a statement of any special capacity in which the petitioner is presenting the petition. (See also *obiter* comments of Lord Hope, in *Somerville v Scottish Ministers* [2007] UKHL 44 (at para [65]), noting that 'the core requirement is simply this. The factual history should be set out succinctly and the issues of law should be clearly identified.')

In terms of the content, RCS 100.7(1) regulates a petition under the 2010 Act and, in a similar fashion, requires a petitioner to set out the facts and circumstances on which the petition is founded, and the relief claimed. Under RCS 100.7(3) the following matters should be identified: (a) the parties to the cause and the arbitration from which the cause arises; (b) the relevant rule of the Scottish Arbitration Rules or other provision of the 2010 Act under which the petition or note has been lodged; (c) any special capacity in which the petitioner or noter is acting or any special capacity in which any other party to the proceedings is acting; (d) a summary of the circumstances out of which the application or appeal arises; (e) the grounds on which the application or appeal proceeds; (f) in the case of an appeal under rule 67(1), whether the appellant seeks the variation or the setting aside of an award (or part of it); (g) in the case of an appeal under rule 69(1), whether the appeal is made with the agreement of the parties to the arbitration; and (h) any relevant requirements of the Scottish Arbitration Rules which have been met.

The RCS do, however, make special provision for some types of petition where some rules are disapplied and other requirements are added. Certain RCS 14 rules are disapplied (RCS 100.3). Other requirements are added. Under RCS 100 the petitioner will have to seek (in most cases – witnesses are an exception) under the Act, permission to intimate and serve the petition and the court can make such order as it considers appropriate in the circumstances (RCS 100.5(3) and RCS 14.7). Other than that, it would appear that arbitration applications in terms of RCS 100 will be in terms of RCS 14 in standard form and there are no special provisions for arbitration petitions other than those noted above.

Summarising all of this, Lord Glennie in *Arbitration Application No 3 of 2011* [2011] CSOH 164 observed:

> All applications and appeals under the Act are governed by RC100. In terms of RC100.5, all such applications and appeals must be made by petition (or, if proceedings are already depending before the court, by a note in that same petition procedure). This is not intended to introduce the formality often associated with petition procedure. Many of the rules relating to petition procedure are disapplied by RC100.4. The intent is to make the procedure as flexible as possible. RC100.7 sets out the matters which should, so far as is necessary, be identified in the petition. Apart from those requirements, it should not be necessary to set everything out at length in the petition. The basis of the challenge, placed (so far as relevant) in the context of the underlying dispute and what has happened in the arbitration, should be set out as simply as possible. By the time an application or appeal comes to be made, the underlying dispute will usually (though not always) be very familiar to both parties.
>
> Upon lodging a petition seeking relief (of any kind) under the Act, the petitioner will enrol a motion for intimation and service: RC100.5. Except in the case of a legal error appeal where leave to appeal is required ... the order for intimation and service will normally provide for answers to be lodged by the respondent. After service, and after expiry of the requisite period for lodging answers, the petitioner must then enrol a motion for further procedure. This enables the court to take hold of the case and ensure that it is dealt with as expeditiously and economically as possible. The motion for further procedure is an essential case management step. On the hearing of the motion, the court will order such further procedure as is appropriate in the circumstances: see RC100.3. The order made will clearly depend upon the nature and subject matter of the application ... Further pleading, or adjustment of pleadings, is to be discouraged. However, in the case of a challenge which potentially raises disputed issues of fact (e.g. a serious irregularity challenge), then, depending always on the particular issue raised in the petition, it might be necessary to have an exchange of further pleadings (possibly restricted to the particular

issue) followed by an exchange of witness statements, leading up to a proof or other hearing to determine the application. There is no one right way to proceed. The important thing, in line with the founding principles set out in section 1 of the Act, is that the procedure be simple and flexible, framed (with the assistance of the parties) to deal with the particular issues before the court, and designed to enable the dispute to be resolved as expeditiously and economically as possible, so far as is consistent with fairness.

Appeal time limited

As a discouragement to parties using the procedure for dilatory tactics, and to prevent them from making vexatious objections in applications to the court to delay the whole process, the tribunal can elect to continue the arbitration while the Outer House is determining the jurisdiction appeal (see further rule 23(3)). Paragraph (2) of rule 21 provides that the arbitral proceedings may continue until the court comes to a decision on the objection to jurisdiction.

As another 'delay prevention mechanism', there is no appeal (called a reclaiming motion in the Court of Session) from the Outer to the Inner House. Rule 21(3) provides that the Outer House's decision on the appeal is final.

Bearing in mind the founding principle in s 1 as to the avoidance of delay, this is a sensible measure and can only be an attraction to those considering arbitration as opposed to litigation with levels of appeal.

'No later than'

There are cases which have commented upon the judicial meaning of 'not later than' although there does not appear to be any authority on the meaning of 'no later than'. See, eg, *Main v City of Glasgow District Licensing Board* 1987 SLT 305 where the expression 'not later than five weeks before the day of the meeting' was held to mean not later than five weeks before the inception of the day on which the meeting takes place and *Ritchie v Maersk* 1994 SCLR 1038 in the court context. Also see D C Coull, 'Not later than defined' 1987 SLT 353, and 'Time' in *The Laws of Scotland: Stair Memorial Encyclopaedia*, vol 22, paras 819–23.

Lodging a petition

What constitutes 'lodging' a petition? The Rules of the Court of Session state in the annotations that it is 'an ex parte application addressed to the Lords of Council and Session and seeks their aid for some purpose or other, by exercising some statutory jurisdiction or the *nobile officium* in a variety of matters'; *Tomkins v Cohen* 1951 SC 22 affirmed by the Inner House in *Drika BVBA v Giles* CSIH 42 at para [44] per the Opinion of the court).

In *Tor Corporate AS v Sinopec Group Star Petroleum Corpn Ltd* mentioned above, the Inner House gave guidance. A petition is the court document requesting the court to do something. In contradistinction to a 'summons' which is the court document used where a party asserts a legal right, a petition is a request to the court, seeking the exercise of its inherent discretion to grant a remedy which in all the facts and circumstances of the case is considered to be equitable or fair.

In the *Tor Corporate* case (in a pre-2010 Act arbitration), one of the parties was founding on and making an application to set aside an arbitral award within the period permitted by Art 34(3) of the Model Law. The argument was whether the petition (being the application) was lodged within the period of time required by the Model Law. (It was held that it was.)

A petition is made to the Petition Department of the Court of Session. If there are time limits for lodging the petition, then failure to meet them will result in the petition not being 'lodged' (cf *Tor Corporate*).

Discretion vested in tribunal to continue proceedings pending court's decision

The Scottish provisions allow the tribunal to continue pending the determination of the appeal. Although this acts as a discouragement for a party to instigate delaying tactics by objecting then appealing, there is of course a risk that the court will decide against the tribunal and in favour of the party, leaving difficult questions of expenses to be determined by the tribunal later. Of course, the tribunal for these very reasons may determine that it will not continue the proceedings and suspend (or in the language of Scots law 'sist') those proceedings until the court has made its determination; and would be wise to do so if that is the joint decision of the parties.

In England, the emphasis is on a discretion vested in the tribunal to 'stay' the proceedings (as opposed to a discretion to continue them) while an application is made to the court for a determination of a preliminary point of jurisdiction (1996 Act s 31(5)).

Under default rule 22 the parties can, subject to conditions, refer a jurisdictional question directly to the Outer House rather than objecting and then appealing. Note that this is different from an appeal on the grounds of substantive jurisdiction in terms of mandatory rule 67 which relates to an 'award'.

The procedure to be adopted in the application to the Outer House is provided for in rule 23 and if rule 22 is not disapplied then the rule 23 procedure is mandatory.

Thus, to be allowed to proceed under this head there will have to be agreement between the parties (which seems unlikely to occur very often, with both parties considering that jurisdiction is uncertain) or the tribunal has consented and the court is satisfied of the three issues specified in rule 23(2)(b)(i), (ii) and (iii).

The decision of the Outer House as to the validity of the application under rule 22 and its determination of the question as to jurisdiction under the same rule is final and cannot be reclaimed by reclaiming motion.

Again, the tribunal can elect to proceed with the arbitration (presumably even having given its consent to the application) and, on one view, under its Part 3 duties is bound to do so.

Again also, the determination of the Outer House is final including any decision as to the validity of the application.

These strict requirements suggest an intention in the Act to encourage parties to adopt the first course and permit the tribunal to rule on its own jurisdiction under rules 19 and 20 with the safeguards under rule 67. It is of course open to the parties to make the court application.

For examples of the types of case which have proceeded straight to court for a determination of a preliminary point of jurisdiction under the 1996 Act s 32, see *Trafigura Beheer BV v Yieh Phui (China) Technomaterial Co Ltd* [2009] EWHC 2054 (Comm); *Esso Exploration & Production UK Ltd v Electricity Supply Board* [2004] EWHC 723 (Comm); *Film Finance Inc v Royal Bank of Scotland* [2007] EWHC 195 (Comm).

However, the recent case of *HC Trading Malta Ltd v Tradeland Commodities SL* [2016] EWHC 1279 (Comm) is illustrative. In that case the claimant intended to make a claim under the contract against the defendant in a London arbitration and asked the defendant to agree to accept service of the arbitration notice at the office of its London solicitors. The defendant declined to do so on the basis that it denied that there was any contract in existence. In the event that the claimant commenced arbitration in London, the respondent advised that it would contest the arbitrator's jurisdiction. Proceedings for a declaration that there was a binding arbitration agreement were then issued by the claimant.

The court held that once an arbitration had been commenced, the ability of a party to apply to the court for declaratory relief as to jurisdiction or anything else was circumscribed by the express provisions of the Act. It continued, in the first place, that it was for the arbitrator to rule on its own jurisdiction. There could be recourse to the court, but that was subject to the conditions in s 32 of the 1996 Act. The court considered that where the 1996 Act 'laid down an extensive code for the governance of arbitrations from start to finish the very fact of this scheme is highly relevant when considering the scope of the court's powers prior to commencement.' The court held that it would be wrong in principle for the court to entertain any such application by a claimant where there are at least the following three factors: (1) the claimant asserts that there is a binding arbitration agreement; (2) the claimant has a claim which it wishes to assert and which therefore (on the claimant's own case) can only be litigated by way of arbitration; and (3) the claimant is clearly able to commence an arbitration in pursuance of that agreement whether or not he has yet done so, and whether or not it is imminent. It considered that the general intention of the Act was that the courts should usually not intervene outside the specific circumstances specified in Part I.

The court also observed that it might have had jurisdiction to consider the existence of an arbitration agreement in the context of an anti-suit injunction, especially where a claimant had no intention of commencing an arbitration; but that did not mean that the court would be right to entertain an application for a declaration where the party seeking it was about to enter into the scheme provided by the Act (following *AES Ust-Kamenogorsk Hydropower Plant JSC v Ust-Kamenogorsk Hydropower Plant LLP* [2013] UKSC 35).

It is suggested that Scottish courts would follow suit in connection with it being for the tribunal in the first place to consider matters relating to jurisdiction rather than the courts.

Mandatory rule 23 provides the procedure to be used if there is a referral by any party under rule 22 and, as noted, this procedure is mandatory for a rule 22 application.

The approach to allowing this to proceed is similar to rule 22: ie to be allowed to proceed under this head there will have to be agreement between the parties (which seems unlikely to occur very often, with both parties considering that jurisdiction is uncertain) or the tribunal has consented and the court is satisfied of the three issues specified in rule 23(2)(b)(i), (ii) and (iii). One could see an argument in that scenario for the party seeking to make the application being bound to provide caution for expenses (security for costs) in the event that the application is unsuccessful.

The decision of the Outer House as to the validity of the application under rule 22 and its determination of the question as to jurisdiction under the same rule is final and cannot be reclaimed (appealed to the appellate Inner House of the Court of Session).

Obstacles to making an application

Rule 23 is a mandatory rule and so it will always 'come into operation' when there is an application under rule 22, but it is suggested that it creates a strange limbo in that, while mandatory, it has no effect if default rule 22 has been disapplied. It might have been better to incorporate rules 22 and 23 in a single rule, and make this a default rule, but nothing really turns on this point.

The rule inserts considerable obstacles for a party to overcome in order to make the application to the Outer House.

The time frame here is 'without delay', rather than 'as soon as reasonably practicable'. This therefore means that the application should be made when the jurisdictional issue arises or shortly thereafter. Whether it has arisen or not in the circumstances will be a matter for the court's determination.

This ties in with, and is reinforced by, the general requirement under rule 76 that 'a party who participates in an arbitration without making a timeous objection on the ground ... (d) that the tribunal does not have jurisdiction, may not raise the objection later before the tribunal or a court.'

Again, while the application is proceeding, the tribunal has a discretion to carry on pending the determination of the application by the Outer House (or to presumably not carry on and to sist). See the point above in connection with rule 21 and 22.

No appeal

Like the provisions in Part 8 below, the scheme of the Act – in keeping with modern arbitral good practice – is to avoid appeals to the court which were in the past exploited for dilatory reasons.

Note that the Arbitration Act 1996 takes a different approach with s 32(6) stating that the decision of the court on the question of jurisdiction shall be treated as a judgment of the court for the purposes of an appeal, but that no appeal lies without the leave of the court, which shall not be given unless the court considers that the question involves a point of law of general importance or one which for some other special reason should be considered by the Court of Appeal.

Rule 24 obviously ties in with the founding principles in s 1, namely the requirement that 'the object of arbitration is to resolve disputes fairly, impartially and with unnecessary delay or expense'.

GENERAL DUTIES (PART 3)

Introduction

At an international level, as an extension of the principle of party autonomy, the parties are free to select their arbitrators. So strong is the principle, it is thought, that they need not actually be impartial and independent.

If the tribunal is to consist of three members then each party may choose a 'co-arbitrator' who then chooses a chairman. In previous international practice, the co-arbitrators were sometimes chosen because they were likely to be very sympathetic to their appointing party's cause and might act as additional advocates for that cause. In such cases, a sceptic might consider that the 'co-arbitrators' cancel one another out, and the chairman is, in effect, a sole arbitrator, but with the expenses of three arbitrators' fees. The failure to appreciate that an arbitrator who is appointed as 'co-arbitrator' may intend to act as a neutral, impartial arbitrator, despite being paid by one of the parties, can give rise to what might be politely described as 'interesting dynamics'. In the United States the historical position for domestic arbitrators, party appointed, was that they were to be considered non-neutral unless otherwise indicated. (The presumption is now in favour of neutrality unless otherwise indicated.)

Again, at an international level, various institutions or appointing author-ities or the domestic arbitral law will provide and police what is required of the arbitrators through the operation of party-led challenges.

The position in Scotland is now clear and mandatory rule 24 leaves no room for doubt. The tribunal *must* be impartial, independent, and treat the parties fairly. It is submitted that this is a sensible approach although rule 77 effectively equates independence and impartiality.

This whole subject-matter, though, has been definitively determined in the Supreme Court case of *Halliburton Company v Chubb Bermuda Insurance Ltd (Formerly known as Ace Bermuda Insurance Ltd)* [2020] UKSC 48 (upholding the Court of Appeal decision, but on different grounds).

In that case, Halliburton Company had provided cementing and well monitoring services to BP in the Gulf of Mexico. Transocean Ltd also pro-vided services to BP, including overlapping services to those provided by Halliburton which had entered into a liability policy with Chubb Bermuda Insurance Ltd (formerly known as Ace Bermuda Insurance Ltd) (the 'respondent'). Transocean Ltd was also insured with the respondent.

In 2010, there was an explosion and fire on an oil rig in the Gulf of Mexico, the 'Deepwater Horizon' oil spill. As a result, thousands of civil claims were brought against BP, Halliburton and Transocean. BP also claimed against Halliburton and Transocean.

The facts were these: following a trial in the US in which judgment was given apportioning blame between the parties, the appellant concluded a settlement to agree the amount of damages. Halliburton sought to claim a proportion of this settlement under its insurance policy. The respondent declined to pay Halliburton's claim. Arbitration was commenced. Both parties selected their own arbitrator, but the parties were unable to agree the chairman of the arbitration. This resulted in an application to the High Court, the result of which was that the respondent's first-choice candidate, the arbitrator, was selected.

The appeal arose out of the discovery by Halliburton in 2016 that subsequent to the arbitrator's appointment and without Halliburton's knowledge, the arbi-trator had accepted appointment as an arbitrator in two other references, both of which arose out of the same Deepwater Horizon incident: (i) Transocean's claim against the respondent; and (ii) a nomination by another insurer to arbi-trate another claim by Transocean arising out of the same incident.

The application to remove the arbitrator was unsuccessful, despite the Supreme Court holding disclosure should have been made, but finding that, on the facts, there was no apparent impartiality or bias.

The rule will sit together and interact with rules 8 (mandatory duty to disclose any conflict of interest), mandatory rule 77 (independence of the arbitrator) and default rule 78 (consideration where arbitrator judged not to be impartial and independent).

As discussed in relation to rule 8, there is a connection here between the requirement placed on the arbitrators to be impartial and independent and also to be free from bias. However, considerable caution should be exercised before imposing a burden on litigants to take the initiative in discovering facts which might support an objection to a decision-maker on grounds of bias. It is considered important that primary responsibility should rest with the decision-maker to make full and timely disclosure (*BAA Ltd v Competition Commission* [2009] CAT 35).

English case law suggests that although a complainant is not entitled to turn a blind eye to the obvious, they could not be fixed with knowledge of facts as to bias or lack of independence or impartiality which they could only have ascertained had the necessary research been done: *Millar (David Cameron) v Dickson* [2001] UKPC D4; *Jones v DAS Legal Expenses Insurance Co Ltd* [2003] EWCA Civ 1071; and *R (on the application of Toovey) v Law Society* [2002] EWHC 391 (Admin).

Scots law has long recognised these principles of impartiality and fairness under the Latin tags *nemo judex in sua causa* and *audi alteram partem* (Lord Clyde and D Edwards, *Judicial Review* para 18.01). Lord President Hope in *Errington v Wilson* 1995 SC 550 at 555 said that the duty to act fairly and the duty to act in accordance with the principles of natural justice 'are different ways of expressing the same thing'. It is suggested that in this area, cases from the judicial review arena touching on bias, natural justice, procedural fairness, and justice being seen to be done may all be of use in considering whether an arbitrator can be subject to challenge.

Impartiality, bias and independence

Note here, though, that there is the addition of independence (cf s 1 and rule 77).

Dependency in the sense of not being independent in the context has been generally considered to mean that there is some relationship between an arbitrator and one of the parties, whether financial, familial, or otherwise. The test is thought to be an objective one because it is not related to the arbitrator or prospective arbitrator's state of mind (*Redfern and Hunter on International Arbitration* (6th edn) para 4.77).

The concepts of impartiality and independence and their interrelation have already been discussed above. Impartiality is connected with actual or apparent bias of an arbitrator either in favour of one of the parties or in relation to the issues in or subject-matter of the dispute. It is therefore more subjective and involves the arbitrator's state of mind (*Redfern and Hunter* (6th edn), para 4.77). Impartiality is a primary essential of the judicial function, but it should be understood that lack of impartiality (or, indeed, positive bias) is often a question of the perception of a party, rather than what is really going on.

A well-known case relating to this (and to the furore that followed accusations that Lord Hoffmann, then a Law Lord, would be perceived to have been biased) was *R v Bow Street Magistrates, ex parte Pinochet Ugarte (No 2)* [2000] 1 AC 119. It was never suggested that His Lordship was *actually* biased, merely that an impartial observer might think he was. See also commentary above and commentary to rule 77.

A duty of impartiality connotes a duty on the arbitrator to keep an open mind, decide the case on the merits, only on the evidence and not on the basis of any assumptions or any preconceptions. Bias can occur in a variety of ways. In the most obvious the (potential) arbitrator may have a vested interest in the subject-matter or is motivated to prefer one of the parties over the other. The courts will quash decisions of those who can be demonstrated actually to be biased (even if they themselves have not seen it) but also those decisions made by those persons who show potential impartiality or who give the impression that they are not impartial (Clyde and Edwards, *Judicial Review* para 18.13). In Scots law, at common law, it is well established that a party acting in the role of judge, adjudicator or arbitrator should act without bias. The Latin tag *nemo judex in sua causa* is often used ('no-one may be judge in his own cause'). The test is whether there is a real possibility of bias. In *Helow v Advocate General for Scotland* [2008] UKHL 62, a case about judicial independence and impartiality, the House of Lords provided guidance about the characteristics of the 'fair-minded observer' following its decision in *Porter v Magill* [2001] UKHL 67, [2002] 2 AC 357. (See also comments of the Privy Council in *Yiacoub v The Queen* [2014] UKPC 22; *Bolkiah v Brunei Darussalam (Procedural Issue)* [2007] UKPC 62; *Almazeedi v Penner* [2018] UKPC 3 and most recently the Supreme Court in *Halliburton* at paras 49, 52, 55–62, and 69.)

This freedom from bias was analysed by Lord Clyde in *Millar v Dickson* [2001] UKPC D4 at para [80] into 'distinct considerations of structural independence and objective impartiality, but the two concepts are closely linked, and it may be sufficient to speak simply of independence. Judicial independence … is an indispensible condition for the preservation of the rule of law.' The Court of Appeal has held that the independence of an expert valuer is subject to the 'tribunal test', being the test of apparent bias assessed at the date of the expert's appointment, so that a valuer would not be independent if they had a connection with a party, an interest in the outcome of proceedings or some connection with the property being valued which, viewed objectively, created a real risk that they might act partially in carrying out the valuation (*Re Maximus Securities Ltd* [2016] EWCA Civ 1057).

In *Sierra Fishing Co v Farran* [2015] EWHC 140 (Comm) an arbitrator was removed by the court under s 24 of the 1996 Act for lack of impartiality. The parties had entered into a loan agreement with an arbitration clause. There was a failure to make repayments and the arbitrator was appointed and the arbitration was commenced. The parties continued negotiations about the repayment concurrently and then agreed to suspend the arbitration. They then entered a new agreement for repayment including transfer of shares. The arbitrator became involved and provided the parties with assistance in drafting it. This new agreement failed and the arbitration was revived. The respondent objected to the arbitrator continuing to act as arbitrator, alleging that he could not be impartial because: (i) he had been employed by a bank of which the first respondent was chief executive; (ii) his father still worked for the bank; (iii) his father had acted for the first respondent on personal matters; and (iv) he had a financial interest in his father's law firm. The court held that the arbitrator should be removed as there was a real possibility that the law firm in which the arbitrator had an interest had, through his father, been instructed to act for the first respondent personally, and for the bank of which the first respondent was chairman. The court noted that the firm derived a significant financial income from those instructions, and which were continuing instructions. The court held that all of these connections would 'give rise to justifiable doubts as to [the arbitrator's] ability to act impartially in the dispute. The fair minded observer would take the view that this gave rise to a real possibility that [the arbitrator] would be predisposed to favour [one party] in the dispute in order to foster and maintain the business relationship with himself, his firm and his father, to the financial benefit of all three.' The court also referred to the International Bar Association Guidelines on Conflicts of Interest in International Arbitration. The court noted that the Non-Waivable Red List is where 'the arbitrator regularly advises the appointing party or an affiliate of the appointing party, and the arbitrator or his or her firm derives a significant financial income therefrom' (paragraph 1.4). The Waivable Red list includes the situation where 'the arbitrator currently represents or advises one of the parties or an affiliate of one of the parties' (paragraph 2.3.1) and where 'the arbitrator's law firm currently has a significant commercial relationship with one of the parties or an affiliate of one of the parties' (paragraph 2.3.6). It also noted the Orange List where 'the arbitrator's law firm has within the past three years acted for one of the parties or an affiliate of one of the parties in an unrelated matter without the involvement of the arbitrator' (paragraph 3.1.4). It concluded that the state of the evidence in the case 'would leave the fair-minded observer concluding that there was a real possibility that the relationship between [the arbitrator and the party] fell within these criteria.'

Previous appointments and instructions as counsel

In *ASM Shipping Ltd of India v TTMI Ltd of England* [2005] EWHC 2238 (Comm) a chairing arbitrator, a Queen's Counsel, nominated by the other two arbitrators, had close connections with T's solicitors, having been instructed as counsel in a previous case against one of the parties in which he had attacked the credibility of an individual who would be key witness in the arbitration before him. The court ordered his removal under s 24.

A similar issue arose in *A and others v B and another* [2011] EWHC 2345 (Comm). An arbitrator in an LCIA Arbitration was appointed, and he signed the LCIA Statement of Independence in the usual way. However, previously, in 2004, he had acted as counsel for one of the solicitors instructed in the arbitration before him, in an unconnected litigation. By 2009 (when the arbitration was proceeding) he was retained again to advise in the case. Shortly before completing and issuing an award, the arbitrator disclosed this, advising that he had been instructed by the defendant's solicitors in an ongoing matter which was 'wholly unconnected with the arbitration'. The claimant objected, arguing that a fair-minded and informed observer would conclude that there was a real possibility of 'unconscious bias' as the arbitrator might have an unconscious predisposition towards the opposing party; that the arbitrator had an 'ongoing relationship' with the instructing solicitors, so his decisions might be unconsciously influenced; there was a financial relationship between the opposing party and the arbitrator. The court held that 'unconscious bias' could not be accepted. The fair-minded and informed observer who was presumed to know how the legal profession worked would not consider that there was a real possibility of bias merely because an arbitrator had acted as counsel, whether in the past or simultaneously with the arbitration, for one of the solicitors firms acting in the arbitration. In all the circumstances, the failure by the arbitrator not to disclose his involvement as counsel in the litigation could not give rise to a real possibility of apparent or unconscious bias (applying *Porter v Magill* [2001] UKHL 67). The court held that the test as to when it was appropriate to disclose potential conflicts was lower than the test of apparent bias, following *Taylor v Lawrence* [2002] EWCA Civ 90; [2003] QB 528. Furthermore, disclosure and apparent bias were separate questions and mere failure to disclose did not amount to a real possibility of apparent bias if the fair-minded and informed observer would not have thought there was anything that needed to be disclosed, *Helow v Advocate General for Scotland* [2008] UKHL 62. Once it was explained to the fair-minded and informed observer that the late delay in disclosure on the arbitrator's part was inadvertent, he would not consider that the delay could have any bearing on whether there was apparent or unconscious bias. The court held in this case that the fact that disclosure was late was not a serious irregularity within the meaning of the Arbitration Act 1996 s 68.

In *Cofely Ltd v Bingham* [2016] EWHC 240 (Comm) an arbitrator was removed on the ground of apparent bias where 18 per cent of his appointments and 25 per cent of his arbitrator/adjudicator income over the previous three years had come from cases involving the defendant as a party or as a claims consultant and where the Chartered Institute of Arbitrators' acceptance of nomination form calls for disclosure of 'any involvement, however remote, with either party over the last five years'.

Apparent bias

Following this, a finding of apparent bias in relation to one member of a collective decision- maker has been held in England not to automatically taint the entire group and each member within it (*Director General of Fair Trading v Proprietary Association of Great Britain* [2001] 1 WLR 700 and *ASM Shipping Ltd v Harris* [2007] EWHC 1513 (Comm)), and it is not necessarily the case that where one member of a tribunal was tainted by apparent bias then the whole tribunal is affected (second-hand) by that apparent bias. As such there is no need for those members to recuse themselves, and nor should there be any requirement that they be excluded from the proceedings: see *ASM Shipping Ltd v Harris* (above).

Waiver of a right to object

As discussed above, rule 76(1)(b) provides that where a party does not make a timeous objection about the arbitrator's impartiality and independence timeously, then they are not entitled to raise that objection later before a tribunal or court. However, that must be on known facts, or at least those that might be ascertained with reasonable diligence. It should be remembered, though, that the duty of disclosure will remain on the arbitrator in terms of mandatory rule 8(2) to disclose without delay, and it is a continuing duty in terms of the wording of the rule ('or which become known to the individual before the arbitration ends') (cf English case law in *Halliburton Co v Chubb Bermuda Insurance Ltd* [2020] UKSC 48; *Soletanche Bachy France SAS v Aqaba Container Terminal (Pvt) Co* [2019] EWHC 362 (Comm)).

A party to an arbitration can of course waive any right to have an alternative individual hear his case if apparent or actual bias is demonstrated but that party should be aware of all the material facts, and of the consequences of the choice open to him, and be given a fair opportunity to reach an unpressured decision (*Smith v Kvaerner Cementation Foundations Ltd* [2006] EWCA Civ 242). Waiver might be implied where, say, parties had chosen an arbitrator where they knew or ought to have known that there could be a conflict. (*Fleming's Trustee v Henderson* 1962 SLT 401).

If the tribunal has decided that there is material which should be disclosed, then it should make full disclosure (*Taylor v Lawrence* [2002] EWCA Civ 90).

If the tribunal has disclosed to the parties the relevant facts which might give rise to 'justifiable doubts', the parties must have had the chance to consider them and to decide whether to object (*Locabail (UK) Ltd v Bayfield Properties Ltd* [1999] EWCA Civ 3004; [2000] QB 4510.

Barristers in the same chambers as arbitrators

In England, there were previously arguments that a Head of Chambers could not sit as a judge in a case relating to an arbitration in which fellow members of his chambers appeared. This was because changes in the way that some chambers funded their expenses and the fact that counsel could act under a conditional fee agreement (CFA) meant that, in some cases, there might be grounds for arguing that a recorder (a judge) should not sit in a case in which one or more of the barristers were members of his chambers. It was also argued that a fair trial was put at risk where a recorder was the head of chambers of the barristers appearing before him but was dismissed on the basis that this was at odds with the high professional standards observed by the Bar.

It is also accepted that barristers from the same chambers may appear before judges who were former members of their chambers or on opposite sides in the same case. Lord Woolf considered in *Lawrence v Taylor* (above) that that close relationship has not prejudiced but has enhanced the administration of justice.

In *Watts v Watts* [2015] EWCA Civ 1297 the court held that the observer, knowing the professional standards applied by part-time judges drawn from the legal profession, would understand and expect that if there had been any overlap between the cases, the judge would have recognised the conflict of interest and recused herself.

In *Azumi Ltd v Zuma's Choice Pet Products Ltd* [2017] EWHC 45 (IPEC) the Intellectual Property Enterprise Court held that a judge who did not recuse themself from a hearing, where they normally shared chambers with a party's barrister, was entitled to do so. It held that the notional, fair-minded and informed observer would know about the professional standards which were applicable to practising members of the bar and barristers who served as part-time deputy judges.

The position is less clear in England with regard to barristers from the same chambers. As barristers are self-employed and are not tied as partners in a common scheme (although they will occupy a common building and make common payments as rent towards its administration), it has been suggested that on an objective assessment of impartiality, they are not partial and therefore independent. It has been judicially noted that this arrangement has existed for a long time (*Laker Airways v FLS Aerospace Ltd* [1999] 2 Lloyd's Rep 45) and the test to be applied on an application to remove a barrister from acting as an arbitrator under the Arbitration Act 1996 s 24(1) (power of the court to remove an arbitrator) is an objective one (*R v Gough (Robert)* [1993] AC 646). Actual bias did not have to be proved, but there must be a reasonable suspicion as to the impartiality of the barrister to justify removal under s 24. A loss of confidence as to impartiality would not suffice. It is thought that a conflict of interest only arises where the same person carries out duties that conflict with the interests of different clients or where self-interest conflicts with the duty owed to a client.

It is possible, though, that this is being eroded. In *Smith v Kvaerner Cementation Foundations Ltd* [2006] EWCA Civ 242 the Court of Appeal held that the way that some chambers funded their expenses and the fact that counsel could act under a conditional fee agreement meant that, in some cases, there might be grounds for arguing that a recorder should not sit in a case in which one or more of the advocates were members of his chambers. However, those special considerations did not apply in the instant case. It also held that the assertion that a fair trial was put at risk where a recorder was the head of chambers of the barristers appearing before him was at odds with the high professional standards observed by the Bar.

It reinforced the appoint made above that the party waiving should be aware of all the material facts, and of the consequences of the choice open to him and be given a fair opportunity to reach an unpressured decision. (See also the decisions of the ICSID tribunals in *Hrvatska Elektroprivreda dd v Republic of Slovenia* (ICSID Case No ARB/05/24) and *The Rompetrol Group NV v Romania* (ICSID Case No ARB/06/3) (Decision of the tribunal on the participation of a counsel) and the discussion above.)

What is certain is that some chambers in England have now separated out their barristers from their arbitrators with each having their own dedicated website to demonstrate their 'independence' from the other. Advocates in Scotland do not share a common building as chambers although do increasingly make contributions to the administration of their 'stables'. It remains to be seen how their arrangements stand up to these requirements.

Solicitors

What of solicitors? A real issue in arbitration is where a partner in a law firm may be instructed by a client to appear in an arbitration in which one of the arbitrators is one of his partners. Convention dictates that this would give rise to justifiable doubts as to his independence if he is engaged in a venture to make profits for himself and his partners in the business. It would also, arguably, breach conflict of interest rules in relation to the practice in question (as opposed to the arbitration itself) if the arbitrator-partner was placed in a position where he had to rule against the interests of the firm's client.

Test for bias/impartiality

As will be seen in the case law above, the concern is that a party lacking impartiality will favour one of the parties over the other and will be biased. As touched upon under rules 8 and 12 above, the courts' approach to bias is now found in the House of Lords' decision of *Porter v Magill* [2002] 2 AC 357 in which Lord Hope gave the leading judgment. The test was formulated as 'whether the fair-minded and informed observer, having considered the facts, would conclude that there was a real possibility that the tribunal was biased'.

The courts will often test bias using the test of 'the fair-minded and informed observer'.

The kinds of issues which might disqualify an arbitrator for potential bias include:

- If they have a pecuniary interest in the dispute or a connection with a party. This can include holding shares in a company involved – even tangentially – with the dispute. It is suggested, however, that merely holding a unit or investment trust, or mutual fund, which itself held relevant securities would be unlikely to produce evidence of bias, particularly if the trust or fund was actively managed without any involvement on the part of the arbitrator.

- It can involve having a personal interest in the outcome of the dispute. Obviously, an arbitrator should not sit in an arbitration involving a family member.
- The arbitrator should probably still accept appointment even if they had acted for one of the parties in the past although there are differing views on this. As to apparent or perceived bias, even if there is a lack of partiality any connection with one side may be enough to disqualify or permit a challenge. (On all of this see also Clyde and Edwards, *Judicial Review* paras 18.12 ff.)

This is all picked up in mandatory rule 77 which states that an arbitrator is not 'independent in relation to an arbitration' if their relationship with any party; their financial or other commercial interests; or anything else, gives rise to justifiable doubts as to their impartiality. If the parties do not remove default rule 78, and the arbitrator is judged by the Outer House not to have been impartial and independent they can be removed under rule 12, or the tribunal can be dismissed under rule 13. Note that the court under rule 78 must take cognisance of whether the arbitrator has complied with rule 8 (duty to disclose any conflicts of interest).

It will be obvious that each case will turn on its own facts and circumstances.

Finally, 'apparent bias' to any fair-minded observer could be grounds for a serious irregularity giving rise to a challenge to an award: cf *Sumukan Ltd v Commonwealth Secretariat* [2007] EWHC 188 (Comm).

How might the tribunal protect itself?

The best course for a prospective arbitrator (or indeed at the point of appointment of the arbitrator) is that he discloses all the facts which could reasonably be considered to constitute grounds for challenge. Thus, these would be facts which under rules 8, 24, 77 and 78 could lead to an assumption of bias, lack of impartiality, etc. It follows that if he does so and the parties do not object in the face of that then it would be very difficult for any of the parties, having been advised of those facts and then acquiesced in the appointment, to launch a later challenge, although it would probably make sense for the arbitrator to make a positive request that the parties do not have any objection based on the facts disclosed.

As noted above, the duty of disclosure is a continuing one – if new circumstances arise then they should be disclosed immediately, and the same request for approval made at that stage.

It has been suggested that in practical terms the arbitrator should disclose all the relevant facts to his appointing party and if there is nothing to cause concern then he should accept office and thereafter write to both parties explaining the facts, this time with a view as to how they may be seen through the eyes of the 'other party'. Thus giving on the one hand an objective presentation as to whether the facts would give rise to doubts in the eyes of a third party and then the subjective one seen through the eyes of the parties to this dispute (*Redfern and Hunter on International Arbitration* (6th edn) paras 4.82 and 4.83).

It is crucial to the acquiescence/waiver argument which may have to be used later that all the parties were versed with these facts and so the facts have to be communicated to the parties at this stage, which is best done by writing to all of them.

There is no need for the party-appointed arbitrators having accepted office without challenge to perform the same procedure in the appointment by them of a chairman (if empowered to do so).

A real problem arises in a small jurisdiction such as Scotland where there may be many professional, or even familial, relationships at all levels which could conceivably give rise to such doubts.

As Gillen J commented in the Northern Irish case of *Derry City Council v Brickkiln Ltd, Professor Stephen Willetts* [2012] NIQB 84:

> I pause to observe in conclusion that it is important that arbitrators as well as other judicial officers discharge their duty to sit and do not, by acceding too readily to robustly contrived suggestions of appearance of bias, encourage parties to believe that by seeking the disqualification of an arbitrator they will have their case tried by someone thought to be more likely to decide the case in their favour (although certainly not a consideration in this case) or somehow delay the hearing and thereby incur further costs. (See also *M's Application (Leave Stage)* [2011] NIQB 4 per McCloskey J at paragraph 4.)

IBA Guidelines on Conflicts of Interest in International Arbitration

The IBA Guidelines have already been referred to in respect of the requirements of mandatory rule 8. They can be found online (www.ibanet.org). They are simply a guide to help parties and arbitrators identify those factors which might be disclosed. As mentioned, under rule 8, they provide specific situations where disclosure is made or not as the case may be, separated into a non-waivable Red List; the waivable Red List; the Orange List; and the Green List.

The Guidelines are often 'the first port of call for many international practitioners in dealing with arbitrator challenges' (G Nicholas and C Partasides, 'LCIA Court Decisions on Challenges to Arbitrators: a Proposal to Publish' (2007) 23 Arb Intl 1, 11).

One may note here, however, the comments of the High Court of England and Wales on the Guidelines in *W Ltd v M Sdn Bhd* [2016] EWHC 422 (Comm) (referred to above) although see also *PAO Tatneft v Ukraine* [2019] (unreported) in which the High Court expressed the view that they are a useful cross-check of 'best practice'.

Treating the parties fairly

The obligation of fairness is fundamental to the nature of arbitration and the courts have repeatedly reinforced this over the years. The parties cannot contract out of this mandatory obligation without depriving the decision of its enforceability as an award. However informal proceedings may be, they must be fair. The proceedings must also be conducted in a manner which maintains confidence in their impartiality.

Note that by rule 24(2) treating the parties fairly includes 'giving each party a reasonable opportunity to put its case and to deal with the other party's case'.

The English provisions

Section 33 of the 1996 Act requires the tribunal to conduct itself by 'giving each party a reasonable opportunity of putting his case and dealing with that of his opponent'.

Equal treatment of parties: Model Law Art 18

The Model Law provides (Art 18) that: 'The parties shall be treated with equality and each party shall be given full opportunity of presenting his case.'

This could perhaps be construed as meaning that the tribunal should allow the parties to explore every aspect by use of the word 'full', but it is suggested that this is not an open-ended obligation. The powers of the arbitrator to control the process of the arbitration necessarily dictate that the wilder 'fishing expeditions' or running of hopeless arguments should be actively discouraged.

Consequences of failure to act impartially and fairly

In the English case of *Gbangbola v Smith & Sherriff Ltd* [1998] 3 All ER 730, the court found on the facts there had been a serious irregularity. The arbitrator had not brought matters which were of concern to him to the attention of the parties, therefore those matters could not be addressed by the parties, and the arbitrator had exercised his discretion as to the award of costs inappropriately, all in breach of s 68 of the 1996 Act.

In *O'Donoghue v Enterprise Inns plc* [2008] EWHC 2273 (Ch) the arbitrator was accused of having failed to hold an oral hearing and allow cross-examination, and it was alleged that as a result he had failed to comply with his duty under s 33 to act fairly and impartially as between the parties, such a failure amounting to serious irregularity. In this case the court considered that there was not enough to constitute a serious irregularity as the arbitrator was entitled to exercise a discretion as to whether there should have been an oral hearing. Further, the case should not be taken as authority that oral hearings and cross-examinations are an inevitable occurrence, merely that they must not be refused where to do so would prevent a party from presenting its arguments or interrogating and challenging those of the other party.

Unnecessary delay and expense

The tribunal does not have to follow court procedures slavishly or even at all. Such an approach was deprecated even under the old procedure (*ERDC Construction Ltd v H M Love & Co (No 2)* 1996 SC 523) although there is frequent concern (and not only in Scotland) that arbitrators, and particularly lawyer-arbitrators, tend to fall back on the relevant court rules on the basis that they cannot be challenged seriously as unreasonable.

It is important to remember that if the parties had wanted the full Rules of Court, they would, it might be suggested, have opted for litigation to resolve their dispute. One of the purposes of arbitration is to allow a more relaxed approach, and arbitrators should be encouraged to use whatever method will achieve a result by the most expeditious and cost-effective method, consistent with obligations of natural justice and general fairness.

What is a suitable arbitration procedure?

Following the above, of course an arbitrator can now choose any format for the procedure and it might be suspected that there will still be some arbitrations run in Scotland after 2010 which bear all the hallmarks of a Court of Session or sheriff court action complete with pleadings and debates and procedure rolls and proofs. The courts may not condone this but will look carefully at any decisions arrived at with a Court of Session approach if that is done. An example of that can be seen (under the old procedure) in *Wiltshier Construction (Scotland) Ltd v Drumchapel Housing Co-Operative Ltd* 2003 SLT 443.

This was a stated case under s 3 of the 1972 Act in an arbitration where the arbiter (as then titled) had adopted a very formalistic approach to the pleadings, which the court then considered permitted it to answer the stated case on matters of mere procedure. As Lord Macfadyen (stating the view of the court) said at para 33:

> It seems to us, however, that if an arbiter has chosen (as the arbiter in the present case has done) to proceed by way of conventional pleadings, and has heard a debate on them, a proposed decision by the arbiter on the relevancy (and even the specification) of the pleadings may well depend on questions of law on which it is perfectly legitimate for him to seek the assistance of the Court by way of a stated case. In the present case, we do not consider that we are precluded from considering the relevancy and specification of the pleadings about the additional agreement on the ground that these are matters

of procedure within the arbiter's discretion. We can, however, only properly consider those matters to the extent that it is necessary to do so in order to answer the questions which the arbiter has formulated.

Tension between party autonomy and tribunal's duties

Rule 24 imposes on the tribunal absolute duties. How then does that affect the doctrine of party autonomy? Can the parties ignore directions from the tribunal on the basis that the will of the parties should override the intentions of the tribunal, no matter how honourable? The answer must be that the tribunal is required by statute to act in accordance with these principles and these express rules and this must have been in contemplation of the parties in the appointment of the tribunal (subject of course to the usual default provisions being modified or disapplied). Therefore, it must be open to the tribunal to take strong and coercive measures at times such as to fulfil or obey those express and implied obligations.

This is not a universally held view though. At a practical level, it is more likely that at least one of the parties would adopt or support the tribunal's proposed coercive measure and thus a direct split between the parties on the one side and the tribunal on the other does not arise often. Further, even if in a crisis of confidence the tribunal adopted a course of action proposed by *all* parties which was *contrary* to the express provisions it would have to have some measure of protection at a later stage if challenged that this was contrary to rule 24 or 77 or 78 or the general principles in s 1. The alternative would be simply to resign (see above in respect of the provision in the rules for parties agreeing procedure). Resignation procedure is provided for by mandatory rule 15. A resignation on the part of the tribunal without provision in the agreement would itself be a breach of contract possibly incurring liability by the parties. The tribunal, though, can apply to the court for relief from liability as per mandatory rule 16.

It is probably a better view that the party autonomy relates to the decision to use arbitration, and to select the Scottish Rules. Once having done so, the parties have no more right to total autonomy than they would have to instruct the arbitrator to give a false award for a collateral purpose – for example, to back-date an award to achieve a tax advantage.

Also the tribunal does have extensive Part 5 powers (via default rules) where there is a failure by a party to submit a claim or defence timeously (rule 37); a failure to attend a hearing or provide evidence (rule 38); and a failure to comply with a tribunal direction or arbitration agreement.

Some English examples

In *Pacol Ltd v Joint Stock Company Rossakhar* [1999] 2 All ER (Comm) 778, a 'documents only' arbitration, it was held that arbitrators had to be particularly astute not to introduce into their deliberations issues which were not disputed between the parties. Where the arbitrator had not given sufficient information for a reasonable commercial lawyer to understand that he was planning to reopen the issue of liability, he had failed to act fairly pursuant to s 33 of the 1996 Act since the claimant in this case had not had the opportunity to make submissions or to adduce evidence on the issues which had formed the basis of the award.

In the well-known case of *Vee Networks Ltd v Econet Wireless International Ltd* [2005] 1 Lloyd's Rep 192 the arbitrator's deviation into irrelevant statutory construction while interpreting the memorandum was held to have constituted a serious irregularity under s 68, as it was a failure to comply with s 33. It was held that the arbitrator in this case should have put his points to the parties for their comments (see also *Zermalt Holdings SA v Nu-Life Upholstery Repairs Ltd* [1985] 2 EGLR 14).

In *OAO Northern Shipping Co v Remolcadores de Marin SL (The Remmar)* [2007] 2 Lloyd's Rep 302, an arbitral award was set aside where the tribunal had found against the claimant on a ground which had neither been raised nor seriously disputed by the respondent, and which the claimant had not been invited to address. It was held that the claimant had demonstrated to the requisite standard that there had been a serious irregularity and such irregularity would, if not rectified, cause it substantial injustice. (See also *Omnibridge Consulting Ltd v Clearsprings (Management) Ltd* [2004] EWHC 2276 (Comm).)

But in *Reliance Industries Ltd v Union of India* [2018] EWHC 822 (Comm) the claimant challenged the award under s 68 alleging procedural irregularities and the tribunal's finding on its own jurisdiction. The claimants argued that they had not had an opportunity of addressing 'development costs' within the meaning of the contract, and which costs were the subject of dispute. The arbitration was under the UNICTRAL Rules and the claimants argued that UNCITRAL Rules art15(1) that each party be given a 'full' opportunity of presenting its case, rather than the 'reasonable' opportunity required by s 33(1)(a) of the 1996 Act, imposed a higher burden of procedural fairness on a tribunal. The court disagreed and held that the tribunal was not obliged to put to the parties all aspects of the analysis in support of its conclusion in order to fulfil the s 33 duty of fairness. The court held that there was a distinction between a lack of opportunity to deal with a case and failure to recognise or take such an opportunity.

Other examples of independence/impartiality clauses

The UNCITRAL Arbitration Rules provide:

Article 11

When a person is approached in connection with his or her possible appointment as an arbitrator, he or she shall disclose any circumstances likely to give rise to justifiable doubts as to his or her impartiality or independence. An arbitrator, from the time of his or her appointment and throughout the arbitral proceedings, shall without delay disclose any such circumstances to the parties and the other arbitrators unless they have already been informed by him or her of these circumstances.

Article 12

1. Any arbitrator may be challenged if circumstances exist that give rise to justifiable doubts as to the arbitrator's impartiality or independence.
2. A party may challenge the arbitrator appointed by it only for reasons of which it becomes aware after the appointment has been made.
3. In the event that an arbitrator fails to act or in the event of the de jure or de facto impossibility of his or her performing his or her functions, the procedure in respect of the challenge of an arbitrator as provided in article 13 shall apply.

The ICDR International Arbitration Rules provide:

Article 7 Impartiality and Independence of Arbitrators

1. Arbitrators acting under these Rules shall be impartial and independent. Prior to accepting appointment, a prospective arbitrator shall disclose to the administrator any circumstance likely to give rise to justifiable doubts as to the arbitrator's impartiality or independence. If, at any stage during the arbitration, new circumstances arise that may give rise to such doubts, an arbitrator shall promptly disclose such circumstances to the parties and to the administrator. Upon receipt of such information from an arbitrator or a party, the administrator shall communicate it to the other parties and to the tribunal.
2. No party or anyone acting on its behalf shall have any *ex parte* communication relating to the case with any arbitrator, or with any candidate for appointment as party-appointed arbitrator except to advise the candidate of the general nature of the controversy and of the anticipated proceedings and to discuss the candidate's qualifications, availability or independence in relation to the parties, or to discuss the suitability of candidates for selection as a third arbitrator where the parties or party designated arbitrators are to participate in that selection. No party or anyone acting on its behalf shall have any *ex parte* communication relating to the case with any candidate for presiding arbitrator.

Article 8 Challenge of Arbitrators

1. A party may challenge any arbitrator whenever circumstances exist that give rise to justifiable doubts as to the arbitrator's impartiality or independence. A party wishing to challenge an arbitrator shall send notice of the challenge to the administrator within 15 days after being notified of the appointment of the arbitrator or within 15 days after the circumstances giving rise to the challenge become known to that party.
2. The challenge shall state in writing the reasons for the challenge.
3. Upon receipt of such a challenge, the administrator shall notify the other parties of the challenge. When an arbitrator has been challenged by

one party, the other party or parties may agree to the acceptance of the challenge and, if there is agreement, the arbitrator shall withdraw. The challenged arbitrator may also withdraw from office in the absence of such agreement. In neither case does withdrawal imply acceptance of the validity of the grounds for the challenge.

The LCIA Arbitration Rules Art 5 (Formation of the Arbitral Tribunal) states at 5.3:

All arbitrators shall be and remain at all times impartial and independent of the parties; and none shall act in the arbitration as advocate for or authorized representative of any party. No arbitrator shall give advice to any party on the parties' dispute or the conduct or outcome of the arbitration.

'Unnecessary' delay and expense

Rule 25 is a mandatory rule. As a corollary to the previous rule, it imposes a general duty on the parties to ensure that the arbitration is conducted without unnecessary delay and without incurring unnecessary expense.

The onus is on the parties to co-operate and this rule, it is suggested, complements the previous one.

'Without unnecessary delay' recognises the possibility of delay for the purposes of the arbitration, and 'unnecessary expense' recognises that the tribunal and the parties may need to incur expense where necessary. The concept of necessary is open-ended and, unlike the English provision, there are no subsectional examples to give colour to the word. It will therefore be for the court or the individual tribunals to make determinations on what is and what is not necessary by virtue of the operation of the other sections and rules under the Act.

In England, the type of things which have been considered 'necessary' for the expeditious conduct of the arbitration have included: pursuing the claim without 'inordinate or inexcusable delay'; attending hearings; preparing and lodging written submissions when required; and complying with the tribunal's orders and directions including those in connection with evidence and procedure. The English provision requires the parties to take these particular steps 'without delay'.

Application to arbitration?

The 1996 Act s 40(1) provides that the parties 'shall do all things necessary for the proper and expeditious conduct of the arbitral proceedings'.

In *Elektrim SA v Vivendi Universal SA* [2007] EWHC 11 (Comm) it was held that the obligations placed on the parties by the 1996 Act s 40 (general duty of the parties) did not constitute an implied term of the arbitration agreement. The mandatory provisions of the Act, which includes s 40, apply as statutory obligations, and in English law and under the 1996 Act the fact that the parties could shape the powers of the arbitral tribunal to deal with breaches of the s 40 duties does not turn the nature of the duties imposed by that section into an implied term of the arbitration agreement. The court also held that, were those duties to be imposed as implied terms, the court would need the power to intervene to award damages for breach and it has neither the express nor the implied power so to do, its only power being to intervene as set out by s 42 of the Act. Finally, to say that the s 40 duties were imposed as implied terms would be inconsistent with other parts of the structure of Part I of the Act.

There are no Scottish cases on this point, but reference may be made to *Rolls-Royce plc v Riddle* [2008] IRLR 873, a Scottish case before Lady Smith sitting as employment tribunal judge, where there was provision in the Employment Tribunals (Constitution and Rules of Procedure) Regulations 2004 (SI 2004/1861) Sch 1 para 18 for the making of a striking-out application. Lady Smith held that where a claimant failed to appear at a full hearing of which he was notified, that amounted to a failure to actively pursue his claim and was an 'intentional and contumelious default justifying the striking out of his claim'. It would not usually be difficult to conclude that where a claimant had failed to appear at a full hearing of which he had been notified, that amounted to a failure to actively pursue his claim. Case law demonstrated that cases of failure to actively pursue a claim fell into one of two categories: the first was where there had been intentional and contumelious default by a claimant and the second was where there had been inordinate and inexcusable delay which gave rise to a substantial risk that a fair trial would not be possible, following *Birkett v James* [1978] AC 297 and *Evans v Commissioner of Police of the Metropolis* [1993] ICR 151.

Duty to ensure

Once again, the principle of party autonomy suggests that it is open to the parties to agree how their arbitration is to proceed, even to the exclusion of the duties imposed on the tribunal which can cause tensions (see rule 24 above). Thus, the obligation placed on the parties is 'to ensure' that the arbitration is conducted without unnecessary delay and without incurring unnecessary expense. However, it is suggested that, if *both* parties agreed, for example, to postpone a hearing, and to pay the arbitrator's costs as a result, it would be difficult to see how (or why) the arbitrator could (or would) take action against both parties for delaying the process. If this was carried to ridiculous lengths, the tribunal might consider resignation, but otherwise, and assuming no nefarious reason for the delay, this seems to be within the scope of party autonomy.

Default rule 26 and the concept of confidentiality in arbitral proceedings

The parties in their arbitration agreement can make provision for their proceedings to be kept confidential. That is one of the main advantages encouraging businessmen to use arbitration in preference to an open court procedure. There may be reasons of technical secrecy or competition or share price sensitivity which makes keeping the proceedings private and confidential an important consideration. Therefore, the parties can insert into their agreement that they and the arbitrators must abide by an obligation of confidentiality and may even specify what element and aspects of the arbitration should not be disclosed to any outside person. They may even extend that to witnesses of fact who may come along to give evidence at a hearing or in writing as well as experts who give evidence for the parties. These latter groups would have to sign confidentiality agreements such that any breach by them of the contractual obligation of confidentiality could give rise to an action for damages or interim interdict (although issues remain as to the enforceability of that!).

Normally, if the parties leave it to the rules of arbitral institutions then those rules will dictate (if applicable) the privacy and confidentiality of the proceedings. So, the ICDR Rules (Art 34) apply confidentiality to the arbitrators and administrators and not to the parties. The ICC Rules (Art 20(7)) provide that the arbitral tribunal may take measures for protecting trade secrets and confidential information.

There will also be some necessary exceptions where statutory or other provisions (eg Stock Exchange Rules) require disclosure.

The new Scottish approach

Rule 26 provided for a new approach in Scotland. It is still a default rule and so the parties must not modify or disapply it in the agreement if it is to have effect.

This rule sets out expressly the obligations of confidentiality on the arbitral tribunal and the parties and an obligation on both to take reasonable steps to prevent unauthorised disclosure by third parties involved in the arbitration (which would cover experts, witnesses to fact, clerks, administrative support staff, etc) and what the consequences are for such a breach.

Rule 26 starts by providing that the arbitrator(s) and the parties must not disclose confidential information as defined in rule 26(4) relating to the arbitration. There are various exceptions to this. The effect is that disclosure will be a breach of an obligation of confidentiality unless the parties agree otherwise. The confidential information definition is wide and means any information which is not, and never has been, in the public domain relating to the dispute; the arbitral proceedings; the award or any civil proceedings relating to the arbitration in respect of which an order has been granted under s 15 (relating to anonymity in public proceedings – see above).

The parties' obligation of confidentiality is owed both to each other and to the tribunal. This is the language of contract, not delict, and so it must be the purpose of the Act to make it an express term of the arbitration that there is such an obligation. There is no room for arguing for implied terms if the parties have agreed that default rule 26 will apply.

The tribunal itself is also placed under an obligation of confidentiality to the parties.

Note also that the tribunal is placed under a duty to inform the parties at the outset of the arbitration of the obligations which this rule imposes on them (rule 26(3)).

It is suggested that this contractual obligation of confidentiality may be capable of being enforced by interdict in order to restrain any actual or threatened breach, subject to the normal tests of a *prima facie* case, and the balance of convenience between granting an interdict, as judged by the prejudice suffered by the pursuer in not granting it as against the other party in doing so. (In England, this is referred to as the *American Cyanamid* test after *American Cyanamid Co v Ethicon Ltd* [1975] 2 WLR 316, although the considerations are very slightly different.)

The confidential information

Rule 26(4) is wide and makes it clear that *any* information *relating to* the dispute, the proceedings, the award or any civil proceedings is 'confidential information'.

It is still open to the parties to agree to disclose this information if they expressly or impliedly authorise that disclosure. Some institutional rules make provision that an award may only be made public with the consent of the parties and the Scottish rule here follows that approach. (See various levels of protection in the LCIA Rules Art 30; ICDR Rules Art 34; and UNCITRAL Rules Art 32(5).) Sometimes, though, the information has to be made public such as when the award is to be enforced by a national court. In England, following *Hassneh Insurance Co of Israel v Stuart J Mew* [1993] 2 Lloyd's Rep 243, it may not be a breach of confidentiality to disclose an award to a third party if it is reasonably necessary for the establishment or protection of an arbitrating party's legal rights vis-à-vis the third party (the exception to the duty of confidentiality applying equally to the reasons for the award). Sometimes the awards will be published if the identifying information has been removed or redacted and with the consent of the parties (see ICDR Rules Art 27(8)). The rule in the 2010 Act also permits this.

Can an award be used by a successful party in another arbitration under the same agreement? The possibility that an award could be used as set-off to defend a counterclaim has been discussed under r 19. This leads to the question as to whether there is a continuing obligation of confidentiality.

Continuing obligation of confidentiality?

Whether there is a continuing obligation of confidentiality does not appear
to have been determined, as the Act is silent on the point. The use of the
present tense 'is' in rule 26(1) might suggest that confidentiality is an ongoing obligation perhaps beyond the life of the tribunal itself. It is suggested
that this must be the correct view, as otherwise the confidentiality provisions
would be of limited value.

Confidential information in relation to the arbitration is defined as 'any
information relating to the dispute itself, the arbitral proceedings, the award
or any civil proceedings in relation to the arbitration in respect of which an
order has been granted under section 15'. It is only confidential information
if it is not, and has never been, in the public domain.

Section 15(1) (discussed above) deals with Anonymity in Legal Proceedings
and provides that a party to any civil proceedings may apply to the court for
an order prohibiting the disclosure of the identity of a party to the arbitration
in any report of the proceedings. By virtue of s 31(1), the court in this context
means any court rather than just the sheriff court or the Outer House of the
Court of Session. Section 15(2) states that the court must grant the order
unless satisfied that disclosure would fall into one of a number of exceptions,
and by s 15(3), the decision of the court on the application is final, ie not
subject to an appeal.

A party would have to make the application under RCS 100.9 and the
application or appeal is referred to, as previously mentioned, as 'Arbitration
Application' or 'Arbitration Appeal' with a designated number and the year
in order to preserve confidentiality.

Lord Glennie explained the procedure in *Arbitration Application No 3 of
2011* [2011] CSOH 164 (paras [21] and [22]):

> The Rules aim to protect confidentiality in and relating to the arbitration: see
> Rule 26. That confidentiality may, however, be put at risk if one or other of
> the parties takes proceedings in court under the Act. S.15 of the Act seeks to
> address this by entitling a party to civil proceedings relating to an arbitration
> (other than proceedings for enforcement under s.12) to apply to the court for an
> order prohibiting disclosure of the identity of a party to the arbitration in any
> report of the proceedings ... The practical problem of how to protect that ano-
> nymity pending such an application is addressed in RC100.9. It provides that
> any application for anonymity shall be made not later than the hearing of the
> motion for further procedure under RC100.5(5), i.e. by the end of the hearing of
> that motion. Until then, the petition will not be available for inspection, except
> by court staff and the parties, the petition shall be referred to publicly, e.g. in
> the Rolls of Court, as 'Arbitration Application' or 'Arbitration Appeal' and by
> number and year. Hence this petition is referred to as Arbitration Application
> No.3 of 2011; and that anonymity is preserved in the heading of this Opinion.
> In giving my decision I have tried to avoid setting out any details which
> might betray the identity of the parties. Explanation of the points at issue is
> necessarily lacking in particulars.

In any judgment decided by the Court the parties may first have the opportunity to review it prior to publication. In *Arbitration Application No 2 of 2011* [2011] CSOH 186, Lord Glennie explained (para [31]) how this might operate practically:

> At the motion for further procedure, I granted a motion for anonymity in terms of s.15 of the 2010 Act and Rule of Court 100.9. In setting out and explaining my decision, I have attempted to respect both the letter and spirit of this requirement for anonymity, though the subject matter of the lease makes the task somewhat difficult. This difficulty is likely to be encountered to some degree, though possibly not in the acute form in which it arises here, whenever arbitration applications come before the courts, particularly since, subject to the statutory protection of anonymity in arbitration cases where an order is made under s.15, there is a public interest in open justice. It was agreed at the end of the hearing that in the first instance I should issue my Opinion to the parties without publishing it more widely, to enable them to make representations as to whether there should be publication and, if so, whether any details could be omitted without removing from my decision such sense as it might otherwise have.

The interpretation of rule 26, and its interaction with s 15 of the Act arose in the case of *North Lanarkshire Council v Stewart and Shields Ltd* 2017 SLT 741. As noted above, parties may impliedly authorise the disclosure of confidential information in arbitral proceedings. In this case, in the course of an arbitration application against an arbitrator's Pt 5 Award, the council moved for an order in terms of s 15 prohibiting the disclosure of the identity of any party to the proceedings. The facts are discussed above.

The contractor opposed the application on the basis that the information sought to be protected was already in the public domain by reason of its publication on the website and no order could or ought to be granted under s 15 of the 2010 Act.

The court decided that the application should be refused. It noted that rule 26 was subordinated to s 15 by reason of being located in secondary legislation, although there was an express link between the two. It affirmed that if the 'obligation of confidentiality' in the arbitration proceedings was breached, any breach could be actionable unless one of the exceptions applied, and once confidential information had been disclosed, it was no longer confidential and could not be undisclosed under reference to the proviso at the end of rule 26(4) that the confidential information was not, and never had been, in the public domain.

Exceptions

Rule 26(1) permits exceptions to these obligations if the disclosure is authorised – expressly or impliedly by the parties – or if it can reasonably be considered as having been so authorised. It is also authorised if the tribunal considers it required or if the disclosure is made to assist or enable the tribunal to conduct the arbitration. The onus there would be on the tribunal to demonstrate that requirement. Lastly, a disclosure is authorised if it is required in order to comply with any enactment of law; for the proper performance of the discloser's public functions; or to enable a public body or office holder to perform its public functions.

Public interest disclosure

Disclosure can also be made if it can 'reasonably be considered as being needed to protect a party's lawful interests' (eg if the party had to intimate the proceedings to its insurer); if it is in the public interest; if it is necessary in the 'interests of justice' or is made in circumstances in which the discloser would have absolute privilege had the information been defamatory (eg in parliamentary proceedings).

The public interest exception is a nod in the direction of Australian jurisprudence regarding arbitral confidentiality where it has been held that, although the privacy of arbitral proceedings should be maintained and respected, confidentiality was not an essential attribute of arbitrations and, although the proceedings were conducted *in camera*, this did not mean that there was an obligation prohibiting disclosure of documents and information provided in the arbitration especially where there was a public legitimate interest in obtaining information about the affairs of public authorities (*Esso Australia Resources Ltd v Plowman* (1995) 183 CLR 10). In that jurisdiction it is considered that the courts view governmental secrets differently from personal and commercial secrets. On this see also *Commonwealth of Australia v Cockatoo Dockyard Pty Ltd* [1995] 36 NEWLR 662.

Disclosure to protect a party's lawful public interests

Paragraph (1)(d) covers disclosure where this is needed to protect a person's lawful interests. In *Emmott v Michael Wilson & Partners Ltd* [2008] EWCA Civ 184, Lawrence Collins LJ said (at para 101) that:

> ... disclosure was permissible when, and to the extent to which, it was reasonably necessary for the establishment or protection of an arbitrating party's legal rights vis-à-vis a third party in order to found a cause of action against that third party or to defend a claim, or counterclaim, brought by that third party. It would be this exception which would apply where insurers have to be informed about the details of arbitral proceedings.

This argument should, therefore, allow the use of the award to defend other proceedings by way of set-off, since not to do so would produce a manifest injustice.

Preventing unauthorised disclosure by third parties

The duty of confidentiality is not imposed on third parties, for example professional advisers, witnesses to fact and expert witnesses (unless the definition of 'parties' includes their advisers). However, rule 26 provides that the tribunal and the parties must take reasonable steps to prevent such unauthorised disclosure by third parties involved in the conduct of the arbitration (rule 26(2)).

It is expected that the parties or tribunal will enter into collateral private confidentiality agreements with the third parties to the arbitration, or the tribunal could take undertakings from them that they would not disclose any 'confidential information' in so far as that is defined in rule 26(4). If the privacy and confidentiality of the proceedings are to be maintained, then some ancillary arrangement would be required as disclosure by third parties is not a breach of any duty of confidentiality imposed by rule 26 (as it is only disclosures by the tribunal, any arbitrator or a party that is actionable).

Remedies for breach

A breach of the obligation of confidentiality by the tribunal will give rise to an entitlement to raise an action against the tribunal itself or some of its members at the instance of the party or parties to whom the obligation was owed. This would most likely be for the remedy of interdict to restrain further disclosures, or an action for damages for loss and damage sustained by the party arising from the breach. Breach of the duty of confidentiality will also for instance allow removal of an arbitrator by the agreement of the parties under rule 11 or by the court under rule 12 where it leads to substantial injustice.

Failure by the tribunal to comply with any of the duties in rule 26 may also be a ground for a serious irregularity appeal where non-compliance causes substantial injustice.

Disapplication or modification of rule 26

Finally, what happens if the parties modify default rule 26 or disapply it? Is there still a lingering obligation of confidentiality or is it removed completely? It is suggested that this could give rise to two constructions – that the removal or modification means that the parties intended it not to be an issue, or they have impliedly agreed there is an implied obligation of confidentiality similar to the English position.

English position

As already discussed, in England and Wales arbitrations are considered private as the parties have agreed to submit the dispute arising between them – and only between them – to arbitration (*Oxford Shipping Co Ltd v Nippon Yusen Kaisha (The Eastern Saga) (No 2)* [1984] 3 All ER 835).

This agreement carries with it an implied obligation on their part not to disclose matters relating to that arbitration. That includes documents and evidence adduced in the course of the arbitration (*Hassneh Insurance Co of Israel v Stuart J Mew* [1993] 2 Lloyd's Rep 243).

In *Dolling-Baker v Merrett* [1990] 1 WLR 1205, Parker LJ noted (pp. 1213–14):

> As between parties to an arbitration, although the proceedings are consensual and may thus be regarded as wholly voluntary, their very nature is such that there must ... be some implied obligation on both parties not to disclose or use for any other purpose any documents prepared for and used in the arbitration, or disclosed or produced in the course of the arbitration, or transcripts or notes of the evidence in the arbitration or the award, and indeed not to disclose in any other way what evidence had been given by any witnesses in the arbitration, save with the consent of the other party, or pursuant to an order or leave of the court. That qualification is necessary, just as it is in the case of the implied obligation of secrecy between banker and customer ... that the obligation exists in some form appears to me to be abundantly apparent. It is not a question of immunity or public interest. It is a question of an implied obligation arising out of the nature of arbitration itself.

So, the obligation of non-disclosure may be waived (impliedly or explicitly – cf rule 26(1)(a)) or ordered by the court. Other exceptions to the confidentiality requirement may include the situation where it is 'reasonably necessary for the protection of the interests of a party to the arbitration' (*Hassneh Insurance Co of Israel v Stuart J Mew* [1993] 2 Lloyd's Rep 243; *Ali Shipping Corp v Shipyard Trogir* [1998] 2 All ER 136; *Webb v Lewis Silkin LLP* [2015] EWHC 687 (Ch); cf rule 26(1)(d)) or the public interest or that the interests of justice require it (*Milsom v Ablyazov* [2011] EWHC 955 (Ch); cf rule 26(1)(e) and (f)).

Questions have arisen as to confidentiality when the courts have been called upon to assist the arbitral process. This might be in interim applications or where proceedings subsequently arise in court in, for example, challenges to awards, or applications to make use of materials in previous arbitrations.

But confidentiality will likely be maintained against 'non-parties' to the arbitration unless the parties to that arbitration consent. In *Glidepath BV v Thompson* [2005] EWHC 818 (Comm), legal proceedings were commenced contrary to an arbitration agreement. The court granted freezing injunctions and disclosure orders and then stayed the proceedings. A third party and a non-party to the arbitration sought information relating to the injunctions and orders on the basis of it being reasonably necessary to protect or establish a wrongful dismissal claim or otherwise in the interests of justice. The court found that it had failed to do so, the parties did not consent to release of that information and therefore it was protected by the confidentiality attaching to arbitral proceedings.

In *Emmott v Michael Wilson & Partners Ltd* [2008] EWCA Civ 184 the question for the Court of Appeal was whether pleadings in a London arbitration could be properly disclosed to the defendants in proceedings abroad. Noting the implied obligation, arising out of the nature of arbitration itself, on both parties to an English arbitration not to disclose or use for any other purpose any documents prepared for and used in the arbitration, when a dispute had arisen as to the applicability and extent of confidentiality it had normally in the past been resolved by an application to the court for an injunction to restrain disclosure. In this case the court considered that the disclosure could be made on the basis of the exception of the 'interests of justice.'

Issues have arisen with confidentiality and whether an application in arbitration proceedings should be in open court and the position with publication of any decision thereafter.

In *Symbion Power LLC v Venco Imtiaz Construction Company* [2017] EWHC 348 (TCC) an issue was taken in connection with the s 68 challenge application that any publication of the Court's decision on the application would cause the disclosure of confidential information and that one of the parties would suffer prejudice as a result. The court (Jefford J) drew a distinction between the hearing of such an application and the publication of the judgment. She noted that under CPR a s 68 application will be heard in private, but that the judgment thereafter is another matter. She considered that the strong public interest in the publication of judgments, including those relating to arbitrations, must be balanced against the parties' legitimate expectation that arbitration proceedings and awards will be confidential to the parties. The court therefore needed to weigh up the various factors and consider whether either party would suffer real prejudice from the judgment being made public. In the circumstances of the case, it was held that the underlying award was already in the public domain and thus it was unrealistic of the claimant to argue that it had a legitimate expectation of confidentiality in it.

In *Chung v Silver Dry Bulk Co Ltd* [2019] EWHC 1479 (Comm) the court had to consider whether a challenge to the substantive jurisdiction of an arbitrator under the Arbitration Act 1996 s 67 should itself be in public following *Department of Economic Policy and Development of the City of Moscow v Bankers Trust Co* [2004] EWCA Civ 314. The court considered that there were cases where the judgment should be in public. The court acknowledged that the starting point was that an arbitration involved a situation where the parties had elected to arbitrate confidentially and privately. However, it was different where parties brought arbitration claims to court where they could not rely on that confidentiality or privacy as there is a public interest in allowing scrutiny to be given to judgments. The court held that this applied to applications under s 67 and s 68.

The position may be different if an award has entered the public domain. In *UMS Holdings Ltd v Great Station Properties SA* [2017] EWHC 2473 (Comm), the s 68 challenge itself had taken place in public. The court read the entire award before the hearing, parts of it were read out in open court, counsel made detailed submissions as to its content, and parts of the award were quoted and referred to by the court in its judgment. As a result, the court held that the award was in the public domain. It couldn't be said that there was at that point an ongoing express contractual obligation to keep it confidential. However, the court did not seek to fetter its discretion in cases like these and held that it possessed an inherent jurisdiction to regulate the 'consequences of an order to hear a s 68 challenge in public'. Parties therefore did not have a discretion themselves as to what could be made of the award and the court held that the award retains its confidentiality further to the original agreement to arbitrate unless the party could demonstrate to a court in an application what further use they wished to make of it.

The English courts have also dealt with the situation where a party to an arbitration has brought legal proceedings against legal advisers for a breach of confidentiality in earlier arbitral proceedings. In *Webb v Lewis Silkin LLP* [2015] EWHC 687 (Ch) a party to arbitration proceedings brought a claim against the defendant, a firm of solicitors, for breach of confidentiality and misuse of her private information in the arbitration. She had been a partner in another firm of solicitors, had left in dispute and referred the dispute to arbitration. The court held that ordinarily arbitration proceedings were held in private and were confidential to the parties and the claimant owed the firm an ongoing duty to keep the arbitration proceedings confidential but that, although arbitral confidentiality will normally apply, it is not absolute, and in some circumstances can be lifted.

The position is different, it is suggested, where the breach of confidentiality is by a non-party, in which case the tribunal will not have jurisdiction or any power to impose a sanction against that non-party.

There have been cases dealing with attempts by parties to use arbitral awards in subsequent arbitral proceedings. In a decision of the Privy Council, in *Associated Electric & Gas Insurance Services Ltd v European Reinsurance Co of Zurich* [2003] UKPC 11, the court held that while an arbitration award should remain confidential and not be disclosed to third parties, it could not be relied on to prevent the award creditor in the arbitration from enforcing the award in a later private arbitration of the same two parties.

In *Party E v Party C* BT/109/2016; [2018] 1 WLUK 108, a decision of the Lands Tribunal of Northern Ireland, a tenant in a lease applied to court for disclosure of an arbitration award which had involved the landlord and a third party and in which the tenant claimant had had no interest or involvement. The Lands Tribunal noted that there was no authority in existence to justify such an application and concluded that it was bound by law to protect the privacy interests of the landlord unless 'the tenant could demonstrate that it was reasonably necessary, rather than merely convenient,' for it to have details of the arbitration award.

Finally, in *Chartered Institute of Arbitrators v B* [2019] EWHC 460 (Comm) the court had had to deal with the situation where disclosure of confidential material from an arbitration was said to be necessary for internal disciplinary proceedings under the disciplinary rules of an institution (the CIArb). The court held that the 'interests of justice' exception included public interest (cf rule 26(e)) and there was a general public interest in maintaining the quality of and standards of arbitrators and that extended beyond the interests of the parties in a particular case to the wider section of the public who chose to refer their disputes to arbitration.

Tribunal's deliberations

Rule 27 is a default rule which provides that the tribunal is not required to share its deliberations with the parties but must advise them if an arbitrator fails to participate in any of the deliberations. It is unclear what effect this failure has on any award made.

Deliberations are different from the end product – the final award. It is open also to an arbitrator or a tribunal not to participate in the deliberations in the writing of the award, hence these provisions, or, indeed, they may write a dissenting opinion.

ARBITRAL PROCEEDINGS (PART 4)

Power of the tribunal to determine procedure

Rule 28 is a default rule that, in the absence of agreement between the parties, the arbitrator or the tribunal can determine the procedure to be followed in the arbitration as well as any evidential matters. Note that the parties can choose to adopt part of the rule and reject the other parts for example, rule 28(2) – a default rule applies only in so far as the parties have not agreed to modify or disapply that rule or any part of it).

Courts will be slow to interfere with procedural decisions of a tribunal unless there has been lack of due process and serious irregularity.

In *K v S* [2019] EWHC 2386 (Comm) the claimant lodged an accountancy expert report. The respondent objected to it on the basis that the report referred to a number of factors which had not been pleaded, or pleaded adequately, or sufficiently particularised, and applied for it to be struck out. The tribunal agreed.

The claimant then made an application to set aside the decision of the tribunal for procedural impropriety under s 68 on the basis that it had wrongly excluded the expert report. The court held (after noting s 33 and the general duty of the tribunal to act fairly and impartially) that the decision had fallen within s 34, which concerned procedural and evidential matters and that this application was not really a s 68 case. Section 68 deals with due process and, in the present case, the tribunal had ruled out expert evidence which had not been pleaded sufficiently, even where the applicant had been given every opportunity to put its case as to why it should be allowed to adduce that evidence. The court reiterated that it is not the function of the court to assess whether the tribunal had reached a correct decision in the exercise of its arbitral functions provided that due process had been followed in reaching that decision.

This rule is designed to cater for situations which can become 'flashpoints' in international arbitration. Because of the international elements in the process, parties and indeed arbitrators frequently come from different legal 'families' and thus expect to do things in different ways when it comes to procedure and evidence.

In addition, and as touched upon elsewhere, domestically there has been complaint over the years that arbitrators have been too ready merely to adopt the relevant Rules of Court as their procedure – simply 'cutting and pasting' procedure designed for formal litigation into a process in which there is supposed to be flexibility and manoeuvrability and even ingenuity. This wholesale adoption has been difficult to challenge traditionally, even in the face of judicial criticism. The words of Lord Prosser relating to pre-2010 procedure in *ERDC Construction v HM Love & Co (No 2)* 1996 SC 523 remain relevant:

> Pleadings of the type currently used in ordinary court procedure are frequently, and indeed normally, ill-suited to their true function, failing to put essentials in sharp focus, and often putting in sharp focus inessential matters of detail, which then become the subject of pointless procedural scrutiny. Even with careful adaptation to the quite different context of arbitration, I do not consider that court pleadings will normally provide a useful model in that context; and if, as in this case, the model appears to have been adopted without the appropriate adaptation, there is an even greater risk of running into a quite unreal – and unnecessary – procedural quagmire. In my opinion, far from copying 'formal' court models in this manner, arbiters will usually do better if they require in writing the kind of notice of issues which they in their own good sense feel they need, and which indeed any competent practitioner could set out in a relatively brief letter. If that were the practice in arbitrations, it may well be that the courts could learn from it.

The theme was developed by Lord Glennie in *Arbitration Application No 2 of 2011* [2011] CSOH 186 in respect of a legal error appeal, in which he noted:

> The legal error appeal proceeds entirely upon the findings of fact found by the arbitrator in his award. Despite that, the case has become somewhat bogged down in pleadings, involving detailed averments in the answers and adjustments to the petition and answers thereafter. For my part, while different considerations may well apply to other appeals and applications under the SAR, I would not wish to encourage detailed pleading on a legal error appeal. In a legal error appeal, unless one party or the other wishes to assert facts relevant to the exercise by the court of any of its powers under the Act, for example the power under Rule 71(8) of the SAR to order the tribunal to state its reasons in greater detail to enable the appeal to be dealt with properly, there is no scope for either party to make averments of fact about the underlying dispute, and extensive

pleading will be unnecessary and, being unnecessary, is likely to be conducive of unnecessary delay. It will normally be sufficient for the respondents in their answers to make clear that they seek to support the award. Adjustment to the petition and answers will seldom, if ever, be required. The hearing of the appeal itself will usually proceed on a basis of written notes of argument lodged in advance of the hearing, rather than on the basis of the formal pleadings.

That said, it is understood (admittedly on apocryphal grounds) that many arbitrators are now taking a more radical approach and provisions such as rule 28 – if adopted by the parties – would permit them to do so. This, it is suggested, is to be encouraged, and the rule makes it clear that arbitrators are entitled, and probably required, to do so and, bearing in mind overriding principles as well as their mandatory duty in terms of rule 24, to operate without unnecessary delay and unnecessary expense. Rule 28 allows them to seek to evolve and create a procedure suitable to the arbitration and the parties thereto with the qualification that it should be remembered that, where the parties agree a different course (by individual agreement or institutional reference) that obviously takes precedence under the principle of party autonomy.

It is suggested that the tribunal should seek to avoid technical or court expressions which may be easily translated concepts to a lawyer but are barriers to understanding for the lay users of the system.

The tribunal should encourage the parties to define the issues and consider breaking the arbitration into manageable parts in appropriate cases. It is also suggested that use should be made of statements of agreed facts and/or law, and, where necessary, a common expert is used, reporting to the tribunal, rather than two 'hired guns' acting as advocates for the parties, as is often the case.

A real issue for the tribunal may be that which has vexed the courts in Scotland – how pro-active should the decision-maker be? Note that in *Field v Network Rail Infrastructure Ltd* [2020] EWHC 3440 (Ch) the court allowed an arbitrator to act in a manner which might be thought to be inquisitorial.

This is particularly apposite as some countries adopt a very 'hands off' adversarial function (traditionally common law systems) while civilian jurisdictions would expect a far more 'inquisitorial' or 'pro-active' decision-maker. This can cause particular problems in international arbitration where the parties are from different traditions (cf the Prague Rules discussed below).

The pro-active arbitrator

The basic structure of dispute resolution in the Scottish courts and arbitrations is, in reality, adversarial, notwithstanding the civil law influences on the Scottish system. While the Act is wide enough to allow a more inquisitorial approach, it seems unlikely that most tribunals will want to move away from a position where the two parties argue their cases and the arbitrator(s) provide(s) a decision.

That having been said, arbitrators should be able and willing to take a more pro-active approach when this seems to be in the interests of a speedier and/or cost-effective resolution of the issues. For example, the tribunal could issue directions requiring that a particular issue be the subject of a report from an independent expert, even if the parties were not addressing the issue, if the arbitrator(s) considered that resolving this point could shorten the proceedings.

While it would be wrong for a tribunal to force the parties to incur costs that they considered unnecessary, there will be cases where a bold approach will be appropriate. In practice, it is suggested that the tribunal should discuss its ideas with the parties and seek to obtain their agreement, rather than proceeding directly to mandatory directions.

It has become relatively common practice for experts in English litigation to meet outwith the hearings. This would seem to be an appropriate approach in arbitration, in cases where a joint expert is not possible or desirable. However, this should, it is suggested, be merely a meeting between the experts to agree a common approach to the greatest extent possible. It would, for example, be generally inappropriate for the tribunal to meet with the experts in the absence of the parties or their legal advisers, as to do so would amount to the tribunal receiving evidence of which the parties were unaware, and the necessary transparency of the process would be lost.

Of course, the tribunal could simply suggest to the parties that they meet and agree lists of documents and productions and witnesses that they intend to rely on. Such an approach was endorsed by the English courts in *Petroships Pte Ltd of Singapore v Petec Trading & Investment Corpn of Vietnam (The Petro Ranger)* [2001] 2 Lloyd's Rep 348 where the court observed that in major arbitrations arbitrators ought to consider directing those representing the parties to liaise with the aim of coming up with an agreed list of the important issues of fact and law; in a separate section of such a document, a list could be provided of what was common ground between the parties. This case supports the approach of getting experts to meet, but also suggests there can be no criticism in getting the legal advisers to take a similar approach to the legal issues.

There is some guidance from other English cases. The analogous section in the 1996 Act is s 34. That and s 33 have been held to give arbitrators a broad discretion in matters of procedure and evidence (*Sonatrach v Statoil* [2014] EWHC 875 (Comm), *New Age Alzarooni 2 Ltd v Range Energy Natural Resources Inc* [2014] EWHC 4358 (Comm)).

In *Checkpoint Ltd v Strathclyde Pension Fund* [2003] EWCA Civ 84, the court determined that there had been no 'procedural irregularity' in the conduct of an arbitration hearing to determine a rent review of business premises where the arbitrator had relied on his own experience and knowledge of local lettings in the same area. Furthermore, the arbitrator had not exercised inquisitorial powers, although caution is perhaps required in the Scottish context on analogy with *SGL Carbon Fibres Ltd v RBG Ltd* [2011] CSOH 62 where an adjudicator was held to have made use of his own knowledge and experience to make factual determinations for which there was no evidence and without giving the parties an opportunity to comment thereon and was therefore in breach of the requirement of natural justice.

In *Warborough Investments Ltd v S Robinson & Sons (Holdings) Ltd* [2003] EWCA Civ 751 the claimant contended that the arbitrator had failed to give the parties an opportunity to make submissions before adopting an approach to the valuation which neither party had advocated, consequently breaching his duty of fairness under s 33 of the 1996 Act. The court rejected that and sided with the arbitrator. It considered that the arbitrator's failure to invite further submissions did not constitute a breach of his statutory duty of fairness under s 33 and concluded that the arbitrator was entitled to apply the figures he had on the basis of the material before him.

Note that while the arbitrator was supported here, the judgment does seem to be on the basis that the approach taken *was* an irregularity, but the court determined that it was not of such a serious nature as to merit over-turning the award. It is suggested that the approach advocated above would reduce the risk of challenge and uncertainty in this area.

Lastly, it is increasingly common in international arbitration for the expert witnesses to give their evidence concurrently – sometimes referred to as 'joint conferencing hot-tubbing' It was used in a long-running Scottish proof, *SSE Generation Ltd v Hochtief Solutions AG and another* [2016] CSOH 177. Lord Woolman explained in the judgment that the court heard 'concurrent evidence from the experts' and went on (at para 156): 'This procedure, known colloquially as "hot-tubbing", involved several experts being present in court at the same time. I chaired a discussion between them with a view to crystallising their respective positions. I found it a valuable way of focussing on the main issues and assessing the quality of their contributions.'

The common law and the civil law traditions

There is always a risk of over-generalisation in seeking to draw a distinction between common law and civil law systems, but, if there are 'fault lines', they are often seen in international arbitrations. In summary, traditionally the central tenets of the Anglo-American adversarial system were that it was the parties who initiated the action; framed the pleadings; selected the material facts; selected the bases in law upon which the suit proceeded; and determined to a large extent the progress of the suit, the conduct of the trial and any appeal thereafter. The pleadings and the procedure pre-trial were all directed towards a set piece, single session trial at which each side would confront the other before the presiding judge and the jury. Thus, justice would be best served if the advocate and the decision-maker were different persons. The task of the judge throughout was to ensure the due administration of justice between the parties, not necessarily the ascertainment of truth. The judge was the referee and the parties were the competitors. As Lord Denning commented in *Burmah Oil Co v Bank of England* [1979] 1 WLR 473 at 484:

> In litigation, as in war. If one side makes a mistake, the other can take advantage of it. No holds are barred.

'Continental' or 'civil law' systems are said to be 'inquisitorial'. What is meant by this, at its simplest, is that the civil law procedural systems do not possess a jury, do not rely so heavily upon written pleadings and the judge is vested with greater powers to investigate the 'truth' of the parties' contentions and is bound to question, inform, encourage and advise the parties, lawyers and witnesses so as to get a true and complete picture. The judge is normally a trained professional. He may even make findings on legal grounds not advanced by the parties. Previous cases on similar facts do not necessarily determine the dispute in the present, civil law systems placing a greater store on the elucidation of principle from institutional writers, codes and principles encapsulated in previous decisions.

Separately but related to this, Lord President Cooper saw differences between the two systems in the modes of reasoning employed in each:

> A civilian system differs from a Common Law system much as rationalism differs from empiricism or deduction from induction. The civilian naturally reasons from principles to instances, the common lawyer from instances to principles. The civilian puts his faith in syllogisms, the common lawyer in precedents; the first silently asking himself as each new problem arises, 'What should we do this time?' and the second asking aloud in the same situation, 'What did we do last time?' The civilian thinks in terms of rights and duties, the common lawyer in terms of remedies. The civilian is chiefly concerned with the policy and rationale of a rule of law, the common lawyer with its pedigree. The instinct of the civilian is to systematise. The working rule of the common lawyer is *solvitur ambulando*. (Rt Hon Lord Cooper of Culross, 'The Common Law and the Civil Law – A Scot's View' in *Selected Papers 1922–1954* (Edinburgh, 1957) 201 at 204. Note, though, that he added that this was 'a deliberate overstatement of the position'.)

In conclusion, it might be said that the two systems approach reasoning and 'fact-finding' in different ways. The common law tradition 'perceives fact-finding as a "lay" activity separate from, and generally anterior to, the "judicial" activity of interpreting and applying the law' whereas the civil law tradition sees 'fact-finding as an integral part of the process by which a dispute between laymen is submitted for determination by a trained professional judiciary'.

It has been said that there is also a psychological distinction in this approach to fact-finding, the adversarial system assuming a witness will be unlikely to tell the truth unless he testifies in open court and is challenged by the party against whom he is testifying, and the inquisitorial procedure assuming that a witness will be inhibited by the prospect of challenge and is more likely to tell the truth in private to a judge who questions him from a neutral standpoint.

In reality, these two classifications are probably more misleading than helpful as they presuppose two parallel procedural systems which can be directly compared point by point. Broad comparisons can of course be made but, in practice, continental systems differ amongst themselves and there are elements of adversarialism in all. Sometimes inquisitorial systems do not actually employ all of the elements which the common lawyer would perceive as inquisitorialism in civil (ie non-criminal) actions. So also, common law systems have retreated from the standards of adversarialism and for some time have adopted, in part, so-called 'inquisitorial' approaches.

Scots law is said to be a 'mixed system' of law. What is meant by this, very simply, is that Scots law, as a result of its development, has one foot in the English common law system and the other in the civil law tradition. This is so in the context of civil procedure. In *Thomson v Glasgow Corporation* 1961 SLT 237 at 245–46, LJ-C Thomson said:

> A litigation is in essence a trial of skill between opposing parties conducted under recognised rules, and the prize is the judge's decision. We have rejected inquisitorial methods and prefer to regard our judges as entirely independent. Like referees at boxing contests they see that the rules are kept and count the points.

In *Duke of Argyll v Duchess of Argyll* 1962 SLT 333 at 338, however, the First Division (a year later) commented that:

> [If] litigations in these courts were just games of skill and ingenuity that argument [by counsel of the defender] might have some force: but the object of a litigation is to enable the court to ascertain the truth, not to give either scope or, indeed, encouragement to tactical manoeuvring.

Documents and electronically stored information (ESI)

Since the tribunal has control over the process, and does not have to follow any court or other rules unless necessary or desirable, it will not usually be necessary to produce original documents or certified copies unless there is some special reason for the tribunal (or the other party) to have sight of the original (cf enforcement and award and agreement) or the parties have adopted the provisions of the Civil Evidence (Scotland) Act 1988 or imposed an 'original' or 'best' evidence requirement.

The parties will produce the documents upon which they seek to rely early on in the arbitration, and documents in their possession which are not subject to any valid claim for privilege, and which might tend to cast doubt on their case.

Electronically stored information (ESI) has become a major issue in international arbitration in recent years particularly regarding compliance with

GDPR regulations and for obvious cybersecurity reasons. The practice of sending information by USB with log in details separately has fallen away and parties and tribunals increasingly use 'platforms' where information can be filed. This leads to a greater coherent level of security. Associated with this is 'e-disclosure' for use in cases in which some disclosable documents are in electronic form.

Some institutions and arbitral bodies have promulgated guides and protocols to assist parties and tribunals. For example, the CIArb: *Protocol for E-Disclosure in International Arbitration* (2008); AAA/ICDR: *Guidelines for Information Disclosure and Exchange in International Arbitration Proceedings*; CPR *Protocol on Pre-Hearing Disclosure of Documents and Information in Arbitration* (2008); ICC Commission Report: *Information Technology in International Arbitration* (2017); ICCA-New York City Bar-CPR Institute *Protocol on Cybersecurity in International Arbitration* (2020).

Evidence

Admissibility, relevancy, materiality and weight to be attached to evidence led before a tribunal are all 'legal' considerations in the sense that as concepts they developed in the law of evidence. The concepts, however, are also very much part of arbitral practice. It is noticeable Art 27.4 of the UNCITRAL Rules 1976 (Revised 2010 and 2013) states, in similar wording that:

> The arbitral tribunal shall determine the admissibility, relevance, materiality and weight of the evidence offered.

Importantly, those issues are issues for the arbitral tribunal and a court will not interfere lightly, if at all. In *Arbitration Application No 3 of 2011* [2011] CSOH 164, Lord Glennie noted (at para [29]):

> It is for the arbitrator to decide questions as to the admissibility, relevance, materiality and weight of any evidence: Rule 28(1)(b). It is not to be assumed that the absence of averments directly on the point will mean that evidence relating to it is inadmissible. Even if the averments are excluded, the evidence may still be admitted. That is for the arbitrator. The petitioners complain that the arbitrator misunderstood the potential relevance of the evidence. If so, so be it. That is not a complaint which the court can entertain. They can try again, at an appropriate stage, to persuade him of its relevance. The exclusion of the averments from the pleadings seems to me to be irrelevant to that question, though ultimately that is for the arbitrator to decide, not the court.

'Admissibility'

Admissibility is whether the evidence can be 'admitted' or allowed to be led before the tribunal. Sometimes evidence is improperly obtained and may be refused to be heard for that reason.

'Relevancy' is a legal test to be applied by the tribunal as to whether the evidence should be used as relevant evidence or having a connection with the subject-matters in dispute.

'Materiality' of evidence looks to the substance of it.

'Weight' means how the tribunal will assess the evidence in the round or the whole evidence, perhaps placing more emphasis on some of it over other parts. So, for example, the tribunal may prefer the oral evidence of an individual whom it hears over a document or, alternatively, it may do the opposite if it thinks that the documentary record is a better or more reliable source than the human memory.

These are legal concepts and, to that extent, intrude into a private dispute resolution mechanism which can cause problems where the arbitrator fails to apply these legal concepts in a proper legal way. Can his/her award be challenged if he/she fails to understand the concepts or misapplies them? What if the award turns on evidence which was irrelevant (in the legal sense) or was inadmissible (in the legal sense)? What is the status of the final award? Some of these concepts are discussed later in consideration of challenges to and appeals of awards.

Approach of the appellate courts

It should be appreciated that appellate courts are very reluctant to overturn or interfere with a lower court or tribunal's findings in fact. This is because the original court or tribunal is and was in the best position to consider the evidence as it heard it in original form. An appellate court is not in that position. Also in civil procedure, where an application requires to be made for an appeal to be allowed, the law will assume that the parties are accepting the findings in fact for the purposes of that appeal (*Geogas SA v Trammo Gas Ltd (The Baleares)* [1993] 1 Lloyd's Rep 215).

It is suggested that if the arbitrator has taken account of something he ought not to or has failed to take account of something he ought to, then that may be tantamount to an error of law and permit an appeal under rule 69. 69, although *Arbitration Appeal No 4 of 2019* [2020] CSOH 46 makes it clear that the incorrect application of the correct legal principles is not an error of law.

It should also be remembered that these 'legal' concepts are most applicable in the courts, and arbitral tribunals may approach matters in a completely different way.

In respect of the admissibility of evidence, in practice a tribunal tends to be fairly pragmatic, and will likely err on the side of caution in excluding evidence. The main concern of the tribunal is to seek to establish the facts necessary for the determination of the issues between the parties. Tribunals tend not to be limited by highly technical rules of evidence that might prevent them from achieving this goal. Also, in practice the tribunal will admit evidence and then deal with a dispute in connection with it on the basis of 'weight' as opposed to the original objection as to 'admissibility'.

Sometimes lawyers from a common law background tend to forget that and think that they have a challenge to evidence produced or adduced by the other side by relying on highly technical rules deployed in their own jurisdiction. On the other hand, civilian lawyers, more used to evidence being allowed in, should be aware that some tribunals will exclude evidence as inadmissible.

In respect of the burden of proof, *each* party has to prove the facts it alleges – not just the claimant. An example of this can be seen stated explicitly in the UNCITRAL Rules 1976 (as revised 2010, 2013) Art 27: 'Each party shall have the burden of proving the facts relied on to support its claim or defence.'

The standard of proof will normally be close to the balance of probability – the standard used in civil proceedings in this country. That may change if there are serious allegations in relation to fraud, in which case the tribunal may elect to 'raise' the standard to 'beyond all reasonable doubt' or something approximating to that standard.

As to weight, as *Redfern and Hunter on International Arbitration* (6th edn) explains at para 6.86:

> The practice of arbitral tribunals in international arbitrations is to assess the weight to be given to the evidence presented in favour on [sic] any particular proposition by reference to the nature of the proposition to be proved. For example, if the weather at a particular airport on a particular day is an important element in the factual matrix, it is probably sufficient to produce a copy of a contemporary report from a reputable newspaper, rather than to engage a meteorological expert to advise the tribunal.

One sees in modern arbitral practice tribunals giving greater weight to the contents of contemporaneous documents than to oral evidence. This is because a document prepared at the time is often considered 'best evidence'. On this point, Redfern and Hunter note (para 6.90):

> Modern international arbitral tribunals accord greater weight to the contents of contemporary documents than to oral testimony given, possibly years after the event, by witnesses who have obviously been 'prepared' by lawyers representing the parties. In international arbitration, the best evidence that can be presented in relation to any issue of fact is almost invariably contained in the documents that came into existence at the time of the events giving rise to the dispute.

When and where

Hearings or meetings do not necessarily have to take place at the 'seat' – for example, one can have a venue in another place if section 1 prevention of delay and expense considerations apply. Thus, the arbitration can be seated in Edinburgh but the hearing(s) take place in Inverness.

It is suggested that the tribunal should be prepared to be very flexible on this matter – it may, for example, save considerable time to hold a hearing at the site of a property or construction dispute, to allow the tribunal to see the subject-matter of the dispute, rather than merely receive third party evidence.

In the absence of an agreement between the parties, it is suggested that the tribunal should propose the most efficient location for hearings, whether at the seat or elsewhere. In default of agreement, it must be for the tribunal to choose this matter of procedure, but party autonomy means that there must be very good reason for the tribunal to override the wishes of the parties.

The Act does not address the question of facilities for the arbitration, on the sensible basis that this is entirely for the parties and the tribunal to determine.

Recording of evidence

It would be open to the parties or the tribunal to determine that evidence be recorded, either by digital recording or by the traditional method of short-hand writer. This is likely to be an expensive process, and it is suggested that it should take place only where the amount in dispute or the importance of the outcome justifies such expenditure. In addition, the taking of notes of evidence can, unless competent court stenographers are used, cause delay in the process. Another drawback is that witnesses, knowing that their words are being recorded verbatim, can sometimes produce stilted responses. As a matter of good practice, parties, their advisers and witnesses should be advised in advance if recording of any type is to take place, and be offered the chance to correct errors in such a record (but not to modify what was actually said).

A further difficulty can sometimes arise where there is no formal agreement to record or transcribe the evidence yet one of the parties will attempt to surreptitiously record the proceedings. This is made easy in the modern era of digital recording devices. If the other party objects, the tribunal will have to make a ruling as to whether the recording should be stopped, and the material recorded deleted, or whether digital copies or transcripts of the evidence or proceedings already recorded should be provided.

Who may appear?

It should be noted that, as the tribunal is a master of procedure, it would be a matter for it (or, of course, for the parties) to agree who can appear before it as counsel (although take careful note of the provisions of rule 33).

There is nothing in principle against a party itself appearing on its own behalf. In that situation, however, the arbitral tribunal would have to be very careful in being seen to assist that party who had little or no experience of arbitral proceedings whilst observing the principle of impartiality and independence.

The situation may be more complicated where the party in question is a limited liability company or other corporate entity. Here Scottish court practice has been to require the company to retain solicitors and, where appropriate, counsel. (See *Equity and Law Life Assurance Society v Tritonia Ltd* 1943 SC (HL) 88; *Secretary of State for Business, Enterprise and Regulatory Reform v UK Bankruptcy Ltd* [2010] CSIH 80; *Apollo Engineering Ltd v James Scott Ltd* [2012] CSIH 4.)

Arbitrators do not, of course, have to follow the same practice and, where a 'close company' is involved (ie one controlled by a single person, or a small group, for example a family company), there would appear to be merit in allowing the owners to represent the company, subject to suitable authorisation by the board of directors and/or the company in general meeting.

Claims and defences and 'pleadings'

The courts have been consistent that arbitrations should not be an imitation of court proceedings – at least as a default position.

Unless parties agree otherwise, the arbitrator can direct that cases be heard without pleadings. If formal (and in most cases it will be written) pleadings are needed, then these need not be carbon copies of initial writs or summons and defences or answers. As Lord Glennie said in *Arbitration Application No 3 of 2011* [2011] CSOH 164 (at para [29]), 'Pleadings in arbitration need not, indeed normally should not, follow the form of pleadings in common use in the Court of Session'.

There is, it is suggested, no need for 'craves' or 'conclusions' or 'condescendences' or 'averments' or 'pleas-in-law' or any of the other formal procedure in the court system in Scotland.

However, any claim or defence will need to set out what the party concerned expects the tribunal to do, and why it considers the tribunal has power to do it (which may in the end resemble a simplified version of court practice). It seems unlikely that an arbitration will not require at least a basic (written) statement of case and a response in order to crystallise the issues. Modern practice has developed (at least internationally) for there to be, sequentially, a Statement of Claim, Statement of Defence, Reply to Defence and a Response to the Reply or similar such wording. For the respondent there may also be 'counterclaims', sometimes referred to as 'cross-claims'.

A fuller document with evidence and submissions may make it easier for the tribunal thereafter to make orders for directions. It is important to bear in mind the general duty on the tribunal to conduct the proceedings in an efficient way, and to avoid what is often a time-consuming and costly game in the Scottish courts of revising pleadings again and again. Lay parties can feel frustrated by the process of fine-tuning through adjustment of pleadings, and arbitrators should be discouraged from following the same route, unless some major new issue arises.

Revisiting *ERDC Construction v HM Love & Co (No 2)* cited above, in that case there had been a stated case by an arbiter in a building contract dispute to the Court of Session under the Administration of Justice (Scotland) Act 1972 s 3. The claimants, following an earlier decision of the court that they could not claim remuneration *quantum meruit*, sought to amend to introduce a new case in respect of damages for breach of contract. The arbiter allowed the amendment which decision the respondents objected to. The arbiter's decision to allow a minute of amendment by the claimants resulted in what the court referred to as a 'muddled' series of questions put to it in the stated case.

Out of all of this procedural morass the court commented that questions of law could and should be referred to the court for answers but that it was inappropriate for matters of fact or procedure to be included in the stated case as these were matters for the arbiter's complete discretion and control (in terms of the then applicable rules to this arbitration). The court considered that the stated case procedure should not be used to frustrate the arbitration process and bring it into disrepute.

It is suggested that it is likely that the Outer House is going to proceed in line with these sentiments in respect of any allegations of misuse of procedure or any attempts to bring rule 68 or 69 challenges based on procedural issues. While precise procedure will vary from case to case, it is suggested that the tribunal should require the parties to agree a single bundle of documents for use at any hearing. Where relevant, the tribunal should also take pro-active steps to reduce the volume of paper used by issuing directions to restrict unnecessary copying of irrelevant documents. It may also be possible to restrict the volume of paper by encouraging the parties to agree facts so as to avoid the need for these to be proved by the production of documents. There have been a number of recent court cases in London where, despite intervention by judges in case management, the parties have managed to produce enormous quantities of paper in trial bundles, much of it never referred to at trial. Arbitrators should consider specific expenses orders penalising parties who waste time and costs with excessive bundles which are then never used.

Disclosure of documents (or recovery or even discovery?)

It is interesting to note that the reference in rule 28 is to disclosure and this is very much a recognised term in international arbitration. In Scottish court procedure, reference is made to 'recovery of documents' under the authority of the court by 'commission and diligence'.

The English practice in respect of the disclosure of documents has tended to require parties to produce the documents on which they will rely (and those that may damage their case) at a relatively early stage in the proceedings.

This has the laudable aim of making sure that all issues are on the table as soon as possible, but does, of course, mean that the costs of proceedings tend to be front-end loaded, and will be wasted if the case settles. Litigation in the United States can also get bogged down in early discovery and disclosure, including third party depositions, sometimes amounting to little more than fishing expeditions at great cost. Against this, the Scottish practice of leaving proof hearings until legal arguments have been exhausted removes the early costs of the English approach but can also mean that several years of entertaining (for the lawyers) legal argument turns out to have been wasted when a 'smoking gun' memo appears (or fails to appear) at a later stage.

As an extreme example, after disclosure had taken five years, an arbitrator was entitled to strike out a claim on the ground of 'inordinate and inexcusable delay' on the part of the claimant: see *TAG Wealth Management v West* [2008] EWHC 1466 (Comm). (See also the discussion below.)

Examination in chief, cross-examination and re-examination

How, if at all, the parties and their witnesses should be questioned is also a matter for the tribunal and can be one of the flashpoints mentioned at the start of this rule. Oral evidence is obviously permitted, but the use of written interrogatories could be appropriate, and might be very helpful if combined with the witness providing a written statement of his evidence in chief.

Issues have arisen in arbitration hearings where a party has failed to cross-examine a witness led by the other side. A question will then arise as to how the tribunal should proceed. In *P v D* [2019] EWHC 1277 (Comm) the defendant's counsel chose not to cross-examine a witness on a material matter, even when the tribunal gave an indication that he should do so. The tribunal thereafter made a decision, finding that there was no agreement or estoppel on that material matter even though that witness had not been cross-examined on it. They also made a finding concerning the parties' 'common assumption' that there had been no cross-examination.

The claimant made an application to the court arguing that the arbitrators had breached their duty under s 33 to 'act fairly and impartially as between the parties, giving each party a reasonable opportunity of putting his case and dealing with that of his opponent', and in respect of the 'common assumption' such a case was not addressed adequately or at all by the first defendant, nor was it ever argued or dealt with during the hearing before the arbitrators. The court agreed that there had been a breach on both grounds. As no challenge was made to the witness's evidence, no case had been put to him as to the material issue. The court added that witnesses must have a fair opportunity to counter allegations made and here the witness was given no opportunity to explain his case on those matters or to meet what the arbitrators subsequently concluded was the 'proper analysis of his evidence' and for these reasons there had been a breach of duty; and granted the application.

It will also be a matter for a tribunal as to whether evidence is taken on oath, but it is suggested that it is unlikely to be appropriate to exclude the use of oath or affirmation in any case where the evidence is, or may become, contentious. Accordingly, witness statements may require to be by way of affidavit unless the witness is going to attend a hearing and swear to their truth.

The nature of any oath may need to be considered where witnesses are not of the Christian faith, but it is probably unreasonable to expect arbitrators to know precisely which oath is binding in each case, and affirmation may be more appropriate in some cases. Care should be taken where the *lex arbitri* incorporates civil procedure of that seat and that procedure requires an oath in a particular form. This is discussed further on page 219.

Each party should indicate to the tribunal which witnesses will attend. Tribunals can also indicate which witnesses they would like to hear, and should be prepared to encourage the parties to agree evidence and to exclude those witnesses whose evidence does not seem germane to the issues. This latter power should, however, be exercised with great caution, as preventing a party from leading evidence could be seen as restricting his right to a fair trial, or demonstrating bias, particularly if only one party's witnesses are excluded.

While it may be sensible for the tribunal to allow requests for 'further and better particulars' or for greater 'specification' of any pleading it permits, and to allow, for example, a defence to any counterclaim made by the respondent, many issues can be dealt with at a hearing, rather than by lengthy pleadings.

There would seem no reason why a party cannot be a witness, although some jurisdictions do not allow this and, similarly, there would not seem to be any bar to a spouse or other relative giving evidence, although the tribunal may decide to attach less weight to it than to the evidence of a truly independent witness where such evidence is challenged. (See the discussion above in connection with 'weight of evidence'.) This will depend on the circumstances, and the tribunal's impression of the witness's performance under oath – his credibility (whether he is telling the truth) and his reliability (how well he remembers), and no 'hard and fast rule' can, or should, be set. Issues may arise concerning taking evidence overseas, which, in this context, might include other jurisdictions within the UK. The tribunal will not generally have subpoena powers and so will have to request the assistance of the courts. (See also the commentary to mandatory rule 45 below.)

Hearings, arguments, documents

It is clear from the language that there is no need for an actual hearing and so 'virtual' hearings would be allowed. In litigation, the concept is that the cases are advanced in written pleadings with a view to disposing of the matters in issue either at a debate (which is a hearing on the law) or in a proof (which is a hearing on the facts) or a proof before answer (which is a combination of the two, the facts being required to be led before the legal arguments can be advanced). So everything in litigation is geared towards these hearings and, because this is a significant expenses burden, parties can manoeuvre tactically to achieve settlements without actually having to run them: approximately 90–95 per cent of cases in the courts will settle extra-judicially – without the hearing taking place.

Although the courts have had procedures in place for determinations on the pleadings alone, for example on the meaning of a document under commercial procedure or some procedures for written submissions to take the place in part only of oral submissions, these are not used heavily, either in Scotland or England.

Having regard to the duties imposed upon the tribunal it may be that in small low-value arbitrations there is no need for hearings, but documents-only arbitrations are also not uncommon in trade disputes in the commodities and other markets, and in consumer disputes. It is suggested that such an approach would make arbitration attractive for business people where the issues were relatively clear, and neither party had any particular desire to have its 'day in court'.

In *Boulos Gad Tourism & Hotels Ltd v Uniground Shipping Co Ltd (The Serenade)* 16 November 2001 (QBD (Comm)) Thomlinson J remarked though that:

> There will be many cases in which, having regard to the amount at stake and other matters related to the issues, it will be entirely appropriate to proceed in that way without an oral hearing. Many hundreds of arbitrations are disposed of in that manner every year in the City of London. Indeed, I suspect that, taken year on year, many more arbitrations are disposed of without oral hearings than are disposed of with oral hearings. However, in a case in which there is a substantial amount of money involved, as there was here, arbitrators would, in my judgment, be wise to hesitate long before denying to the parties the oppor-tunity to present their arguments orally. As Mr Page observed, and as I would endorse, the opportunity for presentation of oral argument can often serve not just to clarify the issues, but also can serve to lessen the prospect of any later misunderstanding as to the basis upon which matters were proceeding. I would therefore respectfully suggest that the arbitrator may here have been unwise to have proceeded without an oral hearing, though he was acting well within his discretion in doing what he did.

It would be quite possible to have part of the arbitration in written form and another part in an oral hearing and, of course, even if there is a hearing then it need not necessarily be conducted in accordance with court procedures.

Even the order of speeches or submissions can cause disputes. It will depend on the home jurisdiction of those participating as to what they can expect and what the tribunal will determine. Thus, in Scotland counsel would expect the pursuer (claimant) to commence the submissions followed thereafter by those for the defender (respondent) with no right of reply thereafter (unlike England).

In *Margulead Ltd v Exide Technologies* [2004] EWHC 1019 (Comm) at paras [28] ff the court noted that:

> At the end of the third day the arbitrator had made it very clear to those appearing at the hearing what procedure was to operate on the last day of the hearing. That procedure involved just two oral closing submissions, the first by Mr Daly on behalf of Margulead and the second by Mr Haubold on behalf of Exide. There was no provision for Margulead to have the last word as would have been the case under English court procedure. But it must or ought to have been clear to all concerned that the arbitrator was following an order of speeches combined with written submissions which did not correspond with that in this court. Indeed, at the commencement of the hearing Exide's counsel had given the first oral opening, notwithstanding Exide was respondent.
>
> There was nothing wrong with this form of procedure, provided always that it gave each party 'a reasonable opportunity of putting his case and dealing with that of his opponent', in accordance with section 33(1)(a), and represented in all the circumstances of the case a fair means for the resolution of the matters falling to be determined in accordance with section 33(1)(b). The proposition that, because Margulead had the burden of proof as claimant, it would necessarily be denied a reasonable opportunity of putting its case or a fair hearing unless its counsel had the last word is not sustainable.

Written pleadings and submissions

Submissions or pleadings are traditionally used to allow the parties to present their respective cases, and to either agree or disagree, and thereby take issue, with the arguments of the other side. The written material presented can take a wide variety of forms. There can be full arguments of fact and law and documents lodged and experts' statements, with legal authorities produced or pleadings or submissions providing an overview and the cases ripen and mature as the arbitration goes on.

The Scottish system allows time for pleadings to be adjusted – that is changed and refined and later in the procedure 'amended' (ie changed only with permission of the court) – but it is suggested that this may not be necessary in arbitration. If, however, amendment and adjustment are required, then the tribunal needs to consider how this should be managed. In practice it is likely to be manageable in sequential, rather than simultaneous, exchanges.

Counterclaims

It may, of course, be that the initial claim is met not only with a defence, but also with a cross-claim – usually referred to in Scotland as a counterclaim. It can even be the case that there is no defence raised to the claim itself, but merely a counterclaim that is said to overtop the claim, and which can, as a matter of law, be set off against the same. The law on set-off is not straightforward and is particularly complex where one of the parties is insolvent. (See the discussion under r 19 above.)

In arbitration, an additional issue arises. If the counterclaim arises out of another contract or remedy and is not part of the contract containing the agreement to arbitrate, then the tribunal may lack jurisdiction, and may, therefore, have to exclude it. Of course, the parties could agree to the other issue being added as, in effect, a joined *ad hoc* arbitration and this might be an attractive solution when compared with the prospect of two sets of proceedings, and then trying to set one off against the other at the stage of enforcement, or, more likely, having to persuade a court to stay execution of the first judgment or award until the second proceedings are concluded.

As mentioned above, it should be noted that the right to set off one claim against another is not absolute. Generally, the right to set off claims within the same contract is relatively non-controversial, but claims between different contracts, or between a contractual claim and one in delict or tort, or between an unliquidated and a liquidated claim, can be more problematic. The rights vary between legal systems, and the contract may also restrict the right to contractual set-off (sometimes by means of a 'pay first, argue later' provision), so the tribunal will need to be careful in considering whether it can set off a counterclaim against a claim, or whether, as a matter of law, such a purported counterclaim actually acts as a defence to the claim itself.

New claims at later stages?

If one of the parties seeks to raise a new claim after the arbitration process is well advanced, the first test must be whether the dispute is, in fact, covered by the agreement to arbitrate. If it is, then the tribunal has to consider whether the late presentation of such a claim amounts to an abuse of process, or whether it should be allowed.

Such decisions will turn on the particular facts, including whether the party concerned was aware, or should have been aware, of the possible claim earlier. However, the tribunal may consider that the need to try and resolve all issues between the parties expeditiously, and in a cost-effective manner, may militate in favour of allowing new claims in some circumstances. If it is felt that the party concerned has acted unreasonably, for example in delaying presentation of the new claim, it would be possible to compensate the other party to some extent with an order for expenses in any event (ie irrespective of the outcome of the arbitration).

It should always be borne in mind that expenses are not the only issue and if a significant delay is going to be incurred, then the award of expenses to the innocent party is only partial compensation.

'Scott Schedules'

Scott Schedules are used in many common law jurisdictions and have been in use in England since at least the days of the old Official Referees Court (which preceded the Technology and Construction Court). In such a schedule, similar items in dispute are grouped together in a series of columns: one for the item; one for claimant; one for respondent; and then arbitrator's award or judge's decision. It provides a useful way of understanding the issues between the parties, and of having a view on their relative values and the delta between the parties' positions.

The Act and the Rules do not specifically require that Scott Schedules have to be produced, but there seems no reason why this technique cannot be used in any arbitration where there are multiple issues, not least as a control mechanism to aid the tribunal and the parties in seeing where the issues stand at any particular time. It is helpful if the Schedule is dynamic, and shared by the parties and the tribunal, so that everyone has the same understanding of the issues at any one time.

Language

It is suggested that most arbitrations under the Act are likely to be conducted entirely in English, but there is no requirement that such be the case. Indeed, it is one of the positive advantages of arbitration that the parties can agree to arbitrate in any language or set of languages they desire. In contrast, courts generally conduct cases in the ruling language or languages of the country concerned.

The tribunal will have to take account of any statements made in the arbitration agreement as to the governing language, and also to any provisions in the contract itself. However, in order to ensure fairness to all parties, it may be necessary to allow evidence to be given in different languages, with the use of translators. It should be emphasised that the parties should, wherever possible, be involved in the selection of translators, including understanding the need for a translator with a strong technical background in the issues in dispute and also, if relevant, an understanding of legal terminology. It is important that the individual is translating, rather than interpreting and adding their own 'spin' on the words used.

Where documents are produced in a foreign language, the tribunal can (and should) order the party relying on the same to provide proper translations (including details of the translator and his qualifications) into the language of the proceedings. If the translation is controversial, it may be necessary to seek notarisation or even a second opinion, but this should be relatively rare.

The civil and common lawyer compromise?

One option open to the parties is to use the IBA Rules on the Taking of Evidence in International Arbitration (2010). As the foreword explains:

> The IBA issued these Rules as a resource to parties and to arbitrators to provide an efficient, economical and fair process for the taking of evidence in

international arbitration. The Rules provide mechanisms for the presentation of documents, witnesses of fact and expert witnesses, inspections, as well as the conduct of evidentiary hearings. The Rules are designed to be used in conjunction with, and adopted together with, institutional, *ad hoc* or other rules or procedures governing international arbitrations.

The parties may adopt the Rules in whole or in part (Preamble 2). The tribunal may 'determine to apply them'. Article 3 deals with documents; Article 4 with witnesses of fact; Article 5 with party-appointed experts; and Article 6 with tribunal-appointed experts. Article 8 deals with the 'evidentiary hearing' and states that 'The Arbitral Tribunal shall at all times have complete control over the Evidentiary Hearing.' Article 9 provides provisions for the admissibility and assessment of evidence.

The Rules on the Efficient Conduct of Proceedings in International Arbitration (the 'Prague Rules')

The IBA Rules on the Taking of Evidence in International Arbitration have been examined above. These have, it is suggested, generally worked well in practice, at least with parties used to proceedings in the common law tradition. However, in recent times a perception developed, among those parties more conversant with civil law systems, that the IBA Rules were too 'common law centric', biased in favour of the common law adversarial style, and permitted an overly expansive approach to the taking of evidence, with resultant delays and cost. This was considered problematic, even though it had been the intention of the Rules to bridge the gap between different legal systems and their respective procedures in the taking of evidence, 'when the parties come from different legal cultures' (IBA Rules, Foreword). Some in the civil law community put this down to a general lack of proactivity or a failure to adopt an inquisitorial approach by international arbitrators, more familiar with the common law adversarial style.

A Working Group was formed of representatives from predominantly civil law-based jurisdictions, which produced a draft of what were to become known as the Prague Rules. These were signed on 14 December 2018 and became available to be adopted by parties in their arbitration proceedings from that date, to be used in conjunction with any institutional or *ad hoc* rules chosen by them or, in a departure from the IBA approach, to be imposed upon them by the tribunal. (Article 1.1 states that 'The parties may agree on the application of the Prague Rules before arbitration is initiated or at any stage of the arbitration' and Art 1.2 provides that 'The arbitral tribunal may apply the Prague Rules or any part thereof upon the parties' agreement or at its own initiative after having heard the parties'.) This is consistent with the approach in the 2010 Act to encouraging arbitrators to take control of the process, although it is difficult to square this with client autonomy if the parties were, jointly, to oppose the use of the Prague Rules.

Whereas the IBA Rules comprise a comprehensive set of rules which were drafted to 'provide an efficient, economical and fair process for the taking of evidence in international arbitrations, particularly those between Parties from different legal traditions', the Prague Rules seek 'to increase the efficiency of arbitral proceedings' *per se* by encouraging 'tribunals to take a more active role in managing the proceedings' and, central to this, to adopt an inquisitorial approach to the production and assessment of evidence, and taking the initiative in the ascertainment of the law.

There are common areas in each set of Rules relating to documents and witnesses and the drawing of adverse inferences for non-compliance. The main differences between the two sets of Rules are in the following areas:

(1) *Pro-activity of the arbitral tribunal.* The Prague Rules require that arbitrators should be pro-active both in the taking of evidence and in fact finding in order to speed up proceedings. So, Art 2 requires that the tribunal will hold a Case Management Conference (CMC) without any unjustified delay after receiving the case file. This, it is suggested, seems a sensible practice whether or not these Rules are being used. In Art 3.1, the tribunal is entitled and encouraged to take an active role in the establishing of the facts of the case; and Art 3.2 provides that the tribunal may, after hearing the parties, at any stage of the arbitration and at its own initiative: (a) request any of the parties to produce relevant documentary evidence or make fact witnesses' testimony available during the hearing; (b) appoint one or more experts, including on legal issues; (c) order site inspections; and/or (d) for the purpose of fact-finding take any other actions which it deems appropriate. Article 3.3 empowers the tribunal to consider a cut-off date for production of evidence.

One might compare the provisions in the IBA Rules: cf IBA Art 3.10 (request parties to produce evidence); Art 5.4 (organise meeting between party-appointed experts); Art 6 (appoint one or more tribunal appointed experts); Art 7 (require inspections); and Art 9.2 (at request of party or on own motion, exclusion of evidence).

While this all makes sense in relation to the target of speedy process, it may sit uncomfortably with those from common law jurisdictions (and hybrid ones such as Scotland) where such an inquisitorial approach is not what is expected. It may, therefore, be sensible for arbitrators to make it clear that they intend to use the Prague Rules (most safely with the agreement of the parties), before the arbitration commences.

(2) *Document production.* The Prague Rules limit document production. So, Art 4.2 provides that, generally, the arbitral tribunal and the parties are encouraged to avoid any form of document production, including e-discovery. Article 4.3 states, however, that if a party believes that it would need to request certain documents from the other party, it should indicate this to the arbitral tribunal at the case management conference and explain the reasons why the document production may be needed in this particular case. If the arbitral tribunal is satisfied that the document production may

be needed, it should decide on a procedure for document production and make an appropriate provision for it in the procedural timetable. Under Art 4.4 a party can request the arbitral tribunal to order document production at a later stage of the arbitration only in exceptional circumstances. Such a request should be granted only if the arbitral tribunal is satisfied that the party could not have made such a request at the case management conference. Article 4.5 provides that, subject to Arts 4.2–4.4, a party may request the arbitral tribunal to order another party to produce a specific document which: (a) is relevant and material to the outcome of the case; (b) is not in the public domain; and (c) is in the possession of another party or within its power or control. This represents a significant reduction in the lengthy and expensive processes that can apply in common law jurisdictions, notably those in the United States.

One might compare the provisions in the IBA Rules: cf IBA Art 3.1 (within the time limit ordered by the tribunal parties will submit all documents available to it upon which it relies); Art 3.3 (a request to produce shall contain a description in sufficient detail of a narrow and specific requested category of documents that are reasonably believed to exist); and Art 3.10 (at any time before the tribunal is concluded, the arbitral tribunal may (i) request any party to produce documents, (ii) request any party to use its best efforts to take or (iii) itself take any step that it considers appropriate to obtain documents from any person or organisation).

(3) *Number of witnesses.* Both sets of Rules contain provisions as to the identification of fact witnesses, the submission of witness statements and the power of the tribunal to order the appearance of a fact witness for testimony at a hearing (Art 5.2 Prague Rules and Art 4.10 IBA Rules.) But the tribunal under the Prague Rules will have the final say regarding the number of witnesses to be heard throughout the proceedings. Under the IBA Rules this is a matter for the parties.

(4) *Examination of witnesses.* The Prague Rules retain cross-examination in the new Rules. However, under Art 5.2, the arbitral tribunal, after having heard the parties, will decide which witnesses are to be called for examination during the hearing subject to further provisions in Art 5; Art 5.3 states that the arbitral tribunal may decide that a certain witness should not be called for examination during the hearing, either before or after a witness statement has been submitted, in particular if it considers the testimony of such a witness to be irrelevant, immaterial, unreasonably burdensome, duplicative or for any other reasons not necessary for the resolution of the dispute; Art 5.7, however, provides if a party insists on calling a witness whose witness statement has been submitted by the other party, as a general rule, the arbitral tribunal should call the witness to testify at the hearing, unless there are good reasons not to do so. It is not clear how to square Arts 5.3 and 5.7, given that, if the tribunal considers evidence not required under Art 5.3, this would, presumably, be a 'good reason' for rejecting a request under Art 5.7.

Again comparing the provisions in the IBA Rules: cf IBA Art 8.2 (the arbitral tribunal shall have complete control over the evidentiary hearing and may limit or exclude any question to, answer by or appearance of a witness); Art 8.5 (the tribunal may request any person to give oral or written evidence on any issue that the arbitral tribunal considers to be relevant to the case and material to its outcome – any witness called and questioned by the tribunal may also be questioned by the parties).

(5) *The requirement for an evidential hearing.* The Prague Rules suggest there should not necessarily be an evidentiary hearing at all (Art 8.1): 'In order to promote cost-efficiency and to the extent appropriate for a particular case, the arbitral tribunal and the parties should seek to resolve the dispute on a "documents only" basis.' The extent to which this is acceptable to the parties may well be determined by the usual practice in the sector concerned.

(6) *Experts.* Parties may appoint experts (Art 6.5: the appointment of any expert by the arbitral tribunal does not preclude a party from submitting an expert report by any expert appointed by that party) but the preferred approach would appear to be for the tribunal to appoint the expert(s) (Art 6.1: at the request of a party or on its own initiative and after having heard the parties, the arbitral tribunal may appoint one or more independent experts to present a report on disputed matters which require specialised knowledge) and the tribunal itself may elect to call that expert for examination (Art 6.4: at the request of a party or on the arbitral tribunal's own initiative, the expert shall be called for examination at the hearing).

Under the IBA Rules, tribunal-appointed experts can be appointed with the consent of the parties, but this method is not promoted above party-appointed experts.

Innovations not found in the IBA Rules

The Prague Rules include two other provisions which are not usually found in common law arbitral systems:

(i) *The 'Iura Novit Curia' principle (Article 7).* This permits a pro-active arbitral tribunal to identify and determine the applicable law on its own initiative and, with safeguards, to apply provisions not set out by the parties. (Article 7.2 provides: 'However, the arbitral tribunal may apply legal provisions not pleaded by the parties if it finds it necessary, including, but not limited to, public policy rules. In such cases, the arbitral tribunal shall seek the parties' views on the legal provisions it intends to apply. The arbitral tribunal may also rely on legal authorities even if not submitted by the parties if they relate to legal provisions pleaded by the parties and provided that the parties have been given an opportunity to express their views in relation to such legal authorities.') It is suggested that, subject to the safeguards about allowing the parties to comment, there is nothing in this provision that would cause issues in an arbitration under the 2010 Act.

(ii) *Assistance in Amicable Settlement (Article 9)*. The tribunal may assist the parties in reaching an amicable settlement and this can be done at any stage of the proceedings. Article 9.1 provides: 'Unless one of the parties objects, the arbitral tribunal may assist the parties in reaching an amicable settlement of the dispute at any stage of the arbitration.' Article 9.2: 'Upon the prior written consent of all parties, any member of the arbitral tribunal may also act as a mediator to assist in the amicable settlement of the case.' Article 9.3: 'If the mediation does not result in a settlement within an agreed period of time, the member of the arbitral tribunal who has acted as mediator: (a) may continue to act as an arbitrator in the arbitration proceedings after obtaining written consent from all parties at the end of the mediation; or (b) shall terminate his/her mandate in accordance with the applicable arbitration rules if such written consent is not obtained.'

The IBA Rules make no provision for members of the tribunal to act in the capacity of mediator (which, it is suggested, is what the provisions of Art 9 amount to), nor to thereafter re-assume the capacity of arbitrator. Although common law practitioners may not be familiar with this mechanism, it is used in parts of the continental Europe (Germany and Switzerland) and also in Asia. See, for example, the HKIAC Rules 2018 (Art 13.8: 'Where the parties agree to pursue other means of settling their dispute after the arbitration commences, HKIAC, the arbitral tribunal or emergency arbitrator may, at the request of any party, suspend the arbitration or Emergency Arbitrator Procedure, as applicable, on such terms as it considers appropriate') and also the rules of the China International Economic and Trade Arbitration Commission (CIETAC) (Art 47 Combination of Conciliation with Arbitration – Art 47.1: 'Where both parties wish to conciliate, or where one party wishes to conciliate and the other party's consent has been obtained by the arbitral tribunal, the arbitral tribunal may conciliate the dispute during the arbitral proceedings. The parties may also settle their dispute by themselves'; Art 47.2: 'With the consents of both parties, the arbitral tribunal may conciliate the case in a manner it considers appropriate'). The Singapore International Arbitration Centre has its SIAC-SIMC Arb-Med-Arb Protocol but proposes the appointment of a different person as the arbitrator and the mediator.

While commendable as incorporating civil law practices from other jurisdictions, the Prague Rules in terms of the 'arb-med-arb' provisions may not sit easily with the core requirement for the impartiality and independence of arbitrators as required by *lex arbitri* and institutions (eg LCIA Rules (Art 5.3) and ICC Rules (Art 11(1)) and, in particular, any express prohibitions on arbitrators advising any party on the parties' dispute or the outcome of the arbitration (eg LCIA Rules Art 5.3).

It is suggested that the Prague Rules are generally compatible with the Arbitration (Scotland) Act 2010 although, if Scotland was the seat, the mandatory provisions would apply and many of the powers given to an arbitral tribunal in the Rules would sit comfortably with the founding principles in section 1 and the general duties on the tribunal in mandatory rule 24.

However, applying the point above, the requirements in mandatory rule 24 of impartiality and independence as well as those in mandatory rule 77 in connection with independence of an arbitrator if 'anything' gives 'rise to justifiable doubts as to the arbitrator's impartiality' could be problematic if the parties had chosen a Scottish seat and used the Prague Rules, availing themselves of the procedure under Art 9.

If the parties attempted a mediation which did not result in a settlement, even after obtaining written consent from all parties at the end of the mediation, could the member of the arbitral tribunal who has acted as mediator continue to act as an arbitrator in the continued arbitration proceedings, and also continue to fulfil the duties in these mandatory rules? Would any confidential or privileged information they had acquired in the private mediation sessions cause problems for them in the continuing arbitration where there would be a continuing duty under mandatory rule 8 to disclose 'any circumstances known' to them 'or which become known to the individual before the arbitration ends which might reasonably be considered relevant when considering whether the individual is impartial and independent?' While it is acknowledged that anything in the mediation is private without prejudice to the concurrent arbitration, it remains a question whether anything acquired by the arbitrator as mediator would give rise to the justifiable doubts.

In addition, it might raise the question as to whether the proceedings in the mediation are confidential or privileged in the subsequent arbitration? Recital 23 of the EU Directive provides:

> Confidentiality in the mediation process is important and this Directive should therefore provide for a minimum degree of compatibility of civil procedural rules with regard to how to protect the confidentiality of mediation in any subsequent civil and commercial judicial proceedings or arbitration.

In England and Wales, the courts recognise that what happens in a mediation cannot be referred to in court subsequently, and they are treated in law as being akin to 'without prejudice' meetings. In *Brown v Rice* [2007] EWHC 625 (Ch) the court said that mediation takes the form of 'assisted without prejudice negotiation'. In *Aird v Prime Meridian Ltd* [2006] EWCA Civ 1866, the Court of Appeal said that, with some exceptions, 'what goes on in the course of mediation is privileged, so that it cannot be referred to or relied on in subsequent court proceedings if the mediation is unsuccessful.'

In *British Sky Broadcasting Plc v Virgin Media Communications Ltd (formerly NTL Communications Ltd)* [2008] EWCA Civ 612, the Court of Appeal held that where confidential information was acquired by the lawyers in the course of a mediation from the other side, this might prevent them from accepting new instructions from another client in a dispute to which such information is relevant.

In *Glencairn IP Holdings Ltd v Product Specialities Inc (t/a Final Touch)* [2019] EWHC 1733 (IPEC), the Intellectual Property Court had to consider whether the defendant's solicitors should be restrained from acting further for the defendant because they had participated in past mediation proceedings with the claimant on behalf of another party that had resulted in a settlement agreement in a similar claim. It held that no fiduciary relationship existed with the claimant. (Note that this case is being appealed.)

There is also case law holding that, on occasion, what has occurred in a mediation may not attract privilege. In *Farm Assist Ltd (in Liquidation) v Secretary of State for the Environment, Food and Rural Affairs (No 2)* [2009] EWHC 1102 (TCC), Ramsey J held that in exceptional circumstances, the confidentiality provisions between the parties and the mediator can be set aside in the interests of justice, if the parties waive that privilege. The privilege is the parties' not the mediator's. In terms of the confidentiality of the proceedings, it was held that the mediation proceedings themselves were confidential as between the parties and between them and the mediator. As a result, the mediator themself could enforce the confidentiality provision (even if the parties agreed to refer to matters outside the mediation) and the court would generally uphold it (except in the interests of justice).

Returning to the Scottish position, it will be possible under the Prague Rules for the parties to appoint an arbitrator, consent to their acting as mediator, but if the mediation fails, for the parties to then terminate the appointment. The question is then, what would happen with the ongoing arbitration under the Scottish Rules? If not modified or disapplied, default rules 9 and 11 would presumably apply. The arbitrator can be removed by the parties acting jointly in terms of default rule 11(1), removal is effected by notifying the arbitrator (rule 11(2)) and the arbitrator's tenure would be treated as 'removed by the parties' in terms of default rule 9(c), although there might have to be an application to the Outer House in terms of the arbitrator's liability (mandatory rule 16), if not agreed by the parties.

In terms of default rule 17, where an arbitrator's tenure ends, the 'tribunal must be reconstituted (a) in accordance with the procedure used to constitute the tribunal, or (b) where procedure fails, in accordance with rules 6 and 7'. That reconstituted tribunal would then have to 'decide the extent, if any, to which previous proceedings (including any award made, appointment by or other act done by the previous tribunal) should stand' (rule 17(2)). They would presumably have to do so also in terms of the provisions of s 1 and rule 24.

The 2010 Act provides that a reconstituted tribunal's decision under this default rule 'does not affect a party's right to object or appeal on any ground which arose before the tribunal made its decision' – but it may do so if the tribunal has already issued an award (see *Emirates Trading Agency LLC v Sociedade de Fomento Industrial Private Ltd* [2015] EWHC 1452 (Comm) where, under s 27 of the 1996 Act, it was held that there is nothing in that Act permitting the reconstituted tribunal to review or change a decision which had been reached by the tribunal on an issue and which was final and binding as to the matters it decided – in that case the tribunal had issued a partial award determining its own jurisdiction).

Reference has already been made in the text to what happened in the case of *Sierra Fishing Co v Farran* [2015] EWHC 140 (Comm) where the parties continued negotiations about repayment terms which had been the original cause of dispute, concurrently agreeing to suspend the arbitration. They then entered a new agreement for repayment including transfer of shares, with which agreement the parties were assisted by the arbitrator. This was unsuccessful and the arbitration was revived, leaving the arbitrator conflicted and ultimately removed by the court.

These provisions in the Rules are probably the most difficult ones for practitioners (either arbitrators or legal advisers) from traditionally common law jurisdictions. It may be better in such cases for the arbitration to be sisted to allow for mediation to be attempted and to be conducted by a separate mediator (cf the SIAC-SIMC Arb-Med-Arb Protocol) rather than the arbitrator.

Place of arbitration

Rule 29 says that the tribunal may meet, and otherwise conduct the arbitration, anywhere it chooses (in or outwith Scotland).

Default rule 29 is in connection with the meetings in the arbitration and the conduct of the arbitration itself and is not to do with the seat. The tribunal may determine when and where the arbitration is to be conducted (default rule 28(2)(a)). Reference is made elsewhere in the text in connection with the seat under s 3 and the difference with venue and 'place' as used in UNCITRAL Model law and Rules. Place would also incorporate, it is suggested, an online arbitration.

As to location of the hearings or meetings, the view has already been stated (and is confirmed) that, while the seat of the arbitration will remain in Scotland, there is no impediment to holding hearings out of the jurisdiction. One caveat is to ensure that such hearings do not fall foul of local law or custom. It is suggested that any final hearing at which an award is to be made should normally take place in Scotland, although this does not appear to be a mandatory requirement under the Rules.

The tribunal needs to consider the practical issues in deciding where to actually hold a hearing. For example, is there adequate space for everyone? If any party, adviser or witness suffers from any disability, is there adequate and easy access to the room or rooms being used? Are there facilities to allow parties and their advisers to hold private meetings during the arbitration if appropriate, or for the tribunal to retire in order to consider matters?

Are there facilities for handling charts, drawings, plans, voluminous documents, experts, shorthand writers, translators, interpreters (and has additional time been allowed)? If presentations are to be made, are there suitable projection facilities? If documents are being produced in electronic format, are there enough computer screens, and has the software used been rigorously tested to ensure all parties can access the data without difficulty, delay or general irritation!

Have any necessary provisions been made for an instantaneous, verbatim, transcript (permanent record of the proceedings), real-time transcription or synchronising transcription software with 'written' or 'graphical' evidence? Is there agreement to use e-bibles; e-bundles; video conferencing in examining witnesses from all over the world; automatic logging and time-stamping of what is shown and when; legal coding; interactive video; graphics; audio streams and so on?

It might be considered whether to employ some ways of displaying material such as flip charts to allow parties (or the tribunal) to record issues agreed, or to be resolved later, in a prominent and open fashion. PowerPoint presentations, it would seem, have become more common.

Clearly much of this has little or no relevance for the vast majority of arbitrations, but is intended to provide a useful basic checklist, since every arbitration will need to consider at least a few of these items.

Useful guidance can also be found in UNCITRAL Notes on Organizing Arbitral Proceedings (2016) and the CIArb Guidelines on Managing Arbitrations and Procedural Orders (2016).

It is to be recommended that the accommodation is secured for the whole period of the arbitration. In hotels, for example, there is a risk that the rooms will be used for evening functions and it will, therefore, be necessary to strip the room every night, and set it up again the next day. In addition to the obvious extra work, this vastly increases the risk of leakage from this private process, since there is always the chance that someone will leave confidential information behind in error.

Overall control of the arbitration

Among the other practical issues, a tribunal may wish to consider as part of its overall control of the proceedings are:

- Use of a chess clock to show time expended in the hearing, particularly if the tribunal has required time-limited speeches etc. In any event, a prominent wall clock is useful for the efficient control of time.
- Fixing the periods for sitting in advance – allowing suitable breaks. These should allow for refreshments for the parties (and the tribunal!), but also provide a useful opportunity for reflection. The tribunal should try and ascertain whether any party, witness or adviser has particular issues to be considered – perhaps a medical condition, religious observance, etc.
- Breaks about every one-and-a-half to two hours seem to work well, although longer periods may be needed to allow a flow of evidence on a particular point.

Tribunal decision-making

Rule 30 is a default rule and so the parties must rule it in or out of their arbitration. Its use, it is suggested, is in making it clear from the outset how a decision will be arrived at by the tribunal. All members of a tribunal should participate in the decision making, even if unanimity is not possible (*European Grain v Johnston* [1982] 2 Lloyd's Rep 550). Where that is not possible, then this rule will regulate how the tribunal will come to a decision. If the decision is not unanimous then a majority view will prevail. (This does not stop the dissenting arbitrator from providing his own opinion as an addendum to the final award.) If that majority is not possible or cannot be arrived at, the chairman is empowered to make the decision or, where there is no chairman, then the person last appointed or, if consisting of two arbitrators, by an 'umpire' appointed by the tribunal or, if that is not met in the time limit by either party, any arbitrator or any arbitration appointment referee at their (either) request.

It is suggested that rule 30(2)(b), giving tie-breaking power to the last arbitrator appointed, is arbitrary, and its use should be avoided, either by having an odd number of arbitrators or by appointing a chairman.

As has been mentioned before, it is recommended that a tribunal with an odd number is used, and to appoint a chairman to enable the use of rule 30(2)(a).

Tribunal directions

Default rule 31 provides:

(1) The tribunal may give such directions to the parties as it considers appropriate for the purposes of conducting the arbitration.
(2) A party must comply with such a direction by such time as the tribunal specifies.

Rule 31 is an important default rule giving the tribunal the power to give directions to the parties for the purposes of conducting the arbitration and requiring the parties to comply with these directions in the time specified. In practical terms the tribunal has to move the arbitration along from the first procedural order 'Procedural Order No 1' to orders or directions forcing parties to comply in the best interests of the expedition and cost saving for the arbitration itself.

Procedural orders normally contain directions as to dates for lodging or producing documents or witness statements etc, times for hearings, delivery of memorials or pleadings, expert reports, and provisional dates for witness hearings. The administrative day-to-day proceedings will be contained in procedural orders.

It is suggested that, in any case with reasonable complexity, it may make sense for the tribunal to send the parties a pre-prepared procedural questionnaire. This can then lead to a draft Procedural Order No 1, possibly without the need for a preliminary hearing.

Preliminary issues

Many arbitrators have their own checklists and model forms of procedural orders (commonly referred to as PO1). These will deal with such matters as:

- bifurcation (splitting the hearing or determination of issues, eg liability and quantum or time bar and case on the merits)
- jurisdiction
- applicable law to the substantive issues between the parties.

Power to appoint clerk, agents or employees etc

Default rule 32 states that:

(1) The tribunal may appoint a clerk (and such other agents, employees or other persons as it thinks fit) to assist it in conducting the arbitration.
(2) But the parties' consent is required for any appointment in respect of which significant expenses are likely to arise.

Rule 32 is a default rule that an arbitrator can appoint a clerk (and others) to assist in the arbitration. However, the parties' consent will be required for the appointment of clerks and other staff if significant costs are likely to arise. The tribunal will have to be cognisant of its obligations under mandatory rule 24 to conduct the arbitration without incurring 'unnecessary expense'. The Scottish practice in the past seems to have been to appoint a legally qualified clerk almost as a matter of course in any relatively large or complex arbitration.

The appointment of a clerk or equivalent is relatively uncommon in practice in England and Wales and indeed internationally, and as mentioned under rule 5 it is hoped that this change of emphasis will reduce the additional costs of such an appointment in Scotland, and restrict appointments to cases where the addition of a clerk adds real value.

In contrast, in large arbitrations it may be necessary to appoint a 'tribunal secretary' or 'administrator' or 'administrative co-ordinator' or 'registrar'. Here the function is not to provide legal advice and support, but to take steps such as to open a bank account in the name of the chairman or arbitrator; take equal monies from parties; arrange an interest-bearing bank account from which the fees and expenses of the arbitration are paid; organise attendance of witnesses; make arrangements for delivery of transcripts; and manage the paper or electronic documents. However, such a person does not take part in deliberations. Some or all of this support would normally be provided by an institution, or an arbitration centre, and it may be that, if arbitration in

Scotland develops as is hoped, organisations will appear that will offer such services on a case-by-case basis.

The very helpful UNCITRAL Notes on Organizing Arbitral Proceedings 1996 state this:

26. Administrative services might be secured by engaging a secretary of the arbitral tribunal (also referred to as registrar, clerk, administrator or rapporteur), who carries out the tasks under the direction of the arbitral tribunal. Some arbitral institutions routinely assign such persons to the cases administered by them. In arbitrations not administered by an institution or where the arbitral institution does not appoint a secretary, some arbitrators frequently engage such persons, at least in certain types of cases, whereas many others normally conduct the proceedings without them.

27. To the extent the tasks of the secretary are purely organizational (eg obtaining meeting rooms and providing or coordinating secretarial services), this is usually not controversial. Differences in views, however, may arise if the tasks include legal research and other professional assistance to the arbitral tribunal (eg collecting case law or published commentaries on legal issues defined by the arbitral tribunal, preparing summaries from case law and publications, and sometimes also preparing drafts of procedural decisions or drafts of certain parts of the award, in particular those concerning the facts of the case). Views or expectations may differ especially where a task of the secretary is similar to professional functions of the arbitrators. Such a role of the secretary is in the view of some commentators inappropriate or is appropriate only under certain conditions, such as that the parties agree thereto. However, it is typically recognized that it is important to ensure that the secretary does not perform any decision-making function of the arbitral tribunal.

Tribunal secretaries in arbitration

Care should be exercised in appointing and using tribunal secretaries. It is important from the outset to get agreement amongst the parties and the tribunal as to the scope and function of such an individual. The concern is that the secretary might go beyond his or her position as an assistant to the tribunal and become a decision-making 'fourth arbitrator' thereby leaving any award by the tribunal open to challenge. In *Yukos Universal Ltd v Russian Federation*, UNCITRAL, PCA Case no 2005-04/AA227 there was an application to the Hague District Court, seeking to annul an award, alleging, *inter alia*, that the arbitrators did not fulfil their mandate personally because the tribunal's assistant played a significant role in analysing the evidence and legal arguments, in the tribunal's deliberations, and in the drafting of the award. (The decision of the District Court on this and other matters was reversed by the Dutch Appeals Court in 2020, but for reasons unconnected with this issue. This award is probably one of the largest ever, understood to be at least $50 billion.)

The issue has also come before the English courts. In *P v Q* [2017] EWHC 194 (Comm) the English High Court considered an application for the removal of two co-arbitrators in an LCIA arbitration in terms of s 24(1)(d) (i) of the 1996 Act, ie on grounds that the arbitrator(s) has/have refused or failed to properly conduct the proceedings.

The parties had appointed them as co-arbitrators and, in the usual way, the chairman was nominated by them. With the parties' agreement, a lawyer was appointed as tribunal secretary.

The tribunal issued three procedural decisions, relating to document sharing with another arbitration, a stay application, and document production. The chairman then sent an email to the tribunal secretary but accidentally sent it to the claimant. The email was a request for the secretary's reaction to an email from the claimant.

As a result, the claimant filed an LCIA challenge seeking the tribunal's removal. The co-arbitrators replied explaining that there had been no delegation of any of the tribunal's functions or responsibilities. The LCIA court dismissed the challenge regarding the co-arbitrators but upheld the challenge to the chairman on different grounds. The chairman resigned. A reconstituted tribunal upheld the original three decisions.

The court held that the co-arbitrators could not be criticised for the performance of their functions of deciding the matters. It was proper, it held, where a decision on a procedural matter was required, for co-arbitrators to consider submissions, let the chairman draft a decision, consider the draft, and thereafter approve or revise it all with a view to them having an input in that decision but also avoiding unnecessary delay or expense. The court noted that this was how international arbitration panels commonly functioned and, in any event, under the LCIA rules the co-arbitrators were entitled to delegate authority to the chairman to make procedural rulings alone. As this was an LCIA arbitration, the parties had agreed that the chairman could take the lead in proposing draft decisions.

On the question of the tribunal secretary involvement, the court expressed the opinion that views differed amongst practitioners and commentators on their appropriate use, but the 'critical yardstick for s.24' was that tribunal members could not 'abrogate or impair their personal decision-making function'. The court noted that the parties in the present case had agreed to the appointment of the tribunal secretary. Best practice would be to avoid asking for the views or opinions of the secretary, but failure to do so was not tantamount to a failure to properly conduct proceedings. It held that that was particularly so where the chairman was an experienced judge used to reaching independent decisions without being influenced by suggestions from junior legal assistants. The court observed that it was normal and appropriate for a secretary to work under the chairman's direct supervision and with an experienced tribunal, for the co-arbitrators to make the assumption that the secretary would be tasked appropriately, unless they were alerted otherwise. Note that LCIA 2020 Rules Art 14A makes detailed provision for Tribunal Secretaries.

Some guidance is available from arbitral organisations and institutions.

For example, the Young ICCA Guide on Arbitral Secretaries 2014 ('Guide') provides in Article 3 a non-exhaustive list of the arbitral secretaries' roles, many of which are of a purely administrative or organisational nature (for example, Articles 3(2)(a), (c) and (d) of the Guide) and the role of an arbitral secretary may go beyond purely administrative tasks, subject to 'appropriate direction and supervision by the arbitral tribunal'.

The IBA Guidelines on Conflict of Interest in International Arbitration 2014 recognise tribunal secretaries as they provide that both 'secretaries and assistants to the Arbitral Tribunal are bound by the same duty of independence and impartiality (including the duty of disclosure) as arbitrators' (IBA Guidelines, General Standard 5(b)).

The ICC has a 'Note to Parties and Arbitral Tribunals on the Conduct of Arbitration under the ICC Rules of Arbitration, effective 1 January 2019 with 'Duties of administrative secretaries' (paras 183–188) and LCIA has Art 14A.

Delegation not permitted

The tribunal must not delegate its duties – duties entrusted to it by the parties (*National Boat Shows Ltd v Tameside Marine* [2001] WL 1560826) – and must decide itself the issues placed before it (*Agrimex Ltd v Tradigrain SA* [2003] EWHC 1656). In English law, to do otherwise could be considered as tantamount to a 'serious irregularity': see *Brandeis Brokers Ltd v Black* [2001] 2 Lloyd's Rep 359.

Note also that an arbitrator bound by the Code of Professional and Ethical Conduct of the Chartered Institute of Arbitrators must comply with rule 7, which states that: 'A member shall not delegate any duty to decide to any other person unless permitted to do so by the parties or applicable law.'

See also the discussion above in connection with tribunal secretaries.

Party representatives

Default rule 33 deals with this issue on the basis that:

(1) A party may be represented in the arbitration by a lawyer or any other person.
(2) But the party must, before representation begins, give notice of the representative –
    (a) to the tribunal, and
    (b) to the other party.

Rule 33 is a default rule which provides that a lawyer or any other person can appear before the tribunal.

This issue is addressed under rule 28, but it should be emphasised that, under the Rules, 'any other person' means just that, and there is no requirement for a legal adviser. In England and Wales, a person as a litigant in person may appear in their own cause but may not delegate or assign that function, nor will granting a power of attorney give rights of audience in court (*Fulton v AIB Group (UK) Plc* [2018] NICh 11).

Having said that, the tribunal does, it is submitted, retain the right to ensure the efficient disposal of proceedings, and thus would be entitled to ask if the representative proposed had relevant qualifications and experience. It could not, however, reject such representative merely because he was not legally qualified, since to do so would be to render the phrase 'or any other person' ineffective, and defeat the clear purpose of the clause.

There might be difficult decisions for a tribunal to take in connection with this provision. On the one hand, parties may simply want to present their case themselves (or not), as is their right, or engage someone to do so who is not a lawyer or who is simply much cheaper. The problem for the tribunal, it is suggested, is twofold. First, it has its obligations to obey under rule 24 in respect of fairness and impartiality, which could be sorely tested if an individual who is making representations is not aware of or clear about the Act and arbitral procedure. Secondly, also as part of its obligations under rule 24, the tribunal must not permit anything to be done which would incur unnecessary delay. Educating a party's representative on arbitral practice, procedure and law would cause delay and thus expense to the other party. Pleadings or claims and defences improperly drawn will cause delay and expense to the other party.

Another real issue is in relation to the applications made to the court under the various provisions in the Act. It was formerly unusual for the Court of Session to entertain appearances from those who claimed to be 'party representatives' but who did not possess any rights of audience (sometimes called 'McKenzie friends' after the English procedure and the case (*McKenzie v McKenzie* [1971] P 33) which permitted this in the first place. (In England and Wales there is court guidance: see Practice Guidance (McKenzie Friends: Civil and Family Courts) [2010] 1 WLR 1881).

This has now changed. There is a procedure under the Rules of Court whereby a party litigant and his proposed representative can apply to the court for 'law support' (see Form 12A-A), where they must state the representative's name, relationship to the litigant and relevant experience, and declare whether he has any financial interest in the result of the litigation and whether he is remunerated, and provide an undertaking to the court that the proceedings will be kept confidential by them. Note that the lay supporter assists the litigant but does not speak for the litigant. LCIA 2020 Art 18 and ICC 2021 Art 17 also provide guidance on this issue.

Experts and the tribunal

These matters are dealt with under default rule 34, which states that:

(1) The tribunal may obtain an expert opinion on any matter arising in the arbitration.

(2) The parties must be given a reasonable opportunity –
   (a) to make representations about any written expert opinion, and
   (b) to hear any oral expert opinion and to ask questions of the expert giving it.

Rule 34 is a default rule, which if not disapplied will permit the tribunal to instruct expert opinion 'on any matter arising in the arbitration'. The parties are afforded a 'reasonable' opportunity to make representations in connection with any expert written opinion (so it would have to be exhibited to them in order to make such representations) and they are entitled to hear any oral expert opinion (not necessarily 'evidence' as it does not make mention of any expert taking the oath and providing the tribunal with that evidence under oath in a formal hearing setting, even if the parties are permitted to ask questions).

The question of 'tribunal appointed experts' is a vexed one in international arbitration presently. The issue frequently arises as a topic at conferences and seminars, particularly in connection with the Prague Rules and tribunal efficiency (see above).

In England it has been held that the tribunal should not meet and discuss the case with an expert appointed by it without obtaining the consent of the parties: *Hussmann (Europe) Ltd v Al Ameen Development & Trade Co* [2000] 2 Lloyd's Rep 83.

Note that the parties will be severally liable to pay the expenses of the expert appointed by the tribunal under the provisions of mandatory rule 60(1)(b)(ii).

Rule 34 does not, of itself, remove the right of the parties to present expert evidence, subject to the directions of the tribunal. While the Act is actually silent on whether parties may instruct their own experts and lead that evidence at a hearing, the rules do not expressly prohibit it. As mentioned in relation to rule 28, this area can be a 'flashpoint' between parties from different jurisdictional backgrounds. Common lawyers expect to instruct their own experts whose evidence they lead in the course of a hearing on evidence. The civil lawyer will not expect to have his own expert and will be much more comfortable with a court or tribunal appointed expert.

The main purpose of the rule appears to be to allow the tribunal to access expertise it does not possess itself, but it could also allow the appointment of a single expert to assist the tribunal, as already suggested, rather than allowing both parties to engage experts whom they consider are likely, genuinely, to favour their position.

The provisions in rule 34(2) provide the parties with protection against the abuse of this provision, and somewhat restrict any attempt by the tribunal to take an uncontrolled inquisitorial approach. It also makes it clear that the expert's reports need to be given to all parties, and any oral evidence in the presence of the parties. This would, in our view, have been the case even without these provisions, but their inclusion brings welcome clarity and certainty to the issue.

As a practical solution, the tribunal could direct the parties to prepare draft instructions to the prospective expert or, at least, be involved in the production of such instructions. While this does not seem to be a requirement of the rule, it would draw the teeth on any argument that the tribunal was going beyond its powers (albeit that the powers under this rule are widely drawn).

Rule 34 is, of course, a default rule, and it will be interesting to see whether parties seek to disapply the provision, so as to prevent the tribunal taking this course (which will, it must be appreciated, be at the parties' expense).

Powers of the tribunal relating to property

Under default rule 35 the tribunal may direct a party –
  (a) to allow the tribunal, an expert or another party –
      (i) to inspect, photograph, preserve or take custody of any property which that party owns or possesses which is the subject of the arbitration (or as to which any question arises in the arbitration), or
      (ii) to take samples from, or conduct an experiment on, any such property, or
  (b) to preserve any document or other evidence which the party possesses or controls.

Rule 35 is an important default rule empowering the tribunal to direct parties to allow it or an expert (presumably a tribunal-appointed expert under rule 34) or another party to take steps in respect of property which is the subject-matter of the arbitration. That party may inspect it, photograph it, preserve it, take custody of it, take samples from it or other evidence or preserve any document or other 'adminicle' of evidence.

This rule should not be underestimated. The interim possession of property in litigation can be a very contested matter. In the Court of Session under the Court of Session Act 1988 s 47(2), the court can make such order regarding the interim possession of any property to which the cause relates, or regarding the subject-matter of the cause, as it (in its discretion) may think fit.

Very often the seizing of property at an early stage in proceedings can convey a considerable tactical advantage. This rule provides scope for the exercise of a similar power.

There is also the simple truth that in adversarial situations one party may be tempted to remove or destroy evidence or property which is not helpful to its cause. There must be a mechanism for the other party to protect itself and that property and evidence should the need arise. This rule does so and sits in conjunction with the provisions of default rule 46 (court's other powers in relation to arbitration).

Parties in disputes should be very conscious to preserve any evidence which is the subject-matter of the dispute and, at the very least, should take steps to record it in some way such as to permit the leading of evidence on the point at a later stage. Using these provisions or those under rule 46 (if applicable and if those default rules are not disapplied or modified) should be a key priority in the early stages. If the rules are not retained then s 47(2) orders might be an option (although note that there has to be a 'cause depending' – ie an action has been raised in the court, albeit that this can be done extremely quickly).

Oaths or affirmations

Under default rule 36, the tribunal may –
   (a)   direct that a party or witness is to be examined on oath or affirmation, and
   (b)   administer an oath or affirmation for that purpose.

See comments made on this subject in the commentary to rule 28 and above in connection with the role of the *lex arbitri* and incorporation of substantive law of evidence at the seat. Rule 36 does not actually specify the nature of the oath, but it can be safely assumed that the normal oaths and affirmations used in Scottish courts would suffice. The normal oath on the Bible is:

I swear by Almighty God that I will tell the truth, the whole truth, and nothing but the truth.

If the witness does not wish to swear an oath on the Bible, he or she may make an affirmation in the following terms:

I solemnly, sincerely and truly declare and affirm that I will tell the truth, the whole truth and nothing but the truth.

One might think that persons giving such evidence on oath or affirmation would render themselves open to charges of perjury for giving false evidence in the same way as in court proceedings. However, this rule merely permits the administration of an oath or affirmation, and the taking of evidence on this basis. We do not see that the tribunal can compel a witness to take the oath, although it could, presumably, then exclude the witness's evidence, or treat it as less compelling. This seems to be correct, since such powers of compulsion of non-parties would sit uncomfortably with the private non-judicial nature of arbitration. The rule is also silent on the compulsion of the parties, but the view must be that, although they have consented to the arbitral process, the same logic must apply, and they cannot be compelled to swear or affirm, although their evidence might then be validly excluded (and, potentially, their case lost).

In cases involving allegations of fraud, the arbitrator should proceed with caution.

Failure to submit claim or defence timeously

This matter is dealt with under default rule 37. In international arbitration a considerable practical cause of delay arises where one or other party does not submit pleadings or documents, which results in delays in the whole process. This rule is an admirable attempt to resolve that difficulty by giving the tribunal powers to try to prevent 'unnecessary delays' caused by a party not submitting or pursuing a claim. The tribunal has to consider that there is 'no good reason' for the delay and must be 'satisfied' that the delay may cause a 'substantial risk' that the claim will not be resolved 'fairly' or it is likely to cause 'serious prejudice' to the other party.

Where there is delay in submitting a defence and the tribunal considers that there is no 'good reason' then the tribunal proceeds (although the delay is not to be treated as an admission).

These are tough tests and they will *all* have to be met before the tribunal is forced to take action (see 'and' at the end of rule 37(1)(b)). In many cases there will be 'good reasons' or the tribunal will not be 'satisfied' or there may be a 'risk' but it is not 'substantial' or there is prejudice, but it is not 'serious'. Nevertheless, in the extreme cases this rule will allow the tribunal to take action. With claims the tribunal, if it considers that the requisite above tests have been met, 'must' (ie presumably with no discretion) end the arbitration and make an award (including expenses) as it considers 'appropriate'.

Rule 37, on one view, leaves the tribunal with no discretion but to end the arbitration if the tests are met. The tests are value-loaded and one could see many arguments which could be deployed to avoid the drastic imposition of ending a claim without a final award on the merits. This can be avoided by meeting time limits imposed by the arbitrator and not engaging in any 'dragging of feet' in the prosecution of the claim. Expedition will avoid any allegation of causing 'unnecessary' delay and the claimant should avoid imitating any 'empty chair' defence tactics or attempts by the respondent to derail the arbitral process.

In *TAG Wealth Management v West* [2008] EWHC 1466 (Comm) the English courts allowed a tribunal to debar a party where disclosure had taken five years.

In *Grindrod Shipping Pte Ltd v Hyundai Merchant Marine Co Ltd* [2018] EWHC 1284 (Comm) the tribunal dismissed the claims on the basis of inordinate and inexcusable delay of four years. The claimant then applied to set aside the award under s 68, arguing that it had not been treated fairly under s 33 as its claims had been dismissed on grounds not argued by the respondent. The tribunal had found the delay had caused serious prejudice to the defendant under s 41(3)(b) because it resulted in a significant increase in costs in defending the claim. The court refused to set aside the arbitral award, noting that it would be a 'retrograde step in international arbitration' if a tribunal could not dismiss a claim on the basis of the increased costs of an inordinate or inexcusable delay.

In *Dera Commercial Estate v Derya Inc* [2018] EWHC 1673 (Comm), a party commenced an arbitration claim and later provided particulars of the claim within the statutory six-year limitation period; the court held that the claim could nevertheless be struck out for inordinate delay under the Arbitration Act 1996 s 41(3) where the parties had contractually agreed a shorter limitation period.

Rule 37 goes beyond this point and gives the tribunal a wide discretion to prevent a party from defeating the purpose of the arbitration by unjustified delay. It is hoped that tribunals will seize this power and use it robustly, but fairly, to offer a speedy method of resolving disputes. As the courts seek to streamline their procedures, following Lord Gill's Scottish Civil Courts Review, it will be important for arbitrators to show that they can be at least as quick. This rule is one of the main weapons in the armoury.

Failure to attend a hearing or provide evidence

Under default rule 38:

> Where –
> (a) a party fails –
>   (i)   to attend a hearing which the tribunal requested the party to attend a reasonable period in advance of the hearing, or
>   (ii) to produce any document or other evidence requested by the tribunal, and
> (b) the tribunal considers that there is no good reason for the failure,
> the tribunal may proceed with the arbitration, and make its award, on the basis of the evidence (if any) before it.

The rule is a default rule which provides that, in the absence of agreement to the contrary, if a party fails to attend a hearing (on reasonable notice) or produce any document or other evidence as requested by the tribunal and there is no good reason for not doing so, the tribunal can proceed and make an award based on the information it has.

Failure to comply with tribunal direction or arbitration agreement

Rule 39 is a default rule which in paragraph (1) provides the tribunal with power to order a party breaching a direction of the tribunal or the Rules and arbitration agreement governing the arbitration to comply. In the past, it was very difficult for a tribunal to order one of the parties to do something which was then backed up with some kind of sanction for default (unless the tribunal had actually been conferred a power to do so by the parties at the beginning).

Rule 39(1)(b) means that a tribunal does not have to take the formal step of directing the defaulting party to comply with its direction or the arbitration agreement or the Rules or any other agreement of the parties relating to the conduct of the arbitration (eg an agreement as to procedures to be used) before making a compliance order.

Rule 39(2) gives the tribunal a number of powers when a party does not comply with an order. This rule follows parts of the 1996 Act s 41.

Failure to comply?

One issue which arises is to what extent must the party have failed to comply with the direction or other provisions? Can there be a 'reasonable excuse' for failure or, as some commentators have suggested, following the English provisions, should this be read as inserting the wording 'without sufficient cause'.

It might be suggested that there should be an allowance made for some explanation to be given by the guilty party for a 'failure'. What standard should be followed as to the reasonableness or sufficiency of the explanation may be an issue for the tribunal and not a textbook. It also seems sensible to allow an explanation and then a reply from the other side and indeed, on one view, the requirements of rule 24(2) ('giving each party a reasonable opportunity to put its case and to deal with the other party's case') would require that.

As to what constitutes a 'failure', it might be suggested that anything less than full compliance will be treated as a failure: ie there will not be partial failures/partial compliances.

Sanctions

The tribunal is empowered to make directions, draw adverse inferences or proceed to make a final award or provisional award. Note that this is discretionary from the use of the word 'may'. Reference is also made to the point above in connection with the very wide discretion vested in a tribunal and the courts' reluctance to interfere with the exercise of it.

Order following direction

The power to make a non-compliance 'order' can follow the situation where a party has not complied with a previous 'direction'.

In *W v X Co* [2017] EWHC 3430 (Comm) the court enforced, under the Arbitration Act 1996 s 42, certain peremptory orders made by arbitration tribunals with regard to arbitral proceedings brought against the alleged buyers of two vessels, where they had failed to comply with the orders within the time prescribed or within a reasonable time.

When to use a non-compliance order

It is suggested that the power to make a non-compliance order should be used only in extreme cases of non-compliance.

A tribunal always has a difficult balancing job of ensuring the expeditious progress of the arbitration and maintaining the respect and compliance of the parties in it. This balance can be easily upset by over-eagerness in imposing sanctions or heavy handedness to the disadvantage of one of the parties.

Withdrawal of a non-compliance order

Can an order be withdrawn? Although the rules are silent, one presumes that this would be possible if both parties consent or are given the opportunity of making representations.

Consolidation of proceedings

Default rule 40 allows the parties to agree to consolidate the arbitration with another arbitration or hold concurrent hearings. There has to be an application or request for this from one of the parties (it cannot be ordered on its own initiative (cf *Oxford Shipping Co Ltd v Nippon Yusen Kaisha (The Eastern Saga) (No 2)* [1984] 3 All ER 835) and one suggests that in most cases agreement of all the parties will be required. This rule is an attempt to provide the parties with some mechanism to prevent expenses being incurred in similar but different arbitrations. Of the well-known codes and sets of arbitral rules, the LCIA has something similar (Art 22A) and ICC 2021 has Art 10.

Contractual provision

Some contracts specifically state that arbitrations arising out of essentially the same facts should be consolidated (even to the extent of requiring sub contractors to join in arbitrations between the main contractor and the ultimate client), and it is suggested that, in such a case, it would have been useful to give the tribunal power to compel such a consolidation. This could not really happen where the same tribunal was not seized of jurisdiction in both/all relevant arbitrations, but it appears that this rule would prevent such a step in any event unless all parties consented. It might be arguable that the signature of the relevant main contractor or subcontractor acted as evidence of such consent, but it seems probable that a tribunal would look at the wording of this rule and suggest the party wanting consolidation sought a court order against the recalcitrant party.

POWERS OF COURT IN RELATION TO ARBITRAL PROCEEDINGS (PART 5)

Referral of point of law

Default Rule 41 allows a party to ask the Outer House to determine any 'point' of Scots law arising in the arbitration. As the rule is a default rule, the parties can exclude the jurisdiction of the court under this rule.

However, this rule has to be read in conjunction with the following rule and, when read together, effectively requires the consent of the other party or parties, or of the tribunal itself in the determination.

Referral

Rule 41 is the replacement for the Administration of Justice (Scotland) Act 1972 s 3, which we have made various references to above as well as to the comments of Lords Hope and Prosser in *ERDC Construction Ltd v HM Love & Co (No 2)* 1996 SC 523. It must of course still be useful to allow the parties to approach and seek the authority of the court in respect of a question of Scots law but without the baggage and the abuses which existed under s 3. The application will be in accordance with the Rules of Court and will therefore proceed as a petition or a note and will come before the arbitration judge.

Any 'point' or 'question'

There is a disparity in language between rule 41 and rule 42 where rule 41 refers to a point of Scots law and rule 42 refers twice to 'the question'. In our view, the only way to give sense and effect to the two interacting provisions is to read the two terms as synonymous.

A 'question of law' is defined in England by s 82(1) of the 1996 Act but there is no need here as the rule specifies this as 'any point of Scots law arising in the arbitration'.

Unlike in England (1996 Act s 45(1)), which provides for the court determining 'any question of law arising in the course of the proceedings which the court is satisfied substantially affects the rights of one or more of the parties', there is no rider in the Scottish provision tying this purely to matters affecting the parties and so, as long as one of the parties makes the application, it could feasibly relate to 'public interest' or 'importance'. While this is theoretically possible, it seems unlikely that such a matter could pass the test in rule 42(2)(b)(i) that resolution will be likely to produce substantial savings in costs in the arbitration, and requests to determine points of law which will not have any immediate practical impact will, presumably, be discouraged.

The party or parties would have to specify what that 'point' or 'question' was though. This would have to be to a fairly high degree of specification given that the court is to be satisfied that determining it is likely to produce substantial savings in expenses as well as whether there is 'good reason' why the 'question' should be determined by the court.

What is a point of law?

The question of what constitutes a point of law was decided by the House of Lords (then the highest civil court in both England and Scotland in civil matters) as long ago as 1956. It had been argued in *Edwards v Bairstow* 1956 AC 14 that there was a difference in meaning between England and Scotland in what amounted to an 'error of law'. This was rejected by Lord Radcliffe. His summary of what he perceived to be the common position in both jurisdictions was in these terms (at 36):

> If the case contains anything *ex facie* which is bad law and which bears upon the determination, it is, obviously, erroneous in point of law. But, without any such misconception appearing *ex facie*, it may be that the facts found are such that no person acting judicially and properly instructed as to the relevant law could have come to the determination under appeal. In those circumstances, too, the court must intervene. It has no option but to assume that there has been some misconception of the law and that this has been responsible for the determination. So there, too, there has been error in point of law. I do not think that it much matters whether this state of affairs is described as one in which there is no evidence to support the determination or as one in which the evidence is inconsistent with and contradictory of the determination, or as one in which the true and only reasonable conclusion contradicts the determination.

This remains sound advice and any potential 'point of law' should be measured against what his Lordship said in this case.

Point of Scots law

It has to be a point of Scots law, not any other law which will fall to be considered as a matter of fact to be proved by evidence before the tribunal.

Discretion

The use of the word 'may' does, of course, make the decision of the court as to whether to hear any application discretionary. In England, the courts have given great weight to the fact that the parties have agreed to incorporate the rule and it has been held that the court does have a discretion in accordance with the same word 'may' in the English provisions: *Taylor Woodrow Holdings Ltd v Barnes & Elliott Ltd* [2006] EWHC 1693 (TCC). That case determined that the court was not simply bound to determine any question of law posed once the threshold conditions had been satisfied: see also *Babanaft International Co SA v Avanti Petroleum Inc (The Oltenia)* [1982] 1 WLR 871.

An example of a point of law in English law can be found in the case of *Goodwood Investments Holdings Inc v Thyssenkrupp Industrial Solutions AG* [2018] EWHC 1056 (Comm), where the court had to consider an application under the Arbitration Act 1996 s 45 for determination of a question of law arising in the course of an arbitration, namely whether the arbitration claim had been settled in 'without prejudice' correspondence between the parties' solicitors. The court noted (at para [1]) that the section 'is relatively little used but ... it has a useful role to play.'

Relationship with rule 42

If under rule 42(2) the parties have not agreed to the inclusion of rule 41, then the court cannot intervene as rule 42(2) cannot come into existence until rule 41 has taken effect and that can happen only if the parties have not disapplied the provision. This is similar to the position in England, where if the parties dispense with requiring reasons in the award it would preclude an appeal under the 1996 Act s 69 against an award on a point of law (cf rule 69). Notice also that rule 42 is mandatory in the event that default rule 41 is adopted by the parties.

Application

Because of rule 42, an 'application' can only be 'valid' if made with the agreement of the parties or the consent of the tribunal and, even then, requires the satisfaction of the court that the determination is likely to produce substantial savings in expenses, *and* that the application has been made without delay, *and* that there is a good reason why the question should be determined by the court. This seems likely to prove a significant series of hurdles to overcome in all but the most serious cases. This approach is to be welcomed and suggests that the courts will not wish to be troubled with 'nice' arguments on points of law that can be properly determined by the tribunal and/or have only peripheral relevance to the dispute.

'Application' is not defined in the Act but in terms of RCS 100.5(1) all applications have to be made to the court by petition or note and, in terms of RCS 100.7(1), the petitioner must set out the facts and circumstances on which the petition or note is founded and the relief claimed (see above).

RCS 100.7(2) also provides that in applications under rules 22, 41, 67, 68 and 69 particular matters should be identified. These are (RCS 100.7(3)):

(a) the parties to the cause and the arbitration from which the cause arises;
(b) the relevant rule of the Scottish Arbitration Rules or other provision of the 2010 Act under which the petition or note has been lodged;
(c) any special capacity in which the petitioner or noter is acting or any special capacity in which any other party to the proceedings is acting;

(d) a summary of the circumstances out of which the application or appeal arises;
(e) the grounds on which the application or appeal proceeds;
(f) in the case of an appeal under rule 67(1), whether the appellant seeks the variation or the setting aside of an award (or part of it);
(g) in the case of an appeal under rule 69(1), whether the appeal is made with the agreement of the parties to the arbitration; and
(h) any relevant requirements of the Scottish Arbitration Rules which have been met.

It is suggested that these matters are a helpful reminder of what to put into an application in terms of RCS 100.7(1).

See also the commentary on the relevant Rules of Court in Appendix 1.

No appeal

Rule 41 clearly states that only the Outer House has jurisdiction. The matter cannot progress beyond that to the Inner House. So once the Outer House has, in its discretion, determined the question or point as well as the validity of the application then that ends the procedural avenues for the parties, either with the decision of the Outer House or, where it declines to determine the point under rule 42, with the decision of the arbitrators. This is to be encouraged as parties to international commercial arbitrations seek, in particular, finality in the court system without endless rounds of appeals with the attendant expenses and delay. Here the Scottish provisions innovate upon the 1996 Act which permits an appeal, albeit with leave and only on questions of general importance or 'some other special reason'.

No delay

Like all the other rules and sections of the Act, rules 41 and 42 will require to be read in conjunction with the general duties imposed on the tribunal in s 1 and rule 24 and the duty imposed on the parties in terms of rule 25.

From when is a delay to be measured? Arguably the end of the period from which the pleadings or written submissions have been prepared. If the tribunal is well on its way to determining the issues between the parties, the court may refuse to be 'satisfied' that there was not 'delay' or that the question should be determined by the court.

However, it is suggested that various indications in the Rules and the Act suggest that the parties should proceed with any such application promptly or not at all. It is, therefore, equally possible to argue that the application needs to be made promptly once the issue arises. It is suggested that such an approach would discourage a party from holding on to a possible legal argument to use at a 'convenient' moment to delay the arbitration.

Continuing arbitration

The arbitration may continue while the court is determining the application. In practice, it is hoped that applications can be disposed of quickly and RCS 100 referred to above does provide for a specialised application procedure by petition or note which will go before the nominated arbitration judge.

It might be suggested that continuing the arbitration in the meantime should be encouraged, certainly to the extent that the steps taken are unlikely to be impacted by the decision in the application. Even where this is not the case, the parties could, presumably, indicate their wish to the tribunal that matters should proceed in any event. It would seem to be prudent for the tribunal to hold a meeting with the parties to seek their approval, rather than risking wasting time and costs, although some risks associated with this approach have already been addressed.

Theoretically the tribunal could make an award which would be determinative of the point and leave the parties to decide whether to challenge the award by one of the methods under the Act. Alternatively, the parties may agree that the tribunal should pause, pending the determination (albeit that the power to continue is here provided). This, though, puts the tribunal in an invidious position as the parties' joint action is contrary to its obligations in terms of s 1 and rule 24.

If the tribunal felt completely compromised it may have to consider resignation. The tribunal itself may not agree with the application (it being valid on the basis of the joint application by the parties) and continue anyway.

Variation of time limits set by parties

Under default rule 43, the court may, on an application by the tribunal or any party, vary any time limit relating to the arbitration which is imposed –

    (a) in the arbitration agreement, or

    (b) by virtue of any other agreement between the parties.

As with rules 41 and 42, rule 43 is a default rule and then rule 44 is mandatory; it only comes into effect where rule 43 is not deleted.

In court proceedings, the court may in its discretion sometimes extend time limits for something to be done. This is called a 'prorogation' of the time limit and the same idea is contained in this rule for arbitrations. Seeking a prorogation of a time limit in the court could be made immediately prior to the expiry of that time limit or after it had passed. There is nothing in this rule to suggest that it is any different in this regard.

Time limits

The time limits are 'any time limit relating to the arbitration' and so could, presumably, include those relating to the 'commencement' of the arbitration. (See the notes to s 23 on the prescription and limitation provisions.)

Note also that the court may vary 'any time limit', which would appear to give total discretion on all issues, and not merely those relating to, for example, the making of awards. However, it will not be possible for the parties to use this and the following rule to avoid failures to meet time limits imposed by the arbitral tribunal itself, which are regulated by rules 37–39.

In some of the English cases on the analogous provision, the courts have refused to allow extensions of time on the basis that a point was weak or that there was no reasonable explanation or excuse for allowing time to expire: cf *Buyuk Camlica Shipping Trading & Industry Co Inc v Progress Bulk Carriers Ltd* [2010] EWHC 442 (Comm).

The court and the discretionary nature of the jurisdiction

Applications can be made to the Outer House or the sheriff court. It is anticipated that the former will be the usual route, given that the Court of Session has nominated specialist arbitration judges, whereas sheriff courts are unlikely to see a substantial number of cases in this area and at the time of going to press do not have a specialised procedure.

Note that under these provisions it is the court which can vary time periods. This is a general power provided to the courts. The parties themselves can, of course, also agree to vary the time limits at any time.

Note also that it is a discretionary power. If variation is included by the parties as a default provision in rule 43 then rule 44 automatically takes effect by rule 44(1). The court requires to be satisfied before allowing a variation of a time period that someone would suffer a substantial injustice if no variation was made.

Who may apply?

Theoretically, it is one of the parties, both of the parties or the tribunal itself who may apply, although it will be more likely that it will be one of the parties. If the tribunal finds itself unable to comply with a time limit imposed on it by the agreement of the parties, and the parties will not agree to an extension, it is suggested that an application to the court for extra time will be fairly unattractive, unless the only alternative were to be resignation and a risk of prejudicing arbitral immunity. Clearly only one party would apply, as if both agreed no application would be necessary.

When does that party apply?

The whole approach, as mentioned in relation to rule 42, would appear to be to encourage prompt applications. In any event, the time limits are likely to be relatively short, given the purpose of the application is to extend an existing time limit, and so it seems probable that prompt applications will be needed, and should certainly be encouraged.

'Substantial injustice'?

Guidance on what constitutes 'substantial injustice' may be obtained from the English case of *Equatorial Traders Ltd v Louis Dreyfus Trading Ltd* [2002] EWHC 2023 (Comm). In this case it was held that a party should seek relief as soon as reasonably practicable upon discovery of a missed time limit. The court held that the defendant should have applied promptly for an extension of the time for the service of the statement of case under a time limit contained in the 1996 Act. The legal representatives had failed to consult the appropriate rules and so there was no substantial injustice in holding Dreyfus to the consequences of its representative's deliberate failure.

Some advice as to what might or might not constitute 'substantive injustice' is available from *Gold Coast Ltd v Naval Gijon SA (The Hull 53)* [2006] EWHC 1044 (Comm). In this case the claimant had applied, in terms of (the analogous provision) of the 1996 Act s 79, for a retrospective extension of time to make an application to the arbitrator for him to correct an interim award. It was argued that the claimant would suffer substantial injustice if an extension of time was not granted. It was further agreed that the claimant had a substantial prospect of success in its application to the arbitrator for correction of the award. The court allowed the extension on the basis that the other party would receive a windfall benefit if the application was refused and the claimant was deprived of advancing its 'strong arguments'. The court also held that it had been understandable in all the circumstances why the point had been missed; that there was a good explanation for the delay and no prejudice had been caused to the defendant by the delay or would be caused by the extension of time.

In *Kalmneft JSC v Glencore International AG* [2002] 1 All ER 76, the court (Coleman J) considered the principles which might apply to an extension of time application generally. Here the court held that the considerations likely to be relevant to applications for extension of time might include any of the following seven matters:

    (a)   the extent of the delay;
    (b)   whether a party had acted reasonably in letting a time limit expire and accruing subsequent delay;
    (c)   whether the respondent to the application or the arbitrator had caused or contributed to the delay;

(d) whether irremediable prejudice would be caused to the respondent because of delay if the application was permitted to proceed;

(e) whether the arbitration had continued in the interim and, if so, what impact determination of the application would have upon it;

(f) the strength of the application; and

(g) whether, in all the circumstances, it would be unfair to refuse the applicant the opportunity of a determination.

While, clearly, these are based on a different piece of legislation (the 1996 Act), it would appear to be a reasonable checklist for use in considering matters under rules 43 and 44.

Finally, these principles devised by Coleman J were applied and commented on in *Squirrel Film Distribution v SPP Opportunities Fund LLP* [2010] EWHC 706 (Ch). The court considered that the list was 'non-exhaustive' and added to it by including 'public policy in the due expedition of arbitration' as a further consideration.

It may be that arbitral tribunals will approach this whole issue like courts do in relation to considering whether to grant extensions or interim relief by looking at the reasons given and then seeing where the balance of convenience lies and who would be more prejudiced by allowing the extension or variation over not allowing it, and by including in that whether any prejudice could be alleviated by an award of expenses or other sanction.

Extent

It is for the court alone to determine the extent of any variation. It will no doubt have regard to the fact that there is no other mechanism available and that there would be prejudice and/or injustice in not granting an extension. It might also have regard to the principles above, and should, it is suggested, be encouraged to do so.

Continuing arbitration

Again, the arbitration is entitled to continue while the application for a variation is being sought. This seems less likely to be problematic, but the issues may be less difficult than in applications under rules 41 and 42.

Finality

Again, the Outer House or the sheriff will determine the matter and dispose of it. There will be no appeal to the Sheriff Principal or Inner House as the case may be.

The court's power to order attendance of witnesses and disclosure of evidence

Rule 45 makes it mandatory for the court, on application, to order the attendance of a witness or the disclosure of documents or other material evidence to the tribunal. This is a similar provision to the Model Law Art 27 and the 1996 Act s 43.

Power of the tribunal

The tribunal does not have powers – even if the parties agreed upon it – to coerce third parties to participate in the proceedings. It is important to remember that the tribunal only has power as between the parties. It is not a substitute court and does not have equivalent powers.

Recently there has been some discussion of this general area in international arbitration, with rules being adapted to purport to extend the powers of the tribunal in the area of making interim orders, granting what amount to injunctions etc, but it is difficult to see how this can either be right as a matter of legal theory, or work in practice. The Scottish approach to make clear the limits of the tribunal's authority is to be welcomed.

The decision to make any order under this rule is always a matter for the discretion of the court, and the parties or the tribunal cannot insist on such an order.

Under the jurisdiction of the court

The court can only order a person to attend who is under the jurisdiction of the court. What is missing in this rule is an analogous provision to s 43 of the 1996 Act which provides that the witness must be in the UK and the tribunal proceedings in England and Wales or, as the case may be, Northern Ireland. Otherwise the court may order the attendance but equally it has no compulsive power over any failure to attend, which, in the final analysis, makes the 'order' something more akin to a 'request'. Although the Act is silent on the point, the practical issues are the same. The power of the courts only runs within the jurisdiction, and the ability to enforce an order on foreign residents may be limited, unless they visit Scotland for some reason. The court will be the sheriff court or the Outer House although, as already suggested, it seems likely that the latter court will hear the majority of such applications, at least in international arbitrations, and to that end it is suggested that expertise in dealing with arbitration matters under the Act is naturally likely to build up more quickly before the arbitration judge in the Outer House.

Disclosure of evidence

There is another reference to 'disclose in civil proceedings' at rule 45(2). Disclosure is the English terminology for the production of evidence. In

Scotland, civil procedure speaks of 'recovery of evidence'. As in rule 28, it is suggested that nothing turns on this and the court will clearly entertain arguments that a party should not be coerced into producing or disclosing something which it would be entitled to claim 'privilege' over or which it would not have to produce or disclose in 'civil proceedings'.

'Privileged documents' would seem to include 'without prejudice' correspondence (ie where documents such as letters have been sent to the other side containing concessions clearly made for the purposes of negotiation only and not for use in any other way) and *post litem motam* documents, which is the Latin tag for those documents which have been prepared by a party in anticipation of or for the purposes of litigation. (This is discussed further below.)

That may beg the question as to whether these are Scottish 'civil proceedings' or those of another country or legal system. The rule will clearly include proceedings in Scotland. However, the wording is not so restricted, as the definition of 'arbitration' in the Act is not limited to arbitrations seated in Scotland, and an interesting argument might arise where the party concerned was involved in civil proceedings in another jurisdiction, and, in that jurisdiction, disclosure would not be required. The court should be alert to a party using an application under rule 45 as a fishing expedition to obtain evidence for use in other proceedings that it may have, or intend to take, against the witness concerned. One can envisage a scenario where there are proceedings in a foreign court between parties A and B, and Scottish arbitration proceedings between parties B and C on related matters, and B seeks to obtain evidence from A for use in the Scottish proceedings, which are then also available for use in the foreign civil proceedings. The confidentiality rules under the Act should provide some protection here.

Issues may arise where a claim is made that the documents are privileged in civil proceedings in another jurisdiction, whether in the rest of the UK or elsewhere. It is difficult to see that, under general principles of comity, the Scottish courts would order the disclosure of a document in a Scottish arbitration which would have the effect of defeating valid legal privilege in court proceedings elsewhere.

The rule is not restricted to persons residing in Scotland or (as in the equivalent English provisions – 1996 Act ss 34 and 43) the UK but appears to be worldwide. This is, however, probably misleading as, if the Scottish courts made an order for a foreign party to give evidence, and it declined, it is difficult to see what would happen next.

Application

As discussed under rule 41, in terms of RCS 100.5(1), all applications have to be made to the court by petition or note and in terms of RCS 100.7(1) the petitioner or noter must set out the facts and circumstances on which the petition is founded and the relief claimed.

An application can be made by both the tribunal and the parties (either of them – there is no need here for a joint application in the absence of tribunal consent or without tribunal participation).

It is slightly strange that the consent of the tribunal is not required in this situation. On the one hand, one can see that parties may be experiencing difficulties with compelling witnesses to attend or in obtaining documents, but the first step would seem to be to seek the assistance of the tribunal. It is presumably intended to allow *ex parte* applications (ie made by one party without the knowledge of the other) so the other party would not be aware of the applicant's possible difficulty with witnesses. The rule does not indicate whether *ex parte* applications are possible. Likewise, the relevant RCS 100.5 is also silent on whether this is expressly possible. As referenced above the rule provides:

(1) Subject to paragraph (2), an application or appeal under the 2010 Act shall be made by petition.

(2) If proceedings are depending before the court under paragraph (1) in relation to the same arbitration process, an application under the 2010 Act shall be made by note in the process of the petition.

(3) Upon lodging a petition or note under paragraph (1) or (2), the petitioner or noter must enrol a motion for intimation and service of the petition or note and the court may make such order as is appropriate in the circumstances of the case.

(4) The court may make an order for intimation and service of the petition or note at the address of a party's agent or other person acting for that party in the arbitration process and the service will be effective if carried out in accordance with that order.

(5) Upon expiry of any period of notice following intimation and service of the petition or note, the petitioner or noter shall enrol a motion for further procedure and the court may make such order as is appropriate in the circumstances of the case, including, where appropriate, an order disposing of the petition or note.

Theoretically therefore, while RCS 100.5(3) requires the petitioner or noter to enrol a motion for intimation and service of the petition or note, the court has a discretion to 'make such order as is appropriate in the circumstances of the case' which must include there being no requirement for intimation and service of the petition as the case may be.

If that is so, it is unclear whether *ex post facto* notice/intimation requires to be given to the other party and/or the tribunal once the application has been disposed of by the court. Presumably the latter point is implicit where an order is made, but what if the application is unsuccessful?

The tribunal can continue the arbitration pending an application made by any party and may feel constrained in terms of s 1 and rule 24 to do so; this may imply that applications can be made only with notice to the other party and the tribunal, otherwise there could be no issue, as the tribunal would be unaware that there was any reason not to proceed.

Scope of the court's order

Attendance before the tribunal is clear enough – subject to the points about jurisdiction above.

Alternatively, the approach could be the same as that used in Scottish courts, namely commission and diligence for the recovery of documents/ evidence whereby the parties must specify the class of documents they require for the purposes of preparing their case and providing greater specification in the pleadings or, in the case of evidence, provide reasons why the evidence has to be taken on commission as opposed to being taken in the course of an arbitral full hearing.

It has been held in England that the analogous provision cannot be used to obtain disclosure from a third party, or give the court the power to order third party disclosure, due to the privacy of the arbitration process (*BNP Paribas v Deloitte & Touche LLP* [2003] EWHC 2874 (Comm); *DTEK Trading SA v Morozov* [2017] EWHC 94 (Comm)) but the wording of the rule seems to imply that will be the potential effect in Scotland.

In the English case of *Tajik Aluminium Plant v Hydro Aluminium AS* [2005] EWCA Civ 1218, the Court of Appeal held that there were clear distinctions to be drawn between an order for disclosure made against a third party and a witness summons to produce documents. Whilst it was not necessary to describe documents individually, it was necessary to identify them with sufficient certainty so as to leave no real doubt in the mind of the person to whom the summons was addressed as to what he was required to do.

The English courts have also held in *Travelers Insurance Co Ltd v Countrywide Surveyors Ltd* [2010] EWHC 2455 (TCC) that there is no power to order pre-action disclosure (an English concept to produce documents before the start of legal proceedings) where the dispute is covered by an agreement to arbitrate. (See also *Mi-Space (UK) Ltd v Lend Lease Construction (EMEA) Ltd* [2013] EWHC 2001 (TCC).)

English and Scottish practices are not identical in this area, and there seems no reason why the Scottish courts should not take a wider view than their English colleagues, given the wording of the rule. It must be open to the parties in the first instance to phrase their applications as they see fit. Likewise, the tribunal.

Finality

Again, the Outer House or sheriff court will determine the matter, without further right of appeal.

Other material evidence

Other material evidence will include evidence which goes beyond documents – including physical evidence.

Entitled to refuse

There is a concept of 'privilege' or 'confidentiality' when discussing documents which a party must disclose to the other party or the tribunal in litigation and this has been applied now to arbitration through this rule. This is part of the Scots law of evidence. We have touched upon this above in the discussion of *post litem motam*, ie those documents prepared in contemplation of litigation. A 'privileged' document is one which the party is not compelled to (using the words of the 2010 Act) 'disclose or give in civil proceedings'.

RCS 35.8(1) provides:

> Where confidentiality is claimed for any document or other property sought to be recovered under any of the following rules, such document or other property shall, where practicable, be enclosed in a sealed packet.

Confidentiality and/or privilege is explained in *Greens Annotated Rules of the Court of Session* (RCS 35.2.7) as including the following:

- Communications between solicitor and client for professional purposes (subject to exceptions where fraud or illegality is alleged).
- Communications between solicitors with a view to achieving settlement of litigation are confidential and not recoverable (including 'without prejudice' communications).
- Communications *post litem motam* are in general not recoverable.
- Public policy (public interest immunity) where a document or property may be withheld on the ground of public policy or immunity or public interest where the interest is a national one put forward by the Crown.
- Communications between spouses are confidential.
- Communications which would self-incriminate the person holding the document (the 'haver', pronounced 'havver') are privileged.
- Communications made as a matter of duty (moral or social) to another who also has a corresponding duty, although it is always a balancing exercise.

It is suggested that these points may be of some assistance if a party wishes to claim that a document or a piece of evidence is confidential or privileged as it would be in 'civil proceedings', therefore entitling them to refuse to give it or disclose it in the face of a court order under rule 45.

The court's other powers in relation to arbitration

Rule 46 is an important provision giving the sheriff or the Court of Session powers relating to arbitrations seated in Scotland whether such arbitrations have actually commenced or where a dispute may give rise to an arbitration in the future in terms of an arbitration agreement (rule 46(4)(b)(i)).

The Scottish Government's Explanatory Notes to the Arbitration (Scotland) Bill stated that:

> [T]he court has the same power in arbitration proceedings as it would have in ordinary civil proceedings. The rule retains the existing law and sets out a range of powers including making an order under section 1 of the Administration of Justice (Scotland) Act 1972 to order the inspection, photographing, preservation, custody and detention of documents and other property (including land) which appear to the court may be relevant to the arbitration proceedings.

Analogous provisions

Rule 46 is similar to s 44 of the 1996 Act. See also the UNCITRAL Model Law as amended in 2006, Art 17.

Note that, in relation to s 44, the English Court of Appeal has indicated (*obiter*) that, while it is possible for the parties to grant the courts wider powers than those contained in s 44, and to remove the restrictions in that section (in the case in question, in relation to the right of appeal), very clear language will be needed (*SAB Miller v East African Breweries Ltd* [2010] EWCA Civ 1564). As rule 46 is a default rule, there seems no reason why a similar approach could not be taken in Scotland, albeit that the specific issue on appeal rights does not arise under this rule.

Default provision

It is for the parties to agree whether to disapply this rule. Conceivably the court could be precluded from interfering in respect of what the English law would term interlocutory relief – ie interim orders – but it is difficult to see how this would be advantageous.

Court

'Court' here will mean the Outer House or the sheriff court in terms of s 31(1).

Finality?

Unlike the other provisions in this Part, there is no prohibition here on appealing against the court's interlocutor in respect of the granting of any 'application' by any party either to the Sheriff Principal or the Inner House as the case may be.

It is uncertain whether this is an oversight or by design. One can see in the granting of interim remedies that the court may have to rely on *ex parte* submissions or statements from a party or counsel and thus is reluctant to permit the interim remedy becoming permanent without further court intervention. It is possible under this rule that one party can approach the court without disclosing this to the other side or the tribunal if it can make its case that an arbitration has begun or a dispute has arisen or might arise and that an arbitration agreement provides that such a dispute is to be resolved by arbitration, and satisfy the court that the case is one of urgency and thus should be heard by the court in the same way as motions for interim interdict and interim suspension.

Pre-conditions

The court can grant such orders only if the application is made by any party (presumably to the arbitration) and, where the arbitration has commenced, with the consent of the tribunal or where the court is satisfied that the case is urgent. It would seem likely that the 'urgency' test is to be used primarily where the party concerned does not wish to seek the approval of the tribunal, perhaps for fear of alerting the other party. It would seem unlikely that the tribunal could consider an application for consent under this rule on an *ex parte* basis for fear of apparent bias. Indeed, it is suggested that it is difficult to see how an arbitrator could ever entertain an *ex parte* application. The court is, of course, very used to dealing with these types of interim applications.

If an application is sought to be made without alerting the other side, best practice might be that this should be taken to the court, rather than the tribunal. This will, of course, always be the case where the concern is in relation to alerting the tribunal itself.

Relief at the start of the process

If the tribunal has yet to be established, the rule allows a party to seek relief right at the start of the process. (See the terms of the Administration of Justice (Scotland) Act 1972 s 1 below.) The court can deal with the matter and thereafter hand over control to the newly established tribunal. It would seem that the tribunal will then be bound by a ruling or rulings made by the court, which may not be the best possible start to an arbitral process. It is, therefore, suggested that such an approach is only worth considering in extreme situations where there is a real risk of prejudice to the position of the party concerned, or the matter is likely to be non-controversial so far as the tribunal is concerned.

Power to make an order under Administration of Justice (Scotland) Act 1972

It is worth setting out the full terms of the 1972 Act s 1 (as amended). The Act conferred the following powers to Scottish courts and the courts will have the same powers in relation to arbitrations (see also *Anderson v Gibb* 1993 SLT 726):

Extended powers of courts to order inspection of documents and other property, etc

(1)   Without prejudice to the existing powers of the Court of Session and of the sheriff court, those courts shall have power, subject to the provisions of subsection (4) of this section, to order the inspection, photographing, preservation, custody and detention of documents and other property (including, where appropriate, land) which appear to the court to be property as to which any question may relevantly arise in any existing civil proceedings before that court or in civil proceedings which are likely to be brought, and to order the production and recovery of any such property, the taking of samples thereof and the carrying out of any experiment thereon or therewith.

(1A)   Without prejudice to the existing powers of the Court of Session and of the sheriff court, those courts shall have power, subject to subsection (4) of this section, to order any person to disclose such information as he has as to the identity of any persons who appear to the court to be persons who –

(a)   might be witnesses in any existing civil proceedings before that court or in civil proceedings which are likely to be brought; or

(b)   might be defenders in any civil proceedings which appear to the court to be likely to be brought.

(2)   Notwithstanding any rule of law or practice to the contrary, the court may exercise the powers mentioned in subsection (1) or (1A) of this section –

(a)   where proceedings have been commenced, on the application, at any time after such commencement, of a party to or minuter in the proceedings, or any other person who appears to the court to have an interest to be joined as such party or minuter;

(b)   where proceedings have not been commenced, on the application at any time of a person who appears to the court to be likely to be a party to or minuter in proceedings which are likely to be brought;

unless there is special reason why the application should not be granted.

(3)   The powers conferred on the Court of Session by section 16 of the Administration of Justice (Scotland) Act 1933 to regulate its own procedure and the powers conferred on that Court by section 32 of the Sheriff Courts (Scotland) Act 1971 to regulate the procedure of the sheriff court shall include power to regulate and prescribe the procedure to be followed, and the form of any document to be used, in any application under the foregoing provisions of this section in a case where the application is in respect of proceedings which have not been commenced, and such incidental, supplementary and consequential provisions as appear appropriate; and without prejudice to the said generality, the said powers shall include power to provide in such a case for the application to be granted *ex parte*, for the intimation of the application to such persons (if any) as the court thinks fit, and for the finding of caution where appropriate for any loss, damage or expenses which may be incurred as a result of the application.

(4)   Nothing in this section shall affect any rule of law or practice relating to the privilege of witnesses and havers, confidentiality of communications

and withholding or non-disclosure of information on the grounds of public interest; and section 47 of the Crown Proceedings Act 1947 (recovery of documents in possession of Crown) shall apply in relation to any application under this section in respect of a document or other property as it applied before the commencement of this section to an application for commission and diligence for the recovery of a document.

Court powers to appoint a person to safeguard interests of person lacking capacity

The requirements of the Adults with Incapacity (Scotland) Act 2000 have been discussed above and the safeguards that are built into that Act (see mandatory rule 4 and rule 68).

The process in default rule 46(1)(a) would appear to be similar to the concept of a guardian *ad litem*, and would, presumably, involve an independent third party being instructed to act in the interests of the party concerned. If such a party is the applicant, this would, presumably, require the court to investigate the claim and determine whether there was a reasonable likelihood of success before allowing the action to proceed. If the party is the respondent, then the position may be relatively straightforward, in that the person appointed could carry out this review to determine if it was worth defending the arbitration.

It would seem unlikely that this power would be required very frequently, since the party would have had to have mental capacity to enter into the arbitration agreement in the first place, but would be relevant where, for example, the party had suffered mental illness or brain injury after the arbitration agreement had been entered into.

Court powers to order the sale of any property in dispute in the arbitration

While rule 46(1)(b) uses the word 'any', must the property be registered in the name of a party to the proceedings? It is difficult to see how property not owned by a party could be the subject of the dispute. If it had been transferred to a third party improperly, the first order would be to reverse the unlawful transfer, and then order the sale.

It is instructive to compare the default rule 35 powers of the tribunal in relation to property. The powers of the tribunal are limited to allowing an expert or another party to inspect, photograph, preserve or take custody of any property which that party owns or possesses which is the subject of the arbitration (or as to which any question arises in the arbitration) or to take samples from or conduct an experiment on or to preserve any document or other evidence which the party possesses or controls. The tribunal under that provision is restricted to producing orders or directions whereas here the court's interlocutor ordering it will have coercive effect in that the party will have a period to comply after which the court will effect the sale in any event.

Power to make an order securing any amount in dispute

In court proceedings where a party is concerned as to the liquidity or solvency of the other party it may apply to the court for the grant of 'caution' (pronounced 'kay-shun'). If the court ordains a party to find caution it must provide to the court a monetary security in the sum ordered. It is calculated as a percentage of the sum sought and will be granted only where there are reasonable prospects of success for the party applying. Caution can only be ordered where there are court proceedings underway. Lastly, the party can satisfy the order for caution by consigning the money to the court (by lodging it in court).

If a party is concerned as to the dissipation of assets or the imminent insolvency of a party before or just as the proceedings are about to commence, it may apply to the court for what is called 'diligence on the dependence', ie on the dependence of the action about to be raised. There are strict legal tests applied but if the court considers that diligence should be granted it can have the effect of stopping a party from using or consuming its own assets pending the determination of the litigation.

Note that in both cases the parties apply and implement the court's order (interlocutor). The court itself does not do so.

If the parties obtain diligence, then they can prevent the dissipation or conveyance of moveable or heritable assets.

Thus, the court is here empowered (if the rule is not disapplied) to deploy these remedies in sub-paragraphs (c) and (e).

Power to preserve evidence and allow recovery pre-litigation

The court has the power to order the preservation of evidence, but can this extend to an order which will have the effect of disclosure of documents by a third party, ie non-party? (See *Assimina Maritime v Pakistan National Shipping Corpn (The Tasman Spirit)* [2004] EWHC 3005 (Comm).) It is suggested that this could only be to the extent that the court would be willing to order the evidence in question to be disclosed in the arbitration, as discussed above.

It is suggested that the court is likely to know exactly what evidence is to be preserved, rather than using this as a device for a fishing expedition to determine whether there is any such evidence. It is unlikely to be best practice to seek such an order without a reasonably precise list of the evidence to be protected, in order to demonstrate that protection is needed. There will also, presumably, be a need to demonstrate, on the balance of probabilities, that there is a risk that evidence will not be preserved in the absence of an order. It is interesting to note that a number of jurisdictions, including some in Australia and the United States, have started to consider a tort of, in effect, disposing of evidence. (The Australian case related to evidence in a tobacco suit, although this action was dismissed on appeal.) If a party to a commercial arbitration, particularly one who is sophisticated enough to understand the rules of court in respect of production of evidence, is the respondent to such an application, there may be a difficult intellectual argument to overcome. If the party knows disposal of the evidence to be unlawful, then why make an order? The test may almost move to the criminal standard to obtain an order in such circumstances, since there would seem no point in making an order which seems unnecessary.

Power to grant warrant for arrestment or inhibition

An arrestment is a diligence against moveable property in the hands of a third party. Inhibition is a diligence against Scottish heritable property held by another.

Power to grant interdict

The court has the equivalent powers to grant interdicts (or interim interdicts) in respect of arbitration proceedings. An interdict is a court order restraining or preventing someone from carrying out an act which is deemed to be illegal or harmful. The act must be ongoing or a future one and also be reasonably anticipated. The reference to interim is that these orders are often sought as a matter of urgency and thus the court will determine, in the first instance, whether there is a case in law and will then balance the convenience of granting the order between the two parties, measuring the prejudice caused to one in granting it over the prejudice caused to the other in not granting it. If granted, the interdict is an interdict *ad interim* or interim interdict. It is a holding position sometimes said to preserve the 'status quo'. It is open later for one of the parties to lead evidence and for the court to explore the full merits of what was sought on an interim basis. If it agrees it may grant a permanent interdict.

It is thought that a court would be very reluctant to grant a permanent interdict where the dispute is governed by the arbitration. As seen below, default rule 49(b) gives the tribunal the power to order a party to do or refrain from doing something which is akin to this power. Where the arbitration has not yet begun (and thus rule 49 is not yet available) parties may want to consider deploying rule 46.

Powers of the Court in England and Wales

In England and Wales, it is possible for a court to grant worldwide injunctions restraining the disposal of assets, so-called Mareva injunctions (named after the case of *Mareva Compania Naviera SA v International Bulkcarriers SA*

[1975] 2 Lloyd's Rep 509) and now often referred to as Worldwide Freezing Orders (WFO)) in support of the arbitration.

Where there is a risk of disposal of assets, courts can 'freeze' assets in order to preserve the *status quo* pending enforcement proceedings, in the form of an extra-territorial freezing order, either over particular assets located outside the territorial jurisdiction of the court or a WFO applying to all foreign jurisdictions (*Cogentra AG v Sixteen Thirteen Marine SA* [2008] EWHC 1615 (Comm); *Emmott v Michael Wilson & Partners Ltd (No 2)* [2009] EWHC 1 (Comm)).

The court will have to be satisfied: that there is a good arguable case as to the merits of claim; whether an order will be effective over the respondents' assets; whether there is a real risk of dissipation; and whether the granting of an order is just and convenient (*Belair LLC v Basel LLC* [2009] EWHC 725 (Comm)).

The natural court for the granting of interim injunctive relief must be the court of the country of the seat of arbitration, especially where the curial law of the arbitration is that of the same country (*Econet Wireless Ltd v Vee Networks Ltd* [2006] EWHC 1568 (Comm)) but English courts have been more willing to intervene in international fraud cases where there is a strong case of serious wrongdoing on a large scale and/or bad faith (*Haiti v Duvalier (No 2)* [1990] 1 QB 202; *Mobil Cerro Negro Ltd v Petroleos de Venezuela SA* [2008] EWHC 532 (Comm); *ArcelorMittal USA LLC v Essar Steel Ltd* [2019] EWHC 724 (Comm)).

The most common basis on which freezing injunctions are sought under s 44 is urgency. The requirement for urgency will be satisfied where there is a risk of dissipation (*Mobil Cerro Negro Ltd v PDVSA* [2008] 1 CLC 542), but if urgency is not pleaded or assets or evidence are not sought to be preserved, then the court can only consider an application if it is made with the permission of the tribunal or with the agreement in writing of the other parties (*Petroleum Investment Co Ltd v Kantupan Holdings Co Ltd* [2002] 1 All ER (Comm) 124; *Cetelem SA v Roust Holdings Ltd* [2005] EWCA Civ 618).

The court may refuse to so act if there are already effective remedies through the tribunal itself or any administering institution (*Gerald Metals SA v Timis* [2016] EWHC 2327 (Ch) – where an application was refused as the emergency arbitrator procedure was available under the LCIA Rules). It may also refuse to act in a subsequent application if the urgency has dissipated and the issues are properly then within the arbitrator's domain (*Schillings International LLP v Scott* [2019] EWHC 1335 (Ch)).

In *Company 1 v Company 2* [2017] EWHC 2319 (QB) the court noted that, as a general rule, there was inevitably significant urgency regarding a freezing order. If there was no mechanism by which that relief could be obtained in the arbitral proceedings, it would only be in unusual circumstances that such an application would not meet the urgency test.

There is nothing in the Act, it is suggested, that would prevent a Scottish court also doing so in support of arbitration. Reference has already been made to the requirements of rule 46(2) for the court to take action on an application by any party and, if the arbitration has begun, with the consent of the tribunal or where the court is satisfied that the case is one of urgency.

Note also that the wording of the rule does not require, as in England under s 44(5), that 'the court shall act only if or to the extent that the arbitral tribunal, and any arbitral or other institution or person vested by the parties with power in that regard, has no power or is unable for the time being to act effectively' and must therefore be deemed to have a wider discretion, albeit it would likely exercise it where there was no effective alternative.

Even greater argument might be needed to secure the draconian provisions of what is sometimes called the 'civil search warrant' of an Anton Piller order, named after the case of *Anton Piller KG v Manufacturing Processes Ltd* [1976] Ch 55.

Power to grant any other interim or permanent order

Other interim or permanent orders might include the panoply of other 'orders' available in the Court of Session.

It is possible to apply to the court for an order *ad factum praestandum*. This is simply an order asking the court to instruct someone to do something – ie a positive order (cf interdict as a negative order). For example, an order that 'the persons occupying the village green should move and vacate by 12 noon on Friday' etc.

Under s 46 of the Court of Session Act 1988, there is a procedure under RCS providing that the pursuer can go to court for an order against a defender where that defender (the person called to the court) has done something which the court could have historically, but has not, prevented by interdict. In that case, the court can order the defender to put the pursuer back in the position he was in in terms of possession or can grant some other relief. This is slightly difficult to follow but simply means that if A committed a wrong against B and B had not prevented it (as a future or ongoing wrong) by interdict, B can still go to the court for the order even though there was no interdict and the wrong has passed.

Under s 47(2) of the Court of Session Act 1988 the court can make any order it thinks fit in terms of 'interim possession' of property in relation to the cause or the subject-matter of the cause. This is a wide-ranging power and often used. The difficulty for application to arbitrations is the reference to 'cause' which presupposes an action already raised in the Court of Session.

It might be possible for the court to make an interim attachment order in terms of the Bankruptcy and Diligence etc (Scotland) Act 2007Act.

For completeness, it might be possible for the court to make orders under the Court of Session Act 1988 s 10 which is specialised procedure in respect of the technicalities of ingathering ('obtaining') evidence.

Tribunal ongoing

Like other provisions in Part 5, the tribunal can continue to sit pending determination of any application to the court.

AWARDS (PART 6)

Rules applicable to the substance of the dispute

Party choice of law

This rule is fundamental to the principle of party autonomy. So, if the parties have a clause in their contract that says: 'The contract shall be governed by the law of Scotland and the Scottish courts shall have jurisdiction', then the substantive law of the contract is Scots law and the parties having chosen it means that the tribunal must enforce it. Rule 47 is a default rule and, if it is not disapplied, it is peremptory in nature with the use of the word 'must'. The dispute will be decided in accordance with the substantive rules decided on by the parties where possible according to the law. If the parties have made no such choice then the tribunal must decide what law applies, applying the conflict of law rules. As explained under s 6 above, there are a number of laws which may govern elements in an arbitration. If the parties have chosen a law to govern the substantive dispute then that is the law that the tribunal must apply.

It must also be possible, from the wording of this rule, for the parties to agree to apply other cadres of law or equity such as 'the dispute will be decided in accordance with the principles of equity' or in accordance with the *'lex mercatoria'* or the tribunal will sit as *'amiable compositeur'*. These principles stray towards those found in 'civilian' systems as opposed to common law systems but note that in international arbitrations they may be enforceable. This is dealt with in more detail below.

Tribunal choice

If the parties have not made the choice of law, or the choice is unlawful (and of course they have not removed this default rule), then it falls to the tribunal to make that election, subject to the terms of the rule. Instead of the parties choosing, the tribunal is given the task of choosing the law applicable to the substance of the dispute and it is to do so in accordance with the conflict of laws rules which it considers applicable. Which conflict of laws rules apply will depend on the nationality of the parties, the *locus* (place) of any dispute, where the contract was created, etc, or even the provisions of the Rome I (Regulation (EC) No 593/2008) and Rome II (Regulation (EC) No 864/2007) regimes if the parties or the subject-matter of the dispute is within the European Union or, where any jurisdiction (such as the UK) has left the EU, what transitional arrangements have been agreed in that regard. Interestingly, the rule appears to allow the tribunal to decide which of the possible rules is applicable. It does not give the tribunal a discretion to choose a law, but the discretion to choose conflict of laws rules may come close to being the same thing in some circumstances.

Justice, fairness or equity

Rule 47(2) is directed at the situation whereby parties make an agreement that their disputes shall be determined by 'equity and good conscience' or 'fairness and justness' or other such general principles. This is what is known in arbitration as an 'equity' clause or the application of the maxim '*ex aequo et bono*' with the tribunal acting as '*amiable compositeur*'. If that is agreed between the parties then, theoretically at least, the tribunal could make its determination and make an award based on these general principles without applying the strict letter of the law. An example of this can be found in certain Institutional Rules such as the LCIA Arbitration Rules 2020 Art 22.4 and ICC 2021 Art 21.3. These clauses are popular in the civilian or continental systems. They are also found in Shari'a law systems. Because law is not to be applied, it follows that a tribunal would not make a decision in terms of law and so there could be no appeal on a point of law on the basis of legal error under rule 69.

The Scottish Rules do not permit this, if rule 47 is incorporated into the parties' agreements. Rule 47(2) expressly prohibits the tribunal from deciding the dispute on the basis of general considerations of justice, fairness or equity *unless* that is part of the law of the substance or unless the parties otherwise agree to it. This last point is circular. If the parties want this right, they can exclude rule 47. If they fail to do so, they can still agree, and the rule has no effect. If the parties have used an 'equity' clause, it is arguable that the tribunal can apply it whether rule 47 is 'in' or not. Accordingly, it could be said that the only purpose of the rule is to prevent the tribunal doing this on its own initiative.

To reinforce this, rule 47(3) provides that the tribunal must have regard to the provisions of any contract relating to the substance of the dispute, and the normal commercial or trade usage of any undefined terms, and any commercial or trade customs or practices relevant to the substance of the dispute and any other matter which the parties agree is relevant in the circumstances. While this appears to be helpful, it does widen the scope somewhat, and could create a clash with rule 47(2) if, for example, trade usage is that a particular law is to apply, but the appropriate conflict of laws rules would reach a different decision.

As an example, it could be reasonably asserted that the trade usage on contracts relating to the offshore oil and gas industry in the UK Sector of the North Sea is that English law is used, whether the work takes place in England or Scotland. In some other types of oil and gas contracts this is modified to, say, the law of Texas. Conflict of laws rules could well say that the law of Scotland should apply in either case but trade usage would suggest otherwise.

Difficult considerations for the tribunal

The job of the tribunal therefore, in the event of the parties not choosing the substantive law, is a difficult one. The parties choosing the substantive law or an alternative law by agreement has much to recommend it, and should be regarded as best practice anyway, even without the issue of dispute resolution by arbitration or otherwise.

But what if the parties choose a law, or the tribunal decides a law is applicable, with which the tribunal is unfamiliar? The rules do, of course, allow the tribunal to appoint a clerk or tribunal secretary, and, while the tradition has been to appoint a lawyer familiar with the law of Scotland, under this new regime (and subject to our comments in connection with the appointment of clerks generally), there would seem to be no barrier to appointing a legal expert in another legal system if appropriate, subject to the agreement of the parties. Alternatively, the parties may agree on the applicable law and simply wish to make submissions on how that applies to the facts. If the parties have not agreed and decline to allow the appointment of an expert or clerk, or to allow the tribunal to obtain expert reports on relevant issues, then the tribunal may be faced with having to resign on the basis that it cannot deliver an award which it is confident complies with the relevant law. Where the tricky legal question is one of Scots law, it is open to one of the parties to the arbitration to begin proceedings in court in accordance with rule 41; albeit regard must also be had to the conditions set out in rule 42.

The pragmatic, alternative approach is to advise the parties that, unless they allow the tribunal to take appropriate advice, the parties will be responsible for ensuring that their legal advisers provide the tribunal with a common position or submissions supported by expert evidence on the relevant law. Finally, some courts (including England) have an assumption that their law is the same as any foreign law used, save to the extent that a party demonstrates that this is not the case.

But what if the tribunal actually decides the matter in accordance with the wrong law? This was considered under the 1996 Arbitration Act, by the Queen Bench, Commercial Court Division, in *B v A* [2010] EWHC 1626 (Comm), where it was asserted that the majority of the tribunal had failed to apply Spanish law as required by the arbitration agreement. The evidence for this assertion seems to have come mainly from the dissenting commentary issued by the third arbitrator, who was of the opinion that his two colleagues had not applied Spanish law and, in particular, had awarded excessive damages that amounted to punitive damages in breach of Spanish law and public policy. The court held (referring to the House of Lords' decision in *Lesotho*

Highlands Development Authority v Impregilo SpA [2005] UKHL 43; [2006] 1 AC 221) that applying the wrong law could only amount to acting in excess of powers under s 68(2)(b) of the 1996 Act, and not to excess of jurisdiction under s 67.

The relevant provisions in the 1996 Act (s 46) are not identical to rule 47, including the interesting change from 'shall' in the 1996 Act to the possibly more determinative 'must' in rule 47. It is suggested that *B v A* might not be resolved in the same way in Scotland on this narrow technical point, on the basis that failure to comply with the selected governing law deprived the tribunal of jurisdiction in cases where default rule 47 was not deleted.

English provisions

English law expressly recognises that arbitral tribunals can, and indeed should, decide disputes in accordance with the law chosen by the parties 'or if the parties so agree, in accordance with such other considerations as are agreed by them or determined by the tribunal' (Arbitration Act 1996 s 46). As stated above, it does not say that they 'must' do so as the Scottish draftsman has included.

The 1996 Act s 46(2) provides that 'the choice of the laws of a country shall be understood to refer to the substantive laws of that country and not its conflict of laws rules', although an English court would stay proceedings brought in breach of the arbitration clause even though some set of principles, not being 'laws of a particular country', had been chosen as the applicable law to govern their disputes – again the principle of party autonomy. It would furthermore enforce an award made by arbitrators applying any 'considerations' agreed between the parties. Thus, if parties wish some form of rules or law not of a country to apply to their contract, then it is open to them to so agree, provided that there is an arbitration clause or some basis of agreement between them. The court will give effect to the parties' agreement in that way. For example, in *Soleimany v Soleimany* [1998] EWCA Civ 285 the parties had agreed to Beth Din arbitration under Jewish law and *Sterling v Rand* [2020] EWHC 2899 (Ch), where the award was enforced five years after it was made.

A challenge to an award may not be successful on the ground that the arbitrators failed to decide the dispute in accordance with the substantive law chosen by the parties as applicable. In *B v A* [2010] EWHC 1626 (Comm), the court found in favour of the defendant and held that there was no realistic prospect of successfully challenging an arbitration award under the Arbitration Act 1996 s 67 or s 68 on that ground as required by s 46.

Shari'a law as a basis

Rule 47 raises an interesting point as to whether arbitration can be used to allow dispute resolution under the Shari'a if that is what the parties agree. The Shari'a is not, of course, a legal system of a country. Shari'a 'courts' (more properly arbitration centres) have been established in a number of locations in England, using the 1996 Act. Prior to the introduction of the 2010 Act, some reports appeared suggesting discussions were taking place with the Muslim Arbitration Tribunal for centres to be established in Glasgow and Edinburgh. This was said to be under the 1996 Act, which did not extend to Scotland. Albeit the Scottish 2010 Act would appear to allow the establishment of such 'courts' in Scotland as arbitration centres, it does not appear that the MAT at least have established such centres in Scotland.

There has been a certain amount of press comment on this issue over the years, much of it fairly unhelpful and often ill-informed. We see no reason why normal civil disputes cannot be resolved in this way if the parties genuinely choose this approach, any more than Islamic banking has created any real problems for the legal systems of the UK. It should also be remembered that English law has long recognised decisions of the Jewish Beth Din as enforceable arbitral awards, and this has not been seen as creating any philosophical or jurisprudential issue. The Act would seem to also allow this approach in Scotland.

Power to award payment and damages

Rule 48 is a default rule and so the parties are free to agree as to what powers the tribunal should have, including as here the power to order payment of a sum of money.

This will be the most common remedy exercised by the tribunal. As mentioned elsewhere, arbitral procedures can sometimes be manipulated by a stronger contracting party and, historically, standard form contracts have contained clauses which removed the power to award damages against that party. This was appreciated by the drafters of the Act and thus this clause is made mandatory. All tribunals will have the power to award damages.

The power is not tied to the powers that a court can have. The tribunal can have greater powers – eg it can award a sum of money in excess of what was sought by one of the parties, which a court cannot do unless the sum sued for in the conclusion or crave is increased. It would, however, be a bold tribunal that awarded more than was requested. English courts do, of course, allow claims for unspecified general damages, and this rule would appear to permit such an approach, but this is not really the same point.

A court does have the power to order payment in a foreign currency (RCS 7.5 and see also *Commerzbank AS v Large* 1977 SC 375) as does the arbitrator here, including the discretion to determine which currency is the 'appropriate' currency. This could have a dramatic effect on the value of an award and parties may wish to consider the merit of seeking an award in a particular currency, having regard to longer term currency fluctuations.

In *Lesotho Highlands Development Authority v Impregilo SpA* [2005] UKHL 43, already referred to under rule 47 in another context, the arbitral tribunal decided to make the award in European currencies as opposed to the Lesotho currency. (The contract was silent on this.) The matter before the court was whether this was an error of law under the 1996 Act s 69 or a substantial injustice point under s 68. It was held in that case that there was nothing in the 1996 Act which empowered arbitrators to disregard the substantive law in relation to foreign currency obligations and it was not left open to arbitrators to approach the currency of their awards, and any questions of currency conversion, simply in accordance with the exercise of their discretion.

The parties can provide the tribunal with whatever powers they wish to bestow and again they are not tied to the types of remedies that a court could exercise. Thus the tribunal could impose 'punitive' damages of the sort found in United States systems. (Although, given the decision in $B \, v \, A$ [2010] EWHC 1626 (Comm), possibly not if the law being applied, Spanish in that case, did not allow such an award on public policy grounds.) This would, however, be an unwelcome development for many users of dispute resolution, and also create problems with insurers. Many insurance policies exclude cover in the United States (and Canada – although the logic of this is unclear) so as to prevent exposure to such awards.

If Scottish arbitrators started to delve into this field, the law of unintended consequences could apply, and commercial parties and their insurers might then steer clear of Scottish arbitration. It is, in practice, difficult to see why parties would agree to such jurisdiction (since the loser would suffer badly), and if one party sought to impose such an agreement on the other, this would seem likely to fall foul of unfair contracts terms legislation.

It is suggested that the powers given to the tribunal should not generally include the power to award damages that are punitive or aggravated in nature and which may exceed those that are compensatory in nature, not least because later enforcement might be difficult on public policy grounds.

Other remedies available to tribunal

Declarator

Like a court, a tribunal could make an award of declarator (declaration in English procedure). This is the determination by the tribunal of the contested rights between the parties. Like in a court action, the declarator may be determinative of the parties' entitlements and therefore remedies thereafter arising. To take a simple example, if one of the parties states that there was a material breach of the contract and it was entitled to terminate (rescind) the contract but the other party claims that there was no breach or, in the alternative, that there was a non-material breach, then the declarator by the tribunal that the breach was material will determine that issue, which in turn confirms that the party was entitled to rescind and will lead to an assessment of the damages which the first party is entitled to following the other's material breach. This could apply to one or more parts or the whole of the case.

Interdict and specific implement

The tribunal has the power under this default rule to order a party to refrain from doing something. It will be recollected that in court that remedy cannot be an attempt to interdict a past wrong or something which has already happened. In order to obtain *interim* interdict, there has to be an ongoing or a future anticipated wrong – hence the usual averments about 'reasonable apprehension'.

Also, before the courts a party cannot be ordered positively to do something by interdict. (Contrast this with England, where a mandatory injunction is possible.)

Rule 49, though, does allow an arbitrator to grant what amounts to a mandatory injunction. A query must therefore arise as to whether the Scottish courts will be comfortable with enforcing such an order, when it is not one that they themselves would have power to grant. (At the Bill stage it was proposed to only provide tribunals with the powers possessed by the Court of Session, but this was abandoned.)

It is submitted, since the Scottish Parliament has stated, in clear terms, that arbitrators have such power, unless excluded by the parties (this is a default rule), then the courts would be bound to enforce such an award in appropriate cases. Ordering a party to do something is often part of what is called specific implement (or in English procedure specific performance). Here a party is ordered to perform its obligations under a contract. In England, this remedy is usually reserved for situations where damages would not be an effective remedy (eg the sale of a unique item, such as a painting). As a recent example, and in another Beth Din case, of *Sterling v Rand* [2019] EWHC 2560 (Ch), the English courts have accepted the right of a tribunal to make what amounted to an award of specific performance although the award was set aside on other grounds.

The only exception to these two categories is probably statutory provisions against the making of any such order (see eg against the Crown under the Crown Proceedings Act 1921 ss 21 and 43).

The rule follows quite closely the English analogous provision in s 48(5)(a) of the 1996 Act allowing the tribunal to 'order a party to do or refrain from doing anything'. As already stated, under English procedure a court may order positively a party to do something, not just to refrain from doing something by injunction. It is empowered to order a mandatory or positive injunction as well as a prohibitory negative injunction.

As the parties are free to so empower the tribunal, then it appears that the tribunal has a power such as this akin to the English courts. In other words, the order should not be seen as a positive interdict but simply as a mandatory order. This may well be a distinction without a difference in practice.

It is suggested that tribunals should be cautious about making these orders on an interim basis if damages would be a suitable remedy or where there is an availability of 'interim interdict' type orders made on a similar basis.

If tribunals are going to go down the road of making orders akin to English courts and tribunals then they should apply the *American Cyanamid* principles (*American Cyanamid Co v Ethicon Ltd* [1975] AC 396) used in the English courts, and seek evidence that irreparable harm will be done which cannot be adequately corrected by an award of damages before interim relief of this type is granted.

Where rule 62 is excluded, it would be possible to agree that the tribunal would not have the power to award costs and expenses, which might be attractive to parties from jurisdictions where 'costs follow the event' is not the norm.

Rectification

Rectification is where a contract or document or deed which does not reflect the actual agreement of the parties can be amended or 'rectified' by the tribunal to bring it into line with what the parties really intended.

As a court-based remedy it can be unilateral or bilateral, ie mistake by one party or both, and the provisions of the Law Reform (Miscellaneous Provisions) (Scotland) Act 1985 ss 8 and 9 apply. (For recent developments on the law relating to rectification and the role of the court in that process, see *Brown v Rysaffe Trustee Company (CI) Ltd* [2011] CSOH 26 per Lord Glennie, albeit this has received positive, neutral and negative judicial consideration (*Cramaso LLP v Viscount Reidhaven's Trustees* 2012 SC 240 per the Inner House regarding duty of care and proximity but not the role of the court).)

It remains to be seen if an award of rectification would be sufficient to rectify a 'record' held in a public register. (This is referred to and discussed earlier, in the commentary to s 11.)

Reduction

Reduction is a remedy available in the Court of Session only (touched on under rule 20) whereby the court can quash the legal effect of a document. Chapter 53 of RCS provides for actions seeking reduction of 'a decree, order, decision or warrant of whatever nature of an inferior court or tribunal'. This is significant power and has traditionally only been exercised by the Court of Session.

Reduction is a powerful tool and through this default rule, if the parties do not disapply it, the tribunal is empowered, like the Court of Session, to reduce documents.

This is only in so far as it does not affect the rights of third parties in these documents and deeds as discussed above in commentary to s 11(2). Also note that the tribunal is not permitted to reduce court decrees.

While all of this makes sense, there is an overriding problem: what happens if the order is ignored? Unlike courts, the tribunal does not have any resources or powers to, for example, imprison a party for contempt. Since the support of the courts will, therefore, be required, these powers are not quite as extensive or impressive as they may first appear, and may, as discussed, prove problematic to the extent that they appear to exceed the powers of the courts themselves in some limited cases.

Interest

Rule 50 is a mandatory rule which gives the right to the tribunal to award interest. At common law the tribunal was not empowered to do so (*John G McGregor (Contractors) Ltd v Grampian Regional Council* 1991 SLT 136 at 137 per Lord Dunpark), and this was seen as a defect in the Scottish system. It is, however, suggested that this is one rule that could properly have been left as default. It provides a problem for arbitrations between parties who may have an objection to the award of interest. The best-known example would be parties who wished to comply with the Shari'a prohibition of *riba* interest which is *'haram'* – that is, forbidden. It is thought that during the Bill stage it was made mandatory for the reasons expressed above in connection with strong contracting parties seeking to remove it in standard form contracts. The tribunal is empowered via this rule to award interest for the period up to the date of the award as well as thereafter.

That power is, however, discretionary – see the use of 'may'. It follows that interest will not automatically accrue on sums awarded and therefore the tribunal should always be alive to this issue of interest. It might also be argued that the parties, while not excluding this mandatory rule, could, nonetheless, indicate in their arbitration agreement that they wished the tribunal to exercise its discretion against the award of interest. In this way the rule remains, but party autonomy allows it to be emasculated. It is unclear how a court would look at a challenge to a decision made on this basis (or an award of interest made in the face of such an instruction).

There are various categories of interest:

(a) interest on the whole or part of any award up to the date of the award;
(b) interest on the whole or part of any amount claimed in the arbitration and outstanding at the commencement of the arbitration but which was paid before the arbitration began; and
(c) interest on the outstanding amount of any amounts awarded (including under (a) and (b) both the pre- and post-award period).

Further, the tribunal has the power to specify the interest rate, how it is to be calculated and the period for which it is payable including any 'rests' which the tribunal considers appropriate. This can be different for different amounts (rule 50(3)). 'Rests' is not defined but is generally taken to mean the frequency at which compound interest is calculated. This is usually annual, but it may be possible to persuade a tribunal to take a different view.

Rule 50(4) preserves any power of the tribunal to award interest otherwise than under this rule. Interest is to be calculated in the manner agreed by the parties or, failing that, in such manner as the tribunal determines.

It would appear therefore that the tribunal could order the payment of interest as compound interest or even interest at a punitive rate – all depending on the terms of the agreement between the parties. However, the wording would need to be clear to allow punitive rates, since the general intent must be to make compensatory awards. (See comments under rule 48 in connection with Scots law and public policy; *City Inn Ltd v Shepherd Construction* 2002 SLT 781 per Lord Macfadyen at para 15 and *Stewart Hill v Stewart Milne Group* [2011] CSIH 50, confirming that, if it is a penalty, then it will be unenforceable.)

Further, it is arguable that an interest rate that is truly punitive could be considered as an unlawful penalty and, therefore, any arbitration agreement which provided for such a rate could be struck down. (See, eg, *Taiwan Scot Co v Masters Golf Co* [2009] EWCA Civ 685 where a statutory rate of interest – amounting to 15 per cent pa – under the Late Payment of Commercial Debts (Interest) Act 1998 was challenged, albeit unsuccessfully on the facts, as an unenforceable penalty, and the Northern Irish case of *Fernhill Properties (Northern Ireland) Ltd v Mulgrew* [2010] NI Ch 20, where a flat interest rate similar to that in *Taiwan Scot* was struck down as a penalty.)

However, any consideration of these issues will have to be reviewed in light of the law developed in the Supreme Court in the conjoined cases of *Cavendish Square Holding BV v Talal El Makdessi, Parking Eye Ltd v Beavis* [2015] UKSC 67, where the law has moved away from the requirement that liquidated damages were a genuine pre-estimate of potential loss and is tested now as to whether they are 'extravagant, exorbitant or unconscionable'. It is likely that the same logic will apply to rates of interest agreed in a contract between the parties or awarded by an arbitrator.

If the contract makes provision for the application of rates of interest on damages then the tribunal must apply those. But if it must apply a substantive law which does not permit the awarding of compound interest or indeed any interest at all (eg Saudi Arabia) then the tribunal is, presumably, precluded from doing so, notwithstanding the mandatory nature of the rule. The other powers to award interest will probably be those relating to any contractual power to award interest as, say, a particular head of damages and, secondly, the implied terms of the Late Payment of Commercial Debts (Interest) Act 1998 and the associated regulations where there is a commercial debt within the meaning of the Act upon which statutory interest will run which will then comprise a head of damages or part of the award for the tribunal.

In Scotland, there is currently a mismatch between the judicial rate of interest (8 per cent) and the market rate of interest; as well as differences between the English and Scottish approaches. The Inner House approved the approach taken by Lord Hodge in the Outer House in *Farstad Supply*

AS v Enviroco Ltd 2013 SC 302 where he exercised his judicial discretion and applied half the judicial rate for part of the period. The Scottish Civil Justice Council plans to reduce the judicial rate within the next year.

Interest as a matter of procedure

As mentioned under rule 48, in *Lesotho Highlands Development Authority v Impregilo SpA* [2005] UKHL 43 the House of Lords considered interest in connection with awards to be a matter of procedural law rather than substantive law. While rule 50 is clear in terms of the circumstances in which interest may be awarded, it should be noted that there is a detailed discussion of interest at common law and under statute by the Inner House in *Wilson v Dunbar Bank plc* 2008 SC 457.

Form of award

Default rule 51 makes provision for the form of a tribunal's award. Put simply, the parties can elect how the award is going to look in form.

The award must be signed, so by implication it must be in writing. It is unclear if an electronic award with suitable electronic signatures would comply, but it is clear that, under this heading, there cannot be an oral award. It has to be signed by all the arbitrators or all of those assenting to the award. Where the award is made by a majority of the arbitrators then it will be those that will sign. It should be noted that there is no requirement to have an odd number of arbitrators, and issues could arise in respect of a two-man panel (see earlier), which supports our view that two-man panels should be avoided, despite being permitted under the Act.

Note that the signing is not the assent. Equally, therefore, the arbitrators could all sign albeit that there were dissenting opinions in the minority.

Seat and date

The juridical seat is important for enforcement of international awards, as has already been discussed.

Equally, the date of the award and when it takes effect are important for enforcement, including issues of limitation and prescription in different jurisdictions.

The date will also be important in connection with any challenge to the award or appeal to the Outer House under Part 8 of these Rules. It will also be relevant in respect of the tribunal's award of interest under rule 50 above.

Reasons

Reasons for the award are now required by rule 51 and this is an innovation on the previous Scottish practice of simply making an award without necessarily explaining the basis of the underlying reasoning on the part of the tribunal. It is, however, consistent with Art 31(2) of the Model Law.

Rule 51 is, of course, a default rule, and the parties could decide to revert to the previous practice, although, as explained elsewhere, this may give problems in enforcement and, indeed, in mounting challenges to the award. It is not explained here to what depth a tribunal has to go in providing reasons. The analogous English provisions in s 52 of the 1996 Act also require that 'The award shall contain the reasons for the award' and case law in that jurisdiction has provided guidance on the extent of this duty on the tribunal. The tribunal does not have to set out each step by which it reaches its conclusion or deal with each point made by the parties (unlike in court proceedings). It should deal with issues but that is different from failing to reason. The award should contain reasons to show why the arbitrator reached his decision on the 'essential issue' (*Pakistan v Broadsheet LLC* [2019] EWHC 1832 (Comm)). There has been further case law in England and Wales dealing with 'sufficient' reasons but as a generality the tribunal does not require to provide further explanations as to how it assessed the evidence and arrived at its conclusion.

In *Gordian Runoff Ltd v Westport Insurance Corpn* [2010] NSWCA 57, the New South Wales courts have made it clear that, while reasons were required by s 29(1) of their Commercial Arbitration Act 1984 and Art 31(2) of the Model Law, the depth of reasoning was not to be equated with that of a judge in court proceedings.

In *Van der Giessen-de-Noord Shipbuilding Division BV v Imtech Marine & Offshore BV* [2008] EWHC 2904 (Comm) it was held that the court's power to set aside an arbitration award in whole or in part was not available simply because the tribunal had made a mistake of fact or law or because the arbitrators had not dealt with all of the points made. However, where arbitrators had failed to deal with all essential issues raised by the claimant in arbitration proceedings, that amounted to a serious irregularity that had caused substantial injustice within the meaning of the Arbitration Act 1996 s 68. It is, of course, often virtually impossible to determine this in the absence of reasons.

Once some points have been determined, others will not always require to be (*Checkpoint Ltd v Strathclyde Pension Fund* [2003] EWCA Civ 841). There is English authority that tribunals do not even have to deal with every possible argument on the facts of a case nor explain why they attach more weight to some evidence than to other evidence (*World Trade Corporation Ltd v C Czarnikov Sugar Ltd* [2004] EWHC 2332 (Comm)).

Reasons would not, however, be needed with an 'agreed award' (see below). The court retains the power to order reasons under rule 71(8) to enable it to dispose of an appeal.

Award made

Under rule 51(3) the award is made by delivering it to each of the parties in accordance with rule 83. This is subject to the power of the tribunal to withhold the award in case of non-payment of the fees and expenses of the arbitration (rule 56). Delivery presumably requires physical delivery, but the parties could agree that it should include transmission by electronic means.

Previous provisional or part awards

Unless the parties modify or disapply this rule, the award must reference any previous provisional or part awards made as well as the extent to which any such award has been superceded.

Award treated as made in Scotland

An award is to be treated as having been made in Scotland even if it is signed at, or delivered to or from, a place outwith Scotland (r 52).

It may not always be possible or convenient to sign the award in the place where the arbitration was held and we have discussed before (s 18) the effect of cases like *Hiscox v Outhwaite* [1992] 1 AC 562. In that case the award was held by the House of Lords to have been made in Paris because that was where it had been signed even though the proceedings had all taken place in London. Rule 52 effectively means that this case has no application to Scottish arbitrations. This is a simple, practical solution and avoids the situation which previously existed in other jurisdictions, eg Dubai, where formerly the arbitrator had to travel to the jurisdiction simply to sign the award.

Provisional awards

Rule 53 provides that the 'tribunal may make a provisional award granting any relief on a provisional basis which it has the power to grant permanently'. It is a default provision, which the parties can modify or disapply if they want to restrict the tribunal to making only final awards (or part awards which are not provisional in their effect).

Different types of award

The 'final and binding' nature of arbitral awards has already been discussed in relation to section 11. That is in connection with the 'end' or final award that the parties are seeking to get to. There is also the requirement in the New York Convention that the award has to be 'binding'. Again, that is a reference to a final award which is an award that will finish the task the parties set for the tribunal – it will dispose of all (or the remaining) issues in dispute.

If it reflects a settlement agreement reached in the course of the arbitration, ie they are no longer in dispute or contesting the terms, then it is known as a 'consent award' or an 'agreed award'. This award is final in the sense of being the last award. Issuing the final award terminates the duties of the tribunal, which ceases to have any jurisdiction over the dispute – it is *functus officio*. The tribunal should therefore be careful to ensure all issues in dispute are disposed of.

However, the moment when the tribunal ceases to have powers was considered in the English case of *Dawes v Treasure and Son Ltd* [2010] EWHC 3218 (TCC). Here the parties concluded a settlement agreement, but did not terminate the arbitration. Following the settlement, an issue arose as to costs (expenses) and it was held that the tribunal still had power to consider this issue. It was not *functus officio*.

At this juncture, it is appropriate to examine both provisional and part awards under this and the following rule for comparative purposes.

Partial, part or interim?

As a preliminary matter of terminology, in international practice the terms 'partial' and 'interim' were often used interchangeably. The UNCITRAL Rules 1976, for example, refer to 'interim, interlocutory or partial awards' (Art 32(1); see now Art 34.1 as revised in 2010), and the ICC Rules used to make reference to 'interim, partial or final awards'. (See also *Final Report on Interim and Partial Awards* ICArb Bul vol 1/2 p 26 (Dec 1990).) The LCIA Rules 2020 state that the tribunal may make separate awards on different issues at different times' (Art 26.1).

The Arbitration Act 1996 s 47 states:

(1) Unless otherwise agreed by the parties, the tribunal may make more than one award at different times on different aspects of the matters to be determined.

(2) The tribunal may, in particular, make an award relating –
   (a) to an issue affecting the whole claim, or
   (b) to a part only of the claims or cross-claims submitted to it for decision.

(3) If the tribunal does so, it shall specify in its award the issue, or the claim or part of a claim, which is the subject matter of the award.

Strictly it is possible to differentiate the two on the basis that partial awards go to substantive claims while interim awards go to issues such as jurisdiction or applicable law. It is, however, likely that the terms will continue to be used interchangeably, and the real issue is to address what the award says it does in order to determine its effect, rather than the label applied (or, sometimes, misapplied) by the arbitrators.

So a part or interim award should dispose of part of the case. A good use of such an award would be to determine jurisdiction or to determine which laws or rules are to apply to the merits of the case. Or it might be possible to 'bifurcate' (ie split into two) the issues in the case into those relating to liability and those to quantum or the assessment of damages. It might be more cost effective and least susceptible to delay if liability were disposed of first. Or there may be a limitation issue between the parties which could be disposed of before going further to examine the merits or substance of the disputed claim. It can also be used to reduce the scope of large, complex disputes into more manageable proportions, although this is only viable where the dispute raises issues that are distinct on the law or facts. All of these situations could be disposed of by the tribunal determining the issues and issuing, in the language of rule 54, a 'part' award.

Note that these awards dispose of those parts to which they relate entirely. They are not 'Final' in the sense that other issues will remain outstanding and they are not the last act of the tribunal in discharging its whole function, and are thus perhaps better thought of as binding interim awards. Note that it should be referred to in the final award in terms of rule 51(2)(d) (unless disapplied) as noted above.

A tribunal operating under these rules should be alive to the effective use of these awards in terms of its overall duty under s 1 and rule 24 to minimise delay and expense. The appropriate exercise of these powers could simplify the whole procedure and produce a much shorter, more efficient and potentially more economical arbitration.

Provisional awards

Rule 53 focuses on provisional awards, which are awards whereby the tribunal can give a party provisional relief. It can do so only if the parties have not excluded this right, this being a default rule. From this rule the tribunal has the power to grant relief to a party by making a provisional award, limited to relief which could be granted in the final award, but on a provisional or temporary basis.

It is not clear what the draftsman had in mind, but the analogous provisions of s 39 of the 1996 Act provide for provisional orders: 'The parties are free to agree that the tribunal shall have power to order on a provisional basis any relief which it would have power to grant in a final award' (s 39(1)). It gives examples in s 39(2), namely a provisional order for the payment of money or the disposition of property as between the parties or, secondly, an order to make an interim payment on account of the costs of the arbitration. No indication is given as to how the tribunal is to make such awards in Scotland. Indeed the use of 'award' infers a finality in itself (unlike the English use of 'order') which really cannot be correct, given that the rule makes it clear that such 'awards' are not intended necessarily to be the final word on the subject in question. It has been suggested by some commentators on the 1996 Act that a tribunal may wish to tread with caution as an 'order' on a provisional basis in the course of the arbitration may be unfair in the longer term if it cannot be unpicked or reversed in the final analysis for whatever reason (Harris, Planterose and Tecks, *The Arbitration Act 1996: A Commentary* (5th edn) pp 204–7, paras 39A–39H; and see in particular para 39D).

It is considered that this applies to arbitrations in Scotland under the Act. This is, it is suggested, more so with a provisional award which, to the authors' view, must be final and binding in respect of that provisional award of relief, at least unless and until it is superseded in accordance with default rule 51(2)(d). We have also already addressed the difficulties and dangers in making interim mandatory orders, save in exceptional cases.

Part awards

Rule 54 is a mandatory rule which provides a general power to the tribunal to make, in the absence of agreement between/among the parties, more than one award at different times and on different aspects of the matters to be determined. This may be a 'part award' which is stated to be an award which decides some (not all) of the matters to be decided. Given the discussion on this subject in relation to the preceding rule, it will be apparent that the tribunal could not decide all of the matters before it in an interim or part award, as that would constitute a final award. A part award must specify the matters to which it relates (rule 54(3)).

Draft awards

Rule 55 is a default rule. Before the tribunal takes the formal step of 'making' the award it may (but does not have to) issue an award in draft to the parties but then it must allow the parties to make representations before the award is actually made.

It is thought that it has been a particularly Scottish practice to issue awards in draft for comment. There is the 'slip procedure' under rule 58 to correct errors, but this is in anticipation of the finalising of the final award. Draft awards are not known to English practice, nor to the Model Law, nor generally to *ad hoc* international practice in the authors' experience although they are known to institutional arbitrations where the institution will review the award in draft before it is sent to the parties, eg ICC awards. The ICC will make sure that it deals with all the issues which were before the tribunal and that costs, and interest apportionments in all their manifestations are provided for (which can be easily forgotten). The ICC does not interfere with the merits nor the reasoning and it is more of a quality control matter.

This is of course a default rule and so could be disapplied but, if it is not, under this rule, the parties are the ones who are given the opportunity of making representations. On the whole it must be a good thing to allow the parties themselves to check that everything is disposed of in the technical sense as well as having the opportunity to point out any ambiguities and to correct any obvious errors and 'typos'. Any representations should not, in our view, be addressed to the merits in an attempt to re-open matters and the tribunal should limit the period of time for these representations. However, rule 55(b) does not contain any limitation on the nature of the representations to be made (although, in practice, the arbitrator may place limitations), but the arbitrators will be bound to consider anything they receive as stipulated in that part of the rule.

A scheme operates in Scotland in the Court of Session, and in England and Wales in the High Court and the Court of Appeal, whereby judgments are issued under embargo to the parties' legal advisers for the correction of any obvious errors before finally being issued publicly as the judgment in the case. The terms of the embargo mean, however, that the parties themselves do not see the draft, and cannot be advised of its contents (although, in practice, the sight of broad grins on the faces of the winning legal team has been known to provide a clue). This is a helpful way of preventing minor practical glitches (eg wrong spelling of names, arithmetical errors, etc). The situation here under the 2010 Act is different, in that the draft is specifically stated as being issued to the parties (rule 55(a)), and there is, as discussed, no restriction on the types of representation.

Power to withhold award on non-payment of fees or expenses

Rule 56 is a mandatory rule, presumably to protect arbitrators from the removal of what is, in reality, their only sanction to ensure payment of their final fees.

This rule is a powerful tool in the armoury of the tribunal in order to ensure payment of its fees and expenses which the parties are liable for under rule 60. As it is mandatory, the parties cannot collude or agree to remove this important piece of protection from the tribunal.

Previously an arbiter could withhold his award for payment of his fees although it was a practice which was tolerated rather than condoned. In statutory adjudications under the Housing Grants, Construction and Regeneration Act 1996 (as amended), attempts were made to do so but came unstuck due to the time limits imposed therein. So, in *St Andrews Bay Development Ltd v HBG Management Ltd* 2003 SLT 740 an adjudicator acting in an adjudication under the Housing Grants, Construction and Regeneration Act 1996, who had reached a decision but did not intend to release it until her fee had been paid, found herself in difficulties as to whether she had actually delivered her decision. This rule does away with that kind of difficulty.

The rule is similar to (and it seems was based on) the Arbitration Act 1996 s 56. In essence the tribunal will be able to exercise a lien over the award pending payment of its outstanding fees and expenses. Where this situation arises, the payment and the release of the award will take place through the court, rule 56(2) providing for any party to apply to the court for delivery of the award, but only on the applicant paying into the court an amount equal to the fees and expenses demanded (by the tribunal) or a lesser amount as ordered by the court; and that amount has to be 'paid into court' for payment of those sums, any remainder after determination by the court to be returned to the applicant. (This is English phraseology, and the Scottish equivalent would be 'consigned' or paid (found) as 'caution'.) This is all subject to the applicant exhausting any available arbitral process of appeal or review of the fees and expenses.

As in other parts of the Act, the decision of the court (here the sheriff or Outer House as the case may be) is final. Note also that this provides a remedy to the party which wants to take up the award but considers the tribunal's fees are excessive and wants them reviewed, although it will not assist a party who considers the fees to be excessive where the other party has already paid the tribunal's fees (in which case the remedy would be an application under rule 60). The 'award' must mean the actual signed, reasoned award and not a copy of it as that would render this protective measure nugatory.

The words in brackets in rule 56(2)(a) are a little difficult to understand. The whole structure of the rule appears to be that the amount claimed is paid into court, and the court will then review the fees, and only release the amount assessed to the tribunal (with any balance, by implication, being returned to the parties). However, the provision for a lesser sum than that claimed being paid into court reduces the value of the lien, and implies the court will make an assessment of the correct level of costs and expenses which will have the effect of being final, not only because the 'horse will, by then, have bolted', but, also, because rule 56(4) would seem to have this effect. This should, in our view, be used only in the most egregious cases where it is obvious, and effectively unanswerable, that the amount claimed is excessive.

While the rule only allows for payment into court, in appropriate cases it may be that some other security such as an on-demand bond (ie a monetary security) could be negotiated to protect the tribunal, but it could not be ordered under this rule, and would need to be a matter of consent. The terms of any such bond would also pre-suppose that a review of the costs and expenses claimed was to take place, and it is difficult to see that a tribunal, which is already in what is likely to be an acrimonious and adversarial situation, would welcome swapping cash for a bond dependent on the outcome of later proceedings.

Arbitration to end on last award or early settlement

Rule 57 covers this and is a default rule – it is up to the parties to incorporate it or not. Rule 57(1) provides that the end of an arbitration, when the arbitral tribunal's powers are to cease, will be when the last, or terminating, award to be made in the arbitration is made. (See the discussion of final awards in relation to s 11.)

It follows that neither party can thereafter attempt to re-open the arbitration as it is *res judicata*, and nor can the tribunal as it is *functus officio* on rendering the award. This is, however, subject to rule 57(2) which provides exceptions in cases of objection to the arbitrator's jurisdiction (rule 20(3)) or failure to submit a claim (rule 37(1)).

Rule 57(3) provides that the parties may end the dispute by notifying the tribunal that they have settled, which could result (if the parties wished it) in the tribunal making a consent or agreed award (see rule 53) and as provided for by rule 57(4). In the latter case, such an award would be a final award, and the settlement provisions of this rule would then become redundant. The rule would of course still apply in respect of any residual matter arising thereafter and does not affect the operation of other rules.

Continued operation of the Rules

Even when the arbitration has ended, the Rules will continue to have effect in accordance with rule 57(5) in order to regulate enforcement, fees, expenses, etc.

Correcting an award

Rule 58 is a default rule which provides for the circumstances in which a tribunal may correct a clerical, typographical or other error arising by virtue of accident or omission, or to clarify or remove any ambiguity (rule 58(1)) but there must be an actual ambiguity (see *Arbitration Appeal No 2 of 2019* [2020] CSOH 51).

It is a sensible provision, similar in form to s 57 of the 1996 Act and Art 33 of the Model Law. It is sometimes called a 'slip rule'. It gives arbitrators a power to correct certain defects in any final award they make. This also applies to part awards and provisional awards.

Note that it must be a clerical mistake, error arising from an accidental slip or omission or any ambiguity in the award and not an error by the arbitrator in misunderstanding the evidence (*No Curfew Ltd v Feiges Properties* Ltd [2018] EWHC 744 (Ch)).

Some institutional rules also permit a tribunal to correct or clarify the award (eg LCIA Rules 2020 art 27) and as such would disapply or modify this default rule. Where correction or clarification is sought to correct an 'an error of expression' in the award, the court is likely to look favourably upon that (*Xstrata Coal Queensland Pty Ltd v Benxi Iron and Steel (Group) International Economic and Trading Co Ltd* [2016] EWHC 2022 (Comm); *Mobile Telecommunications Co KSC v HRH Prince Hussam Bin Saud Bin Abdulaziz Al Saud* [2019] EWHC 3109 (Comm)).

Interaction with rule 55

The need for rule 58 is likely to be much reduced where the tribunal has made use of the ability to issue a draft award under rule 55, even allowing for the problems with the wording of that rule. Indeed, it may be difficult for a party to use rule 58 to seek a correction in circumstances where it has failed to avail itself of the opportunity to correct a draft under rule 55 (assuming that it and this rule were not disapplied). That being said, if the matter is agreed to be an error, and a timely objection is made, good practice would seem to be to make the correction in any event.

Error or ambiguity

Error and ambiguity are two separate concepts. The first implies that the award is simply incorrect. As discussed in relation to rule 55, this is not merely that a party disagrees with the award, but rather that it contains an error of fact. Slip rules in other contexts (eg court proceedings) are commonly used to correct spelling mistakes, dates, calculations, etc. They are not there to allow a re-run of the proceedings. It is anticipated that arbitrators will apply rule 58 in the same way.

Ambiguity is a different issue. Here it is not that the award is inaccurate, but that ambiguity has crept in, leaving the meaning of the award unclear. This allows the tribunal to clarify the intended meaning. As with errors, this is not intended to change the award, merely to make sure the award is properly understood. It is also important if enforcement may be required, since courts are likely to be reluctant to enforce an award where they cannot be certain as to what it actually means. However, it is submitted that there does really need to be an ambiguity – something which could cause confusion in the minds of an intelligent third party – not merely a created position based on an overly legalistic interpretation of language. Although they are legal documents, in many cases awards may be written by non-lawyers and such awards should be given a sensible interpretation wherever possible.

Application or tribunal initiative

The rule provides that the tribunal can act on its own initiative to correct an error or ambiguity, or an application may be made by a party. It is suggested that, where minor corrections are needed and no draft has been issued under rule 55, a party may simply wish to bring the matter to the attention of the tribunal, and let it correct the matter on its initiative, without making a formal application. Any arbitrator wishing to make such a correction, will be well advised to seek comment from both parties (rule 58(5)).

Conditions of validity

If the tribunal corrects on its own initiative, it must, as mentioned under rule 55, give the parties the right to make representations. If the matter follows an application by a party, then the obligation to invite representations still applies in respect of any other party. Importantly, where the arbitrator holds the award until the fees are paid, then the time limit for correction runs from the date of delivery under rule 51(3).

The time limit for making corrections is broadly 28 days from the making of the award where the tribunal is acting on its own initiative (rule 58(6)(a)) or 28 days after an application is received from a party (rule 58(6)(b)). Such application must itself be made within 28 days of the making of the award (rule 58(4)(a)), giving a maximum time for corrections of 56 days from the award. It should be noted that the award is made on delivery (rule 51(3)) and not, for example, necessarily on the day it is signed. There is scope for the court (either sheriff court or the Outer House) to extend that time on the application of a party (but not the tribunal), such decision to be final (rule 58(4)(b)). While the rule is silent, it is suggested that such an extension will only be granted in cases where there is a risk of substantial injustice (eg a serious irregularity within the terms of rule 68) and the applicant party can give a good explanation as to why the matter was not dealt with within the time limits allowed. This is likely to be a particularly difficult threshold to cross where a draft was issued under rule 55.

Reasonable opportunity

As explained, rule 58(5) allows parties to make representations in respect of any proposed correction, and they have to be given a 'reasonable opportunity' to do so. Such period cannot be longer than the time limits in rule 58(6), unless an extension of such period is granted by the court under rule 58(4)(b). A potential problem arises if a very late application is made, just before the expiry of the time limits. This could produce the slightly difficult position that a 'reasonable opportunity' to comment might render the correction impossible without a court order extending the time. Accordingly, best practice would dictate that applications be made as soon as possible.

It should be remembered that correction of errors should, at least in theory, be relatively non-controversial, and thus very limited time will be needed for comment. Ambiguity may, however, be a different matter.

Corrections

The correction may be obvious or trivial and it is open to the tribunal to correct the award itself. In addition, if required, the tribunal may make consequential corrections to any other part of the award, or any other award (rule 58(7)). Although this sounds non-controversial, if the other award was delivered more than 28 or 56 days earlier, as the case may be, it is not clear whether rule 58(7) authorises such corrections even if they are out of time in respect of an application for correction under rule 58 related solely to that earlier award. Such a provision does not appear in the 1996 Act or the Model Law.

English examples

In addition to the cases mentioned above, in *YCMS Ltd (t/a Young Construction Management Services) v Grabiner* [2009] EWHC 127 (TCC) an arithmetical error in an adjudicator's award was capable of being corrected under the slip rule, but the adjudicator had gone further than correction and had recalculated the sums due using a different method by which he introduced a further error. As a result the revised award was invalid. This is clearly not a 'correction' of an error, and the issue here was not an ambiguity (where it might be argued that a different approach to achieve the same result in a clearer fashion could be justified in extreme cases).

In *Buyuk Camlica Shipping Trading & Industry Co Inc v Progress Bulk Carriers Ltd* [2010] EWHC 442 (Comm) it was held that the analogous s 57(3)(a) of the 1996 Act did not apply in relation to an issue which had not been dealt with by the tribunal within the meaning of s 68(2)(d). There was no ambiguity in the reasons or awards that required clarification or removal. This emphasises that there must be a real ambiguity, ie the possibility that the award can be interpreted in more than one way.

O'Donnell Developments Ltd v Build Ability Ltd [2009] EWHC 3388 (TCC) was another adjudication case where an adjudicator was asked to correct a slip and accepted that he had made an error within the slip rule. The court would not interfere with the exercise of the adjudicator's powers, which were within his jurisdiction. It is suggested that the courts in Scotland may well take a similar view under the Act, so long as the decision to correct: is not obviously unsupportable; or does not go beyond a slip rule correction of an error or ambiguity.

ARBITRATION EXPENSES (PART 7)

Arbitration expenses

Rule 59 is a default rule and is the definition section for Part 7. It would, therefore, be possible for the parties to substitute a different definition. If not, this rule will apply and expenses will mean the fees and expenses of the arbitrator; any expenses incurred by the tribunal in conducting the arbitration; the parties' legal and other expenses; the fees and expenses of any arbitral appointments referee; and any other third party to whom the parties give powers in relation to the arbitration. It should be noted that the Act maintains the standard Scottish usage of 'expenses' rather than the term 'costs' used in England and elsewhere. There is, however, no practical difference between the terms.

Arbitrator's fees and expenses

Reading rules 59 and 60 together, the 'arbitration expenses' are the arbitrator's fees and his own expenses which rule 60 explains as:

- the arbitrator's fees for conducting the arbitration and the expenses incurred by him (the expenses incurred by the tribunal while conducting the arbitration including the fees and expenses of any clerk, agent, employee or other persons appointed pursuant to s 60(1)(b)(i));
- the fees and expenses of any expert;
- any expenses incurred in determining recoverable expenses (for a definition see rule 61);
- the appointments referee's fees and expenses; and
- the fees of any third party given powers in relation to the arbitration.

It will be seen therefore that this is where the cost of an arbitration can really start to mount up. The difference in expenses terms between arbitrations and litigation is that the fees and expenses of the arbitrator and the other 'actors' in the arbitration have all to be paid for directly by the parties, which is an extra level of expenditure when compared with litigation. Traditionally in litigation the bulk of the costs (judges, court rooms) was paid for out of general taxation, although recent increases in fees have tended to move more of the cost onto the parties. The Scottish Government has a current policy to make the courts self-funding, which has caused a significant rise in court fees in the Outer House and Inner House in recent years. There is also a cost for the staging of the arbitration, including the hire of the room, lunches, transcription, travelling costs, use of video-conferencing equipment, etc. These would constitute 'other expenses', although they are costs some of which parties to litigation do not generally have to pay.

Both parties will, of course, have to pay for their legal teams and their own experts (as opposed to those instructed by the tribunal) subject to any agreement that there will be an award in their favour where 'expenses follow success', ie the other side pays in whole or in part (in England this is called 'costs follow the event'). In litigation, parties may recover their judicial expenses only, which is not all of the cost of the litigation. This is what it is reasonable to expect the losing side to pay. A common level of recovery is 55–60 per cent of the overall expenses.

The parties' legal and other expenses

What of the costs incurred in seeking injunctory relief in another jurisdiction. Are these expenses of the arbitration? Harris, Planterose and Tecks (*The Arbitration Act 1996: A Commentary* (5th edn) p 291, para 59C) consider that they will not be, in terms of the analogous provisions of the 1996 Act s 59, and we tend to agree. On the wording used, there is no mention of

'ancillary' or 'supportive' proceedings or litigation so it would suggest that
the proper construction of this clause must be that the expenses of those
types of proceedings are not part of the arbitration expenses and will fall
to be dealt with by the court concerned in the usual way, unless, of course,
the parties have modified default rule 59 to substitute a different definition
of arbitration expenses. If they were to do so, this raises the interesting
concept of an arbitrator being asked to reverse or modify a ruling of the
court, which, it is suggested, is not an attractive proposition, or particularly
practical.

One issue that is not completely certain is whether the old pre-Act common
law rule exemplified by *Apollo Engineering Ltd v James Scott Ltd* [2009] CSIH
39 still applies. This held that an arbiter was entitled to make awards of
expenses as the arbitration proceeded, in the same manner as a judge. It is
suggested that there is nothing in the Act to say that this does not remain
good law, and arbitrators should be encouraged to use this method to deal
with clear issues of liability for expenses as the matter proceeds. This has
the advantage of bringing home to parties how the cost of the proceedings
is racking up, and may encourage early settlement. Rule 66 now permits the
arbitrator to make a separate award and so could do so 'as the arbitration
proceeded' on an application by one of the parties.

Arbitrators' fees and expenses

Rule 60 is a mandatory rule which, under s 8, cannot be modified or disapplied and follows the previous default rule 59, which can be changed by
the parties, and which specifies what will comprise the arbitrators' fees and
expenses; the tribunal expenses; and the fees and expenses of the arbitral
appointments referee and any other third party to whom the parties give
powers in relation to the arbitration.

Several liability

Rule 60 provides that the parties to the arbitration are to be severally liable
to the arbitrator(s) for payment. 'Several liability' means that arbitrators can
recover the full amount of fees and expenses from either party in the first
instance – not just the winner or loser. The tribunal may still decide how
recoverable expenses are to be split (r 60), and whichever party actually pays
the arbitrator, one may have a 'right of contribution' against the other. The
parties are not made 'jointly' liable between themselves as rule 60 is mandatory and liability between the parties may not be joint at all times, either
because they have agreed something different, or because that tribunal has
made an award of expenses. This will not be a concern for the *tribunal*, since
it will be entitled to fees on a several basis, and it will then be for the parties
to argue among themselves as to how the sums are to be divided (possibly
in accordance with an award made by the tribunal, or if no such award has

been made, and there is no other agreement, equally under default rule 62(3), if that has not been modified or deleted).

Agreed fees and expenses

Rule 60(3) allows the parties and the tribunal (or the arbitration appointments referee or other third party as the case may be) to agree the amount of costs, possibly including fee rates and even a cap on expenses, and payment terms, but if they fail to do so, all such matters ultimately fall to be determined by the Auditor of the Court of Session. This is highly unattractive given the cost of having matters determined by the Auditor (who charges a percentage of the total overall Account of Expenses regardless of the number of fees in dispute).

The parties themselves may make provision for what the expenses position will be in the various eventualities, following the award, or they can authorise the tribunal to determine the same. However, rule 63 means that a device such as a 'Tolent' clause (*Bridgeway Construction Ltd v Tolent Construction Ltd* [2000] CILL 1662), purporting to make one party liable whatever the outcome, would not survive challenge in much the same way as the eponymous clauses have been effectively eliminated in adjudication in England. (See *Yuanda (UK) Co Ltd v WW Gear Construction Ltd* [2010] EWHC 720 (TCC); [2011] 1 All ER (Comm) 550 and the Local Democracy, Economic Development and Construction Act 2009 s 141; but see in Scotland *Profile Projects Ltd v Elmwood (Glasgow) Ltd* [2011] CSOH 64; 2011 SLT 975.)

Taxation of accounts

The detail of court taxation of expenses is outwith the scope of this book. However, the procedure and authority relevant to Taxation (meaning checking and approval) of Accounts in Judicial Proceedings can be found under RCS Chapter 42 which is published in *Greens Annotated Rules of the Court of Session* and the *Scottish Law Directory Fees Supplement*.

Diet of taxation

In litigation, such matters are determined by the Auditor at a diet of taxation, which is a hearing conducted by the Auditor in his chambers at which the receiving and paying parties attend personally, or at which they may be represented by their respective solicitors or such other persons as the Auditor may allow. The Auditor appoints a day and time for the taxation. This is notified to the receiving and paying parties, who are required to attend the diet under certification that if the paying party does not appear to state any objections to the account, the Auditor may proceed to tax the account as lodged. It is unclear whether the Auditor will use the same process in arbitration cases under this rule, but it seems likely that he would. As practitioners will be aware, this has implications for the costs of taxation for the paying-party, as cancellation within four days of the diet will incur increasing expense. Given the Auditor's lack of experience in the field of arbitration compared with litigation, the parties should be prepared to provide evidence as to appropriate rates for arbitrators of the seniority and experience of those in the case in question.

The Explanatory Notes state that the purpose of allowing the Auditor to determine the fee is to cover the situation where a party who has not agreed the level of fees with the tribunal (because it is claimed the tribunal's demands are excessive) is unable to obtain delivery of the award without paying those fees in full because the tribunal refuses to deliver the award pending full payment. This is, in fact, only one possibility. It may equally be that the parties have made payment (perhaps on a 50/50 basis) to obtain the release of the award, but one (or even both parties) wishes to challenge the fees and expenses, or that the tribunal has awarded expenses to one party, who wishes to have the level of such expenses that it has been ordered to pay taxed – this latter scenario is analogous with the common reason for taxation in litigation.

The matter is complicated in arbitration in that the parties can select whoever they want to act on their behalf, and there seems no reason why the fees of a non-lawyer or, at least, a non-practising adviser may not fall to be taxed in the same way. It is unclear how the Auditor would assess such costs, given that his experience is in dealing with the cost and pricing structures of legal firms and counsel.

Power to order repayment of fees already paid

Rule 60(5) gives the Auditor the right to require fees already paid, but which he considers to be excessive, to be repaid. In practice, the Auditor only has jurisdiction under rule 60(3)(b) where the parties have failed to agree on fees or payment terms etc. Accordingly, this provision in rule 60(5) would seem to have application only where the parties and the tribunal fail to agree, but the parties make payment to the arbitrators (possibly under protest) to allow matters to proceed. In our view, it is not open to the Auditor to review prior agreements made under rule 60(3)(a) on the basis that such agreement provided for an excessive fee. In the circumstances, it would be prudent for any party concerned with the level charged, to record that payments made are under protest, and that they reserve their rights to refer the issue to the Auditor under rule 60(3)(b) and, in appropriate cases, to require a repayment under rule 60(5).

It should be noted that there is no provision in the Act or the Rules for appeals from the decision of the Auditor. Again, it is likely that appeals would generally be dealt with by the Objection Procedure under RCS 42.4.

Increasing costs in arbitration

Various initiatives have been launched at an international level to try to restrict the costs and delays in arbitration, driven by the concern that the system was frequently modelling itself too much on litigation, with the inevitable effect of also mimicking the associated costs and delays – the avoidance of which was, of course, one of the reasons why arbitration was developed in the first place. There have been, for example, the CEDR Rules for the Facilitation of Settlement in International Arbitration; the ICC Task Force and report *Techniques for Controlling Time and Costs in Arbitration*; the ICDR Guidelines for Arbitrators Concerning Exchanges of Information; the CPR Global Rules for Accelerated Commercial Arbitration; and the DIS Rules for Expedited Arbitration, etc and even private initiatives (see Debevoise & Plimpton LLP Protocol to Promote Efficiency in International Arbitration).

These efficiency initiatives take various forms. One approach is a general gravitation towards the civil law approach of presenting a fully developed statement of claim (with supporting documentary evidence) with the request for arbitration, rather than skeletal initial pleadings. Another is the use of witness statements as evidence in chief, proceeding directly to cross-examination so as to avoid time in oral hearings. The 2010 Act allows considerable flexibility with procedure and allows parties to be more creative than litigation in terms of organising the proceedings to suit themselves and prioritise efficiency.

Recovery of arbitration expenses

Default rule 61 provides for which expenses will be 'recoverable', ie capable of being recovered from the other side. It could, of course, be deleted in the event that the parties did not wish the tribunal to have the power to award expenses.

Unfortunately, the drafting in this part of the Rules is not as clear as it could be. There is confusion between 'arbitration expenses' in rule 59, and 'arbitrator's fees and expenses' forming part of arbitration expenses under rule 59(a), and also with 'parties' legal and other expenses' under rule 59(c). It should be noted, for example, that rule 60 only deals with arbitrators' fees and expenses, and not the other elements of 'arbitration expenses' in rule 59. Rule 61(2) provides for the determination of the amount of the parties' 'other arbitration expenses' – which, in the context of rules 59–61 would seem to encompass the parties' legal and other expenses under rule 59(c), since this is the only sub-paragraph of rule 59 not covered in rule 61(1). It is unfortunate that this is not made clear, and the phrase 'other arbitration expenses' in rule 62(2)(a) is not defined, and is not precisely the same wording as rule 59(c).

Such 'other arbitration expenses' which are recoverable, as opposed to the arbitrator's fees and expenses etc (dealt with in rule 61(1)), will be determined by the tribunal or the Auditor where the tribunal refers the matter for determination (presumably by the process of taxation) and, unless they decide otherwise, this will, under rule 61(3), be on the basis of a reasonable amount for reasonably incurred expenses. Any doubt when determining the amount of other expenses recoverable must be resolved in favour of the person liable to pay them.

The basic structure is that expenses are to be 'reasonable'. It is accepted that it is difficult to see how else the draftsman could have dealt with this point, but it must be remembered that this is not an absolute test, and elements of subjectivity will often be involved. The tribunal (or, in default, the Auditor) will, of course, be expected to apply an objective assessment.

It may be helpful to give some examples. What if a party uses a lawyer or expert witness (perhaps a surveyor) who is far more experienced than is necessary for the case in point? Can all of his or her actual costs be recovered from the other party, or merely the likely fees of a suitably qualified individual? Conversely, what if the person concerned has too little experience, and therefore burns huge numbers of extra hours researching what an experienced practitioner would have known already? What if the individual charges fees much higher than those of his or her peers? All of these practical matters, and many more, can fall within the ambit of 'reasonableness'. This would be akin to the test for sanction of counsel in the Sheriff Court which is based on reasonableness and considers the difficulty and complexity and value of the cause (Courts Reform (Scotland) Act 2014, s 108).

Recoverable arbitration expenses

Recoverable arbitration expenses are the expenses incurred in the arbitration in terms of an award or within the parties' agreement which one side (normally, but not always, the loser) will pay to the other (normally the winner). They include the fees and expenses of the arbitral tribunal – both the arbitrator's fees and expenses as well as any expenses incurred by the tribunal when conducting the arbitration – and the fees and expenses of the arbitral appointments referee.

While it will commonly be the loser who pays some or all of the winner's costs and expenses, it will be open to the tribunal to make different orders if, for example, it considers that the winner caused unnecessary additional costs by an unreasonable approach to the arbitration including potentially an unreasonable refusal to mediate.

Basis of determination

As for the basis of the determination of other arbitration expenses under default rule 61(3), in a court situation in Scotland there are various permutations of fees and expenses bases: eg 'agent–client' or 'agent–client, client paying', etc. The Act avoids these types of calculations by specifying the basis – simply that 'a reasonable amount is to be allowed in respect of all reasonably incurred expenses'. That 'reasonableness' test will be applied in favour of the person found liable to pay the expenses, and it is thus for the receiving party to prove that sums claimed are reasonable, both in the nature of the expense and its amount. However, in practice, if the receiving party can demonstrate a *prima facie* argument as to the reasonableness of the sums claimed it will often fall to the paying party to show why this is not correct.

Obviously, as this is a default rule, the parties themselves could make different arrangements for the determination of the expenses. If they do not do so, then the tribunal will become the point of first reference or they can refer the matter to the Auditor. It makes sense for the tribunal to be involved, as it will be fully conversant with all aspects of the arbitration from start to end and is therefore in the best place to make determinations as to what was reasonable.

There are two other advantages that follow from this: first, that the tribunal will thereby be in the best position to determine what parts of the procedure and the evidence were required and which parts perhaps were otiose or redundant or not really adding anything to the party's case. That will have knock-on consequences for that party even if it does succeed. It may find that portions of its expenses will be disallowed. Secondly, the tribunal will be able to dispose of the whole issue of expenses more quickly than anyone else. Also the tribunal will do that through an award and again there is no delay in making it if it can carry out the determination itself without waiting for others to do so.

It is worth repeating that this is a default rule, and the parties could decide to use a totally different method of determination from that set out in rule 61(3). Indeed, the wording of rule 61(3) is such that this is only a default position itself, and the tribunal or the Auditor, as the case may be, appear to have unfettered power to depart from the default 'reasonable' position under rule 61(3). This seems to the authors to be a strange position, in that rule 61(3) may, on the face of it, simply be ignored. It is, however, suggested that if the tribunal or the Auditor wished to depart from the default position under rule 61(3), then the basis to be used should be disclosed in advance, and the parties should at the very least be invited to make submissions on this basis. Accordingly, where the tribunal is required to make a determination of 'other arbitration expenses' under rule 61(2), then it would seem to be best practice to follow the 'reasonable' test under rule 61(3)(a), and the 'burden of proof' test in rule 61(3)(b) unless the parties agree otherwise. Such an approach should make the determination difficult to challenge.

English provisions

Rule 61 is similar to the provisions of s 63 of the 1996 Act in respect of recoverable costs, although, as already discussed, the practices of the English and Scottish courts in this area are not identical, and it may well be that arbitrators will also take different views as to how to exercise their powers under the Act. There is, in our view, nothing to stop them applying the practices of the Scottish courts but, equally, nothing requiring them to do so either.

Liability for recoverable arbitration expenses

Apportionment

Default rule 62 allows the tribunal to allocate liability for the recoverable expenses (or any part of those expenses) between the parties. What this means is that the tribunal can determine that one party is liable to pay, say, 75 per cent of the arbitration expenses which it will then determine separately (as per rule 61). The default position is, however, a 50/50 split of the common expenses (eg the fees of the arbitrators), with each side paying its own costs and expenses (rule 62(3)).

The reason for this is that arbitrations have to be paid for by the parties, unlike litigation which was traditionally partly paid for from court dues, and otherwise from the state but which position is changing with the state contribution decreasing. So, at the start, the parties may have paid an equal amount towards the ongoing costs of the arbitration with the view that there will be an apportionment following the decision of the tribunal. To take the above 75 per cent award, if each paid equally then on that determination there will be a payment of 25 per cent of the total expenses from the losing party to the winning party, but each party would continue to pay its own costs unless the tribunal was authorised to make an award related to such costs, and did so.

Award

The expenses will be dealt with by way of award ('when making an award'). Therefore the tribunal will have to follow the requirements of the mandatory rules in Part 6, and such of the default rules in that Part as have not been disapplied or modified by the parties.

There has been some debate as to whether the use of the singular 'an' precludes the making of more than one award in this area. As explained under rule 59, the common law position was set out in *Apollo Engineering Ltd v James Scott Ltd* [2009] CSIH 39; 2009 SC 525, where a series of awards of expenses was permitted. There is some assistance in rule 54(2) which allows part awards, but possibly not in rule 54(1) which allows multiple awards, but only on 'different' matters.

In rendering the award, the tribunal must have regard to the principle 'that expenses should follow a decision made in favour of a party'. Lawyers will recognise this as 'expenses follow success' (or 'costs follow the event' in England). In other words, the winner should get at least a portion of his expenses. This is part of the Scottish (and English) common law systems.

There is, however, clear provision for amending this base position if it is 'inappropriate'. For example, where the winning party has not behaved well in the course of the arbitration or has delayed or obstructed the process or in some other way failed to assist the tribunal in coming to its decision, the arbitrators may decide to award that party less in expenses than would otherwise have been the case, as is the case in litigation. A party who ran a series of hopeless arguments in addition to the valid one on which it succeeded could be exposed to such a decision. Further it may be that the party has not fulfilled its obligations under the Act in terms of mandatory rule 25 to ensure that the arbitration was conducted without unnecessary delay and without incurring unnecessary expense.

It may be different if the tribunal considers that the winning party has a valid legal argument, but a less attractive moral position. The wording of the Rules would seem wide enough to allow the tribunal to condemn such a party in expenses, but it is suggested that this is not really the function of arbitration, and a tribunal should be cautious before altering the usual expenses order out of distaste for a party's position.

In addition, it is open to the tribunal to take account of a tender made by one party to settle the matter, which is not accepted, but is not beaten in the final award. This could be by way of a sealed offer, or an offer made without the tribunal's knowledge that is 'without prejudice', save as to expenses. The offering party could then produce evidence of such offer after the making of the award, and argue that the receiving party, while successful on the face of it, had wasted the time of the arbitration in not accepting a reasonable offer. Rule 62(3) imposes joint liability (see 'equal share') on the parties for the recoverable arbitration expenses until the award is made or in any event if there is no determination, as well as being liable for their own legal and other expenses. While this latter point is probably self-evident, it is nonetheless confirmed in rule 62(3)(b).

This will also apply in relation to any arbitration expenses in respect of which the tribunal does not allocate liability by award (and so makes each liable, as between themselves, for a 50 per cent share). This is a useful safety net in the event that the tribunal fails to deal with some minor issue in the award, but the parties do not wish to take this issue further.

These provisions operate independently of the requirements under rule 60. Rule 62(4)(a) provides that parties' liability to each other in respect of rule 60 tribunal fees and expenses still applies including in respect of other recoverable third party expenses. It also makes clear that the rule does not affect any liability of any party to a third party. As the Explanatory Notes state, it does not create a *jus quaesitum tertio*, ie a right vested in a third party enforceable as such, but merely preserves whatever rights that third party might have had in any event.

It should be noted that rule 62(1) is permissive, in that the tribunal 'may' make an award. However, this needs to be read with default rule 57(1), which makes it clear that (subject to certain exceptions, which are not relevant here) the arbitration does not end until all issues, including expenses, are the subject of an award.

Ban on pre-dispute agreements about liability for arbitration expenses

Any agreement allocating the parties' liability between themselves for any or all of the arbitration expenses has no effect if entered into before the dispute being arbitrated has arisen. Mandatory rule 63 provides that a party can only be liable to pay the whole or any part of the expenses of arbitration if such agreement on expenses is made *after* the dispute in question arises. This is an important protection for parties in an unequal bargaining position. It reflects the prior English law and follows the present English position in the 1996 Act s 60. The mischief at which this rule is aimed is the situation whereby the parties may sign a contract (whether standard form or negotiated) which provides, for example, that in the event of a dispute arising, 'all costs shall be borne by Party X or Party Y irrespective of the tribunal's determination and final award'. As a matter of public policy a party should at least have knowledge of the nature and extent of the dispute in question and indeed to assess the reasonable prospects in doing so. Consistent with this approach, the rule is made mandatory.

It might be thought that no sensible, well-advised, person or organisation would enter into such an agreement after the dispute had arisen (or even after the arbitration had commenced). However, one can envisage a situation where one party wished to resolve an issue through arbitration, and agreed to pay the costs in any event where the other party was impecunious. This does happen in litigation, but the difference, of course, is that an arbitral award would not amount to binding precedent, unlike a court judgment.

This rule also eliminates any argument as to whether so-called 'Tolent' clauses (see rule 60 above) as used in adjudication are effective. They are not, and the uncertainty created in relation to adjudication by the decision in *Profile Projects Ltd v Elmwood (Glasgow) Ltd* [2011] CSOH 64; 2011 SLT 975 does not apply to Scottish arbitration. The authors believe this was the right decision, and prevents the problems caused to adjudication while the law on this point was corrected. In addition, it is understood that some property leases include predetermined apportionments of arbitrators' fees. It would seem to us that such clauses may fall foul of rule 63 in the event that the arbitration is seated in Scotland and governed by the Act.

If a lease includes, for example, a rent review clause which provides for arbitration in the event of a dispute, any purported pre-allocation of arbitration expenses will be void under mandatory rule 63. The rest of the clause will, however, remain effective. It will be open to the parties to re-agree the allocation, but only after the dispute has crystallised (ie it is clear that the new passing rent is not agreed). Note also that it is probably a good idea not to disapply default rule 62 in such a case, as otherwise the tribunal will have no right to make an award allocating expenses. Where rule 62 is disapplied, rule 63 is still in effect and, it seems to us, the only solution is that each party bears its own expenses.

Security for expenses

Rule 64 is a default rule. In the absence of agreement to the contrary, an arbitrator has the power to order a claimant or counterclaimant to provide security for the expenses of the arbitration and, if that order is not complied with, to make an award dismissing any claim by that party. The nature and amount of the security will be at the arbitrator's discretion.

The security is for the recoverable arbitration expenses in terms of rule 61. Thus, as seen, it will also incorporate the arbitrator's fees and expenses, the fees and expenses of any arbitral institution and the expenses of the parties. Note that it is the arbitrator and not the court that makes this decision.

Note also that it is the 'party making a claim' who is to provide the security. A defendant will not be required to provide such security irrespective of its financial position unless, perhaps, it is making a counterclaim (or, conceivably, appealing against an award already made). 'Claim' is defined as including a 'counterclaim'. A 'counterclaim' is a claim for a remedy made as a positive request by the party defending as opposed to its position in rebuttal of the claimant's position.

While this is a common approach, it is suggested that it could produce unsatisfactory results if a defendant not raising a counterclaim obstructs the arbitration and seeks to run up costs which, if awarded against it, it would be unable to pay. In such cases the tribunal may wish to make use of its wide powers to case manage the arbitration, so as to defeat such a process, but may have to use its powers to dismiss all or part of any defences, rather than order security under this rule. Claimants will still need to consider the possibility of the defendant not paying an expenses award before embarking on an arbitration, in the same way as they already do in litigation.

It is, however, arguable that the court (as opposed to the tribunal) could be asked to order that the defendant (or the claimant) provide security under rule 46(1)(c) on the grounds that the expenses are amounts 'in dispute' in the arbitration and therefore fall to be secured. Rule 46 is not precise on this point, but there seems no reason why the power should be limited to the main subject-matter. Interestingly, rule 46 has no restriction as in rule 64(2) preventing the order of security for costs merely because the claimant is outside the jurisdiction. However, it seems unlikely that a court would fail to take notice of these provisions, and order security for costs against a foreign defendant which could be ordered against a foreign claimant.

Attached to the order for security, in the event of non-compliance, the tribunal has the draconian power to make an award dismissing any claim (and, by implication, any counterclaim) made by that party.

Outwith the UK

The order cannot be made *only* on the ground that the party is outwith the UK (although this implies that it could be one of a number of reasons). This is to avoid the argument that just because a party or body incorporated is based outside the UK, that is sufficient reason to obtain security for the recoverable arbitration expenses from the tribunal. As this is a default rule, it might be thought that parties could defeat this provision in its entirety by deleting the same. The position in relation to EU or EEC countries remains uncertain at the time of writing until Brexit arrangements have been finalised.

As for the 'non-UK' provision in rule 64(2), this also has its origins in the 1996 Act s 38. Like that provision, it is not a good ground to order security just because the party is 'foreign'. This all reflects a move away from previous practice in both jurisdictions that often led to requests for security for costs being based on little more than evidence that the party concerned was 'foreign', in circumstances where no such security would have been required from a British party. (Cf RCS 33.2(1) (Form of application).)

The ordering of caution, meaning security, for expenses cannot be required of foreigners seeking redress under certain International and European Conventions. In Scottish procedure a resident abroad is usually required to 'sist a mandatory' (ie bring in a local party to represent the interests of the person abroad which ensures the proper conduct of the proceedings within the jurisdiction) rather than provide security for expenses. With respect to the process, this has always seemed to miss the point. The Scottish party is concerned about receiving payment of an award of expenses, rather than just the proper conduct of proceedings, and the procedure of sisting a mandatory, apart from being a phrase that is unintelligible to foreign parties, really does not address this at all. The focus appears to be on ensuring the efficient administration of justice, rather than the interests of the parties. While the former is of great importance, there can sometimes be a feeling in the minds of lay users of the system that the latter is not regarded as of sufficient significance.

However, rule 64(2), it is suggested, will reassure foreign parties not based in the UK that there will not be provision for security for expenses just because they are based outwith the UK and without the requirement for 'mandatories' (ie those exercising a mandate) as in the Court of Session. That in itself will not therefore be a deterrent to arbitrating in Scotland. They can still be found liable for security on different valid grounds of course, but only on the same basis as a Scottish party.

The bases for the exercise of that discretion will be for the tribunal to determine and it will have to decide whether the grounds that would apply under RCS 33 would also have a bearing in the consideration of an order under rule 64. For example, would it be a valid basis for an order for security if the claimant was only the 'nominal claimant' (what the Scottish courts would recognise as not being the true *dominus litis* or master of the litigation, or what insolvency law would see as a party controlled by shadow directors) or if the only assets of the claimant or counterclaimant were located abroad? We consider that it will be for the tribunal to determine these types of circumstance on a case-by-case basis and arbitrators should not be tied solely to the grounds which would permit 'caution' for expenses in a court context.

The question of assets abroad may be a complex one, and depend on the enforceability of any award in the relevant country, possibly under the New York Convention. In such cases, there may be detailed argument not only as to the legal position, but also as to the practical likelihood of enforcement in certain circumstances. Again, the test should, we submit, be that the position is looked at in the same way as if the party in question was in Scotland, and similar issues arose as to the availability of assets to meet any award.

In England, in connection with the analogous provisions of the 1996 Act, this has been interpreted as giving the arbitrator a great deal of flexibility to decide on what basis the security should be ordered subject to similar general duties on the tribunal, including the power to order security for its own costs. (See 1996 Act s 38(3) discussed above.)

Can the tribunal itself order security?

It seems that the tribunal could *ex proprio motu* (of its own motion or on its own decision) order security to be provided given that rule 64(1) does not seem to require an application by the other party. In addition, it is arguable that this falls within the general duty of the tribunal under rule 24. However, care needs to be taken that the tribunal is acting in an impartial and fair manner in ordering security for one party over the other on its own decision. This may be particularly the case where the purpose is to provide security for its own fees. The English courts have held that such an award is possible under analogous provisions of the 1996 Act (s 38(3)), but that this should only be done of its own motion in circumstances where a court would award security for costs (*Wicketts v Brine Builders* [2001] CILL 1805).

Sealed offers and security

In England, where a sealed offer has been submitted, the claimant can say 'look I have been made an offer (tender) which, even though the court/tribunal does not know the terms, shows the other side they think I have some sort of case, so no security against me please'. This is always a tricky area, since the sealed offer might, of course, be derisory, and intended only to reflect the 'nuisance value' of the action. For that reason, the arbitrator may be cautious before making a decision solely on the existence of such an offer.

Dismissal of the claim

Dismissal of a claim is probably akin to dismissal in the technical sense used in Scottish civil procedure whereby the party can re-raise the issue at a later stage. The sanction for failing to provide security is the dismissal (ie rejection) of the claim and not a sist (or English stay) given that the tribunal will have made a final award to dismiss, and the arbitration itself will, therefore, be at an end if this covers the entire claim. It may be analogous to what, in American jurisdictions, is referred to as 'dismissal without prejudice', since there has been no decision on the merits. It is, however, suggested that, if a party sought to raise the same issue again, even with the security previously required, this would be met with the argument that it amounted to an abuse of process.

While the rule gives power to dismiss, it is suggested that the general duties which rule 24 gives the arbitrators would allow for the proceedings to be sisted/stayed in appropriate circumstances pending compliance with the order for security. (Cf LCIA Rules 2020 Art 25.2: permits a stay in the face of non-compliance.) However, we believe that any sist should be of finite duration, and, if compliance is still not achieved, dismissal should become inevitable. To do otherwise leaves the innocent party in limbo, and the tribunal in existence when it may no longer be required although no final award has been made. It may also prevent a time bar falling under limitation or prescription rules, which would be unjust to the other party.

Limitation of recoverable arbitration expenses

Rule 65 is equivalent to the Arbitration Act 1996 s 65. The Explanatory Notes to the Arbitration (Scotland) Bill explain that rule 65 is also a default rule 'which gives the tribunal the power to make a provisional or part award to cap a party's liability for arbitration expenses. This is a power which could for instance be used if one of the parties has enough financial resources that they could take advantage of their financial position against another party with more limited resources'.

This rule should also encourage the parties to exercise restraint in their deployment of resources in running the arbitration and hopefully to avoid incurring unnecessary expense. If they know that there is a 'cap' then they will know from the outset that that will be the maximum that is recoverable. So they may expend greater sums but only in the knowledge that they will have to bear the cost. This does not, therefore, totally prevent an 'inequality of arms' but at least means that such inequality has to be paid for by the richer party.

The rule can be seen also as part of the general duty of the tribunal in terms of mandatory rule 24 to ensure fair play between the parties and to avoid unnecessary expense.

While this is probably not the motivation behind the rule, similar provisions in court rules have been used to encourage litigation by relatively impecunious claimants on issues which might be said to be of general public importance. As already discussed, arbitration does not lend itself to such disputes, because of the confidentiality, and the inability to create precedent, but it does provide a reserve power in appropriate circumstances, perhaps where a private individual wishes to arbitrate against a government body, but is frightened off by the risk of expenses awards if he loses. This will be relatively easy to do if both parties are in agreement (indeed, and would get round the problems of rule 63 in relation to pre-agreed costs), but will be more challenging for the tribunal if the more powerful party objects.

Awards on recoverable arbitration expenses

An expenses award (under rule 62 or 65) may be made together with or separately from an award on the substance of the dispute (and these rules apply in relation to an expenses award as they apply to an award on the substance of the dispute).

Rule 66 is a default rule which removes any doubt that expenses awards can be made by the tribunal separately from final awards. This makes sense as the tribunal may want to have the flexibility to make its award on expenses in respect of a part of the procedure and not have to wait until a final award. Alternatively, the tribunal may wish to invite submissions on a final award of expenses after the final award on the issues themselves (or, perhaps a draft of that award) has been issued.

CHALLENGING AWARDS (PART 8)

This part is very much at the core of the thinking within the Act, in that it contains the rules representing the limited extent to which the courts will entertain appeals against arbitrators' decisions. Rule 67 and rule 68 are mandatory and, accordingly, appeals on the grounds of substantive jurisdiction or serious irregularity cannot be excluded by agreement of the parties. The positions regarding challenges on the grounds of error of law, however, differ. Rule 69 is a default rule and can be excluded by agreement of the parties.

In their format and wording these rules follow the correspondingly numbered sections of the English Arbitration Act 1996, and it might be thought that the positions in the two jurisdictions are identical. However, an English decision suggests this may not be completely true. *Shell Egypt West Manzala GmbH v Dana Gas Egypt Ltd* [2010] EWHC 2097 (Comm) has generally been discussed as an authority on termination of contracts, but also included an argument on whether a statement that an arbitration award was 'final and binding' precluded the use of the appeal processes in the 1996 Act where those would otherwise be available. It was held that it did not, and that if such rights were to be excluded, this needed to be clearly stated in unequivocal terms. The logical corollary of this is that, in England at least, it is potentially possible to remove any right of appeal to the courts (save, one assumes, for matters such as fraud). Under the Scottish Act, however, the appeal rules (except for rule 69) are mandatory and cannot, therefore, be excluded.

Useful guidance was provided to those considering bringing a challenge in the Outer House by Lord Glennie in *Arbitration Application No 3 of 2011* [2011] CSOH 164.

Challenging an award: substantive jurisdiction

Rule 67 is a mandatory rule. It allows an appeal against the tribunal's award on the basis of a lack of jurisdiction on the part of the tribunal to make all or part of an award. Under this rule, the focus is on an award having been made in excess, or want, of jurisdiction, even if the tribunal itself is validly constituted.

The wording of rule 67 appears also to permit a challenge to an award in a situation where there is any challenge to jurisdiction to make the award, and this produces a theoretical conflict between rules. Rule 67(1) provides that a party can apply to the court to challenge the arbitrator's jurisdiction and rule 67(2) gives the court powers in relation to the award made. These powers are either to confirm, vary or set aside the award (and, in relation to varying or setting aside, part of the award). Reference should be made to the discussion on the meaning of 'setting aside' under rule 20. We believe that this term must be read as equivalent to reduction under Scots law, since otherwise this rule would require the ability to confirm part of the award, when only part had been 'set aside' in terms of the usual Scottish terminology. (Cf Lord Glennie's comments in *SGL Carbon Fibres Ltd v RBG Ltd* [2011] CSOH 62; 2011 SLT 417 at para [47] discussed above in relation to rule 20.)

Where the setting aside of part of the award means that part no longer exists, then confirmation of the balance is not problematic. There is another provision in the Rules (rule 19) for the arbitrator to rule on their own jurisdiction (and further procedural provisions on this point in rules 20–23), and an appeal under rule 67 is also subject to the limits on review in rule 71(2) and (4) (including the requirement to use any available arbitral process of review). It is, however, necessary to make provision for an appeal after the final award has been made since it may only be at that stage that it becomes apparent that the arbitrator has acted outwith their jurisdiction. Rule 67(3) provides that any variation in the award has effect as part of the tribunal's award.

Once the Outer House has determined the appeal, rule 67(4) provides that an appeal against the Outer House's decision on a jurisdictional appeal may be made to the Inner House, but only with leave of the Outer House. Leave may be given only where there is an important point of principle or practice or another compelling reason for the Inner House to consider the appeal (rule 67(5)) and the Outer House's decision on whether to grant such leave is final (rule 67(6)). If leave is granted, any decision of the Inner House is final (rule 67(7)).

In *G1 Venues for Orders under Schedule 1 of the Arbitration (Scotland) Act 2010 to set aside a decision of an 'arbiter' dated 10 May 2013* [2013] CSOH 202 an appeal had been taken against a decision of an arbitrator who held that he had no jurisdiction to proceed with the arbitration. He had accordingly ended the arbitration in terms of rule 20(3). The petitioners sought to over-turn that decision and appealed to the Outer House (in terms of rule 21). The court held that the arbitrator had misdirected himself.

While the basic thrust of the Act is to limit the involvement of the courts, this rule is the first of three ways in which the Act permits a challenge to be made to the award of a tribunal. As noted above, rules 67 and 68 are mandatory, whereas rule 69 is default. The first two rules provide non-controversial reasons why the court should become involved, and this is the reason why they are mandatory. The third (rule 69) is a matter of choice for the parties, replacing the old, discredited 'stated case' procedure under the Administration of Justice (Scotland) Act 1972 s 3.

Any challenge on the basis that the tribunal had no jurisdiction whatso-ever should fall to be dealt with by the tribunal under rule 19 or objection under rule 20 or a challenge to such decision under rule 21, all mandatory rules, or by application for a determination by the Outer House under rule 22 (default) and requiring leave. The wording of rule 67 makes it clear that it only applies to a lack of jurisdiction in relation to the making of the award itself (rule 67(1) and the limited remedies in rule 67(2)). Accordingly, if the challenge is to the jurisdiction of the tribunal itself under one of the three matters set out in rule 19 (valid arbitration agreement; proper constitution; matters submitted in accordance with agreement), then the challenge should be made to the tribunal itself in accordance with the objection procedure in rule 20 (mandatory). If this decision is not accepted, an appeal to the Outer House is made under rule 21 (mandatory). In other circumstances, a direct application to the Outer House can be made under rule 22 (default), with leave.

Such objections must be made timeously (generally as soon as reasonably practicable), or rights to object will be lost under rule 76. It is suggested that, in such a case, rule 67 cannot be used to revisit the *same* issues in order to challenge the making of an award where a decision has already been made, either by the tribunal or the court, that jurisdiction exists. It remains possible to raise new jurisdictional issues relating to the award itself.

The matter is complicated by the tribunal being given power under rule 20(4) to delay a ruling until the making of an award on the merits (normally a final award). In such a case, the process for challenging jurisdiction would seem to be under rule 67, although arguably a right still exists under rules 21 and 22 and the latter may be appropriate if the entire basis of the tribunal, rather than merely the award in question, is what is being challenged. The latter approach might be attractive if, for example, the award on the merits was limited to part of the dispute, but the party wished to challenge the entire jurisdiction of the tribunal, since rule 67 only allows the court to take steps in relation to the award itself.

In applications under rule 67, RCS 100.3 states that the judge shall deter-mine procedure, including, presumably, whether there is to be a rehearing, oral evidence etc. RCS 100.7 sets out the circumstances, relief sought, and the matters to be identified by the appellant, including whether the remedy sought under rule 67(2) is variation of the award or setting it aside, or part of the award in either case (RCS 100.7(3)(f)).

It is important for any party seeking to challenge an award under rule 67 to consider the appropriate timing for making such a challenge. If the challenge is under one of the three headings in rule 19, we recommend that it should be done promptly at the time the matter becomes apparent, and not left to the end for a 'challenge to any award' under rule 67. While the possibility of a challenge under rule 67 remains, doing so would risk the Outer House being reluctant to accept such a challenge at the very last stage of the process, unless there were good reasons why the challenge under the relevant rules 19–23 was not appropriate at the earlier stage. This may become even more of an issue if seeking leave to appeal to the Inner House under rule 67(5 (b) since there is a requirement that the reason for allowing an appeal is 'compelling'. (Note that such an appeal to the Inner House is not available for challenges under rule 19 and following.)

Once a ruling under rule 19 is received from the tribunal, the party needs to either accept the same, or make a challenge to the Outer House under rule 21 within 14 days of the decision under rule 19. Failure to do so would seem to the authors to risk a party losing any right to challenge an award under rule 67 at a later date on the same grounds. While the position is not free from doubt, particularly if a party fails to participate in the arbitration for some reason, proceeding promptly under rules 19, 20 and 21 is the safest course of action. There also remains scope for a direct application to the Outer House under rule 22, but the same logic applies. If the tribunal exercises its right under rule 20(4) to delay a decision on jurisdiction, then the party objecting should decide either to make a direct application under rule 22, or reserve its position to challenge after the award on the merits, either under rule 67, 21 or 22.

Challenging an award: serious irregularity

Like rule 67, rule 68 is a mandatory rule. It allows an appeal against the tribunal's award to the Outer House on the basis of serious irregularity. Like rule 67, no leave is required to appeal to the Outer House.

Rule 67 sets out comprehensive grounds which include both pre-existing remedies under Scots law and new procedures (in rule 68(2)) on which an award may be challenged for serious irregularity and gives the court appropriate powers in relation to any award made in such circumstances. The procedure is only available in cases of 'serious irregularity', so as to avoid the rule being used in unmeritorious cases to delay the enforcement of awards. To be a serious irregularity, there has to be substantial injustice.

The circumstances include: (a) the tribunal failing to conduct the arbitration in accordance with (i) the arbitration agreement, (ii) these rules (in so far as they apply), or (iii) any other agreement by the parties relating to conduct of the arbitration; (b) the tribunal acting outwith its powers (other than by exceeding its jurisdiction); (c) the tribunal failing to deal with all the issues that were put to it; (d) any arbitral appointments referee or other third party to whom the parties give powers in relation to the arbitration acting outwith powers; (e) uncertainty or ambiguity as to the award's effect; (f) the award being (i) contrary to public policy, or (ii) obtained by fraud or in a way which is contrary to public policy; (g) an arbitrator having not been impartial and independent; (h) an arbitrator having not treated the parties fairly; (i) an arbitrator having been incapable of acting as an arbitrator in the arbitration (or there being justifiable doubts about an arbitrator's ability to so act); (j) an arbitrator not having a qualification which the parties agreed (before the arbitrator's appointment) that the arbitrator must have; or (k) any other irregularity in the conduct of the arbitration or in the award which is admitted by (i) the tribunal, or (ii) any arbitral appointments referee or other third party to whom the parties give powers in relation to the arbitration. We will dealt with these in more detail below.

The responsibility of the court is to review the *process* by which the tribunal came to its decision. It is also subject to the limits set out in rules 68(2) and (4). It is not the function of the court under this rule to substitute its own view of the correct decision, merely to determine whether the decision was arrived at in breach of the matters set out in the rule.

Rule 68(5) permits an appeal to be made to the Inner House against the Outer House's decision on a serious irregularity appeal, but only with the leave of the Outer House. Leave may be given only where there is an important point of principle or practice or another compelling reason for the Inner House to consider the appeal (rule 68(6), following the same approach as rule 67(5)). The decision of the Outer House as to whether to grant leave is final (rule 68(7)), as is the decision on any such appeal by the Inner House (rule 68(8)).

Serious irregularity and substantial injustice

This mandatory rule relates to 'serious irregularity', which is defined by way of an exclusive list of potential irregularities deemed to be sufficiently 'serious' in this context. Note that these do not generally appear to be mere examples, as they are stated to be a definition of 'serious irregularities' as being 'any' of the 'kinds' of irregularity listed. The only exception to this is in rule 68(2)(k), referred to below. There is, also, a second test in rule 68(2) that such irregularity must have 'caused, or will cause, substantial injustice to the appellant'. Accordingly, it is not enough to see whether your 'irregularity' appears on the list – this mechanism is only intended to rectify matters where a *substantial* injustice is likely to occur. In other cases, the decision of the tribunal is final, notwithstanding any irregularities, even if these are within this list.

In *Minister of Finance (Inc) v International Petroleum Investment Co* [2019] EWCA Civ 2080, the Court of Appeal overturned a decision granting a stay of applications pursuant to s 67 and s 68 on the basis the lower court had failed to recognise the appellants' statutory right to challenge a consent award under ss 67 and 68. The consent award had been complied with initially but was challenged on the grounds of, *inter alia*, fraud, having been procured by Malaysia's prime minister in his own interests and only challenged after he left office. The court decided the appellants had the right to challenge the consent award for lack of substantive jurisdiction and serious irregularity.

Guidance on what amounts to a 'serious irregularity' has been given by Lord Woolman in *Arbitration Application No 1 of 2013* [2014] CSOH 83 at para [18]:

> Three general points can be made about serious irregularity appeals. First, they are designed as 'a long stop available only in extreme cases where the tribunal has gone so wrong in its conduct of the arbitration that justice calls out for it to be corrected': Departmental Advisory Committee on Arbitration Report on the Arbitration Bill 1996. That passage has been quoted with approval in several cases, see for example *Walsall Metropolitan Borough Council v Beechdale Community Housing Association Ltd* [2005] EWHC 2715. Second, the court will not intervene on the basis that it might have done things differently, or expressed its conclusions on the essential issues at greater length. Third, such an appeal can only succeed if there has been substantial injustice. If the result of the arbitration would have been likely to be the same or very similar, then there is no basis for overturning the award: *Checkpoint Ltd v Strathclyde Pension Fund* [2003] EWCA Civ 84. Accordingly a dissatisfied party has to meet a high test.

A failure to meet this high test will result in refusal of the appeal or the grounds which rely on a serious irregularity at least. (See *Arbitration Appeal No 2 of 2017* [2018] CSOH 12.)

Rule 68 allows an appeal against an award. It should be noted that it does not appear to sanction appeals against orders (directions, etc) short of awards. It does, presumably, catch interim, probably provisional (if taken effect), part and final awards, since these must all be considered as 'awards' for this purpose.

The tribunal's consent is not required for such an application, and this is particularly relevant when the final award has been delivered, since the tribunal is then said to be *functus officio*, that is it no longer has any powers. It is also important to remember that whether or not 'substantial injustice' has occurred, or is likely to occur, is a matter for the court, and not the tribunal or the aggrieved party.

While it will obviously be a matter to be determined on the facts in each case, some guidance can be derived from English decisions on the equivalent wording in s 68 of the 1996 Act, such as *Checkpoint Ltd v Strathclyde Pension Fund* [2003] EWCA Civ 84; *Margulead Ltd v Exide Technologies* [2004] EWHC 1019 (Comm) and *Newfield Construction Ltd v Tomlinson* [2004] EWHC 3051, which, taken together, indicate that the appropriate test to be used is to ask what action the appellant party would have taken 'but for' the irregularity complained of, and, if he cannot show that he suffered substantial prejudice as a result of the irregularity, it would seem that he is unlikely to succeed in his application. To take an example, if the irregularity has led to the award being made in favour of the wrong party, then this will clearly meet the injustice test. However, if it is suggested that the tribunal has rounded down numbers so that an award is made for £50,000 which should clearly have been for £50,005, then there is 'injustice', but it is difficult to see that this could ever be considered 'substantial' in context. It is also important to recognise that the first step is to determine if there is an irregularity, and then apply the 'but for' test and that the injustice must flow from the irregularity complained of by the appellant.

Kinds of 'serious irregularity'

Rule 68 sets out a comprehensive list of examples which are recovered. Scottish authorities do not yet exist on all of these examples, but there are a large number of English examples which deal with challenges on these grounds. Scottish practitioners would be entitled to have regard to the English cases and to rely on the reasoning in these, given the comments of Lord Glennie and Lord Woolman. In *Arbitration Application No 3 of 2011* [2011] CSOH 164 per Lord Glennie at para [8]:

> Since the Act was closely and unashamedly modelled on the English Act, and reflects the same underlying philosophy, authorities on the Act (and its predecessor, the Arbitration Act 1979) in relation to questions of interpretation and approach will obviously be of relevance. There is no point in re-inventing the (arbitration) wheel. In the written submissions relating to this application, both parties have helpfully referred to authorities on the approach to granting leave to appeal under the English Act.

In *Arbitration Application No 1 of 2013* [2014] CSOH 83 per Lord Woolman at para [10]:

> The 2010 Act is modelled on the Arbitration Act 1996. Much of the wording is similar or identical. I agree with Lord Glennie's observations in *Arbitration Appeal No 3 of 2011* 2012 SLT 150 that English decisions provide helpful guidance in this area.

The listed 'irregularities' in rule 68(2) are as follows:

(a) Failure to conduct the arbitration in accordance with the agreement; the Rules; or any other agreement of the parties relating to the conduct of the arbitration

This is a very broad statement and may well be the first port of call for any party looking to make an application under this rule. In this context 'these rules (in so far as they apply)' means all the mandatory rules plus those default rules which have not been disapplied and those that have been modified. There is some duplication between this provision and some of the kinds of irregularity listed in later sub-clauses (eg impartiality is specifically covered by rule 68(2)(g) and, because of mandatory rule 24(1)(a), is also included in the wording of rule 68(2)(a)). Accordingly, on this point, the same facts could give rise to two distinct grounds of appeal under rule 68(2) (a) and (g). Nothing turns on this.

(b) Tribunal acting outwith its powers (other than by exceeding its jurisdiction)

This clearly overlaps to some extent with (a) above, since such action might well also amount to a breach of the arbitration agreement conferring the powers in question, or of the Rules. Challenges where jurisdiction is exceeded are brought under rules 19–23 and/or rule 67 above, which is why they are excluded here.

It is difficult to see how this will generally differ from the powers in (a). It has been suggested that this sub-clause is intended to cover interim orders short of awards, but this seems to sit uneasily with the fact that the only power in rule 68(1) is to appeal against 'an award'.

Where the tribunal was acting outwith its powers (other than by exceeding its jurisdiction as per rule 67 above) any party considering a challenge under this ground may wish to consider the following: *Lesotho Highlands Development Authority v Impregilo SpA* [2005] UKHL 43, [2006] 1 AC 221 at paras [48]–[49]; as applied in *Warborough Investments Ltd v S Robinson & Sons (Holdings) Ltd* [2003] EWCA Civ 751 and mentioned in *Arbitration Application No 1 of 2013* [2014] CSOH 83. In *Margulead Ltd v Exide Technologies* [2004] EWHC 1019 (Comm), [2004] 2 All ER (Comm) 727; *Newfield Construction Ltd v Tomlinson* [2004] EWHC 3051; *Van der Giessen-de-Noord Shipbuilding Division BV v Imtech Marine & Offshore BV* [2008] EWHC 2904 (Comm), [2009] 1 Lloyd's Rep 273; *UMS Holding Ltd v Great Station Properties SA* [2017] EWHC 2473 (Comm), [2018] 1 All ER (Comm) 856.

(c) Tribunal failing to deal with all the issues put to it

This is intended to prevent the tribunal from making what purports to be a final award without having addressed all issues. This clearly covers all issues included in the original submission to arbitration, including, for example, the making of awards for interest and/or expenses. However, it would also seem to capture any issues which all of the parties specifically require the tribunal to decide as the arbitration process progresses (although presumably only where such issue is arbitrable).

This is not the same as the question of whether the tribunal has to address every *argument* raised by or on behalf of the parties, since it only refers to the issues themselves. In England *Petroships Pte of Singapore v Petec Trading & Investment Corpn of Vietnam (The Petro Ranger)* [2001] 2 Lloyd's Rep 348 makes it clear that mere failure to address every argument is not an irregularity and that it is not necessary to sacrifice brevity in order to avoid a charge of breach of duty.

While this is a short and apparently simple sub-clause, the issues it raises have often proved contentious in practice in the analogous English law provision, which has approached this by determining whether the issue is 'essential' or 'subsidiary', with only the former having to be addressed: see *Van der Giessen-de-Noord Shipbuilding Division BV v Imtech Marine & Offshore BV* [2008] EWHC 2904 (Comm) in which the pleadings alone ran to 17 volumes, and the hearing bundles to over 80 lever arch files.

Arbitration tribunals should check carefully that they have addressed each issue that has been raised. In addition, the parties or their advisers need to ensure that all matters they wished to see resolved have been dealt with, and be alive to the fact that an appeal may be available to the other party if any point which that party wanted resolved goes unanswered.

In complex cases, a tribunal might consider issuing a checklist to the parties before preparing its award setting out the issues it believes it has been asked to address, in order to ensure that nothing relevant has been missed.

In cases where the obligation to provide reasons under default rule 51(2)(c) has not been disapplied, and where there are a substantial number of arguments put forward by one or both parties, it may be prudent for the tribunal to state specifically that it has addressed all matters it considers to be necessary to reach its decision, and that it had also considered all other arguments, but did not consider it was necessary to address them, as they would not have altered the decision made. It cannot be said that this is necessarily watertight, but it removes any argument that the tribunal has failed to address arguments by incompetence or oversight.

(d) Arbitration appointments referee or other third party to whom the parties give powers acting outwith powers

Where any arbitral appointments referee or other third party to whom the parties give powers in relation to the arbitration is acting outwith powers (rule 68(2)(d)), again there would need to be some reliance on English authorities: *Lesotho* above; *Gao Haiyan v Keeneye Holdings Ltd* [2011] HKEC 514; *Orascom TMT Investments SRL v Veon Ltd* [2018] EWHC 985 (Comm), [2018] Bus LR 1787.

On the face of it, this sub-clause appears to deal with failures in the process of appointing the tribunal, whether by an approved arbitration appointments referee (see s 24) or by a body selected by the parties, but not on the list approved under s 24. However, the sub-clause does not restrict itself to these powers, although it is difficult to envisage what other powers might be caught by its provisions. In practice, it is difficult to see how the fact that an AAR had acted outwith its powers when making an appointment would only become apparent after an award had been made. This is just about conceivable, but it is suggested that this sub-clause will have limited application in practice.

Examples of successful challenges on this ground can be found in the following cases. In *Transition Feeds LLP v Itochu Europe plc* [2013] EWHC 3629 (Comm) the Board had been guilty of a serious irregularity within s 68(2)(d) by failing to deal with two issues before it. The court held that the Board's failure to address those two issues had caused substantial injustice. In *Lorand Shipping Ltd v Davof Trading (Africa) BV (Ocean Glory)* [2014] EWHC 3521 (Comm) the threshold under s 68 was very high. However, it was important to consider the dicta in that case in the context of other relevant authorities. Where a tribunal wished to adopt a course not advocated by either party, a failure to give the parties a chance to make representations on that course before adopting it might amount to a serious irregularity.

If such a challenge is successful, in deciding whether to remit or set aside, the court must consider all the circumstances and background facts relating to the dispute, the award, the arbitrators and the overall desirability of remission and setting aside, as well as the implications of the respective remedies in terms of costs, time and justice. Where the court has formed the view, following a finding of serious irregularity under s 68(2)(d), that a reasonable person would no longer have confidence in the arbitrators' ability to come to a fair and balanced conclusion on the issues if remitted, that view might well underpin a conclusion that it would not be appropriate to remit as in *Secretary of State for the Home Department v Raytheon Systems Ltd* [2015] EWHC 311 (TCC).

In addition it should be noted that s 24 does not in any way limit the powers of an AAR. Accordingly, it is difficult to see how an AAR (or indeed a third party appointing body) has powers, unless those powers have been given by the parties. If, however, the appointing body exceeds the powers granted to it, this would be a different matter. For example, in the event that the Law Society of Scotland had been requested, in its capacity as an AAR, to appoint three solicitor-advocate QCs and appoints three arbitrators, two of whom do not hold that rank, then they are acting outwith their powers. This is clearly an irregularity, and is a 'serious irregularity' for the purposes of rule 68 because it is within this sub-clause (d). However, if the entire arbitration has been conducted without complaint, and no obvious injustice can be shown, it would seem likely to be an uphill task to persuade the Outer House arbitration judge to accept an appeal, because of a combination of delay, acquiescence, personal bar, the provisions of mandatory rule 76, and, in the context under discussion, lack of evidence of injustice. (It should be noted that this particular example could also be attacked under rule 68(2)(j), but the same problems could well arise.)

But what if the parties and the tribunal agree that part of the arbitration should be referred to mediation, conciliation, etc? A mediator or conciliator has no 'power' of determination, and this sub-clause could only apply if they purported to make what amounted to an award and this was treated as being part of the arbitration. This is a complex point, since it is unclear whether such a purported award could ever be considered as an arbitration award that required to be challenged, as it would be unenforceable in any event and, as it would not be a lawful arbitration, the Act would have no application.

Care should also be taken where arbitration and mediation are mixed, in what is called arb/med or med/arb. Interestingly, the courts in Hong Kong, in *Gao Haiyan v Keeneye Holdings Ltd* [2011] HKEC 514 refused to enforce an arbitration award where some (but not all) of the tribunal had tried to effect a settlement outside the arbitration itself. This is understood to be fairly common practice in China, and the court did not condemn the whole concept of arb/med, but ruled that the process in this case was inappropriate and was lacking in transparency and independence. In other jurisdictions, arb/med and med/arb are commonplace: for example, Switzerland and Singapore.

(e) Uncertainty or ambiguity as to the award's effects

Where the award is uncertain or ambiguous it is worth remembering that if default rule 58(2)(b) is in force, the tribunal has power to correct the terms of the award, and failure to use this process, where it has not been disapplied, will remove the right to appeal (see rule 71(2)). Parties may also wish to invite the arbitrator to give them sight of a draft award prior to issue of the final award.

Where there is uncertainty or ambiguity as to the award's effect (rule 68(2)(e)), again there are no Scottish authorities, but in the English case of *General Feeds Inc v Slobodna Plovidba Yugoslavia* [1999] 1 Lloyd's Rep 688 at 695 the court indicated that it would afford awards with the most favourable construction.

If, despite all of these techniques, an award is issued which is considered to be uncertain or ambiguous, the burden of demonstrating this must lie with the appellant. The test to apply would appear to be whether the award is incapable of interpretation or is open to more than one interpretation, not that the party or the court might have expressed matters more elegantly. It is also suggested that the inability to interpret has to be real, and that the court should be hesitant to intervene on the basis of fanciful alternative interpretations of awards which are, in reality, perfectly clear.

(f) Contrary to public policy; obtained by fraud or in a way contrary to public policy

Where the award was said to be contrary to public policy or obtained by fraud or in a way which is contrary to public policy (rule 68(2)(f)(i) and (ii)) consideration may be given to: *Elektrim SA v Vivendi Universal SA* [2007] EWHC 11 (Comm), [2007] 1 Lloyd's Rep 693 at para [79]; *Profilati Italia SrL v Painewebber Inc* [2001] EWHC 24 (Comm), [2001] 1 Lloyd's Rep 715 at para [17]; and *Celtic Bioenergy Ltd v Knowles Ltd* [2017] EWHC 472 (TCC), [2018] 1 All ER (Comm) 608. Although there are areas of commonality in Scotland and England on the topic of fraud, they are not identical, so consideration of English cases involving allegations of fraud should be treated with caution. Having said that, the leading case in Scotland, *Boyd & Forrest v Glasgow & South Western Railway Co (No 1)* 1912 SC (HL) 93, followed the leading English decision in *Derry v Peek* (1889) 14 App Cas 337. (See also *Soleimany v Soleimany* [1998] EWCA Civ 285.)

Awards obtained by fraud are always going to be capable of challenge, whether under the Act or the principles of Scots common law. Different jurisdictions do not have identical views on what constitutes fraud, or its effects, or how it must be proved. As an example, the comprehensive updating of fraud law in England and Wales and Northern Ireland as per the Fraud Act 2006 does not apply to Scotland.

There appear to be two distinct grounds related to public policy, namely that the award itself is contrary to such policy, or that the way the award was obtained is offensive to such policy. An example of the latter might be the obtaining of an award by bribery, although this would also seem to breach a raft of other provisions within the Act, and wider legislation.

The 'public policy' applicable in this case is presumably that of Scotland, on the basis that the seat is Scottish. While no immediate issues present themselves as examples, it is fair to say that this is Scottish legislation, and if any issue of public policy arose where the position in Scotland differed from that of the rest of the UK, it would seem that the former's public policy would prevail, save in cases where the area of public policy has not been devolved.

Rule 68 does not specify what is meant by 'public policy', and this is likely to vary from year to year as the courts consider how public policy develops. An example from English law, which has already been cited, is *Soleimany v Soleimany* [1998] EWCA Civ 285 where the courts refused enforcement on the basis that the award related to an agreement, the purpose of which was to breach the law of Iran. For an example from another jurisdiction, see Swiss Supreme Court's decision 4A_490/2009, of 13 April 2010, in *Club Atlético de Madrid SAD v Sport Lisboa E Benfica – Futebol SAD and Fédération Internationale de Football Association (FIFA)* where an attempt to circumvent a court decision by a second arbitration was suppressed on public policy grounds. It is instructive that this is believed to be the first time public policy has been used successfully as an argument in an arbitration dispute in the Swiss courts. This does emphasise that it is unlikely to be a common issue.

(g) Arbitrator not being impartial and independent

These are mandatory obligations on any arbitrator under the Act, and indeed one of the founding principles in s 1 is that the object of arbitration is to resolve disputes impartially. It is thus unsurprising that, if these standards are not met, the award is open to challenge. The issues of impartiality and independence have already been addressed in relation to s 24, but we would merely comment that the rule uses 'and' rather than 'and/or' which might give rise to the argument that both failures have to apply. This could be problematic where, for example, an arbitrator acts wholly independently of the parties, but favours one of them. However, rule 77 makes it clear that lack of impartiality is itself a badge of lack of independence and, thus, the two words may have become virtually synonymous for this purpose in many cases. In all events, we consider that rule 68(2)(a)(ii) would apply, since the arbitration would be conducted outwith the terms of the Rules, and in particular rule 24(1)(a).

Where an arbitrator has not been impartial or independent (rule 68(2) (g)), again there are numerous examples in the English cases: *Groundshire v VHE Construction* [2001] BLR 395 at paras [34]–[35]; *ASM Shipping Ltd of India v TTMI Ltd* [2006] 1 Lloyd's Rep 401 at para [39]; *Oldham v QBE Insurance (Europe) Ltd* [2018] 1 All ER (Comm) 1044.

(h) Arbitrator not having treated the parties fairly

This is consistent with the founding principle in s 1 of 'fairly resolving' disputes and the general duty imposed on the tribunal by mandatory rule 24.

Where an arbitrator has not treated parties fairly (rule 68(2)(h)): *Bandwidth Shipping Corp v Intaari* [2008] 1 Lloyd's Rep 141 per Waller LJ at para [38], who observed that a party alleging unfairness of this ground faces a 'high hurdle'.

In other fields, where issues of fairness arise, then the appropriate remedy is often judicial review. However, since judicial review is specifically excluded by the Act (s 13(2)), this sub-clause would seem to bring in this type of remedy by another route. It does, however, only apply to appealing an award.

The Act does not define 'fairness', which is understandable, but means that this will also be an area where judicial interpretation will be required to assist the parties. In this context, decisions in judicial review proceedings as discussed before may be of some assistance particularly in respect of issues of 'fairness' and 'bias'.

(i) Arbitrator having been incapable of acting as such (or there being justifiable doubts about arbitrator's ability to so act)

While mandatory rule 4(b) states that an individual is ineligible to act as an arbitrator if he is an incapable adult under the Adults with Incapacity (Scotland) Act 2000 s 1(6), this does not seem to be the total definition of 'incapable' for this purpose, and the word is used again in rule 12, but without a further definition. For example, rule 4(a) renders anyone under the age of 16 'ineligible' to act as an arbitrator, but does not say they are 'incapable' of so doing. In practice, if someone under 16 were appointed, any award would fall to be challenged under rule 68(2)(a), and the distinction here may be that an arbitrator cannot be validly appointed and then become too young later, but can be validly appointed and later lose capacity for reasons of physical or mental health.

It does not appear that the word 'incapable' (which is not defined in the 2010 Act) relates to the competence of an arbitrator. There will be other ways to challenge an award that is itself incompetent, or to remove an incompetent arbitrator during the arbitration, but this is not the relevant provision for dealing with this problem.

The words in brackets in this sub-clause make it clear that it is not necessary to prove incapability, the obligation being merely to raise 'justifiable doubts'. We would add that the word 'ability' in this sub-clause relates to the ability to act as an arbitrator in the arbitration, and not, as already explained, to the general competence of the arbitrator.

(j) Arbitrator not having a qualification which the parties agreed before appointment that the arbitrator must have

This appears to be a simple and non-controversial provision, and an example is given above in relation to appointment of QCs. The matter was, however, thrown into some doubt by the decision of the English Court of Appeal in *Jivraj v Hashwani*, but the Supreme Court ruling reversing that decision ([2011] UKSC 40) has removed the risk that the appointment of arbitrators is subject to employment and associated equality laws.

(k) Any other irregularity in the conduct of the arbitration or in the award, which is admitted by the tribunal or any AAR or third party given powers in relation to the arbitration

Sub-clause (k) refers to 'any other irregularity', which would seem to imply an irregularity that is *not* included in (a)–(j). This, therefore, seems to be the one place where the list of kinds of irregularity is open-ended, but only so long as it is admitted by one of the parties named in the sub-clause. The wording mirrors s 68(2)(i) of the 1996 Act. If our view is correct, then this must be an irregularity not included in (a)–(j), albeit the other provisions will cover most real-life examples. This does provide an avenue open to a party, to challenge the award under this rule, where the circumstances are highly unusual and may not have been envisaged by the drafters.

As drafted, it would seem that an admission of an irregularity which is already listed is not caught by this sub-clause. This has some basis, since the admission would merely be conclusive evidence to support an appeal under (a)–(j) as the case may be. However, it does mean that any admission that states that there has been an irregularity, however trivial, creates a 'serious irregularity' under the rule, but this could only be where the irregularity in question is not one of those listed in the preceding paragraphs and was indeed serious.

Further, the question arises as to when the admission has to be made. The provisions of rule 68(2)(k)(i) allow the tribunal to make an admission. However, once the award has been made (and rule 68 only applies to appealing an award), if that award is final, the tribunal is *functus officio*, and no longer exists for the purpose of making an admission. If the admission was made before the final award, it is difficult to see why the tribunal would not correct the irregularity at that stage or, if it could not or would not, why a party would refrain from taking action. Where the irregularity is capable of remedy, a prompt remedy may prevent a challenge under rule 68(2)(k) after an award.

The provisions of rule 68(2)(k)(ii) allow admissions to be made by an AAR or another party to whom the parties give powers in relation to the arbitration. This would cover appointing bodies who are not on the AAR list (and therefore approved under s 24) but, while it is wider than this, it is difficult to see what it would cover in practice. It is also difficult to see what admission could be made by an AAR or such other party that would allow an award to be challenged, particularly bearing in mind that rule 68 does not deal with want of jurisdiction (see rule 67).

It is considered that this is not a sub-clause which is likely to be used frequently, and even its equivalent in England does not appear to have generated very much case law.

Outer House – options

The Outer House may decide to confirm the award, order the tribunal to reconsider the award, or a part thereof, or set aside the award or part thereof. The issues of confirmation and setting aside have already been addressed, for example in relation to rule 67(2), and the question of reconsideration is addressed below in relation to rule 69 appeals and the procedures under rule 70(8). In relation to remitting to the tribunal where a challenge has been successful, see *Secretary of State for the Home Department v Raytheon Systems Ltd* [2015] EWHC 311 (TCC) above.

Arbitrators' expenses

The Outer House is given power, in any case where it does not merely confirm an award, to sanction the arbitrator or arbitrators by making any order it thinks fit as to entitlement to, or repayment of, fees and expenses, but only where the grounds for 'serious irregularity' are those set out in rule 68(4). These are, in effect, the grounds under rule 68(2)(a), (g) or (h). Interestingly, an admission by the arbitrator of irregularity under rule 68(2) (k), where the irregularity was not one of those set out in the preceding sub-paragraphs of rule 68(2) would appear not to allow sanction, however serious the irregularity.

It would seem consistent with principles of natural justice that the arbitrator be given the opportunity to appear or be represented before any final order is made under this rule.

Further appeal

There is the possibility of an appeal to the Inner House, but only with the leave of the Outer House. In the event that such leave is granted (in respect of which the decision of the Outer House is final), the decision of the Inner House on such appeal is final. The basis for granting leave is the same as in rule 67 (important point of principle or practice, or another compelling reason).

For any party considering an application under rule 68, they must do so within 28 days of the award (rule 71). With regard to the merits, they must (i) consider that the irregularity complained of comes within the list of examples given in the rule; (ii) consider whether there is a strong case to prove substantial injustice; and (iii) have evidence available to support these arguments. Any application is made to the Outer House under RCS 100.7(2)(b).

Challenging an award: legal error

Unlike rule 67 and 68 challenges, a challenge under rule 69 is a default rule. The 2010 Act repeals the Administration of Justice (Scotland) Act 1972 s 3 (the so-called 'stated case' procedure) and replaces it with a default rule for appeals for error on a point of Scots law.

This rule only allows appeals for errors under Scots law. If the arbitration, although seated in Scotland, is to be conducted under another law, then this rule appears to be intended to have no application, and no possible appeal will lie. While this is not specifically stated, it is suggested that it is implicit that, in such a case, a party cannot complain about the award being in error under Scots law, even if it would also be an error under the law of the arbitration. On a similar point, if the arbitration is conducted under a law other than the law of Scotland, but the parties fail to produce adequate evidence as to that law, the tribunal may apply Scots law on the presumption that it is the same as the law selected. This does not, however, seem to us to mean that Scots law itself is being applied. It is still an arbitration under the law agreed, but it has been assumed that such law is identical to the law of Scotland. This is not, therefore, a mistake under Scots law capable of being appealed under this rule. For guidance, see *Arbitration Application No 3 of 2011* [2011] CSOH 164; 2012 SLT 150.

The cross-reference to rule 51(2)(c) is sensible from a practical point of view, since, without reasons, the court's position would be nearly impossible without reverting to the stated case procedure which the 2010 Act was intended to bring to an end.

It will, clearly, be a matter for the parties whether they wish the arbitration to be final and binding on legal issues, in which case this rule should be disapplied as it is a default rule.

Rare as they are, examples of successful legal error appeals can be found in *Manchester Associated Mills Ltd v Mitchells & Butler Retail Ltd* [2013] CSOH 2; 2013 SCLR 440 per Lord Malcolm; *Millchris Developments Ltd v Waters* [2020] 4 WLUK 45; and *Nobiskrug Gmbh v Valla Yachts Ltd* [2019] EWHC 1219 (Comm).

Legal error appeals: procedure etc

The procedure should discourage frivolous or timewasting attempts at appealing to the Outer House under the rules. The consent of both parties is needed, or the leave of the Outer House (rule 70(2)). The circumstances in which the winning party consents to an appeal on a point of law are fairly difficult to envisage, and it is suggested that most cases will require an application for leave, allowing the court to set clear detailed guidelines as to when such appeals will be allowed, within the terms of rule 70(3). A detailed explanation of procedure has been usefully given by Lord Glennie in the opinion section in *Arbitration Application No 3 of 2011* [2011] CSOH 164; 2012 SLT 150.

Rule 70(3) itself makes it clear that appeals are only likely to be approved where the decision will substantially affect a party's rights (rule 70(3)(a)); it was within the matters the tribunal was asked to decide (rule 70(3)(b)); and it was obviously wrong, based on the findings of fact made by the tribunal (rule 70(3)(c)(i)). The last point (but not the others) can be overcome on the basis that the decision was on a matter of general importance, although it still needs to be subject to 'serious doubt' as to its correctness (rule 70(3)(c)(ii)).

None of these tests seems likely to be particularly easy to overcome, as with the identical 'obviously wrong' test in English law. In *Draco of Doune Wind Farm (Scotland) Ltd v Alfred McAlpine Business Services Ltd* [2008] EWHC 426 (TCC); [2008] 2 All ER (Comm) 493 the court determined that it was not enough that a part of the arbitrator's reasoning in his decision was wrong, or that conceivably another tribunal might respectably have reached the opposite conclusion (Akenhead J at para [28]).

It is worth pointing out that rule 70(3)(c)(i) means that, so long as the law is applied correctly to the facts as determined by the tribunal, a challenge will be impossible, even if the determination of the facts is challenged. This is consistent with the general rule in court proceedings that the determination of fact by the court of first instance is generally final.

The procedural requirements for an application for leave are set out in rule 70(4) and (5). Rule 70(4) requires the application to identify the point of law concerned, and why the applicant considers leave should be granted.

The fairly limited requirements suggest that the Outer House is unlikely to be looking for voluminous submissions, not least since the preceding paragraphs of this rule make it clear that leave is only likely to be granted in cases where the position is reasonably obvious. The provisions of rule 70(5) make it clear that a hearing is not normally required, although the wording is slightly strange, stating that, in effect, proceeding without a hearing is mandatory, unless the Outer House decides it is not. Accordingly, the decision is actually discretionary, but the use of 'mandatory' will likely give the judge pause for thought and the default position is that no hearing is required. The Outer House's determination is final (rule 70(6)) and any leave granted expires seven days after it is granted (rule 70(7)), although the rule makes it clear that an appeal remains possible after that date with the consent of the parties under rule 70(2)(a). It has to be said that, given the difficult hurdles to cross, proceeding to the Outer House on the basis of party consent when leave has been refused looks to require an heroic level of confidence, and it is difficult to see why a party that refused consent prior to the application for leave is likely to change its position after the applicant has been refused leave.

Once any appeal is determined, the outcomes are set out in rule 70(8) as (a) confirmation of the award (in effect refusing the appeal); (b) ordering the tribunal to reconsider all or part of the award; or (c) setting aside all or part of the award. The last option applies only where the court considers that reconsideration under rule 70(8)(b) is inappropriate. It is presumed that this last option could apply where, for example, the whole issue had been rendered moot by some further development outside the appeal, or where the issues remaining in dispute did not justify the costs of reconsideration. (This might particularly apply where only a small part of the award required reconsideration).

Strangely, while rule 70(8)(b) and (c) specifically address the possibility of only part of an award being set aside or sent for reconsideration, rule 70(8) (a) only allows confirmation of the whole award. However, as mentioned above, we consider that it is implicit that, if only part of the award is sent for reconsideration or set aside, the Outer House has power to confirm the balance of the award.

The effect of remission must effectively reconstitute the tribunal, which might otherwise be considered *functus officio*. The process for reconsideration by the tribunal is covered by rule 72.

If the decision of the Outer House does not resolve the matter, there remains the possibility of an appeal to the Inner House (rule 70(9)). This can only take place with the leave of the Outer House (the ability or willingness of the parties themselves to consent, does not apply at this level). Such leave will only be given in respect of an important point of principle or practice or for 'another compelling reason' (rule 70(10)). The decision of the Outer House on whether to grant leave is final (rule 70(11)), as is any decision of the Inner House on the appeal (rule 70(12)). Accordingly, no appeal to the

UK Supreme Court is possible. This provides the interesting possibility of different lines of authority developing on broadly similar wording in the 1996 and 2010 Acts, but we consider that the courts are likely to treat one another's decisions as highly persuasive and, in any event, that there is nothing inherently wrong in Scotland's distinct laws developing in line with the thinking within the country.

Rule 70 is a mandatory rule, so long as rule 69 has not been disapplied (in which case no appeal on a point of law is possible), and it is not open to the parties to agree different appeal processes. However, an interesting issue is what happens if rule 69 is disapplied, but the parties substitute a bespoke right of appeal on a point of law, but not as a replacement rule 69. In such a case, rule 69 would not apply, and nor would rule 70 (see rule 70(1)). It is our view that it must be the case that the process in rule 70 would still have to be followed, since to do otherwise would allow the parties to evade the mandatory nature of rule 70 and for the parties to write rules for the Outer and Inner Houses to follow, which cannot be correct. We therefore think that rule 70(1) should be read to include not only the application of the precise wording of rule 69, but also any equivalent amendment or restatement of such rule agreed by the parties.

Challenging an award: supplementary

The mandatory nature of rule 71 is applicable to appeals on a point of law only if default rule 69 has not been disapplied (rule 71(1)(c)). Similar comments apply as in relation to rule 70(1) above, where rule 69 has been disapplied, but theoretically replaced by a bespoke provision.

The rule provides a number of detailed procedural provisions, many of which are self-explanatory, and which, taken together, are intended to ensure any appeal process is disposed of promptly, so that the overall intent of the Act to assist in the rapid resolution of disputes is not defeated at the last hurdle, and to deter frivolous applications.

Rule 71(2) makes it clear that any arbitral appeal processes, whether under the Rules (particularly correction under rule 58) or, presumably, any institutional rules and/or bespoke rules agreed by the parties, have to have been exhausted.

The rules clarify that it is not possible to appeal against a provisional award (rule 71(3)).

Time limits under rule 71(4) mean that there is a 28-day limit for commencing appeals, running from the latest of (a) the date of the award in question, (b) the date on which the tribunal decides whether or not to correct the award under rule 58 (interestingly, not the date of actual correction, if different), and (c) the date of the notification to the applicant of any other appeal or review process. The final paragraph of rule 71(4) merely states that a legal error appeal is to be treated as having been made for the purposes of this rule if an application for leave is made. This seems to ignore the possibility of such an appeal being made on the basis of the consent of the parties under rule 70(2)(a), in which case no such application for leave would be required, but, in such a case, the appeal by consent must, presumably, be presented within the time limits in rule 71(4)(a)–(c). In the very limited range of appeals to the Inner House, rule 71(5) provides an equivalent 28-day time limit to that in rule 71(4), and also provides that any leave granted expires after seven days in line with rule 70(7).

In *Terna Bahrain Holding Co WLL v Al Shamsi* [2012] EWHC 3283 (Comm) an application to extend time was made almost 17 weeks after expiry of the 28-day period provided by the Arbitration Act 1996 s 70(3) was refused. The court held that this was a very substantial delay in the context of the statutory period. The 'overwhelming inference from the evidence' was that a deliberate tactical decision was taken by R to challenge the award in Sharjah rather than in England and that that deliberate choice was maintained until it became apparent that the English proceedings initiated by Terna to enforce the award would be irresistible unless an application was made in England. It was a case of deliberate and tactical delay.

Once the time limit for any appeals has passed, the award will be enforceable. In the circumstances, best practice requires a party to make all applications within the time limits set out in the rules.

Since the rules specifically deal with variations of time limits under rules 43 and 44, and these do not apply to appeals, it is difficult to see that the intention of Parliament was to allow the time limits to be extended.

Some hope may be available as shown in *Haven Insurance Co Ltd v EUI Ltd (t/a Elephant Insurance)* [2018] EWHC 143 (Comm): a motor insurer had misunderstood the requirements under the Motor Insurers' Bureau's articles of association as to when time began to run for notifying the MIB of its intention to appeal against a decision and the appeal was out of time. Despite this the court took the view that it was 'just' to extend time where the MIB itself had been under a misapprehension as to when time began to run. The court held that it could extend time under s 12 it if would be 'just to do so and if the circumstances were outside the reasonable contemplation of the parties when they had agreed to the provision in question'.

The appellant has to give notice of appeal both to the other party (which is to be expected) but, it should be noted, also to the tribunal (rule 71(6)). It should also be noted that rule 71(7) specifically states that an arbitration may proceed notwithstanding the fact that a part award is being appealed. The operative word is 'may', and it is suggested that a tribunal could be reluctant to proceed where the appeal is an attack on its jurisdiction, or alleges a serious irregularity in the process.

The provision of rule 71(8) is interesting, in that it allows the Outer or Inner House, as the case may be, to require the tribunal to provide reasons for the award, and (in rule 71(8)(b)) to provide for any additional expenses, if it thinks fit. This provides a slight concern. If the parties have disapplied default rule 51(2)(c), this means that the tribunal is not required to provide reasons. While the disapplication of rule 51(2)(c) effectively precludes an appeal on a point of law under rule 69 (see rule 69(2)), rule 71 is not, unlike rule 70, applicable only to such appeals. This therefore seems to allow the court to override the decision of the parties, and the basis on which the tribunal agreed to conduct the arbitration. While it may be that rule 71(8) will mainly apply to legal error appeals in practice, we foresee problems if, for example, a tribunal is made up of arbitrators from overseas, who have delivered their award on the basis that no reasons were required, and are then faced with something akin to a stated case approach requiring retrospective reasons. In such a case, it is not clear what the court would, or could, do in the event of refusal, since the persons constituting the tribunal could be beyond its jurisdiction.

Note also that the court retains the power to 'make any other order' regarding additional expenses arising from the order. Feasibly, that could include the additional expenses incurred by a tribunal in stating its reasons or providing the 'sufficient detail' if the original requirement was for an award 'without reasons'. There is a potential problem where all or part of an award is set aside, and the arbitration agreement provides, as is often the case, that no legal proceedings are permitted, that a party might be left without a remedy where the tribunal was *functus officio*. This is resolved by rule 71(9), which allows the Outer or Inner House, as the case may be, to declare the provision prohibiting other legal action void.

The practical rules continue with rule 71(10), which allows for a security for expenses order against the appellant (but not any other party) in respect of appeals, or applications for leave to appeal, to the Outer House, or any further appeal to the Inner House. If any order is not complied with, the application or appeal may be dismissed (rule 71(10)(b)). This provision is, presumably, intended to ensure that parties presenting applications, or appeals where no leave is needed, without obvious merit, can be deterred, but it may be difficult to justify such security where leave to appeal has been granted on the limited grounds set out in the rules. Such security cannot be ordered merely on the grounds that the appellant (whether a natural person or a company) is from outside the UK (rule 71(11)).

As a further development of this point, the court may require the bringing into court or otherwise securing of the amount in dispute, and again the application or appeal can be dismissed if the appellant fails to comply with the order (rule 71(12)). Interestingly, the requirement to pay money into court or provide security under rule 71(12)(a) is not stated to be limited to the appellant and, theoretically, if the respondent was ordered to bring the subject-matter into court and failed to comply, the appellant's appeal or application could be dismissed under rule 71(12)(b). It is, however, assumed that this latter provision should be read as only applying to situations where it is the appellant who is in breach. Similar provisions exist in England and Wales at s 70(7) of the 1996 Act: *Erdenet Mining Corpn LLC v ICBC Standard Bank plc* [2017] EWHC 1090 (Comm). The authorities identify an approach which should apply whether or not the case involved commercial funding: *Progas Energy Ltd v Pakistan* [2018] EWHC 209 (Comm).

While it is understood that rule 71(13) (providing any appeal from the Outer House to the Inner House under rule 71 requires the leave of the Outer House) is necessary, it is suggested that the whole intent of the legislation does not appear to encourage appeals to the Inner House on procedural points relating to appeals against arbitration awards. It is hoped that a robust line will be taken and any attempt to drag out proceedings on technical grounds prevented. Having agreed to go to arbitration, if the award is against you, the court would expect you to honour this, unless compelling reasons exist to appeal. This view appears to be supported by rule 71(15), which limits the granting of such leave to situations where there is (a) an important point of principle or practice, or (b) another compelling reason. This repeats earlier language. In the event that any such applications for leave are made, rule 71(14) mirrors earlier provisions requiring the application to be made within 28 days, and any leave to be utilised within seven days after being granted. The Outer House's decision on leave is final (rule 71(16)), as is any appeal decision by the Inner House (rule 71(17)).

Reconsideration by tribunal

Rule 72 appears to be a practical and straightforward provision specifying the time within which the tribunal must reconsider any award, or part of an award, remitted to it by the court. The default period is three months, although the court can order a different date, at its discretion.

It is, however, suggested that there could be a practical issue, in that the tribunal may have other commitments by this stage, particularly where senior, perhaps international, figures are involved. Difficulties may arise, if members resident outside the jurisdiction of the court refuse to comply.

It is also assumed that the Outer or Inner House (as the case may be) will ensure that it provides guidance to the tribunal to assist in the reconsideration, and prevent the risk of a further round of appeals once the reconsidered award is issued.

Interestingly, there is no provision for dealing with the expenses of such a reconsideration, as there is in rule 71(8)(b) in relation to provision of reasons. Presumably it was felt that, where this procedure applied, it was implicit that the tribunal had made a mess of things, but this could be harsh if, for example, a three-person panel had issued a defective award on a 2–1 majority, and the minority member is supported by the court. It is suggested that, in such a case, the court might utilise more general powers on expenses to ensure the innocent minority was not prejudiced.

The tribunal has to be given notice of any appeal under rule 71(6), and it is suggested that the court could ask for the thoughts of the tribunal members, in advance, even if they do not seek to appear.

RECOGNITION AND ENFORCEMENT OF AWARDS IN SCOTLAND

The majority of awards are honoured by the side against whom the award was made (89 per cent according to research carried out by the Queen Mary University of London, School of International Arbitration in 2015; Blackaby and Partasides, with Redfern and Hunter, *International Arbitration* (6th edn) p 606, footnote 3). For the remainder, the successful party will be forced to consider recognition and enforcement of the award in the country where the losing side's assets are held. Many international companies, particularly oil and gas, banking and construction, have a place of business in Scotland and in those circumstances recognition and enforcement may be necessary in Scotland.

Recognition and Enforcement are distinct processes. Blackaby and Partasides, with Redfern and Hunter, *International Arbitration* (6th edn) para 11.23 use an analogy of a shield and a sword. Recognition of an award is a useful mechanism to defend proceedings which have been raised elsewhere, such as to support a *res judicata* defence. However, enforcement of the award means applying legal sanctions, as are available in the jurisdiction, to compel the party, against whom the award was made, to comply with the order(s).

For the purposes of recognition and enforcement in Scotland, the power to enforce an award is set out in s 12 of the Act, which states at s 12(1): 'The court may, on an application by any party, order that a tribunal's award may be enforced as if it were an extract registered decree bearing a warrant for execution granted by the court.'

When considering enforcement in Scotland, it matters not whether the award was seated in Scotland (s 11). The essential issue is whether or not the state is a signatory of the New York Convention. For 'Convention' awards, the applicable sections are ss 18 to 22 of the 2010 Act. Section 18(1) of the 2010 Act draws a distinction between arbitral awards made in connection with a written arbitration agreement in the territory of a state (outwith the UK) that is a signatory to the New York Convention and those that are not.

If the award is a Convention award, the court will recognise that as binding on the persons as between whom it was made and it may be relied on by those persons in any legal proceedings in Scotland (s 19(1)). The court may order that a Convention award may be enforced as if it were an extract registered decree bearing a warrant for execution granted by the court (s 19(2)).

For those awards not falling within the definition of Convention awards, the party must rely on s 12 of the 2010 Act for recognition and enforcement. This applies whether the award was seated in Scotland or abroad and also allows the party to rely on common law. The case of *Politakis v Spencely* [2017] ScotSAC Civ 19, is an unedifying example of arbitral procedure prior to the 2010 Act and an award which was challenged on the grounds of bad faith.

Once recognition and enforcement are granted, the award is akin to a court order and the usual diligence may be exercised.

The list of NYC signatories is available online at: http://www.newyork convention.org/countries and the list as at date of publication is found in Appendix 3.

When embarking on recognition and enforcement proceedings in the Court of Session in Scotland, they should be by petition and the form can be found in the Rules of the Court of Session 1994, as amended in Form 14.4.

Where the award is from outwith Scotland, the party must also produce the following to the court: a translation (rule 62.3); a certificate of currency conversion (rule 62.2) as per Form 62.2. The party must also produce an affidavit stating: (i) the full name, title, trade or business and the usual or last known place of residence or, where appropriate, of the business of the petitioner or noter and the party against whom the Convention award was made; (ii) the amount of the Convention award which is unsatisfied; and (iii) that the Convention award has become binding on the parties and has not been set aside or suspended by a court of the country which, or under the law of which, the award was made (rule 62.57(2)(d)).

Section 21 of the 2010 Act also requires the party to lodge a duly authenticated original award (or a duly certified copy of it), and the original arbitration agreement (or a duly certified copy of it); and a translation of any award or agreement (certified by an official or sworn translator or by a diplomatic or consular agent).

Rules of Court

Albeit it remains possible in Scotland for parties to agree that the award can be registered and enforced at common law, by registering in the Books of Council and Session (*Baillie v Pollock* (1829) 7 S 619) it is much more likely that in practice, where dealing with a Convention award, the procedure set out in the Rules of the Court of Session 1994, as amended, rule 100 will be used; alongside rule 62.

The procedure is very flexible. The Rules are subject to the provisions of the Scottish Arbitration Rules, but provide that the procedure in any cause shall be 'as the judge shall determine' (rule 100.3). Any application under the 2010 Act is by petition (rule 100.5(1)); unless proceedings are extant, when any application is by note in process (rule 100.5(2)) and the court has the power to make 'such order as is appropriate in the circumstances' (rule 100.5(3) and rule 100.5(5)).

For those awards not falling within the definition of Convention awards, the party must rely on s 12 for recognition and enforcement and the Rule of the Court of Session 100.10 applies and the requirements are minimal.

Grounds for refusal of recognition and enforcement

Recognition and enforcement of an award will not be ordered if the court is satisfied that the award is the subject of an appeal under Part 8 of the Scottish Arbitration Rules; an arbitral process of appeal or review; or the process of correction under rule 58 of the Scottish Arbitration Rules, which has not been finally determined (s 12(2)).

The court will make no order if satisfied that the tribunal did not have jurisdiction, or the court may restrict the extent of the order if satisfied that the tribunal did not have jurisdiction to make a part of the award (s 12(3)).

Where the award was seated in Scotland and the Scottish Arbitration Rules applied, there is an important exception to the above rule. Even if the tribunal did not have jurisdiction to make the award (or part of the award) the court may still make the order for recognition and enforcement, if the party has lost the right to raise that objection by virtue of rule 76. If that situation arises, some assistance may be gleaned from the comments of Lord Collins in the Supreme Court in *Dallah Real Estate v Government of Pakistan* [2010] UKSC 46 at para [98].

Otherwise, an application for recognition and enforcement of a Convention award, seated in Scotland or outwith Scotland, can be implemented in the Court of Session by following the Rules set out on Enforcement of Arbitral Awards under the New York Convention on the Recognition and Enforcement of Foreign Arbitral Awards in rules 62.56 to 62.60. These Rules will apply automatically to the majority of awards given the definition of a Convention award (s 18(1)).

Recognition and enforcement of a Convention award may be refused under the 2010 Act in certain circumstances only (s 20(1)) and these mirror those found under the New York Convention 1958.

In particular, it may be refused if: the person against whom it is invoked proves that a party was under some incapacity under the applicable law (s 20(2)(a)); the arbitration agreement was invalid under the law which the parties agree should govern it (or, failing any indication of that law, under the law of the country where the award was made) (s 20(2)(b)); the person (i) was not given proper notice of the arbitral process or of the appointment of the tribunal, or (ii) was otherwise unable to present their case (s 20(2)(c) (i) and (ii)); the tribunal was constituted, or the arbitration was conducted, otherwise than in accordance with (i) the agreement of the parties, or (ii) failing such agreement, the law of the country where the arbitration took place (s 20(2)(d)).

An interesting example can be found in *ST Group Co Ltd and others v Sanum Investments Ltd and another appeal* [2019] SGCA 65. The Singapore Court of Appeal held that once an arbitration is incorrectly seated (ie not chosen by the parties), any subsequent award would not be recognised and enforced by the court. In this case, after Sanum commenced arbitration proceedings under SIAC rules, the claimants formally objected to the arbitration and did not participate further. The Singapore Court of Appeal ruled in favour of the claimants and held Macau had been chosen as the arbitral seat and the SIAC arbitration was incorrectly seated. The objection by the claimants and 'non-participation' had not waived the use of the wrong seat and accordingly the award could not be enforced.

There is no Scottish authority on the issue of incapacity under s 20(2)(a) but Professor Davidson has commented (F Davidson, *Arbitration* (2nd edn) at para 20.25):

> … cases … suggest that difficult issues may arise in relation to corporate enti-ties and public bodies, the capacity of which might be regarded as determined by the law of the state in which they were incorporated or created. Thus there have been cases where an award has been refused enforcement because the act of entering into the agreement was ultra vires a corporate party,[146] or because such a party was not properly incorporated.[147] A number of awards have also been denied enforcement on this ground on the basis that the individual seek-ing to bind the corporation to the arbitration agreement lacked the power or authority to do so.[148] It is suggested that this is a matter affecting the validity of the arbitration agreement or the jurisdiction of the tribunal and not an issue of capacity at all, and this is the view of the Cour de Cassation in *Tresor Public v Galakis* 1966 Revue de l'Arbitrage 99.

It is essential that any person, even where they refuse to engage with the arbitral proceedings or do not attend, should in any event have proper notice throughout the process or the party seeking recognition and enforcement may find that the order is refused on the basis of s 20(2)(c). Where the court is considering whether the person was able to present their case, the party seeking the order may wish to put before the court issues regarding what the party resisting did or did not do at the arbitration, with a view to arguing personal bar.

Under s 20(2)(d) the court must first consider the agreement of the par-ties and, if no answer can be found, to consider the law where the arbitra-tion took place. This could give rise to an interesting dilemma, where the agreement conflicts with mandatory rules of the seat of the arbitration. Following the mandatory rules of the seat would appear to be a pragmatic solution to the problem given the bias towards enforcement as demon-strated in *RBRG Trading (UK) Ltd v Sinocore International Co Ltd* [2018] EWCA Civ 838.

Recognition or enforcement of a Convention award may also be refused if the person against whom it is invoked proves that the award: deals with a dispute not contemplated by or not falling within the submission to arbi-tration (s 20(3)(a)); contains decisions on matters beyond the scope of that submission (s 20(3)(b)); is not yet binding on the person (s 20(3)(c)); or has been set aside or suspended by a competent authority (s 20(3)(d)).

These mirror Article V(1) and (2) of the New York Convention 1958. In regard to s 20(3)(a), Lord Steyn in the House of Lords confirmed that it should be 'construed narrowly' in *Lesotho Highlands Development Authority v Impregilo*

SpA [2005] UKHL 43, [2006] 1 AC 221. Section 20(3)(d) should also be read alongside s 20(7) of the 2010 Act, which defines 'competent authority'.

Section 20(4) provides that recognition or enforcement of a Convention award may also be refused if: (a) the award relates to a matter which is not capable of being settled by arbitration; or (b) to do so would be contrary to public policy. Issues of arbitrability and public policy are normally judged by the place of enforcement, albeit this is not spelled out in the legislation. Certainly the English courts have adopted such an approach (*Soleimany v Soleimany* [1998] EWCA Civ 285, [1998] 3 WLR 811 at 821G). This catch-all provision does not permit the court to simply take a different view, as was recently reinforced by the Court of Appeal in *RBRG Trading (UK) Ltd v Sinocore International Co Ltd* [2019] 1 All ER (Comm) 810 at para [26] per LJ Hamblen:

> There are sound justifications for taking a different approach to substantive claims and enforcement claims, reflecting the different role performed by the court in each circumstance … This is illustrated by the authorities referred to above and by the following comments of Waller LJ at [36] of his judgment in *Westacre Investments Inc v Jugoimport-SPDR Holding Co Ltd* [2000] QB 288 (CA):
>
> > '… It is legitimate to conclude that there is nothing which offends English public policy if an Arbitral Tribunal enforces a contract which does not offend the domestic public policy under either the proper law of the contract or its curial law, even if English domestic public policy might have taken a different view'.

Finally, a Convention award containing decisions on matters not submitted to arbitration may be recognised or enforced to the extent that it contains decisions on matters which were so submitted, which are separable from decisions on matters not so submitted (s 20(5)).

Scottish authority is limited on s 20, but includes *Partners of Dallas McMillan, Petitioners* [2015] CSOH 136 per Lord Philip where the five partners sought reduction of an arbitral award and interdict and interdict *ad interim* against enforcement. The arbiter had found in favour of a former partner of the firm but the court found that the arbiter had acted *ultra vires* and contrary to natural justice in certain regards and her award to the former partner fell to be reduced.

MISCELLANEOUS (PART 9)

Immunity of tribunal etc
Rule 73, which is a mandatory rule, provides:

(1) Neither the tribunal nor any arbitrator is liable for anything done or omitted in the performance, or purported performance, of the tribunal's functions.

(2) The rule does not apply –
    (a) if the act or omission is shown to have been in bad faith, or
    (b) to any liability arising from an arbitrator's resignation (but see rule 16(1)(c)).
(3) That the rule applies to any clerk, agent, employee or other person assisting
    the tribunal to perform its functions as it applies to the tribunal.

An obvious way to compromise the tribunal would be to allege misconduct or negligence (or breach of contract) coupled with a threat to raise an action of damages in the court. Thus the unscrupulous claimant or respondent could derail the arbitration process leaving the arbitrators compromised by a pending action in the court. It would be a 'back-door' method of trying to get the decisions and awards of the tribunal reviewed or reopened. Such a course is prevented, in part, by giving the arbitrator and the tribunal limited immunity. It is mandatory and will apply in all cases. It will also apply to those who assist the arbitrator, namely any 'clerk, agent, employee or other person assisting'.

The rule follows the 1996 Act s 29, there being no liability for 'anything done or omitted' in the performance or purported performance of the tribunal's functions. Similar provisions appear in other jurisdictions (eg International Arbitration Act 1974 s 28 in Australia).

Further, if such immunity did not exist, it could be difficult to persuade individuals to act as arbitrators in high-value disputes, particularly with adversarial parties, if they risked personal ruin in the event of an actual or perceived error of judgment.

Finally, this provision is consistent with the immunity offered to others acting in a judicial or quasi-judicial capacity.

Limited immunity?

The immunity is limited because bad faith on the part of the tribunal will disapply the rule. This is consistent with general principles that a person should not be able to hide behind statutory or contractual immunities when they have acted dishonestly or otherwise in bad faith. Equally, subject to rule 16(1)(c) any liability arising from an arbitrator's resignation may also disapply the rule. 'Bad faith' is not defined. There have not been any decisions in respect of the 1996 Act s 29 that provide any guidance. There have been some earlier English cases under the common law, such as *Sutcliffe v Thackrah* [1974] AC 727 relating to construction contracts where it was held that an architect had to act in a 'fair and unbiased manner' in applying the contract. While not a case on arbitration, the analogy is clear, and genuine bias (as opposed to a party's perception of the same) could be argued as amounting to bad faith. It is suggested, however, that the courts would be likely to require that an arbitrator had acted in a way that was more than unwitting bias before depriving him of this statutory immunity. In *Arenson v Casson Beckman Rutley & Co* [1977] AC 405 it was held that a party acting as what might be thought of as a 'quasi-arbitrator', resolving a dispute but not formally appointed as arbitrator, still had immunity for his actions 'although not for fraud or collusion' (Lord Simon of Glaisdale considered that the 'essential prerequisite ... to claim immunity as an arbitrator is that, by the time the matter is submitted to him for decision, there should be a formulated dispute between at least two parties which the decision is required to resolve' (at 424). Note that the Scottish judges also expressed views on the immunity of the arbitrator. Lord Kilbrandon considered under the then common law, and the then applying Arbitration Acts that arbitrators did not have full immunity (at 431A–B and 432D) and Lord Fraser of Tullybelton considered that 'it may be that a person, even if formally appointed as an arbitrator, ought not in all cases to be accorded immunity' (at 442D).

In England, in the context of the tort of misfeasance in public office, or, as it is sometimes called, deliberate abuse of power, the term 'bad faith' has had a restricted meaning. Traditionally a moral element has been an essential ingredient. Lack of good faith connotes either (a) malice in the sense of personal spite or a desire to injure for improper reasons, or (b) knowing that one does not actually have the power to make the decision in question. It remains to be seen whether 'bad faith' under the Arbitration Act 1996 and Construction Acts will be interpreted more widely by the courts, but it is suggested the courts should be cautious about removing immunity, save in the most egregious cases. (See also the discussion under rule 75 in connection with *Jones v Kaney* [2011] UKSC 13.)

If the arbitrator has resigned, then he is not protected from any claims in breach of contract. Rule 16(1)(c) provides that where an arbitrator has resigned, the Outer House may on an application by any party or the arbitrator concerned make such order as it thinks fit about the arbitrator's liability in respect of acting as an arbitrator. That could encompass an order from the court finding that he was entitled to relief from liability together with an order regarding his entitlement to fees and expenses. The parties could, of course, agree to extend the immunity on a contractual basis where the resignation was consensual.

It remains the advice that an arbitrator considering resignation should either get the parties to agree that they should continue to enjoy immunity, or, if they do resign, consider applying to the court to grant them immunity, rather than exposing themself to potentially ruinous litigation.

Immunity of appointing arbitral institution

Rule 74 goes on to provide that an arbitral appointments referee, or other third party who the parties ask to appoint or nominate an arbitrator, is not liable –

(a) for anything done or omitted in the performance, or purported performance, of that function (unless the act or omission is shown to have been in bad faith), or

(b) for the acts or omissions of –
   (i)   any arbitrator whom it nominates or appoints, or
   (ii) the tribunal of which such an arbitrator forms part (or any clerk, agent or employee of that tribunal).
The rule applies to an arbitral appointments referee's, or other third party's, agents and employees as it applies to the referee or other third party.

Rule 74 provides immunity likewise for appointing institutions and will apply in all cases, being mandatory. Similar considerations apply as to the reasons why immunity is granted to arbitrators, and there can be no attempt to reopen or revisit an arbitral award by alleging vicarious liability on the part of the appointing institution.

This has relevance as there may be situations (eg under rule 7 (failure of appointment procedure)) where the arbitrator is appointed by an appointing body (eg under s 24). Such body will actually appoint the arbitrator and thereby might be taken to be warranting or in some way vouching for the performance of the arbitrator or tribunal. This is in contrast to a nominating body which simply recommends names for the parties themselves to then appoint.

For similar considerations as under rule 73, as a matter of policy such institutions, including an arbitration appointments referee, other third parties, agents and employees as it applies to the referee or other third party, shall be immune.

Note that if the referee or institution were to have an administrative function beyond the appointment then rule 74 would not provide immunity for that function, although they might be treated as a 'person assisting the tribunal' under rule 73(3), and therefore obtain immunity under that provision.

Immunity of experts, witnesses and legal representatives

Further mandatory rule 75 states that '[e]very person who participates in an arbitration as an expert, witness or legal representative has the same immunity in respect of acts or omissions as the person would have if the arbitration were civil proceedings.'

The Explanatory Notes to the Arbitration (Scotland) Bill provide:

> As arbitration is a private version of judicial proceedings, the Bill places experts, witnesses and legal representatives in no more vulnerable a position if they are taking part in arbitration proceedings than if they are taking part in civil court proceedings.

Rule 75 makes mandatory provision for immunity for experts, witnesses and legal representatives in arbitration as traditionally set out in *Karling v Purdue* 2004 SLT 1067. When a witness gives evidence before a court, he will have immunity from any civil action in negligence in respect of the things said or done by him during those proceedings.

The position on immunity for expert witnesses is currently in flux, at least in England. The established law was the decision in *Stanton v Callaghan* [2000] QB 75, which provided blanket immunity. However, following the removal of blanket immunity for advocates under *Arthur J S Hall & Co v Simons* [2003] 3 WLR 543, the Supreme Court was asked to reconsider the extent of immunity in *Jones v Kaney* [2011] UKSC 13. The decision has, in effect, reversed the *Stanton v Callaghan* ruling. This was on the basis that the logic was the same as the removal of advocates' immunity, but two justices disagreed, and it must be said that it is not clear that the position of advocates and expert witnesses is necessarily identical. However, since the rule restricts the immunity of expert witnesses to that enjoyed in legal proceedings, this ruling would appear to restrict such immunity to protection from defamation proceedings (which is understood to remain). The Supreme Court stated that advocates had not been deterred by the decision in *Arthur J S Hall & Co v Simons*, but time will tell if the same is true for expert witnesses. It should be remembered that advocates appear in court for their living, whereas many expert witnesses only appear infrequently, and may well be deterred by the prospect of getting dragged into satellite litigation by losing parties. It is anticipated that they will either seek indemnities or insurance (or both), and the impact of this decision on the willingness of expert witnesses to participate in arbitration is uncertain. However, rule 75 only grants expert witnesses the same protection as they have in court proceedings, and *Jones v Kaney* would appear to have removed the bulk of such protection.

Expert witnesses and, indeed, others involved in arbitration, need to be alive to the ongoing developments in the law in this area.

Loss of right to object

Mandatory rule 76 is directed towards supporting the founding principle in s 1(a) of avoiding unnecessary delay and expense, and preventing parties seeking to delay proceedings or avoid the effect of an award by objecting on the basis of lack of jurisdiction or irregularity but doing so late in the day.

The rules set up the concept of a 'timeous objection' defined in subparagraph (2) as being 'as soon as reasonably practicable'. Reasonable practicability is not defined in the Act, but guidance can be obtained from the English Court of Appeal decision in *Edwards v National Coal Board* [1949] 1 KB 704, which stated that 'reasonably practicable' is a narrower term than 'physically possible'. (*Edwards* was followed in *Austin Rover Group Ltd v HM Inspector of Factories* [1990] 1 AC 619, and thereafter in *Baker v Quantum Clothing Group* [2009] EWCA Civ 499, which was reversed by the Supreme Court [2011] UKSC 17, but not on this point.) For Scottish dicta see *Mains v Uniroyal Englebert Tyres Ltd (No 1)* 1995 SC 518 and *Beggs v Motherwell Bridge Fabricators Ltd* 1998 SLT 1215. This issue has already been discussed in relation to the use of the same phrase in mandatory rule 20 (objections to tribunal's jurisdiction).

Those failing to take timeous action to object and participating lose the right to object. Making a timeous objection will be a question of fact.

'Participates in an arbitration'

One could envisage a party being involved in the arbitration nominally and thereby 'participating' within the meaning of the rule but thereafter losing the right to object. Thus, if a respondent had a problem with the arbitrator for one of the grounds in sub-paragraph (1) and did nothing about it, then it seems that from the time of the appointment of the arbitrator the clock would start ticking on the timeous element of any potential objection. If a party did not participate at all and the final award was made, that party would have lost the right to object as any objection at that point would not be timeous as it would not have been made 'as soon as reasonably practicable after the circumstances giving rise to the ground for objection first arose' – ie here the appointment. The right would be reacquired only if provision is made in the arbitration agreement or if allowed by the other party (or the rules) or where the tribunal itself considers that there is justification and allows a late objection under rule 76(2)(c) (cf *Rustal Trading Ltd v Gill & Duffus SA* [2001] 1 Lloyd's Rep 14).

The party should raise any relevant issue as soon as it is, or reasonably ought to be, aware of the objection and the rule will not apply only where that party shows (ie bearing the burden of proof) that it did not know of the ground for objection and could not with reasonable diligence have discovered the ground.

The time bar will not, however, fall where the party was unaware of the ground for the objection, and could not have become aware with reasonable diligence (rule 76(3)). It should be noted that this relates to lack of knowledge of the ground of objection, not, for example, failure to appreciate the legal position. It may, however, be that a tribunal would exercise its discretion under rule 76(2)(c) where an unrepresented party was unaware of the legal significance of a potential ground for objection.

English provisions

Section 73 of the 1996 Act provides for objections being made 'forthwith' or 'within the prescribed period of time'. The body of case law on the meaning of 'forthwith' is considered not to be totally helpful to a definition or guidance towards 'reasonable practicability' under rule 76(2)(a).

Independence of arbitrator

Mandatory rule 77 states that an arbitrator is not independent in relation to an arbitration if –
   (a) the arbitrator's relationship with any party,
   (b) the arbitrator's financial or other commercial interests, or
   (c) anything else,
gives rise to justifiable doubts as to the arbitrator's impartiality.

It is rather strange that these very important mandatory provisions find themselves in the miscellaneous part at the back of the Rules, particularly as the themes such as impartiality run throughout the entire Act (eg rules 8(2), 10(2)(a), 12(a), 24(1)(a)). Indeed there has been quite a bit of reference to them throughout the commentary. Rule 77 sets out when an arbitrator will not be taken to be independent in relation to an arbitration. The key is whether his relationship with any party, his financial or other commercial interests or anything else gives rise to justifiable doubts as to his impartiality.

It should be noted that it is not whether he actually *is* impartial, but whether the relationship gives rise to justifiable doubts. This issue has already been considered in relation to rule 24(1)(a) which introduces the obligation of impartiality, which these rules then explain.

It should be noted that rule 77 equates lack of impartiality with lack of independence. In reality an arbitrator could be impartial while not being independent, and could be partial while being independent. They are really distinct concepts, but the purpose of this rule is to prevent an arbitrator acting where there must be doubts as to whether he can make a fair decision between the parties. Accordingly, the distinction may be academic.

Consideration where arbitrator judged not to be impartial and independent

Mandatory rule 24 requires the arbitrator to act independently, and rule 77 lays down the requirements for such independence. Default rule 78 provides for what happens if an arbitrator has been removed under rule 12 for lack of impartiality and independence; when the entire tribunal has been dismissed under rule 13 for failure to comply with its duty to be impartial and independent; or where the tribunal's award (or part of it) is returned for reconsideration or is set aside or either under rule 68.

In those circumstances the Outer House (and only the Outer House) can consider whether an arbitrator has complied with rule 8 when considering whether to make an order under rules 16(1) or 69(4) about the arbitrator's entitlement to fees or expenses and whether there should be a repaying of fees or expenses already paid to an arbitrator.

It is interesting that rule 78 implies that there are two distinct tests to be passed, namely lack of independence *and* lack of impartiality, whereas rule 77 defines lack of independence as lack of impartiality. Rule 78 could, therefore, have merely used 'independence'.

It will be recalled that mandatory rule 8 provides that an arbitrator is under a duty to disclose any conflict of interest, rule 8(2) requiring the disclosure 'without delay'. Mandatory rule 16 deals with the liability of the arbitrator when his tenure is at an end and rule 16(1) in particular provides that the Outer House (and only the Outer House) may, on an application by any party or the arbitrator, make an order as it thinks fit about the arbitrator's entitlement to fees and expenses, about the repaying of fees or expenses already paid and, where the arbitrator has resigned, about the arbitrator's liability in respect of acting as an arbitrator.

It will be recalled that mandatory rule 68(4) provides that in a 'serious irregularity' appeal the Outer House may make such orders as it thinks fit about any arbitrator's entitlement (if any) to fees and expenses and such an order may provide for the repayment of fees or expenses already paid to the arbitrator.

Death of arbitrator

Under mandatory rule 79, an arbitrator's authority is personal and ceases on death.

Sometimes in law rights vested in a party at death can transmit to his executors (ie those persons administering his estate). Mandatory rule 79 makes clear that an arbitrator's authority ceases on his death, which is consistent with the role of arbitrator being a personal appointment. The fact that bodies corporate cannot be arbitrators is also consistent with this approach. This is a mandatory rule and applies in all cases.

Rule 79 complements the following rule which provides for whether an arbitration agreement is discharged by the death of a party. It also complements the fact that an arbitrator must be a natural person under mandatory rule 3, and can no longer be, for example, a partnership.

This provision is similar (in part) to the 1996 Act s 26.

In long-running arbitrations with a single arbitrator, particularly when significant sums are involved, it is sometimes the practice to insure the arbitrator's life. While this does not solve the problem of having to restart the arbitration, it can, at least, prevent the duplication of costs. It is, however, a matter to be handled with some delicacy when asking the arbitrator to submit to an insurance medical …

Death of party

Default rule 80 deals with what happens with the death of a party. First, an arbitration agreement is not discharged by the death of a party and may be enforced by or against the executor or other representative of that party, and, secondly, the rule does not affect the operation of any law by virtue of which a substantive right or obligation is extinguished by death.

As a corollary to rule 79 above, on the death of one of the parties, the arbitration agreement is not discharged and his interests in the arbitration will transmit to his executors or personal representatives on death. It will be for the executors or representatives then to determine whether to continue in it. If a party dies and is either intestate and his next of kin do not seek to be appointed as executors under the relevant law, or his executors named in a will decline to confirm to the estate of the deceased, the matter could still grind to a halt unless the other party sought appointment as an executor-creditor, and would then be in the slightly bizarre position of being on both sides of the arbitration. In England under the 1996 Act s 8 where a corporate body ceases to exist, any arbitration in which it was involved will fall (*Morris v Harris* [1927] AC 252) and cannot be revived, unless the company is restored to the register having been struck off rather than being dissolved.

The 2010 Act employs almost identical wording and a similar case for this might be argued here.

Likewise, presumably in bankruptcy if the trustee adopts a contract containing the agreement then it will be enforceable by or against him on the basis that he is stepping into the shoes of the bankrupt. If, however, the trustee declines to adopt the contract, then it will fall.

Unfair treatment

Default rule 81 provides that, subject to the agreement of the parties, the unfair treatment of any party by the tribunal will be deemed to be unfair treatment of the parties which may resonate with the other provisions in the Act. It is difficult to see why this is a default rule, as the only reason for a party not to want it included would seem to be if it was certain it was only the other party who would be treated unfairly. Further, since treating one party unfairly would seem likely to amount to evidence of impartiality, it is difficult to see why this rule is required at all.

Rules applicable to umpires

Mandatory rule 82 clarifies the application of certain specific rules to umpires. Sub-paragraph (2) clarifies that the parties cannot choose to disapply mandatory rules in relation to umpires, but can modify or disapply the default rules.

Formal communications

Default rule 83 covers the important topic of communications and the rule is replicated here.

(1) A 'formal communication' means any application, award, consent, direction, notice, objection, order, reference, request, requirement or waiver made or given or any document served –
    (a) in pursuance of an arbitration agreement,
    (b) for the purposes of these rules (in so far as they apply), or
    (c) otherwise in relation to an arbitration.
(2) A formal communication must be in writing.
(3) A formal communication is made, given or served if it is –
    (a) hand delivered to the person concerned,
    (b) sent to the person concerned by first class post in a properly addressed envelope or package –
        (i) in the case of an individual, to the individual's principal place of business or usual or last known abode,
        (ii) in the case of a body corporate, to the body's registered or principal office, or
        (iii) in either case, to any postal address designated for the purpose by the intended recipient (such designation to be made by giving notice to the person giving or serving the formal communication), or
    (c) sent to the person concerned in some other way (including by email, fax or other electronic means) which the sender reasonably considers likely to cause it to be delivered on the same or next day.
(4) A formal communication which is sent by email, fax or other electronic means is to be treated as being in writing only if it is legible and capable of being used for subsequent reference.
(5) A formal communication is, unless the contrary is proved, to be treated as having been made, given or served –
    (a) where hand delivered, on the day of delivery,
    (b) where posted, on the day on which it would be delivered in the ordinary course of post, or
    (c) where sent in any other way described above, on the day after it is sent.
(6) The tribunal may determine that a formal communication –
    (a) is to be delivered in such other manner as it may direct, or
    (b) need not be delivered,
    but it may do so only if satisfied that it is not reasonably practicable for the formal communication to be made, given or served in accordance with this rule (or, as the case may be, with any contrary agreement between the parties).
(7) This rule does not apply in relation to any application, order, notice, document or other thing which is made, given or served in or for the purposes of legal proceedings.

Default rule 83 provides for the often crucially important area of the means of intimating certain formal notices or documents under the arbitration agreement or in the course of arbitral proceedings, in the event that this is not already agreed between the parties.

Rule 83(1) provides the definition for 'formal communication'; sub-paragraph (2) requires it to be in writing as defined in rule 79(1); sub-paragraph (3) makes provision for the delivery of a formal communication, but seems to assume that all such communications will take place within the UK (eg the reference to first class mail, and the implied assumption that letters will arrive the next day); and rule 83(4) provides that any electronic communication will be treated as being in writing only if it gets to its destination in a readable state and can be used as a record. This is fine in practice, but how can a sender prove, for example, that a fax or email received by the other party was in a readable form? It was noted under rule 1 that this provision appears not to take full account of current practices in communications.

While rule 83 requires communications to be in writing, it does not say they should be signed. This is, however, good practice for formal communications, and may give rise to a further requirement to agree methods of verified electronic signatures that may be acceptable, or whether faxed or scanned copies of signed documents will be enough.

Rule 83(5) provides for where formal communication is to be deemed to have been made, given or served; rule 83(6) provides that where it is not reasonably practicable for formal communication to be made, given or served, the arbitrator will have the power to determine that another means of intimation is used or may dispense with intimation which will allow the arbitrator to expedite the process while also reducing court involvement.

Specific provision for review by the court on this matter has not been made but in some cases the general provisions in Part 8 on challenging the decision of an arbitrator might be relevant.

Rule 83(7) means that the rule only applies to documents which are being produced under the arbitration agreement or as part of the arbitration proceedings. If the documents relate to proceedings of the court, then the rules of court in relation to delivery and service of documents will apply.

Notices, and the method of communicating them to the other party, are important – much can depend on them. In *Muir Construction Ltd v Hambly Ltd* 1990 SLT 830 the court held that a notice (in this case of termination) was invalid because it had been delivered by hand, and not by registered or recorded delivery post as required in the contract. In *Ben Cleuch Estates Ltd v Scottish Enterprise* [2008] 2008 SC 252 a key issue related to the service of a notice in the exercise of a break option in a commercial lease. The tenant was held not to have validly exercised the option when it had served the notice on the landlord's agents (a surveyors' firm) and not at the address of the landlord which was required under the lease.

Periods of time

In the Act, under default rule 84, periods of time are to be calculated for the purposes of an arbitration as follows –

    (a) where any act requires to be done within a specified period after or from a specified date or event, the period begins immediately after that date or, as the case may be, the date of that event, and

    (b) where the period is a period of 7 days or less, the following days are to be ignored –

        (i)   Saturdays and Sundays, and

        (ii) any public holidays in the place where the act concerned is to be done.

The Explanatory Notes to the Arbitration (Scotland) Bill stated that this rule 'provides default provisions for calculating time periods in the absence of agreement between the parties'.

There is little to add to this sensible provision, other than noting that, in Scotland at least, 'public holidays' can be a bit of a challenge, especially when the concept of local holidays needs to be taken into account.

The rules also provide a useful index as follows:

Index of interpretation of terms

The words and other expressions listed in the following index are defined or otherwise explained for the purposes of these rules by the provisions indicated in the index.

Expression	Interpretation provision
arbitral appointments referee	section 24
arbitration	section 2
arbitration agreement	section 4
arbitration expenses	rule 59
arbitrator	section 2
claim	section 31(1)
court	section 31(1)
default rule	section 9(1)
dispute	section 2
independent	rule 77
Inner House	section 31(1)
mandatory rule	section 8
Outer House	section 31(1)

Expression	Interpretation provision
part award	rule 54
party	sections 2 and 31(2)
provisional award	rule 53
recoverable arbitration expenses	rule 61
rule	section 2
statutory arbitration	section 16(1)
tribunal	section 2

Conclusion

The Arbitration (Scotland) Act 2010 represented a completely new start for both domestic and international arbitration law in Scotland. In the first edition of this book, it was commented that the success or failure of the Act would very much depend upon the willingness of those involved to use arbitration in the future. Almost a decade later, it has proved to be correct that the Act was the start Scottish arbitration needed to increase in prominence and profile. The numbers of arbitrations in Scotland has increased and is increasing as more parties are willing to resolve their disputes by arbitration. The increase of stepped or tiered dispute resolution clauses in contracts has also added to this, requiring non-litigation methods of resolution to be considered.

The Scottish Government has continued to be supportive, and continues to give consideration to using arbitration, but, where statutory arbitration is required, the provisions of the 2010 Act remain dormant and require to be brought into force. It is also hoped that further refinements will be made to the Act such as additional tribunal powers including emergency powers.

Scotland does in fact have a considerable number of factors in its favour. Apart from being a pretty pleasant place to conduct an arbitration, it has competent arbitrators and lawyers, good places to hold arbitration hearings, international connections and good support facilities. Costs are significantly lower than in the nearest major international arbitration centre, London, or in other European centres such as Paris, Geneva, Zurich or Stockholm.

A particular sales point Scotland has is being something of a 'bridge' jurisdiction between the common law and civil law worlds. It also has what is an advantage in many disputes, of being an English-speaking jurisdiction that is neither England nor the United States. However, the biggest selling point is that it has a modern, up-to-date, high-quality piece of legislation in the Arbitration (Scotland) Act 2010 and is able to draw on a vast body of English arbitral case law in support. It is up to all those involved in dispute resolution to promote Scottish arbitration in appropriate cases, both domestic and international.

Finally, a new chapter in the development of Scottish arbitration may shortly open following the ICCA Congress meeting in Edinburgh originally planned for 2020, but now postponed as a result of the COVID-19 pandemic. This will put Scottish Arbitration front and centre in the international marketplace and may provide further opportunities for Scotland to exploit into the future. This will require the same willingness on the part of those with an interest in, and involvement with Scottish arbitration going forwards.

Appendix I

Arbitration (Scotland) Act 2010

2010 ASP I

The Bill for this Act of the Scottish Parliament was passed by the Parliament on 18th November 2009 and received Royal Assent on 5th January 2010

An Act of the Scottish Parliament to make provision about arbitration.

Introductory

I Founding principles

The founding principles of this Act are—

- (a) that the object of arbitration is to resolve disputes fairly, impartially and without unnecessary delay or expense,
- (b) that parties should be free to agree how to resolve disputes subject only to such safeguards as are necessary in the public interest,
- (c) that the court should not intervene in an arbitration except as provided by this Act.

Anyone construing this Act must have regard to the founding principles when doing so.

2 Key terms

(1) In this Act, unless the contrary intention appears—

"arbitration" includes—

- (a) domestic arbitration,
- (b) arbitration between parties residing, or carrying on business, anywhere in the United Kingdom, and
- (c) international arbitration,

"arbitrator" means a sole arbitrator or a member of a tribunal,

"dispute" includes—

- (a) any refusal to accept a claim, and
- (b) any other difference (whether contractual or not),

"party" means a party to an arbitration,

"rules" means the Scottish Arbitration Rules (see section 7), and

"tribunal" means a sole arbitrator or panel of arbitrators.

(2) References in this Act to "an arbitration", "the arbitration" or "arbitrations" are references to a particular arbitration process or, as the case may be, to particular arbitration processes.

(3) References in this Act to a tribunal conducting an arbitration are references to the tribunal doing anything in relation to the arbitration, including—

    (a) making a decision about procedure or evidence, and

    (b) making an award.

3   Seat of arbitration

(1) An arbitration is "seated in Scotland" if—

    (a) Scotland is designated as the juridical seat of the arbitration—

        (i) by the parties,

        (ii) by any third party to whom the parties give power to so designate, or

        (iii) where the parties fail to designate or so authorise a third party, by the tribunal, or

    (b) in the absence of any such designation, the court determines that Scotland is to be the juridical seat of the arbitration.

(2) The fact that an arbitration is seated in Scotland does not affect the substantive law to be used to decide the dispute.

Arbitration agreements

4   Arbitration agreement

An "arbitration agreement" is an agreement to submit a present or future dispute to arbitration (including any agreement which provides for arbitration in accordance with arbitration provisions contained in a separate document).

5   Separability

(1) An arbitration agreement which forms (or was intended to form) part only of an agreement is to be treated as a distinct agreement.

(2) An arbitration agreement is not void, voidable or otherwise unenforceable only because the agreement of which it forms part is void, voidable or otherwise unenforceable.

(3) A dispute about the validity of an agreement which includes an arbitration agreement may be arbitrated in accordance with that arbitration agreement.

6   Law governing arbitration agreement

Where—

    (a) the parties to an arbitration agreement agree that an arbitration under that agreement is to be seated in Scotland, but

    (b) the arbitration agreement does not specify the law which is to govern it, then, unless the parties otherwise agree, the arbitration agreement is to be governed by Scots law.

Scottish Arbitration Rules

7   Scottish Arbitration Rules

The Scottish Arbitration Rules set out in schedule 1 are to govern every arbitration seated in Scotland (unless, in the case of a default rule, the parties otherwise agree).

8   Mandatory rules

The following rules, called "mandatory rules", cannot be modified or disapplied (by an arbitration agreement, by any other agreement between the parties or by any other means) in relation to any arbitration seated in Scotland—

rule 3 (arbitrator to be an individual)
rule 4 (eligibility to act as an arbitrator)
rule 7 (failure of appointment procedure)
rule 8 (duty to disclose any conflict of interests)
rules 12 to 16 (removal or resignation of arbitrator or dismissal of tribunal)
rules 19 to 21 and 23 (jurisdiction of tribunal)
rules 24 and 25 (general duties of tribunal and parties)
rule 42 (point of law referral: procedure etc.)
rule 44 (time limit variation: procedure etc.)
rule 45 (securing attendance of witnesses and disclosure of evidence)
rule 48 (power to award payment and damages)
rule 50 (interest)
rule 54 (part awards)
rule 56 (power to withhold award if fees or expenses not paid)
rule 60 (arbitrators' fees and expenses)
rule 63 (ban on pre dispute agreements about liability for arbitration expenses)
rules 67, 68, 70, 71 and 72 (challenging awards)
rules 73 to 75 (immunity)
rule 76 (loss of right to object)
rule 77 (independence of arbitrator)
rule 79 (death of arbitrator)
rule 82 (rules applicable to umpires)

9   Default rules

(1) The non-mandatory rules are called the "default rules".
(2) A default rule applies in relation to an arbitration seated in Scotland only in so far as the parties have not agreed to modify or disapply that rule (or any part of it) in relation to that arbitration.

(3) Parties may so agree—
  (a) in the arbitration agreement, or
  (b) by any other means at any time before or after the arbitration begins.
(4) Parties are to be treated as having agreed to modify or disapply a default rule—
  (a) if or to the extent that the rule is inconsistent with or disapplied by—
      (i)   the arbitration agreement,
      (ii) any arbitration rules or other document (for example, the UNCITRAL Model Law, the UNCITRAL Arbitration Rules or other institutional rules) which the parties agree are to govern the arbitration, or
      (iii) anything done with the agreement of the parties, or
  (b) if they choose a law other than Scots law as the applicable law in respect of the rule's subject matter. This subsection does not affect the generality of subsections (2) and (3).

Suspension of legal proceedings

10   Suspension of legal proceedings

(1) The court must, on an application by a party to legal proceedings concerning any matter under dispute, sist those proceedings in so far as they concern that matter if—
  (a) an arbitration agreement provides that a dispute on the matter is to be resolved by arbitration (immediately or after the exhaustion of other dispute resolution procedures),
  (b) the applicant is a party to the arbitration agreement (or is claiming through or under such a party),
  (c) notice of the application has been given to the other parties to the legal proceedings,
  (d) the applicant has not—
      (i)   taken any step in the legal proceedings to answer any substantive claim against the applicant, or
      (ii) otherwise acted since bringing the legal proceedings in a manner indicating a desire to have the dispute resolved by the legal proceedings rather than by arbitration, and
  (e) nothing has caused the court to be satisfied that the arbitration agreement concerned is void, inoperative or incapable of being performed.
(2) Any provision in an arbitration agreement which prevents the bringing of the legal proceedings is void in relation to any proceedings which the court refuses to sist. This subsection does not apply to statutory arbitrations.
(3) This section applies regardless of whether the arbitration concerned is to be seated in Scotland.

Enforcing and challenging arbitral awards etc.

11   Arbitral award to be final and binding on parties

(1) A tribunal's award is final and binding on the parties and any person claiming through or under them (but does not of itself bind any third party).

(2) In particular, an award ordering the rectification or reduction of a deed or other document is of no effect in so far as it would adversely affect the interests of any third party acting in good faith.

(3) This section does not affect the right of any person to challenge the award—
   (a) under Part 8 of the Scottish Arbitration Rules, or
   (b) by any available arbitral process of appeal or review.

(4) This section does not apply in relation to a provisional award (see rule 53), such an award not being final and being binding only—
   (a) to the extent specified in the award, or
   (b) until it is superseded by a subsequent award.

12   Enforcement of arbitral awards

(1) The court may, on an application by any party, order that a tribunal's award may be enforced as if it were an extract registered decree bearing a warrant for execution granted by the court.

(2) No such order may be made if the court is satisfied that the award is the subject of—
   (a) an appeal under Part 8 of the Scottish Arbitration Rules,
   (b) an arbitral process of appeal or review, or
   (c) a process of correction under rule 58 of the Scottish Arbitration Rules,which has not been finally determined.

(3) No such order may be made if the court is satisfied that the tribunal which made the award did not have jurisdiction to do so (and the court may restrict the extent of its order if satisfied that the tribunal did not have jurisdiction to make a part of the award).

(4) But a party may not object on the ground that the tribunal did not have jurisdiction if the party has lost the right to raise that objection by virtue of the Scottish Arbitration Rules (see rule 76).

(5) Unless the parties otherwise agree, a tribunal's award may be registered for execution in the Books of Council and Session or in the sheriff court books (provided that the arbitration agreement is itself so registered).

(6) This section applies regardless of whether the arbitration concerned was seated in Scotland.

(7) Nothing in this section or in section 13 affects any other right to rely on or enforce an award in pursuance of—
   (a) sections 19 to 21, or
   (b) any other enactment or rule of law.

(8) In this section, "court" means the sheriff or the Court of Session.

13   Court intervention in arbitrations

(1) Legal proceedings are competent in respect of—
    (a)   a tribunal's award, or
    (b)   any other act or omission by a tribunal when conducting an arbitration,only as provided for in the Scottish Arbitration Rules (in so far as they apply to that arbitration) or in any other provision of this Act.

(2) In particular, a tribunal's award is not subject to review or appeal in any legal proceedings except as provided for in Part 8 of the Scottish Arbitration Rules.

(3) It is not competent for a party to raise the question of a tribunal's jurisdiction with the court except—
    (a)   where objecting to an order being made under section 12, or
    (b)   as provided for in the Scottish Arbitration Rules (see rules 21, 22 and 67).

(4) Where the parties agree that the UNCITRAL Model Law is to apply to an arbitration, articles 6 and 11(2) to (5) of that Law are to have the force of law in Scotland in relation to that arbitration (as if article 6 specified the Court of Session and any sheriff court having jurisdiction).

14   Persons who take no part in arbitral proceedings

(1) A person alleged to be a party to an arbitration but who takes no part in the arbitration may, by court proceedings, question—
    (a)   whether there is a valid arbitration agreement (or, in the case of a statutory arbitration, whether the enactment providing for arbitration applies to the dispute),
    (b)   whether the tribunal is properly constituted, or
    (c)   what matters have been submitted to arbitration in accordance with the arbitration agreement,and the court may determine such a question by making such declaration, or by granting such interdict or other remedy, as it thinks appropriate.

(2) Such a person has the same right as a party who participates in the arbitration to appeal against any award made in the arbitration under rule 67 or 68 (jurisdictional and serious irregularity appeals) and rule 71(2) does not apply to such an appeal.

15   Anonymity in legal proceedings

(1) A party to any civil proceedings relating to an arbitration (other than proceedings under section 12) may apply to the court for an order prohibiting the disclosure of the identity of a party to the arbitration in any report of the proceedings.

(2) On such an application, the court must grant the order unless satisfied that disclosure—
    (a)   is required—

      (i)   for the proper performance of the discloser's public functions, or

      (ii) in order to enable any public body or office-holder to perform public functions properly,

  (b) can reasonably be considered as being needed to protect a party's lawful interests,

  (c) would be in the public interest, or

  (d) would be necessary in the interests of justice.

(3) The court's determination of an application for an order is final.

Statutory arbitration

16 Statutory arbitration: special provisions

(1) "Statutory arbitration" is arbitration pursuant to an enactment which provides for a dispute to be submitted to arbitration.

(2) References in the Scottish Arbitration Rules (or in any other provision of this Act) to an arbitration agreement are, in the case of a statutory arbitration, references to the enactment which provides for a dispute to be resolved by arbitration.

(3) None of the Scottish Arbitration Rules (or other provisions of this Act) apply to a statutory arbitration if or to the extent that they are excluded by, or are inconsistent with, any provision made by virtue of any other enactment relating to the arbitration.

(4) Every statutory arbitration is to be taken to be seated in Scotland.

(5) The following rules do not apply in relation to statutory arbitration—

      rule 43 (extension of time limits)

      rule 71(9) (power to declare provision of arbitration agreement void)

      rule 80 (death of party)

(6) Despite rule 40, parties to a statutory arbitration may not agree to—

  (a) consolidate the arbitration with another arbitration,

  (b) hold concurrent hearings, or

  (c) authorise the tribunal to order such consolidation or the holding of concurrent hearings, unless the arbitrations or hearings are to be conducted under the same enactment.

17 Power to adapt enactments providing for statutory arbitration

Ministers may by order—

  (a) modify any of the Scottish Arbitration Rules, or any other provisions of this Act, in so far as they apply to statutory arbitrations (or to particular statutory arbitrations),

  (b) make such modifications of enactments which provide for disputes to be submitted to arbitration as they consider appropriate in consequence of, or in order to give full effect to, any of the Scottish Arbitration Rules or any other provisions of this Act.

Recognition and enforcement of New York Convention awards

18   New York Convention awards

(1)   A "Convention award" is an award made in pursuance of a written arbitration agreement in the territory of a state (other than the United Kingdom) which is a party to the New York Convention.

(2)   An award is to be treated for the purposes of this section as having been made at the seat of the arbitration.

(3)   A declaration by Her Majesty by Order in Council that a state is a party to the Convention (or is a party in respect of any territory) is conclusive evidence of that fact.

19   Recognition and enforcement of New York Convention awards

(1)   A Convention award is to be recognised as binding on the persons as between whom it was made (and may accordingly be relied on by those persons in any legal proceedings in Scotland).

(2)   The court may order that a Convention award may be enforced as if it were an extract registered decree bearing a warrant for execution granted by the court.

20   Refusal of recognition or enforcement

(1)   Recognition or enforcement of a Convention award may be refused only in accordance with this section.

(2)   Recognition or enforcement of a Convention award may be refused if the person against whom it is invoked proves—

(a)   that a party was under some incapacity under the law applicable to the party,

(b)   that the arbitration agreement was invalid under the law which the parties agree should govern it (or, failing any indication of that law, under the law of the country where the award was made),

(c)   that the person—

(i)   was not given proper notice of the arbitral process or of the appointment of the tribunal, or

(ii)   was otherwise unable to present the person's case,

(d)   that the tribunal was constituted, or the arbitration was conducted, otherwise than in accordance with—

(i)   the agreement of the parties, or

> (ii) failing such agreement, the law of the country where the arbitration took place.

(3) Recognition or enforcement of a Convention award may also be refused if the person against whom it is invoked proves that the award—

    (a) deals with a dispute not contemplated by or not falling within the submission to arbitration,

    (b) contains decisions on matters beyond the scope of that submission,

    (c) is not yet binding on the person, or

    (d) has been set aside or suspended by a competent authority.

(4) Recognition or enforcement of a Convention award may also be refused if—

    (a) the award relates to a matter which is not capable of being settled by arbitration, or

    (b) to do so would be contrary to public policy.

(5) A Convention award containing decisions on matters not submitted to arbitration may be recognised or enforced to the extent that it contains decisions on matters which were so submitted which are separable from decisions on matters not so submitted.

(6) The court before which a Convention award is sought to be relied on may, if an application for the setting aside or suspension of the award is made to a competent authority—

    (a) sist the decision on recognition or enforcement of the award,

    (b) on the application of the party claiming recognition or enforcement, order the other party to give suitable security.

(7) In this section "competent authority" means a person who has authority to set aside or suspend the Convention award concerned in the country in which (or under the law of which) the Convention award concerned was made.

21 Evidence to be produced when seeking recognition or enforcement

(1) A person seeking recognition or enforcement of a Convention award must produce—

    (a) the duly authenticated original award (or a duly certified copy of it), and

    (b) the original arbitration agreement (or a duly certified copy of it).

(2) Such a person must also produce a translation of any award or agreement which is in a language other than English (certified by an official or sworn translator or by a diplomatic or consular agent).

22 Saving for other bases of recognition or enforcement

Nothing in sections 19 to 21 affects any other right to rely on or enforce a Convention award in pursuance of any other enactment or rule of law.

Supplementary

23   Prescription and limitation

(1) The Prescription and Limitation (Scotland) Act 1973 (c. 52) is amended as follows.

(2) In section 4 (positive prescription: interruption)—
   (a) in subsection (2)(b), after "Scotland" insert "in respect of which an arbitrator (or panel of arbitrators) has been appointed",
   (b) in subsection (3)(a), for the words from "and" to "served" substitute "the date when the arbitration begins",
   (c) for subsection (4) substitute—
      "(4) An arbitration begins for the purposes of this section—
         (a) when the parties to the arbitration agree that it begins, or
         (b) in the absence of such agreement, in accordance with rule 1 of the Scottish Arbitration Rules (see section 7 of, and schedule 1 to, the Arbitration (Scotland) Act 2010 (asp 1)).".

(3) In section 9 (negative prescription: interruption)—
   (a) in subsection (3), for the words from "and" to "served" substitute "the date when the arbitration begins",
   (b) in subsection (4), for "preliminary notice" substitute "the date when the arbitration begins".

(4) After section 19C, insert—
   "19C A Interruption of limitation period: arbitration
      (1) Any period during which an arbitration is ongoing in relation to a matter is to be disregarded in any computation of the period specified in section 17(2), 18(2), 18A(1) or 18B(2) of this Act in relation to that matter.
      (2) In this section, "arbitration" means—
         (a) any arbitration in Scotland,
         (b) any arbitration in a country other than Scotland, being an arbitration an award in which would be enforceable in Scotland.".

(5) In section 22A(4), for the words from "and" to "served" substitute "the date when the arbitration begins (within the meaning of section 4(4) of this Act)".

(6) After section 22C, insert—
   "22C A Interruption of limitation period for 1987 Act actions: arbitration
      (1) Any period during which an arbitration is ongoing in relation to a matter is to be disregarded in any computation of the period specified in section 22B(2) or 22C(2) of this Act in relation to that matter.
      (2) In this section, "arbitration" means—
         (a) any arbitration in Scotland,
         (b) any arbitration in a country other than Scotland, being an arbitration an award in which would be enforceable in Scotland.".

24 Arbitral appointments referee

(1) Ministers may, by order, authorise persons or types of person who may act as an arbitral appointments referee for the purposes of the Scottish Arbitration Rules.

(2) Ministers must, when making such an order, have regard to the desirability of ensuring that arbitral appointments referees—

(a) have experience relevant to making arbitral appointments, and

(b) are able to provide training, and to operate disciplinary procedures, designed to ensure that arbitrators conduct themselves appropriately.

(3) Despite subsection (2)(b), an arbitral appointments referee is not obliged to appoint arbitrators in respect of whom the referee provides training or operates disciplinary procedures.

25 Power of judge to act as arbitrator or umpire

(1) A judge may act as an arbitrator or umpire only where—

(a) the dispute being arbitrated appears to the judge to be of commercial character, and

(b) the Lord President, having considered the state of Court of Session business, has authorised the judge to so act.

(2) A fee of such amount as Ministers may by order prescribe is payable in the Court of Session for the services of a judge acting as an arbitrator or umpire.

(3) Any jurisdiction exercisable by the Outer House under the Scottish Arbitration Rules (or any other provision of this Act) in relation to—

(a) a judge acting as a sole arbitrator or umpire, or

(b) a tribunal which the judge forms part of, is to be exercisable instead by the Inner House (and the Inner House's decision on any matter is final).

(4) In this section—

"Judge" means a Judge of the Court of Session, and

"Lord President" means the Lord President of the Court of Session.

26 Amendments to UNCITRAL Model Law or Rules or New York Convention

(1) Ministers may by order modify—

(a) the Scottish Arbitration Rules,

(b) any other provision of this Act, or

(c) any enactment which provides for disputes to be resolved by arbitration, in such manner as they consider appropriate in consequence of any amendment made to the UNCITRAL Model Law, the UNCITRAL Arbitration Rules or the New York Convention.

(2) Before making such an order, Ministers must consult such persons appearing to them to have an interest in the law of arbitration as they think fit.

27 Amendment of Conveyancing (Scotland) Act 1924 (c. 27)

In section 46 of the Conveyancing (Scotland) Act 1924—
    (a) in subsection (2), for "This section" substitute "Subsection (1)", and
    (b) after subsection (2) insert—
"(3) Where—
    (a) an arbitral award orders the reduction of a deed or other document
        recorded in the Register of Sasines (or forming a midcouple or link of
        title in a title recorded in that Register), and
    (b) the court orders that the award may be enforced in accordance with
        section 12 of the Arbitration (Scotland) Act 2010 (asp 1), subsection
        (1) applies to the arbitral award as it applies to a decree of reduction
        of a deed recorded in the Register of Sasines.".

28 Articles of Regulation 1695

The 25th Act of the Articles of Regulation 1695 does not apply in relation to arbitration.

29 Repeals

The repeals of the enactments specified in column 1 of schedule 2 have effect to the extent specified in column 2.

30 Arbitrability of disputes

Nothing in this Act makes any dispute capable of being arbitrated if, because of its subject-matter, it would not otherwise be capable of being arbitrated.

Final provisions

31 Interpretation

(1) In this Act, unless the contrary intention appears—
"arbitral appointments referee" means a person authorised under section 24,
"arbitration" has the meaning given by section 2,
"arbitration agreement" has the meaning given by section 4,
"arbitrator" has the meaning given by section 2,
"claim" includes counterclaim,
"Convention award" has the meaning given by section 18,
"court" means the Outer House or the sheriff (except in sections 1, 3, 10, 13
    and 15, where it means any court),
"default rule" has the meaning given by section 9(1),
"dispute" has the meaning given by section 2,

"Inner House" means the Inner House of the Court of Session,

"mandatory rule" has the meaning given by section 8,

"Ministers" means the Scottish Ministers,

"New York Convention" means the Convention on the Recognition and Enforcement of Foreign Arbitral Awards adopted by the United Nations Conference on International Commercial Arbitration on 10 June 1958,

"Outer House" means the Outer House of the Court of Session,

"party" is to be construed in accordance with section 2 and subsection (2) below,

"rule" means one of the Scottish Arbitration Rules,

"Scottish Arbitration Rules" means the rules set out in schedule 1,

"seated in Scotland" has the meaning given by section 3,

"statutory arbitration" has the meaning given by section 16(1),

"tribunal" has the meaning given by section 2,

"UNCITRAL Arbitration Rules" means the arbitration rules adopted by UNCITRAL on 28 April 1976, and

"UNCITRAL Model Law" means the UNCITRAL Model Law on International Commercial Arbitration as adopted by the United Nations Commission on International Trade Law on 21 June 1985 (as amended in 2006).

(2) This Act applies in relation to arbitrations and disputes between three or more parties as it applies in relation to arbitrations and disputes between two parties (with references to both parties being read in such cases as references to all the parties).

32 Ancillary provision

(1) Ministers may by order make any supplementary, incidental, consequential, transitional, transitory or saving provision which they consider appropriate for the purposes of, or in connection with, or for the purposes of giving full effect to, any provision of this Act.

(2) Such an order may modify any enactment, instrument or document.

33 Orders

(1) Any power of Ministers to make orders under this Act—
  (a) is exercisable by statutory instrument, and
  (b) includes power to make—
    (i) any supplementary, incidental, consequential, transitional, transitory or saving provision which Ministers consider appropriate,
    (ii) different provision for different purposes.

(2) A statutory instrument containing such an order (or an Order in Council made under section 18) is subject to annulment in pursuance of a resolution of the Scottish Parliament. This subsection does not apply—
  (a) to orders made under section 35(2) (commencement orders), or
  (b) where subsection (3) makes contrary provision.

(3) An order—
   (a)   under section 17 or 32 which adds to, replaces or omits any text in this or
         any other Act,
   (b)   under section 26, or
   (c)   under section 36(4), may be made only if a draft of the statutory instrument
         containing the order has been laid before, and approved by resolution of,
         the Scottish Parliament.

34   Crown application

(1)   This Act binds the Crown.
(2)   Her Majesty may be represented in any arbitration to which she is a party
      otherwise than in right of the Crown by such person as she may appoint in
      writing under the Royal Sign Manual.
(3)   The Prince and Steward of Scotland may be represented in any arbitration to
      which he is a party by such person as he may appoint.
(4)   References in this Act to a party to an arbitration are, where subsection (2) or
      (3) applies, to be read as references to the appointed representative.

35   Commencement

(1)   The following provisions come into force on Royal Assent—
         section 2
         sections 31 to 34
         this section
         section 37
(2)   Other provisions come into force on the day Ministers by order appoint.

36   Transitional provisions

(1)   This Act does not apply to an arbitration begun before commencement.
(2)   This Act otherwise applies to an arbitration agreement whether made on,
      before or after commencement.
(3)   Despite subsection (2), this Act does not apply to an arbitration arising under
      an arbitration agreement (other than an enactment) made before commence-
      ment if the parties agree that this Act is not to apply to that arbitration[1].
(4)   Ministers may by order specify any day falling at least 5 years after commence-
      ment as the day on which subsection (3) is to cease to have effect.
(5)   Before making such an order, Ministers must consult such persons appearing to
      them to have an interest in the law of arbitration as they think fit.
(6)   Any reference to an arbiter in an arbitration agreement made before com-
      mencement is to be treated as being a reference to an arbitrator.
(7)   Any reference in an enactment to a decree arbitral is to be treated for the
      purposes of section 12 as being a reference to a tribunal's award.
(8)   An express provision in an arbitration agreement made before commencement

which disapplies section 3 of the Administration of Justice (Scotland) Act 1972 (c. 59) in relation to an arbitration arising under that agreement is, unless the parties otherwise agree, to be treated as being an agreement to disapply rules 41 and 69 in relation to such an arbitration.

(9) In this section, "commencement" means the day on which this section comes into force.

37   Short title

This Act is called the Arbitration (Scotland) Act 2010.

SCHEDULE 1
Scottish Arbitration Rules

(introduced by section 7)
Mandatory rules are marked "M".
Default rules are marked "D".

Part 1
Commencement and constitution of tribunal etc.

Rule 1 Commencement of arbitration D

An arbitration begins when a party to an arbitration agreement (or any person claiming through or under such a party) gives the other party notice submitting a dispute to arbitration in accordance with the agreement.

Rule 2 Appointment of tribunal D

An arbitration agreement need not appoint (or provide for appointment of) the tribunal, but if it does so provide it may—

    (a) specify who is to form the tribunal,

    (b) require the parties to appoint the tribunal,

    (c) permit another person to appoint the tribunal, or

    (d) provide for the tribunal to be appointed in any other way.

Rule 3 Arbitrator to be an individual M

Only an individual may act as an arbitrator.

Rule 4 Eligibility to act as arbitrator M

An individual is ineligible to act as an arbitrator if the individual is—

    (a) aged under 16, or

(b) an incapable adult (within the meaning of section 1(6) of the Adults with Incapacity (Scotland) Act 2000 (asp 4)).

Rule 5 Number of arbitrators D

Where there is no agreement as to the number of arbitrators, the tribunal is to consist of a sole arbitrator.

Rule 6 Method of appointment D

The tribunal is to be appointed as follows—
  (a) where there is to be a sole arbitrator, the parties must appoint an eligible individual jointly (and must do so within 28 days of either party requesting the other to do so),
  (b) where there is to be a tribunal consisting of two or more arbitrators—
      (i) each party must appoint an eligible individual as an arbitrator (and must do so within 28 days of the other party requesting it to do so), and
      (ii) where more arbitrators are to be appointed, the arbitrators appointed by the parties must appoint eligible individuals as the remaining arbitrators.

Rule 7 Failure of appointment procedure M

(1) This rule applies where a tribunal (or any arbitrator who is to form part of a tribunal) is not, or cannot be, appointed in accordance with—
  (a) any appointment procedure set out in the arbitration agreement (or otherwise agreed between the parties), or
  (b) rule 6.
(2) Unless the parties otherwise agree, either party may refer the matter to an arbitral appointments referee.
(3) The referring party must give notice of the reference to the other party.
(4) That other party may object to the reference within 7 days of notice of reference being given by making an objection to—
  (a) the referring party, and
  (b) the arbitral appointments referee.
(5) If—
  (a) no such objection is made within that 7 day period, or
  (b) the other party waives the right to object before the end of that period, the arbitral appointments referee may make the necessary appointment.
(6) Where—
  (a) a party objects to the arbitral appointments referee making an appointment,
  (b) an arbitral appointments referee fails to make an appointment within 21 days of the matter being referred, or
  (c) the parties agree not to refer the matter to an arbitral appointments

referee, the court may, on an application by any party, make the necessary appointment.

(7) The court's decision on whom to appoint is final.

(8) Before making an appointment under this rule, the arbitral appointments referee or, as the case may be, the court must have regard to—

    (a) the nature and subject-matter of the dispute,

    (b) the terms of the arbitration agreement (including, in particular, any terms relating to appointment of arbitrators), and

    (c) the skills, qualifications, knowledge and experience which would make an individual suitable to determine the dispute.

(9) Where an arbitral appointments referee or the court makes an appointment under this rule, the arbitration agreement has effect as if it required that appointment.

Rule 8 Duty to disclose any conflict of interests M

(1) This rule applies to—

    (a) arbitrators, and

    (b) individuals who have been asked to be an arbitrator but who have not yet been appointed.

(2) An individual to whom this rule applies must, without delay disclose—

    (a) to the parties, and

    (b) in the case of an individual not yet appointed as an arbitrator, to any arbitral appointments referee, other third party or court considering whether to appoint the individual as an arbitrator,

any circumstances known to the individual (or which become known to the individual before the arbitration ends) which might reasonably be considered relevant when considering whether the individual is impartial and independent.

Rule 9 Arbitrator's tenure D

An arbitrator's tenure ends if—

    (a) the arbitrator becomes ineligible to act as an arbitrator (see rule 4),

    (b) the tribunal revokes the arbitrator's appointment (see rule 10),

    (c) the arbitrator is removed by the parties, a third party or the Outer House (see rules 11 and 12),

    (d) the Outer House dismisses the tribunal of which the arbitrator forms part (see rule 13), or

    (e) the arbitrator resigns (see rule 15) or dies (see rule 79).

Rule 10 Challenge to appointment of arbitrator D

(1) A party may object to the tribunal about the appointment of an arbitrator.

(2) An objection is competent only if—

    (a) it is made on the ground that the arbitrator—
        (i)   is not impartial and independent,
        (ii)   has not treated the parties fairly, or
        (iii) does not have a qualification which the parties agreed (before the arbitrator's appointment) that the arbitrator must have,
    (b) it states the facts on which it is based,
    (c) it is made within 14 days of the objector becoming aware of those facts, and
    (d) notice of it is given to the other party.
(3) The tribunal may deal with an objection by confirming or revoking the appointment.
(4) If the tribunal fails to make a decision within 14 days of a competent objection being made, the appointment is revoked.

Rule 11 Removal of arbitrator by parties D

(1) An arbitrator may be removed—
    (a) by the parties acting jointly, or
    (b) by any third party to whom the parties give power to remove an arbitrator.
(2) A removal is effected by notifying the arbitrator.

Rule 12 Removal of arbitrator by court M

The Outer House may remove an arbitrator if satisfied on the application by any party—
    (a) that the arbitrator is not impartial and independent,
    (b) that the arbitrator has not treated the parties fairly,
    (c) that the arbitrator is incapable of acting as an arbitrator in the arbitration (or that there are justifiable doubts about the arbitrator's ability to so act),
    (d) that the arbitrator does not have a qualification which the parties agreed (before the arbitrator's appointment) that the arbitrator must have,
    (e) that substantial injustice has been or will be caused to that party because the arbitrator has failed to conduct the arbitration in accordance with—
        (i)   the arbitration agreement,
        (ii)   these rules (in so far as they apply), or
        (iii) any other agreement by the parties relating to conduct of the arbitration.

Rule 13 Dismissal of tribunal by court M

The Outer House may dismiss the tribunal if satisfied on the application by a party that substantial injustice has been or will be caused to that party because the tribunal has failed to conduct the arbitration in accordance with—
    (a) the arbitration agreement,
    (b) these rules (in so far as they apply), or
    (c) any other agreement by the parties relating to conduct of the arbitration.

Rule 14 Removal and dismissal by court: supplementary M

(1) The Outer House may remove an arbitrator, or dismiss the tribunal, only if—
    (a) the arbitrator or, as the case may be, tribunal has been—
        (i) notified of the application for removal or dismissal, and
        (ii) given the opportunity to make representations, and
    (b) the Outer House is satisfied—
        (i) that any recourse available under rule 10 has been exhausted, and
        (ii) that any available recourse to a third party who the parties have agreed is to have power to remove an arbitrator (or dismiss the tribunal) has been exhausted.
(2) A decision of the Outer House under rule 12 or 13 is final.
(3) The tribunal may continue with the arbitration pending the Outer House's decision under rule 12 or 13.

Rule 15 Resignation of arbitrator M

(1) An arbitrator may resign (by giving notice of resignation to the parties and any other arbitrators) if—
    (a) the parties consent to the resignation,
    (b) the arbitrator has a contractual right to resign in the circumstances,
    (c) the arbitrator's appointment is challenged under rule 10 or 12,
    (d) the parties disapply or modify rule 34(1) (expert opinions) after the arbitrator is appointed, or
    (e) the Outer House has authorised the resignation.
(2) The Outer House may authorise a resignation only if satisfied, on an application by the arbitrator, that it is reasonable for the arbitrator to resign.
(3) The Outer House's determination of an application for resignation is final.

Rule 16 Liability etc. of arbitrator when tenure ends M

(1) Where an arbitrator's tenure ends, the Outer House may, on an application by any party or the arbitrator concerned, make such order as it thinks fit—
    (a) about the arbitrator's entitlement (if any) to fees and expenses,
    (b) about the repaying of fees or expenses already paid to the arbitrator,
    (c) where the arbitrator has resigned, about the arbitrator's liability in respect of acting as an arbitrator.
(2) The Outer House must, when considering whether to make an order in relation to an arbitrator who has resigned, have particular regard to whether the resignation was made in accordance with rule 15.
(3) The Outer House's determination of an application for an order is final.

Rule 17 Reconstitution of tribunal D

(1) Where an arbitrator's tenure ends, the tribunal must be reconstituted—
  (a) in accordance with the procedure used to constitute the original tribunal, or
  (b) where that procedure fails, in accordance with rules 6 and 7.
(2) It is for the reconstituted tribunal to decide the extent, if any, to which previous proceedings (including any award made, appointment by or other act done by the previous tribunal) should stand.
(3) The reconstituted tribunal's decision does not affect a party's right to object or appeal on any ground which arose before the tribunal made its decision.

Rule 18 Arbitrators nominated in arbitration agreements D

Any provision in an arbitration agreement which specifies who is to be an arbitrator ceases to have effect in relation to an arbitration when the specified individual's tenure as an arbitrator for that arbitration ends.

Part 2
Jurisdiction of tribunal

Rule 19 Power of tribunal to rule on own jurisdiction M

The tribunal may rule on—
  (a) whether there is a valid arbitration agreement (or, in the case of a statutory arbitration, whether the enactment providing for arbitration applies to the dispute),
  (b) whether the tribunal is properly constituted, and
  (c) what matters have been submitted to arbitration in accordance with the arbitration agreement.

Rule 20 Objections to tribunal's jurisdiction M

(1) Any party may object to the tribunal on the ground that the tribunal does not have, or has exceeded, its jurisdiction in relation to any matter.
(2) An objection must be made—
  (a) before, or as soon as is reasonably practicable after, the matter to which the objection relates is first raised in the arbitration, or
  (b) where the tribunal considers that circumstances justify a later objection, by such later time as it may allow,
  but, in any case, an objection may not be made after the tribunal makes its last award.
(3) If the tribunal upholds an objection it must—

(a) end the arbitration in so far as it relates to a matter over which the tribunal has ruled it does not have jurisdiction, and

(b) set aside any provisional or part award already made in so far as the award relates to such a matter.

(4) The tribunal may—

(a) rule on an objection independently from dealing with the subject-matter of the dispute, or

(b) delay ruling on an objection until it makes its award on the merits of the dispute (and include its ruling in that award),

but, where the parties agree which of these courses the tribunal should take, the tribunal must proceed accordingly.

Rule 21 Appeal against tribunal's ruling on jurisdictional objection M

(1) A party may, no later than 14 days after the tribunal's decision on an objection under rule 20, appeal to the Outer House against the decision.

(2) The tribunal may continue with the arbitration pending determination of the appeal.

(3) The Outer House's decision on the appeal is final.

Rule 22 Referral of point of jurisdiction D

The Outer House may, on an application by any party, determine any question as to the tribunal's jurisdiction.

Rule 23 Jurisdiction referral: procedure etc. M

(1) This rule applies only where an application is made under rule 22.

(2) Such an application is valid only if—

(a) the parties have agreed that it may be made, or

(b) the tribunal has consented to it being made and the court is satisfied—

(i) that determining the question is likely to produce substantial savings in expenses,

(ii) that the application was made without delay, and

(iii) that there is a good reason why the question should be determined by the court.

(3) The tribunal may continue with the arbitration pending determination of an application.

(4) The Outer House's determination of the question is final (as is any decision by the Outer House as to whether an application is valid).

Part 3
General duties

Rule 24 General duty of the tribunal M

(1) The tribunal must—
    (a) be impartial and independent,
    (b) treat the parties fairly, and
    (c) conduct the arbitration—
        (i)   without unnecessary delay, and
        (ii) without incurring unnecessary expense.
(2) Treating the parties fairly includes giving each party a reasonable opportunity to put its case and to deal with the other party's case.

Rule 25 General duty of the parties M

The parties must ensure that the arbitration is conducted—
    (a) without unnecessary delay, and
    (b) without incurring unnecessary expense.

Rule 26 Confidentiality D

(1) Disclosure by the tribunal, any arbitrator or a party of confidential information relating to the arbitration is to be actionable as a breach of an obligation of confidence unless the disclosure—
    (a) is authorised, expressly or impliedly, by the parties (or can reasonably be considered as having been so authorised),
    (b) is required by the tribunal or is otherwise made to assist or enable the tribunal to conduct the arbitration,
    (c) is required—
        (i)   in order to comply with any enactment or rule of law,
        (ii) for the proper performance of the discloser's public functions, or
        (iii) in order to enable any public body or office-holder to perform public functions properly,
    (d) can reasonably be considered as being needed to protect a party's lawful interests,
    (e) is in the public interest,
    (f) is necessary in the interests of justice, or
    (g) is made in circumstances in which the discloser would have absolute privilege had the disclosed information been defamatory.
(2) The tribunal and the parties must take reasonable steps to prevent unauthorised disclosure of confidential information by any third party involved in the conduct of the arbitration.
(3) The tribunal must, at the outset of the arbitration, inform the parties of the obligations which this rule imposes on them.

(4) "Confidential information", in relation to an arbitration, means any information relating to—
   (a) the dispute,
   (b) the arbitral proceedings,
   (c) the award, or
   (d) any civil proceedings relating to the arbitration in respect of which an order has been granted under section 15 of this Act,
   which is not, and has never been, in the public domain.

Rule 27 Tribunal deliberations D

(1) The tribunal's deliberations may be undertaken in private and accordingly need not be disclosed to the parties.
(2) But, where an arbitrator fails to participate in any of the tribunal's deliberations, the tribunal must disclose that fact (and the extent of the failure) to the parties.

Part 4
Arbitral proceedings

Rule 28 Procedure and evidence D

(1) It is for the tribunal to determine—
   (a) the procedure to be followed in the arbitration, and
   (b) the admissibility, relevance, materiality and weight of any evidence.
(2) In particular, the tribunal may determine—
   (a) when and where the arbitration is to be conducted,
   (b) whether parties are to submit claims or defences and, if so, when they should do so and the extent to which claims or defences may be amended,
   (c) whether any documents or other evidence should be disclosed by or to any party and, if so, when such disclosures are to be made and to whom copies of disclosed documents and information are to be given,
   (d) whether any and, if so, what questions are to be put to and answered by the parties,
   (e) whether and, if so, to what extent the tribunal should take the initiative in ascertaining the facts and the law,
   (f) the extent to which the arbitration is to proceed by way of—
      (i) hearings for the questioning of parties,
      (ii) written or oral argument,
      (iii) presentation or inspection of documents or other evidence, or
      (iv) submission of documents or other evidence,
   (g) the language to be used in the arbitration (and whether a party is to supply translations of any document or other evidence),

    (h) whether to apply rules of evidence used in legal proceedings or any other rules of evidence.

Rule 29 Place of arbitration D

29 The tribunal may meet, and otherwise conduct the arbitration, anywhere it chooses (in or outwith Scotland).

Rule 30 Tribunal decisions D

(1) Where the tribunal is unable to make a decision unanimously (including any decision on an award), a decision made by the majority of the arbitrators is sufficient.
(2) Where there is neither unanimity nor a majority in favour of or opposed to making any decision—
    (a) the decision is to be made by the arbitrator nominated to chair the tribunal, or
    (b) where no person has been so nominated, the decision is to be made—
        (i) where the tribunal consists of 3 or more arbitrators, by the last arbitrator to be appointed, or
        (ii) where the tribunal consists of 2 arbitrators, by an umpire appointed by the tribunal or, where the tribunal fails to make an appointment within 14 days of being requested to do so by either party or any arbitrator, by an arbitral appointments referee (at the request of a party or an arbitrator).

Rule 31 Tribunal directions D

(1) The tribunal may give such directions to the parties as it considers appropriate for the purposes of conducting the arbitration.
(2) A party must comply with such a direction by such time as the tribunal specifies.

Rule 32 Power to appoint clerk, agents or employees etc. D

(1) The tribunal may appoint a clerk (and such other agents, employees or other persons as it thinks fit) to assist it in conducting the arbitration.
(2) But the parties' consent is required for any appointment in respect of which significant expenses are likely to arise.

Rule 33 Party representatives D

(1) A party may be represented in the arbitration by a lawyer or any other person.
(2) But the party must, before representation begins, give notice of the representative—

(a) to the tribunal, and
(b) to the other party.

Rule 34 Experts D

(1) The tribunal may obtain an expert opinion on any matter arising in the arbitration.
(2) The parties must be given a reasonable opportunity—
    (a) to make representations about any written expert opinion, and
    (b) to hear any oral expert opinion and to ask questions of the expert giving it.

Rule 35 Powers relating to property D

The tribunal may direct a party—
    (a) to allow the tribunal, an expert or another party—
        (i) to inspect, photograph, preserve or take custody of any property which that party owns or possesses which is the subject of the arbitration (or as to which any question arises in the arbitration), or
        (ii) to take samples from, or conduct an experiment on, any such property, or
    (b) to preserve any document or other evidence which the party possesses or controls.

Rule 36 Oaths or affirmations D

The tribunal may—
    (a) direct that a party or witness is to be examined on oath or affirmation, and
    (b) administer an oath or affirmation for that purpose.

Rule 37 Failure to submit claim or defence timeously D

(1) Where—
    (a) a party unnecessarily delays in submitting or in otherwise pursuing a claim,
    (b) the tribunal considers that there is no good reason for the delay, and
    (c) the tribunal is satisfied that the delay—
        (i) gives, or is likely to give, rise to a substantial risk that it will not be possible to resolve the issues in that claim fairly, or
        (ii) has caused, or is likely to cause, serious prejudice to the other party,
    the tribunal must end the arbitration in so far as it relates to the subject-matter of the claim and may make such award (including an award on expenses) as it considers appropriate in consequence of the claim.

(2) Where—
    (a) a party unnecessarily delays in submitting a defence to the tribunal, and
    (b) the tribunal considers that there is no good reason for the delay,
the tribunal must proceed with the arbitration (but the delay is not, in itself, to be treated as an admission of anything).

Rule 38 Failure to attend hearing or provide evidence D

Where—
    (a) a party fails—
        (i) to attend a hearing which the tribunal requested the party to attend a reasonable period in advance of the hearing, or
        (ii) to produce any document or other evidence requested by the tribunal, and
    (b) the tribunal considers that there is no good reason for the failure,
the tribunal may proceed with the arbitration, and make its award, on the basis of the evidence (if any) before it.

Rule 39 Failure to comply with tribunal direction or arbitration agreement D

(1) Where a party fails to comply with—
    (a) any direction made by the tribunal, or
    (b) any obligation imposed by—
        (i) the arbitration agreement,
        (ii) these rules (in so far as they apply), or
        (iii) any other agreement by the parties relating to conduct of the arbitration,
the tribunal may order the party to so comply.
(2) Where a party fails to comply with an order made under this rule, the tribunal may do any of the following—
    (a) direct that the party is not entitled to rely on any allegation or material which was the subject-matter of the order,
    (b) draw adverse inferences from the non-compliance,
    (c) proceed with the arbitration and make its award,
    (d) make such provisional award (including an award on expenses) as it considers appropriate in consequence of the non-compliance.

Rule 40 Consolidation of proceedings D

(1) Parties may agree—
    (a) to consolidate the arbitration with another arbitration, or
    (b) to hold concurrent hearings.
(2) But the tribunal may not order such consolidation, or the holding of concurrent hearings, on its own initiative.

Part 5
Powers of court in relation to arbitral proceedings

Rule 41 Referral of point of law D

The Outer House may, on an application by any party, determine any point of Scots law arising in the arbitration.

Rule 42 Point of law referral: procedure etc. M

(1) This rule applies only where an application is made under rule 41.
(2) Such an application is valid only if—
  (a) the parties have agreed that it may be made, or
  (b) the tribunal has consented to it being made and the court is satisfied—
    (i) that determining the question is likely to produce substantial savings in expenses,
    (ii) that the application was made without delay, and
    (iii) that there is a good reason why the question should be determined by the court.
(3) The tribunal may continue with the arbitration pending determination of the application.
(4) The Outer House's determination of the question is final (as is any decision by the Outer House as to whether an application is valid).

Rule 43 Variation of time limits set by parties D

The court may, on an application by the tribunal or any party, vary any time limit relating to the arbitration which is imposed—
  (a) in the arbitration agreement, or
  (b) by virtue of any other agreement between the parties.

Rule 44 Time limit variation: procedure etc. M

(1) This rule applies only where an application for variation of time limit is made under rule 43.
(2) Such a variation may be made only if the court is satisfied—
  (a) that no arbitral process for varying the time limit is available, and
  (b) that someone would suffer a substantial injustice if no variation was made.
(3) It is for the court to determine the extent of any variation.
(4) The tribunal may continue with the arbitration pending determination of an application.
(5) The court's decision on whether to make a variation (and, if so, on the extent of the variation) is final.

Rule 45 Court's power to order attendance of witnesses and disclosure of evidence M

(1) The court may, on an application by the tribunal or any party, order any person—
  (a) to attend a hearing for the purposes of giving evidence to the tribunal, or
  (b) to disclose documents or other material evidence to the tribunal.
(2) But the court may not order a person to give any evidence, or to disclose anything, which the person would be entitled to refuse to give or disclose in civil proceedings.
(3) The tribunal may continue with the arbitration pending determination of an application.
(4) The court's decision on whether to make an order is final.

Rule 46 Court's other powers in relation to arbitration D

(1) The court has the same power in an arbitration as it has in civil proceedings—
  (a) to appoint a person to safeguard the interests of any party lacking capacity,
  (b) to order the sale of any property in dispute in the arbitration,
  (c) to make an order securing any amount in dispute in the arbitration,
  (d) to make an order under section 1 of the Administration of Justice (Scotland) Act 1972 (c. 59),
  (e) to grant warrant for arrestment or inhibition,
  (f) to grant interdict (or interim interdict), or
  (g) to grant any other interim or permanent order.
(2) But the court may take such action only—
  (a) on an application by any party, and
  (b) if the arbitration has begun—
    (i) with the consent of the tribunal, or
    (ii) where the court is satisfied that the case is one of urgency.
(3) The tribunal may continue with the arbitration pending determination of the application.
(4) This rule applies—
  (a) to arbitrations which have begun,
  (b) where the court is satisfied—
    (i) that a dispute has arisen or might arise, and
    (ii) that an arbitration agreement provides that such a dispute is to be resolved by arbitration.
(5) This rule does not affect—
  (a) any other powers which the court has under any enactment or rule of law in relation to arbitrations, or
  (b) the tribunal's powers.

Part 6
Awards

Rule 47 Rules applicable to the substance of the dispute D

(1) The tribunal must decide the dispute in accordance with—
- (a) the law chosen by the parties as applicable to the substance of the dispute, or
- (b) if no such choice is made (or where a purported choice is unlawful), the law determined by the conflict of law rules which the tribunal considers applicable.
(2) Accordingly, the tribunal must not decide the dispute on the basis of general considerations of justice, fairness or equity unless—
- (a) they form part of the law concerned, or
- (b) the parties otherwise agree.
(3) When deciding the dispute, the tribunal must have regard to—
- (a) the provisions of any contract relating to the substance of the dispute,
- (b) the normal commercial or trade usage of any undefined terms in the provisions of any such contract,
- (c) any established commercial or trade customs or practices relevant to the substance of the dispute, and
- (d) any other matter which the parties agree is relevant in the circumstances.

Rule 48 Power to award payment and damages M

(1) The tribunal's award may order the payment of a sum of money (including a sum in respect of damages).
(2) Such a sum must be specified—
- (a) in any currency agreed by the parties, or
- (b) the absence of such agreement, in such currency as the tribunal considers appropriate.

Rule 49 Other remedies available to tribunal D

The tribunal's award may—
- (a) be of a declaratory nature,
- (b) order a party to do or refrain from doing something (including ordering the performance of a contractual obligation), or
- (c) order the rectification or reduction of any deed or other document (other than a decree of court) to the extent permitted by the law governing the deed or document.

Rule 50 Interest M

(1) The tribunal's award may order that interest is to be paid on—
- (a) the whole or part of any amount which the award orders to be paid (or which is payable in consequence of a declaratory award), in respect of any period up to the date of the award,

    (b) the whole or part of any amount which is—
       (i)   claimed in the arbitration and outstanding when the arbitration began, but
      (ii) paid before the tribunal made its award,
    in respect of any period up to the date of payment,
    (c) the outstanding amount of any amounts awarded (including any award of arbitration expenses or pre-award interest under paragraph (a) or (b)) in respect of any period from the date of the award up to the date of payment.
(2) An award ordering payment of interest may, in particular, specify—
    (a) the interest rate,
    (b) the period for which interest is payable (including any rests which the tribunal considers appropriate).
(3) An award may make different interest provision in respect of different amounts.
(4) Interest is to be calculated—
    (a) in the manner agreed by the parties, or
    (b) failing such agreement, in such manner as the tribunal determines.
(5) This rule does not affect any other power of the tribunal to award interest.

Rule 51 Form of award D

(1) The tribunal's award must be signed by all arbitrators or all those assenting to the award.
(2) The tribunal's award must state—
    (a) the seat of the arbitration,
    (b) when the award is made and when it takes effect,
    (c) the tribunal's reasons for the award, and
    (d) whether any previous provisional or part award has been made (and the extent to which any previous provisional award is superseded or confirmed).
(3) The tribunal's award is made by delivering it to each of the parties in accordance with rule 83.

Rule 52 Award treated as made in Scotland D

An award is to be treated as having been made in Scotland even if it is signed at, or delivered to or from, a place outwith Scotland.

Rule 53 Provisional awards D

The tribunal may make a provisional award granting any relief on a provisional basis which it has the power to grant permanently.

Rule 54 Part awards M

(1) The tribunal may make more than one award at different times on different aspects of the matters to be determined.

(2) A "part award" is an award which decides some (but not all) of the matters which the tribunal is to decide in the arbitration.
(3) A part award must specify the matters to which it relates.

Rule 55 Draft awards D

Before making an award, the tribunal—
    (a) may send a draft of its proposed award to the parties, and
    (b) if it does so, must consider any representations from the parties about the draft which the tribunal receives by such time as it specifies.

Rule 56 Power to withhold award on non-payment of fees or expenses M

(1) The tribunal may refuse to deliver or send its award to the parties if any fees and expenses for which they are liable under rule 60 have not been paid in full.
(2) Where the tribunal so refuses, the court may (on an application by any party) order—
    (a) that the tribunal must deliver the award on the applicant paying into the court an amount equal to the fees and expenses demanded (or such lesser amount as may be specified in the order),
    (b) that the amount paid into the court is to be used to pay the fees and expenses which the court determines as being properly payable, and
    (c) that the balance (if any) of the amount paid into the court is to be repaid to the applicant.
(3) The court may make such an order only if the applicant has exhausted any available arbitral process of appeal or review of the amount of the fees and expenses demanded.
(4) The court's decision on an application under this rule is final.

Rule 57 Arbitration to end on last award or early settlement D

(1) An arbitration ends when the last award to be made in the arbitration is made (and no claim, including any claim for expenses or interest, is outstanding).
(2) But this does not prevent the tribunal from ending the arbitration before then under rule 20(3) or 37(1).
(3) The parties may end the arbitration at any time by notifying the tribunal that they have settled the dispute.
(4) On the request of the parties, the tribunal may make an award reflecting the terms of the settlement and these rules (except for rule 51(2)(c) and Part 8) apply to such an award as they apply to any other award.
(5) The fact that the arbitration has ended does not affect the operation of these rules (in so far as they apply) in relation to matters connected with the arbitration.

Rule 58 Correcting an award D

(1) The tribunal may correct an award so as to—
 (a) correct a clerical, typographical or other error in the award arising by virtue of accident or omission, or
 (b) clarify or remove any ambiguity in the award.
(2) The tribunal may make such a correction—
 (a) on its own initiative, or
 (b) on an application by any party.
(3) A party making an application under this rule must send a copy of the application to the other party at the same time as the application is made.
(4) Such an application is valid only if made—
 (a) within 28 days of the award concerned, or
 (b) by such later date as the Outer House or the sheriff may, on an application by the party, specify (with any determination by the Outer House or the sheriff being final).
(5) The tribunal must, before deciding whether to correct an award, give—
 (a) where the tribunal proposed the correction, each of the parties,
 (b) where a party application is made, the other party,
 a reasonable opportunity to make representations about the proposed correction.
(6) A correction may be made under this rule only—
 (a) where the tribunal proposed the correction, within 28 days of the award concerned being made, or
 (b) where a party application is made, within 28 days of the application being made.
(7) Where a correction affects—
 (a) another part of the corrected award, or
 (b) any other award made by the tribunal (relating to the substance of the dispute, expenses, interest or any other matter),
 the tribunal may make such consequential correction of that other part or award as it considers appropriate.
(8) A corrected award is to be treated as if it was made in its corrected form on the day the award was made.

Part 7
Arbitration expenses

Rule 59 Arbitration expenses D

"Arbitration expenses" means—
 (a) the arbitrators' fees and expenses for which the parties are liable under rule 60,

(b) any expenses incurred by the tribunal when conducting the arbitration for which the parties are liable under rule 60,

(c) the parties' legal and other expenses, and

(d) the fees and expenses of—

   (i) any arbitral appointments referee, and

   (ii) any other third party to whom the parties give powers in relation to the arbitration,

for which the parties are liable under rule 60.

Rule 60 Arbitrators' fees and expenses M

(1) The parties are severally liable to pay to the arbitrators—

  (a) the arbitrators' fees and expenses, including—

    (i) the arbitrators' fees for conducting the arbitration,

    (ii) expenses incurred personally by the arbitrators when conducting the arbitration, and

  (b) expenses incurred by the tribunal when conducting the arbitration, including—

    (i) the fees and expenses of any clerk, agent, employee or other person appointed by the tribunal to assist it in conducting the arbitration,

    (ii) the fees and expenses of any expert from whom the tribunal obtains an opinion,

    (iii) any expenses in respect of meeting and hearing facilities, and

    (iv) any expenses incurred in determining recoverable arbitration expenses.

(2) The parties are also severally liable to pay the fees and expenses of—

  (a) any arbitral appointments referee, and

  (b) any other third party to whom the parties give powers in relation to the arbitration.

(3) The amount of fees and expenses payable under this rule and the payment terms are—

  (a) to be agreed by the parties and the arbitrators or, as the case may be, the arbitral appointments referee or other third party, or

  (b) failing such agreement, to be determined by the Auditor of the Court of Session.

(4) Unless the Auditor of the Court of Session decides otherwise—

  (a) the amount of any fee is to be determined by the Auditor on the basis of a reasonable commercial rate of charge, and

  (b) the amount of any expenses is to be determined by the Auditor on the basis that a reasonable amount is to be allowed in respect of all reasonably incurred expenses.

(5) The Auditor of the Court of Session may, when determining the amount of fees and expenses, order the repayment of any fees or expenses already paid which the Auditor considers excessive (and such an order has effect as if it was made by the court).

(6) This rule does not affect—
   (a) the parties' liability as between themselves for fees and expenses covered by this rule (see rules 62 and 65), or
   (b) the Outer House's power to make an order under rule 16 (order relating to expenses in cases of arbitrator's resignation or removal).

Rule 61 Recoverable arbitration expenses D

(1) The following arbitration expenses are recoverable—
   (a) the arbitrators' fees and expenses for which the parties are liable under rule 60,
   (b) any expenses incurred by the tribunal when conducting the arbitration for which the parties are liable under rule 60, and
   (c) the fees and expenses of any arbitral appointments referee (or any other third party to whom the parties give powers in relation to the arbitration) for which the parties are liable under rule 60.
(2) It is for the tribunal to—
   (a) determine the amount of the other arbitration expenses which are recoverable, or
   (b) arrange for the Auditor of the Court of Session to determine that amount.
(3) Unless the tribunal or, as the case may be, the Auditor decides otherwise—
   (a) the amount of the other arbitration expenses which are recoverable must be determined on the basis that a reasonable amount is to be allowed in respect of all reasonably incurred expenses, and
   (b) any doubt as to whether expenses were reasonably incurred or are reasonable in amount is to be resolved in favour of the person liable to pay the expenses.

Rule 62 Liability for recoverable arbitration expenses D

(1) The tribunal may make an award allocating the parties' liability between themselves for the recoverable arbitration expenses (or any part of those expenses).
(2) When making an award under this rule, the tribunal must have regard to the principle that expenses should follow a decision made in favour of a party except where this would be inappropriate in the circumstances.
(3) Until such an award is made (or where the tribunal chooses not to make such an award) in respect of recoverable arbitration expenses (or any part of them), the parties are, as between themselves, each liable—
   (a) for an equal share of any such expenses for which the parties are liable under rule 60, and
   (b) for their own legal and other expenses.
(4) This rule does not affect—
   (a) the parties' several liability for fees and expenses under rule 60, or
   (b) the liability of any party to any other third party.

Rule 63 Ban on pre-dispute agreements about liability for arbitration expenses M

Any agreement allocating the parties' liability between themselves for any or all of the arbitration expenses has no effect if entered into before the dispute being arbitrated has arisen.

Rule 64 Security for expenses D

(1) The tribunal may—
   (a) order a party making a claim to provide security for the recoverable arbitration expenses or any part of them, and
   (b) if that order is not complied with, make an award dismissing any claim made by that party.
(2) But such an order may not be made only on the ground that the party—
   (a) is an individual who ordinarily resides outwith the United Kingdom, or
   (b) is a body which is—
      (i) incorporated or formed under the law of a country outwith the United Kingdom, or
      (ii) managed or controlled from outwith the United Kingdom.

Rule 65 Limitation of recoverable arbitration expenses D

(1) A provisional or part award may cap a party's liability for the recoverable arbitration expenses at an amount specified in the award.
(2) But an award imposing such a cap must be made sufficiently in advance of the expenses to which the cap relates being incurred, or the taking of any steps in the arbitration which may be affected by the cap, for the parties to take account of it.

Rule 66 Awards on recoverable arbitration expenses D

An expenses award (under rule 62 or 65) may be made together with or separately from an award on the substance of the dispute (and these rules apply in relation to an expenses award as they apply to an award on the substance of the dispute).

Part 8
Challenging awards

Rule 67 Challenging an award: substantive jurisdiction M

(1) A party may appeal to the Outer House against the tribunal's award on the ground that the tribunal did not have jurisdiction to make the award (a "jurisdictional appeal").

(2) The Outer House may decide a jurisdictional appeal by—
 (a) confirming the award,
 (b) varying the award (or part of it), or
 (c) setting aside the award (or part of it).
(3) Any variation by the Outer House has effect as part of the tribunal's award.
(4) An appeal may be made to the Inner House against the Outer House's decision on a jurisdictional appeal (but only with the leave of the Outer House).
(5) Leave may be given by the Outer House only where it considers—
 (a) that the proposed appeal would raise an important point of principle or practice, or
 (b) that there is another compelling reason for the Inner House to consider the appeal.
(6) The Outer House's decision on whether to grant such leave is final.
(7) The Inner House's decision on such an appeal is final.

Rule 68 Challenging an award: serious irregularity M

(1) A party may appeal to the Outer House against the tribunal's award on the ground of serious irregularity (a "serious irregularity appeal").
(2) "Serious irregularity" means an irregularity of any of the following kinds which has caused, or will cause, substantial injustice to the appellant—
 (a) the tribunal failing to conduct the arbitration in accordance with—
  (i) the arbitration agreement,
  (ii) these rules (in so far as they apply), or
  (iii) any other agreement by the parties relating to conduct of the arbitration,
 (b) the tribunal acting outwith its powers (other than by exceeding its jurisdiction),
 (c) the tribunal failing to deal with all the issues that were put to it,
 (d) any arbitral appointments referee or other third party to whom the parties give powers in relation to the arbitration acting outwith powers,
 (e) uncertainty or ambiguity as to the award's effect,
 (f) the award being—
  (i) contrary to public policy, or
  (ii) obtained by fraud or in a way which is contrary to public policy,
 (g) an arbitrator having not been impartial and independent,
 (h) an arbitrator having not treated the parties fairly,
 (i) an arbitrator having been incapable of acting as an arbitrator in the arbitration (or there being justifiable doubts about an arbitrator's ability to so act),
 (j) an arbitrator not having a qualification which the parties agreed (before the arbitrator's appointment) that the arbitrator must have, or
 (k) any other irregularity in the conduct of the arbitration or in the award which is admitted by—
  (i) the tribunal, or

       (ii)   any arbitral appointments referee or other third party to whom the parties give powers in relation to the arbitration.

(3) The Outer House may decide a serious irregularity appeal by—

    (a) confirming the award,

    (b) ordering the tribunal to reconsider the award (or part of it), or

    (c) if it considers reconsideration inappropriate, setting aside the award (or part of it).

(4) Where the Outer House decides a serious irregularity appeal (otherwise than by confirming the award) on the ground—

    (a) that the tribunal failed to conduct the arbitration in accordance with—

       (i)   the arbitration agreement,

       (ii) these rules (in so far as they apply), or

       (iii) any other agreement by the parties relating to conduct of the arbitration,

    (b) that an arbitrator has not been impartial and independent, or

    (c) that an arbitrator has not treated the parties fairly,

it may also make such order as it thinks fit about any arbitrator's entitlement (if any) to fees and expenses (and such an order may provide for the repayment of fees or expenses already paid to the arbitrator).

(5) An appeal may be made to the Inner House against the Outer House's decision on a serious irregularity appeal (but only with the leave of the Outer House).

(6) Leave may be given by the Outer House only where it considers—

    (a) that the proposed appeal would raise an important point of principle or practice, or

    (b) that there is another compelling reason for the Inner House to consider the appeal.

(7) The Outer House's decision on whether to grant such leave is final.

(8) The Inner House's decision on such an appeal is final.

Rule 69 Challenging an award: legal error D

(1) A party may appeal to the Outer House against the tribunal's award on the ground that the tribunal erred on a point of Scots law (a "legal error appeal").

(2) An agreement between the parties to disapply rule 51(2)(c) by dispensing with the tribunal's duty to state its reasons for its award is to be treated as an agreement to exclude the court's jurisdiction to consider a legal error appeal.

Rule 70 Legal error appeals: procedure etc. M

(1) This rule applies only where rule 69 applies.

(2) A legal error appeal may be made only—

    (a) with the agreement of the parties, or

    (b) with the leave of the Outer House.

(3) Leave to make a legal error appeal may be given only if the Outer House is satisfied—
    (a) that deciding the point will substantially affect a party's rights,
    (b) that the tribunal was asked to decide the point, and
    (c) that, on the basis of the findings of fact in the award (including any facts which the tribunal treated as established for the purpose of deciding the point), the tribunal's decision on the point—
        (i) was obviously wrong, or
        (ii) where the court considers the point to be of general importance, is open to serious doubt.

(4) An application for leave is valid only if it—
    (a) identifies the point of law concerned, and
    (b) states why the applicant considers that leave should be granted.

(5) The Outer House must determine an application for leave without a hearing (unless satisfied that a hearing is required).

(6) The Outer House's determination of an application for leave is final.

(7) Any leave to appeal expires 7 days after it is granted (and so any legal error appeal made after then is accordingly invalid unless made with the agreement of the parties).

(8) The Outer House may decide a legal error appeal by—
    (a) confirming the award,
    (b) ordering the tribunal to reconsider the award (or part of it), or
    (c) if it considers reconsideration inappropriate, setting aside the award (or part of it).

(9) An appeal may be made to the Inner House against the Outer House's decision on a legal error appeal (but only with the leave of the Outer House).

(10) Leave may be given by the Outer House only where it considers—
    (a) that the proposed appeal would raise an important point of principle or practice, or
    (b) that there is another compelling reason for the Inner House to consider the appeal.

(11) The Outer House's decision on whether to grant such leave is final.

(12) The Inner House's decision on such an appeal is final.

Rule 71 Challenging an award: supplementary M

(1) This rule applies to—
    (a) jurisdictional appeals,
    (b) serious irregularity appeals, and
    (c) where rule 69 applies to the arbitration, legal error appeals,
and references to "appeal" are to be construed accordingly.

(2) An appeal is competent only if the appellant has exhausted any available arbitral process of appeal or review (including any recourse available under rule 58).

(3) No appeal may be made against a provisional award.
(4) An appeal must be made no later than 28 days after the later of the following dates—
    (a) the date on which the award being appealed against is made,
    (b) if the award is subject to a process of correction under rule 58, the date on which the tribunal decides whether to correct the award, or
    (c) if there has been an arbitral process of appeal or review, the date on which the appellant was notified of the result of that process.
    A legal error appeal is to be treated as having being made for the purposes of this rule if an application for leave is made.
(5) An application for leave to appeal against the Outer House's decision on an appeal must be made no later than 28 days after the date on which the decision is made (and any such leave expires 7 days after it is granted).
(6) An appellant must give notice of an appeal to the other party and the tribunal.
(7) The tribunal may continue with the arbitration pending determination of an appeal against a part award.
(8) Outer House (or the Inner House in the case of an appeal against the Outer House's decision) may—
    (a) order the tribunal to state its reasons for the award being appealed in sufficient detail to enable the Outer House (or Inner House) to deal with the appeal properly, and
    (b) make any other order it thinks fit with respect to any additional expenses arising from that order.
(9) Where the Outer House (or the Inner House in the case of an appeal against the Outer House's decision) decides an appeal by setting aside the award (or any part of it), it may also order that any provision in an arbitration agreement which prevents the bringing of legal proceedings in relation to the subject-matter of the award (or that part of it) is void.
(10) The Outer House (or the Inner House in the case of an appeal against the Outer House's decision) may—
    (a) order an appellant (or an applicant for leave to appeal) to provide security for the expenses of the appeal (or application), and
    (b) dismiss the appeal (or application) if the order is not complied with.
(11) But such an order may not be made only on the ground that the appellant (or applicant)—
    (a) is an individual who ordinarily resides outwith the United Kingdom, or
    (b) is a body which is—
       (i) incorporated or formed under the law of a country outwith the United Kingdom, or
       (ii) managed or controlled from outwith the United Kingdom.
(12) The Outer House (or the Inner House in the case of an appeal against the Outer House's decision) may—
    (a) order that any amount due under an award being appealed (or any associated provisional award) must be paid into court or otherwise secured

pending its decision on the appeal (or the application for leave to appeal), and

(b) dismiss the appeal (or application) if the order is not complied with.

(13) An appeal to the Inner House against any decision of the Outer House under this rule may be made only with the leave of the Outer House.

(14) An application for leave to appeal against such a decision must be made no later than 28 days after the date on which the decision is made (and any such leave expires 7 days after it is granted).

(15) Leave may be given by the Outer House only where it considers—

(a) that the proposed appeal would raise an important point of principle or practice, or

(b) that there is another compelling reason for the Inner House to consider the appeal.

(16) The Outer House's decision on whether to grant such leave is final.

(17) A decision of the Inner House under this rule (including any decision on an appeal against a decision by the Outer House) is final.

Rule 72 Reconsideration by tribunal M

(1) Where the Outer House or, as the case may be, the Inner House decides a serious irregularity appeal or a legal error appeal by ordering the tribunal to reconsider its award (or any part of it), the tribunal must make a new award in respect of the matter concerned (or confirm its original award) by no later than—

(a) in the case of a decision by the Outer House—

(i) where the decision is appealed, the day falling 3 months after the appeal (or, as the case may be, the application for leave to appeal) is dismissed or abandoned,

(ii) where the decision is not appealed, the day falling 3 months after the decision is made, or

(iii) such other day as the Outer House may specify,

(b) in the case of a decision by the Inner House—

(i) the day falling 3 months after the decision is made, or

(ii) such other day as the Inner House may specify.

(2) These rules apply in relation to the new award as they apply in relation to the appealed award.

Part 9
Miscellaneous

Rule 73 Immunity of tribunal etc. M

(1) Neither the tribunal nor any arbitrator is liable for anything done or omitted in the performance, or purported performance, of the tribunal's functions.

(2) This rule does not apply—
  (a) if the act or omission is shown to have been in bad faith, or
  (b) to any liability arising from an arbitrator's resignation (but see rule 16(1 (c)).
(3) This rule applies to any clerk, agent, employee or other person assisting the tribunal to perform its functions as it applies to the tribunal.

Rule 74 Immunity of appointing arbitral institution etc. M

(1) An arbitral appointments referee, or other third party who the parties ask to appoint or nominate an arbitrator, is not liable—
  (a) for anything done or omitted in the performance, or purported performance, of that function (unless the act or omission is shown to have been in bad faith), or
  (b) for the acts or omissions of—
    (i) any arbitrator whom it nominates or appoints, or
    (ii) the tribunal of which such an arbitrator forms part (or any clerk, agent or employee of that tribunal).
(2) This rule applies to an arbitral appointments referee's, or other third party's, agents and employees as it applies to the referee or other third party.

Rule 75 Immunity of experts, witnesses and legal representatives M

Every person who participates in an arbitration as an expert, witness or legal representative has the same immunity in respect of acts or omissions as the person would have if the arbitration were civil proceedings.

Rule 76 Loss of right to object M

(1) A party who participates in an arbitration without making a timeous objection on the ground—
  (a) that an arbitrator is ineligible to act as an arbitrator,
  (b) that an arbitrator is not impartial and independent,
  (c) that an arbitrator has not treated the parties fairly,
  (d) that the tribunal does not have jurisdiction,
  (e) that the arbitration has not been conducted in accordance with—
    (i) the arbitration agreement,
    (ii) these rules (in so far as they apply), or
    (iii) any other agreement by the parties relating to conduct of the arbitration,
  (f) that the arbitration has been affected by any other serious irregularity,
  may not raise the objection later before the tribunal or the court.
(2) An objection is timeous if it is made—

    (a) as soon as reasonably practicable after the circumstances giving rise to the ground for objection first arose,

    (b) by such later date as may be allowed by—

        (i)   the arbitration agreement,

        (ii) these rules (in so far as they apply),

        (iii) the other party, or

    (c) where the tribunal considers that circumstances justify a later objection, by such later date as it may allow.

(3) This rule does not apply where the party shows that it did not object timeously because it—

    (a) did not know of the ground for objection, and

    (b) could not with reasonable diligence have discovered that ground.

(4) This rule does not allow a party to raise an objection which it is barred from raising for any reason other than failure to object timeously.

Rule 77 Independence of arbitrator M

For the purposes of these rules, an arbitrator is not independent in relation to an arbitration if—

    (a) the arbitrator's relationship with any party,

    (b) the arbitrator's financial or other commercial interests, or

    (c) anything else,

gives rise to justifiable doubts as to the arbitrator's impartiality.

Rule 78 Consideration where arbitrator judged not to be impartial and independent D

(1) This rule applies where—

    (a) an arbitrator is removed by the Outer House under rule 12 on the ground that the arbitrator is not impartial and independent,

    (b) the tribunal is dismissed by the Outer House under rule 13 on the ground that it has failed to comply with its duty to be impartial and independent, or

    (c) the tribunal's award (or any part of it) is returned to the tribunal for reconsideration, or is set aside, on either of those grounds (see rule 68).

(2) Where this rule applies, the Outer House must have particular regard to whether an arbitrator has complied with rule 8 when it is considering whether to make an order under rule 16(1) or 68(4) about—

    (a) the arbitrator's entitlement (if any) to fees or expenses,

    (b) repaying fees or expenses already paid to the arbitrator.

Rule 79 Death of arbitrator M

An arbitrator's authority is personal and ceases on death.

Rule 80 Death of party D

(1) An arbitration agreement is not discharged by the death of a party and may be enforced by or against the executor or other representative of that party.

(2) This rule does not affect the operation of any law by virtue of which a substantive right or obligation is extinguished by death.

Rule 81 Unfair treatment D

A tribunal (or arbitrator) who treats any party unfairly is, for the purposes of these rules, to be deemed not to have treated the parties fairly.

Rule 82 Rules applicable to umpires M

(1) The following rules apply in relation to an umpire appointed under rule 30 (or otherwise with the agreement of the parties) as they apply in relation to an arbitrator or, as the case may be, the tribunal—

> rule 4
> rule 8
> rules 10 to 14
> rule 24
> rule 26
> rules 59, 60 and 61(1)
> rule 68
> rule 73
> rules 76 to 79

(2) But the parties are, in so far as those rules are not mandatory rules, free to modify or disapply the way in which those rules would otherwise apply to an umpire.

Rule 83 Formal communications D

(1) A "formal communication" means any application, award, consent, direction, notice, objection, order, reference, request, requirement or waiver made or given or any document served—

(a) in pursuance of an arbitration agreement,

(b) for the purposes of these rules (in so far as they apply), or

(c) otherwise in relation to an arbitration.

(2) A formal communication must be in writing.

(3) A formal communication is made, given or served if it is—

(a) hand delivered to the person concerned,

(b) sent to the person concerned by first class post in a properly addressed envelope or package—

(i) in the case of an individual, to the individual's principal place of business or usual or last known abode,

    (ii) in the case of a body corporate, to the body's registered or principal office, or

    (iii) in either case, to any postal address designated for the purpose by the intended recipient (such designation to be made by giving notice to the person giving or serving the formal communication), or

  (c) sent to the person concerned in some other way (including by email, fax or other electronic means) which the sender reasonably considers likely to cause it to be delivered on the same or next day.

(4) A formal communication which is sent by email, fax or other electronic means is to be treated as being in writing only if it is legible and capable of being used for subsequent reference.

(5) A formal communication is, unless the contrary is proved, to be treated as having been made, given or served—

  (a) where hand delivered, on the day of delivery,

  (b) where posted, on the day on which it would be delivered in the ordinary course of post, or

  (c) where sent in any other way described above, on the day after it is sent.

(6) The tribunal may determine that a formal communication—

  (a) is to be delivered in such other manner as it may direct, or

  (b) need not be delivered,

    but it may do so only if satisfied that it is not reasonably practicable for the formal communication to be made, given or served in accordance with this rule (or, as the case may be, with any contrary agreement between the parties).

(7) This rule does not apply in relation to any application, order, notice, document or other thing which is made, given or served in or for the purposes of legal proceedings.

Rule 84 Periods of time D

Periods of time are to be calculated for the purposes of an arbitration as follows—

  (a) where any act requires to be done within a specified period after or from a specified date or event, the period begins immediately after that date or, as the case may be, the date of that event, and

  (b) where the period is a period of 7 days or less, the following days are to be ignored—

    (i) Saturdays and Sundays, and

    (ii) any public holidays in the place where the act concerned is to be done.

SCHEDULE 2
REPEALS

(introduced by section 29)

Enactment	Extent of repeal
Arbitration (Scotland) Act 1894 (c.13)	The whole Act
Arbitration Act 1950 (c.27)	The whole Act
Administration of Justice (Scotland) Act 1972 (c.59)	Section 3
Arbitration Act 1975 (c.3)	The whole Act
Law Reform (Miscellaneous Provisions) (Scotland) Act 1980 (c.55)	Section 17
Law Reform (Miscellaneous Provisions) (Scotland) Act 1990 (c.40)	Section 66 Schedule 7

Commencement

Sch. 2 para. 1: June 7, 2010 except for the purposes of statutory arbitration; not yet in force otherwise (SSI 2010/195 art. 2)

Extent

Sch. 2 para. 1: Scotland

Appendix 2

The Rules of Court

The Act of Sederunt (Rules of the Court of Session Amendment No 4) (Miscellaneous) 2010 (SSI 2010/205) makes changes to the Rules of the Court of Session 1994 (as amended) ('RCS'). The new provisions came into force on 7 June 2011. Paragraph 10(2) substitutes the provisions in respect of the Enforcement of Arbitral awards (Convention awards).

PART IX
ENFORCEMENT OF ARBITRAL AWARDS UNDER THE NEW YORK CONVENTION ON THE RECOGNITION AND ENFORCEMENT OF FOREIGN ARBITRAL AWARDS

62.56 Interpretation and application of this Part

(1) In this Part—
'the 2010 Act' means the Arbitration (Scotland) Act 2010;
'the Convention' means the New York Convention on the Recognition and Enforcement of Foreign Arbitral Awards;
'Convention award' means an award made in pursuance of a written arbitration agreement in a territory of a state (other than the United Kingdom) which is a party to the Convention.
(2) This Part applies to an application under section 19 of the 2010 Act (recognition and enforcement of New York Convention awards).

62.57 Applications for enforcement of a Convention award

(1) An application for enforcement of a Convention award under section 19(2) of the 2010 Act shall be made by petition or, where there are proceedings depending before the court under the 2010 Act in relation to the same arbitration process, by note in the process of the petition.
(2) There shall be produced with such a petition or note—
  (a) the duly authenticated original award or a certified copy of it;
  (b) the original agreement referred to in article II of the Convention or a certified copy of it;
  (c) a translation of any award or agreement which is in a language other than English, certified by an official or sworn translator or by a diplomatic or consular agent;

(d) an affidavit stating—
   (i)   the full name, title, trade or business and the usual or last known place of residence or, where appropriate, of the business of the petitioner or noter and the party against whom the Convention award was made;
   (ii) the amount of the Convention award which is unsatisfied; and
   (iii) that the Convention award has become binding on the parties and has not been set aside or suspended by a court of the country which, or under the law of which, the award was made.

62.58   Registration of Convention award

(1) The court, on being satisfied that the Convention award may be registered, shall grant warrant for registration.
(2) Where the court pronounces an interlocutor under paragraph (1), the Deputy Principal Clerk shall enter the Convention award in a register of Convention awards.
(3) Where the Keeper of the Registers receives from the petitioner or noter the documents referred to in paragraph (4), he or she shall register them in the register of judgments of the Books of Council and Session.
(4) The documents are—
   (a) a certified copy of the interlocutor of the warrant of registration,
   (b) a certified copy of the Convention award to be registered, and any translation of it, and
   (c) any certificate of currency conversion under rule 62.2(1)(b).
(5) An extract of a registered Convention award with warrant for execution shall not be issued by the Keeper of the Registers until a certificate of service under rule 62.59 (service on party against whom Convention award made) is produced to him or her.

62.59   Service on party against whom Convention award made

On registration under rule 62.58, the petitioner or noter shall forthwith serve a notice of registration on the party against whom the Convention award was made in Form 62.59.

62.60   Application for refusal of recognition or enforcement of a Convention award

(1) An application under article V of the Convention (request by party against whom Convention award made for refusal of recognition or enforcement) shall be made by note.
(2) A note referred to in paragraph (1) may crave—
   (a) suspension or interdict of any past or future steps in the execution of the

       Convention award, including registration or enforcement of the award; and

   (b) recall of the interlocutor pronounced under rule 62.58(1) (registration under the Convention).

(3) The note shall be supported by affidavit and any relevant documentary evidence.

(4) Where any interlocutor pronounced under rule 62.59(1) is recalled, a certificate to that effect issued by the Deputy Principal Clerk shall be sufficient warrant to the Keeper of the Registers to cancel the registration and return the documents registered to the petitioner or noter on whose application the interlocutor under that rule was pronounced.

Paragraph 10(4) of the Act of Sederunt inserts into the Rules of Court a new Chapter 100 (Arbitration) in respect of arbitration applications.

CHAPTER 100
ARBITRATION

100.1   Interpretation and application

(1) In this Chapter—

     'the 2010 Act' means the Arbitration (Scotland) Act 2010;

     'Convention award' means an award made in pursuance of a written arbitration agreement in a territory of a state (other than the United Kingdom) which is a party to the New York Convention on the Recognition and Enforcement of Foreign Arbitral Awards;

     'Scottish Arbitration Rules' means the Scottish Arbitration Rules set out in schedule 1 to the 2010 Act;

     'tribunal' means a sole arbitrator or panel of arbitrators.

(2) Subject to paragraph (3), this Chapter applies to applications and appeals made under the 2010 Act (including applications and appeals made under the Scottish Arbitration Rules).

(3) Rules 100.5 and 100.7 do not apply to an application under section 19(2) of the 2010 [Act] for enforcement of a Convention award.

100.2   Proceedings before a nominated judge

All proceedings in the Outer House in a cause to which this Chapter applies shall be brought before a judge of the court nominated by the Lord President as an arbitration judge or, where no such judge is available, any other judge of the court (including the vacation judge).

100.3   Procedure in causes under the 2010 Act

Subject to the provisions of the Scottish Arbitration Rules and this Chapter, the procedure in a cause under the Scottish Arbitration Rules shall be such as the judge dealing with the cause shall determine.

100.4   Disapplication of certain rules

The following rules shall not apply to a cause under this Part—
  rule 6.2 (fixing and allocation of diets in Outer House);
  rule 14.5 (first order in petitions);
  rule 14.6 (period of notice for lodging answers);
  rule 14.8 (procedure where answers lodged).

100.5   Application or appeal under the 2010 Act

(1)   Subject to paragraph (2), an application or appeal under the 2010 Act shall be made by petition.
(2)   If proceedings are depending before the court under paragraph (1) in relation to the same arbitration process, an application under the 2010 Act shall be made by note in the process of the petition.
(3)   Upon lodging a petition or note under paragraph (1) or (2), the petitioner or noter must enrol a motion for intimation and service of the petition or note and the court may make such order as is appropriate in the circumstances of the case.
(4)   The court may make an order for intimation and service of the petition or note at the address of a party's agent or other person acting for that party in the arbitration process and the service will be effective if carried out in accordance with that order.
(5)   Upon expiry of any period of notice following intimation and service of the petition or note, the petitioner or noter shall enrol a motion for further procedure and the court may make such order as is appropriate in the circumstances of the case, including, where appropriate, an order disposing of the petition or note.

100.6   Application for attendance of witnesses or disclosure of evidence

In relation to a petition or note lodged under rule 45 of the Scottish Arbitration Rules (court's power to order attendance of witnesses and disclosure of evidence), intimation and service of the petition or note is not required.

100.7   Averments in petitions and notes under the 2010 Act

(1) The petitioner or noter must set out in the petition or note the facts and circumstances on which the petition or note is founded and the relief claimed.
(2) In particular, any—
   (a) application under rule 22 (referral of point of jurisdiction) or rule 41 (referral of point of law) of the Scottish Arbitration Rules, or
   (b) appeal under rule 67(1) (jurisdictional appeal), rule 68(1) (serious irregularity appeal) or rule 69(1) (legal error appeal) of the Scottish Arbitration Rules, should, so far as is necessary, identify the matters referred to in paragraph (3).
(3) The following matters should be identified—
   (a) the parties to the cause and the arbitration from which the cause arises;
   (b) the relevant rule of the Scottish Arbitration Rules or other provision of the 2010 Act under which the petition or note has been lodged;
   (c) any special capacity in which the petitioner or noter is acting or any special capacity in which any other party to the proceedings is acting;
   (d) a summary of the circumstances out of which the application or appeal arises;
   (e) the grounds on which the application or appeal proceeds;
   (f) in the case of an appeal under rule 67(1), whether the appellant seeks the variation or the setting aside of an award (or part of it);
   (g) in the case of an appeal under rule 69(1), whether the appeal is made with the agreement of the parties to the arbitration;
   (h) any relevant requirements of the Scottish Arbitration Rules which have been met.

100.8   Appeals against arbitral award on ground of legal error

(1) In addition to complying with rule 100.5(3) and (5), upon lodging a petition or note under rule 69 of the Scottish Arbitration Rules (legal error appeal), the petitioner or noter shall at the same time—
   (a) except in a case where an appeal is made with the agreement of the parties, enrol a motion for leave to appeal; and
   (b) lodge any documents that the petitioner or noter intends to rely on in the application for leave (if applicable) and in the appeal.
(2) A motion for leave to appeal under paragraph (1) shall—
   (a) identify the point of law concerned; and
   (b) set out the grounds that are relied on for the giving of leave.
(3) Within 14 days of service of the petition or note, or such other time as the court may allow, a respondent may lodge and intimate to all other parties grounds of opposition, including any evidence to be relied upon in opposition to the application for leave.
(4) The application for leave to appeal shall be dealt with without a hearing unless the court considers that a hearing is required.

(5) Where the court considers that a hearing is required, it may give such further directions as it considers necessary.

(6) Rule 41.2 (applications for leave to appeal), rule 41.3 (determination of applications for leave to appeal) and rule 41.3A (competency of appeals) do not apply to an application for leave to appeal under this rule.

100.9 Anonymity in legal proceedings

(1) Where a petition or note is lodged under the 2010 Act, any application to the court under section 15 of the 2010 Act (anonymity in legal proceedings) shall be made not later than the hearing of a motion for further procedure under rule 100.5(5).

(2) Until an application under section 15 of the 2010 Act has been determined or, where no such application has been made, the time at which a motion for further procedure is made under rule 100.5(5) and, thereafter, if the court grants an order under section 15 of the 2010 Act—

    (a) the petition or note shall not be available for inspection, except by court staff and the parties;

    (b) the petition or note shall be referred to publicly, including in the rolls of court, as 'Arbitration Application' or 'Arbitration Appeal' (as the case may be) and by reference to a number and the year in which it was lodged;

    (c) the court proceedings shall be heard in private.

(3) Unless the court grants an order under section 15 of the 2010 Act, all applications and appeals made under the 2010 Act shall be heard in public.

100.10 Applications for enforcement of a tribunal's award under the 2010 Act

(1) A petition or note under section 12 of the 2010 Act for enforcement of a tribunal's award shall—

    (a) Identify the parties to the cause and the arbitration process from which the cause arises;

    (b) specify that the award is not currently the subject of—

        (i) an appeal under Part 8 of the Scottish Arbitration Rules (challenging awards);

        (ii) any arbitral process of appeal or review; or

        (iii) a process of correction under rule 58 of the Scottish Arbitration Rules; and

    (c) specify the basis on which the tribunal had jurisdiction to make the award.

(2) There shall be produced with such a petition or note—

    (a) the original tribunal's award or a certified copy of it; and

    (b) the documents founded upon or adopted as incorporated in the petition or note.

Appendix 3

New York Convention States

The following countries are Convention States for the purposes of the New York Convention 1958, as at the date of publication. Note that some countries have reservations in respect of some provisions of the Convention, and that the Appendix uses the common names for some countries, rather than the formal name recorded by UNCITRAL (eg South Korea rather than Republic of Korea) for ease of reference by users. Please also note that the Convention may have been ratified at an earlier date, but the date of accession or succession has been used, although the precise date of coming into force (typically about three months later) in the country concerned should always be checked.

Country	Accession or Ratification date	Country	Accession or Ratification date
Afghanistan	30/11/04	Albania	27/6/01
Algeria	7/2/89	Andorra	19/6/15
Angola	6/3/17	Antigua and Barbuda	2/2/89
Argentina	14/3/89	Armenia	29/12/97
Australia	26/3/75	Austria	2/5/61
Azerbaijan	29/2/00	Bahamas	20/12/06
Bahrain	6/4/88	Bangladesh	9/5/92
Barbados	16/3/93	Belarus	15/11/60
Belgium	18/8/75	Benin	16/5/74
Bhutan	25/9/14	Bolivia (Plurinational State of)	28/4/95
Bosnia and Herzegovina	1/9/93	Botswana	20/12/71
Brazil	7/6/02	Brunei Darussalam	25/7/96
Bulgaria	10/10/61	Burkina Faso	23/3/87
Burundi	23/6/14	Cabo Verde	22/3/18
Cambodia	5/1/60	Cameroon	19/2/88
Canada	12/5/86	Central African Republic	15/10/62
Chile	4/9/75	China	22/1/87
Colombia	25/9/79	Comoros	28/4/15
Cook Islands	12/1/09	Costa Rica	26/10/87
Cote D'Ivoire	1/2/91	Croatia	26/7/93
Cuba	30/12/74	Cyprus	29/12/80

Country	Accession or Ratification date	Country	Accession or Ratification date
Czech Republic	30/9/93	Democratic Republic of the Congo	5/11/14
Denmark	22/12/72	Djibouti	14/6/83
Dominica	28/12/88	Dominican |Republic	11/4/02
Ecuador	3/1/62	Egypt	9/3/59
El Salvador	26/2/88	Estonia	30/8/93
Ethiopia	24/8/20	Fiji	27/9/10
Finland	19/1/62	France	26/6/59
Gabon	15/12/06	Georgia	2/6/94
Germany	30/6/61	Ghana	9/4/68
Greece	16/7/63	Guatemala	21/3/84
Guinea	23/1/91	Guyana	25/9/14
Haiti	5/12/83	Holy See	14/5/75
Honduras	3/10/00	Hungary	5/3/62
Iceland	24/1/02	India	13/7/60
Indonesia	7/10/81	Iran (Islamic Republic of)	15/10/01
Ireland	12/5/81	Israel	5/1/59*
Italy	31/1/69	Jamaica	10/7/02
Japan	20/6/61	Jordan	15/11/79
Kazakhstan	20/11/95	Kenya	10/2/89
Kuwait	28/4/78	Kyrgyzstan	18/12/96
Lao People's Democratic Republic	17/6/98	Latvia	14/4/92
Lebanon	11/8/98	Lesotho	13/6/89
Liberia	16/9/05	Liechtenstein	7/7/11
Lithuania	14/3/95	Luxembourg	9/9/83
Madagascar	16/7/62	Malaysia	5/11/85
Maldives	17/9/19	Mali	8/9/94
Malta	22/6/00	Marshall Islands	21/12/06
Mauritania	30/6/97	Mauritius	19/6/96
Mexico	14/4/71	Monaco	2/6/82
Mongolia	24/10/94	Montenegro	23/10/06
Morocco	12/2/59	Mozambique	11/6/98
Myanmar	16/4/13	Nepal	4/3/98
Netherlands	24/4/64	New Zealand	6/1/83
Nicaragua	24/9/03	Niger	14/10/64
Nigeria	17/3/70	North Macedonia	10/3/94
Norway	14/3/61	Oman	25/2/99
Pakistan	14/7/05	Palau	31/3/20

Country	Accession or Ratification date	Country	Accession or Ratification date
Panama	10/10/84	Papua New Guinea	17/7/19
Paraguay	8/10/97	Peru	7/7/88
Philippines	6/7/67	Poland	3/10/61
Portugal	18/10/94	Qatar	30/12/02
Republic of Korea	8/2/73	Republic of Moldova	8/9/98
Romania	13/9/61	Russian Federation	24/8/60
Rwanda	31/10/08	San Marino	15/5/79
Sao Tome and Principe	20/11/12	Saudi Arabia	16/4/94
Senegal	17/10/94	Serbia	12/3/01
Seychelles	3/2/20	Sierra Leone	28/10/20
Singapore	21/8/86	Slovakia	28/5/93
Slovenia	6/7/92	South Africa	3/5/76
Spain	12/5/77	Sri Lanka	9/4/62
St Vincent and the Grenadines	12/9/00	State of Palestine	2/1/15
Sudan	26/3/18	Sweden	28/1/72
Switzerland	1/6/65	Syrian Arab Republic	9/3/59
Tajikistan	14/8/12	Thailand	21/12/59
Tonga	12/6/20	Trinidad and Tobago	14/2/66
Tunisia	17/6/67	Turkey	2/7/92
Uganda	12/2/92	Ukraine	10/10/60
United Arab Emirates	21/8/06	United Kingdom of Great Britain and Northern Ireland	24/9/75
United Republic of Tanzania	13/10/64	United States of America	30/9/70
Uruguay	30/3/83	Uzbekistan	7/2/96
Venezuela (Bolivarian Republic of)	8/2/95	Viet Nam	12/9/95
Zambia	14/3/02	Zimbabwe	29/9/94

NOTE – The official names are used for all countries.
For Congo see Democratic Republic of Congo
For South Korea see Republic of Korea
For Moldova see Republic of Moldova
For Palestine see State of Palestine
For Tanzania see United Republic of Tanzania

Appendix 4

Recognition and Enforcement of Convention Awards

Form 62.59 below is inserted into the Rules of Court by the Act of Sederunt (SSI 2010/205) para 10(3).

FORM 62.59

Rule 62.59
Form of notice of registration of award under the New York Convention on the Recognition and Enforcement of Foreign Arbitral Awards

REGISTRATION OF AWARD UNDER THE NEW YORK CONVENTION ON THE RECOGNITION AND ENFORCEMENT OF FOREIGN ARBITRAL AWARDS

Date: (*date of posting or other method of service*)
To: (*name and address of person on whom service executed*)

TAKE NOTICE

That on (*date*) [Lord/Lady (*name*) in] the Court of Session, Edinburgh, granted warrant for the registration of (*identify award to be registered*) on the application of (*name and address of petitioner or noter*).

The above award was registered in the Books of Council and Session on (*date*) for execution (enforcement). An application will be made to the Keeper of the Registers of Scotland for an extract of the registered award with warrant for execution.

> (*Signed*)
> Messenger-at-Arms
> [*or* Solicitor [*or* Agent] for petitioner or noter]
> (*Address*)

Appendix 5

United Nations Convention on International Settlement Agreements Resulting from Mediation (the 'Singapore Convention on Mediation')

Introduction

Although mediation as a dispute resolution mechanism has a long history, it is in the last couple of decades that it has started to be used seriously in commercial disputes, both domestically and internationally. Policy decisions by the courts to encourage mediation, use by parties in dispute resolution clauses, and increased general public awareness have, it is suggested, all contributed to this. The interrelationship between mediation and arbitration (often in the past grouped together and referred to, together with other processes, as ADR) has been redefined and both are now recognised methods of resolving disputes.

Increasing interest in this area can be seen in the promulgation of policy papers and reports by interested pressure groups and Scotland is no different. At the time of writing, an interest group called Scottish Mediation has published (in July 2019) a paper called *Bringing Mediation into the Mainstream in Civil Justice in Scotland* which proposes, among other things, more encouragement for mediation by the courts and the introduction of a Scottish Mediation Act. The Scottish Government has formally responded that it intends to launch a public consultation on mediation and wider dispute resolution reforms in 2020 and to collaborate with key stakeholders within a 'Collaborative Partnership on Dispute Resolution' to establish a new 'Scottish Dispute Resolution Delivery Group' as part of developing its policy on dispute resolution. The Justice Committee of the Scottish Parliament has also published a report: 'I Won't See You in Court: Alternative Dispute Resolution in Scotland' (2018).

It is submitted therefore that it will be vital for lawyers generally to be aware of mediation as a dispute resolution mechanism as well as arbitration and litigation. Solicitors must comply with the Rules and Guidance issued by the Law Society of Scotland, which require that Solicitors 'must communicate effectively with ... clients and others. This includes providing clients with any relevant information ... and which is necessary to allow informed decisions to be made by clients ... Information must be clear and comprehensive and, where necessary or appropriate, confirmed in writing' (Rule 1.9.1). Solicitors are also required to:

have a sufficient understanding of commonly available alternative dispute resolution options to allow proper consideration and communication of options
to a client in considering the client's interests and objectives. A solicitor providing advice on dispute resolution procedures should be able to discuss
and explain available options, including the advantages and disadvantages
of each, to a client in such a way as to enable the client to make an informed
decision as to the course of action and procedure he or she should pursue to
best meet their needs and objectives, and to instruct the solicitor accordingly
(Guidance B1.9).

Reference has been made in the text to Practice Note No 1 of 2017 in relation
to Commercial Actions, which states (at Note 11) that, before bringing a
case in the commercial court of the Court of Session, 'Both parties should
consider carefully and discuss whether all or some of the dispute may be
amenable to some form of alternative dispute resolution.'

This may be the start of greater use of mediation (and arbitration) in
the Scottish civil justice system and lawyers in Scotland will have to be
conversant with these as well as the enforcement elements in the Singapore
Mediation Convention.

At a European level, for over 10 years now the UK has had the benefit of
the Mediation Directive 2008/52/EC (implemented in the UK by the Cross-
Border Mediation (EU Directive) Regulations 2011 (SI 2011/1133) and in
Scotland by the Cross-Border Mediation (Scotland) Regulations 2011 (SSI
2011/234)), which allows the enforcement of cross-border mediated settlement agreements through the national courts of other Member States. Indeed,
in EU law it has recently been held that in disputes involving consumers,
and where the law of the Member State permits it, mandatory mediation
should take place before any court proceedings (*Menini v Banco Popolare
Società Cooperativa* (C-75/16) European Court of Justice (First Chamber)
EU:C:2017:457 EU) (2017)).

In terms of the Singapore Convention, the United Kingdom and other EU
countries, however, are yet to sign (the EU, for its part, has been engaged in
discussions as to whether to sign *en bloc* or to leave it to individual member
states, and following Brexit, the UK will presumably now make its own
decision). It is worthy of note though, that even without ratification, the
citizens of the UK and Member States could still benefit from the Singapore
Convention as, under the Convention, there is no requirement for reciproc-
ity, so a settlement agreement signed in the UK or a Member State can still
be enforced in another jurisdiction which is a signatory.)

At an international level, mediation holds the same attractions for parties
in terms of confidentiality, as dispute resolution incorporated into transnational agreements, as well as those of speed and flexibility. But the problem
of enforcement of such mediation agreements has remained, where, for
example, the parties have mediated a settlement, but where one party has
later reneged on it.

In terms of enforcement, at a domestic level, if all the parties to the mediated agreement were in one jurisdiction, then a party wanting to enforce the terms of a mediated settlement could bring court proceedings in that jurisdiction for implementation of that agreement or for breach of contract. That is the position in the England and Wales (*Pedriks v Grimaux* [2019] EWHC 2165 (QB)) and would likely be followed in Scotland.

The problem lay with international agreements where the parties were situated in different jurisdictions. This has become more acute as more and more trade and commerce is cross-border and transnational and the additional requirement of contracts increasingly demanding mediation as a step in a tiered or escalation dispute resolution clause. Parties could agree to arbitration, but an arbitral final award would be needed first before it could be enforced by an Award Creditor under the New York Convention in the courts of the place of the assets. There was no framework for enforcing mediation settlement agreements internationally. The Singapore Mediation Convention attempts to remedy that.

Lastly, some individual jurisdictions themselves have taken active steps to incorporate mediation into dispute resolution, alongside arbitration. As mentioned in the text, there have been initiatives from the Singapore International Arbitration Centre, CIETAC and the Hong Kong International Arbitration Centre, specifically focused on resolving disputes by arbitration and mediation. Singapore, in particular, has in recent years brought forward a number of initiatives in international mediation, including the Singapore International Mediation Centre (SIMC) (which offers mediation services), establishing the Singapore International Mediation Institute (which sets professional standards for the sector) and enacting the Mediation Act (which allows parties to record their mediated settlement agreements as Singapore court orders in order to enjoy the benefits of enforcement, and provides legal clarity around certain issues such as confidentiality).

The Convention

The United Nations Convention on International Settlement Agreements Resulting from Mediation was signed on 7 August 2019. It is to be known as the 'Singapore Mediation Convention'.

Mediation is defined in Art 2(3) of the Convention as 'a process, irrespective of the expression used or the basis upon which the process is carried out, whereby parties attempt to reach an amicable settlement of their dispute with the assistance of a third person or persons ("the mediator") lacking the authority to impose a solution upon the parties to the dispute.'

The Convention provides a process for the direct enforcement of cross-border settlement agreement between parties resulting from mediation and such an agreement may be enforced directly by the courts of a State. As in arbitration, a party may seek enforcement to apply directly to the courts of the State where the assets are located.

As at the present time, 53 States, including the US, South Korea, China, Malaysia, the Philippines, India, Saudi Arabia and Qatar, are now signatories. As it is an International Convention, it requires both signature and ratification and if a State has done so, a mediated settlement agreement can be enforced in that State, provided the settlement falls within the scope of the Convention. As with arbitration, it can also be invoked as a defence to a claim relating to an issue already decided by the mediated agreement.

The main provisions of the Convention

Article 1 provides that the Convention applies to international settlement agreements resulting from mediation, concluded in writing by parties to resolve a commercial dispute. Like the New York Convention, but unlike the 2010 Act, the agreement must be 'in writing'. This is defined in Art 2(2) as being in writing if 'its content is recorded in any form'. The requirement that a settlement agreement be in writing is met by an electronic communication 'if the information contained therein is accessible so as to be useable for subsequent reference'.

It must also be 'international', so that 'at least two parties to the settlement agreement have their places of business in different States or the State in which the parties to the settlement agreement have their places of business is different from either the State in which a substantial part of the obligations under the settlement agreement is performed or the State with which the subject matter of the settlement agreement is most closely connected' (Art 1(a) and (b)).

Article 1 also lists the exclusions, namely: 'settlement agreements concluded by one of the parties as a consumer for personal, family or household purposes' (Art 1(2)(a)), or relating to family, inheritance or employment law (Art 1(2)(b)). Article 1(3) states that the Convention does not apply to 'settlement agreements that have been approved by a court or concluded in the course of proceedings before a court and are enforceable as a judgment in the State of that court' (Art 1(3)(a)), or 'settlement agreements that have been recorded and are enforceable as an arbitral award' (Art 1(3)(b)).

This is presumably to prevent overlapping in enforcement provisions among settlement agreements, judgments (which already fall under the Convention on Choice of Court Agreements (2005) and the Convention on the Recognition and Enforcement of Foreign Judgments in Civil or Commercial Matters (2019)), and arbitral awards (regulated of course by the New York Convention on the Recognition and Enforcement of Foreign Arbitral Awards (1958)).

Article 3 contains the 'General Principles': namely, 'Each Party to the Convention shall enforce a settlement agreement in accordance with its rules of procedure and under the conditions laid down in this Convention' (Art 3(1)); and 'If a dispute arises concerning a matter that a party claims was already resolved by a settlement agreement, a Party to the Convention shall allow the party to invoke the settlement agreement in accordance with its rules of procedure and under the conditions laid down in this Convention, in order to prove that the matter has already been resolved (Art 3(2)).

Article 4 covers the formalities for relying on a settlement agreement, providing that the party relying on a settlement agreement 'shall supply to the competent authority the settlement agreement signed (including electronic signature) by the parties' (Art 4(1)(a)), and 'evidence that the settlement agreement results from mediation' (Art 4(1)(b)). The competent authority 'may require any necessary document in order to verify that the requirements of the Convention are complied with' (Art 4(4)).

The Convention defines in Article 5 the grounds upon which a court may refuse to grant relief at the request of the party against whom relief is sought. Echoes of the New York Convention can be seen here.

They fall into four main categories: (1) the 'incapacity' of the disputing parties (Art 5(1)(a); (2) that the settlement agreement is 'null and void, inoperative or incapable of being performed' or is 'not binding, or is not final, according to its terms' (Art 5(1)(b)); (3) the mediation procedure itself (serious breach by the mediator (Art 5(1)(e)) or a 'failure by the mediator to disclose to the parties circumstances that raise justifiable doubts as to the mediator's impartiality or independence and such failure to disclose had a material impact or undue influence on a party without which failure that party would not have entered into the settlement agreement'); and (4) where the competent authority where relief is sought finds that the agreement is contrary to the public policy of that country where enforcement is sought or that the subject-matter is not capable of settlement by mediation under the law of that country (cf arbitrability) (Art 5(2)). Note here that the court may, on its own motion, refuse to grant relief.

If an application or a claim relating to a settlement agreement has been made to a court, an arbitral tribunal or any other competent authority which may affect the relief being sought under Article 4, Article 6 empowers the competent authority of the Party to the Convention where such relief is sought, if it considers it proper, to 'adjourn the decision and may also, on the request of a party, order the other party to give suitable security.'

With the aim to provide for the application of the 'most favourable framework for settlement agreements' (analogous to ISDS Arbitrations and the Washington Convention 1960), Article 7 envisages the application of the more favourable law or treaty.

Article 8 includes the reservations that are permitted to be made by a signing state. A first reservation permits a party to the Convention 'to exclude from the application of the Convention settlement agreements to which it is a party, or to which any governmental agencies or any person acting on behalf of a governmental agency is a party, to the extent specified in the declaration'. A second reservation permits a party to the Convention 'to declare that it will apply the Convention only to the extent that the disputing parties have agreed to its application' (Art 8(1)).

Article 9 provides that 'the Convention and any reservation or withdrawal thereof shall apply only to settlement agreements' which have been 'concluded after the date when the Convention, reservation or withdrawal thereof enters into force for the Party to the Convention concerned.'

Mediation in a UK context and the effect of the Convention if ratified

Mediation in dispute resolution is increasingly used in England and Wales and Scotland as an alternative to litigation and arbitration, or as a pre-cursor to either as imposed by escalation clauses in contracts, and so, in the event that the UK signs the Convention, the provisions will be an interesting addition to the law that has developed in this area.

The interrelationship of mediation and litigation has developed significantly in the last 10 years and a growing body of case law (in English law at least) has built up. These cases have predominantly related to the interaction between mediation (and refusals to mediate) and litigation costs. The courts themselves have actively encouraged mediation and provisions can now be found in court rules and protocols (see the Civil Procedure Rules, Technology and Construction Court Guide and Pre-Action Protocol for Construction and Engineering Disputes, and Scottish Commercial Court per Practice Note No 1 of 2017 (note 11)).

It remains the case that a court cannot compel parties to resolve their disputes through mediation (*Halsey v Milton Keynes General NHS Trust* [2004] EWCA Civ 576, although see *Shirayama Shukusan Co Ltd v Danovo Ltd* [2003] EWHC 3006 (Ch)) and the position has not yet been reached where the mere presence of ADR means it is not reasonable to litigate (*Briggs v First Choice Holidays* [2017] EWHC 2012 (QB)). All considerations have to be taken into account (*Lahey v Pirelli Tyres Ltd* [2007] EWCA Civ 91). (Cf *Lomax v Lomax* [2019] EWCA Civ 1467 where it was held that a court had the power pursuant to CPR rule 3.1(2)(m) to order Early Neutral Evaluation even though one party had not consented to it. It was held that the rule did not impose a limitation to the effect that consent of all the parties was necessary as the power to do so came from the CPR themselves and therefore incorporated the overriding objectives.)

The courts have consistently ruled that an unreasonable refusal to mediate prior to or during litigation may result in later adverse costs findings (*BXB v Watch Tower and Bible Tract Society of Pennsylvania* [2020] EWHC 656 (QB); *DSN v Blackpool Football Club* [2020] EWHC 670 (QB); *Richard Wales (t/a Selective Investment Services) v CBRE Managed Services Ltd* [2020] EWHC 1050 (Comm)).

The overriding objective is that the courts must deal with cases justly and at proportionate cost and that entails consideration of the use of mediation, as opposed to litigation. In *Northrop Grumman Mission Systems Europe Ltd v BAE Systems (Al Diriyah C4I) Ltd* [2014] EWHC 3148 (TCC) the High Court considered that mediation could have a positive effect, even if a claim had no merit, as a mediator could bring a new independent perspective, and not every mediation ended in a payment to a claimant. It noted that a skilled mediator could find middle ground by analysing the parties' positions and making each reflect on its own and the other's position and a mediator might find solutions that the parties had not considered, by bringing other commercial arrangements or disputes into the discussion, or by finding future opportunities for the parties.

The issue regarding costs is whether there has been an adequate justification for not engaging in the mediation process. Where one party has offered mediation and that is refused without adequate justification, or unreasonably, the courts have reflected that fact in awards of costs (*Imperial Chemical Industries Ltd v Merit Merrell Technology Ltd (Costs)* [2018] EWHC 1577 (TCC); *Reid v Buckinghamshire Healthcare NHS Trust* [2015] EWHC B21).

The courts have been prepared, *ex post facto*, to consider for the purposes of costs, whether the mediation was one which had a 'reasonable chance of success' (*Laporte v Commissioner of Police of the Metropolis* [2015] EWHC 371 (QB)). Further, where one party has attempted to use mediation as a dilatory tactic, this might constitute reasonable refusal (*Parker Lloyd Capital Ltd v Edwardian Group Ltd* [2017] EWHC 3207 (QB)) albeit in the older authorities it was held that the fact that a party reasonably believes that it has a watertight case might be sufficient justification for a refusal to mediate (*Daniels v Commissioner of Police of the Metropolis* [2005] EWCA Civ 1312).

Courts have awarded costs on both a normal and an indemnity basis (*Imperial Chemical Industries Ltd v Merit Merrell Technology Ltd (Costs)* [2018] EWHC 1577 (TCC). They have also held that costs incurred in an abortive mediation can be recovered as incidental wasted costs in subsequent litigation (*Roundstone Nurseries Ltd v Stephenson Holdings Ltd* [2009] EWHC 1431 (TCC)) and intra-litigation mediation costs can be considered to be part and parcel of the costs of legal proceedings for the purposes of legal aid certificate (*Edmunds' Application for Judicial Review, Re* [2019] NIQB 50).

It is to be noted that recently the courts have been prepared to take steps in support of mediation agreements entered into by parties (akin to arbitration and arbitration agreements). They have been prepared to stay litigation proceedings for mediation (*King Berebon v Shell Petroleum Development Co of Nigeria Ltd* [2018] EWHC 1377 (TCC)). Where a contract has included a dispute resolution clause containing an escalation procedure with mediation required before arbitration, that has been held as a condition precedent to litigation, the litigation proceedings being stayed: *Ohpen Operations UK Ltd v Invesco Fund Managers Ltd* [2019] EWHC 2246 (TCC). It was noted in that judgment (paras [58]–[59]) that there is a clear and strong policy in favour of enforcing alternative dispute resolution provisions and in encouraging parties to attempt to resolve disputes prior to litigation. Where a contract contains valid machinery for resolving potential disputes between the parties, it will usually be necessary for the parties to follow that machinery, and the court will not permit an action to be brought in breach of such agreement. The Court must consider the interests of justice in enforcing the agreed machinery under the Agreement. However, it must also take into account the overriding objective in the Civil Procedure Rules when considering the appropriate order to make.

In terms of enforcement of mediation agreements, this is simply treated as a breach of contract (*Pedriks v Grimaux* [2019] EWHC 2165 (QB)). The courts have had to rule on whether 'heads of terms' agreed in mediation are enforceable as a binding contract (*Abberley v Abberley* [2019] EWHC 1564 (Ch)). Indeed, the courts have responded to mediation enforcement actions in a manner not unlike that adopted in arbitration. In *Beauty Star Ltd v Janmohamed* [2014] EWCA Civ 451 the parties had agreed to the appointment of an accountant in a mediation which was reflected in their Mediation Agreement and the court ordered parties to appoint the accountant under that agreement rather than by court order. There have also been cases where a party has entered into a mediation without the power or *vires* to do so. In *The Serpentine Trust Ltd v HMRC* [2018] UKFTT 535 (TC) the court found that there were constraints imposed on an HMRC mediation as a non-departmental government agency and whilst it had purported to enter a mediation agreement and that was held to constitute a contract, it was, nevertheless, *ultra vires* HMRC's powers and therefore the court held that it was void.

Conclusion

The Singapore Convention has been lauded as 'completing the circle' and 'being the last piece of the international enforcement jigsaw' and indeed, to a large extent, it fills that gap. It has been suggested that the Singapore Convention will do for mediation what the New York Convention has done for international arbitration. Time will tell, but the adoption of mediation as the preferred method of dispute resolution increasingly in civil law based systems and also in South East Asia (China, Singapore, Hong Kong) may mean that its use will grow globally as China's vast infrastructure programme takes hold (in particular the Belt and Road Initiative). As a testament to that, international contractors are said to be already including dispute resolution clauses in their contracts which include mandatory mediation provisions.

Its success will depend on how many States sign and ratify the Convention. The success of the New York Convention is due largely to its widespread acceptance and it currently has in excess of 160 State signatories. But it should be remembered that there were only 10 States which first signed the New York Convention in June 1958; so far, 53 States have already signed the

Singapore Mediation Convention. It may also be important if those States adopt a reservation under the Convention.

Its success may also depend on how parties and courts interpret the grounds for refusing enforcement under Art 5. Arbitration case law may yet have a part to play in that interpretation given the similarities in concept and wording between the New York Convention and the Singapore Convention.

In the Preamble to the Convention it is recognised that mediation has a 'value for international trade as a method for settling commercial disputes' and it is noted that 'mediation is increasingly used in international and domestic commercial practice as an alternative to litigation'.

If one of the primary objectives of the Convention is to give parties confidence in the mediation process and the international enforcement of mediated settlements in cross-border disputes, it is a right step in the right direction. Mediation, as a more time and cost efficient method than arbitration or court proceedings, with its non-adversarial approach and greater likelihood of preserving parties' commercial relationship, may yet become more important in dispute resolution and, if so, the Singapore Convention will play a key part in that. It will also be an important factor in arbitration if Arb-Med (as opposed to Arb-Med-Arb or Med-Arb) models become more common in Scotland, and if such models have the final resolution as a mediated agreement, as opposed to a consent award. On this issue, it is suggested that a consent award might be a safer option presently, where international arbitration is concerned, given that the New York Convention is well established, and the Singapore Convention is in its infancy.

Index

abuse of power, 126, 309
abuse of process, 59, 200, 280
adults with incapacity, 95, 114, 240, 293–4
adversarial approach, 185, 187–9, 202, 218
affidavits, 197, 304
affirmation, 197, 219
age, arbitrators, 95–6
agricultural holdings, 76–7
Agricultural Industries Confederation, 81
alternative dispute resolution, 41, 47–8, 384–5, 390–1; *see also* **mediation**
anonymity
  arbitration proceedings, 73–5
  Rules of Court and, 75
  UNCITRAL Model Law, 73–4
  see also **confidentiality**
anti-suit injunctions, 42–6, 59, 155
appeals
  adults with incapacity, 240
  applications, 226–7
    procedures, 233–4
    standing, 229, 234
    time, 230–1
  arbitration time limits and, 228–9
  awards *see* **appeals against awards**
  beginning of arbitration process, 238
  continuing arbitration, 153–6, 228, 231, 245
  court intervention principles, 12–14
  court jurisdiction, 12–13, 229–30
    choice of court, 229
    discretion, 229
  court powers, 12, 236–7
    arrestment and inhibition, 242
    cautions, 241
    England and Wales, 242–4
    evidence, 232–3, 235–6, 244

    inspection orders, 239–40
    interdicts, 242
    interim orders, 244
    Mareva injunctions, 242–3
    permanent orders, 244
    preservation of evidence, 241–2
    sale of property, 240–1
  delay and, 227
  discretion, 225–6
  evidence, 191–2
    gathering, 244
    powers, 232–3, 241–2
    preservation, 241–2
    privileged documents, 233
    scope, 235
    witnesses, 232–3
  finality, 227, 231, 235, 237–8
  interim remedies, 237–8
  jurisdiction of tribunals, against, 66, 150–3
    continuing arbitration, 153–6
    Form 14.4, 150
    lodging petitions, 152–3
    petitions, 150–2
    time limits, 152
  meaning of court, 40, 61, 237
  minimum court intervention, 12, 283
  overview, 224–45
  points of law, 224–5, 226, 296–9
  restrictions, 5, 12–14, 65–6
  time limits, 230–1
  tribunal powers, 232
appeals against awards
  arbitrators' expenses, 295–6
  continuing arbitration proceedings, 228
  empty chairs, 68–72
  expenses, 301, 302
  foreign jurisdictions, 63
  fraud, 70, 286, 291–2

appeals against awards (*cont.*)
　further appeal, 296
　legal errors, 296–9
　　time limits, 299–300
　mandatory rules, 36, 281
　Outer House options, 295, 301, 314
　overview, 281–302
　procedures, 299–302
　provisional awards, 299
　reasons for awards, 300–1
　reconsideration by tribunal, 302
　restrictions, 15, 65–6
　serious irregularity, 284–95, 314
　　AARs, 289–91, 295
　　against arbitration agreements,
　　　287–8
　　ambiguities, 291
　　arbitrators' lack of qualifications,
　　　294
　　examples, 287–95
　　exceeding powers, 288
　　fraud, 291–2
　　inability to act as arbitrator, 293–4
　　lack of impartiality/independence,
　　　292–3
　　not dealing with issues, 288–9
　　other irregularities, 294–5
　　public policy, 291–2
　　substantial injustice, 284–7
　　third parties acting outwith powers,
　　　289–91, 295
　　unfair treatment, 293
　time limits, 299–300
　timing, 283, 284
　tribunal jurisdiction lacking, 66, 282–4
applicable law *see* **conflict of laws**
arbitrability of disputes
　comparative law, 84–5
　Crown disputes, 86
　employment rights, 86
　family law, 85
　New York Convention and, 307
　overview, 84–7
　personal injuries, 85–6
arbitral appointment referees (AARs)
　see **referees**
arbitration, definition, 6, 18, 233, 318
arbitration agreements
　agreement to arbitrate, 23
　appointment of arbitrators, 93
　　number, 97
　　removal, 125
　assignation, 93, 139–40

　binding nature, 40–1
　clauses, 23
　commercial element, 28
　death of parties and, 315
　definition, 23, 318
　failure to comply with, 221–2, 287–8
　frustration, 139
　governing law, 34
　incorporation by reference, 29, 140
　intentions, 28–9
　loss of right to arbitrate, 31–2
　no mention of arbitration, 28–9
　novation, 93, 140
　one-stopness, 29–31
　overview, 23–39
　pathological clauses, 28
　registration, 64
　related agreements, 140
　removal of arbitrators and, 114
　Scottish Arbitration Rules, 35–8
　separability, 32–4, 136–7, 139
　service of notice, 89, 91, 92
　signatures, 27
　submission agreements, 23
　time limits, 81
　validity
　　inoperative agreements, 56
　　jurisdiction of tribunals and, 137,
　　　139
　　New York Convention and, 53
　　sist and, 50–3, 56
　written v oral, 24–7
arbitration proceedings
　commencement, 88–93
　consolidation, 223
　legal development, 1–2
　Scottish approach, 2–3
　termination, 145, 149, 262–3
　see also specific procedures
arbitrators
　age, 95–6
　appointment, 93–116
　　challenges, 109–12, 129–31, 144
　　failure of procedure, 100, 127, 310
　　immunity of appointing
　　　institutions, 127–8, 309–10
　　appointment methods, 93–4, 98–9
　　AARs, 100–1
　　agreement appointees, 125
　　court appointment, 100–1
　　procedural failures, 100, 127. 310
　　time limits, 101
　bad faith, 125, 126–7, 308–9

bankruptcy, 96
bias *see* **bias**
breach of contract, 125
choices, 100
conflicts of interests, 101–8
  IBA Guidelines, 107–8
death, 122, 133, 314
definition, 18, 318
discrimination, 16–17
duties, 156–8
  party autonomy and, 169–70
  see also specific duties
eligibility, 94–5, 114
employment status, 14
end of tenure, 122–4
  finality, 123–4
  grounds, 122–3
  liabilities, 122, 123
  repayments, 123
expenses *see* **expenses**
fairness *see* **fairness**
identity, 16–17
immunity, 125–9, 307–9
  appointing institutions, 127–8,
    309–10
  restrictions, 125, 126–7
impartiality *see* **impartiality/
    independence**
individuals, 36, 94, 133, 314
judges as, 83–4
legal capacity, 95–6
life insurance, 133
nationality, 104
negligence, 125
numbers, 18, 96–8
objections to appointment, 109–12
  allegations, 111
  grounds, 109, 110–11, 129
  loss of right to, 129–31
  notices, 109
  reconstituted tribunal, 124
  resignation, 120–1
  standard of proof, 111
  time limits, 109, 111–12, 129, 130,
    131
  waiver of right to, 162
qualifications, 82, 109, 110, 114, 294
religious beliefs, 16–17
removal, 35, 36, 112–17
  agreement appointees, 125
  breach of confidentiality, 179
  by court, 114–15
  continuing arbitration, 119–20

failure to conduct proceedings,
    117–18
  finality, 123–4
  grounds, 114, 116
  illegal purposes, 113
  methods, 112
  notification, 118
  party applications, 115–16, 117
  representations, 118–19
  substantial injustice, 114–15
  sufficient grounds, 119
resignation, 120–2
  breach of contract, 169, 309
  expenses, 121
  liabilities, 121, 125, 127
sole arbitrators, 96–8
tenure, 109, 122–4
terminology, 18
arrestment, 242
**assignation, arbitration agreement
    rights,** 60, 93, 139–40
audi alteram partem, 158
Australia, disposal of evidence, 242
autonomy *see* **party autonomy**
awards
  agreed awards, 257–8
  ambiguities, 264, 266, 291
  assignation of interests, 60
  binding nature, 257
  challenging *see* **appeals against
    awards**
  conflict of laws, 245, 247–8
  consent awards, 257–8
  continuation of Rules, 263
  correcting, 263–6
    English cases, 266
    time limits, 265
  date, 255
  delivery, 256
  draft awards, 260–1, 263
  enforcement *see* **enforcement of
    awards**
  errors, 263–6
  expenses, 274–5, 281
    appeals, 295–6
  final awards, 146, 147
  finality, 57–9, 61, 146, 257–8
  foreign currencies, 249–50
  form, 255
  interest, 253–5
  interim awards, 258–9
  jus quaesitum tertio, 60
  justice, fairness and equity, 246–7

awards (*cont.*)
  lack of jurisdiction, 146–7, 149
  made in Scotland, 257
  making, 256–7
  overview, 245–66
  part awards, 146–7, 257, 258–9, 260,
    319
  provisional awards, 58, 61, 146, 257
    definition, 319
    no appeal, 299
    overview, 259–60
  reasons, 255–6, 300–1
  reconsideration by tribunal, 302
  rectification, 252
  registration, 64
  remedies, 250–3
    damages, 249–50
    declarators, 250
    interdicts, 251–2
    reduction, 252–3
    specific implement, 251–2
  seat of arbitration and, 255, 257
  subrogation, 59–60
  termination of arbitration, 262–3
  third parties and, 58, 59–61
  through and under parties, 59–61
  tribunal jurisdiction and, 145
  tribunal powers, 249–50
  types, 257–61
  withholding, 257, 260–1

bad faith
  arbitrators, 125, 126–7, 308–9
  enforcement of foreign awards, 303
bankruptcy
  arbitrators, 96
  parties, 134, 315
barristers, impartiality as arbitrators,
    162–3
bias
  apparent bias, 161–2, 165
  arbitrators, 102, 103, 104–8, 115,
    157–72
  objections to arbitrators, waiver of
    right to, 162
  previous appointments and
    instructions as counsel, 160–1
  test, 164–6
breach of contract, 169, 308, 309, 391
Brexit, 3, 33, 42

Canada, 31, 250
capacity *see* **legal capacity**

case management, 5, 9, 10, 117–18, 151,
    195, 203–4, 277
cautions, 155, 241, 277–80
Centre for Effective Dispute
    Resolution (CEDR), 47, 271
Chartered Institute of Arbitrators
  AAR, 81
  appointment of arbitrators, 99
  conflicts of interest and, 161
  e-disclosure, 190
  guidelines, 100, 138
  international survey of costs, 9
  members as arbitrators, 110–11
  membership categories, 95
  non-delegation principle, 215
  organisation of hearings, 210
China
  ADR, 391
  arbitrability of disputes, 84–5
  carriage of goods at sea, 59
  competence/competence and, 138
  mediation, 291
  Singapore Convention signatory,
    387
China International Economic and
    Trade Arbitration Commission
    (CIETAC), 74, 206, 386
choice of law *see* **conflict of laws**
civil law systems, 185, 187–9, 320
civil search warrants, 244
claims, definition, 318
clear language, 12
clerks, 98, 125, 174, 212
commencement of arbitration
  appeals at the start, 238
  notice, 89–92
  overview, 88–93
  standing, 88, 93
communications
  electronic communications, 25–7, 90,
    135, 316
  formal communications, 134–6,
    316—17
competence/competence, 136–9
conditional fee agreements, 162, 163
confidentiality
  advantage of arbitration, 86
  arbitration proceedings, 73
  continuing obligation, 176–7
  exceptions, 177–8
    interests of justice, 181
    public interest, 178
  fair trial and, 15

information, 175–8
mediation and, 207, 385
new Scottish approach, 174–5
privileged information, 207
appeals, 233, 236
remedies, 179
Rule 26, 174–83
disapplication, 179–83
third party disclosures, 179, 182
tribunal deliberations, 183
waivers, 180
conflict of interests
acquiescence, 166
arbitrators, 101–8
barristers in same chambers,
162–3
IBA Guidelines, 107–8, 166
previous appointments and
instruction as counsel, 160–1
disclosure, 165–6
test, 164–6
UNCITRAL Model Law, 170–1
waivers, 166
conflict of laws
arbitration agreements, 34
awards and, 247–8
considerations, 247–8
Conventions, 387
English provisions, 248
European Union, 33
jurisdiction of tribunals and, 141
lex arbitri, 38–9
party choice, 245
Prague Rules, 205
preliminary issues, 212
seat of arbitration, 19
Singapore Convention and, 388
tribunal choice, 245–6
consolidation of proceedings, 223
consumer arbitration
limitation periods, 80–1
prescription, 80
unfair clauses, 17–18
Convention on Choice of Court
Agreements (2005), 387
Convention on the Recognition
and Enforcement of Foreign
Judgments in Civil and
Commercial Matters (2019), 387
costs *see* expenses
counterclaims, 142, 175, 178, 194, 197,
199–200, 277
court intervention *see* appeals

courts
definition, 40, 61, 237, 318
self-funding policy, 267
COVID-19, 320
CPR (International Institute for
Conflict Prevention and
Resolution), 190, 271
Crown proceedings, 86, 240, 251

damages, tribunal powers to award,
249–50
death
arbitrators, 122, 133, 314
parties, 133–4, 314–15
decision-making procedures, 211
declarators, 68, 154, 250
defamation, 79, 128, 311
default rules, 4, 37–8, 88, 318
definitions, 18–19, 318–19
delay
appeals and, 227
fairness and, 168–9
inordinate delay, 196
judges as arbitrators and, 84
lay representatives, 216
minimising, 5, 7, 8–10, 48, 98, 146,
172–3
new later claims, 200
prevention mechanisms, 152
removal of arbitrators and, 119
timeous objections, 311–12
timeous submissions, 220–1
directions
failure to comply, 221–2
non-compliance orders, 222–3
tribunal procedures, 211–12
disability, 80, 95, 209
disputes, definition, 18–19, 318
documents
appeals
inspection orders, 239–40
privileged documents, 233
disclosure, 195–6
electronically stored information,
189–90
formal communications, 134–6,
316–17
importance, 192
Prague Rules, 203–4
tribunal procedures, 189–90

electronic communications, 25–7, 90,
135, 316

electronic signatures, 135, 255, 317, 388
email *see* **electronic communications**
employment, arbitrability of disputes,
    86
empty chair, 60, 68–72, 149
enforcement of awards
    appeal time limits and, 300
    applications, 62–3
    diligence, 63
    empty chair defence, 60, 68–72
    foreign awards, 64–5, 303–7
    interlocutors, 63
    jurisdiction of tribunals and, 62, 63–4
    New York Convention and, 65
    ordinary actions, 63
    overview, 61–5
    public policy and, 62
    registration of awards, 64
equality legislation, 16–17
equity, awards, 246–7
European Convention on Human
    Rights, 9, 14–16
European Union
    choice of law, 33, 245–6
    GDPR Regulations, 190
    mediation, 96, 207, 385
    primacy of law, 33
evidence
    admissibility, 190, 191–2
    appeals, 191–2, 232–3, 235–6
        preservation, 241–2
    best evidence, 189
    disposal, 242
    documents, 189–90, 192
    failure to provide, 221
    IBA Rules, 201–2, 203, 204, 205–6
    materiality, 190, 191
    Prague Rules *see* **Prague Rules**
    property inspections, 218–19
    recording, 193
    relevancy, 190, 191
    tribunal procedures, 190–3
    weight, 190, 191
expenses
    agreed fees and expenses, 269
    ancillary proceedings, 267–8
    appeals against awards, 301, 302
    apportionment, 274
    arbitrators, 267, 268, 295–6
    awards, 252, 274–5, 281
        appeals, 295–6
    capping, 269, 280–1
    caution for, 155, 277–80

conditional fee agreements, 162, 163
consolidation of proceedings and, 223
definition, 266, 318
determination, 272–3
end of arbitrators' tenure, 122
    repayments, 123
    resignation, 121
following success, 267, 274–5
increasing costs, 270–1
joint liability, 275
mediation, 390
minimising, 5, 7, 8–10, 48, 98
    case law, 172–3
    removal of arbitrators and, 119
new later claims and, 200
non-payment, 257, 260–1
overview, 266–81
participating parties, 149
pre-dispute agreements, 36, 269, 276
pro-active procedures and, 186
recoverability, 271–2, 319
repayment of fees already paid, 122,
    270
sealed offers and, 279
security for, 155, 277–80
    appeals, 301
    dismissal of claims, 279–80
    outwith UK, 277–9
    tribunal orders, 279
several liability, 268–9, 275
taxation of accounts, 269–70
terminology, 266
Tolent clauses, 36–7, 269, 276
unnecessary expense, fairness and,
    168–9
wasted costs orders, 123
expert evidence
    confidentiality, 174
    IBA Rules, 205
    immunity of witnesses, 128–9, 310–11
    joint conferencing hot-tubbing, 187
    Prague Rules, 203, 205
    procedures, 186, 216–18
    property inspections, 218–19
    resignation of arbitrators and, 120, 121
extra-judicial settements, 198

Facebook, 90, 106
Faculty of Advocates, 81, 101, 104, 110,
    111
fairness
    arbitrators, 114, 116, 156–72
        appeals against awards, 293

fair treatment of parties, 134, 167,
    315
  party autonomy and, 170
  audi alteram partem, 158
  awards, 246–7
  consequences of failure of, 167–8
  ECHR, 9, 14–16
  founding principle, 7–8
  hearing procedures, 196
  object of arbitration, 5
  representatives and, 216
  UNCITRAL Model Law, 167
  unnecessary delay/expense and,
    168–9
family law arbitration, 85
Family Law Arbitration Group
    Scotland (FLAGS), 85
Family Law Arbitration Scheme, 85
fax, 25–6, 90, 135, 316, 317
force majeure, 139
foreign awards
  Convention awards, 27, 305–7
  Conventions, 387
  documentation, 304
  Form 14.4, 304
  Form 62.2, 304
  Form 62.28, 150
  Form 62.59, 375, 383
  grounds for refusal to enforce, 305–7
  non-participating parties, 306
  notices, 306
  petitions, 304
  public policy and, 307
  recognition and enforcement, 303–7
  Rules of Court, 304
  see also **New York Convention;
    Singapore Convention**
foreign currencies, 249–50
foreign parties, security for expenses,
    277–9
formal communications, 134–6, 316–17
forum *see* seat of arbitration
fraud, 70, 219, 286, 291–2
frustration, 139

Gill Review (2009), 31, 221
guarantors, 60
guardians *ad litem*, 240

hearings
  amendments of pleadings, 195
  cross-examinations, 196–7, 204
  doing without, 197–8, 205

examinations in chief, 196–7
failure to attend, 221
location, 192–3, 209–10
order of submissions, 198–9
overall control, 210
pleadings, 194–5, 197–9
re-examinations, 196–7
Reply to Defence, 194
representation, 193–4
Response to Reply, 194
Statements of Claims, 194
Statements of Defence, 194
time limits, 210
venue facilities, 209–10
witnesses, 196–7
Hong Kong, 391
Hong Kong International Arbitration
    Centre (HKIAC), 206, 386
hot-tubbing, 187

IBA *see* International Bar Association
ICC *see* International Chamber of
    Commerce
ICDR *see* International Centre for
    Dispute Resolution
illegal contracts, 62
immunity
  appointing institutions, 127–8, 309–10
  arbitrators, 125–9, 307–9
    bad faith, 308–9
    restrictions, 125, 126–7
  experts, 128–9, 310–11
  legal representatives, 128, 310–11
  overview, 307–11
  public interest immunity, 236
  witnesses, 128, 310–11
impartiality/independence
  arbitrators
    appeals against awards, 292–3
    barristers in same chambers, 162–3
    case law, 102–3
    considerations, 313–14
    objections, 109
    overview, 156–72
    previous appointments and
      instructions as counsel, 160–1
    removal, 114, 116
    requirements, 313–14
    rule 81, 134
    rules 77/78, 131–3
    solicitors, 164
    waiver of right to objections, 162
  consequences of failure of, 167–8

impartiality/independence (*cont.*)
definition, 132, 318
disclosures and, 165–6
founding principle, 7–8
hearing procedures, 196
IBA guidelines, 108–9
ICDR Rules, 171–2
LCIA Rules, 171
object of arbitration, 5
Singapore Convention, 388
test, 164–6
UNCITRAL Model Law, 171
incapable adults, 95, 114, 240, 293–4
independence *see* **impartiality/**
independence
India, 27, 387
inhibition, 242
Inner House, definition, 318
Institution of Civil Engineers, 81
insurance
arbitrators, 133
marine insurance, 103
punitive damages and, 250
subrogation of awards, 59–60
interdicts
appeal court powers, 242
awards, 251–2
breach of confidentiality, 179
interim interdicts, 251
sisting legal proceedings, 42
interest
awards, 253–5
categories, 253
compound interest, 254
judicial v commercial rate, 254–5
procedural law, 255
punitive rate, 254
Shari'a law, 253
International Bar Association (IBA)
Guidelines on Conflicts of Interest in
International Arbitration, 107–8,
166
Green List, 108, 166
Orange List, 108, 160, 166
Red List, 107, 160, 166
tribunal secretaries, 215
Rules on the Taking of Evidence in
International Arbitration (2010),
201–2, 203, 204, 205–6
International Centre for Dispute
Resolution (ICDR)
anonymity, 74
confidentiality, 174, 175

e-disclosure, 190
exchanges of information, 271
impartiality and independence, 171–2
International Chamber of Commerce
(ICC)
anonymity, 74
confidentiality, 174
controlling time and costs, 271
draft awards, 260
e-disclosure, 190
impartiality and independence, 206
interim awards, 258
minimising delay and expense, 9
party autonomy, 10
tribunal secretaries, 215
International Council for Commercial
Arbitration (ICCA), 190, 214–15,
320
International Institute for Conflict
Prevention and Resolution
(CPR), 190, 271
Internet, 26, 54
investor-state dispute settlement
(ISDS), 388

judges, as arbitrators, 83–4
judicial review, 65, 158, 293
jura novit curia **principle,** 205
jurisdiction of tribunals
appeals against, 66, 150–3
challenging awards, 282–4
continuing proceedings pending
decisions, 153–6
Form 14.4, 150
petitions, 150–3
time limits, 152
competence/competence, 136–9
constitution issues, 139, 142
determination
delay, 149
time limits, 147
timing, 145–6
empty chairs and, 68–72
end of tribunal, 145, 149
enforcement of awards and, 62,
63–4
governing law, 141
lex arbitri, 136
no jurisdiction options, 142
objections
awards and, 146–7, 149
late objections, 148
loss of right to, 148–9

non-participating parties, 144, 149
procedures, 143–9
timing, 144–5
tribunal options, 145
ruling on jurisdiction only, 141–2
separability and, 136–7, 139
service and, 72
subject matters, 142
types of challenge, 139–41
jus quaesitum tertio, 60, 275

Land Court, 76
language
clear language, 12
foreign languages, 201
non-technical language, 185
tribunal procedures, 201
Law Society of Scotland, 82, 101, 111, 384
law support, 216
legal capacity
adults with incapacity, 95, 114, 240, 293–4
arbitrators, 95–6
New York Convention and, 305, 306
Singapore Convention, 388
legal representatives *see* representatives
liens, 85, 261–2
life insurance, arbitrators, 133
limitation periods, 79–81, 86, 89, 112, 221
LinkedIn, 106
litigants in person, 215–16
local government, 74, 95
London Court of International
Arbitration (LCIA)
anonymity, 74
appointment of arbitrators, 99
confidentiality, 175
consolidation of proceedings, 223
correcting awards, 263
expenses, 280
impartiality and independence, 171, 206
party autonomy, 10
principles, 246
procedural rulings, 214
separate awards, 258
London Maritime Arbitrators
Association (LMAA), 24

McKenzie friends, 216
Malaysia, 387

mandatory injunctions, 86, 251
mandatory rules, 35–6, 88, 318
Mareva injunctions, 44, 242–3
marine insurance, 103
Mather, Jim, 88
mediation
awards and, 290–1
breach of agreements, 391
confidentiality, 207–8, 385
costs, 390
definition, 386
enforcement, 385–6
European Union, 96, 385
non-compellable procedure, 389
objectives, 389–90
Prague Rules, 206–8
Scottish solicitors and, 384–5
significance, 384–6
Singapore Convention, 384–92
mental disorder *see* adults with
incapacity
misfeasance in public office, 126, 309
money laundering, 62, 113, 114–15, 121, 147
Muslim Arbitration Tribunal, 249

nationality, arbitrators, 104
negligence, arbitrators, 125, 308
nemo judex in sua causa, 102, 158, 159
New York Convention (1958)
application, 6
arbitrability of disputes, 84
binding awards, 257, 303
binding nature of arbitration
agreements, 40
Convention awards
grounds for refusal, 305–7
meaning, 27
Convention states, 7, 303, 304, 380–2
due process paranoia, 9
enforcement requirements, 65
narrow interpretation, 306–7
Singapore Convention and, 387
stay of proceedings, 46
success, 391–2
validity of arbitration agreements, 53
written agreements, 24, 25, 26–7
non-compliance orders, 222–3
non-participating parties, 69, 100, 106, 144, 149, 309

notices
communications, 90, 134–6, 316–17
proceedings notices
electronic communications, 90
English law, 91–2
New York Convention and, 305
service, 89–92
time, 91
requirement of writing, 135
service, 135
signatures, 135
novation, arbitration agreements, 93,
140

oaths, 197, 219
objections
arbitrators' appointments *see*
arbitrators
jurisdiction *see* **jurisdiction of
tribunals**
loss of right to, 311–12
participants, 312
timeous objections, 311–12
Outer House, definition, 318

parties
autonomy *see* **party autonomy**
bankruptcy, 134, 315
conflicts with tribunals, 147
death, 133–4, 314–15
definition, 319
fair treatment, 134, 167, 315
legal capacity *see* **legal capacity**
non-participating parties, 69, 100, 106,
144, 149, 309
party litigants, 215–16
standing *see* **standing**
party autonomy
2010 Act, 3
choice of law, 245
default rules and, 37
founding principle, 5, 10–11, 93, 146,
156
location of hearings and, 193
procedural choices, 173, 185
restrictions, 36
statutory tribunal duties and, 169–70
UNCITRAL and, 66
personal injuries, 79, 80, 85–6
Philippines, 387
pleadings
adjustment, 199
hearings, 194–5

time limits, 220–1
written pleadings, 197–8, 199, 205
Prague Rules
amicable settlement, 206–8
applicable law, 205
compatibility with Scots law, 206–7
document production, 203–4
doing without hearings, 205
expert evidence, 203, 205
jura novit curia principle, 205
objectives, 203
origins, 202
overview, 202–7
pro-active tribunals, 203
witnesses, 204–5
preliminary issues, 153, 154, 212
prescription
commencement of arbitration and, 89
consumer arbitration, 80
negative prescription, 78–9
objections to arbitrators, 112
overview, 77–81
positive prescription, 77–8
principles
English arbitration, 5–6
founding principles, 5–16
justice, fairness and equity, 246–7
see also specific principles
procedural orders, 210, 211–12
procedures *see* **tribunal procedures**
property
appeal court powers
arrestment, 242
inhibition, 242
inspections, 239–40
interim orders, 244
sale, 240–1
inspections, 218–19
appeal court powers, 239–40
tribunal powers, 240–1
public interest
anonymous proceedings and, 73
arbitration principles and, 5, 6, 93
confidentiality and, 177, 178, 180, 181,
183, 240
party autonomy and, 93
public interest immunity, 236
questions of law, 224
public policy
arbitrable disputes and, 85, 86
avoiding delay, 146, 231
awards and, 62, 250, 285, 291–2
concept, 62

Convention awards and, 307
immunities, 310
Prague Rules and, 205
pre-dispute expenses agreements and,
    276
public interest immunity, 236
punitive damages and, 248–9, 250
Singapore Convention and, 388
punitive damages, 247–8, 250

Qatar, 387

recognition and enforcement *see*
    enforcement of awards; foreign
    awards
rectification, 252
reduction, 148, 252–3, 282
referees (AARs)
acting outwith powers, 289–91, 295
appointment powers, 81–3
definition, 318
fees and expenses, 267
functions, 94, 100–1
immunity, 309–10
legal capacity and, 96
list, 81–2
serious irregularities, 289–91, 294–5
use of appeal process, 113
religious discrimination, 16–17
representatives
fairness and, 216
immunity, 128, 310–11
litigants in person, 215–16
notice of, 215
rule 33, 215–16
tribunal hearings, 193–4
res judicata, 56, 58, 262, 303
Royal Incorporation of Architects in
    Scotland, 82
Royal Institution of Chartered
    Surveyors, 82, 111
rule of law, 102, 159
Rules of Court
anonymity and, 75
text, 374–9

Saudi Arabia, 254, 387
Scott Schedules, 200–1
Scottish Agriultural Arbiters and
    Valuers Association, 82
Scottish Arbitration Centre, 38, 82
Scottish Arbitration Rules
default rules, 4, 37–8, 88, 318

mandatory rules, 35–6, 88, 318
meaning, 3
text, 343–72
Scottish Mediation, 384
seat of arbitration
arbitration agreements, 38–9
awards and, 255, 257
designation
    by agreement, 20, 22
    by court, 20, 22–3
    by tribunal, 20
enforcement of awards and, 64–5
English position, 20–2
lex arbitri, 38–9
location of hearings and, 192–3, 209
New York Convention and, 306
place, 19–20
principles, 19–23
Scottish advantages, 320
sisting and, 57
statutory arbitration, 76
secretaries, 212, 213–15
service of notice, 89–90
set-off, 142, 175, 178, 199–200
setting aside
awards, 116, 149, 151, 227, 282, 298
lack of jurisdiction, 147–8, 149
meaning, 147–8
reduction and, 148
settlement, amicable settlement,
    Prague Rules, 206–7
Shari'a law, 246, 248–9, 253
sheriff court, appeals to, 229
ship liens, 85
signatures, 27, 135, 223, 255, 317, 388
Singapore
ADR, 391
arbitration agreements, 25
Singapore Convention (2019)
assessment, 391–2
choice of law, 388
definition of mediation, 386
enforcement, 386, 388
entry into force, 389
European Union and, 385
formalities, 388
impartiality and independence, 388
legal capacity, 388
main provisions, 387–9
New York Convention and, 387
objectives, 392
overview, 384–92
Preamble, 392

Singapore Convention (2019) (*cont.*)
  principles, 387–8
  procedural breaches, 388
  public policy and, 388
  refusal to enforce, 388
  reservations, 388–9
  scope, 387
  signatories, 387, 391–2
  United Kingdom and, 385, 389–91
Singapore International Arbitration
    Centre (SIAC), 206, 209, 305–6,
    386
Singapore International Mediation
    Centre (SIMC), 386
Singapore International Mediation
    Institute, 386
sisting, arbitration proceedings
    pending jurisdiction appeals,
    153–5
sisting legal proceedings
  anti-suit injunctions, 42–6, 59, 155
  any matter under dispute, 48–9
  applications
    multiple applications, 56–7
    notices, 54
    standing, 53–4
  binding nature of arbitration
    agreements, 40–1, 47
  court's inherent jurisdiction, 40
  existing arbitration agreement, 47–8
    validity, 50–3, 56
  losing entitlement, 55
  meaning, 41–6
  meaning of court, 40
  meaning of legal proceedings, 49–50
  mediation agreements and, 390–1
  no contracting out, 57
  overview, 39–57
  procedural considerations, 39–40
  recalling sist, 41, 56–7
  reference to European Court, 41–2
  s 10 structure, 46–53
  seat of arbitration and, 57
site inspections, 203, 237, 239
social media, 54, 90, 106–7
solicitors
  ADR and, 384–5
  as arbitrators, impartiality, 160–1, 164
South Korea, 387
specific implement, 251–2
standard form contracts, 249, 253, 276
standing
  appeal applications, 229, 234

  applications for sist, 53–4
  through or under parties, 50, 88, 93
stated cases, 1, 2, 3, 14, 66, 168, 195, 283,
    296–7
statutory arbitration
  definition, 319
  overview, 75–7
  seat of arbitration, 76
stay of proceedings *see* **sisting**
Stock Exchange, 73, 174
subject matters, arbitrability of
    disputes, 84–7
subrogation of awards, 59–60
suspension of legal proceedings *see*
    sisting

taxation, 113, 169
taxation of accounts, 269–70
time limits
  computation of periods, 136, 318
  see also specific actions
Tolent clauses, 36–7, 269, 276
trade usage, 246–7
tribunal procedures
  see also specific procedures
  common v civil law, 185, 187–9
  decision-making, 211
  deliberatons, confidentiality, 183
  directions, 211–12
  documents, 189–91
  evidence, 190–1
  hearings *see* **hearings**
  language, 201
  new later claims, 200
  New York Convention and, 305–6
  non-delegation principle, 215
  overall control of arbitration, 210
  Prague Rules, 202–7
  preliminary issues, 212
  pro-active arbitrators, 185–7, 203
  representatives, 215–16
  Scott Schedules, 200–1
  timely submissions, 220–1
  transparency, 186
  tribunal power to determine, 183–5,
    202
tribunals
  agents and employees, 212–13
  appointment, 93–16
  awards *see* **awards**
  clerks, 98, 125, 174, 212
  conflicts with parties, 147
  definition, 319

dismissal
    continuing arbitration, 119–20
    failure to conduct proceedings, 118
    finality, 123–4
    grounds, 116–17
    liabilities, 122, 123
    notification, 118
    party applications, 117
    reconstitution, 124
    representations, 118–19
    sufficient grounds, 119
immunity, 125–9, 307–9
jurisdiction see **jurisdiction of
    tribunals**
powers, 232
procedures see **tribunal procedures**
proper constitution, 139, 142
reconstitution, 124
secretaries, 212, 213–15
see also **arbitrators**
Turkey, arbitrability of disputes, 85
Twitter, 90

umpires, 36, 83–4, 97, 102, 134, 211, 315
UNCITRAL
    1976 Rules see **UNCITRAL Rules
    (1976)**
    Model Law see **UNCITRAL Model
    Law**
    Notes on Organizing Arbitral
        Proceedings (1996), 210, 213
UNCITRAL Model Law (1985)
    appeals, 65, 153, 237
    application, 66–7
    appointment of arbitrators, 99
    correcting awards, 263
    court intervention, 12
    electronic communications, 25
    equal treatment, 167
    introduction, 1, 3
    jurisdiction of tribunals, objections,
        143, 144–5, 149
    meaning, 339
    number of arbitrators, 97

party autonomy, 10
    reasons for awards, 256
    Scots law and, 5–6, 66
    stay of legal proceedings, 46, 47, 55
    written arbitration agreements, 25
UNCITRAL Rules (1976)
    anonymity, 73–4
    burden of proof, 192
    confidentiality, 175
    conflicts of interests, 170–1
    evidence, 190
    fairness, 170
    impartiality and independence,
        170–1
    interim awards, 258
    meaning, 339
    relevance, 11
    separability of arbitration clauses, 32
unfair treatment see **fairness**
United States
    disposal of evidence, 242
    insurance policies, 250
    neutrality or arbitrators, 156
    punitive damages, 250
    Singapore Convention signatory, 387
    tribunal procedures, 196

Washington Convention (1960), 388
witnesses
    affidavits, 197
    appeals, 232
    exclusions, 197, 204
    immunity, 128, 310–11
    number, 204
    oaths and affirmations, 197, 219
    Prague Rules, 203, 204–5
    tribunal hearings, 196–7
    see also **expert evidence**
Woolf Review (1996), 31
**World Intellectual Property
    Organization (WIPO),** 74
worldwide freezing orders (WFO), 44,
    242–3
written pleadings, 197–8, 199, 205